IRISH NATIONALISM AND THE BRITISH STATE

Irish Nationalism and the British State

From Repeal to Revolutionary Nationalism

BRIAN JENKINS

McGill-Queen's University Press
Montreal & Kingston • London • Ithaca

Legal deposit second quarter 2006
Bibliothèque nationale du Québec

Printed in Canada on acid-free paper that is 100% ancient forest free
(100% post-consumer recycled), processed chlorine free.

This book has been published with the help of grants from the
Canadian Federation for the Humanities and Social Sciences, through
the Aid to Scholarly Publications Programme, using funds provided by
the Social Sciences and Humanities Research Council of Canada, and
from Bishop's University, Office of Research Services.

McGill-Queen's University Press acknowledges the support of the
Canada Council for the Arts for our publishing program. We also
acknowledge the financial support of the Government of Canada
through the Book Publishing Industry Development Program (BPIDP)
for our publishing activities.

Library and Archives Canada Cataloguing in Publication

Jenkins, Brian, 1939–
    Irish nationalism and the British state : from repeal to revolutionary
nationalism / Brian Jenkins.

    Includes bibliographical references and index.
    ISBN 0-7735-2971-3

    1. Nationalism – Ireland – History – 19th century.   2. Ireland –
Politics and government – 19th century.   I. Title.

DA950.J46 2006   941.5081   C2005-905908-7

Typeset in 10/13 Sabon by True to Type

In memory of Ivo Lambi and Karl Kuepper

Contents

Preface

This examination of Irish nationalism during the first half of the nine-teenth century was originally intended merely as a short introduction to a study of a liberal state's response to the challenge of revolutionary nationalism. However, as my interest in the topic developed and the text expanded, I elected to have it stand alone. In seeking to explain the strength of nationalism in Ireland itself and in the emigrant communities of North America, I was impressed with the central but not exclusive importance of religion. There is always a danger that even implied criticism of a particular body of clergymen will be erroneously construed as sectarian hostility to their faith. Philip Bagenal, in his *The Priest in Politics* (1893), recognized this, and I wish to reaffirm for myself his prefatory declaration: "My last desire has been to attack in any way the tenets or religious convictions of Roman Catholics, and I wish to deprecate in the strongest possible manner any idea that such is the aim or scope of this publication." Yet, as Bagenal observed, and at least one member of the hierarchy conceded, a number of clergy did not always appear to "appreciate the trend and logical result" of their words and actions.

The volume concludes with the emergence of a new strain of revo-lutionary nationalism, widely known as Fenianism. A follow-on study will examine the response of a liberal state, the United Kingdom, to a disruptive force that took the form of raids into British North America, attempted rebellion in Ireland, and a series of terroristic incidents, the most sensational of which took place in Britain. It is in the context of Fenian activities that I will discuss Irish migration to Britain, British popular attitudes towards the Irish and the Irish problem, and, with the attempted assassination of the Duke of Edinburgh, the Irish in the

Australian colonies. This explains, I trust, the absence of material whose omission might otherwise perplex readers.

The current work is essentially one of synthesis and reinterpretation, and for this reason the text is supported by detailed endnotes. These represent an attempt to do justice to those authors whose books and articles were particularly helpful at specific points in the argument. The analysis of the vital contribution of the Roman Catholic Church to the development of Catholic Irish and Irish American nationalism is also rooted in significant manuscript collections. I wish to express my thanks to the Archdiocese of Dublin for access to and permission to quote from the Papers of Cardinal Cullen; to All Hallows College, Dublin, for access to its archives; to the Archdiocese of Westminster for permission to quote from the Papers of Cardinal Wiseman; to the American Catholic Historical Society, Philadelphia, for access to its collections; to the Archdiocese of Baltimore for permission to quote from the Papers of Archbishops Kenrick and Spalding; to the Catholic University of America for the use of its microfilm copies of the Papers of Archbishop Hughes and the correspondence of American bishops with the Irish College, Rome, and for permission to quote from the Papers of O'Donovan Rossa; and to the Archdiocese of Toronto for permission to quote from the Papers of Archbishop Lynch. The Papers of Archbishop Leahy are available on microfilm at the National Library of Ireland, along with copies of the O'Donovan Rossa collection held by the New York Public Library. The National Library of Ireland is also the deposit of the Richmond, Larcom, Mayo, Smith O'Brien, John O'Mahony, and Richard Lalor Sheil Papers. The Public Record Office of Northern Ireland holds the John Mitchel and Thomas O'Hagan Papers and a fragmentary collection of those of James Stephens. The Papers of the Earls of Derby are on deposit at the Liverpool Central Library; those of Odo Russell are at the Public Record Office, Kew, along with the Cairns Papers; the Peel and Wellesley Papers are part of the British Library's immense manuscript collection; those of Whitworth are to be found at the Centre for Kentish Studies, Maidstone; and those of Goulburn at the Surrey Record Office. The Papers of Wellesley-Pole are quoted with the permission of the Earl of Harrowby.

Finally, I wish to thank the Social Sciences and Humanities Research Council of Canada for its support of the research of this project.

Brian Jenkins
Bishop's University

IRISH NATIONALISM AND THE BRITISH STATE

I

A Less than Perfect Union

"The people of Ireland and of Great Britain are among the most dissimilar nations in Europe," wrote a contributor to the *Edinburgh Review* in the autumn of 1846. "They differ in race, in religion, in civilization, and in wealth. To extend similar laws and institutions to countries not merely widely different but strongly contrasted, is to act in violation of all sound legislation and wise government." Yet, less than a half century earlier, the dawn of a new millennium had brought the formal establishment of a new state, the United Kingdom of Great Britain and Ireland. A response to the Irish rebellion of 1798 and to the rebels' alliance with Britain's most dangerous and relentless continental enemy, France, it had the appearance of a long-delayed but natural constitutional evolution. The union of England and Wales effected by the Tudors had been followed, with the death of the last of that house in 1603, by monarchical union with Scotland. Legislative union was to follow barely a century later. James I had made an ambitious if premature attempt to create a "perfect Union" out of his joint thrones soon after he succeeded Elizabeth on that of England. Describing them as the United Kingdom of Great Britain, he hoped eventually to embrace the third of his multiple kingdoms, Ireland. What was missing then and for long afterwards was a master plan to bring all of the Crown's "outer provinces" under closer central control, notwithstanding Oliver Cromwell's short-lived British republic. With the demise of the protectorate, Irish Protestants recovered an Irish parliament, but it was "little better than a cypher" and met only "infrequently" after 1661. The advantages, even necessity, of a more unified state were freely acknowledged during the following century. The miseries afflicting Switzerland, Germany, Poland, and Italy "for want of union either in opinions or in manner of acting," together with the proven vulnerability of the British Isles to invaders when merely a collection of petty states, convinced some reflective observers of the merits of an all embracing union. The legislative union effected with Ireland in 1800 was even "more promising of good effects" than that negotiated with Scotland almost a century earlier, one provincial newspaper declared early the following year, for the Irish plainly stood more in need of the connection than had the Scots.[1]

The arrogant assumption that Irishmen would gratefully come to think of themselves as Englishmen indicated optimism over the development of an enlarged civic or official nationalism. Why would the Irish differ from the Welsh and Scots, who had apparently embraced Britishness? Led by the luminaries of the Scottish Enlightenment, such as William Robertson, who in his *History of Scotland* (1759) argued that the distinctions between the two peoples were gradually disappearing, many Scots referred to themselves as "North Britons." In the case of the Irish, however, the confidence not only was misguided but was reflected in a deeply rooted and frequently nurtured English conviction of Irish inferiority. Contempt for a civilization they considered "backward and barbarian" and horror at its "savagery," had long ago armed the English with the missionary's moral justification for the neighbouring island's conquest. Her constitutional status as a dependent was formally established by law in 1494, and there followed a form of colonization in the shape of plantations first under the Tudors and then most famously in Ulster under James I. Although the introduction of the common law and the establishment of an "imperial economic order" appeared to confirm her colonial status, as did the seemingly ingrained English notion of ethnic superiority, Ireland was unlike any other colony. She was a kingdom with her own Parliament. Moreover, occasional efforts were made, especially by promoters of plantations, to enhance the English popular image of the Irish, which had never been entirely negative. They were described as "prompt, pleasing, decently dressed" human beings, as much victims of misguided English policies as of their own benighted customs. Their salvation was still possible. Prolonged peace and good government would surely modify their "crude and barbaric environment." Unhappily, one such attempted literary rehabilitation of the Irish character was put to the sword in the rebellion of 1641. Although an "anti-popery English Parliament" had helped provoke Ulster Catholics into a pre-emptive strike, which was never a "great Catholic nationalist uprising" against the British "plantations," the

wildly exaggerated accounts of the barbarity with which Roman
Catholic or "native Irish" had tortured and slaughtered "English settlers" served as ammunition for those who disputed the capacity and
worthiness of the Irish ever to be truly one with the English. They
were stigmatized as too untrustworthy, too prone to a peculiar disposition to cruelty, too determined to recover lands lost in earlier
confiscations, and too subservient to their priests. The rising served
to remind Anglicans in particular of their vulnerability. They were
convinced that Irish Catholics were ever willing to unite in order to
subvert Protestantism. Catholicism was thus a "religion of rebellion,
sedition and oppression," for had not the rebels received the blessing
of the Catholic hierarchy?[2]

The rebellion "made religion for the first time the main justification for dispossession," and the substitution of English and Protestant landowners for Catholics was adopted as a policy for making
Ireland secure. John Temple's *The Irish Rebellion* (1646) powerfully
made the sectarian and ethnic case, and the later action of James II's
Irish Parliament – a body almost as exclusively Catholic as it was
soon to be Protestant – in proclaiming the book a seditious libel, simply enhanced its sectarian popularity. It had gone through more than
ten editions by the first years of the nineteenth century and stood as
"an infallible witness against Irishness." Meanwhile, the Catholic
Irishman as both brute and buffoon had become a fixture in English
popular culture. To contradict the contemptuous English dismissal of
him as a species of savage, Irish antiquarians sought for their country a gloriously sophisticated past and blamed England for its loss
and the corruption of a parallel tradition of liberty. They were able
to draw upon the influential work of a seventeenth-century Catholic
priest, Geoffrey Keating, whose account of Ireland from the Creation
to the arrival of the Normans was circulating in manuscript form in
the mid-1630s. Quickly translated into English and subsequently
printed, it was guaranteed a wider readership. Keating rejected
charges of Irish barbarity. On the contrary, they were "an honourable
people" whose history had been distorted by "unreliable, usually foreign, writers." The ancient Irish society he described was "one of
moral order as exemplified by the saints, of social order as revealed
in respect for the law, and of political order underpinned by the proper
recording of history." Not that any of this altered English opinion.
Eighteenth-century visitors admired Dublin's elegant architecture
and acknowledged the outstanding natural beauty of much of the

countryside, but were inclined to ridicule Ireland's claim to have been, before the arrival of the English, a "grand seat of learning." The "degraded people" of this "starving land could not organize their own survival," one prominent visitor dismissively observed. Thus, English advocates of legislative union insisted that such a union was essential if the Irish were ever to be rescued from primitiveness, ignorance, superstition, and slavish respect for a "despotic and intolerant" Catholic Church.[3]

Irish unionists were more impressed with the arrangement's material as opposed to its supposed ethereal benefits. Early in the eighteenth century, Irish parliamentary enthusiasm for a union not unlike that negotiated with England by the Scots had been rooted in a similar commercial ambition – free access to a large mainland and expanding imperial market. Chilled by English indifference, the Irish subsequently experienced a warm glow of self-confidence generated by refreshingly robust domestic economic growth. This helped foster a Protestant Irish patriotism, if not nationalism, that presented unexpected obstacles when English interest in the constitutional integration of the western kingdom was awakened. Protestant patriots no less than antiquarians drew strength not only from a natural and national resentment of commercial ill-treatment at the hands of Britain but also from English notions of Irish inferiority. Yet many Protestant critics of the relationship with Britain remained both scornful and fearful of their far more numerous Catholic countrymen. They identified civilization with Protestantism, accepted Protestant superiority as an article of faith, and sought greater independence for an exclusively Protestant parliament in order better to defend their liberty and property. They conceived of Ireland as a separate kingdom, not a separate nation. A vulnerable minority in their own land, they felt more secure as part of the larger British Protestant majority. Nevertheless, at a time of peculiar imperial stress, the people of Ulster in particular were exposed to "extreme anti-government propaganda," which included attacks on the concept of British rule in Ireland. Facing the loss of the American colonies, the British government made concessions to Ireland's limited nationalists in 1782. Sixteen years later, the alliance of radical and dissident United Irishmen, many of them Protestants, with France and the enlistment of violently anti-English and anti-Protestant Catholic 'Defenders' in the army of rebellion concentrated minds as never before on the constitutional relationship.[4]

The union with Scotland had seemingly simplified the means by which England controlled the northern kingdom, and this illusion encouraged a belief that the same strategy would work on Britain's exposed western flank. In 1707, mollified by concessions, leading Scottish opponents of union made little effort to exploit the popular hostility it aroused. After all, the Act of Union did not legislate a genuinely unitary British state. Great Britain embraced three historic nations, three different languages, a multiplicity of mutually unintelligible dialects, and multiple cultures. The British Parliament, when it found time to legislate for a Scotland whose representation in both houses was small, did so separately and not always coherently. The northern kingdom continued to be governed "almost as a separate polity" by its landed elite and had "a civil society which was largely self-governed." Distinctive institutions remained in place, not least a different national church, which was Presbyterian, not Anglican; a different system of education; and a distinct legal code, which was Roman, not case law, in its acknowledged ancestry. Yet legal uniformity and religious unity had long been regarded as indispensable for political cohesion. Henry VIII had been careful in the much earlier union with Wales to extend English law and administration into the principality while seeking to throttle the Welsh language, and he had endeavoured to destroy the Irish language by banning its use. His second daughter, Elizabeth, had drifted off this linguistic course by authorizing the translation of the Bible into Welsh and donating the font necessary for the printing of an Irish Bible. Although a partial translation was published in 1603 and the Anglican Church of Ireland decided in 1634 to permit parts of divine service to be performed in Irish, many Irish Protestants scorned the vernacular as the "barbarous language of a backward people." Less than twenty years later, in response to the Protestant challenge, the Catholic Church made knowledge of Irish a requirement for priests coming to three of the provinces. Leinster was excepted.[5]

Great Britain survived the early disillusionment of Scottish unionists, discouraged by economic difficulties, and Jacobite rebellions. By the time union with Ireland was under serious consideration, that with the northern kingdom was being paraded as a triumph of far-sighted statesmanship and hailed as "perfect, absolute and irrevocable." Scotland's agriculture was undergoing modernization, her finances were stable, while industrial and urban development was rapidly progressing, as was anglicization. A "sense of Britishness" appeared to be growing among two peoples who shared a common if distinctive Protestantism, were united in a life or death struggle with France, and experienced a swelling pride in, and extracted a mounting profit from, the vastly enlarged empire. Consequently, promoters of union with Ireland fell prey to the seductive notion that history was on their side. However, they ought to have given more thought to the length of time it had taken to transform the Scots, in English minds, from a "lazy, improvident, ignorant, semi-barbarous, lawless, disorderly, seditious, hopelessly miserable, incurably disaffected" tribe into "industrious, thrifty, intelligent, self-reliant, persevering, law-loving and law abiding [subjects], devotedly loyal to the Throne and the Constitution." This sterling reputation owed much to selective amnesia. Neither radical conspiracy and violence nor labour militancy was unknown to the North Britons. More to the point, enthusiasts of the larger union who cited the Scottish experience to illustrate the certainty of Irish cultural accommodation and political assimilation overlooked the Scots' tendency to offset Britishness with a cultivated national distinctiveness rooted in the "myth-history and heritage (of a Highland 'Celtic Race')." Equally, they glossed over the awkward and obvious differences between the experiences of the two countries. In Scotland, the land had not been thrice confiscated as a result of devastating civil wars; a colony of English invaders had not usurped dominion of almost the whole country; a dominant native landed elite was committed to economic growth as a national objective; there existed in abundance the resources required for industrial development and the resultant diversified economy was no mere colony of England's; an alien church that seized all ecclesiastical property and maintained itself as a garrison of the English interest through the tithe system had not been forced on the Scots as the Establishment; and the people, or by far the greater proportion of them, had not been subjected to a religious discrimination more or less systematic. In Ireland, the penal laws enacted by the protestant Parliament at the turn of the eighteenth century, following the defeat and exile of James II, had "asserted by implication that the Catholic religion was inimical to the institutional, intellectual and social norms of English culture." The laws may not have been the "unhuman tyranny – the blackest known to history," as described in the textbooks issued to Irish Catholic children two centuries later, but they did foster an "undercurrent of sullen Catholic resentment, and swaggering, if insecure, Protestant imperiousness." The Catholic Irish evidently had more to forget, if not forgive, if following the union they were ever to consider themselves West Britons. Assimilation would necessarily be a lengthy if not tortuous process, one that demanded a loss of historic memory and the soothing of well-developed national antipathies.[6]

The formidable – even daunting – problems of integration were in no way eased by the surging nationalism of the era. An already well-developed sense of national identity on the part of the English had deepened in intensity during the course of the eighteenth century. A smug belief in the superiority of their form of government was merely one manifestation of it, and it was a British government that they controlled through an overwhelming national dominance of both houses of Parliament. The English were a chosen people, they believed, hence their "overriding loyalty to one, British state" fell far short of full acceptance of a common British identity. They rarely described themselves as Britons, while Scottish immigration simply sharpened the edges of an "Englishness" that found expression in "Scottophobia." If English arrogance and ill-disguised national contempt were deeply resented by the Scots and the Welsh, their derision of the Irish had always been more vocal and vitriolic. The reactive anger it aroused contributed to the Irish Protestant nationalism and Presbyterian radicalism that were given further fillips by the American and French revolutions. The dissidents found allies among the Catholic middle classes, whose sense of "alienation and victimhood" was nourished by sectarian discrimination.[7]

The United Irishmen hoped to create "the common name of Irishman in the place of the denominations of Protestant, Catholic and Dissenter" and saw in national unity the stepping stone to national independence. Although they failed to achieve the "popular imagined" community expressed in their name, and their rebellion was scarred by sectarian atrocities and a brutal suppression, they succeeded not only in eroding "the Catholics' traditional deference" to authority but also in persuading them that "the entire structure of government" was a fundamental grievance. Moreover, the concept of the nation as "a willed political union of fellow-feeling and culturally similar 'citizens'" survived. There was widespread resistance in Europe to French imperialism, and in Latin America a mounting challenge to colonial rule, while the struggle of the Greeks against the Ottoman Empire was soon to prove an even more romantic source of inspiration. Robert Peel, in 1815 a precocious politician marked for advancement, observed "that Ireland is a country separated by nature from that to which she is united by law; a country having once had an independent existence – having within twenty years had an independent legislature – having still her separate courts of justice, and distinct departments of executive government." The Irish Executive was a graphic and grandiose reminder of Ireland's anomalous position within the United Kingdom, as was her retention of a Privy Council, her own legal structure, and for several years her own chancellor of the Exchequer and Treasury. Day-to-day administration was supervised by more than a score of departments employing a legion of public servants. Preserving as it did so much of the historic Irish nation, thus duplicating in this sense the earlier arrangement with Scotland, the Union was perpetuating institutions that might ultimately be its undoing. Lording it over this territory was a viceroy whose office dated back seven centuries and whose full title, "Lieutenant General and Governor General of that part of the United Kingdom called Ireland," suggested the degree of imagined unity. However, his chief secretary was steadily emerging from the shadows of viceregal pomp into the sunlight of far greater circumstance. It was he who supervised the large Irish administration and journeyed to London for the parliamentary year to pilot legislation through the Commons and help formulate as well as defend policy.[8]

British ministers failed to heed the advice of observers who identified British ignorance of Ireland as a grave danger to the United Kingdom. If Ireland was "less than equally treated," Thomas Newenham wrote in *A View of the Natural, Political, and Commercial Circumstances of Ireland* (1809), "then 'the union will surely be regarded, by all reflective and unbiased men, as a vain, illusive, nugatory, and even mischievous measure.'" Three years later, in his monumental *An Account of Ireland Statistical and Political,* Edward Wakefield warned that so long as Ireland was administered like some "distant province," national spirit, jealousy, and prejudice would thrive there. But the Irish did not enjoy the effective self-administration exercised by the North Britons, for the Englishmen who invariably headed the Executive tended to view Ireland more as an imperial possession than as an integral region of the United Kingdom. Her history had been one of invasion, settlement, and a form of colonial rule. Even the progress towards greater legislative autonomy during the American Revolutionary War had stalled well short of parliamentary independence. After 1782 Ireland continued to be a separate kingdom only in name. The legislature remained under the control of the viceroy, who received his instructions from London, and the first of these orders was to maintain Ireland as "a subordinate part of the imperial system." As for the Union, it was designed, in the words of its author, the Younger Pitt, "to integrate Ireland more closely and firmly within the empire." This mindset reflected a period of dramatic overseas expansion that had both altered the concept of empire and inculcated in the British an even more powerful sense of their destiny as civilizers. Of the three most influential early occupants of the chief secretary's chair, the single Irishman belonged to a family that had earned fame and garnered a fortune in India, while the other pair were transferred to Dublin directly from the Colonial Office. Ireland could not be governed, they assumed, in the same manner and on the same principles as England. "The circumstances of the two countries were extremely different," one of them later reminded the House of Commons, and "if gentlemen imagined that what was the rule in England, could be uniformly applied to Ireland, or that the difference of the habits and situation of the people did not require a separate mode of concluding the affairs of each, they would grievously err." Yet her significant representation in the 'Imperial' Parliament, along with the fact that in domestic matters the home secretary's writ formally extended to Ireland, meant that Ireland could not be treated as another colony. This recognition of Irish exceptionalism left unanswered a question: How was it to be acknowledged "within the parameters and culture of the Union"? Eventually, William Gladstone was to talk of governing Ireland according to Irish ideas, but this implied pluralistic concept of the United Kingdom was not one espoused by ministers earlier in the century.[9]

Religion further bedevilled the relationship, central as it was to the identity of Britons and Irishmen. England, Wales, and Scotland shared a common Protestantism, however distinctive their respective versions of the reformed faith and the persistence of sectarian tensions. They were at least united in hostility towards the papacy and Catholicism. But the great majority of the people of Ireland remained true to Rome and considered Protestantism "a cultural import, legitimising conquest, dispossession and discrimination." After all, it had in the seventeenth century rejected Gaelic ways. Catholicism, on the other hand, in compromising with those ways, created a powerful and enduring image – the "organic unity" of Gaelic past and Catholicism. Texts in wide circulation long before their publication in the nineteenth century identified Roman Catholicism as Ireland's "ancestral religion." This Catholic faithfulness was interpreted by British Protestants as further evidence of Irish obduracy, primitiveness, and disinclination to assimilate. Consequently, the decision to unite in the articles of union the Church of England with that of Ireland's small Protestant Ascendancy was a fateful if not fatal one, for it placed at the heart of the new state the anomaly of a church establishment that was anathema to most of its Irish citizens. Equally embarrassing, and yet another formidable obstacle to Irish assimilation, was Britain's virulent and popular anti-Catholicism. Having helped launch the good ship Great Britain in 1707, Protestantism now threatened to be the reef on which the United Kingdom foundered. Had not another page in the sad saga of Irish sectarianism been written in blood in 1798, while a less gory but chronic religious antagonism heightened the tension that customarily existed between owners and occupiers of the land? Ireland stood as an exception to the rule of other countries where "the church establishment followed the creed of the population," the prime minister acknowledged. There, "the church and property" were on one side and the great mass of the people on the other. Would sectarian animosity overwhelm social deference in the Irish countryside? This was an unnerving question for isolated and predominantly Protestant Irish landlords confronted by recurrent outbreaks of agrarian violence and the emergence of a class of "underground gentry" who claimed descent from the old, dispossessed Catholic proprietors.[10]

Merited or not, Ireland had a dark reputation for exceptional and brutal lawlessness. Much of it was the work of agrarian secret societies largely unknown in Britain. Sympathetic observers who denied that the Irish were either incurably bad or vicious were frequently contradicted by sensational press reports of "intemperate and savage behaviour." Others admitted the violence but attributed it to the island's exceptional poverty and resultant human misery. Great social and political evils go far to explain Irish conduct and would produce their form of barbarism even among the most cultivated people in the world, one commentator wrote. Theirs was a "civilized barbarity," he added ironically. The widely recognized general causes of unrest were present in Ireland to a singular degree – economic pressure of want, social and political aspirations, and religious differences. Of course, the Younger Pitt had given an assurance that union would ameliorate if not solve these problems.[11]

The American rebellion had served as a painful reminder to the British of the limits of their hegemony over "outlying provinces" – hence the nervousness with which ministers regarded expressions of a

Protestant Irish desire for greater political autonomy. A concern to "add to the strength and power of the empire" by enhancing national security inevitably turned Pitt's attention to Ireland. Her long coastline, exposed ports, good roads, and disturbed society made her an inviting and vulnerable target of the enemy. The "internal treason" of 1798 had merely "ingrafted [French] jacobinism on those diseases which necessarily grew out of the state and condition of Ireland," he argued. She needed to be rescued from "great and deplorable evils" rooted "in the situation of the country itself – in the present character, manners and habits of its inhabitants – in their want of intelligence, or, in other words, their ignorance – in the unavoidable separation between certain classes – in the state of property – in its religious distinctions – in the rancour which bigotry engenders and superstition rears and cherishes." Here was an analysis at once eloquent and supercilious, founded as it evidently was on the traditional national conceit that only English values could redeem the Catholic Irish from their barbarism. Echoing Adam Smith in *The Wealth of Nations*, Pitt promised that closer "connection and intercourse with Great Britain" through the agency of an "impartial legislature" would be the means of channelling to Ireland, as earlier to Scotland, the English capital investment needed to spur economic development. An increase in Irish national wealth, an infusion of "English manners and industry," the cultivation of those middle classes who united "the highest and lowest orders of the community without a chasm in any part of the system," would so "improve the temper and manners, as well as the understanding of the people of Ireland," that "barbarism and ignorance" would be eradicated and "internal tranquillity" reign. In a sentence, the way to make the empire "more powerful and secure" was to make "Ireland more free and more happy."[12]

Like many another prenuptial pledge of marital bliss, this one did not long survive the wedding breakfast. Few eyebrows ought not to have been raised in surprise, given the numerous Irish witnesses to the union who spoke out against it and were therefore under no moral obligation forever to hold their peace. The Dublin Corporation declared its opposition, as did municipal trade organizations, an assembly of merchants and bankers, county gatherings of freeholders and freemen, "and twenty-five counties and eighteen corporate and commercial interests." Members of the legal professions were conspicuous and industrious naysayers. In Dublin's reduction from capital to provincial centre they saw the loss of wealthy clients, profitable briefs, and social status. They founded the *Anti-Union* newspaper, which was allowed to lapse but was successfully revived as The *Constitution; or Anti-Union Evening Post*. They wrote many of the widely circulated pamphlets disputing the legitimacy of the Union. The Irish Parliament lacked the competency and constitutional right to vote itself out of existence, they charged, and its compliance had been corruptly purchased by the government. Thus "a popular refusal to accept the act would be justifiable and legal." More surprising was the opposition of a body of Roman Catholics to the abolition of an exclusively Protestant national legislature. Pitt responded by skilfully angling for the support of leading Roman Catholics with the bait of speedy emancipation from religious discrimination. He expressed a desire to liberate the Irish from "the blind zeal and phrenzy of religious prejudices," mused on the need to relieve the Roman Catholic lower orders "from the pressure of tithes," and spoke of eventually making "effectual and adequate provision" for their clergy. Hearing in such remarks an implied promise of religious equality and fearful of a revolutionary France, which they associated with irreligion, a conservative Catholic hierarchy and the Catholic gentry signed on to union. They did so without any great display of enthusiasm for fear of widening the breach within the ranks of their own denomination and jeopardizing the government's campaign to convince Protestants that union would ensure their security. But Pitt's talk of Catholic emancipation was as tactical as it was principled. He was keen to raise more troops in Ireland. Intellectually, he may have understood that emancipation was both desirable and an important instrument of Irish integration into the United Kingdom, yet his personal commitment proved less than absolute. This Henry Grattan recognized. The patriot statesman reminded his countrymen that relief was only to be introduced "when the conduct of the Catholics shall be such as to make it safe for the government to admit them to the participation of the privileges granted to those of the established religion, and when the temper of the times shall be favourable to such a measure." If the elasticity of these conditions permitted British politicians, in deference to a monarch of precarious mental health who saw in union the means of slamming the door on additional concessions to his Roman Catholic subjects, to defer emancipation with an easy conscience, their inaction perpetuated the "sectarian character of Irish political life" and convinced a great many Irishmen that the Union was founded on a deception.[13]

Irish Catholic disillusionment proved a less immediate threat to the Union than its association with economic hardship. Important sectors of Britain's more developed economy were soon struggling with the consequences of Bonaparte's Continental System and an American trade embargo. The resultant misery was worsened by a rash of bank failures and a poor harvest that drove up the price of food even as artisans were put on short time or thrown out of work. Ireland experienced similar difficulties, and the painful and stark contrast between current hard times and the last few golden years of the Irish Parliament was fresh meat for the anti-unionist grinder. An arrangement that "was to have given freedom to the Catholic, and extension to our commerce," had produced neither benefit, the *Dublin Evening Post* complained bitterly. Instead, "our artisans are existing on public charity; our manufacturers and shopkeepers are bankrupt; our exports consist of more than two millions sterling [in the form of rents] to absentees; [and] our imports are principally of that very raw material manufactured by English hands." Ireland had been injured, insulted, and reduced to a form of "colonial servitude." This inflammatory accusation again distinguished Ireland from Scotland, for on the eve of the earlier union Scots had believed their economy to be contracting, not expanding.[14]

Irish industries had retained a substantial, if temporary, measure of protection against British competition, while the prospects of industrial expansion and economic diversification had been far less rosy before 1800 than the Union's critics now alleged. Ireland lacked readily utilizable sources of power, and her rapidly swelling population produced no correspondingly sharp expansion of the domestic market for manufactures. All too many of her people were trapped in the ranks of the rural and subsistence poor. Yet fundamental weaknesses had been temporarily masked by wartime prosperity. Heavy British demand for Irish foodstuffs, which prompted a huge increase in grain exports, combined with inflation and a succession of inferior harvests, had driven up prices. The lion's share of profits were harvested by the large landowners at the top of the social hierarchy, but the girth of its middle was fattened with affluence as substantial farmers joined professionals and successful merchants. Unfortunately, they were not the piers of that bridge Pitt had wished to see constructed over the chasm separating wealth from poverty. Many farmers grasped the easy profits made from the subdivision and subletting of land they held on long leases. By this broadening of the rural subsistence stratum, they were further distorting the island's social structure. Then, at the beginning of the second decade of the new century, came the sudden and sharp deterioration in the economy that excited unflattering comparisons with its performance during the final months of the Irish Parliament. Critics demanded repeal of the "accursed union." In the midst of the deadly struggle against Napoleonic France, they found themselves accused of disloyalty if not treachery. To this they made an ominous rejoinder: "We never received a particle of power or privilege from the gen-erosity, nothing whatever from the liberality of England." All concessions had been "wrung from her capitulating fears" at times of external danger. Britain's emergencies were Ireland's opportunities.[15]

Discreet public loans to industries in difficulty, the exertion of subtle but persistent pressure on the discontented, and the unwillingness of disgruntled Protestants to campaign more aggressively at a time of constitutional uncertainty (there had been another collapse of the monarch's health and preparations were being made for a regency) saw the Union weather this storm. Victory over France at last beckoned, and a native Irishman in the person of Arthur Wellesley was cast in the role of military hero while his Catholic fellow countrymen were conspicuous within the other ranks of his command. In Ireland, as elsewhere in the United Kingdom, there was a surge in patriotic British sentiment. Pride stirred by battlefield triumphs and the dramatic expansion of the empire – now the largest the world had ever seen, including more than forty colonies in five continents – briefly diverted attention from the problems inherent in the relationship with Britain. The hierarchy wrote to the Pope in praise of "glorious Britain." She had repulsed despotism and given back "peace to the world at large" by expanding her "immense resources, and the blood of her population," sending forth "invincible armies of which brave Irish Catholic legions formed a part." The "measure of Catholic gratitude, due to such an Empire, is no other than that, which may be claimed upon mankind by the *deliverers of the human race*," the prelates concluded. Unfortunately, victory, however glorious, had proven extraordinarily expensive. War's end found Ireland virtually bankrupt. Although her contribution to the expenses of the United Kingdom had in 1800 been calculated with considerable care and a concern for equity, the long conflict with France had resulted in her over-taxation. The accelerating pace of expenditures had obliged the Irish Exchequer to borrow heavily, and the quadrupling of the debt in little more than a decade meant that by the time Napoleon was banished to St Helena all but a fraction of annual revenues were being applied to its servicing. Here was another crisis to nourish the Irish belief that, with union, their interests had been subordinated and even sacrificed to those of Great Britain. The corrosive conviction that Ireland was being exploited like a colony, not treated as an equal, threatened any evolving all-embracing British civic nationalism.[16]

The imminence of peace had inspired measures intended to cushion its economic blows. The Irish Executive vetoed a proposal of the Board of Trade to remove the duty on foreign linens, one native industry showing strong potential for growth. Irish members of Parliament lobbied vigorously for the protection of their country's substantial share of Britain's cereals market and ridiculed Adam Smith's "vain philosophy" that corn ought to be purchased wherever it could be obtained at the cheapest price. They expected Ireland to be a principal beneficiary of the new, highly protectionist Corn Laws. Did she not possess "incalculable" advantages, in the form of fertile soil and cheap labour? Her legions of small farmers were subsequently conceded a major share of the British market for butter, and the heavily laden vessels clearing Irish ports for Britain were cited as visible proof of economic success. The consolidation of the two Exchequers in 1817, together with debts and revenues, promised to lighten the crushing burden of debt under which Ireland was staggering. Nonetheless, as the Irish quickly realized, they were running faster but on the same spot. The boom in agricultural exports barely compensated Ireland for a sharp postwar decline in prices. Moreover, whenever Britain's far larger economy caught a chill, hers almost immediately required intensive care. Many Irish industries were exhibiting telltale signs of infirmity, and the relatively healthy agricultural sector was unable to reinvigorate an economy in desperate need of diversification. Instead, the very policies working to the farmers' benefit simply compounded the problem of an excessive dependence on the land at a time of a rapidly expanding population.[17]

Recurrent food shortages and grinding poverty lent a certain plausibility to the dismal analyses of Ireland's predicament and prospects inspired by Thomas Malthus. Ireland had too many mouths to feed. Modest experiments with state-assisted emigration, as a means of easing the perceived population pressure on provisions, ran afoul of demands for postwar retrenchment and were further discouraged by sectarian concerns. Ministers had no desire to facilitate the departure of the Protestants they credited with holding Ireland "fast to the British connexion." Another response to the suffering was private philanthropy. Subscriptions were launched in Britain to alleviate acute – as distinct from chronic – Irish distress, motivated in part by a hope that such help would finally convince the Irish of the Union's benefits. "Read the extracts from the Irish papers, and then refuse or hesitate any longer if you can," a Welsh newspaper challenged its readers. Suffering was especially severe in 1817 and 1822 following partial failures of the potato crop, on which the multiplying rural poor were dangerously dependent, drawing attention to Ireland's lack of a poor law safety net. Should private charity ever prove insufficient, one chief secretary had earlier warned,"it must be for consideration whether Government shall advance money for the maintenance of the Poor."[18]

State intervention violated the new mantra of political economy, but on occasion political pragmatism trumped economic fundamentalism. Ministers thought they detected a strange phenomenon in Ireland, one at odds with English experience. Disturbances appeared to be less common where distress was most acute. Evangelicals in the Cabinet were further constrained by the fear that state assistance to the needy impugned the "dispensations of Providence" by encouraging them to trust in an earthly power to free them from want and dependence. For their own good, the poor of Ireland, even more than those of Britain, needed to learn that self-help was the only sure way to escape chronic want. Was it not a well-established maxim that no government could "provide food for the whole population of any country"? The Christian's duty to succour the helpless was conditional on the availability of the means. On the other hand, the Union would surely be strengthened if on occasion the government was brought "into contact with the public through the medium of kind offices." From such a jumble of ideology, concerns, and commonplaces, Robert Peel during his term as chief secretary constructed a surprisingly coherent and enduring model for the delivery of public relief. The Executive would establish a central relief commission ostensibly free of sectarian bias (this effectively meant the inclusion of a Catholic or two) to assess the extent and depth of distress. Government aid would then be provided discreetly. There must be no discouragement of private giving or encouragement of the idea that Britain was "about to undertake the subsistence of Ireland." Public funds were first to be made available in the form of advances, not grants, and for the purpose of supplementing local subscriptions in those areas where landowners had shouldered their primary responsi-

bility to provide relief. However, wherever people were "actually starving" or were "without hope of relief from other quarters," considerations of "general policy and principle" were to be set aside and food
provided to them at public expense. Thus were provisions quietly
imported, duties on them suspended, seed potatoes and biscuit discreetly distributed, and supervisory agents despatched to areas that
lacked local gentry or local means. These agents were under orders to
provide relief as cheaply as possible, whether through soup kitchens or
the employment of the helpless poor on a wide and often imaginative
range of public works. To the extent that there was a guiding principle
of public assistance, it was that "the more employment and less gratu-
itous relief" given the better. In 1822 this system at least ensured there
was no repetition of the heavy death toll that had marked a pair of
earlier famines.[19]

The extraordinary lengths to which the state went to mask the
extent of its involvement in relief subverted the objective of bringing
it into contact with the people through "the medium of kind offices."
Instead, the premature and precipitate termination of its operations,
often at the cost of much suffering, and the chilling rhetoric of political economy created a popular impression of hard-heartedness.
Henry Goulburn ruefully observed as chief secretary that he was supposed to be "the most inhuman and unfeeling of men" because he
declined to give public assurances that the Irish administration would
"feed all the people." The assistance doled out was deliberately
miserly, and the release in 1823 of a parliamentary report on the condition of the Irish poor prompted an incredulous British newspaper
to calculate that in County Clare twenty-six thousand persons had
been supported at the per capita rate of slightly less than a penny a
day. A witness giving testimony to a committee investigating the
plight of Irish farm labourers likened their condition unfavourably to
that of West Indian slaves. What was needed in Ireland was work for
her people, the committee concluded. It would improve their moral
condition and by promoting peace and tranquility advance the
general interest of the United Kingdom.[20]

Peace and tranquility were widely regarded as rare commodities in
Ireland. They were as scarce, or so it seemed to many contemporaries,
as readily exploitable sources of industrial power that might alleviate
social tensions by providing abundant employment off the land. Disturbances appeared to be a permanent feature of rural life. Secret societies such as the Ribbonmen, often given the generic name of White-

boys, were active, spawned by traditional grievances, such as excessive taxation, the tithe exacted by clergy of an alien church, sectarian injustice suffered at the hands of Protestant magistrates, and disputes over access to land. Within these societies lay a larger ambition, the protection of a peasant economy from "the pressures of capitalistic agriculture." Members brutally resisted the consolidation of holdings and the conversion of tillage to pasturage. If the objectives of most of these "marauders" were local and limited, they nevertheless "presented a direct challenge to the government and the primacy of the law" and signalled "the refusal of the suppressed to accept the legitimacy of the 'stranger.'" In short, on occasion they hinted at political subversion. The reports of endemic and savage agrarian violence in Ireland led the English to draw unflattering comparisons with Scotland. They contrasted a turbulent, ignorant, and disloyal Irish peasantry with "instructed and peaceable" Scots. While the latter were far from being paragons of passivity, northern eruptions occurred with less frequency and were less extensive and less ferocious than those across the Irish Sea. Moreover, there was a reassuring belief that in Scotland criminals rarely escaped punishment. This made a deep impression on those many Englishmen who considered the apprehension and punishment of lawbreakers a yardstick of civilization. Here, then, was another measurement against which the Irish came up short. In the words of one observer, "a system which consists in defying the laws is a systematic waging of war against the very element that binds men in society, it is a casting off of civilization, a return to a miserable dependence on animal strength alone, on brutish cunning, or midnight hiding in the dark."[21]

Richard Lalor Sheil was one political agitator who urged his fellow countrymen to be "sensible of the extent of the calamity which follows the indulgence of that disastrous predilection for tumult which characterizes the mass of the population." Was it any wonder, therefore, that a perception of the Irish as a peculiarly violence-prone people went far to shape the attitudes of so many of those Britons – and they were usually Englishmen – despatched to Dublin to govern the island. Robert Peel inveighed against the "wretched depravity and sanguinary disposition" of the Irish lower orders. They had, in his opinion, "'a natural predilection for outrage and a lawless life'" which he doubted anything could control. An "honest Englishman" knew about as much of the state of Ireland as he did of the state of "Kamchatka," and Peel thought it "really fit" that members of Parliament recognize the "difference between England and Ireland." In the same vein, his close friend and a successor in the office, Henry Goulburn, likened the island to the dark and primitive continent of Africa, while the prime minister under whom they both served, Lord Liverpool, wearily allowed that the Irish were a political phenomenon "not influenced by the same feelings as appear to affect mankind in other countries." Nor was this opinion the exclusive preserve of illiberal Tories of an unreformed age. The 1860s were to find the popular and smugly liberal *Daily Telegraph* describing the Irish as "much too fond of taking the law into their own hands, instead of waiting for the slow remedies provided by English jurisprudence. It is a bad habit," the newspaper commented, "for which centuries of misery afford no palliation." They were addicted to a lawlessness "utterly alien to English ideas," it concluded, much as Peel had done two generations earlier. Consequently, even administrators not given to exaggerating the political significance of agrarian "atrocities" suppressed their constitutional qualms and sponsored draconian countermeasures. Severity was absolutely necessary, Goulburn explained, "otherwise men would be taught to believe either that mere Whiteboyism ... is not a capital crime or that Government are afraid to punish with severity."[22]

The Tory Ministry led by Liverpool between 1812 and 1827 established three fundamentals for Ireland's better government – the suppression of lawlessness, the uprooting of the causes of evil, and the identification and correction of "the real grounds of complaint." Coercive legislation (first descriptively entitled the "insurrection act" but later reintroduced time and again in modified form with the more euphemistic heading of "peace preservation"), the suspension of *habeas corpus,* and a large military garrison were the state's initial weapons of choice in the battle against lawlessness. But frequent resort to the army to uphold civil power was an acute embarrassment to a nation proud of its liberal reputation. Therefore, successive Irish Executives progressively created a large armed police force. Robert Peel formed flying squadrons, but Goulburn eventually supplemented these with a national regular force of county constabularies, totalling four thousand men, who were able to call on the assistance of stipendiary magistrates in the event that local gentry failed to shoulder their law enforcement responsibilities. As a result, by the 1820s, there was "an efficient police in every county of Ireland." Only time would tell whether these new policemen could establish and maintain law and order.[23]

What of the causes of evil? The Executive quickly fastened on elements of the press, which the consciously propagandist United Irishmen had so skilfully exploited barely two decades earlier. They had reached both the illiterate and the poor who were unable to afford newspapers by staging public readings, often at chapel gates, a practice consistent with a Gaelic oral culture. If this fastening on the press as an instrument of subversion was another example of the politicians' inclination to blame the messenger, popular organs such as the *Dublin Evening Post* invited scrutiny. It repeatedly claimed to be the Irishman's only "one great and powerful engine of salvation left" and promised to speak his wrongs until justice was obtained. Chief Secretary William Wellesley-Pole, Wellington's brother, railed against such "villainy." He accused the press of the "most foul and personal abuse" and of the encouragement of "licentiousness and disaffection." His immediate successor, the precocious Robert Peel, was of a like mind. Even as Napoleon's empire crumbled, he persuaded himself that Irish journals were increasing their circulations by making out a case for the French enemy and writing down the United Kingdom's victories in battle. This was certainly true of Walter Cox's monthly *Irish Magazine*, yet the popularity of such journals said as much about patrons as it did about publishers. To counter this "malign influence," a "Castle press" was subsidized, yet its editors proved so indiscreet and inept that they quickly became less an asset than a liability. More successful were the Executive's efforts to disrupt or sabotage the distribution systems of the "factious prints." Another ploy was the harassment and intimidation of editors and publishers with prosecutions for seditious libel, but it was not one that could be resorted to indefinitely, given the costs in terms of time, cash, and political credit. A campaign against the muzzling of the press, led by radicals, who identified censorship with tyranny, was gaining popular momentum. Emboldened by an Executive in full retreat, a hostile and unrepentant press re-emerged to be welcomed as an ally by agitators such as Daniel O'Connell, who had noted the United Irishmen's use of newspapers as a tool of mass propaganda.[24]

The most constructive response to the Irish problem was to determine and remedy the "real grounds of complaint." Force had to be repelled by force, Robert Peel observed, "but the more we can soothe the better for the future at any rate." This spirit guided a series of measures entirely consistent with a conservative commitment to evolutionary change. The ambitious intent was to halt, if not reverse, Irish alienation. "We must modify and adapt our theories to the conditions of that national compact [the Union] which we cannot infringe," Peel announced. Elementary education held promise as a means of rescuing the Irish lower orders from ignorance while improving their character. Properly instructed, they would surely be less "easily misled" and better disciplined. In the opinion of the Executive, too many of the existing schools were controlled by the Catholic clergy and too many children were being taught by a "disloyal and bigoted set of men." The fact that these schools also charged fees, however modest, effectively excluded from schoolrooms the largest and most turbulent section of the population. Thus, the Kildare Place Society, founded in 1811 to establish schools divested of sectarian distinctions, was adapted to the administration's needs and provided with public funds. Here was an opportunity to promote national unity and the "value system of the state." Not that schools avowedly committed to "mixed" education were welcomed by a Catholic hierarchy that naturally preferred denominational education under its "complete controul." Nor were the bishops' suspicions of them as instruments of Protestant proselytism entirely unfounded. As Goulburn explained to his evangelical wife, "[I]f you educate the people of Ireland on Christian principles you work effectually for the overthrow of the Roman Catholic persuasion. It cannot stand against the light of the Gospel. If however you attempt directly to convert them you arouse every feeling of the parents against you and I am anxious therefore on all occasions to disclaim any proselytizing or direct attempt at conversion."[25]

The Tories tinkered with the justice system in an effort to mollify critics of its sectarianism. The state promised to "purify" the selection of sheriffs, monitor more closely the conduct of sub-sheriffs, remove incompetent and inert magistrates from the bench, and appoint more Irish Catholics to office. None of this stilled the criticism, for purification of the magistracy was conducted neither thoroughly nor consistently, while the promising innovation of petty sessions, to finesse the partisanship of individual justices of the peace, had not been made permanent. Equally, the pitiful number of Catholic officeholders remained a scandal. Meanwhile, difficulties in finding private prosecutors of the agrarian marauders, along with reliable jurors and witnesses willing to testify, brought a centralization of the forces of law as well as of those of order. Public prosecutions were instituted and quickly became the norm in Ireland, an innovation that again distinguished her from England. Crown solicitors were appointed to conduct cases before Assize courts, but decisions to prosecute rested with the attorney general in Dublin. A centralized system for the vetting of jurors was also put in place. If with these innovations the Executive was endeavouring "to ensure that arrest, trial and verdict under English law would be insulated, so far as possible, from the hostilities of Irish society," it was at the same time tying itself to prosecutions. Now, every failure of justice, every unpopular attempt to uphold law and order, would provide a reasonable excuse to attack the "English Government." In the eyes of the Irish, William Gladstone was later to admit, the law wore "a foreign garb."[26]

The most sectarian of Catholic fiscal grievances, the tithe, was also fiddled with, while the most sectarian of loyalist organizations, the Orange Order, which by its aggression during the 1790s had driven many Catholics into the arms of the United Irishmen and was then employed as an agent of "counter-subversion," was reluctantly suppressed. Unfortunately, the sore of Catholic emancipation continued to fester. Indeed, the Union's failure to generate the capital investment so necessary for the island's economic development was tied by some critics to Parliament's continuing refusal to grant Roman Catholics genuine civic equality. The sense of oppression common to Catholics, they argued, ignited the disturbances that paralysed "all exertions" and intimidated "English capitalists from embarking their money in Ireland." Seven centuries of misgovernment, Protestant tyranny, and Catholic enslavement were increasingly cited causes of the island's "'wretched, barbarous, anarchical, burthensome, and dangerous condition.'"[27]

The disabilities under which Irish Catholics lived and laboured had greatly increased as a result of their support of the hapless James II. The Protestant minority emerged from the "Glorious Revolution" grimly resolved to ensure its future security and political control by rendering the Catholic majority virtually powerless. The end of the seventeenth century saw the laying of the foundation stones of an Anglican Ascendancy, for Protestant Dissenters received scant reward for their considerable contribution to the Williamite victory. The fact that the Penal Laws were not rigorously enforced may have been a case of discretion being the better part of prejudice. In England, loose enforcement of penal legislation directed against the small and vulnerable Catholic community may have been a case of tolerance being the better part of a greater sense of security. But, as Edmund Burke informed a fellow member of Parliament who made much of the laws' lax

enforcement, connivance was "the relaxation of slavery, not the definition of liberty." Elements of Ireland's Catholic gentry managed to survive the restrictive and destructive measures governing land ownership
and leaseholds. A Catholic merchant class emerged thanks to the
opportunities still open in the world of commerce, while the Catholic
clergy continued to function and even expand its influence among a
laity that looked to their church rather than the state for leadership.
Indeed, the Catholic Church developed an elaborate and complex
national structure during the second half of the eighteenth century.
Episcopal succession was maintained with the collusion of the authorities. They recognized the need for disciplinary figures who commanded
the respect of the turbulent lower orders. Reforming clergy laid the
groundwork for the far-reaching changes of the following century, able
as they were, ironically, to operate with an independence rarely permitted to colleagues in countries where Catholicism was the established religion. With the passage of time, increasingly confident
Catholics sought removal of their secular disabilities. Ever more rest-
less in a state that was exclusively and oppressively Protestant, they
made considerable gains in this direction during the lengthy period of
turmoil that opened with the American colonial rebellion and culmi-
nated in the French Revolution.[28]

The progressive relaxation of the sectarian restrictions on landownership and the admission to Catholics to the bar further expanded the
middle classes. The establishment of a seminary at Maynooth, partially
funded by the state, amounted to a form of indirect recognition of the
Roman Catholic Church, while the admission of Catholic Irishmen to
the franchise on the same terms as it was exercised by Protestants had
far-reaching political consequences. The vote had been given to "the
poorest and most ignorant peasantry in the world," spluttered one outraged Tory, referring to the forty-shilling freeholders. The decision
threatened the Protestant Ascendancy, another charged. Predictably,
enfranchised freeholders increased sharply in number as landlords
endeavoured to bolster their personal political influence by multiplying
the electors seemingly at their beck and call. But enfranchisement fell
far short of emancipation. Catholics remained ineligible for certain distinctions and continued to be legally excluded from a number of senior
and important offices, including membership of Parliament. These disabilities were a measure of the suspicion and fear with which Ireland's
nervous Protestants regarded the fast multiplying and increasingly
politicized Roman Catholic majority. Commemorative sermons on the

annual anniversary of the rising of 1641 revealed "an essential continuity in the Protestants' fears about their vulnerability." Nor was this
simple paranoia. Recent events at home and abroad had seemingly
reawakened the "Anti-English, anti-Protestant and anti-authority
sentiments" of the Catholic community. The restraint exhibited by
Protestant patriots in pursuit of genuine legislative independence during the American Revolution had reflected their belief that the British
connection was vital to their personal security. Subsequently, persistent prodding from London had been required to cajole the Protestant Irish Parliament into permitting the enfranchisement of
Catholics and then their admission to the ranks of the militia.
William Pitt and his Cabinet colleagues were hoping in this way to
promote "Catholic loyalty to the state" and thus strengthen the
Anglo-Irish relationship, but the militia quickly became too Catholic
for Protestant peace of mind.[29]

The knowledge that the preponderance of parliamentary seats were
located in boroughs into which the freeholder franchise did not extend
had made it easier for the Irish Protestant Parliament to enfranchise
Catholics in 1793. Yet sectarian contempt for Roman Catholicism
infected several of the leaders of the United Irishmen, whose calls for
Irish national unity were more firmly rooted in political expediency
than in religious toleration. Certainly, a great many other Protestants
saw in the rebellion of 1798 a reprise of 1641 notwithstanding the initial heavy involvement of Ulster Presbyterians. Sir Richard Musgrave's
Memoirs of the Different Rebellions in Ireland (1801) served as a
sequel to Temple's account of the earlier rebellion, and both tragedies
were depicted as manifestations of "Popish bigotry." Musgrave
declared Protestantism "'the only bond of union between the two kingdoms'" and pronounced Ireland's Catholics peculiarly perfidious, with
a propensity for violence, rebellion, and hatred. They could never be
trusted. The major roles played in 1798 by a relatively small number
of priests – the conduct of several Presbyterian ministers and the extent
to which most Catholic shepherds had followed, not driven, their
flocks being conveniently overlooked – served only to reinforce mis-
conceptions of the extraordinary reach of priestly influence and deepen
convictions of clerical disloyalty. Robert Emmet's postscript rebellion
in 1803 was promptly distorted into another Catholic conspiracy, and
one of which the hierarchy had foreknowledge. Against this background of rebellion and sectarian enmity, resistance to further Catholic
relief stiffened. The Executive gave priority instead to the sensibilities

and interests of the loyal Protestants, and nervous Anglicans finally threw open the doors of the Ascendancy to fellow adherents of the reformed faith.[30]

Union further complicated the Irish problem to the extent that it created additional obstacles to Catholic emancipation. The Irish "were now governed 'by a state & people notoriously prejudiced'" against their religion and "'particularly hostile to Irish Catholics,'" Archbishop Troy, the most influential member of the hierarchy, commented in 1809. However, the restructuring of Irish parliamentary representation along largely county as opposed to borough lines, now that a reduced number of members sat in the Imperial Parliament, further enhanced the political influence of the overwhelmingly Catholic forty-shilling freeholders. Here was an electorate that the issue of emancipation might galvanize. In 1808 the Catholic clergy and laity definitively rejected a Crown veto over the appointment of Irish Catholic bishops as the price of relief. Provocatively, Daniel O'Connell ascribed the rejection to Irish hatred of England, but this imprudent declaration was ignored by those British advocates of emancipation who ridiculed demands for Protestant securities. Had not the rights to hold property and to vote already been conceded to Ireland's Catholics "without any security against their being turned to the destruction of the Establishment"? Were those liberal and rational concessions to be unmasked as merely a cynical reaction to foreign crises and ministerial difficulties? The Reverend Francis Wrangham in his assize sermon at York Minster in 1810 advanced another argument. To withhold emancipation was to dishonour the sacrifice of the many Catholic dead who had fallen fighting Bonaparte.[31]

Yet Roman Catholicism continued to be feared and despised, especially by those evangelical Protestants who identified "Papal superstition" as the source of Ireland's many evils. Such bitter resistance to emancipation often went beyond naked bigotry. Suspicion of the Catholics' allegiance to a "foreign earthly potentate" was constantly nourished by their refusal or inability to define its limits. Not that this concern carried much weight with those observers alive to the selectivity with which the Irish frequently followed papal instructions. Nevertheless, the chronically disturbed state of rural Ireland constantly replenished the well of doubt of Catholic loyalty and sharpened the perception that the Catholics were merely awaiting the opportunity to strike. Would the opening of the doors of Parliament to them jeopardize a constitution under which Britain's citizens had "so long enjoyed security and happiness"? Would Catholics as members of Parliament seek to influence the government of the state church? What was in question, Lord Liverpool declared in 1815, was "whether a Protestant dynasty, and a Protestant ecclesiastical establishment should be supported by a Protestant Parliament, and a Protestant Administration." Would concession not only undermine the Church Establishment but also confirm the supremacy in Ireland of a well disciplined and secretive Catholic clergy, for it was an article of Protestant faith that even "the first Roman Catholics" were little more than "puppets" of their priests? Would an emboldened and empowered hierarchy then demand the re-Establishment of their church? Similarly disconcerting was the prospect of Roman Catholics ceasing to be content merely with the right to sit in Parliament. Would they eventually demand a proportionate share both of the Irish representation and all offices, civil, military, and political? The great majority of Ireland's counties were dominated electorally by a Catholic interest in the person of the freeholder, and a number of Irish members of Parliament were already allowing this to shape their conduct. Some were plainly putting electoral discretion before Establishment valour. These Protestant bugbears helped account for the sensitivity of successive occupants of the chief secretary's chair to any Catholic agitation that manifested "a thorough contempt for the legitimate Government" by organizing a competitive and parallel administrative structure. It was illegal for any organization to assume a representative character, yet one Catholic committee seeking emancipation behaved in just such a manner. It set up for business within the very shadow of Dublin Castle, the headquarters of the Irish Executive, adopted procedures reminiscent of those of the House of Commons, and staged something approximating a country-wide election of delegates. The committee was suppressed, as was a successor Catholic board.[32]

Ireland's Protestants were struggling to defend their religion, their property, their existence, and the Union, many Britons believed. They were just as deeply convinced of the Irish Catholics' ambition to undo the constitutional arrangement. The popular *Dublin Evening Post* fed this suspicion. "The Catholic should feel that his Emancipation can only be attained through the 'Emancipation of his country,'" it proclaimed. In much the same spirit, an assertive generation of Catholic historians and writers continued the work of the earlier antiquarians, who had contrasted a golden age of ancient Irish civilization with contemporary "enslavement." Against this background, the Executive grimly resisted any compromise with the growing sentiment in the House of Commons in favour of emancipation. It did so in the knowledge of the popularity of this resolute stand in Britain. Robert Peel airily insisted that toleration of Catholicism while maintaining Anglicanism as the religion of the state was "more likely to preserve, inviolate, the union between the two countries – more likely to provide for the stability of the Protestant church establishment in Ireland – and to ensure harmony between Roman Catholic and Protestant inhabitants of the country." The dubious validity of all three propositions was eventually exposed by O'Connell.[33]

British opponents of emancipation had long been hamstrung by their inability to form a government committed to resistance. They were obliged to share power with sympathizers, if not supporters, of the cause – hence the adoption of a shabby expedient whereby individual ministers voted their consciences while the Cabinet avowed collective neutrality. The sorry figure the government cut on this important issue became more apparent still with the formation of a divided Irish Executive. The conservative, business-like, and evangelical Henry Goulburn was appointed chief secretary largely as a counterweight to a liberal and indolent viceroy, Richard Wellesley. With characteristic hyperbole, Daniel O'Connell hailed the latter as the "harbinger" of emancipation and excoriated the former, more accurately, as its inveterate adversary. The appointment of Robert Peel as the home secretary to whom both men reported further complicated the situation. Tiring of the inevitable stalemate, O'Connell helped to found the Catholic Association, which quickly developed into a formidable and intimidating popular pressure group. He sought and received the cooperation of the hierarchy and the support of the priesthood. Catholic clergy naturally sympathized with the organization's principal objective and responded even more enthusiastically when O'Connell gave an assurance that a portion of its revenues would be reserved for the construction of manses, churches, and denominational schools and the funding of overseas missions. He was equally astute in his appeal to the masses. To secure their support, he persuaded them that they had much to gain from the seating of Catholic gentlemen in the House of Commons. The peasants' traditional grievances were placed on the association's agenda, and they were promised legal aid to fight evictions. This advocacy of their causes, together with the establishment of a special minuscule weekly subscription for associate members, brought huge numbers into the association and with them a swollen treasury from which to fund a sophisticated agitation. In this way O'Connell bound the lower orders more securely to the campaign for emancipation, though his task was simplified by their violently sectarian and anglophobic attitudes.[34]

Before long a nervous Executive was fretting over the Catholic Association's capacity to communicate directly through its agents with most regions of the country and thus direct "simultaneously to one object the great mass of the people." Accused of aping and assuming "the Authority of Parliament," the association was suppressed on the orders of the Cabinet. Not that ministers expected the intelligent and innovative O'Connell to be seriously inconvenienced or so easily silenced, which may explain their initial hesitation to act. A new association was announced and quickly began to behave much like its predecessor. "No country can be satisfactory to the Government in which a power exists stronger than that of the Government, independent of the Government, and in which that power can at any moment direct against the Government a mass of poor, ignorant, unemployed, and discontented population," an exasperated Goulburn grumbled in October 1826. He might also have given careful thought to what the existence of such a discontented mass revealed about Irish popular opinion.[35]

Almost two centuries earlier, in his influential history of Ireland, Geoffrey Keating had identified Catholicism as the heart and soul of Irishness. But the sectarianism on which Musgrave dwelt so selectively in his account of the United Irish rebellion dominated both sides of the religious divide. In 1798 loyalists and rebels had been united only in their identification of the other in nakedly sectarian terms, and atrocity begat atrocity. Before long, "Catholics sought to forget and were even ready to distort or deny the sectarian excesses of their forbears in 1798." Walter Cox's "very influential" *Irish Magazine,* which spoke to and aspired to speak for the lower orders of society and was read publicly to the illiterate, assailed the "whimsical and wicked" notions of religion that the English would impose upon the Irish. Cox ridiculed their "Irish Crusade" for the "extirpation of Popery and Pike making," singling out Methodism for its "beastly enthusiasm and persecuting character" and warning that this "modern spirit of Puritanism" would, unless checked, do "much injury to Ireland, particularly to Catholics, as could be expected from the hands of the most vandal invader." He stood Musgrave on his head, declaring that in 1798 "every species of cruelty, oppression, and tyranny, were inflicted, throughout the unhappy land, upon the Roman Catholic inhabitants." Orange murderers had driven "Irishmen to America to enjoy a liberty and abundance unknown to any other nation," while those who remained at home had been compelled to form Ribbon societies to defend themselves, their houses, and their families. "We say that it is a first principle in law, in social order, to resist oppression," the *Irish Magazine* informed readers and listeners, "and we further say, when it is notorious that none of the public money is applied to stop orange depredations, the terms on which society are formed become dissolved, as no man will bear with murder, or the whimsical nonsense, that he ought to submit to the murderers, rather than violate the law."[36]

Cox waged an unrelenting campaign against the "oppressor." He charged English ministers, "acting on the laid-down principle of hatred" that their countrymen bore the Catholic Irish, with endeavouring to deprive the latter of "every remnant of independence." Tyranny, treason, or fraud had seen the Irish robbed of the "memorials" of their "intrepid and pious ancestors" and condemned to a personal wretchedness and degradation worse even than that of the Russian peasantry. Ireland had been sacrificed not to English "cruelty and ambition alone, but to jealousy and avarice." Furthermore, the English "passion for domination" ensured that persecution disavowed under "the apprehension of danger" would be resumed whenever it could be "prosecuted with impunity." Ireland's millions were begging for "repose, protection and deliverance, from a savage penal code, at the Bar of a *strange* senate," and thus the Union "*must be repealed.*" But anxious to demonstrate that Irish Catholics were not being "led by the nose by their clergy," Cox excoriated prelates and priests willing to accept a British government veto of episcopal appointments in exchange for Catholic emancipation. Those who would surrender to the British the independence of the Irish branch of the Catholic Church were public enemies who endangered Catholic unity. The *Irish Magazine* was equally harsh in its condemnation of the priesthood's inability to function in Irish, which Keating had named another indelible mark of Irishness. All too many parish priests could only hear confessions and administer the sacraments in English or Latin, yet Methodist missionaries were "preaching heterodox doctrine in the language of the country to the catholics of Ireland." Nor was there any likelihood of the seminary at Maynooth reversing this trend. "Is it to be imagined that the Irish language can be had by inspiration? Is it to be supposed that two or three lectures a year, can qualify to preach and teach in it," Cox asked.[37]

A "shared belief in Protestant oppression and its impending destruction" as predicted in the so-called Pastorini prophecy "reduced the sharpness" of Catholic class antagonism during the early 1820s. Distributed in penny handbills or broadsheets throughout the countryside, repeated orally by schoolmasters and peddlers, the promise of Protestantism's imminent doom was, in the opinion of senior police officers, widely known and believed, at least by the Catholic "lower orders." The result was a wave of rural violence more serious than any since the rebellion, which targeted Protestant churches, gentry and the military. Following a tour of southern Ireland during the waning days of this Rockite eruption, named for its mythical leader, Tom Moore published a "remarkable prose satire," the *Memoirs of Captain Rock* (1824). The work had as its premise the existence of a "trans-generational principle of misrule and consequent reactive violence at the heart of Irish history," and one by-product of this was a "traumatic tradition of peasant remembrance." Certainly, contemporary songs, street ballads, and poems in both Irish and English suggested an Irish poor who, deeply infected with racial and sectarian hatred of the Saxons and heretics, wished to expel "the foreigners and free Ireland." The hopes expressed in these forms of popular culture reflected the fact that "the audience for political songs in Irish now consisted almost entirely of the rural poor, whose survival was tied to the level of rents and tithes." They continued to perceive of their enemies in "sectarian even more than class terms," while their own identity was "articulated more and more through a resurgent Catholicism." In short, the popular memory of 1798 had not faded and it "combined lamentation for defeat" with a bloodthirsty "quest for vengeance."[38]

As Rockite violence subsided on the very eve of the date named for the fulfilment of the prophecy, so the agitation for Catholic emancipation gathered momentum and recruits. Daniel O'Connell was surprisingly slow to exploit the freeholder electorate as an instrument of political pressure. Instead, in 1825 he agreed to trade it away in return for a relief bill. He had every reason for acute embarrassment, therefore, when with this and another concessionary "wing" emancipation still failed to get off the ground. The following year several of his colleagues organized a freeholder political revolt that inflicted a handful of stunning electoral defeats on the landlord interest. Here was proof that the people had finally been taught to know their rights, one of the New Catholic Association's leading lights excitedly concluded. O'Connell required no further prompting. The New Year of 1828 found him charging to the fore. He engaged in an intimidating flexing of popular muscle by staging simultaneous meetings in a multitude of Ireland's Catholic parishes. Equally important, membership dues were pouring into his coffers. Flush with cash and confidence, he committed the association to oppose the return to Parliament of any supporter of the government now headed by the Duke of Wellington. O'Connell justified the decision by pointing to the long-standing opposition to emancipation professed by the prime minister and several senior members of his Cabinet. Prominent among them were Peel at the Home Office and Goulburn at the Exchequer. However, the Iron Duke exhibited unexpected flexibility by naming the liberal Marquis of Anglesey as Irish viceroy and endorsing repeal of the legislation that formally discriminated against Protestant Dissenters. This retreat established "a clear precedent for alterations to the Constitution in the interests of religious toleration." Nevertheless, Wellington's promotion of fellow Irishman Vesey Fitzgerald to the Cabinet, necessitating his re-election for County Clare, saw O'Connell contest the seat even though the new minister was a long-time supporter of Catholic emancipation. The Catholic leader's dramatic victory at the polls obliged Wellington, who had planned only to advance stealthily towards the concession, to launch a cavalry charge.[39]

The opening of the doors of Parliament to Catholics did not usher in that era of Anglo-Irish harmony predicted by overly optimistic liberal Protestants. "The thunder-cloud, whose pressure took away our breath, is gone," an ecstatic *Edinburgh Review* mistakenly announced, for the popular Protestant world view had not undergone a dramatic modification. This tens of thousands of Britons signalled by putting their names to petitions opposing emancipation. O'Connell's anglophobic rhetoric, meanwhile, was continuing to anger even his English fellow religionists. His aggressiveness and assertiveness attracted the backing of only a small faction led by the most intransigent vicar apostolic, who happened to be the English agent of the Irish hierarchy. A larger party of English Catholics, more conciliatory in their response to Protestant concerns and seeking the limited end of the removal of the remaining disabilities, as distinct from O'Connell's lengthy list of grievances, allowed the conduct of the Irish to aggravate the ethnic distaste with which they already viewed them. They had received, or so English Catholics muttered, too little Irish recognition and credit for undertaking the heavy intellectual spadework of educating British opinion in the political wisdom of emancipation. Among those so educated were liberal Protestants, but they now went to considerable lengths to deny any respect for Catholicism, resurrecting the hoary charge that it contributed "to the backwardness and barbarism of Ireland." Debasing superstition, childish ceremonies, and "profound submission to the priesthood," they declared, would ever prevent Ireland "from becoming as free, as powerful, and as rich as the sister kingdom."[40]

The charge so often on the lips of emancipation's opponents, that Roman Catholic priests controlled far more than the spiritual lives of their flocks, had seemingly been proven by the astonishing and dramatic events in County Clare. Even before that sensational by-election, priests had in several other contests organized Catholic freeholders as electoral rebels against the very landlords who had multiplied them with such "rash and reckless" abandon. An estimated 150 clergy had been active in Clare in summoning the faithful to a species of religious warfare, browbeating those hesitant to enlist in the sectarian army, and marshalling and marching voters to the poll. All of this O'Connell's counsel, Richard Lalor Sheil, faithfully recorded and published. Hence the victory was widely interpreted as fresh proof of priestly political power. Inevitably, the rank and file suffered the heaviest casualties in this political rebellion. The freeholders were subsequently disenfranchised, principally on the grounds that they were commanded by priests. Yet almost as disquieting to the authorities as the columns of well-marshalled Catholic voters on polling day in Clare were the seemingly spontaneous victory parades held in neighbouring Tipperary. Did these aftershocks presage another political earthquake? The calls by O'Connell and other association leaders for an end to faction fighting during the election had apparently been understood by some peasants as a sly instruction to ready themselves for "the greatest Whiteboy insurrection of all." Although the authorities remained blissfully unaware of this, they were unnerved by evidence of a loss of control of the Tipperary demonstrations by their erstwhile clerical organizers. Priests were beating a hasty retreat from these pseudo-military displays. The alarming incidents in Tipperary and another eruption of agrarian violence in Clare inevitably deepened British doubts of Irish loyalty. O'Connell's immediate announcement of a movement to repeal the Union served to confirm them. The opponents of emancipation, who had warned that it was merely a stalking horse for separation, could claim vindication.[41]

The British response to emancipation served to harden the Catholic Irish opinion that this large step towards civic equality had not been taken willingly but had resulted from a powerful Hibernian push. Consequently, it failed to fill some deep well of Irish gratitude. Instead, the delay of almost thirty years since Ireland's entrance into the United Kingdom solidified the case advanced by Keating two hundred years earlier, that Catholicism was the essence of Irishness. Furthermore, sectarianism remained at the heart of Irish politics. A population astutely politicized by O'Connell had every reason to continue to think of itself as an "essentially Catholic nation." Nor had emancipation mollified the Catholic clergy. The Established Church remained in place. Richard Lalor Sheil, who in 1825 had assured a parliamentary committee that the "single act of justice" of emancipation would remove the priests from politics, now added abolition of the tithe as a precondition for their withdrawal. Nor had emancipation reconciled occupiers of the land to the existing regime. Indeed, both O'Connell and Peel had long doubted that it would. But the collapse of the Wellington government in 1830 and its replacement by Whigs, who had long voiced sympathy for Ireland from the opposition benches, appeared to herald the turning of an important page in the evolution of the United Kingdom.[42]

Whigs had insisted that Ireland was "the vital and urgent question for England" in comparison to which all other questions, whether domestic or foreign, "shrank into insignificance." However, on taking office, ignoring the demands made by the likes of John MacHale, coadjutor Bishop of Killala, that they first address the food shortages, amounting to famine in western Ireland, by preventing the export of Irish produce to England and making fundamental changes to Ireland's system of land tenure, the new government gave priority to parliamentary reform, which excited far greater interest in England. Final passage of the Reform Bill did allow the Irish question to come to the fore as "the most definitive party issue" of the decade. Whig disparagement of the cautious and modest efforts of the Tory administrations to govern Ireland more effectively and somewhat more fairly had been accompanied by an assurance: they would correct the "faults and follies" of the seven centuries of oppression and misgovernment that had not simply "generated a deep rooted and cordial hatred of the English name and nation in the minds of the vast majority of the Irish people," but had "depraved and vitiated their characters, and fitted them for the commission of every crime." Here was an admission of English responsibility for much of what ailed Ireland, but one still rooted in an unflattering view of the Irish. The Whigs had welcomed emancipation as the indispensable ground-clearing step that would permit them to concentrate on the task of raising the peasantry "from their present state of poverty and destitution," but longer on promise than performance, the Whig administration initially exhibited a greater tactical interest in cultivating O'Connell and his parliamentary coterie than in aggressively redressing the many grievances of the Irish tenantry and peasantry.[43]

Radical reform was inhibited by Whig divisions. These extended into the leadership, pitting liberal ministers against more conservative colleagues. Eventually, several of the latter resigned and found their way into the Conservative Party as rebuilt by Robert Peel. The Tories, although a minority in the Commons, were able to obstruct Whig legislation, and they could derail it in the Lords, which they dominated. They were greatly assisted by alarming reports from the Irish countryside. The virtual peasants' war being waged there against the tithe was interpreted as an assault on sacred property rights, and this convinced "enlightened Englishmen" that the Irish had yet to attain "a state of civilization." The Whigs, as much as they desired to govern Ireland without resort to extraordinary measures, were reduced to adopting a form of martial law. Nor was this the only way in which their Irish policy resembled that of the Tories. The reforms they implemented were in some sense merely variations on the modestly progressive themes of the previous decade. They created an even larger, more centralized, and more para-military constabulary, which by the end of the decade exceeded eighty-five hundred armed men. Admittedly, it enjoyed greater popular respect than the earlier far more heavily Protestant force and it was credited with the reduction in rural violence, but sectarian tension bedevilled its ranks and complicated relationships between Catholic policemen and Protestant magistrates. The Whigs did press on assiduously with the purification of the magistracy and supervised more closely its conduct; they exhibited greater diligence than their Tory predecessors in seeking to exclude Orangemen from office and appointing Roman Catholics to vacancies; they finally withdrew public support from the Kildare Place Society schools and created a system of national education that was avowedly non-sectarian and mixed; and they tackled the tithe in a more forthright manner, eventually reducing it, converting it into a rent charge, and forgiving arrears.[44]

Tithe reform reflected the Whigs' willingness to grapple with the related but more profound Irish Catholic grievance of the Established Church. Of course, they were not unmindful of the partisan benefits of action. Any erosion of that institution's privileged position promised to solidify their support among the swelling ranks of Protestant dissent in Britain. On the other hand, this sensitive and passionate issue exposed the divisions on the Treasury bench. The most advantageous arrangement in Ireland, several ministers believed, was the establishment of religious equality through the concurrent endowment of the Anglican and Catholic churches. One problem was the certain refusal of British Protestants to swallow such bitter medicine. Another was this arrangement's lack of appeal for the Irish Catholic hierarchy. Other Whigs argued for the diversion of the alleged surplus revenues of the Established Church to worthy secular purposes. Lay appropriation, as this expedient was dubbed, repeatedly proved too controversial for a majority of the members of Parliament. Instead, the Church of Ireland underwent surgery. A number of bare branches were lopped off, while others were more neatly trimmed. Now a slightly less egregious sectarian anomaly, the Anglican Church received a new lease on life. Since this dismayed far more Irishmen than it delighted, the day of reckoning had merely been postponed. As one indefatigable campaigner against the Establishment later remarked, reforms "do but aggravate the evil by really increasing the aggressive power of the Church in proportion as its more prominent scandals are diminished." The legislation had given "permanence, with augmented powers of mischief, to that most anti-social engine of denationalization."[45]

Inevitably, there was disillusionment in Ireland with the Whigs. Richard Lalor Sheil was one of the prominent Irishmen bitterly disappointed with their reforms. Although a fiery agitator in the cause of emancipation and a founder of the Catholic Association, he had always been less of a nationalist than O'Connell and had broken with him in 1830 on the issue of repeal of the Union. On one occasion, Sheil urged his fellow countrymen to strive to convince the people of England that they were worthy of incorporation in "the great and free community of British citizenship." However, he and the Liberator now patched up their differences and he returned to Parliament in 1833 as a repealer. There, he delivered an emotional and sweeping indictment of the Union. "The mass of the [Irish] people," he declared, "are in a condition more wretched than that of any nation in Europe; they are worse housed, worse covered, worse fed, than the basest boors in the provinces of Russia." The survival of serfdom in Russia suggests a predilection for rhetorical overstatement, and it was one to which many of Sheil's countrymen succumbed in their criticisms of the Union.

All of this misery exists, he went on, in a country "teeming with fertility, and stamped with the beneficent intents of God." The implication was clear – the nationalism of repeal was a product of the Union's failure to deliver on Pitt's promise that it would improve the quality of Irish life.[46]

Following the defeat of a short-lived Conservative ministry headed by Peel during the winter of 1834–35, the Whigs returned to office. In return for the informal support of O'Connell, they renewed their commitment to justice for Ireland. Led by Lord Melbourne, who less than ten years earlier had been serving in Dublin as chief secretary, the government planned to "civilize" the neighbouring island. To that end, it completed the reform of the police and the modification of the tithe, resolutely purged Orangemen from office and filled vacancies with Catholics, placed more Catholics on the bench, and destroyed the Protestant monopoly of municipal corporations at the price of dissolving most of them. At stake here was control of thousands of jobs and the ability to influence the administration of justice, the management of prisons, and the conduct of parliamentary elections. Ten new municipal councils were created, though they had a more restricted electorate than the reformed municipalities in England and were entrusted with substantially less authority. The Whigs finally erected an Irish poor law safety net, but in this instance it was at one and the same time too similar to and too different from that which they had recently restrung in England. The new workhouses, John MacHale charged, were "prison-houses of the poor."[47]

The Irish Poor Law Unions embraced far larger populations than those of England, which did not bode well for their effective and efficient management. Moreover, the utility of the English deterrent model, given Ireland's broader and deeper endemic poverty, had been disputed by an investigating commission that inconveniently proposed a general program of economic development. Even the carefully selected author of a second report, who did recommend the introduction of deterrent workhouses, was moved to warn that the system would not be able to manage a famine. Unlike in England and Wales, relief in Ireland was to be exclusively provided within the workhouses and the absence of a legal right to relief meant that whenever a building was full, applicants might be rejected. However, the measure served a political purpose. It appeased English critics who were demanding an assimilation of the law of Ireland to that of the mainland. An ever rising tide of Irish immigrants to Britain had seemingly threatened to see the natives drown in a flooded labour market. The Irish were held responsible for unemployment, short time, and low wages. Similarly, the fact that Irish farmers had on hand an abundant supply of cheap labour and had until this time escaped payment of poor rates provided a handy explanation of their ability to sell produce "at prices which will not keep the English farmer out of jail, or English farms in cultivation." One substantial Welsh farmer calculated that his labour costs were triple those of his Irish competitors, while the booming coal trade between South Wales and Ireland allowed the latter to ship their produce at cheap rates in vessels making the return journey. As for Irish landlords, it was alleged that they had been "enabled to screw extortionate rents from the miserable tenantry, whom they thrust upon England for maintenance." Indeed, one of the principal merits of the Irish Poor Law in many an English eye was the likelihood that it would finally oblige Irish landowners, whether absentee or resident, "to set seriously to work in the regeneration of that country, by the employment of its poor, the introduction of work, capital, manufactures and middle class."[48]

After a decade of Whiggery, Ireland had changed. "By 1840 much Protestant privilege had been stripped away." The power of the Protestant Ascendancy, at least in the person of the landlord, had evidently been weakened as a result both of Catholic agitation and administrative reform. The dispensaries established shortly after union to provide free medical attention to the poor had by 1840 increased in number to six hundred, and together with county infirmaries, fever hospitals, and regional mental hospitals, they offered the rudiments of a health service. A new board of works had throughout the 1830s sponsored a variety of constructive projects, improving communications and promoting land reclamation. Religious discrimination was now less egregious; the country had a generally sound and honest administration; the national schools were steadily increasing literacy in English, which by mid-century was the boast of more than half the population; and legislation with respect to the Church Establishment, the tithe, municipal corporations, and the Poor Law confirmed the willingness of the British to address serious Irish problems. Here was a record of achievement that surely confirmed Whigs in the opinion that it was less the British connection than a succession of Tory regimes that had been the source of Irish disenchantment with the Union. And while the Whigs' inability to enact more far-reaching reforms could be conveniently ascribed to the caution and essential conservatism of most members of

Parliament, Daniel O'Connell's ambivalence with respect to social leg-islation had played its part. He might have made much more than he did of the Whigs need of him and his coterie to maintain their grip on power.[49]

An era of reform had failed to reconcile Irish opponents of the Union. One young intellectual, Thomas Davis, complained that Ireland had gotten little from the British Parliament apart from "'coercion bills, arrears bills, disfranchising bills, stipendiaries, – special commis-sions, – and fraudulent juries." Moreover, in a number of instances, remedial measures further complicated the very problems they were intended to alleviate. For example, the national system of education did not deliver the mixed schooling of Catholic and Protestant children that might have promoted greater social harmony. Instead, it illustrated Ireland's deepening sectarianism. Many schools effectively became publicly funded Catholic institutions largely as a result of the refusal of Protestants to attend them. Nor did they all promote the "value sys-tem" of the state. In many areas Catholic clergy served as their man-agers, thus becoming even more influential locally, much to the chagrin of those who had hoped to curtail priestly power. Neither the reform of the Anglican Church nor the masking of the tithe appeased Catholics demanding religious equality. This was another cause in which priests were prominent, and one that enhanced their popular prestige. They grew further in stature as a result of an era of Catholic Church reform that was eventually to blossom as a 'devotional revolu-tion' especially marked among the swelling ranks of the middle classes. Consequently, the interest and involvement of priests in politics did not diminish. Suggestions from Rome that they confine themselves to pas-toral duties went unheeded even though "the Catholic Church in Ire-land had more freedom from state political control than in almost any other country in the world." Finally, the Irish Poor Law was a ticking human time bomb, having put in place an English system of relief ill-suited to the island's problems and needs.[50]

Ireland's incomplete integration into the United Kingdom con-tributed to the dangerously fragile condition of her economy. An inability to diversify meant that by the 1840s there was still all too lit-tle alternative employment off the land for a population that over the preceding half-century had continued to increase dramatically despite a slackening in the pace of growth. The likelihood of disaster grew with the failure of agriculture to modernize and the bloating of a rural population dangerously dependent on a single source of food, the potato.

All of this lent weight to the accusation that Britain had deliberately impeded Ireland's industrial growth in order to be able to exploit her as an economic colony. Britons, on the other hand, were inclined to blame Irish economic backwardness on an exceptional, if not unique, proclivity for violence. And no matter the degree to which the lawlessness was on occasion exaggerated and sensationalized by the British press and politicians, there were areas of Ireland that had developed a culture of violence. Equally ominous was the seeming success of rural terror. The victorious tithe war and the widespread reluctance of many landowners and substantial farmers to confront agrarian secret societies by seeking to dispossess inefficient smallholders were but two examples of the seeming efficacy of violence. A weapon that came so readily to hand in social and economic relations was likely to be employed to advance political causes. This danger was heightened by the oratorical recklessness of some opinion leaders. Words commonly associated with aggression have a tendency to increase a listener's levels of aggression. To describe the United Kingdom as tyrannical, a despotism, and to liken the plight of the Irish people to slavery was irresponsible. Those who did so were subscribing, whether consciously or not, to Thomas Hobbes's observation that "[t]he end of Rhetoric is Victory, which consists in having gotten belief." Among the obvious perils of verbal violence was its threat to social peace. Irishmen were being taught, and by those they respected and to whom they looked for instruction and guidance, that the state lacked legitimacy.[51]

Seemingly oblivious to this danger and arrogantly scornful of humility as a virtue, the Whigs were confident by 1840 that they had rung down the curtain on seven centuries of oppression and misgovernment of Ireland. From the Catholic Irish they expected gratitude, and they pointed to the island's unusual tranquility as proof of their success in reconciling the Irish people to the Union. The belief that Irish Catholics were finally beginning to think of themselves as West Britons rather than Irishmen was an illusion, however. How were they to do so when a once and future Tory lord chancellor gave voice to a common enough English sentiment with his dismissive labelling of Irish Catholics as aliens in blood, language, and religion? At best, they were "British subjects with a difference." Meanwhile, Daniel O'Connell responded to a revival of conservatism under "Orange" Peel by reactivating the agitation for repeal of the Union that he had suspended on entering into his tactical arrangement with the Whigs. His objective was a form of national political autonomy, one he backed with appeals to Irish nationalism. But it was a demand most Britons rejected out of hand. In their minds, it smacked of rank ingratitude and betrayed "an extraordinary defect in the Celtic character." Solid proofs of British "generosity" were all "so easily forgotten, while the past brutalities of Anglo-Norman chiefs [were] so keenly remembered," they grumbled. To "trumpet complaint when they ought to have been expressing gratitude" was the very essence of Irishness.[52]

2

Holy Nationalism

Writing in the spring of 1842 to Paul Cullen, rector of the Irish College in Rome, Daniel O'Connell rejected Britishness: "British!!! I am not British. You are not British." Ireland was "a separate nation," he went on, having successfully preserved her "separate existence" through centuries of English persecution. British meddling with the Irish Catholic Church, even by fellow religionists, had to be opposed, as did "British intermeddling" with Irish temporal concerns. The answer to the Irish question was a single word – repeal. Terminating the Union would be "an event of the most magnificent importance to Catholicity," O'Connell assured his sympathetic clerical correspondent. It was for this very reason, he added, that he did not present the demand "in its true colours to the British people least [*sic*] it should have its effect in increasing their hostility to that measure." He had launched repeal campaigns in 1830, in 1834, and then far more energetically during the waning months of the Whig administration at the beginning of the 1840s. The Precursor Society was followed by the National Repeal Association, the latter modelled on the extraordinarily successful Catholic Association, and it in turn by the Loyal National Repeal Association. Members were required to take an oath of allegiance to the monarch and were issued with a button that bore a pair of inscriptions: "God Save the Queen" and "Repeal of the Union." Perhaps expressions of O'Connell's loyalty to the Crown, the name and the oath were more likely adopted as a first line of defence against accusations of disloyalty. Thus O'Connell's loyalty "to Queen Victoria and to the institution of monarchy itself" did not prevent him from insulting both in 1845. Victoria's failure to visit the island that year, as had been expected, saw O'Connell stage his own regal visits to Dublin and Cork in his assumed role as Ireland's uncrowned king.[1]

Fervent protestations of loyalty could not "disguise the high degree of autonomy" O'Connell was seeking for his native land, though they did obscure the question of sovereignty. His objective was a measure of national self-determination – the preservation of an Irish "nation" – and he offered a string of arguments in its support. Ireland was an island, physically separate from Britain. Her land mass exceeded that of a full handful of European states. She had for centuries possessed her own parliament, which barely a half century earlier had achieved a measure of legislative independence, and O'Connell contrasted the prosperity of that era with the hard times following union and the ending of the French Wars. He repeated the charges of the Union's trenchant literary critics, that it had only been effected by "'intimidation, bribery, corruption, treachery and blood.'" Consequently, it could never be binding on Irishmen. As for the Protestant minority, he gave an airy assurance that nothing was to be feared from a restored parliament dominated by Catholics. In private, he was candidly sectarian. He forwarded to Cullen a string of arguments with which the rector might secure Vatican support for Irish political autonomy. He denied, not entirely accurately, that Catholics had been parties to the Union. He cavalierly dismissed Protestants as mere politicians, not true religionists, who would quickly be absorbed into the overwhelming majority of Catholics following repeal. Once liberated from the expense of maintaining "the useless protestant Church" and able to "disengage" the former lands of the Church from Protestant hands, a more affluent faithful would make generous provision for their clergy. Further, the means would be available not only to underwrite a dramatic expansion of the number of priests, who remained a minority of Ireland's clergy, but also to construct and support Catholic educational institutions. Finally, O'Connell gave Cullen an assurance that the nationalism he espoused was not simply Catholic but also ultramontane. A truly Irish parliament would be "devoted to Religion, to Catholic truth in doctrine, discipline and submission to authority, with an undeviating attachment to the authority of the Holy See." This represented a subtle modification of his position during the veto controversy almost three decades earlier. Then, in response to an unwelcome papal rescript that endorsed the veto clauses in a recent Catholic relief bill, he had publicly declared: "I am sincerely a Catholic but I am not a papist. I deny that the Pope has any temporal authority, directly or indirectly, in Ireland."[2]

The passage of two years found O'Connell stipulating in a letter to a well-meaning Englishman the measures that "would mitigate the present ardent desire for Repeal." The list was short, daunting, and dis-couraging – perfect religious equality, which seemed unobtainable without disestablishment of the Church of Ireland; the re-establish-ment of a more equitable balance on the land between landlords and tenants (upset by the passage since 1801 of at least seven statutes, by O'Connell's reckoning, that enhanced "the landlords' power"); a more popular and representative Irish presence in Parliament, where repeal-ers, their number severely limited due to a disproportionately small Irish electorate, were "swamped and overwhelmed" by the "great and prejudiced English majority"; a revisiting of municipal reform; and the fiscal punishment of absentee landowners so memorably accused by Richard Lalor Sheil of extracting millions of pounds annually "which, instead of circulating through Ireland, swell the overflowings of the deep and broad Pactolus of British opulence." This was not an agenda likely to be adopted by a people infected with a "national antipathy" to the Irish, O'Connell remarked. "You have injured us too deeply, too cruelly, ever to forgive us," he chided his English correspondent. "And then there is a bigoted anti-Catholic spirit embittering, enhancing and augmenting English hatred of the Irish nation." Privately, he acknowl-edged that the ethnic hostility was reciprocal. The Irish expected noth-ing from an "English Parliament" for whose proceedings they had "vivid contempt" and they felt only "hatred of England." In short, there was no alternative to repeal.[3]

O'Connell's well-publicized coquetting with federalists, who sought the restoration of an Irish legislature restricted to a severely limited number of domestic matters, was surely more tactical than serious. Espousal of federalism might draw the more timid nationalists into the fold, among them an estimated seventeen members of Parliament. Revealingly, O'Connell expected them to take the repeal pledge. When queried about this, he took refuge in a classic political fudge. He was seeking "federative Repeal," he lamely explained. But he remained convinced that his fellow countrymen, in looking only to themselves, would neither revolt nor rebel. Instead, they would "avail themselves of the first day of peril to England to require conciliation." The implied notion here, that justice had to be extracted from Britain and would rarely if ever be freely conceded, was not without its own perils. Too much turned on the definition of justice. Nor was it entirely consistent with recent developments. One highly respected Irish member of Par-liament had lavished praise on the Whigs for their acceptance of his native land as a genuine partner in the United Kingdom. Orangemen had been suppressed, a Catholic appointed attorney general of Ireland, others named to the bench and to the new police force, education improved, municipal reform initiated if not completed, institutional sectarianism curtailed, and franchise extension at least attempted. Thus O'Connell's vitriolic assaults on the "English Parliament" and its six hundred "scoundrels" smelt of demagogy, as did his tendency to coat his political frustration with ever thicker layers of ethnic if not racial hostility. He recognized the symbiotic relationship between nationalist politics and popular support, but to blame the English for all of Ireland's ills and misfortunes was a dangerous if not treacherous tactic of mass mobilization.[4]

Ireland's most charismatic political figure frequently larded his speeches with coruscating criticisms of the "Saxon," thereby exploiting the traditional Irish "resentment of outsiders." The English, or persons of English origin, were seen less as individuals than as members of a "resented race." O'Connell was implying the existence of an ethnic hierarchy, using "racialism" as a "supplement to nationalism." As one observer later remarked, the wealthy Saxon and the prosperous Protestant were viewed as invaders who "'notwithstanding the prescription of three hundred years,'" ought to be "'deprived of [their] possessions, and expelled from the soil of Ireland.'" Ironically, O'Connell's vanity led him privately to express an "almost quasi-racial dislike" of the masses he led. They were, he informed one friend, a "'species of animals,'" "'crawling slaves.'" Nevertheless, his "strident" and "raucous" rhetoric was "calculated to arouse the passions of his audiences," confirming their belief that they and the British were irreconcilable. By heightening ethnic consciousness, if not inflaming racial antipathies, O'Connell was erecting a formidable barrier to Ireland's political integration into the British state. Even the English Catholic community was on occasion dismissed as unworthy of the faith, its leading peer publicly disparaged as a "Saxon and a stranger," and the designation "true Catholics" reserved for Irish nationalists. Of course, the English were in a poor position to complain given the undisguised scorn with which they regarded the Irish.[5]

Surprisingly, expressions of Irish nationalism failed to inspire a systematic counteroffensive on behalf of an all-embracing concept of British nationality. Instead, just as the architects of the Union failed to draft a "pragmatic blueprint" for making the Union work over the long term, so successive British governments appeared to trust in the growth of "official nationalism" by osmosis. The disproportionately large Irish contribution to the British Army offered some reassurance in this regard, for military service was viewed as "an antidote to particularism and other divisive influences within the state" and a means of promoting "communal solidarity." The steady advance of English as the vernacular literature and the contribution of Irish writers to its glory, the wide circulation of national newspapers, and the rapid decline in the use of Irish were evidence of anglicization, which many in Britain confused with Britishness. A dramatic improvement in national communications provided another bond. The construction across the Menai Straits of Thomas Telford's bridge, which completed the road link between the ferry port of Holyhead on the Isle of Anglesey and the mainland, the introduction of steam ferries on the Irish service, the upgrading of trunk roads, the progressive extension of the railways, the completion in 1850 of Robert Stephenson's tubular railway bridge within sight of Telford's architectural wonder, and the electric telegraph, together with the standardization of Greenwich mean time, seemed certain to knit the peoples of the islands progressively more closely together. These improvements had done more to promote the amalgamation of England and Ireland than all the legislation passed since 1800, a conservative and unionist Irish periodical confidently announced as the second half of the century opened. It was now possible to take the train from London to the ferry terminals and then a steam vessel to Dublin. Meanwhile, the inexpensiveness of the crossing for those willing to brave primitive conditions on far less glamorous vessels was facilitating the seasonal migrations of Irish harvest workers to Britain and the arrival of more permanent residents. The resultant ethnic intermingling would surely foster a much greater and stronger sense of common identity. Had not the Welsh and the Scots already been successfully incorporated if not fully assimilated? "Experience proves," wrote Britain's most distinguished living philosopher, John Stuart Mill, "that it is possible for one nationality to merge and be absorbed in another: and when it was originally an inferior and more backward portion of the human race the absorption is greatly to its advantage." The historian John Acton agreed. "The combination of different nations in one State is as necessary a condition of civilized life as the combination of men in society," he wrote in the *Home and Foreign Review*. "Inferior races are raised by living in political union with races intellectually superior."[6]

There was a strong whiff of mid-Victorian complacency and English conceit in Acton's assertion that states like the British, which "include various distinct nationalities without oppressing them," were "substantially the most perfect." He may have been more concerned with developments in Europe, reacting as a Catholic to the struggle for Italian unity and critical of Giuseppe Mazzini, the father of the Young Italy movement, yet neither he nor Mill could have been oblivious to what was happening in Ireland. "A State which is incompetent to satisfy different races condemns itself," the historian conceded, before adding that the "national impulse" was only awakened where there was "an alien element, the vestige of foreign dominion, to expel." Mill, fully convinced that free institutions were next to impossible in a country made up of different nationalities, believed their successful development in such alien circumstances depended on the presence of an overpowering nationality more numerous and more advanced than the subdued. Further, to be genuinely reconciled to integration, the latter had to abandon all hope of ever achieving independence. To this end, the subdued needed to be governed with "tolerable justice" and denied any reason to consider themselves the victims of discrimination at the hands of the "more powerful nationality." Unlike the nationalist icon Mazzini, who simply denied that the Irish possessed two essentials of nationhood – a national language and an historic mission – and counselled them to accept absorption into the United Kingdom, as did Count Cavour, the future agent of a united Italy, Mill admitted that the Irish were "sufficiently numerous to be capable of constituting a respectable nationality by themselves." This fact and a sorry history of English misgovernment explained to his satisfaction their "bitter resentment" of "Saxon rule."[7]

Irish dissatisfaction with the Union, and O'Connell's skilful marshalling of it into a formidable popular force, might well have prodded a prudent central government into activity. The promotion of a concept of Britishness that ensured an equality of rights of all those it legally embraced, no matter their ethnicity, national identity, and culture, would have been a wise response to the dramatic growth of the Repeal Association, for the philosophical foundation of British citizenship was essentially contractual and a potent foreign impetus to domestic unity had been lost with the ending of the long French Wars. On the other hand, the triumph over France had bequeathed ample excuse for patriotic ceremonies and provided a number of national symbols. These might readily have been put to good use in a territorial nation on whose disparate national identities the concept of Britishness still rested lightly. Of the great professions, only medicine was organized as an all-embracing association, and not until the 1860s was the United Kingdom represented as "a single culture" by the "members of the influential National Association for the Promotion of Social Science." This multi-ethnic state also lacked the reinforcement of a uniform system of secondary education, and ethnic hostility remained a problem for the Catholic Irish who settled in Britain. Few of them found welcome mats on the mean streets of industrial Britain. Instead, the increased contact between peoples with distinct cultures threatened to aggravate existing antagonisms. Civic solidarity had yet to be achieved, and one important reason for its retardation was the strength of English nationalism. Here was a powerful force whose transmutation was going to be difficult to effect, for England could claim to be "the prototype of both nation and nation state." Her people had long since defined their identity as one uniquely blessed by liberty, the rule of law, and a balanced constitution. It was underpinned by "a sense of the transcendent virtues of English Protestantism and the prophetic historical position of the English people." Englishmen devoutly believed they "enjoyed a peculiar covenant with the deity." In the words of one sixteenth-century divine, "God is English." Even the conservative patriotism so assiduously cultivated by Robert Southey in prose and poetry during and after the French Wars had continued to stress the Englishman's blessings, prominent among which was the Church of England. Southey isolated English heroes as personifications of the national character, and the Duke of Wellington could be embraced as such, given his notorious refusal to be identified by his place of birth.[8]

Thomas Macaulay boasted in 1849 that England was so great that Englishmen cared little for what others thought or said of her. This example of national arrogance was not another example of the careless use of English for British but a reflection of the fact that many if not all Englishmen still did not think "in 'British' terms." This many Irishmen understood. The English cried down "nationality in the mouth of an Irishman," one organ of the immigrant Irish in Britain later charged, even as they gloried in their English nationality "as if no other people had a nation but themselves." Rare was the Englishman who could truthfully repeat after William Cobbett: "I have never been able, for a single moment, to view an Irishman as other than as my countryman." More common was the disdainful and casual dismissal of Ireland's Catholics as "an inferior and degraded *caste*." One Catholic Irishman who had embraced Britishness protested that "the spirit of eminence and masterdom" was "so fixedly settled" in the English that they could never bring themselves to regard the Irish as their equals. The Irish were at best "domestic foreigners," a species of internal aliens within not only Britain but also the United Kingdom. O'Connell and his followers responded in kind with their scornful references to the Saxons, while resentment of the remnants of Ireland's Protestant Ascendancy became in his hands another instrument with which to mould Irish national consciousness into "full-fledged national demands." In the words of one anonymous pamphleteer, the Union, in reality, was "Ireland governed by foreigners, to her own prejudice, and for their profit only." Yet as the Irish were fully aware, they were members of an historic state that had once boasted a golden age and an independent existence. Before the Union, they "felt that they had a country; they acted under the influence of that instinct of nationality, which for his providential purposes, the author of nature has implanted in [them. They] were then a nation," Sheil declared. In Ireland, "particularistic nationalism" was assured of a powerful following.[9]

"A portion of mankind may be said to constitute a Nationality," John Stuart Mill lectured contemporaries, " if they are united among themselves by common sympathies, which do not exist between them and any others." As a result, they would cooperate with each other more willingly than with others and demonstrate a desire to live under a government exclusively their own. This "feeling of nationality" might be rooted in an identity of race or descent, a common language or religion, and geography, but the most powerful spur, in Mill's opinion, was "the possession of a national history, and consequent community of recollections; collective pride and humiliation, pleasure and regret, connected with the same incidents in the past." This was a definition similar to that now offered for ethnicity – "a shared, conscious or subconscious, feeling of peoplehood, based on common referents of racial, religious, national, and/or regional identification." When it came to dating the emergence of "nationality," the historian Acton was an early modernist. It had been called into existence by the French Revolution of 1789, he concluded, only to be subsequently expanded by a second French upheaval almost sixty years later. The Revolution of 1848 had made popular sovereignty a fundamental of nationalism. In Mill's succinct phrase, "the question of government ought to be decided by the governed," while "the boundaries of government should coincide in the main with those of nationalities." Herein lay a potential threat to the territorial integrity of a multinational state such as the United Kingdom, and it was one Mill sought to finesse with his insistence that the blending of different nationalities in a common union was "a benefit to the human race." Acton went further, dismissing as regressive a "congruence of national and political boundaries." Nationality would be a "retrograde step" if it sacrificed liberty and prosperity "to the imperative necessity of making the nation the mould and measure of the State."[10]

In lauding the United Kingdom, which he revealingly described as the "English" system, the Catholic Acton chose to ignore English nationalism and thus the extent to which it had been either religiously inspired or infused with fresh zeal "from contact with Roman Catholic resisters and Protestant dissidents in the Celtic fringe." He identified "race" as an engine of nationalism, though his definition of it as merely a natural and physical connection, amounting to "a community of affections and instincts infinitely important and powerful in savage life, but pertaining more to the animal than to civilized man," suggests a synonym for ethnicity. Race was also employed as a synonym for nation, encouraging the idea "that each nation was homogeneous and therefore complete in itself." It was a use O'Connell was promoting. But in the shadows of Acton's references to superior and inferior races, even if the historian referred to "social" races as distinct from "biological," there lurked the contemporary "scientific racism" popularized by Robert Knox, who insisted that "in human history race is everything."[11]

A powerful sense of common identity among a people occupying a well-defined territory and determined to secure a greater degree of autonomy, if not a state of their own, was frequently rooted in a conviction of their distinctive ethnicity. This was certainly true of Ireland, where the seeds of national distinctiveness had been sown by Gaelic bardic poets. Their "elaborate descriptions" of the island fostered a sense of it as "a perceived *entity*, an integrated place," a national territory. The poets imagined Ireland as an anguished woman defiled by foreign invaders, and their sense of nationality became ever more strongly Irish, as opposed to Gaelic, during the Reformation and the English campaigns and plantations of the Tudor and early Stuart years. That these "New English" were unable to understand the Irish language was one reason why Geoffrey Keating valued it so highly as an identifier of national identity. Moreover, in a semi-literate society he considered the priesthood the community's natural storyteller and arbiter of standards "in terms of social and political order" and language as well as morality. In short, Keating personified a transfer of intellectual leadership from a Gaelic intelligentsia of bards and poets to the "Counter-Reformation Catholic clergy." Their productions, designed with an eye to the broadest appeal, included learned treatises on theology, philosophy, and history for the educated elite, while popular poetry and "scurrilous gossip about Luther's relations with nuns" catered to the masses.[12]

Keating profoundly influenced many later antiquarians and historians of the Irish past. He had looked back to an ancient Ireland uniquely blessed with saints, an illustrious centre of learning from which missionaries were despatched to enlighten the English, the Scots, and hosts of Europeans. Abbé MacGeoghegan, in his three-volume *History of Ireland Ancient and Modern* (1758-1763), did not stray from this increasingly well trodden path. The Catholic Irish were an ancient and civilized people, he wrote, not the "barbarous and unhistoried race described by their enemies and traducers." The torch was subsequently taken up and held aloft by Father John Lanigan, a member of the Faculty of Maynooth and a founder of the Gaelic Society. His multi-volume *Ecclesiastical history of Ireland from the first introduction of Christianity to the beginning of the thirteenth century* (1822) described the land of the saints and scholars Ireland had once been. Like Keating before him, he fused religion and nationality. So did James Hardiman, whose partial loss of sight prevented him from entering the priesthood. The "copious notes" of his *Irish minstrelsy* (1831) offered a "passionate defence of the Irish language and its traditional culture; denunciation of 'Anglo-Ireland' and a deeply held belief in the indissoluble bond between Gaelicism and Catholicism." In one of his own poems, he wrote:

> The shrines of our faith are destroyed and polluted
> By treacherous wolves that assailed us;
> The race of our might is fall'n and uprooted –
> Oh weep, for our high hope has failed us

Here was a nationalist, inspired by language and religion, praying for an end of foreign domination. But the placing of a golden age of Christian Ireland at the very heart of the country's historical identity strengthened the claim of the Roman Catholic Church to the position of its custodian.[13]

Nurtured and fertilized by an historic memory and a culture considered authentic and unique, the seeds of Irish national distinctiveness were further propagated by the rise in literacy and the explosion of the written word in books and newspapers, which greatly facilitated the dissemination of ideas. Schools served as hothouses, where pupils might be taught "the glories of the past, the opportunities of the present, and the destiny of the future." Often, the most zealous cultivators of "myths, memorials, symbols [and] values" were intellectuals and professionals struggling to persuade a seemingly passive people that they were members of a distinct community. These missionaries and proselytizers, clergy prominent among them, seized on injustices or oppression suffered at the hands of foreigners to arouse the masses with a summons to "corporate consciousness and cohesion." They paraded the "Joys of Hatred" under the banner of nationalism. The call to the colours proved all the more irresistible whenever claims of ethnic and cultural distinctiveness were reinforced if not defined by religion, a vital element of culture in pre-industrial societies. Religion possessed a peculiar capacity to unite strangers, establishing "communion through common practice and a sort of brotherhood" and transmitting "the communal memory" through the ecclesiastical structure. In this respect the Roman Catholic Church enjoyed a number of advantages, not the least of which was an elaborate network of communications. This greatly facilitated the widespread dissemination of a "social and political message." Moreover, in Ireland, as elsewhere, the national hierarchy commanded "considerable political resources." These were the clergy and, through them, a laity who in Ireland were believed almost to worship their priests.[14]

Nationalism possessed messianic properties even if its "revolutionary messianism" usually stopped well short of establishing the kingdom of God on earth. It was frequently "suffused with religious terms." Imagery of self-sacrifice, death, martyrdom, and resurrection, the message of deliverance through suffering and victimhood, the link imagined and provided between past and future, dead and unborn, the inspiration of reverence as "an effective bonding force," contributed to its "quasi-sacred" character, as did the concept of "ethnic election," of being a "chosen people," even a "Holy Nation." The Bible provided "a developed model of what it means to be a nation – a unity of people, language, religion, territory and government." It elevated the community "to the level of a transcendent moral entity" and served as the "prime lens through which the nation is imagined by biblically literate people." Nationalism was "'a soul, a spiritual principle.'" Just as faith binds people to an image "unchanging and eternal," so nationalists believe "they are mystically connected to the past, in some form of communion, without any need for veridical warrant." Their "'transvaluation' and politicisation" of religion's values have therefore been "profoundly significant for the mobilization of the people and the character of the subsequent nationalism." Richard Lalor Sheil had given voice to a belief that the "instinct of nationality" was divinely inspired, a conviction commonly identified with the most famous contemporary apostle of nationalism, Mazzini, who declared the nation "consecrated" and ultimately "a holy entity." The Protestant Reformation had in some instances drawn strength from resistance to the foreign control exercised by the papacy, and Protestantism frequently became an intimate ally of the state. England provided a prime example of this close relationship – hence religion's description as "a sixteenth-century word for nationalism." It certainly "reinforced ethnic consciousness and nationalism." Religious festivals were frequently celebrated with processions that made conspicuous use of national symbols, such as St Patrick's Day festivities, and thus the "points of intersection between religion, nationalism and notions of identity [were] many and varied." Catholic Irishmen had the assurance of priests as well as poets that they, no less than the English, were a chosen people. In Ireland they were the "chosen people in captivity." Similarly, the legions of Catholic Irish emigrants were fulfilling a divine mission. They had been selected by God to carry the true faith to the far corners of the world.[15]

"Centuries of oppression and misgovernment have generated a deep-rooted and cordial hatred of the English name and nation in the minds of the vast majority of the Irish," and infected them with a "strong nationality," a contributor to the *Edinburgh Review* reminded its readers in 1825. The Irish had no need to invent or imagine that "subjective sense of discrimination" so "intrinsic to the construction of a separate identity." Herein lay a peculiar danger, especially for a state professing a civic or contractual nationalism. To differentiate among citizens on the basis of "'race,' or cultural traits such as religion," was to provide the "backward region or population" with a powerful incentive to think of itself as a separate nation. Recognizing this, Irish liberal unionists argued that a wise government would "conciliate and tranquillize a great body of the community, who not only have the power of acquiring wealth and intelligence, but have actually acquired both." Richard Lalor Sheil, who abandoned his flirtation with repeal and became one of their most eloquent spokesmen, repeatedly condemned the "detestable distinctions" drawn by Parliament between the two countries. Ireland was being practically reduced to "a colonial dependency," he charged, that made a mockery of the United Kingdom. He was giving voice to a bitterness deeply imprinted on the Irish historic memory, and advised Britons anxious to understand his native land's "excesses" to scan the pages of her history. Had Scotland been portioned out amongst "merciless adventurers," had a "code of debasement of the Presbyterian population been enacted," had Presbyterians "been shut out of every honourable employment, and debarred from every creditable pursuit," had an episcopal establishment been maintained "amongst a degraded Calvinistic people," could there be any doubt, he asked, that long after this repressive regime had been "partially abolished" the northern kingdom would have presented "the same spectacle" as contemporary Ireland. Even the single great victory of Catholic emancipation belonged entirely to the Irish themselves, Sheil claimed. It represented a triumph of "indefatigable energy," "indissoluble union," and "undaunted and indomitable determination." Who were the Irish people? They were "the mighty masses." What was the Irish nation? It was "the Catholic millions" who constituted "the enormous majority of the people."[16]

Roman Catholicism had been fundamental to Irish national and ethnic consciousness ever since the English Reformation. Resentment of plantations, colonial-style rule, and religious persecution had, in nourishing Catholic Irish hostility towards Protestantism and the English, prepared the ground for an exclusive popular nationalism. The United Irishmen had striven to repudiate the religious factor while exploiting the national, only to see their cause supported and suppressed with sectarian ferocity. Following union, British governments made a greater effort to maintain at least "a posture of religious neutrality," given the immense size of an Irish Catholic population that soon constituted more than one quarter of the total population of the United Kingdom. Nevertheless, critics identified Orangeism as "the fatal engine" by which ministers split the ranks of the Irish people in order to maintain "a monopoly of power in the country, under the imposing term *Protestant ascendancy*, which their predecessors more modestly termed *English interest*." The resultant equation seemed simple enough to many Irishmen. "Our country suffered for being Catholic; our people suffered for being Irish; the bond between our Nationality and our Faith is, therefore, One for ever." The sanctification of ethnicity was being matched by the ethnization of religion, and the integration of Irish nationality with Catholicism was further strengthened by persecution and discrimination. One definition of that nationality "excluded everything not Catholic and everything English." This was the thrust of the remarks of a clerical agent of the dominant figure in the Irish Catholic Church. He reminded an impetuous Irish politician that "our nationality and our Catholicity are inseparable" and any attempt to promote the former at the expense of the latter would be disastrous to both. Catholicism was the "mainspring of Irish nationalism."[17]

O'Connell's victorious campaign for emancipation and his preaching on behalf of a broad range of peasant grievances not only produced the first triumphant mass mobilization of popular nationalism but also stamped it with an indelible sectarian mark. Struggling against Protestant sectarianism, he appealed to and reinforced the belief – which the United Irishmen had pragmatically and idealistically attempted to overcome – that Catholicism and Ireland were an organic unit. In the Catholic Association he created what the evangelical Protestant sitting in the chief secretary's chair dubbed a "Popish Parliament." Its representative character, the active participation of priests, and the recruitment of so many Catholic forty-shilling freeholders as constituents quickly convinced the then viceroy, the ineffectually liberal Richard Wellesley, that electoral rebellion was in the offing. During the Clare by-election three years later, the activities and energy of priests alarmed the Executive. Of course, the freeholders were subsequently sacrificed on the altar of emancipation, and far fewer political sermons were delivered on the topic of peasant hardships, but O'Connell had demonstrated the power of extra-parliamentary popular pressure and careful electoral organization. Equally significant, in opening to fellow Roman Catholics the previously locked doors of the House of Commons, he was making possible the eventual seating there of a truly popular Irish party. Not that the constitutional pursuit of change was assisted by the Reform Bill of 1832. The resultant Irish electorate, "because of its smallness and lack of social uniformity," was rarely "capable of *sustained* and cohesive political action." Furthermore, there was no great body of potential candidates willing to rally to the banner of repeal, and several of those selected and elected promptly deserted the standard. Hence the Liberator's willingness to cooperate with the Whigs during the 1830s and his revival of the politics of extra-parliamentary mass mobilization to back his renewed demand for repeal following the Tories' return to office in 1841.[18]

Divisions within Ireland, both sectarian and regional, threatened the genuinely national mobilization in support of repeal that would have confirmed the existence of a "community of people" bound together "by a sense of solidarity, a common culture, a national consciousness," and thus a nation. Ulster Protestants were highly suspicious of repeal, for they doubted that the Liberator had them in mind when he spoke of Ireland for the Irish. Sectarian suspicion similarly influenced the response of a number of those liberal Protestants who had been supporters of emancipation, while Dublin's Protestant working people suffering through the agonies of a depression, who ought therefore to have been responsive to the claim that repeal would produce better times, broke ranks with their Catholic fellow artisans. Another source of acute sectarian tension was an aggressive and provocative Protestant crusade to convert the Catholic masses. This goaded priests into bitter denunciations of proselytism and spurred them into a "frenzy of print" that finally saw millions of copies of the Douay Bible put into circulation. On the other side of the ever-deepening and widening religious divide, the construction of Catholic churches to accommodate the faithful alarmed many Protestants. So did the arrival of new religious orders and the new spirit of militancy evident among a clergy convinced that they were members of the one true church and that it alone was entitled to freedom. Protestants also seized upon the growth of ultramontanism, making much of the papacy's recent denunciations of religious liberty as the "poison of indifference" and its history of intolerance in treating those it damned as heretics. All of this made ever more unlikely any substantial Protestant support of repeal. Adding to O'Connell's difficulties was the decision of a number of prominent Roman Catholics, among them the primate, to distance themselves from the cause. Archbishop Crolly, who had supported the Precursor Society, drew the line at repeal. He considered it unattainable, a distraction from other valuable and achievable measures of reform, and an objective certain to aggravate sectarian enmities. Others feared that agitation would severely weaken the position of Britain's Roman Catholics, or deplored the tactic of fomenting ethnic differences in order to impugn the legitimacy of the existing form of government. There could be no mistaking the Repeal Association's underlying messages – government by an alien society did violence "to the unique national spirit" of the Irish and nationalism was "a form of politics."[19]

Local and regional divisions were another threat to repeal's national appeal. Ironically, the task of sublimating parochial identities into at least a sense of Roman Catholic community may have been aided by the massive Irish enlistments in the British Army. Military service reminded Catholic Irishmen both of their national distinctiveness and the sectarian discrimination to which they were subjected. Another bond was provided by the careful construction of O'Connell's public image, including the design of his clothing and headgear, which gave full rein to nationalist symbolism. Massive processions and monster meetings, deliberately staged at historically evocative and emotive sites, served to deepen the participants' sense of national involvement and integration. Prevented by law from flying the green flag of nationalist Ireland, thousands of those in attendance sported the symbolic colour of faith and cause by carrying natural greenery. As a result, vast numbers of Catholic Irish "were able to imagine themselves as part of a vast national community in a way they had never been able to do before." But O'Connell's most important ally in this regard remained his church. It was no mere happenstance that on the platform at repeal meetings and at the high table of political banquets, he was invariably surrounded by clerics.[20]

Political agitators had long regarded the clergy as "the only lever by which they could raise the people." An inquisitive and intelligent French visitor, Alexis de Tocqueville, who toured Ireland the very year his profound insights into *Democracy in America* were published, establishing his enduring reputation as a peculiarly acute analyst of society, was struck by the intimate union of Irish priests and people. As mass was celebrated in Latin, the sermon in English or Irish was the principle vehicle of priestly instruction of parishioners – hence the emphasis many bishops placed upon its importance. If the sermon was an opportunity to explain the essentials of Catholic doctrine, many priests were inclined, during Ireland's recurrent periods of social and political crises, to dilate on less spiritual issues, such as the "relationship between government and religion." Nor was it unknown for some of them to "spur congregations into violent action," although the vast majority behaved far more prudently. Nevertheless, if, as has been argued, an "organic intelligentsia" proved to be the "heroes of nation-building," then Catholic clergy were a dominant element. They blurred the line between religious doctrine and political ideology, thereby "'nationalising' and politicising their 'flocks' with near missionary zeal." The ill-educated poor, listening to the "gospel of nationalism" preached from the altar, "found it difficult to know where the spiritual pronouncements of their religious superiors left off, and where their class preferences and political teachings took over." As the Catholic primate subsequently admitted, churches were used for the purposes of political agitation.[21]

The priests' popularity and influence owed much to their humane concern for the plight of the poor, but they were confirmed as community leaders by institutional reform. The authority that the priest wielded by virtue of his recognized place in that "divinely appointed instrument whereby faith is preserved, truth discovered and the efficacy of the sacraments conveyed," was reinforced whenever the hierarchy ensured that his personal conduct made more credible his claim to be "the living representative of God on earth." Furthermore, priests began to increase in number, especially during the 1840s, although the pace of growth initially lagged behind that of the population. Recruited largely from the ranks of the middle classes, whose interests they instinctively espoused, educated more often than not in Ireland, and required to give due attention to their spiritual and pastoral duties, they waged a determined, if less than completely effective, campaign to overcome superstition and suppress peasant traditions identified with spirituous excess and immorality. There were now more churches in which the faithful might worship, and with the introduction of social agencies, such as the Society of St Vincent de Paul in 1844, and an energetic commitment to denominational education, there were more missions to encourage religious behaviour. This was manifest in the greater number of diocesan and parochial institutions and in the work of the newly founded Christian Brothers. In short, "the social origins and lifestyle of the Catholic priest, his lack of connection with the political and social establishment, the absence of alternative social leaders, the atmosphere of an authoritarian culture" all helped to guarantee him a prominent place in local society. Almost inevitably, his influence in spiritual and civil affairs extended into the world of politics.[22]

The cause of emancipation had inevitably drawn priests ever more deeply into popular politics, where they were regarded as an "almost irresistible force." They had acquired a secular taste, one they were repeatedly to indulge long after that particular cause had triumphed. Opponents of the tithes demanded by an alien and "heretical" established church could count on their support. Occasional episcopal injunctions against political involvement went largely unheeded, for even a moderate and cautious primate publicly defended it. Priests had a duty, Archbishop Crolly insisted, to seek genuine equality for the Irish Catholic citizenry of the United Kingdom and to uphold a moral order of society. Patrick Leahy, Archbishop of Cashel, made much the same case a generation later. He defined electoral politics as a struggle of priest against landlord, a struggle in which the priest used persuasion to convince voters to do what was morally right and to act according to conscience, whereas the landlord employed coercion in an effort to compel them to do what was wrong and thus immoral. The priest exhorted voters to support the candidate who was for "his country," his creed, the greatest good for the greatest number, and for equal rights for all. Here was a heady mixture of religion, nationalism, and utilitarianism. Leahy realized that the extent of this political activity might seem strange to the English and the Scots, but he considered the condition of Ireland so abnormal and unhappy that the Roman Catholic clergy could not remain aloof. Ireland had grievances that demanded redress, and it was to obtain that redress that priests mixed in politics.[23]

There was danger in their political activities, as Alexis de Tocqueville recognized. Following dinner with a party of clergy, the Frenchman concluded that they were "[c]learly as much the heads of a party as the representatives of the church." Similarly, conservative elements of the French Catholic press, whose interest in the plight of Ireland reflected both an "awakening of *pan-celtisme*" and traditional anglophobia, were critical of the active involvement of Irish priests in political life. Such behaviour was, in their opinion, undignified and even vicious. Nor was this a concern restricted to foreigners. One member of the Irish laity who fully accepted that the clergy had "a political *duty*" to serve as "guides and directors of the people in Politics" worried that "if they so far forget their dignity as to become agents of the laity instead of their masters they injure themselves and their people." They could not "command and serve at the same time." Of course, the political power of priests was far from absolute; nor could they simply govern the support of the peasantry.[24]

John MacHale was regarded by the Irish Executive and the British government as the archetypal "agitating priest," but in the eyes of a great many of his countrymen he stood as a fearless patriot. His childhood experiences may have awakened in him an incipient nationalism. He could remember the belated arrival of a small French expeditionary force in 1798 and the execution of his local priest for assisting the invaders. The experience, he later claimed, led him to "'expose the misdeeds of those who ruled Ireland.'" Nor would this sentiment have been extinguised either by his early education in a "hedge school" or training at Maynooth, where the "burden of Ireland's wrongs and woes" would have been impressed upon him. They included in his mind the "disastrous" commercial and social consequences of the recent union with Britain, which he observed for himself during a first visit to Dublin in 1807. On completing his seminary training, he remained at Maynooth to lecture in dogmatic theology – filling a vacant chair in 1820 – and quickly became notorious for practising what he taught. He made swingeing assaults on the heresy of Protestantism and was unsparing in his biting criticisms of the Established Church and those institutions and agencies he suspected of proselytism, such as the Kildare Place Society. His "considerable talents" as a controversialist, which he paraded in a series of "Hierophilos" letters whose authorship was no closely guarded secret, earned him the grudging respect of some adversaries but excited disquiet. There was, after all, a "disconcerting savagery" to his denunciations. What impact was he having on the young men who attended his lectures? Appointed Coadjutor Bishop of Killala in 1825, he broadened the field of his fire to target a system of government that he accused of abandoning the Irish peasantry to a wretchedness without parallel in Europe. "Religion and Country [were to him] the objects of one undivided worship." He dwelt upon the golden age of saints and scholars overthrown by foreign enemies, assailing the English as more insidious and brutal invaders than the Danes. When the archiepiscopacy of Tuam fell vacant, the British government pressed the Vatican to overlook him. The Pope's ignoring of "English" pressure, having received MacHale during his pilgrimage to Rome in 1831, undoubtedly contributed to the explosion of popular triumphalism that greeted the announcement of MacHale's elevation. Celebratory dinners rang with praise of this ardent advocate of Ireland's independence. His personal contributions to such gatherings were often intemperate. He blasted many existing laws as "emanations of racial hatred and religious rancour," and when he burst into song, with renditions of "Down with the Saxon, and up with the Gael," there was no hint of the Christian injunction that hatred of sin be matched by love of the sinner. Instead, there was every likelihood of him being understood by less sophisticated listeners as summoning them to resist the "tyranny of alien rule." He was encouraging his fellow Catholics to see themselves "as a persecuted race of true believers." Hence he gained the reputation among some foreign observers as an "unscrupulous troublemaker." Under the circumstances, the appearance in his province of militant Protestant proselytizers, who were hailed by his Anglican counterpart as disseminators of British influence, was tantamount to waving a red rag before this clerical bull.[25]

A man of courage and dynamism, MacHale was respected by several of his fellow prelates and widely admired by humbler clergy. Yet his was a difficult and abrasive personality. Frequently intolerant, intractable, intransigent, irritable if not insufferable, he was doomed to antagonize and ultimately to alienate many of his peers. Those who crossed him felt the lash of his tongue and were liable to fall victim to his propensity for character assassination. But on the issue of repeal he was as one with a majority of his episcopal brethren. As early as September 1842 MacHale, who had met O'Connell while still at Maynooth, becoming a lifelong friend and supporter of the politician, attended and spoke at repeal rallies, claiming publicly that the great mass of the people and the great majority of the clergy were supporters of the cause; nor was he the only outspokenly nationalist member of the hierarchy. William Higgins, Bishop of Ardagh, had travelled to Paris during the depths of the Napoleonic Wars to train for the priesthood. He had then taught theology at the Irish College in Paris before filling the chair at Maynooth and emerging as one of a clutch of vehement episcopal nationalists. Another was Edward Maginn of Derry, who accused the English of "'panting, as in olden times for the blood of the half starved Celts.'" John Cantwell of Meath was no more discreet or less inflammatory. "'British power abroad and gold at home are bent on affecting [sic] what British cruelty and injustice, assisted by the powers of earth and Hell, has for centuries tried to accomplish," he announced on one occasion in reference to the horrors of "famine and pestilence." These were all men who considered it a sacred duty of every Irishman to advocate "the political interest of his country." Some among them even advanced the radical concept of the people as "the true source" of legitimate political power. In dioceses where this kind of leadership was provided, clergy dutifully followed. Indeed, the Catholic Church appeared to be "permeated by national feeling" and the Union "virtually unsupported by any priests." Revealingly, those bishops who did not support repeal prudently refrained from attacking it. If the Roman Catholic clergy were crucial to the successful mobilization of the people in support of the cause, they had valuable allies. In Dublin, where the clergy played a less significant organizational role, the lay leadership was devotedly Catholic, and it too identified nation and people with their religion. Newspapers were similarly crucial to the success of the campaign. They reprinted O'Connell's speeches in full and laid heavy emphasis on the depressed state of the economy, rising unemployment, and the terrors of the Poor Law. Economic deprivation was a natural instrument of ethno-nationalist agitation and an "exacerbator of national tensions."[26]

The Tory government led by Robert Peel approached the Vatican, seeking a papal rescript deploring and discouraging further involvement of clergy in politics. The response was disappointing, merely a vague call in 1844 for priestly obedience to constituted authority and renewed dedication to spiritual concerns. This evident reluctance to offer anything other than bromides may have been the understandable papal reaction to the reports from Ireland. A freshly installed and ironic Bishop of Cork warned the Vatican that "peremptory prohibition of the electioneering partisanship of the clergy, of their attendance and inflammatory harangues at public meetings, their involvement in factious societies and their individual agency in the collection of funds for the purpose of political agitation, would possibly be resented as an undue interference with the exercise of their civil rights, and might compromise the authority of His Holiness." When the Archbishop of Dublin made a half-hearted attempt to use the limp rescript to rein in his priests, he met fierce resistance from the city's lay repealers, while his clergy casually dismissed the document as inapplicable to Irish circumstances. Characteristically, MacHale issued a forthright rejection of the papal missive. Not surprisingly, disappointed Cabinet ministers concluded that, in the struggle against repeal, the priesthood was their most dangerous and formidable adversary. However, the prominence of priests and the repeated declarations that "Catholicism and nationalism were virtually interchangeable" eventually caused problems for O'Connell. He found himself at odds with one of the most attractive and ardent elements within the nationalist movement.[27]

O'Connell's enthusiastic resort to ethnic stereotypes, his lauding of Celts and denigration of Saxons, created common ground between him and a new generation of cultural nationalists, dubbed Young Irelanders. They were keen "to demonstrate the past traditions" of an Irish nation in order to produce "symbolic evidence of its historic continuity and its authenticity." Young Ireland was an elitist and educational movement committed to the re-creation of a distinctively Irish national civilization and identity. The Celtic revival that they championed might have been traced to the Gaelic bardic poets of the Middle Ages. Then, in the seventeenth century, imbued with Counter-Reformation zeal, the poets justified Roman Catholic resistance to English rule, especially after the Old Irish and the Old English, also Irish speakers and Catholics, coalesced "to create an embattled Irish Catholic nation." Geoffrey Keating signalled the emergence of the priest as the leading literary warrior in this struggle, but the eighteenth century saw Protestant as well as Catholic Irish jointly endeavour to counter British contempt through the further embellishment of a gloriously sophisticated Irish past. The founding in 1785 of the Royal Irish Academy gave another fillip to interest in Irish antiquities, and barely a decade later the United Irishmen seized upon this antiquarian research to support their claim for social and political parity with the British. Through the columns of their newspapers and with the aid of verse and song, such as the ballads collected in the songbook *Paddy's Resource*, they appealed to the "primitive national consciousness" of popular "native Irish culture" and expressed a truly national spirit. If sectarianism and anglophobia remained vital elements of the popular culture long after the suppression of the rebellion of 1798, the founding of the Gaelic Society in 1807, to renew the cultural mission, was later followed by additional non-sectarian efforts "to vindicate Ireland's claim to a separate civilization." The Irish Archeological Society (1840) may have been largely Protestant in membership, but the Celtic Society (1845) included representatives of the Protestant intelligentsia within its heavily Catholic ranks.[28]

The Young Irelanders conceived of themselves as an ethnic "organic intelligentsia" and were inspired by Thomas Davis. Half-British in his family origins and an Anglican, he was idealized by his intimates as the repository of most human virtues. His thought appears to have been strongly influenced by the late eighteenth-century German philosopher Johann Gottfried Herder, who argued that "self-determination and independence [were] indispensable for the development of a country" and that a national spirit exists within peoples who "share the same cultural heritage." Education and language were the means by which a nation's spiritual growth was "catalyzed" and transmitted from generation to generation. Thus Young Irelanders set for themselves the ambitious task of mobilizing and unifying the Irish people. Nationalists were "enjoined to 'saturate' themselves in Irish feeling through absorption in the Irish language, peasant life and Irish history in order to create a distinctive Irish future." Although Davis was of the opinion that a people who lacked a distinctive language were no more than half a nation, Irish was already in decline. By mid-century English had become "the everyday language of the vast majority of the people." It had long since been adopted by the expanding and rising Catholic middle classes as an instrument of opportunity and advancement, and it was the preferred medium of the Irish Catholic Church, although many priests remained fluent in Irish, no thanks to Maynooth, and John MacHale published a partial Irish translation of the Old Testament.

Instruction in the national schools was given exclusively in English, and English was the language of the state and its institutions. So Young Irelanders compromised and allowed that "soul could be expressed in poetry in the English language."[29]

Davis exhorted his countrymen to reject distinctions of sect, blood, and class and evoke a "nationality of the spirit as well as the letter." Several of his acolytes were fellow Protestants, but the "race of men" whom they were seeking to educate in their cultural distinctiveness were Roman Catholics, and with the decline of the Irish language they continued to find in their religion the essential bond. Moreover, Davis's dream may have been, as one thoughtful and sympathetic observer remarked a generation later, "to educate the people of Ireland into an acknowledgment of this race characteristic," but idealistic appeals to non-sectarianism were further subverted by the ethnic distinction he and his associates drew. They echoed O'Connell in their denigration of the English "Saxons" as they sought to impress Irishmen with their country's "historic individuality and thus its right of political autonomy." They provided an ironic echo to Lord Lyndhurst's notorious dismissal of the Irish as aliens. Davis contemptuously dismissed the English as "'the mongrel of a hundred breeds,'" dwelt in his verse on the Saxons' "historic cruelties" in Ireland, lectured on their "'unscrupulous appetite for power and plunder,'" praised France as the "'apostle of liberty,'" condemned England as the world's "'turnkey,'" excoriated the "treacherous" and "savage" system established by the English in Ireland, and mourned the debasing of the latter's heritage by alien Saxon values. The Irish differed from the English in "blood, faith, opinions, social habits, sentiments and traditions," Young Irelanders averred. They found evidence of their country's "distinct nationality" in her scenery, in her climate, and in her people's character, and discovered the elements of a "distinctive destiny" in her records, in ancient relics, and in the language, songs, genius, and spirit of her population. This politicization of ethnicity was contributing to the progressive "de-legitimation" of the United Kingdom in the minds of many Irishmen. They were being taught by clerical and lay nationalists that the existing state was alien to their ethnic and cultural identity and that continued rule by strangers was oppressive and degrading. The "dependence of one people upon another, even for the benefits of legislation, [was] the deepest source of national weakness."[30]

The Young Ireland leadership joined O'Connell's Repeal Association, even though they were less than enamoured of the political nationalists, because they considered the triumph of repeal a necessary precursor to the redress of their country's multiple grievances. Hence the joint focus on a presumed enemy, England, in order to arouse and sustain Irish national consciousness. Nor did the association's leadership differ significantly socially from that of Young Ireland. It was a little older but equally middle class in origins and occupations, if less self-consciously a vanguard intelligentsia. Most had reached manhood and launched careers immediately following emancipation, and all bitterly resented the discrimination to which those of them who were Roman Catholics were still subjected. These nationalist missionaries were alarmed by the progress of anglicization, dismayed by the chronic weakness of the Irish economy, and galled by the virtual exclusion of Irishmen of their class, qualifications, and abilities from the most prestigious and important administrative positions. Repeal would bring first-class citizenship. To lay their case before their countrymen, the Young Irelanders founded a newspaper, the first issue of which appeared in the autumn of 1842. Established by Davis, his friend Charles Gavan Duffy, a northern Catholic and experienced newspaperman, and John Blake Dillon, a middle-class Catholic who had entered Maynooth only to make the discovery that he lacked a priestly vocation, the weekly *Nation* resolved "'to direct the popular mind and sympathies of educated men of all parties to the great end of Nationality.'" Its nationality was intended not only to raise the people "'from their poverty, by securing to them the blessings of a DOMESTIC LEGISLATION, but [to] inflame and purify them with a lofty and heroic love of country." To this end, the newspaper preached self-reliance. Indeed, the poem "Ourselves Alone" appeared in one of the first issues. In short, the *Nation* was conceived as an organ of propaganda, its editors owing a large and acknowledged debt to the United Irishmen, whom they defended as men driven to conspiracy and rebellion by state repression. Davis avowed a profound personal admiration for Wolfe Tone as the "model of the politically engaged intellectual," and one of the newspaper's most popular poems was John Kells Ingram's "The Memory of the Dead." He asked: "'Who Fears to speak of Ninety-Eight?'" As one admirer later recalled, "To be national without exaggeration or boasting, to be separatist without seditious rhetoric, to be energetic without being ungentlemanly in violence, to be pure, and free from mean personality was the boast of *Davis's* Nation." Nevertheless, the admiration expressed for the United Irishmen tapped into popular attitudes, which were violent as well as sectarian and anglophobic, and even songs in Irish in praise of O'Connell, who repeatedly avowed a commitment to constitutional action, celebrated physical force. They suggested that "many of the people expected O'Connell to lead them in an armed revolt."[31]

Within a year the *Nation* boasted a circulation exceeding that of any contemporary and this success was aided by its membership of the association. This ensured that Young Ireland's messages reached a far greater audience than would otherwise have been possible. Although approximately one-half of the population were functionally literate, many of them were unable to afford a subscription. Instead, they became familiar with the *Nation* in reading rooms, where the illiterate might have it read to them. Because private circulating libraries were frequently sponsored by Protestants and thus contained materials offensive to Catholics, the latter were discouraged from patronizing them. Equally, legislation to enable Irish corporations to establish public libraries was not enacted until 1855, and even then almost forty years were to pass before publicly funded libraries were established outside of Dublin and Dundalk. The void was filled by reading rooms, some set up by parishes, others by Mechanics Institutes, but many were sponsored by the burgeoning temperance movement.[32]

The Irish, in all probability, were no heavier drinkers than Scots, but their reputation for drunkenness was firmly established and the available evidence at the time pointed to a "considerable increase" in the consumption of legal spirits. However, the evangelical, Protestant, and English colouring of the early teetotal movement led many Roman Catholics to regard it with suspicion as perhaps another sinister instrument of proselytism. Still, a number of priests in both Dublin and Cork had taken the lead in the establishment of Catholic temperance societies before Father Theobald Mathew threw himself into the cause in 1838. He had an immediate impact, quickly emerging as the driving force in an organization overwhelmingly Catholic in complexion that attracted the support of several bishops and several hundred priests. The result was an exponential growth in membership, from nine thousand in 1839 to, by some estimates, five million three years later. But Mathew encountered powerful enemies. Born into a branch of a family of privilege, surrounded by close Protestant relatives, carefully preserving friendly relations with local Protestants who helped to fund his schools and the construction of his church in Cork, Mathew was too ecumenical and insufficiently nationalist for the likes of John MacHale and William Higgins. The former, never loath to engage in character assassination, accused Mathew of an infamous relationship with a female assistant and of duping innocents out of their hard-earned cash. "'In private and public he has applied the most degrading epithets to me and the Teetotallers,'" Mathew complained unavailingly to Paul Cullen in Rome. And in 1847 enemies within the hierarchy blocked his promotion to the episcopacy. On the other hand, Mathew's steering clear of politics, apart from membership of the Catholic Association, stood him in good stead with the authorities. A number of magistrates and police inspectors did fear that under priestly leadership the huge temperance meetings might be adapted to political ends and that the Irish masses were being infused by the repeal campaign with confidence in their own strength. If sober and disciplined, they would surely prove even more dangerous to "English power." Others detected no subversive purpose, and Mathew had a highly placed friend and admirer in Lord Morpeth, the chief secretary. Nevertheless, his organization attracted the predatory interest of the Liberator.[33]

Although Daniel O'Connell had taken the pledge as early as October 1840, there was some doubt concerning the sincerity of his commitment. His personal embrace of teetotallism had about it the stale odour of a temporarily deserted but much frequented taproom. He had "long been a champion of the drink industry," had invested a substantial sum in a brewery managed by one of his sons, blamed its failure on teetotallism, and eventually announced his return to moderate drinking on doctor's orders. "'The evil that has been caused by the association of drinking Repealers is unutterable,'" Mathew informed a fellow priest in 1844. "'At the great O'Connell banquet in this city, there were over three hundred persons drunk ... The Repeal wardens throughout the country hold their meetings in public houses and many publicans are wardens and hundreds of our own faithful teetotallers have yielded to the temptation.'" Father Mathew established reading rooms where those who had taken the pledge might consult uplifting tracts, books, and newspapers. The popularity of the rooms and the success of the movement in general led him to suspect O'Connell of seeking to quaff the entire enterprise in order to adapt it to his political ends. "'The more the masses are educated the weaker – the more palpable – must become the fraud and villainy of those who have enslaved and plundered them,'" one nationalist newspaper observed. By their self-discipline, sobriety, and education, the Irish would demonstrate their capacity for self-government. Gavan Duffy, an "opportunistic ally" of Father Mathew, urged Thomas Davis to impress upon O'Connell the need for repeal reading rooms, "'to diffuse among the people useful information and early intelligence on all subjects of public interest.'" In some communities, temperance rooms were transformed into repeal rooms, which by 1845 numbered in excess of three hundred. Repealers also co-opted temperance halls and bands, all of which infuriated Mathew, who feared that O'Connell's anti-British rhetoric would alienate Protestant backers of the temperance crusade. Thus, at a repeal meeting in Roscommon, the Liberator bellowed: "'[T]eetotallism is the first sure ground on which rests our hope of sweeping away Saxon domination, and giving Ireland to the Irish.'"[34]

Members of the Repeal Association, together with many Roman Catholics who had shunned the agitation, even a number of liberal unionists, criticized the initial heavy-handed response of the Tory government to the growth of Irish nationalism. Monster meetings were effectively suppressed with O'Connell's meek acceptance of the ban of the meeting set for the historic site of Clontarf in the autumn of 1843. Magistrates considered sympathetic to repeal were removed from the bench, a peculiarly restrictive arms bill pushed through Parliament, while O'Connell, along with several leading colleagues and Gavan Duffy of the *Nation*, found himself in court. The trial, when it opened early in 1844, did not reflect well on the quality of British justice. The accused stood indicted of "unlawfully and maliciously" conspiring to excite popular discontent, class hatred and jealousy, disaffection in the army, and contempt for the institutions of justice, and of seeking to secure the dissolution of the Union by means of "intimidation." The initial empanelling of an exclusively Protestant jury led to protests within and without court, and they were not quieted by the selection of a second panel, which was again essentially Protestant following the suspiciously convenient loss of a list of eligible jurors with Catholic names. Although prosecution witnesses admitted that the mass meetings addressed by O'Connell and others were invariably peaceful and orderly, the Crown made much of their quasi-military character and the implied threat of violence. After thirty hours of deliberation, the jury returned guilty verdicts. O'Connell, in the interval between his conviction and admission to prison, made a triumphant visit to London. There, before a congregation estimated to number almost six thousand, he was invested with the Holy Order of the Guild of St Joseph and Mary. Although he was sentenced to a year's imprisonment and a hefty fine, his detention proved to be not only brief but so extraordinarily comfortable and pleasant that he gained noticeably in weight much to the amusement of the satirical *Punch*. Released on 7 September 1844 after fourteen weeks, following an appeal to the Law Lords, he returned to prison the following day to stage a triumphal procession from there to his Dublin home. His "martyrdom" had profited the repeal coffers to the tune of £600,000 and soured many a mind.[35]

Peel made this discovery when he introduced several progressive measures in a parallel and more sophisticated effort to disrupt the "formidable confederacy" against the British connection. His efforts to conciliate elements of the Roman Catholic middle classes and the moderate if mute minority within the hierarchy encountered unexpectedly resolute and vituperative opposition from a disturbingly disparate body of critics. Perhaps harkening to the advice of liberal unionists, he was seeking to assure middle-class Catholics that they could "practically reap the advantage of their nominal equality as to civil rights." But a proposal to appoint more of them to important and valuable offices was effectively resisted by a less enlightened lord lieutenant whom it would have been impolitic to recall. A modest enlargement of the electorate had to be abandoned in the face of backbench resistance in the Commons, while an investigation led by the mildly liberal Lord Devon of the land problem, one on which O'Connell and Davis had seized with a raft of radical proposals beneficial to tenants, produced little of substance.[36]

The introduction of well-intentioned legislation to facilitate the charitable endowment of the Catholic Church and end the exclusively Protestant control of the board controlling bequests infuriated the bishops largely because of Peel's failure to consult them first. MacHale and Paul Cullen, among others, who included O'Connell, assailed the bill as an insidious attempt to meddle in church affairs. Thirteen bishops and more than six hundred priests promptly signed a circular denouncing the measure, and the clerical signatories eventually approached three times that number. Meanwhile, Archbishops Crolly and Murray, who had exhibited a willingness to work with the government in the matter, were branded its "'paid advocates'" by Bishop Cantwell. An act to establish three non-denominational provincial university colleges was quickly denounced by both sides of the sectarian divide. Ultra-Protestants and the ultra-nationalists within the hierarchy – MacHale, Higgins, Cantwell and Maginn – reviled the institutions as "Godless." MacHale accused the prime minister of seeking under the "shadow" of the Maynooth grant to "'steal on the country a disastrous

and demoralizing measure.'" Once more Crolly and Murray were subjected to the abuse of several of their fellow prelates. O'Connell again
sided with the clerical critics. The bill was "'execrable,'" he declared,
and "'a more nefarious attempt at profligacy and corruption never disgraced any minister.'" Other secular opponents of the measure insisted
that the colleges be boycotted because they were certain to be infected
with an "anti-national ethos." Peel's provision of the more generous
public funding so desperately needed by the Catholic Seminary at
Maynooth, which MacHale dismissed as a bribe to the Catholic clergy,
sundered his ranks in the Commons and incited a furious popular
Protestant backlash throughout Britain. This did little to persuade Irish
Roman Catholics of the benefits of Britishness or of the merits of the
Union. Instead, Peel's attempt to demonstrate that an avowedly Protestant state could transcend sectarian interest had been vitiated.[37]

The prime minister did find a silver lining to the dark and ominous
clouds gathering over his government in the late summer of 1845. He
assured a monarch who rarely thought well of her Irish subjects that
priests were finally proving cooperative in the matter of maintaining
public peace. Equally reassuring, at least from the standpoint of the
Protestant state, was the schism within the Irish hierarchy. With its
nationalist majority at the throats of the three moderates, there seemed
scant likelihood of the bishops patching up their differences any time
soon to make a united challenge to government policies. More encouraging still, repeal appeared to be in a terminal decline. Here again, the
evidence of internal dissension was all too visible. The episcopal flay-
ing of Peel's conciliatory measures had angered Young Irelanders, for
they interpreted the clerical intervention as a return to the sectarian
politics they deplored and further proof of an unwelcome identity of
repeal with Roman Catholicism. They resented clerical charges that the
Nation was un-Catholic and un-Christian, and were outraged by the
innuendo, which they traced to the O'Connell clan, that in publishing
the articles of Thomas Davis and John Mitchel, Protestants both, the
newspaper was promoting writers antithetical to the traditions and
faith of Catholic Ireland. They were exasperated by the Liberator's
opposition to the Charitable Bequests Bill, accusing him of putting
church before nation. They were at odds with him over the university
colleges, which they welcomed as another means of uniting Irishmen of
different persuasions and subduing "the animosities of manhood." In
mixed education they saw a means of restricting the Church's meddling
in affairs of state, and Davis issued an ironic rejoinder to the charge

that communication between students of different creeds would taint "'their faith and endanger their souls.'" He declared: "'They who say so should prohibit the students from associating *out* of college even more than *in* them.'"[38]

Beyond disagreements over the role of the Catholic Church, which Davis regarded as but one of several sects rather than the sole means of man's salvation, the Young Irelanders' differences with O'Connell were increasingly personal. They deplored his *amour propre,* his vulgarity on the stump, and feared that his nepotism and demagoguery were tarnishing the shining cause for which they were crusading. Nor could he match their high-minded integration of the evil of drunkenness into a "full-blooded philosophy of Irish nationalism." Misery and despair drove the people to drink, Thomas Davis insisted, and their moral elevation was the indispensable prerequisite for the achievement of national independence. On the other hand, the Liberator's denunciation of slavery in the United States was far more principled than their somewhat shabby evasion of the issue out of fear of alienating potential transatlantic supporters. Curiously, the Young Irelanders exhibited a lack of pragmatism in their sharp criticism of O'Connell for allowing Richard Lalor Sheil to be returned to Parliament unopposed. He had been appointed master of the Mint in the Whig government formed by Lord John Russell on the fall of the Peel administration in the summer of 1846. Against the background of an ever-deepening human crisis spawned by a fungus that was destroying the potato crops, and given Russell's recent remark that the Union would have become meaningless were Ireland not to be treated in this emergency as an integral part of the United Kingdom, it was but common sense to accommodate the incoming ministry. Russell's vehement opposition to repeal was at this juncture less important than his apparent willingness to deliver generous measures of relief to suffering Ireland.[39]

3

Famine and Nationalism

British confidence that the "material advantages" of union would eventually "wean the Irish from their animosities of race" proved to be misplaced, and not least because the advantages failed to materialize. This Richard Lalor Sheil had emphasized when appearing as the defence counsel of John O'Connell, the Liberator's son, chosen political heir and fellow accused, during their trial early in 1844. Ireland "'might, perhaps, be reconciled to the terms of the Union, bad as they were,'" Sheil declared, "'had the results been beneficial to the country; but travellers stood appalled at the misery she represented.'" The British were quick to deny responsibility for the lamentable state of affairs. They blamed the Irish themselves, whom they accused of wasting "in faction, and political and religious hatred, the energies which should have been devoted to developing the resources of their country." The onset of the Great Famine provided an especially cruel reminder of the continuing failure of the constitutional marriage to produce prosperity as its Irish progeny. O'Connell's demand for an annulment and the politicization of ethnicity by the Young Irelanders, which was a preliminary to divorce, had both drawn strength from economic disillusionment with the match. Indeed, the mass appeal of the Repeal Association turned in part on O'Connell's ability to convince the peasantry that autonomy would significantly improve their lot, for the passage of years had done little to weaken the Irish conviction that this was one union in which the commitment for better or for worse was being applied separately to the partners. This was certainly the complaint of Isaac Butt, a conservative unionist but a "nationally minded Irish Tory." The Irish had been promised a partnership in a "great and opulent nation," he observed, only to discover that for them it was always one of loss and never one of profit. This former editor of one of the most influential voices of Protestant unionism, the *Dublin University Magazine*, reflected an ominous broadening and deepening disillusionment with "the meagre fruits of union." It was now infecting the ranks of Irishmen traditionally regarded as its staunchest supporters.[1]

Economic discontent found one expression in demands for the revival of tariff protection for native industries, even the repudiation of free trade. Daniel O'Connell might on occasion blame militant trade unions for the decline of certain industries, but more commonly he charged the Union with assault and battery of Ireland's industrial sector. The strong growth of Irish exports to Britain, producing not only a favourable balance of trade but prosperity for many farmers, simply provided additional grist for this particular mill. The exports were overwhelmingly agricultural. While several industries, especially textiles, had managed to survive Ireland's absorption into Britain's far more advanced and diversified economy, there could be no mistaking the precipitous decline in domestic flax spinning. This was an especially ominous development for a large segment of the over-abundant rural labour force, which depended heavily on the industry for supplementary income. Tragically, it was the self-same segment in which rapid population growth had been most heavily concentrated. The small pockets of successful industrialization that did exist could not provide sufficient employment off the land to ameliorate the condition of an immense subsistence stratum. Even the success of the temperance movement proved counterproductive in the sense that it adversely affected employment in the brewing and distilling industries and in the distribution and sale of their products. On the other hand, Ireland's rural poor enjoyed relatively good health, for their supplies of food and fuel were usually adequate, and they escaped the diseases of urbanization. It was this vast reservoir of exploitable and cheap labour, usually paid with temporary access to a plot of land on which to grow food (this was dubbed the conacre system), that largely explained the increased productivity of Irish agriculture. The escalating cost of land saw the rural poor steadily reduced to ever-smaller plots and a restricted if still nourishing diet. An ever-greater dependence on potatoes, and increasingly those of inferior if especially productive varieties, together with progressive impoverishment, left millions of them peculiarly susceptible to disaster. "It is the want of manufactures and commerce that reduces the peasantry, whether in Ireland or in England, to the conacre system," wrote one sympathetic English reporter. "An exclusive dependence on agriculture always leaves its dependents to be pursued and overtaken by famine." That the Irish in this perilous position numbered, according to many estimates, more than three million brought readers of Thomas Malthus to the morbid conclusion that Ireland's swelling population was rapidly outgrowing the ability to feed itself.[2]

Dire warnings of the loss of "'considerably more than one-third of the entire of the potato crop'" and of the daily extension of the destruction were being issued by the late autumn of 1845. Police reports and Irish newspaper accounts signalled a catastrophe in the making, while the Dublin Mansion House Committee, chaired by the Duke of Leinster and Lord Cloncurry, declared a famine of "'a most hideous description'" to be "'immediate and pressing.'" In recommending obliquely a halt to the export of Irish grains, the committee was pursuing a liberal political agenda, the repeal of the protectionist Corn Laws. Thus, it protested the continued closure of Ireland's harbours to the importation of corn even as the grain being exported would in quantity have been "'nearly adequate to feed" the island's entire population. The committee was preaching to one of the converted. Robert Peel had already concluded that the remedy for the "'very alarming'" situation in Ireland was "'the total and absolute repeal for ever of all duties on all articles of subsistence.'" However, a government led by him and with Henry Goulburn at the Treasury – both men former occupants of the chief secretary's chair with considerable experience of Ireland and its recurrent food crises – was not about to rush into action without compelling supporting evidence of a truly desperate situation. After all, the British were repeatedly informed by their press that the Irish were ignorant, indifferent to squalor, and seemingly content to live in abject poverty. The initial reports suggested that their condition this year differed little from other years and that the suffering was far from uniform. Moreover, O'Connell's repeal campaign "had generated a good deal of ill will in England, not only towards the leader but also towards his [peasant] supporters as well." The influential *Times* mused that Irishmen "'required some great and terrible calamity to remind them of their common duties and to restore them to commonsense.'" Its tone changed as it rallied to the cause of free trade in corn. Before the end of the year it was admitting the danger of famine in Ireland and criticizing Peel's delay in introducing effective countermeasures.[3]

The importation of maize on the government's account and its sale at cost to local relief committees, the funding with Treasury advances and smaller grants of a broad range of public works as a means of putting money into the hands of the poor to purchase available food, the establishment of soup kitchens, and the launching of private relief subscriptions were the traditional responses to emergencies. This crisis also brought the repeal of the Corn Laws, though in driving the measure through Parliament, with the aid of the Opposition, Robert Peel completed the disruption of the Conservative Party he led. The Whigs took office in June 1846. Before either of these developments, Earl Grey, who within a few months was to enter the Whig Cabinet as colonial secretary, delivered in the House of Lords a remarkable indictment of British government of Ireland. That unhappy country stood as a "'standing disgrace'" of Britain, he informed his fellow peers, and was so regarded "'throughout the whole civilised world.'" All foreign visitors to the island returned home convinced that "'nothing comparable'" to her sorry condition was to be found in their native lands. The evils they witnessed were the result, in his judgment, of misgovernment, and while he considered the government of Ireland before the Union "'the most ingeniously bad that was ever contrived in the face of the world,'" Grey conceded that the many useful measures adopted since the turn of the century had not "'gone to the root of the social disease.'" The people of Ireland had "'experienced no abatement'" of their "'wretchedness and misery.'" Nor did he pull his punches on the political consequences of this sad state of affairs. The "'whole mass'" of the Irish nation was now alienated from the institutions under which they lived. They harboured "'a deep feeling of hostility to the form of government'" under which they were placed. "'This feeling, which is the worst feature of the case,'" he added, "'seems to be rather gaining strength than to be diminishing.'" Of course, it was possible, as one prominent official at the Treasury later remarked, that even the "'poorest and most ignorant Irish peasant'" would in this crisis realize "'the advantage to him of forming part of a powerful Community like that of the United Kingdom the Establishments and pecuniary resources of which are at all times ready to be employed for his benefit.'"[4]

Charles Trevelyan, who as assistant secretary of the Treasury supervised from London the administration of relief in Ireland, repeatedly informed the senior officials in the field that cost what it may, "'the people must not, *under any circumstances*, be permitted to starve.'" Had this principle truly guided British policy throughout the crisis, then the "poorest and most ignorant" of Irish peasants might have been genuinely impressed with the advantages of the Union. Instead, as the situation continued to deteriorate, this "idealism" gave way to a

desire merely to ameliorate the unfolding calamity. People were soon
starving, and more than one million deaths were eventually attributed,
directly and indirectly, to the Famine. Most were victims of the diseases
associated with severe malnutrition and impoverishment. Typhus,
relapsing fever, typhoid, dysentery, and cholera had been frequent visitors to Ireland in the past, where even in rural areas poverty in combination with rapid population growth obliged large families to live in
primitive and cramped conditions. Mobility compounded the problem,
and severely undernourished itinerants made generous hosts for
aggressive organisms. There were all too many carriers of disease wan-
dering the countryside, and the "crowds of dirty, louse-ridden people
ever on the move, crowding together in temporary lodgings or at soup-
kitchens, incessantly begging from door to door," proved a disastrously
efficient means of propagating contagion. Further complicating the
situation was the insufficient number of fever hospitals in which to isolate the evidently ill. Those that did exist, together with the numerous
dispensaries, were starved of adequate funding. Similarly, the accommodation set aside for the sick in the workhouses, to which the desperate poor were compelled to resort in unmanageable numbers, "fell
far short of what was required." As a result of an inability or failure to
separate the diseased from the healthy or maintain reasonable standards of sanitation, these refuges became a primary source of human
misery and tragedy. The Fermoy workhouse had been built to house
eight hundred inmates, but for a period of five months it gave shelter
to three thousand. Almost half of them perished.[5]

As the men employed on public works grew steadily in number,
reaching seven hundred thousand, and with the addition of dependents
the grand total so supported probably exceeding three million, the
Whigs' commitment to this form of relief withered. "'The common
delusion that government can convert a period of scarcity into a period
of abundance is one of the most mischievous that can be entertained,'"
the prime minister observed to a member of the Cabinet in October
1846. Lord John Russell's pessimism could only have deepened with
the receipt of multiplying reports of abuse. The respected Father Mathew privately complained that wherever works were instituted, magistrates granted licences for public houses. Overseers and pay clerks then
set up their offices in these "pestiferous erections," in which some of
them had a pecuniary interest. "'It often happens,'" he advised
Trevelyan, "'that the entire body of labourers, after receiving payment,
instead of buying provisions for their famishing families, consume the

greater part in the purchase of intoxicating drink.'" The Cavan Relief Committee acknowledged the receipt of "numerous complaints" of persons securing employment on public works who did not qualify under the instructions issued by the government, which limited this form of aid to persons destitute of support or "'for whose support such employment [was] actually necessary.'" Henry Goulburn, the former Tory chancellor of the Exchequer, who was still consulted by his Whig successor, believed the new government had made a disastrous mistake in seeking to apply to a widespread famine the means he and his colleagues had utilized to relieve an extensive yet partial dearth. The government could not go on making new roads forever or employ a large portion of the population on them year after year, he argued. Like so many others in Britain, Goulburn feared that vast sums were being wasted and that Irish poverty would be the ruin of Britain. Russell and his Cabinet evidently agreed. In the spring of 1847 expenditures by the Board of Works were running at £1.2 million a month. Continued at this rate for an entire year, they alone would consume more than one-quarter of the total current revenues of the United Kingdom.[6]

Yet the evidence of a truly desperate situation continued to pile up. Father Mathew informed Trevelyan in December 1846 that in Cork women and children were wasting away, reduced to filling their stomachs "'with cabbage leaves, turnip tops and the like to appease the cravings of hunger.'" Another priest claimed that men were working for two days on public works without "'tasting a morsel of food.'" Alexander Somerville, the correspondent of the *Manchester Examiner,* reported that "[n]ever, in the known history of mankind, was there a country and its people so dislocated as Ireland is now; so inextricably ravelled, and its people in such imminent hazard of perishing utterly." They were dying of want and of diseases induced by it, he warned, while many of those who were managing to survive were too feeble to work. Despite this, the Russell Cabinet decided to call a halt to the expensive public works. As a stopgap measure, it secured passage of the Destitute Poor Act in February 1847. Soup kitchens were to be set up, thus greatly extending a form of relief that the Quakers were already employing successfully on a much smaller scale. A noted French chef, Alexis Soyer, was recruited to open a model soup kitchen in Dublin, which he did in April. His culinary concoction failed to scale the heights of *haute cuisine*. Although the correspondent of the *Times* declared it palatable, *Punch* ridiculed it as devoid of nutritional value. Father Mathew implied as much in his correspondence with Trevelyan.

The kitchens were "'affording great relief,'" he wrote, but "'flesh meat, fish and milk'" needed to be introduced into the soup to make it a fit food. The issue of quality aside, a lack of coordination between the termination of public works and the opening of soup kitchens led to a disastrous hiatus in the provision of public relief. Private agencies were active. The British Association for the Relief of Extreme Distress in Remote Parishes of Ireland and Scotland had been founded on New Year's Day, 1847, and within a fortnight a national appeal for funds was made over the Queen's signature. The government contributed £2,000 in her name, and the total amount collected exceeded £430,000. Although it then supplied five steamers to convey to distribution points the £20,000 worth of seeds, principally of oats, for the potato purchased by the association had proven "treacherous," this state contribution was not disclosed for fear of antagonizing the commercial sector. But private relief agencies could not fill the void created by the premature closing of public works, and the result was "the horrendous mortality of 1847."[7]

The cautious and inadequate British response to this unprecedented crisis invited harsh Irish criticism. A new Central Board of Health was established, one with "the right to decide on the extent and nature of local provisions for the sick," but imperial pressure to provide such provisions was rarely if ever accompanied by adequate central government funding. Instead, the additional expenditures were to be a charge on the local rates. Unionists such as Isaac Butt and Richard Lalor Sheil, the latter a member of the Whig government, rejected the argument of British newspapers, such as the *Times*, that the Famine was a "provincial" crisis. Britain would not think twice about entering a war in defence of her national honour, Sheil pointed out in the Commons in May 1847, even though the expenditures in such a conflict would within six months exceed the funds needed to support famine-stricken Ireland for six times that length of time. The Crimean War was soon to vindicate him. He urged British members to follow the noblest of all their "national characteristics," their humanity, and acquiesce in essential relief appropriations, for he made no bones of the fact that there were men in the House "whose national kindness" had been overwhelmed by "their austere political economy." In much the same spirit and frame of mind, Daniel O'Connell had reminded Whig ministers of the £20 million set aside barely a decade earlier, by an administration in which several of them had served, to compensate West Indian slave owners for the legislated emancipation of their human property.[8]

Members of the hierarchy also assailed the policies of a government that appeared to be shirking its responsibilities. The knowledge that the bishops would assemble in Dublin in October 1847 prompted the commissary general, Sir Randolph Routh, to make an attempt to forestall further attacks from so influential a quarter. Many of the bishops were "'as ignorant as they are excited,'" he privately observed, "'and paint every public act in grossest form.'" Through a Catholic member of the Relief Commission, he sought to impress them with the government's expenditures, its seed distribution, and the recent grants for fever hospitals. The bishops' response was an "extraordinary memorial" presented to the viceroy. This located the source of the current tragedy in "unjust penal enactments" that deprived the bulk of the people of "the rights to property thus debarring them from the enjoyment of its fruits." In the name of humanity and social justice, the hierarchy condemned the conduct of the governing Whigs as utterly inadequate and demanded a more interventionist strategy. MacHale was in the vanguard of the clerical critics. In a series of widely circulated letters addressed to Lord John Russell, he framed a typically sarcastic and brutal indictment. "If you are ambitious for a monument," he informed the prime minister, "the bones of a people, 'slain with the sword of famine,' and piled into cairns more numerous than the ancient Pyramids, will tell posterity of the triumph of your brief but disastrous administration." He was laying Famine deaths at the government's door. All it needed to do to halt the tragedy, he insisted, was check the exportation of foodstuffs from Ireland. Here was a simple and easily grasped solution to a complex problem, and one that the rector of the Irish College in Rome discreetly advocated. The ban of such exports from the papal states, and similar interventions by other sovereigns, persuaded Paul Cullen that were Britain to adopt the same policy in Ireland, the suffering would be greatly diminished. William Higgins, the vehemently nationalist bishop of Ardagh, on the other hand, expressed incredulity that any "honest Irishman" still looked to the British Parliament for justice. He went further, accusing landlords of starving the poor with the government's connivance. Public statements such as these were liable to be interpreted as an implied justification of a resort to extra-constitutional methods to secure desperately needed measures of relief.[9]

Secular critics did not pull their punches either. From the outset, the *Nation* seized on the crisis to flay the British connection. The potato was "'an English importation, another method of keeping a conquered race under control, and the great men of Irish history had been fed on corn.'" It poured scorn on the initial relief measures of the Whigs, including the program of public works. The English people were merely doling out to the Irish a pittance of their very own money plundered from them year after year and for which the English were taking "'ample security ... on Irish soil'" so that they could plunder the Irish again in the future. The *Nation* was soon levelling the accusation that other nationalists subsequently elevated into an article of faith: "'The potato blight is the dispensation of Providence – the famine is the work of a foreign Government.'" News that the public works it had earlier disparaged were about to be wound up saw the *Nation* charge the British with the certain death of as many as two million people. As for the soup provided eventually in the kitchens, this it labelled "'dysentery-juice.'"[10]

Daniel O'Connell accused the British of treating Ireland like some foreign farm, whereas an Irish parliament would have kept domestic foodstuffs at home and thus rescued a starving people. Thomas Francis Meagher, one of the most effective Young Ireland orators, ploughed much the same furrow. Exports of agricultural produce were evil, he declared, because they were "so grievously wanted at home." England was able to rob Ireland of food, he went on, because the Irish lacked the power to protect it. The *Nation*, along with other newspapers, repeatedly insisted that Ireland was producing enough food to feed her famine-stricken population but the harvest was being shipped off to already well-stocked English larders. Even the repeal of the Corn Laws was condemned as yet another body blow to Ireland's farmers. Then came legislation to amend the Poor Law and levy the costs of relief on Irish property. Both decisions expressed and exploited traditional British contempt for Irish landlords, who increasingly became the target of the British press as the crisis worsened with successive failures of the potato crop. They were blamed for Ireland's poverty and suspected, if not accused outright, of diverting relief monies into their own pockets. The *Times* led a determined effort, with the support of the *Illustrated London News* and the enthusiastic backing of *Punch*, to depict O'Connell as the classic example of Ireland's negligent and apathetic landlords. Shortly before the first wide-scale failure of the potato crop, the newspaper had despatched a "Commissioner," Thomas Campbell Foster, to Ireland to investigate the condition of her people. He reported that the island's most wretched peasants were to be found on the Liberator's estate, and *Punch* caricatured him as "a gross, lumpy potato, complete with organic Repeal Cap, reclining on a divan." The reputation of Irish landlords in general sank to new depths with reports of their massive evictions of unwanted tenants. Estimates of the number of families forced off the land have varied widely, but they were certainly counted in the tens of thousands. Russell was moved to contrast the conduct of Irish landlords with those of England, observing to the viceroy that the latter did not "'turn out fifty persons at once, and burn their homes over their heads, giving them no provision for the future.'"[11]

The loud demand in a Britain anxious to slash, if not halt, relief expenditures was for Irish landlords to be compelled, if necessary, to do their duty "'by the pressure of a stringent poor-law.'" The trouble was that many landlords, already up to their ears in debt, could not bear a far heavier burden of relief and might be driven to the wall. This did not concern the British press. Far better a class be ruined, the *Times* blithely remarked, than a nation, meaning the British nation, be ruined: "'England must be freed from the drag-chain of Irish improvidence and the contagion of Irish pauperism.'" But as the *Nation* asked, and it was no natural ally of landlords, from whom was money to be raised in a near bankrupt nation? Recalling earlier Whig assurances that the resources of the empire and all the means of the Treasury would be employed to save the Irish from starvation, the *Freeman's Journal* condemned government policy as a positive cruelty and repeatedly insisted that millions were being "deliberately sacrificed" to "a spurious political economy." All that had been required to halt the horrors of famine and demonstrate that Ireland was truly an integral part of the United Kingdom, it added, was political will – the will to provide a starving people with food and employment. Indeed, elements of the Irish press charged the government with a capital crime – "the murder of the people."[12]

Allegations of calculated British indifference to the plight of the Irish people – that the British government was allowing the Irish to starve while food was exported under guard to Britain; that it was permitting its Irish agents, the stone-hearted landlords, to evict masses of small-holders forcing the dispossessed into underfunded and disease-ridden workhouses even though the government was refusing to provide emergency funding to dispensaries and fever hospitals – failed to excite an immediate response from a desperate population whose traditional attitudes, as reflected in street ballads, were anglophobic and violent. Instead, one American visitor found an exhausted people who made plain their gratitude for the assistance they were receiving from imperial authorities. Many of those frantically struggling simply to survive had no surplus energy with which to protest their terrifying plight, nor could they spare the time, let alone the money, to digest newspaper accounts of their abandonment by the government. Moreover, the distribution of the determinedly propagandist *Nation* was concentrated among the comparatively affluent middle classes in the better-off counties, whereas the misery was far worse among the more impoverished and less literate residents of the west and southwest. These victims were undoubtedly preoccupied with the failings of persons much closer to home, as modern folklore studies confirm. Anger was directed more at "landlords, land grabbers, agents, grain dealers and large farmers rather than the British government," which was feeding three million people a day in soup kitchens during the summer of 1847. Popular opinion apportioned a full share of the blame for evictions to tenant farmers who exploited their neighbours' poverty to grab their land by offering its rent to the proprietors. Shopkeepers who did the same by foreclosing on mortgages were also vilified, as were the members of local relief committees accused of diverting food to their relatives and friends or of using it as feed for their livestock. The *Nation* might excuse the discharge of labourers by farmers, for those working ten acres or less could ill-afford to retain help, but men thrown overboard into the sea of grief, denied money wages or access to conacre plots without advance payment, or prosecuted for stealing food from the fields, could see for themselves that many of the farmers working twenty or more acres were finding safe harbours. Thus, in some areas middling farmers became figures of hate. They and merchants were the principal beneficiaries of the government's blinkered reliance on market forces, which at least resulted in the importation of far more food into Ireland than she exported. By 1847 the volume of grain imports was sixfold that of exports. Furthermore, much of the food shipped out was too expensive to be diverted to famine relief, and neither agricultural labourers nor cottiers had the means to buy it, while the five hundred thousand farmers, together with millers, merchants, and labourers dependent on the trade, "would certainly have resisted the lower prices that an export embargo would have brought in its train."[13]

Some contemporaries readily understood that interference with the profitable food trade would be resisted by a large and powerful sector of Irish society. Alexander Somerville certainly emphasized the difficulties in his reports to the *Manchester Examiner*, while attempts by the famished physically to prevent shipments of provisions from their localities usually saw landlords, farmers, and merchants jointly demand police and military protection of their merchandise. Nor would an embargo have solved the acute food shortage created by successive and virtually total failures of the potato crop. At best, it might have mitigated the suffering during the autumn and early winter of 1846 by checking the inflation in prices. Then again, the Famine's principal victims were aware that local dealers in provisions often could not resist the temptation to exploit the crisis; traders as well as farmers engaged in profiteering. Father Mathew, who set up a soup kitchen in his own home, complained to London of the price gouging by traders in corn and flour. Indeed, his plan to open a public bakery to produce a less expensive loaf than that currently on sale in Cork was fought by local bakers. Some merchants opposed the opening of soup kitchens in order to protect their profits. Surveying all of this, an appalled *Galway Vindicator* berated those farmers, merchants, millers, bakers, and provisions hucksters whose conduct was putting "to the blush every feeling of humanity and [was libelling] the very name of Christian." Nevertheless, by its blind and obdurate refusal to undercut the inflated prices, the "English Government" lent additional credibility to the accusation that it was entirely responsible for the tragedy of the Famine.[14]

Nationalists continued to lay the charge. One listener to an O'Connell speech recalled years later that it "turned on the famine, which in some wonderful way was so mixed up with English oppressions that his audience probably ended by believing that the potato blight had come by Act of Parliament." The tens of thousands of pounds sent to Ireland as donations by English Protestants were evidence less of sympathy with than of fear of the Catholic Irish, O'Connell gracelessly asserted. Fresh seeds of anglophobia were being both carefully planted and wildly scattered, and seemed certain to germinate and eventually to propagate. They were to flower in the "overtly political ballads on the Famine" that began to circulate a decade later. By blaming the English or British for the tragedy, the Irish were acquitting themselves of complicity in the crime of failing to do more. The sad truth was that while the British government ought to have done far more to mitigate suffering and thus bore the heaviest responsibility for the tragedy, few sectors of Irish society were entirely free of guilt. The delivery of voluntary relief was frequently impeded by the virulent sectarianism that had discouraged ecumenical cooperation in the decade before 1845 and now manifested itself in a "dreadful competition" between Catholic and Protestant clergy over the administration of assistance to those in need. Accusations of "souperism," of Protestant evangelicals offering relief in exchange for conversion, were levelled. While such cases undoubtedly existed, the legend of its extensive practice which Cullen was to foster in his first pastoral on appointment as Archbishop of Armagh, probably resulted from "the compression of stories over a longer period of time." The "well-meaning" Protestant rector of Kilmoe, County Cork, who provided a sacramental service and confession for the Catholics of his parish following their abandonment by their priest, was subsequently "reviled as a 'souper.'" The Rector of Westport, County Mayo, gave half his stipend to the local relief committee. Bishop Cantwell chose to ignore "the extraordinary and disinterested efforts of Protestant rectors" in Westmeath. His clergy, he declared, "were the only 'assistance which inspired the poor with confidence.'" His small-mindedness appears to have been largely political. This devout nationalist "realised that the crisis represented an opportunity for his clergy to assume a leadership role at this critical juncture." The dedication of Catholic priests, who braved great personal danger to perform their pastoral duties in fever-ridden parishes, was illustrated by the numerous deaths among them. Equally, dependence on the voluntary contributions of their parishioners condemned a great many others to severe hardship. The privations of the vast majority helped to mute criticism of the minority who declined to accept parishes where disease was rampant, who enjoyed relative comfort amidst the destitution, or who backed the demands of successful farmers for a greater police and military presence in those areas where a starving peasantry were driven to steal food or sought to prevent its shipment out. The Catholic Church might have chosen in this crisis to suspend its campaign to raise funds for the ambitious program of church construction – "one priest was even accused of levying contributions on the meagre earnings of his parishioners from public works" – and some members of the hierarchy might have temporarily diverted to the domestic tragedy collections for the propagation of the faith, or the monies raised to aid a pontiff put to flight by Italian nationalists. But these would have been mere drops in the bucket of need. Ironically, the most persuasive rejoinder to any such criticism would have been equally valid as a rebuttal to the bitter condemnation of continued food exports – far more was arriving in Ireland than was leaving the stricken land. The Pope's personal appeal to the Catholic world in March 1847 on behalf of the suffering Irish brought a generous response from Europe, the Americas, and the Antipodes.[15]

Farmers who discharged their labourers, either to pare expenses they could no longer afford or to protect their profit margins, were no more inclined to support them via higher poor rates. The ruthless decision of the Whigs in the summer of 1847 to charge the costs of relief to Irish property, the timing of which they may have rationalized in their own minds following the encouraging reports of a "blight free and prolific" potato crop in the summer of that year, put communities and individuals to a severe test that in many instances they failed. Middle-class repealers, in their capacity as Poor Law guardians, often behaved callously, for the larger the expenditures on the needy, the greater the drain on their own incomes. Even in some relatively affluent areas, guardians refused to provide adequate funding for temporary fever hospitals and turned a deaf ear to pleas to keep open those hospitals in which some separation of the sick from the healthy was attempted. Where Poor Law Union indebtedness resulted in the local guardians being replaced by central officials in the shape of vice-guardians, the restoration of solvency took precedence over humane considerations. Unfortunately, the return of control to the guardians often brought no change of policy or priorities. Instead, on occasion, it resulted in a more "rigorous" interpretation of the Poor Law. The rate-in-aid, which sought to spread the costs of relief more evenly by raising monies in more affluent unions to help defray the heavier expenses elsewhere, excited bitter opposition, especially in Ulster and Leinster. Officials in the northern province protested the taxing of their solvent unions to fund "'the dissolute, uncivilized west.'" In Leinster, the measure was resisted as an unfair burden and an unwelcome shift from local rating to national charge. Nor did opponents overlook the argument that it represented a violation of the principles of the Act of Union. If all of Ireland was to be rated, why should the rest of the United Kingdom escape? The Famine was an imperial crisis. One terrible consequence of such failures, whether communal or imperial, was a sharp rise in deaths in 1849. The potato blight had returned the previous summer, and so did cholera towards the end of 1848. "This is dreadful, I am appalled at the prospects of the next winter," one Irish member of the government had written home on reading reports of all of the potatoes again being "spotted." Meanwhile, a senior relief administrator gave the Treasury fair warning that it was inviting the charge of "slowly murdering the peasantry by the scantiness of relief."

Once again, the Whig government was not the only culprit. Ireland's political leadership, including that of the nationalists, abjectly failed to put aside personal, class, economic, and partisan differences and pull together on behalf of their tormented countrymen.[16]

John Bright, a Radical member of Parliament, confessed to "a personal humiliation" when as an Englishman he considered the condition of Ireland. Yet he was critical of the performance of Ireland's political representatives. Had 105 English members sitting in a parliament that met in Dublin, or even a far smaller number equal only to the current body of repealers, been convinced that their country was a victim of bad legislation, they would in his opinion have responded with far greater energy and effectiveness. By "their knowledge of the case, their business habits, activity, union, and perseverance, [they would] have showed a powerful front, and by uniting together, and working manfully in favour of any proposition they might think necessary to remedy the evils of which they complained, they would have forced it on the attention of the House." It was a severe but far from entirely unfair judgment. The fissures that Robert Peel's Irish policies exposed within his own parliamentary ranks had, during the first year of the Famine, presented Irishmen with a rare opportunity to exert exceptional influence.[17]

Smith O'Brien, a descendant of one of Ireland's historic families, had as a feckless young man suddenly discovered his life's purpose in politics. A former Tory who became a liberal unionist and courageous parliamentary foe of O'Connell, he was dismayed over Parliament's seeming inability, or unwillingness, to legislate properly for Ireland, and as a consequence deserted to the repealers. It was his belief that a solid phalanx of fifty or sixty Irish members could shape an imperial policy far more generous to Ireland. The *Dublin Evening Mail* and the *Freeman's Journal*, one as unionist as the other was nationalist, took up the cry. Nor did the final collapse of the Tory government in 1846 immediately damage the Westminster prospects of an Irish Party. Instead, by the end of that year, Russell's indecisive leadership and minority position in the Commons suggested that a unified and determined body of Irishmen would be able to extract far more in the way of famine relief from the dithering Whigs. To this end, and with the blessing of the physically fading Liberator, a meeting was held in Dublin in mid-January 1847. Thirty-six resolutions were adopted and subsequently endorsed by some eighty peers and members of Parliament. They denied that market forces could provide the Irish with sufficient food and agreed that the Famine was an imperial calamity, that the costs of public works were therefore properly a charge on imperial funds, that the works ought to be as far as was possible genuinely "reproductive," and that evicted tenants should receive compensation for any improvements they had made to their holdings.[18]

This national coalition quickly disintegrated once Parliament reassembled. A Tory proposal for massive public investment in Irish railroad construction was of dubious merit as a make-work project, as Britain's most distinguished railroad engineer privately pointed out, and Russell's threat to resign if it passed the House saw repealers break ranks with the Irish Tories. The dissolution of the Irish Party was completed by the landlords' hostility to the principle of outdoor relief written into the revised Irish Poor Law. Once passage of the measure was certain, they successfully attached a provision – the quarter-acre test for relief – designed to facilitate the removal of the swarms of unwanted smallholders from estates. This response again laid bare the inability of Ireland's political representatives to place the national calamity ahead of personal and partisan interests. Very few Irish members voted against the measure. The intent of the sponsors of the amendment was to bracket the quarter-acre test with a scheme for a truly massive emigration funded both publicly and privately. Inevitably, they underestimated the resistance. Russell's Cabinet objected on grounds of cost, while one prominent repealer from a merchant family protested that the loss through emigration of large numbers of customers would ruin trade. Naturally, he couched self-interest in nationalist terms. English shipowners would carry the emigrants to their new homes, he complained, and English manufacturers would supply them with goods once they were established overseas. Members of the hierarchy and the priesthood were similarly critical, though there was a conspicuous lack of clerical unity. Some priests described emigration as a "Divine destiny" and emigrants as "holy missionaries," while others were moved to "verbal violence." Bishop Maginn refused to consent to the expatriation of millions of his "'co-religionists and fellow countrymen'" at the behest of the "'hereditary oppressors'" of his race and religion who had "'reduced one of the noblest peoples under heaven to live in the most fertile island on earth on the worst species of a miserable exotic, which no humane man, having anything better, would constantly give to his swine or his horses.'" So much for the potato. Emigration was a result of English hatred of the Irish people and their religion. Why should Irishmen quit their native land when they had just title to its soil?[19]

John O'Connell led the repealers out of the Irish Party. His ailing and enfeebled father died in May of 1847 while on a pilgrimage to Rome, but not before he had made his own personal contribution to Irish political disunity. He engineered a break with the Young Irelanders on the contrived issue of physical force, thereby further easing, if unintentionally, the pressure on the Whig administration. John Mitchel provided the excuse for the breach. An Ulster Protestant, a lawyer by profession but a literary firebrand by avocation, radicalized by the terrors of the Famine witnessed first-hand during a walking tour of the west, he returned to Dublin a "grim conspirator" of "cynical severity" and "fervent hater" of all things English. He was convinced that the British government had seized the opportunity of this tragedy finally to subjugate the Irish. He was also something of an ideological paradox. A revolutionary idealist who advocated "national and social revolution in Ireland," he was at the same time a conservative revolutionary who lacked "democratic instincts" yet revelled in his role and reputation as an extremist. "'I propose copious bloodletting,'" he later wrote, but "'upon strictly therapeutical principles.'" As acting editor of the *Nation* during Gavan Duffy's sabbatical to work on a book, Mitchel published one of his own deliberately radical articles in which he explained how easily the railroad network might be sabotaged in order to prevent the rapid deployment of troops in the event of an emergency. Duffy stoutly defended author and article, an act of loyalty that subsequently saw him brought to book on a charge of seditious libel. He was acquitted, thanks to a hung jury, which undoubtedly confirmed the authorities in their dark suspicion that individual jurors were inclined to be governed in political trials by considerations unrelated to the quality of the evidence.[20]

Some Young Irelanders were privately critical of the incendiary and violent tone of their organ during Mitchel's temporary editorship. Ironically, Thomas Davis, whose premature death in September 1845 had robbed the movement of its inspirational leader and created the vacancy on the *Nation*'s staff that Mitchel filled, had exhibited a measure of ambiguity on the issue of physical force. Under certain circumstances he had considered it an imperative, exhibiting a romantic's admiration of military glory and contempt for the "Quaker creed." Moreover, most Young Irelanders, as self-conscious missionaries of a "revolutionary aesthetic" alive to the inherently revolutionary character of their nationalism, balked at the idea of an "unqualified repudiation of physical force in all countries, at all times, and under every circumstance."

Meagher, for one, insisted that there were times when arms alone would suffice and when political improvements called "for a drop of blood, and many thousand drops of blood." But it was on just such a blanket peace resolution that O'Connell effectively expelled the Young Irelanders from the Repeal Association and banned the *Nation* from its reading rooms. There was more than a whiff of hypocrisy in his posturing. As a youth he had witnessed a little of the horror of the French Revolution, and as a young man he had deplored the sanguinary rebellion of 1798. Both experiences contributed to his decision to make the repudiation of violent means a central tenet of his ideology. His commitment to constitutionalism and moderate nationalism, however, had never prevented either the spectre of violence or its frequent harbinger, ethnoreligious enmity, from haunting his platform rhetoric. His personal taste in semi-martial dress, his arch and frequent references to the heavy Irish enlistments in the British armed forces, his boasts that he stood at the head of an army mightier than that commanded by Wellington at Waterloo, his dismissal of the duke and Robert Peel as latter-day Cromwells, his deliberate association of the repeal agitation with the events of 1798, and his threats to resist physically any curtailment of the right to petition for redress of grievances, all smacked at the very least of a willingness to fight a defensive war. Of course, artful politician that he was, O'Connell was usually careful to temper his suggestive remarks with expressions of reverence for the Crown. Ambiguity similarly characterized the remarks of several of the clergy who rushed to second his attack on Young Ireland. Earlier, they had surrounded O'Connell on the platforms from which he bellowed his thinly veiled threats. So what were the faithful to make of the comments of those priests who now held up the rebels of 1798 as a "noble contrast" to Young Irelanders?[21]

Following a tumultuous debate on Daniel O'Connell's peace resolutions, during which Thomas Francis Meagher rhetorically unsheathed the patriot's righteous sword and Smith O'Brien declared his aversion to violence but declined as a matter of personal and national pride to proffer any cast-iron assurances on this score to the British, the Young Irelanders were in the summer of 1846 evicted from the Repeal Association. This did not sit well with the artisan repealers of Dublin, as a substantial majority of the repeal wardens and some fifteen thousand sympathizers demonstrated by signing a remonstrance protesting the purge. There was strife also in Cork, where the Burgess Association dominated by the lower middle class championed Young Ireland against the more affluent O'Connellites of the Chamber of Commerce. Schism at the top took a heavy toll on morale at the base of the nationalist movement, especially as famine and unemployment were already starving the agitation of funds. Indeed, the Liberator may well have privately concluded only months before his death that an Irish parliament would have had great difficulty organizing a more generous program of relief than that implemented by the Whig ministers in London. Nonetheless, as the suffering intensified following a second and total failure of the potato crop, he attacked the insufficiency of their measures. What price nationalist unity now? A belated and hesitant attempt was made to reconcile the adversaries, one to which Daniel O'Connell contributed with a signal of his willingness to make cosmetic amendments to his peace resolutions. But the Young Irelanders were held fast in the grip of their own virtue. They rejected compromise and celebrated the New Year by organizing the Irish Confederation "for the purpose of protecting the national interests and obtaining the Legislative Independence of Ireland, by the force of public opinion, by the combination of all classes of Irishmen, and by the exercise of all political, social and moral influences within their reach."[22]

The lip service paid to Irish unity and an assurance of non-sectarianism could not mask the extent to which the Confederation's governing council reflected a sectarian reality. Nationalism was a cause that drew its popular support almost exclusively from the Catholic community. Ironically, when a delegation of prominent Confederates ventured north to Belfast, they were assaulted and their meetings disrupted, not by the suspicious Protestants they had come to court, but by repealers. Elsewhere, the new nationalist organization did succeed in attracting the support of urban artisans, but in rural Ireland it encountered hostility. Catholic peasants believed that the leading Confederates had harried and hurried the Liberator into his grave. Briefly, the prospects of a nationalist reunification appeared to improve. A call from John O'Connell for Irish members to withdraw from Westminster and reconvene in Dublin as a council of national distress was endorsed by the *Nation*. Hope was quickly dashed. John O'Connell's shameless efforts to exploit for partisan advantage the public sympathy aroused by his father's death, together with a savage attack on the late leader in the *Nation*, the work of a radical priest, further embittered relations. Matters were made worse by the onset of a general election campaign, for this further heightened tensions and spawned excesses. The Irish Confederation called for the formation of a truly independent Irish parliamentary party that would maintain an "absolute independence of all English parties." Such a party, it argued, would be "more formidable than armed insurrection." However, support was largely restricted to an urban class few of whose members had yet been enfranchised. Consequently, the Confederation returned only a pair of members, one of them Smith O'Brien. The repealers, on the other hand, with the conspicuous assistance of the clergy, won thirty-nine seats. Unfortunately, they had little sense of party loyalty and lacked the astute leadership necessary for their development into an effective parliamentary ginger group. Yet again Ireland was denied the resolute and disciplined representation that the deteriorating condition of so many of her people demanded. This was less a failure of constitutionalism than a failure of political class, whether nationalist or unionist.[23]

Irish disunity thus rendered virtually impotent a parliamentary strategy, and this reality contributed in turn to the further enfeeblement of the Confederation as a political force. A group of disenchanted radicals, centred around the mercurial Mitchel, now sowed dissension in its ranks. They found an ideologist in the person of James Fintan Lalor. The son of a highly successful tenant farmer and sometime repealer member of Parliament, Lalor broke from his father's political allegiance. He derided the repeal movement as "a leaky collier smack, with a craven crew to man her and a sworn dastard and forsworn traitor at the helm." On the other hand, he had been impressed with the possibilities of political agitation and was preoccupied with tenant rights and the plight of the legions of smallholders. Initially, he approached Robert Peel in the guise of a self-avowed Conservative with a proposal of thoroughgoing land reform as the sure means of crippling repeal. But the tragedy of the Famine convinced him that little worthwhile could be expected from London. He turned to the Confederation for political support. Hating the Irish aristocracy, heavily influenced by the writings of Sir William Blackstone and John Locke, Lalor argued in a series of public letters that "the entire soil of a country belongs of right to the people of that country, and is the rightful property not of any one class, but of the nation at large." Ireland's landlords were aliens and robbers who by their selfish response to the Famine had demonstrated that they were also traitors to Ireland. He urged Confederates to promise a redistribution of land and a clear definition of tenant rights in order to attract mass support from an independent peasantry on which he believed a secure nation could be erected. He identified the five hundred thousand farmers of ten acres or less who were being driven to the wall during the Famine, or cleared from estates, as the core of that peasantry. More than this, in some mysterious and unexplained way, peasant proprietors would produce the diversified economy Ireland had long needed. Given a seat on the Confederation's council, Lalor quickly discovered that his proposals, which included a rent strike, were far too radical for most of his colleagues. John Mitchel was one member who stood apart from the dominant moderates.[24]

Seeking to expand the base of its popular support, the Confederation began in the summer of 1847 to promote the establishment of local clubs complete with meeting rooms where an ample supply of nationalist reading material was to be found and, in the best Young Ireland tradition, regular lectures might be delivered on Irish history, literature, and economic development. Moderates may have seen the clubs as a defensive force against hostile repealers, but the Confederation's radicals openly declared their purpose to be the destruction of the English interest, the formation of a national government, and the restoration, by legislation and arms, of the country's full integrity. The clubs were not to be mere reading rooms, John Mitchel informed his fellow clubmen, but places of study on how to rid Ireland of English rule and how to "'re-conquer'" it from England. To this end, and given the heartbreaking news from across the land of suffering and death from famine and related diseases, an angry, frustrated, and ever more strident Mitchel advocated ever more radical measures. He urged tenants to hold their produce for domestic consumption and revived the idea of an embargo on food exports; he exhorted ratepayers to withhold that portion of the tax designated as repayment of earlier Treasury advances to finance relief measures, and eventually recommended a rates strike in apparent ignorance of the consequences for the poor; he proposed that the people arm themselves and form militias to resist a recent Whig coercion bill; and he eventually implied that guerilla warfare was a viable alternative to parliamentary action. Denied access to the columns of the *Nation*, Mitchel announced in January 1848 the prospectus for his own newspaper with the meaningful masthead of the *United Irishman*. The very first issue declared: "'Exactly half a century has passed away since the last Holy War waged in this island, to sweep it clear of the English name and nation.'" As the correspondent of a German newspaper observed, Mitchel was "preaching 'resistance against the law and unrest, if not treacherous murder.'" Then, at a meeting of the Confederation in February, Mitchel and Thomas Devin Reilly quit the governing council in disgust when the council reaffirmed a commitment to class unity and constitutional means, leaving them in a minority. They remained members of the Confederation, however, and sought to build support among the clubs. Lalor, still smarting from the rejection of his proposed rent strike, surprisingly refused to contribute to Mitchel's organ.[25]

Mitchel disparaged as illusory all talk of achieving Young Ireland's ends through legal and constitutional means. Only through physical force would Irishmen win their nation's freedom, he insisted, but a rebellion was certain to fail so long as Britain remained at peace. The Irish had to wait for a foreign war or domestic upheaval before striking. Aware of the appeal of Mitchel's radicalism to the rank and file of the multiplying clubs and seduced by a seemingly painless revolution in Paris, which had prompted the firebrand's call for an Irish republic, the Confederation's leading moderates agreed that this was the moment to exert additional pressure on Britain. Smith O'Brien led a delegation to Paris in search of support, a seemingly realistic quest given the reported expressions of sympathy for repeal by leading figures in the new French government. The Irishmen discovered that Gallic Republicans were pragmatists rather than idealists, who placed respect for British power above commitment to revolutionary fraternity. O'Brien and his companions returned home with little to show for their journey, although they had been given an enthusiastic reception by the young theologians studying at the Irish College in France and were carrying a recovered nationalist symbol in the form of a tricolour flag. White in the centre signified a lasting truce between the orange and the green, Meagher explained somewhat unnecessarily to a Dublin audience. There was also a curiously ambivalent appeal for Irish American support, while O'Brien and Gavan Duffy pressed for the establishment of an Irish National Guard. Had not the defection of the French Guard persuaded Louis Philippe to abdicate and retire to England? Indeed, Duffy offered a qualified endorsement of physical force from his editorial chair at the *Nation*. Overtures were also made to the Chartists, both the British and their Irish offshoot, the former undergoing something of a resurgence during the early spring. These radicals were the closest the Confederation was likely to come to British allies, for a number of them had voiced impatience with constitutional agitation and a preference for physical force. Their principal attraction and value was a diversionary force, which in the event of an Irish rising might prevent the rapid concentration of state power. Not that there was long a strong likelihood of any such alliance proving a serious embarrassment to the government, for Chartism's springtime proved distressing brief. Moreover, the long-threatened split in the Confederation had occurred. Mitchel's avowal of republicanism made him even more of a political liability to the leadership and had resulted in his resignation.[26]

The Whig administration was unwilling to leave developments to chance. It sought to cow the Confederation leadership by arresting several of its more prominent figures on the charge of seditious libel, even as a treason-felony bill was being pushed through Parliament. The purpose of the new statute was to facilitate successful prosecutions by defining a serious non-capital crime. Juries would surely be more willing to convict if punishment was restricted to transportation. Failure to secure jury unanimity in the trials of Smith O'Brien and Thomas Francis Meagher on the lesser charge of seditious libel ensured a more careful selection of the jurors before whom John Mitchel was to be tried on the charge of treason-felony. This Protestant nationalist stood before a jury box occupied by his sectarian peers. Although Mitchel did not dispute the charge that he had advocated a resort to physical force, the composition of the jury and the severity of the sentence – transportation for fourteen years – filled fellow nationalists of all stripes with indignation and excited sympathy among many who were in no way identified with his cause. The number of Confederate clubs had grown dramatically, with a total membership of some forty thousand, following the successful revolution in France and the earlier attempted prosecutions. Several of them resolved to stage a rescue in the all too probable event of Mitchel's conviction, only for this plan to be scotched by a leadership that recognized the folly of confronting Ireland's formidable military garrison. Mitchel bitterly resented, as did many clubmen, this putting of discretion before valour. He was swiftly transported. But Gavan Duffy proved to be equally resolute in rejecting a similar rescue plan in his own case when he subsequently found himself again standing in the dock.[27]

An unforeseen consequence of Mitchel's martyrdom was an apparent closing of nationalist ranks. The Confederation reached an understanding with the rump of the Repeal Association and in mid-June of 1848 agreed to form the Irish League. The authorities' nervousness increased with reports of arming and drilling by Confederate clubs, ostensibly as the cadre of the proposed National Guard. The Executive responded by steadily increasing the pressure on the nationalists. First, leading nationalist agitators, beginning with the editors of the three most radical newspapers, were rounded up and detained. Charged with sedition, they enjoyed a curiously liberal detention during which they were permitted to meet and continued to write editorials. The contributors to John Martin's *Irish Felon* now included Lalor, impressed as he had been by the martyrdom of the editor's brother-in-law, Mitchel. Lalor's own call for armed rebellion saw him quickly added to the list of detainees. Next, to simplify the business of arrests, *habeas corpus* was suspended. The ease with which this negation of a fundamental British liberty sped through Parliament, thanks largely to the alarming reports of a massive "semi-military demonstration" in County Tipperary and the invocation there of the "true gospel" as preached by John Mitchel, provided extra-parliamentary nationalists with a stark reminder of the inability of the recently elected repealers to mount a worthwhile constitutional resistance to coercive measures. Finally, the government increased the intimidatory pressure. It leaked news of an imminent strengthening of the military garrison and naval stations in Ireland; issued a proclamation declaring illegal membership in the clubs, to which recruits had recently been flocking; despatched police and soldiers to search for caches of arms; and made fresh arrests. Among those detained was the leading Irish Chartist.[28]

All of this galvanized elements within the Confederation into "defensive" action. An agent was despatched to Scotland to organize a diversionary strike in Glasgow. Convinced that Chartists there were ripe for a rising and that the Scottish city was virtually undefended, the Confederates hoped to create a regiment of rebels out of its thousands of Irish residents. Word of rebellion in Ireland was to serve as the signal for them to seize a vessel and hurry to their native land. There were plans to stage a similar diversion in Liverpool and for a small expeditionary force composed of Liverpool Irish to land at Wexford. In the event, the men who rose with Smith O'Brien at Ballingarry, County Tipperary, on 29 July 1848, surrendered ingloriously after a brief skirmish with a modest detachment of police. The diversions failed to materialize. The hapless leader's *aide-de-camp* was James Stephens, a youthful employee of a railway company. He drew several lessons from the humiliating episode. To have any chance of success, a rising required resolute leadership, "meticulous preparation," a none too scrupulous adherence to "strictly honourable tactics," and a healthy scepticism about clerical support. A second misguided attempt at rebellion in much the same area of the country less than two months later, led by John O'Mahony, proved to be another humiliatingly damp squib. The following year saw Lalor dabble with direct action. Released from prison because of chronic ill-health, he threw himself into the plotting of an uprising that included a scheme to kidnap the Queen during her coming visit to Dublin. However, Lalor suffered cold feet at the last moment and his career as a revolutionary activist ended ignominiously.[29]

The British press gleefully twisted a knife in the self-inflicted Irish wound. Led by a mocking *Times*, they heaped ridicule on O'Brien's "cabbage patch" rebellion. The failure of the Irish people to answer his call was widely credited to the Catholic clergy. On this point, both viceroy and rebels were in agreement. Yet a rudimentary opinion survey circulated by the Executive among magistrates both endorsed the conclusion that the rebellion's failure was attributable to the intervention of the priesthood and confirmed rebel claims that several priests had encouraged subversive organizations only to desert them at the critical moment. Senior churchmen, among them the Archbishop of Dublin, together with the usually well-informed rector of the Irish College in Rome, privately admitted that a number of clergy "had a large share in promoting among the people that excitement of which the calamity which lately impended over us should have been foreseen as the natural growth." Thus, in O'Mahony's area of Tipperary a parish curate, Father Patrick Byrne, was the chief organizer of Confederate clubs. He led the way in the establishment of almost a dozen, which together enrolled perhaps one-third of the community's adult males. The curate of a neighbouring parish founded the club of which O'Mahony became the president, and it provided the model for several others.[30]

Bishops and priests had waged a long and unrelenting campaign of criticism of the government, and this, no less than the ethnopolitics of Young Ireland, often amounted to a denial of the legitimacy of the United Kingdom. Religion was fundamental to the ethnic identity of the vast majority of Irishmen, and priests had long been prominent within the ranks of political entrepreneurs of ethnic consciousness and assertiveness. Pastorals and letters had been circulated to expose "the unparalleled sufferings & miseries of the people of Ireland from bad government." As leaders of their people, they sought to instill a sense of patriotism and remind them of their duty to support Catholic nationalists. The role of priests in election campaigns, and especially on behalf of repeal, had rarely been greater than in 1847. The MacHale-led assault on Peel's conciliatory measures, the repeated if far from unjustified condemnation of the government for stinting on famine relief, the charging of the government with responsibility for the terrifying death toll, the claim that it had banished, drowned, or killed one and a half million terror-stricken emigrants, the unfounded allegation that it had given the cold shoulder to desperately needed foreign aid, all amounted to a sweeping and grim indictment of the existing political and social order. Priests who on occasion acknowledged the generosity of the English people often did so only to contrast their "charities" with the behaviour of a "faithless government." There was every likelihood of listeners interpreting the wholesale criticism as a rejection of the United Kingdom as a "properly constituted authority" and a justification of attempts to overthrow it. The French *chargé d'affaires* had ironically remarked of MacHale's pastorals that they were ill-calculated "to temper his flocks with a spirit of penance and humility." In the words of one modern witness to a priestly accusation from the pulpit that the regime under which his congregation lived was unjust and needed to be kept under constant pressure if it was ever to change, "[t]here were those in that church that night, and in the district outside it, who would adapt that sense to their own methodology: a resurrection of the physical force tradition." It was their nationalism as much as their spiritual leadership that accounted for the clergy's enormous popular influence, the Lord Lieutenant acknowledged. This was an opinion shared by a revolutionary nationalist of the following generation. He recalled that in his youth "the parish priest was looked up to as 'the embodiment of hostility to England,'" for it was often difficult to determine "where the clergy's dislike of Protestantism ended and their loathing for England began." This was equally true of several members of the hierarchy. "Some of us, by our denunciations of the government, drive the people, who reason more logically than canonically, to rebellion," one bishop later conceded.[31]

The use of religion to legitimate a search for national identity raised questions about its relationship to means as well as to ends. Upholding "an ideal against which human performance can be measured," religion provided the dissatisfied with hope for a better life on earth and thus ammunition for an attack on the status quo. It had "frequently spurred revolt, providing the ideology and social cohesion for rebellion against the existing political and social order." St Augustine's gospel of submissiveness, that God appoints rulers "according to the merits of the people," enunciated with an eye to securing temporal assistance to suppress a heresy, had undergone reinterpretation during the medieval period. Peter Abelard drew a clear distinction between the power to rule justly derived from God and the tyranny rooted in a man's evil nature. To resist the latter was not to deny the former. The following century brought Thomas Aquinas's refinement of the right of rebellion against tyrannical regimes. This was a duty "whenever the state infringed upon the religious conscience of its subjects." If this was an important qualification of the legitimacy of revolt, so also was his requirement that a community not suffer greater harm from the upheaval "than it would from a continuance of the former rule." Nor did the somewhat ambiguous condemnation of the doctrine of tyrannicide at the Council of Constance in 1415 discourage Catholic theologians, during the stress and strife of the Reformation, from restating the right of resistance to tyrannical or heretical rulers. These authorities were frequently cited by both the modern minded and the traditionalists during the tumult of the French Revolution, but in the nineteenth century the institutional concerns and authoritarian predisposition of the Catholic Church increasingly shaped its stand on rebellion. Gregory XVI condemned the Belgian and Polish rebels in 1830, even though both were Catholic subjects of anti-Catholic regimes. In truth, the Church had long been allying itself with absolute monarchy, and the humiliations it subsequently suffered at the hands of Italy's liberal nationalists did nothing to liberalize its stance.[32]

Priests still came forward to defend violent change and suffered the disciplinary consequences. A prominent French liberal Catholic made the discovery that there was no place for him within the Church following his defence of the right to rebel. Other clergy were conspicuous in the Mexican revolt, the Neapolitan revolution, and even the Italian nationalist movement the papacy anathematized. A similar state of affairs had long prevailed in Ireland. Thus, in 1798, at a moment when the Holy See was peculiarly dependent on the favour of the British government, it had enjoined the hierarchy to impress upon the faithful the virtues of loyalty and obedience. This the bishops duly did, only to be made painfully aware of their inability "to deflect suggestions that the lower clergy were not only involved in the radical [United Irish] conspiracy, but that they were to a great degree responsible for its direction." While the seventy priests actively involved in the rebellion were a mere fraction of the entire vocation, they proved numerous enough to attract unwelcome notoriety. Moreover, the subsequent and far heavier clerical involvement in the struggle for Catholic emancipation signalled the end of the official policy of "total passivity in the face of temporal authority." Similarly, too much ought not to be read into the effort of priests to suppress ordinary crimes in the name of law and order. Their conduct was entirely consistent with the interests of that class of farmers from which they increasingly came, and it went hand in hand with their political agitation. Some of them, such as John MacHale, with his passionate concern for the socially oppressed, fervent advocacy of nationalism, and excoriation of British tyranny, appeared to be advancing an inchoate form of liberation theology. However, the commitment of the Roman Catholic Church in Ireland to "human liberation from social injustice" was less than ardent, and priests tended to be highly selective when it came to the identification of the oppressors of the "poor and needy." They had no "systematic social philosophy," while their political and economic philosophy was fundamentally conservative.[33]

The dawn of 1848 had seen the Vatican, under British diplomatic pressure, order an investigation of the accusation that Irish churches were still being used as places of political assembly and of the still more sensational claim that clergy were implicated, if only indirectly, in acts of violence and even murder. The Archbishop of Cashel, in a prolix response, traced the root of the problem to a desire by a Protestant and English government to control the Catholic Church. Ireland's ills "were the direct result of the subjugation of Catholic Ireland by Protestant England," he asserted. Here was an explanation calculated to dissuade Rome from allying itself with the government of the United Kingdom. The primate, meanwhile, firmly denied any clerical involvement with murder but did admit that churches were being profaned by political harangues. The admission prompted Paul Cullen, then still rector of the Irish College, to initiate an exercise in damage limitation. Publicly, he declared that such blasphemous conduct must be halted. Privately, he urged MacHale to prod his bishops into despatching a joint letter to the pontiff detailing the "real state of things and protesting against English lies and English interference." Cullen also sought to dress up the clergy's political activities in the familiar humanitarian garb, arguing that it would not be right to prevent them "from advocating the rights of the poor and pointing out to the rich the duties of their station." Indeed, with the arrival of MacHale and a fellow bishop in Rome in mid-April, the critics of "English" policy succeeded in securing a satisfyingly definitive papal ban on the attendance by Catholics at the "Godless" colleges.[34]

A triumphant MacHale returned to Ireland only to find himself under attack for being absent during the rising against English rule, which his detractors maintained he had done much to foment. It was certainly true that the younger clergy who admired him for his nationalism made up that small minority of priests who exhibited revolutionary sympathies. They no less than the secular nationalists had been inspired by the news from Paris and especially by the reports of the active involvement of fellow priests in the virtually bloodless events there. Smith O'Brien, in planning his uprising, may well have been persuaded that nationalist clergy would rally to him and would bring with them a peasant army. John O'Mahony later claimed that in south Tipperary "the originators of the movement were priests" and that the Young Irelanders would never have attempted to lead the people in a rebellion had they not "calculated upon the cordial and active cooperation of those clerical revolutionists" who had declared void the contract between government and people. A Waterford priest had proclaimed "that there is *practically* no government in this kingdom, and, therefore, in conscience, no allegiance is further due." In Limerick, another promised that he and his clerical brothers would do their utmost to rescue their fellow countrymen from "the debasement, destitution, and destruction of foreign rule," and predicted that in the event of a rising the clergy would be with the people "to a man." Instead, priests underwent a late change of heart. Lingering suspicions of the *Nation* and of Protestant influence upon it and Young Ireland played a part in their veering away from radical action. An even more decisive factor was the disturbing turn of events in France – red revolution and the murder of the Archbishop of Paris – and the threats to the Pope from Italian nationalists. If these crises and concerns nurtured serious doubts as to the efficacy of revolutionary violence, the certainty of a rebel defeat in Ireland weighed heavily in the balance of clerical minds and tipped them in favour of discretion. Moreover, the notion that clerical nationalists suddenly reversed course due to the fear that they had helped to create a Frankenstein monster was contradicted by their seeming success in discouraging popular support of the 1848 rising. Of course, a people physically exhausted and psychologically damaged after almost three years of famine had never been truly promising revolutionary material.[35]

The rebels were roundly condemned by senior figures at Maynooth, where most Irish priests now received their training, and this may well have contributed to the seminary's emerging unscathed from a parliamentary investigation of its loyalty. Cullen also denounced the Young Irelanders, describing them as "sowers of dissension and a source of ruin to the Irish cause." Statements such as these angered John Mitchel, who complained that as much as the hierarchy disliked British power, it hated revolution more. The cause of Ireland would never be advanced through an alliance with the Catholic clergy but only over its "fallen power," he insisted. Yet individual clerics continued to exhibit sympathy for the defeated rebels. They urged the viceroy to treat the captured with clemency; a nationalist member of the hierarchy aided the escape of Thomas D'Arcy McGee from Ireland, perhaps unaware that he had been the agent despatched to Scotland to stage a diversionary uprising and recruit an emigrant regiment to support the main event in Ireland; and John Mitchel's eventual flight from his Tasmanian exile to the American republic was effected only with the active assistance of a local Irish priest clearly motivated by nationalist rather than sectarian sympathies. Nevertheless, an investigation of the Church's attitude to rebellion, conducted by a member of the theology faculty at Maynooth, had long since concluded that force might only be resorted to in cases of unbearable tyranny, where submission was morally more costly than resistance, where there was no obvious alternative to violence, and where success was certain and community approval demonstrable. These demanding preconditions clearly made little enduring impression on a number of younger priests. Fifteen years after Ballingarry, a regular and trusted clerical correspondent of the now Archbishop Cullen wrote: "I am shocked at hearing too many young Priests gloating over anticipated rebellion and Revolution through American intervention, losing sight of all the horrors of civil war and forgetful of their divine mission of Peace and that they were sent not as wolves but as sheep to the slaughter." He had heard all too many of them speak of "war & physical force as the only means of righting the country & scoffing at O'Connell & his peaceful policy." Clergy who became "active agitators, often fierce political firebrands," seemingly failed "to appreciate the trend and logical result" of their words and actions.[36]

4

Unholy Nationalism

"England, whether Catholic, Protestant, Ritualistic, or in a state of semi-conversion, is still the Evil Genius of our country and our people." This was the blunt message of the *Irish Catholic Banner* twenty years after the 1848 rebellion and during a period of high tension following another eruption of Irish revolutionary nationalism. The newspaper's disavowal of any sectarian colouring to its nationalism echoed the revolutionary ideal espoused first by the United Irishmen and then by the Young Irelanders. Yet there could be no denying the increased influence and power of the Roman Church and its priests, at times the engine and bogies of Irish nationalism. Their prominence in the repeal campaign, denunciations of inadequate governmental measures of relief during the Great Famine, and even the success of Young Ireland's propaganda war on Britishness had all served to enhance the popular esteem of hierarchy and priesthood. The Catholic clergy's standing and self-confidence were further strengthened by the evident and increasing respect accorded them by a Protestant government anxious to distance the United Kingdom from a narrowly sectarian identity. The Catholic Church had emerged as "a powerful interest group" and was acknowledged as such.[1]

Was it possible that British pragmatism would rescue the Union, allowing it to succeed, not merely survive? The odds had seemingly shortened with the collapse of repeal and the disintegration of Young Ireland. But there remained, as ever with respect to Ireland, grounds for caution if not pessimism. The mass clearances of uneconomic smallholders from estates, and effected only at the cost of much additional misery, thrust "exterminations" to the forefront of Irish national consciousness. Any struggle between landlords and tenants could all too persuasively be reduced to an ethnic and sectarian confrontation. James Fintan Lalor had tied the land issue to the national cause, and he was one of those radicals who turned to journalism to promote their ideas. O'Connell's demagogic appeals had always paled beside the *Nation*'s assiduous advocacy of ethnic nationalism, and that newspaper's enduring influence was reflected in the number of provincial organs committed to raising "the level of awareness regarding the history and culture of Gaelic Ireland." This several of them sought to do by printing at least a little material in Irish, thereby reminding readers, including those who neither read nor spoke the language, of the cultural differences with Britain. Much the same could be said of the Ossianic Society, founded symbolically on 17 March 1853. Its declared purpose was to collect and publish "Gaelic manuscripts with English translations, dealing with the ancient Irish legendary band of hunter-warriors the Fianna," a brave and fearless elite who had protected Ireland from foreign attacks during the pagan era. The nationalists who dominated the society and edited the great majority of its limited publications attributed Ireland's later inability to resist foreign invasions to the destruction of this Fenian militia. Although dedicated to cultural rather than political activity, the Ossianic Society was "a largely nationalist organization" and one that pointed the way "to the potential link between Gaelic folk culture and a more democratic, and possibly revolutionary view of Irish society."[2]

Parish priests and curates were a significant proportion of the Ossianic Society's admittedly small membership. They were similarly prominent in the Celtic Society, which united with the Archeological in 1854. Here was fresh evidence both of their literary interests and cultural nationalism. Nationalism was part of the culture of Maynooth, and clergy were prominent among the Irishmen who believed that during the Famine the starving poor had been treated by the British as aliens. For their part, British observers were in no doubt of "the effect produced by the impassioned declarations of these trusted guides of the people." They found a grain of comfort in the Irish Catholic Church's reaffirmation of an unswerving commitment to constitutionalism. Indeed, this was one of several factors (among the others were the steady erosion of Ascendancy privileges as a result of O'Connell's understanding with the Whigs, the gradual progress of parliamentary reform, and the comparatively liberal attitude of the state with respect to rights of association and assembly, together with its toleration of an often savagely critical if not inflammatory press) that held promise of the safe steering of Irish nationalism "into the realm of open political and parliamentary campaigning."³

The entrance of a new leading player onto the national stage early in 1850 did not appear to presage any radical alterations to the script. Paul Cullen returned to his native land as primate and apostolic delegate. The new Archbishop of Armagh boasted a longer and purer nationalist pedigree than his moderate predecessor, the late William Crolly. Distrust of Protestant government was a Cullen birthright. His family had a rebel history and a tradition of intense Catholicity, his father having been imprisoned in 1798 while other kin forfeited their lives. The elder Cullen had subsequently sent Paul to a Quaker school for his early education, only eventually to pack him off to Rome rather than Maynooth to train for the priesthood. He objected to the seminary's acceptance of state funds and to the related requirement that its students take an oath of allegiance. Placed at the heart of the Universal Church, the young Cullen attracted august patrons in the persons of Leo XII and Gregory XVI. Following ordination, he was appointed first to the faculty of the College of Propaganda and then as rector of the Irish College. He was not yet thirty years of age. The counter-reformation character of both institutions shaped his attitudes and conduct, as indeed did his inherited nationalism. When the Protestant Archbishop of Armagh made a courtesy call on the new Catholic primate, he was curtly informed that he was "not at home." Politically, Cullen's sympathies were with repeal, though always with the proviso that it not be pushed to the point of civil war. Nor did Peel's conciliatory measures persuade him that "Poor Ireland" would ever "get anything from England." It was an article of Cullen faith that English intentions and objectives were invariably sinister, and foremost among them was greater state control of Irish hierarchy and the Catholic Church. Cullen had been deeply suspicious of Russell's proposal to establish "diplomatical relations" with the Vatican, reading into it a larger strategy to "intrigue in ecclesiastical matters" in order to annoy and ultimately enslave the Irish Church. To allow the British government to have any influence in Church affairs, and especially in "the appointment of priests to benefices or bishops to sees," would in his judgment be "most pernicious both to the liberty and other interests" of Ireland. Consequently, he energetically discouraged the Vatican from responding positively to British demands for papal restraints on clerical meddling in politics, and was equally active in the campaign to secure a definitive papal condemnation of "Godless" education. He viewed the new university colleges as part of "a great [Protestant] conspiracy to destroy Catholicity."[4]

Cullen's family upbringing, his years in Rome, his dismissal of the British administration in Ireland as "a heretical authority," and his profound enmity for the British government made him as rector a natural ally of the nationalist members of the hierarchy. As the bishops' Roman agent and their principal link with the Vatican, he was especially valuable. Privately, he dismissed Archbishop Crolly as "a decided government man" whose fear of embarrassing the Ministry had hobbled his effectiveness as a prelate. Thus, Cullen's appointment to the See of Armagh promised to heighten sectarian tensions and add additional strains to the relationship between the national church he now led and the state. In pastorals, he mourned the destruction by foreign enemies of that golden age when Ireland had been chosen to be "'the sanctuary of religion, the seat of sacred law.'" He dilated on England's more recent iniquities, such as the Penal Laws, which had subjected Ireland to "'relentless persecution.'" The English had forcibly despatched eighty thousand Irish Catholics to the West Indies, he reminded the faithful, sacrificing them to disease as they had other Irish Catholics to the sword. Ireland alone could lay claim to the "'proud title of the martyr nation of the Church of Christ.'" There was, in short, an "intimate connection" between "nationality and Catholicism." He identified Protestants as the betrayers of O'Connell and rejected their claims to Irishness. He detected England's sinister hand behind the Italian liberal nationalists who were attacking the Pope's temporal power. Englishmen organized and English money paid the anti-clerical mobs roaming Rome's streets early in 1848, he informed MacHale. Giuseppe Mazzini, a former political refugee in Britain, had in his opinion "not done otherwise than to transfer to Italy the spirit with which he was imbued in England," corrupting the minds of the lower classes to such an extent that all would have become "Mahometans" had he so instructed them. The robbing and desecration of churches, the dispersal of nuns and friars, the murder of priests, the destruction of "fine villas," even the felling of trees, were in Cullen's fevered imagination all evidence of the malign influence of the English. Nevertheless, if events in Rome reinforced his "hearty hatred" of England, they also discouraged him from giving it full play. He emerged from the crisis an inveterate enemy of secret societies and a confirmed opponent of revolutionary violence.[5]

Long before his permanent return to the homeland, Paul Cullen had enunciated a guiding principle for the Irish leaders of the Church. "If all our bishops were united," he wrote to his then ally MacHale, "who could resist our just cause?" Not that the strong-willed and fractious Archbishop of Tuam immediately grasped the implications of this statement for his own future. He lobbied for Cullen's appointment as Crolly's successor, no doubt as confident as the Lord Lieutenant was fearful that he would prove to be a MacHale man. Instead, Cullen was determined to lead if not command. His Roman years equipped him well for the demanding task of establishing a primacy more than nominal. He possessed a subtle, secretive, suspicious, and even devious mind, a morbid fear of conspiracy, which at times bordered on paranoia, and well-developed skills in the arts of manipulation and management. He enjoyed a number of other advantages. He was familiar with, and respected by, powerful figures in the Church's bureaucracy, not least at the Propaganda; he had an admirer on the papal throne; his former deputy and loyal supporter, Tobias Kirby, filled the strategic position of rector of the Irish College; while a transfer from Armagh to Dublin in 1852, following the death of the moderate Murray, placed Cullen at the head of the wealthiest diocese as well as at the centre of power in Ireland.[6]

Ambition served to harden Cullen's resolve to unify and command the Irish division of a militant Roman Catholic Church. He intended to strengthen the bonds of loyalty and obedience to Rome. As rector of the Irish College, he had seen in its swelling student body "the means of introducing Roman maxims in Ireland and uniting that church more closely with the Holy See." There was, in his opinion, altogether too much Gallicanism in his homeland. He was no less grimly resolved to fight any measure that even hinted at an infringement by the state on ecclesiastical authority. Consequently, the Irish Catholic Church quickly "adopted a much more hostile attitude toward the British government." This belligerence had an ironic aspect. The Catholic Church enjoyed in Ireland greater freedom from state control than it did in many a European nation where Catholicism was the establishment. Cullen was similarly unswerving in his commitment to a counteroffensive against the heresy of Protestantism, spurred on by alarming reports of its proselytizing in MacHale's fiefdom. There the enemy had been bolstered by the arrival of a fresh regiment of evangelical shock troops led by a veteran of Waterloo. No less unwelcome was the evidence of increasing Protestant unity in

Ireland. Presbyterians were patching up their internal differences, Anglicans and Dissenters establishing a better understanding on the basis of a common evangelicalism, while a new Protestant political consciousness threatened to be harnessed by a more tightly organized Conservative Party. The explosion in Britain of anti-Catholic hysteria, ignited by the announcement in 1850 of the Pope's re-establishment of a hierarchy for England and Wales, intensified Cullen's counter-reformation zeal. His personal intolerance, which led him to regard with deep suspicion any Catholic – including clergy – who mixed socially with Protestants, and his active discouragement of mixed marriages impelled one former Young Irelander and co-founder of the *Nation*, but devout Catholic politician, to express regret at Cullen's transfer to Dublin. "This religious bigotry is now flaming so high on both sides," John Blake Dillon lamented.[7]

War on heresy went hand in hand with a campaign to promote the devotional life of the faithful. Cullen was helped in this endeavour by the heavy toll the Famine had taken on a peasantry devoted without being orthodox and by the consequent relative increase in strength of a "rural bourgeoisie" who had always been more dutiful in their religious practices. Some successful farmers may have been driven to attend church even more regularly in an effort to expiate a nagging sense of guilt for their failure to do more for those far less fortunate than themselves during that catastrophe. They had long provided many of the priests who Cullen was determined to "romanize" and who were now far more adequate in number to serve the needs of a much reduced population. He quickly summoned a synod at Thurles to build upon the earlier reforms in religious practice and conduct, skilfully masking from the public the divisions within the hierarchy. But near defeat at Thurles on the issue of the "Godless" colleges and blunt episcopal criticism of his plan to found a Catholic university left him more determined than ever to create a loyal majority within the hierarchy. This he was narrowly to achieve with Rome's aid by mid-decade, yet the success proved ephemeral. It was not long before his loyalists were reduced to a large, stable, but permanent minority. Fortunately, a group of independent bishops could usually be relied upon to side with him. Nor in this struggle for power did he overlook Maynooth. Only a few years previously he had described the seminary as well managed and its faculty "a most admirable body of men." Now he suspected it of Gallican sympathies, and his distrust of the institution eventually led him to construct at great expense his own diocesan seminary at Clonliffe. Of course, progress towards the creation of "a strong bureaucratic, authoritarian, centralized, and devotional structure in the Irish Roman Catholic church" alarmed and frightened many Protestants.[8]

Cullen's initial target within a divided hierarchy were those colleagues who had looked to Archbishop Murray for leadership. He had placed Murray in the dock alongside Crolly, charged with complaisance in his dealings with the British government. This English card was one with which Cullen frequently trumped the qualifications of candidates whom he considered unfit for a bishop's mitre. Similarly, his father's ineradicable distrust of Maynooth had been reawakened in him by Peel's generous increase in its public grant, which in his eyes made the faculty dependents of the government. What better example was there of this than that "humiliating" oath of allegiance required of staff and students to which his father had objected so many years earlier? Somewhat inconsistently, he also accused the college of graduating violent Young Ireland priests and on occasion used guilt by association to damage the reputations of other unwelcome episcopal candidates. But his own attitudes bordered on a "messianic nationalism," and his policies sustained the nationalist cause, even if a bitter conflict with the larger-than-life figure who had so long dominated that end of the clerical political spectrum seemed preordained. John MacHale was too volatile, too unmanageable, too unreliable, and too insubordinate to long serve or survive as a Cullen ally. The latter was soon striving to erode MacHale's influence within his own province. There was an irony in this, since Cullen's hostility to the notion of Britishness equalled his adversary's and they were as one in the belief that the Irish Catholic Church and people were victims of uniquely harsh misrule. Both illustrated the extent to which the culture of victimhood and the discourse of oppression were common indulgences of the hierarchy. And Cullen's efforts to unify the Church and promote greater uniformity of religious practice served, however unintentionally, a secondary political purpose. He was further solidifying the sectarian and ethnic unity of Catholic Irishmen across divisions of class and region.[9]

The religious authority that Cullen wished to see rule in Ireland was not only loyal and obedient to Rome but determinedly nationalist. This helps explain his mistrust of his English fellow religionists, whose zeal he dismissed as exclusively ornamental if not frivolous. "Thus the poor have the idea that the churches are only for the rich and those who are well dressed," he complained, "not for the poor who cannot frequent them without dirtying the fine carpets and offending the eyes of the great." The poor he had in mind were Irish immigrants to Britain. Or as another member of the hierarchy had remarked only a few years earlier: "English Catholics – aye and English priests – are the corrupt tools employed by Peel." Yet Cullen soon found himself under attack by fellow nationalists for his appointment of an English Catholic as rector of his Catholic university. Perhaps his choice of the widely admired convert John Henry Newman was motivated in part by the hope that it would enhance the reputation of the institution and facilitate the securing of a charter from the "English" government. It certainly did not indicate any lessening of his distrust of English fellow religionists. He discreetly vetoed Newman's elevation to the rank of bishop and was highly critical of his English appointments to the university's faculty. For his part, Newman was startled by "the hatred felt for England in all ranks in Ireland." The bald truth was, as perhaps he appreciated, nationalism and religion were binding Catholic Irishmen ever more tightly together. The result was an ever-deeper divide "between natives and aliens, Catholics and heretics, the state of the oppressor and the Church of the oppressed."[10]

Cullen naturally placed the concerns of the Church ahead of mere secular issues. His principal concern was the protection of its interests and the enhancement of its status and that of the Catholic community. His answer to the question of "whether religious or national pride" ought to have the greatest influence on the conduct of the Catholic Irish was never in doubt. This goes far to explain his desire to rein in priests whose commitment to political causes threatened the full performance of their pastoral duties. However, the tradition of priestly participation in politics was too well established to be easily curtailed. "No election can take place in Ireland without the clergy giving their advice if not their commands to the people," a French visitor noted. "The priest is changed into the demagogue, and the very tongue which insisted upon the duty of giving to Caesar the things which are Caesar's, proclaims aloud that every good Catholic ought to vote against Protestants." That was, of course, an exaggeration, for liberal Protestants were frequently returned to Parliament with clerical support. Nevertheless, the political dimension of most religious issues, given the Catholicism of the vast majority of Irishmen and the Protestantism of the state, explained the vigour with which many priests engaged in the hurly-burly of electoral contests. Nor was their exclusion from politics part of Cullen's strategy. The synodical address that he composed and issued from Thurles dwelt upon the sufferings of the poor and their victimization by "the most ruthless oppression that ever disgraced the annals of humanity." Here was a ready-made excuse for priests who spoke out violently against the government. "They see their parishes deserted, their parents, their friends and their flocks exterminated and therefore sometimes they cannot restrain their indignation," Cullen informed Rome. "The great lords and the officials of the government would like everyone to remain silent in order to continue their persecution without any opposition." In short, it was neither possible nor desirable to withdraw clergy completely from the political fray. On the other hand, Cullen saw no reason for them to make a great din and every reason for them to avoid being associated with violence.[11]

Despite the mistakes and failures of the previous decade, Irish nationalists had reason to enter the 1850s in a surprisingly confident frame of mind. A conjunction of extraordinary developments and circumstances promised to allow them to make the most of constitutional means to secure redress of perceived national grievances. Catholics were united as rarely before, and Ireland awash with indignation, as a result of the Whig government's ill-advised response to the re-establishment of a Catholic hierarchy in England and Wales. The prime minister's contemptuous public references to Roman Catholicism and the vulgar antics of ultra Protestants in the Commons had been capped by a foolish and inept piece of legislation. The Ecclesiastical Titles Bill, which denied Catholic bishops the use of British place names, was immediately condemned by Paul Cullen, among others, as a Penal Law. MacHale was, as ever, more direct. He addressed another public letter to the prime minister, which he signed "John, Archbishop of Tuam." Although Lord John Russell eventually stripped it of the restrictions most objectionable to the Irish hierarchy – and even those that survived were disregarded in Ireland – he received little Roman Catholic applause for this concession even as he forfeited whatever credit he had stored up with Protestant ultras. In the opinion of one sardonic contemporary, he had conciliated nobody but had alienated everybody.[12]

A spasm of ethnoreligious violence in the Cheshire mill town of Stockport in June 1852 and reports of the desecration of Catholic chapels kept the issue simmering and Irish tempers boiling. "Blood has been shed in torrents – churches have been ransacked – Catholic clergymen openly insulted in the streets; the very tabernacle rifled and its contents scattered on the floor and trampled upon by an infuriated populace," an outraged *Tuam Herald* informed the residents of John MacHale's cathedral city. The *Freeman's Journal* was similarly tempted by hyperbole, describing the Stockport riots as "unparalleled in the records of human infamy." More credible and less hysterical were Irish claims that the government of the United Kingdom had finally thrown off the liberal cloak of recent years to expose its naked sectarianism. The Tory protectionists, who in the early summer of 1852 briefly held the reins of power, were led by the Earl of Derby. An absentee Irish landlord, he held Roman Catholicism responsible for the chronic poverty in Ireland and thus indirectly responsible for the Famine. Although the Tory administration quickly collapsed, the coalition of Whigs and Peelites that replaced it did not dampen down anti-Catholic fires. Russell was a senior member of the new government, and in 1853 he delivered a blistering attack on Irish Catholics. He accused them of ingratitude, questioned their loyalty and their dedication to liberty, and assailed priests for exerting a peculiarly benighted political influence over their congregations.[13]

The recent passage of the Irish Franchise Act had more than trebled the number of voters, finally creating "a coherent constituency chosen on a uniform principle, capable of sustained and consistent political mobilization." A heightened "national politicization of the Irish countryside" seemed inevitable, and it was widely anticipated that priests would be in its vanguard. "Nobody now denies, in Ireland," wrote one critical observer, "that the success of the elections is entirely dependent upon the influence of priests, who hold in their hands the souls of the people." Like many another contemporary, he overstated the case. Farmers constituted more than three-quarters of the enlarged county electorate, and their landlords readily grasped the significance of the revisions to the electoral registers. Not only did many of them still command a measure of social respect and deference, but as proprietors they were able to instill fear into their tenantry without the necessity of constantly resorting to the crudest methods of intimidation. With these advantages, landlords even recovered some of the electoral influence they had lost during the repeal agitation. Irish Tories moved smartly to capitalize on this development, shrewdly creating a more coherent party structure. As a result, they were to perform remarkably well during the ensuing decade even though this was widely regarded as the heyday of the political priest.[14]

Intelligent priests understood the risk they ran if they repeatedly endeavoured to lead their people in a direction they did not wish to travel. Frocked "political godfathers" did make offers that many Catholic voters found difficult to refuse, and several members of Parliament were unseated in 1853 on the grounds that their election had been secured through "spiritual intimidation." But the progress of constitutional nationalism required something more than turning out the vote. Voters and non-voters, the latter organized as an intimidatory offset to landlord pressure on the enfranchised, needed to be harnessed to the support of a parliamentary party that would behave as a solid and disciplined phalanx committed to a number of achievable objectives. Only then would Irish members be sufficiently well positioned to exploit to the full the unstable situation in the House of Commons. The crumbling of the Whig ministry under the insupportable weight of Russell's ineffectual leadership, together with the continuing division of the Tories despite Robert Peel's tragic death following a riding accident, presented an opportunity. An independent Irish party might find itself in a position of power-broker or at least be able to exploit esoteric parliamentary procedures and rules to obstruct business and thus force Irish issues onto the parliamentary agenda. The British might debate and divide but Irishmen would decide which side had the majority, the *Nation* boasted.[15]

At first, the nationalists' universe seemed to be unfolding according to plan. The evidence taken before the Devon Commission had strengthened the general belief that Ireland's economic backwardness was a function of the insecurity that discouraged tenants from investing in agricultural improvements. This Daniel O'Connell and Thomas Davis had recognized in the plan of land reform presented to the Repeal Association, while the mass evictions during the Famine brutally drove home the point. The organization of a league committed to greater tenant rights, especially compensation for improvements, was therefore a logical step and one that seemed capable of bridging sectarian differences. Founded in 1850, the Tenant League rapidly won the endorsement of several members of the hierarchy and a host of parish priests. Similarly blessed by clergy was the Catholic Defence Association. Its declared objectives were repeal of the obnoxious Ecclesiastical Titles Bill, "perfect freedom" for the entire Catholic population of the empire, resistance to Protestant proselytism, denominational education, and improvements in the social condition of Roman Catholics. Paralleling these developments was the re-emergence of avowed political nationalists. Having survived several attempted prosecutions, Gavan Duffy had resumed publication of the *Nation* in September 1849. Before year's end, an English convert to Catholicism and a surprisingly strident Irish nationalist, Frederick Lucas, had quit London for Dublin, bringing with him his Catholic weekly, the *Tablet*. On their left stood Bertram Fullam, who had founded the *Irishman* much earlier that same year to espouse a Mitchelite nationalism and hurl invective at the government. The following year he formed the Irish Democratic Association to link together the political clubs that had survived the wreck of the Confederation and educate workers "in nationally minded radicalism." Although the Democratic Association failed to survive the perils of infancy, a reborn Loyal National Repeal Association seemed certain to enjoy longer life.[16]

Why not bind these disparate nationalist elements together? Once again, hierarchy and priesthood smiled on the endeavour. Under the umbrella of the Independent Irish Party, nationalists captured almost half of the Irish seats in the general election of 1852. Unfortunately, the new party conspicuously failed to define a coherent nationalist policy. Elected members simply pledged themselves to remain "independent of and in opposition to" all governments that failed to adopt the Tenant League's legislative agenda. A self-denying ordinance with respect to office was a very unstable foundation on which to construct a solid parliamentary force out of a large number of ambitious men. In the absence of membership lists, of whips to enforce a measure of party discipline in the division lobbies, of an acknowledged leader, and even of a generally accepted name, the likelihood of members going their separate ways was strong. Nor could the party count upon Cullen's resolute backing. He offered only tepid support, being sceptical of the Independents' ability to exploit the rifts in the British parties despite their significant role in forcing Derby's resignation. The British would, in the archbishop's opinion, eventually close ranks in the face of a militant Irish brigade. So, when two prominent Independents promptly violated the pledge by accepting minor offices in the coalition that replaced the Tories, the leader of the Irish Catholic Church did not join the general nationalist condemnation of their conduct. At this point, he was apparently willing to settle for the advantage of having allies in the government of the day.[17]

Ireland's serried ranks of nationalists were in truth as riddled as ever with disaffection. Sectarianism had swiftly compromised the Tenant

League, while ethnic tension helped undermine the Defence Association. Frederick Lucas's intolerance, that of the convert, his taste in caustic prose, and his brutal anti-Protestantism alienated non-Catholics from the league. Cullen's easing of William Keogh, a personable, clever, nakedly ambitious lawyer and apparent ally of MacHale, out of the secretary's chair of the association, to make room for another English convert, antagonized many nationalists. Neither the appointment of an Irish assistant to the English secretary nor reminders that English Catholics were the principal targets of the Ecclesiastical Titles Bill consoled or appeased them. They bewailed the "national degradation" and discouragement of "that noble nationality which had hitherto been the life and inspiration of the Catholic cause." The Defence Association's response to Lucas's savage assaults – it funded a lower-priced competitor to the *Tablet*, excluded all other publishers and editors from membership, and unsuccessfully attempted to prevent Lucas from being nominated as a parliamentary candidate for County Meath – delivered another body blow to nationalist unity.[18]

Although the Defence Association quietly disappeared from the scene and the fray, there was scant evidence of any genuine reconciliation among leading Catholic nationalists. They appeared unable "to forge any alliance of common purpose among themselves." It was from the divisions of Irish society that the chief obstacles to Irish freedom came, Thomas Meagher had earlier observed. Meanwhile, a conflict of interests between tenant farmers and rural labourers divided the nationalist rank and file. The rural poor, principal victims of the Famine, were now being shortchanged on prosperity as the economy recovered. As their resentment grew, so a number of priests endeavoured to channel it away from their employers and towards alien landlords. This strategy of blame was not entirely successful. Labourers continued to resist efforts to organize them as a pressure group in support of tenant rights. Nor could they have been impressed by a sorry spectacle of personal animosities and ideological differences that further hindered nationalist political effectiveness. Duffy, who had served in the vanguard of the advocates of the Independent Irish Party, was under constant and savage attack by Fullam and his Mitchelite organ, the *Irishman*. Its collapse brought only a brief respite. Duffy was soon locked in a vituperative hand-to-hand combat with Mitchel himself. Following his escape from Van Dieman's Island to the United States, the latter had founded a "militant Irish-American newspaper, the *Citizen*," in which he published extracts from his prison diary that cast Duffy as a sorry and dishonourable figure. Mitchel, who at his trial had made no bones of his commitment to physical force, flailed Duffy for pleading an undying allegiance to moral force whenever he found himself in the dock. The *Nation*'s editor responded with a fierce counterattack. The result was an unedifying exchange between these two leading nationalists. If Duffy's constitutionalism was anathema to Mitchel and his admirers, it ought to have provided a bond with both John O'Connell and clerical nationalists. Instead, his Young Ireland antecedents proved too great a liability in both cases. Hated by the Liberator's son, Duffy was despised by Cullen. The archbishop, darkly suspicious of the *Nation* for its lauding of MacHale as a patriot, and infuriated by its praise of continental anti-clericals, castigated its editor as Ireland's Mazzini.[19]

Conflict between Cullen and the secular nationalists had been inevitable. For Cullen, after all, religious issues had primacy with respect to national objectives. John Mitchel, who likened himself to a Christ-like figure, for had he not stood in the dock between a pair of thieves "'for having dared to aspire to the principles of freedom and manhood'" and then suffered the martyrdom of transportation, concluded from his reading of Irish newspapers that priests were "systematically trying to merge all national feelings in Catholicity." Henceforward, he predicted, their nationality would be "papal nationality only." Certainly, denominational education, religious equality, and an end to Protestant proselytism were the leading items on Cullen's political agenda. Pondering this, one Tory Cabinet minister later suggested that Cullen and the entire priesthood were fixated on a need to foster a "Celtic Ireland, full of national feeling and religious zeal and densely peopled." That the archbishop's overriding concern was religious zeal surely did not surprise secular nationalists. What they objected to was his ambition to control the political agenda. He was not helped in this struggle for influence by the evidence of internal opposition to his control of the Church. The Archbishop of Tuam remained a formidable opponent, and one of the many sources of contention was the proper political role of the priesthood. The Archbishop of Dublin was far more cautious than MacHale "in his interpretation of constitutional opposition." Cullen and other clergy questioned the morality and efficacy of the conduct of some of their colleagues. Not a few churchmen were dismayed by the rhetorical extremism that saw a Catholic Whig member of Parliament publicly vilified by his parish priest as a traitor to his religion and his country for declining to pledge himself to the Tenant League in 1852. Equally scandalous were bouts of priestly pugilism between clergy who found themselves in opposite corners of the political ring. This unseemly resort to fisticuffs might have been avoided had the hierarchy been united and thus in a position to provide coherent and consistent leadership. Alarmed by such indiscipline and determined to ensure that his clerical army marched in step, Cullen persuaded his fellow bishops to endorse a series of decrees designed to curb political activities *within* churches and prevent free-for-alls between priests. The decrees were modestly effective at best, though in some constituencies they provided an excuse to exclude laity from the business of nominating candidates. This was one certain way to prevent them from witnessing priestly brawls.[20]

None of this was welcomed by those nationalists who, echoing the rebels of 1848, complained bitterly that an independent parliamentary party was being betrayed "by those who created it." Both Duffy and Lucas identified Cullen as the chief apostate. In an attempt to secure a papal reversal of the hierarchy's decrees, Lucas travelled to Rome. His was a doomed mission, for there was never any likelihood of the pontiff allying himself with laymen against the friend he had sent home to Ireland as primate. Already, the Propaganda was struggling to heal the deep divisions within the leadership of the Irish Church by attempting to arbitrate the dispute between Cullen and MacHale. Little was achieved. MacHale made himself characteristically obnoxious to the Vatican authorities before returning home to renew his war against Cullen. As for Lucas, his only success was a very modest one. He secured the withdrawal of the decree that had required clergy who wished to address a public meeting in the province of Armagh to secure the prior permission of the priest of the parish where the gathering was to be held. Of course, the Cullen camp had never intended to abrogate "the rights of our Patriot Priests." On the contrary, the intent was to illuminate the means by which priests could "effectively assert their civil and political rights."[21]

The general election of 1857 proved the point, priests being as active as they had ever been. By this time, the Independent Party was a spent force and within two years had expired. Death and emigration had removed Lucas and Duffy respectively from the scene in 1855. Secular nationalists did score a symbolic electoral victory over Cullen. They returned a member of the O'Connell clan, The O'Donoghue, for

County Tipperary, instead of the wealthy Catholic landowner whom the archbishop was backing. But the incessant infighting was rapidly depleting the remaining reserves of nationalist energy. Independents held only a baker's dozen of Ireland's seats after the election. Of the forty-eight victorious Liberals, approximately half were Roman Catholics, while forty-four Tories were Protestants. Yet the nationalists' failure was, as a decade earlier, evidently one of men, not of constitutionalism, as the agency of significant reform and change. The modesty of the gains Ireland had made was a measure of the inability of nationalists to agree among themselves on objectives and means during a confused period in politics, when unity might well have enabled them to extract much more. Their own culpability unacknowledged, they continued to issue statements calculated to undermine public respect for the existing order and the state. Cullen's circular to the Dublin clergy in 1857 was fiercely Irish and Catholic. Commenting on the archbishop's taste in "intolerant and inflammatory language," a later liberal viceroy wearily asked: "What hope is there for religious peace when such a document [with] such a line is issued?" But the Whig/Liberal government was also at fault. It made a parade of its nationalist sympathies with respect to events in Italy and was using its diplomatic influence to undermine the pontiff's temporal power there. What more pointed reminder could Irish Catholics have of the extent to which their religion still separated them from other subjects of the Crown and from Britain? In the words of a former Young Irelander, "the cause of the Irish Catholic Church and the cause of the Irish Catholic people are one and indivisible."[22]

The somewhat more sympathetic attitude towards the Pope as a temporal prince surprisingly adopted by the Tories on taking office again under Derby, in February 1858, persuaded Roman Catholics in Britain, notably Cardinal Wiseman, and even some in Ireland to look upon them with a favour that might not otherwise have been expected. After all, the Conservative Party had long been regarded by Cullen and other Irish Catholics as the political arm of the hated and feared Orange Order. Another promising development was the despatch of the Prince of Wales to Rome early in 1859, to add artistic refinement to his education. During his sojourn there, he was received by the Pope, made several visits to St Peter's, and called at the Irish College. There he met Cullen as well as Tobias Kirby. Perhaps it was no surprise, therefore, that Irish Catholic members on the opposition benches provided the minority Tories with sufficient votes to cling, against expectations, to office until the summer of 1859. Moreover, facing defeat on a reform bill and looking ahead to another general election, Derby applied to Rome for help in securing Irish support. The Earl of Malmesbury, at the Foreign Office, tasked the British representative, Odo Russell, nephew of the former prime minister, to manoeuvre the Vatican's secretary of state into proposing papal assistance of Tory candidates in Irish contests. This he did by playing on Cardinal Antonelli's fears of a return of Palmerston and his own uncle to office, fears "reflected in [the Cardinal's] bilious countenance." He was evidently in terror of Palmerston and regarded Lord John Russell with "profound horror."[23]

Antonelli soon assured Odo Russell that he had done all in his power to persuade British and Irish Roman Catholics to vote Tory. Meanwhile, Derby and his colleagues were announcing decisions and making promises with an eye to the same segment of the electorate. These measures hinted at what Irish nationalists might have achieved had they pulled together and implemented the parliamentary strategy as originally outlined by Duffy. Catholic chaplains and nursing nuns had been permitted to minister to soldiers in the Crimea, and a permanent body of Catholic chaplains was appointed in 1858 on terms of equality with Protestant colleagues. Catholics had been permitted to open their own industrial schools and reformatories, and now priests were authorized to provide instruction to Catholic children in workhouses. There was talk of appointing and paying Catholic chaplains in prisons. Catholic naval ratings were excused from attendance at Anglican services while at sea, higher pay was awarded to Catholic clergy serving with the Indian Army, and a postal subsidy was finally granted to the Galway Packet Line. Here was a direct public stimulus to the development of transatlantic shipping from a region of Ireland notorious for its chronic poverty. The packet station had long been promoted as essential to the creation of local wealth. "All Irishmen felt that at last they had got something more than words." They also got those, of course. Vague promises were given with respect to tenant reform, while the hierarchy was assured that a request for a charter for the Catholic university would receive serious Tory consideration.[24]

Whig policies during the Famine, Whig authorship of the despised Ecclesiastical Titles Bill, and Whig/Liberal enthusiasm for a form of nationalism in Italy that Irish Catholics considered anything but holy had already persuaded one organ of the Irish hierarchy that Whig difficulties were "a providential punishment for their misdeeds against God's Church and God's poor." Egged on by Wiseman, who published a letter of support for the Conservatives, and by the strong signals from Rome, Catholic voters helped Conservatives win more than half of Ireland's seats in 1859. They would surely have enjoyed even greater success had there been a clear directive from the hierarchy and a united army of priests working on the ground. Instead, Cullen, who was absent from Ireland for most of the political campaign, and MacHale remained ambivalent. Both appear to have shared with the strongly nationalist Bishop of Clonfert the opinion that it was impossible to distinguish between the two political parties in their approach to Ireland and that only through "independent armed neutrality" could meaningful concessions be wrung from the British. Both the Whigs and the Tories, McHale believed, wished to "decatholicise and denationalise the Irish Celts." On the other hand, a former Young Ireland sympathizer, David Moriarty, Bishop of Kerry, worked heroically for the Liberals. When the new parliament assembled, Irish members, of whom thirty-six were Catholics, voted heavily with the Tory government on a confidence motion. They were unable to save it, and the Whig/Liberals returned to office in June 1859.[25]

Lord Palmerston headed the new government while Russell, described by Pius IX as "our bitterest enemy in England," went to the Foreign Office. Lord John patronizingly insisted that the Pope, "Poor Man," was much mistaken about him. "I have fought all my life for Catholic privileges," he informed his nephew in Rome, "but not for priestly government by any Church." The return of the two old Whig warhorses to office coincided with revolution in the papal states, and they made plain Britain's support of the successful rebellion in Romagna. The subsequent plebiscites staged there and in Tuscany, Parma, and Modena delivered the desired popular endorsement of annexation to Sardinia. Odo Russell was soon describing the papal government as "rotten and despicable" and disparaging the Pope as "firmly determined to turn a deaf ear to the voice of reason, reform and moderation." These despatches were music to the ears of his uncle, who, while he privately expressed great respect for the virtues of Pius IX and was willing that he be left "undisturbed" in Rome, remained convinced that Italy had simply outgrown the papacy. The pontiff was a temporal "anachronism" who could not be left to govern three million people, condemning them to "perpetual misery." Professing a desire to emancipate several millions of "priestridden" subjects "from ignorance, tyranny and corruption of ecclesiastical rule," the British government favoured limiting the Pope's territories to Rome and its environs. Not surprisingly, one of the most popular and romanticized Italian liberal nationalists, Giuseppe Garibaldi, lauded Britain as the representative of God in a conflict against "tyranny and evil priests." Victor Emmanuel of Sardinia, around whose territories the Kingdom of Italy was now being formed with Britain's blessing, paid his own effusive public tribute to "the long established land of liberty." In the Eternal City, meanwhile, a beleaguered Pius identified the people, Parliament, and Liberal politicians of Britain as the most powerful haters of the papacy. This was an opinion that the most powerful figure in the Irish Catholic Church had long held.[26]

The Pope issued a call to arms early in 1860, urging his bishops to rouse the faithful in defence of the Church and his temporal authority. If this amounted to a legitimization of physical force as a means to suppress popular nationalist uprisings, so also did the enthusiastic Irish episcopal response to the call. Cullen ploughed a narrow ethno-sectarian furrow. He blamed English Protestants but also some English Catholics for the pontiff's plight, insisting that all the former and a number of the latter were supporters of Garibaldi and revolution. Why did England support nationalists in Italy and insurrection in Sicily but extend "no similar understanding to Ireland"? The stock British reply was to insist that only national revolts that promised to enhance the happiness of the world merited support. This was a test few Britons considered the Irish capable of passing. Conversely, how could the Catholic clergy promote nationalism in Ireland but oppose the Italian national movement? The Pope required a territorial base in order to maintain his political independence, the Irish bishops replied. Rome's environs were too small to support a great city and the Universal Church. Without a state large enough to generate a substantial income, the Pope would be unable to pay police, magistrates, and soldiers. Already, he was running an annual deficit of £4 million. But Cullen and some lay Catholics, such as John Francis Maguire, member of Parliament for Cork and publisher of the *Cork Examiner*, were quick to adapt bitter memories of the Famine to a defence of their nationalist inconsistency. The Pope's subjects had not died in their "millions" or been turned off the land by "exterminating agents" and left to perish, Cullen declared in a pastoral, nor were they obliged to live in "that squalid and disgusting poverty" that was all too visible in

Britain's cities. The papal states were veritable and visible models of good government compared to British "misrule" in Ireland.[27]

Appeals to anti-English sentiment delivered an immediate cash dividend. Substantial sums were raised for the papal cause – some £16,000 in the archdiocese of Dublin alone, and Cullen estimated the national contribution at £60,000 – while more than a thousand men "emigrated" to Italy to serve under the papal standard. So many Irishmen volunteered that Cullen feared the Pope would be unable to provide for them. Even as Irish Catholics were making their way to central Italy, hundreds of Britons were heading to Sicily to fight alongside Garibaldi. "British subjects, thus, fought for and financed opposing sides of the papal conflict in Italy." What more graphic illustration could there be of the national and sectarian divisions beleaguering the United Kingdom? Then, as if to rub salt into Catholic wounds, Russell explained his failure to enforce the Foreign Enlistment Act against British volunteers by likening Garibaldi's campaign to that of William of Orange in the Glorious Revolution. Almost inevitably, the developments in Italy, the policy of the government, and the hierarchy's response gave another fillip to "Irish national consciousness." Catholic Irishmen were being encouraged, yet again, to view "their hereditary enemy" the English, as an unrepentant and "deadly foe of their race, their creed, and their nationality." Furthermore, a number of them had acquired both military experience and a taste for physical force as a solution to political problems. But enmity for England was also exploited by the hierarchy in its long-running battle for denominational education, and education was to make a powerful contribution to a revival of revolutionary nationalism.[28]

Most senior members of the hierarchy had been willing in 1858 to postpone agitation for a publicly funded system of separate primary education. Were not the national schools "for the most part exclusively Catholic," thanks to the attitude of Protestants? The Anglicans had launched the Church Education Society in 1839 to establish rival institutions, and this opposition continued until 1860. But Cullen anathematized the national schools as a potential "dreadful engine" against his church and faith, while MacHale denounced them as "an insidious method of proselytism." Cullen continued to suspect "liberal" Protestants of scheming to do "everything possible to get all education of the country into their hands, [in order] to spread 'indifferentism' in the minds of the people." Catholic parents were urged to agitate for a system of education "'free from the dangers of Govern-

ment control and from the deadly poison of irreligion and heresy.'"
The policy of the national schools, he declared, was to keep Catholic
children "'in complete ignorance of the traditions of their country.'"
So, in 1859, the bishops adopted a more assertive policy – the education of Catholics, at all three levels, must be under episcopal control.
They were opposed by the dominant figures on the Board of National
Education, who were keen to ensure widespread instruction in a
humanized version of political economy. This, they fancied, would
ultimately rescue Ireland's economy, and by making the Irish people
"more *rational*" complete their assimilation into the United Kingdom.
Nor had the Palmerston administration any inclination to substitute a
separate system for the ideal of mixed education, though the prime
minister did subsequently agree to establish sectarian parity on the
board. Whatever credit this modest concession might have earned him
and his colleagues among Catholics was tossed away with the
appointment of Sir Robert Peel's son and namesake as chief secretary.
A loud admirer of Garibaldi and something of an evangelical Protestant bull in a Catholic china shop, this Peel was peculiarly ill-equipped
to work harmoniously with Cullen and the hierarchy.[29]

Disappointed by the government's response to their educational
demands, the bishops could still count on the Christian Brothers for
"uncompromising denominationalism." The Brothers drew students
away from the model schools so objectionable to the hierarchy and
earned much Catholic applause for their refusal to accept "the Saxon's
blood money." Competing with national schools in some areas, while
in others, especially urban centres, taking them over or replacing
them, the Brothers had an influence far greater than their modest
number suggested. Barely one hundred strong on the eve of the
Famine, they were to increase tenfold during the second half of the
century. They saw it as a duty to infuse a "Catholic and national spirit" throughout their schools, and one self-described old rebel lauded
them for the national as well as the religious training he received.
Their aim was to make pupils familiar with their native land, to teach
them to love it and to be aware of their national identity. In short, they
taught ethnic identity. Their textbooks rigidly excluded criticism of
Ireland or Catholicism but were free with censure of England and
Protestantism. The history of Ireland as narrated by the Christian
Brothers was a long and painful struggle against English invasion, persecution, and oppression, and a battle to "maintain a distinct nationality." It was a tale "calculated to inflame and exasperate against

England, and against the Protestant religion, and in a way accessible to the meanest capacity," one Anglican bishop had earlier charged. Their view of geography was equally nationalistic, as evidenced in their *Treatise on modern geography* (1842). Britain was to blame for the failure of the Irish to rise in the scale of improvement, despite their enterprise and industry. Thus the Brothers instilled in their charges, not simply love of Ireland, but dislike if not hatred of England or Britain, and by so doing they were making a contribution, however unintentional, to a revival of revolutionary nationalism. Much the same could be said of Cullen, despite his undoubted aversion to revolutionary violence. He privately praised the Brothers' "excellent series of classbooks" and disingenuously dismissed the suggestion that the instruction they provided cultivated hostility. He employed, as one later critic wrote, the "perfunctory sophistry" that pupils were taught the Christians' duty not to hate those who had wronged them, and in his encouragement of the Brothers he "knew exactly what he was doing."[30]

As the archbishop himself illustrated, codes of morality did not always act as neutralizers of hostility. His pastorals were invariably highly critical, if not extraordinary severe, in their judgment of the English. Herein lurked danger, because by its very emphasis on "absolute evaluative judgments" religion often reinforced a people's "tendencies to judge themselves and other people in biased ways: good versus evil, benevolent versus malicious." The Church couldn't "just wash its hands and walk away," one modern revolutionary nationalist has written. "Most of us learned our history from nuns, priests and brothers." Patrick Leahy, a future archbishop of Cashel, founded a reading society having as its avowed purpose the encouragement of popular education but with the "ulterior design" of advancing the "great national struggle." The masters of the old hedge schools had long been accused of being "ministers of treason," and in areas of the west these schools still outnumbered those of the state system. John MacHale had excluded national schools from his province, much to the disadvantage of its children, but St Jarlath's College, Tuam, under the presidency of a noted Gaelic scholar, taught tales of earlier rebels and graduated a generation of young men who went on to become revolutionary nationalists. Even the national schools with their "sapless" and "un-Irish" texts and daily singing of "God Save the Queen," were by no means entirely free of subversive influences. Their purpose had been to produce a literate and numerate population while fostering the "value system of the state," but a minority of national schoolmasters were strongly suspected of giving instruction in nationalism and sedition. Indeed, teachers were of "immense importance in the growth of nationalism." Although those in the national system were prohibited from participating formally in political activities, they, as another old rebel later recalled, gave students "'the naked facts about the English conquest'" and Ireland's "'bondage.'" Many children emerged from such classes "no longer content to grow up 'happy English children.'" Ironically, Cullen distrusted these teachers and cited them as proof of the perils of a "Godless" education, whereas Protestants claimed that in all but a handful of cases the masters arrested for sedition or revolutionary nationalism had been employed in schools of which priests were the patrons.[31]

The Christian Brothers' textbooks received ecstatic reviews in nationalist newspapers, for the fourth estate was the remaining member of nationalism's missionary quintet – politicians, priests, professionals, pedagogues, and pressmen. Unencumbered by false modesty, the Irish press had long regarded itself as the "palladium of Liberty." Young Irelanders, learning from United Irishmen, had grasped the propaganda value of the printed word in a heavily peasant society that accepted it as authoritative. Here was a short and sure means of shaping the popular mind, so long, that is, as literacy continued to advance. The Sunday schools and book clubs founded by the United Irishmen, the hedge schools and the national schools, the temperance and repeal reading rooms, the reading societies, even the ambition for promotion harboured by many of the Irishmen who served in the British army, all acted as stimulants to a level of Irish literacy which, while regionally uneven, was far greater than the notorious poverty of the people suggested. By mid-century more than half of the total population could read, and in the provinces of Ulster and Leinster the figures were higher still. The printed literature was almost exclusively in English. Unlike in Wales, where Protestantism sustained the language, the provocative efforts of Irish Protestants to reach and convert the people through the use of the vernacular was another reason for the Catholic Church to regard with suspicion religious literacy in Irish. It had long since elected to function in English, many of its clergy sharing with O'Connell the opinion that Irish was an impediment to material advance. Similarly, the universal nature of Catholicism and the use of Latin in the Mass told against the vernacular. The national schools simply built upon this foundation, though this did not prevent

MacHale and other nationalists from hurling the accusation that they were entirely responsible for the decline of the Irish language.[32]

By no means all functionally literate Irishmen could afford newspapers. However, the custom of priest or pedagogue reading aloud from selected organs of the press after Mass ensured wide knowledge of their contents. The repeal of the "taxes on knowledge" – those on advertisements and paper, and the stamp duty on newsprint – saw both a cheapening and proliferation of newspapers between 1853 and the middle of the following decade. Far from the tax repeal promoting the distribution of London papers to the four corners of the United Kingdom, as many of its supporters had confidently predicted, thus creating a British "national tone," there was instead a dramatic growth in Ireland of a provincial press. Although approximately "half of the 'political' papers" were Tory organs, the nationalist press wielded considerable influence and was dedicated to the task of fostering "a nationalist Catholic identity." The Church was quick to appreciate the potential for mass mobilization, and some observers were equally quick to connect the priesthood to certain newspapers. The association was a matter of pride for the *Tuam Herald,* which declared itself the hierarchy's "special organ." But journalism was a profession from which political dissidents were able to make a comfortable living. Certainly, editors and publishers had been prominent figures in the Independent Irish Party – for example, Duffy and his eventual successor at the *Nation,* A.M. Sullivan; Frederick Lucas of the *Tablet*; John Francis Maguire of the *Cork Examiner,* formerly the *Cork Total Abstainer*; and Sir John Gray of the *Freeman's Journal,* which was closely identified with Archbishop Cullen despite the Protestantism of its owner. When a disenchanted Duffy emigrated to Australia in 1855, one contemporary extolled him for having given to Irish journalism "a lofty, national tone" and for making the public press "a power in the land." Indeed, the provincial press has been described as "one of the most important agents of nation building in nineteenth-century Ireland." The readers to whom nationalist publishers and editors directed their propaganda were the very same targets as those of the Ossianic Society "with its cheap, popular and entertaining publications" – "respectable wage earners, the skilled workers, and the urban lower-middle class," such as national schoolmasters, shop-boys, mechanics, and tradesmen.[33]

The agricultural depression that brought hardship to much of the country between 1859 and 1864 provided additional grist for nationalist mills. The human tragedy of the late 1840s was not repeated, nor were workhouses again filled to overflowing with desperate labourers and cottiers. By way of explanation, one member of the hierarchy pointed to the better employment of the people, their better wages, which had at least kept pace with inflation, and the existence of many more food stores at which provisions could be purchased or obtained on credit. He might have added that the people were healthier and better housed than a decade earlier. In truth, the ravages of the Famine, together with heavy emigration and a declining birth rate, had by reducing the population given a boost to living standards. Per capita income was at last edging closer to the average elsewhere in the United Kingdom, and life expectancy increasing. Nevertheless, the depression caused much localized distress, especially in the West, where the rural poor had managed to cling to plots of land. Strong farmers, who had survived the Famine and profited in its aftermath, joined the complainants, and as debt increased, so did evictions, although at their peak in 1864 they were merely a fraction of those in 1850. Moreover, during the good years of the 1850s, rents had increased far more slowly than the value of agricultural production, with the result that tenants had retained a large share of the prosperity. Thus the demand for security of tenure was frequently driven less by fear of eviction than by a desire to guard these gains, and one obvious means of their protection was to undermine the landlords' ability to claw them back – hence the farmers' deepening anxiety following passage of the Land Act of 1860, which recognized "the exclusive property of the landlord."[34]

Peter Ward, the parish priest of Williamstown, County Galway, described for the readers of the *Irish Canadian* harrowing scenes of suffering and governmental neglect. The "shrieks of dying fathers, the moans of desolate mothers; the sighs of skeleton children; the nakedness of abandoned orphans, and many hundreds of wretched creatures perishing from hunger and want, could not move to action our iron-hearted authorities," he wrote. Other nationalists invoked far more deliberately heart-rending memories of the Great Famine and reiterated the charge that the English had been to blame for that tragedy. They "came to us then, as now, in the hour of our helplessness and desolation, to proclaim that we should be blotted from the land, and that our race should survive no more in the ancient home of our fathers," the *Nation* intoned. The old indictment – that the Irish had been treated like aliens; that the Queen's coronation oath to protect and defend her subjects had been violated; that Ireland would have been treated with greater compassion had she truly been regarded as an integral part of the United Kingdom, and that the suffering she had experienced would never have been permitted to occur in a region of England – was given new life by the Lancashire cotton famine. The "cold and merciless" attitude of the Palmerston administration towards Ireland's current distress was contrasted with its allegedly generous response to the hardship caused by an interruption of supplies of raw cotton to England's textile mills following the outbreak of the American Civil War. If Irish newspapers were to be believed, the unemployed operatives in England were recipients of money, bedding, clothing, education, daily newspapers, and a rich diet of venison, fish, beef, bacon, flour, sugar tea, plum pudding, and mince pies, and were even provided with the cultural diversions of "musical and dramatic entertainments." The truth was otherwise. The textile workers' widespread and prolonged unemployment meant loss of income, exhaustion of savings, the pawning of clothes, and resort to the Poor Law. Almost one-quarter of the population of the cotton districts were eventually on public relief, often compelled to perform the heavy physical labour for which their normal occupations ill-prepared them, while a deterioration in diets hastened the spread of disease. Still, their suffering could not be compared to the human catastrophe of the Great Famine, and Cullen was one of the Irish critics who also dismissed it as "nothing" compared to the current "Irish destitution." He was especially caustic in his condemnation of those rich Irish people, an allusion to what remained of the Ascendancy, who sent "large contributions" to Lancashire but could not "spare anything for the poor Catholics at home." Even more strident and wildly accusatory was Father Patrick Lavelle, the parish priest of Partry. A notorious clerical nationalist, he relentlessly developed the theme of a heartless and discriminatory government. The "English Government" was looking on "with secret delight, as the angel of death comes to slay his hecatombs to her national malice and hatred," he charged. Lancashire was "starving on beefsteaks" while Munster and Connaught were "to fatten on a half supply of Indian meal and black potatoes."[35]

"If we are poor," went the nationalists' refrain, "it is because we are plundered by England." Deaths from famine in a fertile land, exterminators protected by law, manufacturing deliberately discouraged by legislation, large sums extracted by absentees to add to the glut of wealth in England, masses of Irish obliged to emigrate by a government determined to depopulate their homeland – such was the litany of grievances recited by the *Nation* and other newspapers. "If our people leave the country, and go to foreign nations," the *Dundalk Democrat* insisted, "it is because they fly from poverty created by English rapacity, and the cruelty of British Law." Ireland was "bleeding from every pore in her emaciated and enervated form," the *Tipperary Advocate* claimed. Necessity, not adventure, drove Irishmen to quit their native land, one emigrant wrote to the *Nation*: "[W]e are exiles from no fault of ours." The massive flight from a land "so blessed by nature but so accursed by man" was cited as proof positive of the government's lack of concern for the Irish people. The *Galway American* went further, insisting that it was British policy to keep the Irish "in a perpetual state of slavery and destitution." The old Young Irelander John Martin, widely respected as "a man who would say a good word of the devil himself," advanced a proto-eugenicist interpretation of the consequences of the "ruthless rapacity of English rule." The loss of the young, strong, and spirited to emigration and "the incessant pressure of want and misery among the population who remain" had produced in some regions of the country, he argued, "a sensible deterioration in beauty, in size, in strength, and in moral and intellectual qualities."[36]

Stories of Irish immigrants to Britain being searched on arrival for contraband were offered as illustrations of their treatment as something less than fellow citizens of a single state. In the same sense, Irish visitors to Britain discovered that their banknotes were not legal tender, which meant that they were discounted as if foreign currency. The English who visited Ireland, on the other hand, could oblige locals to accept a Bank of England note. Still more powerful were the examples cited by nationalists of British ethnic contempt for the Irish. The *Nation* plundered England's most influential newspaper, the *Times*, and its most popular contemporary, the *Daily Telegraph*, together with *Punch*, to illustrate "a most rancorous [British] hatred and hostility" towards Irish fellow citizens. The Radical *Morning Star* proved an especially helpful ally, for it was an English newspaper that took the satirical weekly sternly to task for its ceaseless ridiculing of the Irish. The *Star* considered Lord Lyndhurst's infamous dismissal of them "as mild as milk compared with the vitriol of *Punch*." Stories in the Irish press of the "studied insults offered to Ireland and Irishmen" and "the partial enactment and administration of laws" were calculated to make any patriot's blood boil. The *Irishman*, which had been revived, reported how, following his sentencing of a London garrotter to four years of penal servitude, a judge had travelled down to Birkenhead and imposed a sentence of fifteen years on "an unfortunate Irishman" who had merely knocked a policeman down during a street riot. "It is to us a wonder how any nation – even of savages – could have, so long, submitted to such a system of spoliation, insult [and] degradation," the *Connaught Patriot* fumed.[37]

Oppression and tyranny were two of the most overused, provocative, and dangerous nouns in the Irish nationalists' vocabularies. Through their use, nationalists sought to convince fellow countrymen that not only were they victims of these evils but that their victimization was uniquely evil. There was an element of irony in this argument, for the United Kingdom enjoyed an international reputation as a liberal state. Certainly, it was a far from oppressive state. The "law was dominant, the rights of the subject highly regarded, and administration remarkably honest, if limited in scope." The system of government was representative in a restricted but slowly expanding sense, and Ireland's recently enlarged electorate returned approximately one-sixth of the membership of the House of Commons. Moreover, there was mounting pressure for a further and general liberalization of the franchise. This was also a society in which the press enjoyed considerable freedom, and newspapers had been brought within the reach of a significant proportion of an increasingly literate population. Similarly, the Irish Catholic Church exercised a measure of independence from state control that was rare in contemporary societies, and its bishops, as one foreign critic of Britain conceded, possessed great liberty in "treating all questions." Nor was there any evidence of a police state. Ireland was policed by a large, identifiable, and armed constabulary, but there were very few plainclothes policemen to maintain surveillance on individuals or pursue criminals. This reflected an abhorrence of any organization smacking of secret policemen. In short, truly effective supervision of the citizenry was minimal. The people possessed the right of assembly, the protection of *habeas corpus*, and trial by jury – hence Britain's attraction as a place of asylum for foreign political dissidents, which went far to explain the scandal sparked by the revelation that the home secretary had been opening the mail of the most famous of the refugee Italian nationalists.[38]

The drumbeat of Irish nationalist criticism of Britain was persistent, repetitive, hypnotic. "Where on the face of the earth is a parallel to be found for the oppression endured by the Irish people," the *Nation* asked. Britain's reputation as a liberal state was dismissed as a mask behind which she "perpetrated unnoticed, if not unknown," crimes in India and Ireland of such unprecedented enormity that it was impossible to find for them "adequate expression in the language of any people under the sun." Nationalists made much of Ireland's gross under-representation in Parliament. Had she received membership there in the same proportion of representatives to people as had England, they pointed out, the number of Irishmen sitting in the Commons would have more than doubled. They reviled the armed police force as an army of occupation. Expressions of British sympathy for the Poles when they launched an uprising against Russian rule early in 1863, no matter how shallow that support quickly proved to be, provided nationalists with yet another stick with which to beat the drums of dissent. Ireland's persecution by England surpassed in intensity, enormity, and variety that of Poland by Russia, they declared. The Tsar's regime admittedly dealt sternly with every symptom of revolt – a euphemism for repression so brutal that Poles abandoned physical resistance for the remainder of the century – but it protected industry, promoted industrial development, and permitted Poles to spend their revenues at home and to keep the produce of their land. Unlike poor Ireland, there could be no famine in Poland so long as she produced enough food to feed her people. The only emigrants from Poland were "patriotic conspirators or other malcontents" who left in their hundreds each year. The lesson to be drawn from all of this was taught by the *Tablet*: "If there be a God in Heaven to punish great criminals, nations as well as individuals, surely a dark doom awaits England."[39]

The time had come for Irishmen to take the necessary steps "towards compelling England to do justice to their country," the *Nation* announced. The most important of those steps was repeal of the Union, which John Martin promised a new generation of his countrymen meant "food for our hungry, clothes for our naked, comfort for our wretched, industry for our idle, peace and friendship among our factions, justice, honour, and prosperity for Ireland." As one long-term resident later recalled, it was scarcely possible to believe how extravagant were the hopes of the peasantry about the advantages they would derive from the re-establishment of an Irish parliament. Seizing on British support for the cause of Italian unity at the expense of papal sovereignty and of the right of the peoples of the Roman states to choose through plebiscites their own rulers, Irish nationalists embarked on a campaign for a popular referendum on repeal, launching a national petition. A.M. Sullivan of the *Nation* took the lead, and a document bearing more than half a million signatures was duly presented to the Executive. Significantly, Cullen remained aloof. He saw the hand of Young Irelanders behind this endeavour and believed that the Catholic laity was badly divided both on the attainability of repeal and on the means to pursue it. As a result, only a handful of bishops and a minority of priests participated. But the authorities' ignoring of the petition surely reinforced the impression that constitutional representations were pointless. Certainly, "English Constitutionalism" continued to be the butt of the seemingly relentless ridicule of the Irish press. To send members over to Westminster was "little short of a sickening sham" because they were "powerless for any good for the country," the *Tipperary Advocate* bellowed. In short, as John Martin protested in another of his epistles to the *Nation,* the Irish were denied justice under English rule and could never secure "good legislation from the English Parliament."[40]

Where such unrelentingly critical analyses might lead some Irishmen was illustrated by the *Connaught Patriot*. This organ of a former teacher and current confidant of the notorious Father Lavelle affirmed that revolutionary nationalism "must be a holy thing" if it could restore Ireland to her ancient, independent state. Encouraged to think of themselves as victims of unprecedented wrongs and the cruellest of oppressions, as the good in the eternal struggle against evil, and to regard the "English" government as a "monolithic organization dedicated to violating their basic rights," and one that lacked legitimacy as the ruler of their land, it was not surprising that a great many Catholic Irishmen exhibited a "passive alienation" from the state. It manifested itself not only in renewed expressions of the traditional "very deep and far reaching" anti-English sentiment, but also in the hope for a successful rebellion. Even if they were unwilling to rebel themselves, the alienated were prone to sympathize with those of their countrymen whose hostility was far more demonstrative. If "overt behavioral obedience" to state authority was not withdrawn, "the moral allegiance" to it that "undergirds such obedience" was being eroded. This was a development that John Mitchel detected from his distant American refuge. "I believe, or rather I know that the disaffection of a great mass of the people against English law and government is just as intense as ever," he wrote to a friend. "The meaner and more abject is their pretence of loyalty for tacit allowance of that law and government." Publishers and editors, such as Sullivan, and nationalist priests glorified rebels of the past even as they discouraged a resort to physical force by their own contemporaries. There was every likelihood of young men being confused by such ambivalence. Whether or not man's imagination is naturally violent, the young are usually more willing than their elders to defy authority and break society's traditional restraints. Thanks to the passion of the missionaries of nationalism, there was no shortage of moral justification on offer in mid-century Ireland for a resort to political violence. Their aggrieved dwelling on Irish rights long denied by England "supplied the alibi for aggressive conduct." Furthermore, Ireland had a tradition of violence that in some areas had arguably become part of the popular culture, having proven an effective means of correcting perceived injustices.[41]

Addressing an aggregate meeting at Clonmel in 1828, at the height of the fevered popular campaign to secure Catholic emancipation, Richard Lalor Sheil had emphasized "the extent of the calamity which follows the indulgence of that disastrous predilection for tumult which characterizes the mass of the population." A decade later, the presiding judge at the spring assizes held in the same town declared that "the Mass of Violence and Blood" and "Disregard of human life" appeared to mark County Tipperary off not only from other counties but also from "every other part of the civilized world." Several members of the hierarchy were equally frank during conversations with an insatiably curious French visitor. The people threw themselves "at an obstacle with extraordinary violence," some bishops admitted to Alexis de Tocqueville, and they attributed the "rather frequent" acts of violence largely to "drunkenness or political passions." One prelate acknowledged the existence of "a vague instinct of hatred against the conquerors" and laid at the door of "bad government" his countrymen's want of "civil virtues." Inevitably, at least so long as a desperate and famished people possessed the energy necessary to uphold the tradition of rural protest and violence, the Famine brought a spike in the incidence of crimes and acts of intimidation. To obtain employment on public works, to protect wage rates, or to discourage reductions of local relief appropriations, Ireland's peasantry had gathered menacingly. An estimated ten thousand assembled in 1846 outside the extraordinary presentment sessions in Clifden, and the crowd's intimidating presence induced the grand jury to vote a substantial sum for the employment of the poor. There were similar demonstrations to deter shipments of provisions or to influence the amount of food distributed by the soup kitchens. When threats failed, the rural poor rioted, staged ambushes, and on occasion murdered. They had the encouragement of success. Wages were initially kept up on the public works, and close supervision of the labour performed was discouraged. The resistance of Westmeath landlords to the calling of a county meeting to discuss the potato crisis quickly collapsed following an attempt on the life of one of their most prominent figures. Moreover, the successful prosecution of individuals involved in serious crimes continued to be extremely difficult. Popular sympathy for the "midnight marauders," their clandestine organization, and the intimidation of witnesses and jurors went far to explain a rate of acquittals in Ireland double that elsewhere in the United Kingdom. Since punishment was unlikely, those involved in the violence were "given little reason to shun collective action in the future." There was need, one well-connected landowner warned, for a stern effort to bring an end to terrorism in the countryside.[42]

The violence for which Tipperary had become a byword was essentially agrarian. One close observer attributed its eventual decline during the Famine to the "paralysing effects" of that catastrophe and to the fact that the plot of land to which people had formerly clung with such reckless tenacity, because "its possession was synonymous with life," had with repeated failures of the potato become a liability. Earlier, access to land, if only a potato patch; opposition to the tithe, which supported an "alien" and "heretical church"; resistance to the consolidation of holdings, evictions, wage reductions, and the payment of county and church cess (tax); and antagonism to the new police forces; had all sparked trouble if not a resort to "terror." Threatening letters, which one Conservative periodical argued revealed the true feelings of the Irish peasantry, acts of arson, the mutilation of animals, and murder were all employed. Charles Kickham, Tipperary man, poet, and revolutionary nationalist, put into the mouth of a character in his immensely popular novel *Knocknagow* the declaration that "'the dread of assassination'" was the people's sole protection against "'extermination.'" Often the agents of violence were individuals or small groups of men rather than secret societies, but some regions of the country were so frequently visited by "agrarian rebellion" that it constituted a deep-seated tradition. Nor was it ever entirely devoid of political meaning. At the very least, "it articulated a broad refusal to internalize the English legal order." Equally, it was rarely a simple class and ethnic struggle between tenants and landlords. Rural society was riddled with conflicts that pitted tenant against tenant, the landless against the farmer, even labourer against labourer. Nevertheless, landlords and their agents were often prime targets, and it was the willingness and ability to murder, as well as the existence of secret societies, that so clearly distinguished Irish rural dissidents from those elsewhere in the United Kingdom. No less a landlord than the Earl of Derby withdrew under the threat of violence the eviction notices issued to a number of his tenants suspected of being implicated in, or of withholding information about, the murder in broad daylight and before witnesses of the under-agent on his Tipperary estate. More land was provided for conacre, evictions and consolidations were limited, and rents were held down. Violence worked.[43]

Sectarianism stained many an agrarian confrontation, especially in those counties where Catholics and Protestants were both present in substantial numbers. Not that other areas lacked evidence of a Catholic tenantry's ambition to overthrow the dominion of Protestant landlords. Clerical denunciations of outrages were on occasion qualified by understandable expressions of sympathy with the tenants' cause and condition, while the notion that agrarian killings were only homicides in a technical sense "found some encouragement in moral theology for popular consumption." In County Longford, Protestant landlords and Anglican clergy responded in kind. They encouraged the Orange Order, promoted proselytism, and even established sectarian tests for leases. These rarely proved effective countermeasures. Some priests sanctioned the physical intimidation of the proselytisers, and life invariably became more unpleasant for the most vulnerable members of the religious minority. The "desire to escape from violence was second only to the goal of economic independence in explaining why an estimated 500,000 Irish Protestants emigrated during the pre-Famine decades." Others, Catholics as well as Protestants, moved to more secure areas within Ireland. By 1861 County Longford had, within a generation, lost one-third of its Protestant residents. But sectarianism was increasingly colouring, and primarily orange, the urban violence that also bedevilled Ireland. Labour militancy, characterized by the destruction of property and astonishing acts of personal brutality, had been a source of the tension between O'Connell and Dublin tradesmen during the 1830s. This form of violence died out there during the following decade, but northern towns and villages, including Belfast, were increasingly scarred by riots sparked by provocative Orange processions and the sectarian cleansing of Roman Catholics from certain areas of a community. During a particularly bloody clash in the village of Dolly's Brae on 12 July 1849, a number of Catholics were killed. Where they had the numbers, Catholics took revenge.[44]

Sectarianism and brute force on a scale unmatched in England and Scotland remained seemingly ineradicable features of Irish elections. The calling of general elections in 1852 and 1865 during the Orange marching season guaranteed explosions of religious rancour in some northern counties, but it was no stranger elsewhere. Horrific murders were far from uncommon and intimidation all too frequent. The fact that labourers and cottiers often provided the muscle of election mobs suggested a connection between agrarian disturbances and election riots. Some of the rioters were plainly pursuing "agrarian disputes by other means," for a good proportion of the candidates standing for election were landlords. Equally, election riots were evidently another manifestation of political violence. More sinister still were the activities of the secret societies that had long been active in the countryside and had survived the Famine.[45]

Few Irish landowners possessed the "inherited authority" that provided a traditional foundation stone of relative social tranquility. They were widely regarded by a Catholic peasantry as aliens and heretics. Convinced that justice was not to be obtained from a landlord-staffed magistracy, that the legal system was sectarian and oppressive, the Catholic rural poor had long sought through direct action to enforce their own harsh justice. They employed violence and terror to secure a favourable resolution of problems and the redress of grievances. In numbers there was strength and in secrecy a measure of immunity. The character of many townlands, "with the long months of idleness that their marginal economies dictated," and "surreptitious culture" provided an environment conducive to conspiracy. There was also the cohesion provided by the common religious faith of the vast majority of the poor, though Catholic priests were on occasion victims of agrarian secret societies organized to protect peasant interests. Nevertheless, the societies' sectarianism was often celebrated in the oath to wade deep in Orange blood. Few of the early societies had a political agenda, but their antipathies and "experience of organized illegality" made them readily adaptable to political ends. Furthermore, they were resowing the seed of violence deep in the soil of Ireland.[46]

The Defenders, a secret society whose members were from small towns as well as the countryside, had acquired notoriety in 1798 as sectarian rebels. They "postulated ideas of national revolution" even before their association with the United Irishmen. The Ribbon societies of the first half of the nineteenth century appeared to be their natural heirs. "Ribbonism was nationalist, Catholic communalist if not sectarian and vaguely radical in a populist mode with much millenial admixture." Its leadership was drawn heavily from trade, primarily shopkeepers and publicans, but included farmers and artisans. Here was another blend of urban and rural lower-middle and working classes, those segments of the population to which by mid-century nationalist publishers and editors were directing their propaganda, and the Ossianic Society its publications. Thus secret societies ostensibly formed to fight some local injustice might often be led by men imbued with the belief that Ireland was the victim of national injustice, and the Ribbonmen belonged within the tradition of Irish nationalism and were not "just another agrarian secret society." Under a variety of names (the Brotherhood of St Patrick, the Molly Maguires) and a variety of fronts (social clubs and mutual aid societies), with hedge schoolmasters reputedly serving as recruiting agents, they possessed in theory an elaborate hierarchical structure not unlike that of the Church. At the base were pub-centred lodges, the equivalent of a congregation, and above them the parish, county, province, and national boards. In truth, there was little if any effective central direction of local bodies and Ribbonism remained faintly anarchic in an organizational sense. Nevertheless, the Molly Maguires of Roscommon, who waged a brutal campaign during the 1840s against those they accused of tyrannizing the poor, demonstrated yet again the efficacy of violence. They intimidated with relative impunity well-to-do farmers, middlemen, and the unfortunate land agents whose duties included the collection of rents and the supervision of evictions. A pair of landlord murders late in 1847 did result in executions, and one of the cases became a national sensation when a local priest was accused of inciting the deed. The *Nation*, appalled as it declared itself to be by the violence, stirred the pot of controversy by labelling this particular crime an "Ejectment Murder." Indeed, it went further and declared itself unable to "condemn an instinctive rebellion against conventional morality in a time of Famine, and significantly, that it was possible the murders were a manifestation of God's Justice." Although energetic police activity did subsequently thin the ranks of the Ribbonmen in the county, there could be no denying the Molly Maguires' success in highlighting violence as a weapon of first resort in battles against perceived oppression.[47]

The authorities did succeed in penetrating the Ribbon societies, for there was no shortage of self-confessed members ready to volunteer as informers. A series of police raids in the autumn of 1839 netted a rich haul of documents. They indicated the existence of a complex organization centred in both Ulster and Dublin, but one well established also in Britain's Irish communities. Aided by legislation that made it a crime to maintain correspondence with any society that used secret signs or passwords (Freemasons and Friendly Brothers excepted), the Irish Executive secured the conviction and transportation of the Dublin leadership. In Ulster a police inspector infiltrated the leadership only to see the ringleaders, on being brought to trial, sentenced to relatively short periods of imprisonment thanks to "mistaken judicial leniency." Even from behind bars the Ribbonmen managed worryingly to maintain communications and keep the system in operation. Yet the Executive remained uncertain of the political seriousness of this threat. There were suspicions of Ribbon involvement in Dublin's brutal labour violence, and the police eventually came to the conclusion that the Ribbonmen sought repeal of the Union and regarded physical force as the only means by which it would be achieved. But other observers continued to insist that they were organized simply to defend themselves, principally against Orangemen, to provide mutual support in obtaining work, or to raise money for those in need. In short, they amounted to "much ado about nothing." Thomas Drummond, the highly respected and influential undersecretary during the late 1830s, identified forty-five cases of Ribbonism but discounted any threat of a political conspiracy. He was contemptuous of the organizers, dismissing them as low publicans motivated exclusively by hopes of pecuniary gain from the expenditures of members in their houses. Their followers were mere "dupes."[48]

Drummond's disdain for a membership drawn from "the vile lowest class," or at best led in the countryside by farmers' sons, was matched by his distaste for the means by which the state gathered evidence. He was deeply sceptical of the worth of information provided by "approvers," and he stressed the limited usefulness of informers who declined to go into court to give evidence. Nor was he unmindful of the requirement for warrants in order to detain suspects or conduct searches in a state that took pride in the rule of law, and warrants required sworn information. Others expressed ethical reservations over the funding of government agents within the Ribbon societies who then helped with their dues to sustain the branches to which they belonged. Confident by the end of 1840 that it had weakened the Ribbon organization, the administration no longer felt justified in supplying money for such purposes, even allowing that "the result might be the detection of persons engaged in illegal practices, inasmuch as their guilt might and probably would be increased in proportion to the encouragement thus secretly afforded to them." Why risk the damaging and emotive accusation that the state was employing *agents provocateurs*? In this context, the denunciation of secret societies by the Catholic hierarchy provided additional reassurance. Archbishop Murray advised Drummond that "we consider such illegal combinations as strongly censured by Religion as they are condemned by law, and we consider it the indispensable duty of every Clergyman to discountenance and put them down by every means in his power." Before long the Executive was receiving encouraging reports from the countryside of "the beneficial effect of the interference of the Roman Catholic Clergy in putting down the [Ribbon] system."[49]

The continued existence of "felonious associations" whose purposes were poorly defined but plainly unlawful was freely admitted by a number of priests. Some burial societies were suspected of being fronts for Ribbonism, and their members' professions of loyalty merely a "blind." A formal declaration of allegiance was invariably turned down and thus not read when an initiate was sworn, informants warned. There was a similarly simple way to circumvent the religious ban on membership in secret societies. Ribbonmen took advantage of the brief lapse in their good standing as members at the end of each quarter. They then attended church, swore in good conscience that they did not belong to any secret society, and received absolution. Moreover, Drummond's opinion notwithstanding, the Executive concluded after his death that this organization was a "general confederacy" available for local purposes, both offensive and defensive, "but ultimately directed to political objects, and especially to the ascendancy of the Roman Catholic Religion and its professors." Ribbonism evidently provided a substantial force "ready and at hand to political agitators," and the Tory government led by Robert Peel fancied that priests would not cooperate as willingly with it as they had with the Whigs in the suppression of violence. So, the new Irish Executive resolved to spare neither pain nor expense to destroy Ribbonism. It failed, and hence the warning issued by the Whig Lord Lieutenant in the aftermath of the 1848 rising that future treasonous conspiracies could not be prevented "unless some effectual steps [were] taken for the prevention of secret combinations." The early 1850s did not lack for evidence of their continued existence, and while the peasantry seemed submissive enough and behaved with exaggerated respect to their "betters," there were suspicions that they were concealing "a well of bitterness that awaited only a sign of weakness to overflow into violence." An observer who flattered himself that he had an intimate knowledge and understanding of the Irish peasantry warned that their chief hope was for a successful rebellion, aided by the United States or France. These were the people who continued to offer "overt behavioral obedience" to the state and whose alienation remained essentially passive. Nor did this go undetected. In the words of one viceroy, "we have to deal with a population, the masses of which are in their hearts disaffected by British rule. They will, I fear, long continue to be so." The Ribbonmen and their ilk were likely to be more active in their disaffection.[50]

As the decade of the 1860s dawned, there existed in Ireland many of the preconditions necessary for another eruption of revolutionary nationalism. A discontent extending far beyond material concerns had long been politicized, and it sought the state's remodelling. The United Kingdom was under constant attack in a society where the levels of literacy and education were rising, the means of communication improving, and the single most influential institution considered itself the victim of "brutal" discrimination. The existing system of government was disparaged as illegitimate and oppressive, indeed as an alien imposition. Equally inflammatory in this context was the insistence of opinion leaders that the redress of grievances and passage of constitutional reform were unlikely to be achieved through the peaceful means open to the Irish people. What point was there in appeals to the "English Parliament"? Irishmen were being encouraged to regard their social, political, and even physical environment as hostile, and to consider themselves victims of English malevolence. This conviction was likely to move some of them to violence, a choice all the more seductive in a society whose people not only had become accustomed to, but also had reason to believe in, its efficacy and the unlikelihood of punishment. People who find rewards in violence, "either through attainment of their goals or through the satisfaction of acting out their anger without harmful consequences," are increasingly likely to resort to it again. This was especially true of young men who had migrated to towns, perhaps disenchanted with rural life, only to encounter urban deprivation yet find themselves part of a "very dense network of interpersonal relationships." Members of local social groups, both rural and urban, it has been said, "make the best recruits for violent bands." Ireland was rich in such groups – Ribbon societies, Phoenix societies, even the Young Men's Catholic societies founded by Dean O'Brien of Limerick. Here was a tradition of mobilization that helped to preserve a sense of group identity, and in the case of the Ribbonmen the tradition was equally one of violent resistance to perceived oppression. The probability of aggressive behaviour was all the greater given the long campaign waged by nationalism's missionaries to hold the British, and often more narrowly the English, responsible for all of Ireland's woes. "I cannot conceal from myself that we here (every nationalist I know included) believe *only* in arms and believe *only* in French assistance," one Dubliner confided to Smith O'Brien in 1860.[51]

The contributory causes of political violence were therefore present in mid-nineteenth-century Ireland, and to a remarkable degree. Ireland's relationship with the rest of the United Kingdom remained a tormented one. It was bedevilled by ethnic tensions, religious hostility, and a definition of the national culture in which there was scant place for things British despite the triumph of English as Ireland's language. There were also problems of socio-economic deprivation, along with a perception of inequality and injustice. The great majority of Irishmen had yet to be granted full citizenship in the contractual or territorial nation. Catholics were still excluded from the highest offices of state, while most senior positions in the Executive were occupied by Britons and Protestants, all of which contributed to a well-developed sense of oppression. Finally, not only had discontent been politicized, but there existed in Ireland a tradition, if not a culture, of violence. But two other important factors were seemingly absent – deep divisions within the governing elite and a government either too feeble or too inept to maintain law and order. If revolutionary nationalism was to erupt, Ireland needed, as she had in the 1790s, "a revolutionary leadership equipped with a potentially attractive ideology."[52]

One possible source of this leadership was Irish America. North America was home to the large Irish communities formed by the legions who had emigrated there during the first half of the nineteenth century. Had these emigrants, especially the vast numbers of Catholics who had fled the Famine and made new homes for themselves in new lands, carried with them a hatred of England or Britain so intense that they and their children were grimly determined to work for the independence of the old country? Certainly, there developed within Irish America, and to a lesser degree in Irish Canada, a peculiarly virulent strain of Irish nationalism.

5

Emigration, Exile, and Nationalism: British North America

Speaking in Rochdale, early in 1867, John Bright declared that there was no man either in office or in opposition who could prevail upon the House of Commons "to do anything substantial to remedy the grievances of the Irish people." His intent was to harness the chronic Irish problem to the cause of franchise reform. A more truly representative legislature, he argued, would be far more sympathetic to Ireland's plight. For some Irishmen, however, his remarks surely reinforced their even more radical analysis of the situation. After all, Young Irelanders had failed as rebels but they had succeeded in preparing the way for a thoroughgoing separatist challenge to constitutional nationalism. Why be bound by a constitution that denied Irishmen equal rights or remain as citizens of a union in which they continued to suffer discrimination? Even Daniel O'Connell had resorted to an implied threat of violence in his struggle to secure concessions from Britain and, arguably, had inadvertently revealed the shortcomings of a constitutionalist strategy that placed its faith in the ability of a charismatic leader to rouse and organize the masses as an irresistible force for peaceful change. Catholic emancipation had benefited the few at the expense of the many who contributed so much to its eventual triumph, while repeal had been decisively defeated by the state. Thus moral force seemed unlikely to swiftly effect greater Irish political autonomy.[1]

The chronic failure of the constitutional nationalists to pull together long enough during the 1850s to exploit fully the instability of the major political parties could only have reinforced in many minds the argument advanced so forcefully by John Mitchel – that physical force alone could redeem Ireland. This assessment undoubtedly had an impact upon a generation of young men schooled in ethnopolitics.

They had been taught that their own culture had been stolen from them and a foreign one imposed in its place, that they were victims of ethnic tyranny, and that they belonged to an ethnic community that was an organic unit. They were duty bound, therefore, to uphold their distinctive values, if not morally obligated to sacrifice themselves in order "to secure the survival of the collective whole." They could take renewed hope in the late 1850s from Britain's foreign difficulties, which had historically been regarded as Ireland's opportunity. Britain and France, allies in the Crimea against Russia, had with war's end quickly returned to their more familiar relationship of mutual distrust. A "French party" of Irish nationalists now emerged, ever hopeful of assistance from the traditional ally of Irish rebels, only to be reprimanded by Smith O'Brien. He feared an outbreak of sectarian civil war in Ireland. But as both O'Connell and the Young Irelanders had recognized, there was an Irish nation in "exile" to which nationalists might also look for succour. Why was it that the Scots and English who emigrated cherished not the "smallest hostility to the people, to the institutions, or to the Government" of the United Kingdom, some Britons asked themselves, whereas every Catholic Irishman who left his country determined to better his life in North America appeared to carry as part of his baggage "an undying love" of his native land and "an equally vehement hatred for the race whose oppressions" he had been taught to believe had driven him into exile? Were Irish emigrants "constantly preparing, by a secret destiny, the terrible retribution of seven hundred years of persecution"?[2]

In seeking a better life elsewhere, the Irish differed little from other peoples. Europeans had been on the move for centuries, in search of spouses, subsistence, seasonal employment, greater opportunities for advancement, personal improvement, or an escape from political strife and religious intolerance. But the pressures to emigrate mounted in the United Kingdom during the nineteenth century. Rapid population growth; a sharp rise in the cost of land; the contraction of steady, let alone secure, rural employment; the withering, under the challenge of mechanization, of a number of domestic industries that had been an important if not vital source of supplementary income of the Irish rural poor; crop failures that resulted in hunger if not famine; cyclical industrial depressions in Britain's advanced economy; and the lure of higher wages in North America were all powerful inducements to seek to start life anew across the Atlantic. Additional impetus was provided by the ready availability of information on distant lands, by the reassuring existence of overseas communities formed by fellow countrymen and women who had crossed the oceans earlier, by an onrushing transportation revolution that produced less expensive, more comfortable, and normally less perilous passages (though the crossing of the North Atlantic was not an experience many emigrants from the British Isles would wish quickly to repeat, since the great majority of them at least, in the first half of the century, travelled out as human ballast aboard sailing vessels designed for the timber and other trades), and by regulations that were occasionally designed to discourage, but more frequently to promote, the emigrant trade and divert the human stream to colonial shores.[3]

Emigration produced its own psychopathology. Departure from home and homeland was for the great majority of people a traumatic experience. The "loss of one's most meaningful and valued objects: people, things, places, language, culture, customs" was predictably painful and likely to imperil the individual's sense of identity. The idealization of the new society or the devaluation of the old might lessen the anxiety, but damage to the ego, "feelings of uprootedness" and even guilt, left some emigrants peculiarly susceptible to mental or physical illness. Depression, paranoia, and confusion were intensified whenever host communities greeted them with suspicion and hostility, and the process of adjustment and integration was especially difficult for immigrants who considered themselves exiles. They were strongly inclined to idealize the homeland and to be embittered by their "expulsion" from it. Nor was expulsion either narrowly or precisely defined. Persons fleeing "sociopolitical or economic conditions" might legitimately claim that theirs had been a "forced expatriation" by a government that had not left them "room to live," and the Irish were peculiarly susceptible to this interpretation of their experience. The notion of emigration as exile was "rooted deeply in Irish literary and historical tradition," but during the nineteenth century priests and press were two influential and consistent designers of this simple human equation. "Lord John of Tuam" instructed his clergy to denounce one emigration scheme "as a devilish plot to exile the bone and sinew of the country," while Paul Cullen, along with other members of the hierarchy, frequently referred to "our poor exiles ... flying from their native land."[4]

The Irish were not the only residents of the British Isles who concluded that they could do better for themselves overseas. The English left in substantial number, and emigration from Wales and Scotland was proportionately greater still. The Welsh had settled America during the colonial period, many of them Dissenters seeking to escape religious discrimination, political dissidents seeking a larger measure of freedom, and farmers seeking fertile land free of landlord control. Rural discontent long remained the mainspring of Welsh emigration. Insecurity of tenure, landlord oppression, appalling living conditions, and the endemic poverty of a rapidly multiplying peasantry pushed many out of the principality. That Wales did not experience an exodus of biblical proportions was largely attributable to the availability of alternative employment in the industrializing south and neighbouring England. This profile of the Welsh emigrant did change as harsh lives and hard times subsequently drove skilled industrial workers, coal miners, and slate quarrymen to abandon a native land to which they had a mystical attachment. Rare was the Welshman who did not suffer pangs of *hiraeth* (yearning for country and loved ones), yet many still chose to cross the Atlantic rather than the nearby border with England. Those who hoped to return to the land as farmers knew that this ambition was more likely to be realized in the United States, but an incipient nationalism may also have been a factor in the decision. The principality's industrial workers and employers were often separated by language, ethnicity, and nonconformity, as were tenants and peasants from anglicized or English landlords. A desire to escape subordination to England and the English, "to preserve the Welsh nation from oblivion by re-creating a truly Welsh community in the United States," influenced a number of emigrants. Equally, "devotion to Wales, the Welsh language, and the Welsh way of life" led many a Welshman to remain at home.[5]

Scots, like the Welsh, had the domestic option of migrating to rapidly developing industrial centres. Many made their way to the urban centres of the western Lowlands in the mid-nineteenth century, though it was often no more than a brief halt before leaving Britain. Scots, long a peculiarly mobile people, emigrated for much the same reasons as the Welsh. Those from the agricultural Lowlands responded to the possibility of acquiring their own farms in North America, while the skilled and semi-skilled artisans who formed fully one-half of the Scots leaving urban industrial centres for the United States during the century were attracted by higher wages and passages that were increasingly less costly in terms of time and fares. Few had greater cause than Highlanders to be embittered by their experience at the hands of landlords.[6]

Confronted by proprietors determined to extract greater profits from their estates, evicted from their holdings to make room for sheep to graze (or fearful that this fate awaited them), reduced to miserable crofts too small to support their families, compelled to engage in kelping or fishing to eke out a bare existence, living in hovels and increasingly reduced to a diet of potatoes which could support four times as many people to the acre as had the traditional crop of oats, Highlanders and Western Islanders were for several years effectively denied access to the escape hatch of emigration. Afraid of an exodus of cheap labour but operating under the guise of humanitarian concern, the landed interest secured in 1803 regulations governing the transportation of emigrants that priced passages beyond the reach of dispossessed tenants, let alone impoverished crofters. The result, in the opinion of sympathetic visitors, was a people ground into poverty by landlord oppression. They compared the plight of the Highlanders to that of Ireland's cottiers, for both were frequently threatened with famine.[7]

Common dearth and squalor convinced some observers that these two Celtic societies suffered from a common disease – overpopulation. An obvious remedy was large-scale emigration. The collapse of the market for kelp following the end of the Napoleonic Wars, a decline in cattle prices, the suppression of illicit distillation, and the completion of a number of public works projects combined to remove landlord obstacles from emigration's path. Suddenly fearful of being burdened with a peasantry of little economic value and with tenants unable to pay their rents, and keen to effect more clearances to create additional sheep runs, landlords reversed course and launched an energetic and successful campaign for the relaxation of the restrictive regulations they had earlier obtained. There was no shortage of emigrants. Some raised their fares by liquidating what remained of their scanty assets, such as livestock, while others provided the links of a chain migration or benefited from modest experiments with assisted passages. Those who accepted landlord assistance only to refuse to leave at the last moment were on occasion forcibly driven like animals to waiting transports. This shattering experience was all too often followed by a sea passage of "unalloyed horror." Cramped and fetid quarters aboard converted timber vessels that seemed harrowingly unseaworthy in heavy weather ensured that disease was a fellow passenger.[8]

The appearance in Scotland late in the summer of 1846 of the fungus already wreaking havoc in Ireland threatened another tragedy.

Crofters heavily dependent on the potato for food faced disaster. Hunger, along with cold and disease, became a daily companion. The Russell government despatched an investigator to the region who had honed his skills as a relief organizer in southwest Ireland. He bore the unfortunate family name of Coffin. This threat of famine on British as distinct from Irish soil did not induce the government to liberalize the policies adopted in Ireland. The Treasury continued to insist that people not be allowed to starve, but it expected Scots landowners to provide employment for their tenants through estate improvements financed with loans it advanced. State intervention was to be kept to a minimum, avowedly out of concern for the welfare of both the economic system and the moral character of those in need, and terminated at the first opportunity. Thus the government formally withdrew from Scottish relief operations in the summer of 1847, much the same time as it transferred the crushing burden of Irish relief to Irish property. Nonetheless, it continued to exert influence on the policies of the charitable organizations still in the field. Charles Trevelyan at the Treasury, citing the Irish experience, established a miserly "destitution test" of one pound of meal as full payment for an entire day's labour. Furthermore, he insisted that this food allowance be issued in fortnightly dollops as a means of compelling the poor to ration and discipline themselves. Such niggardliness was framed by ethnic and social contempt, for Trevelyan had no higher opinion of the Scots than he did of the Irish. As one mordant Scottish editor put it, the "Highlands upon grounds of Catholic affinity were to be starved after the Irish fashion." Fortunately, the Scots escaped the human catastrophe that famine brought to Ireland.[9]

Death rates rose, primarily among the very young and the old, but the counting of the endangered Highlanders in the tens of thousands made for a more manageable and less daunting crisis than that in Ireland, where the imperilled were numbered in the millions. The Scots utterly dependent on relief had by 1848 fallen below seventy thousand. The strength of the rapidly industrializing and urbanizing Lowlands economy made the relatively short migration there a realistic option for many of those at risk, though Glasgow clergy reported being besieged by destitute Highlanders who added "'much to the existing mass of pauperism and distress there.'" Nevertheless, a more resilient economy, less dependence on the potato, a smaller population in relation to available land, an ongoing revolution in communications that allowed the swift shipment of supplies to especially hard-hit areas, and a social revolution within the landed interest contributed to the avoidance of another human catastrophe. A new capital-rich class had entered the landlord ranks. They were better positioned than their Irish counterparts to shoulder the less onerous relief responsibilities. By the same token, the greater wealth in Scottish society allowed greater play of a powerful commitment to philanthropy, which was spurred by the evangelicalism and social conscience of the two principal Protestant churches. Substantial sums were raised to aid the distressed, initially by the Free Church, but their administration was eventually transferred to a central board. As a result, the landed class escaped much of the financial burden of relief. Furthermore, Scots received a disproportionate share of the donations that poured into the British Association, especially from expatriate communities, to finance aid to stricken areas. The romanticized Highlander was a passive, patient, and loyal figure, and thus credited with being a worthier recipient of charitable assistance than the turbulent Irish Celt. Even so, many Scots complained that the Irish were being rewarded for their tradition of violence with a greater measure of state support.[10]

By no means all Highlanders accepted their fate passively. There had been sporadic resistance to the clearances, but poorly organized and generally bereft of any threatening ideology it had never smacked of the terrorism identified with the Irish countryside. Of course, virtually any part of the United Kingdom "would have seemed relatively 'peaceful' by comparison" to Ireland. Scottish clergymen eschewed the provocative, if not incendiary, rhetoric to which members of the Irish hierarchy on occasion gave voice, and they tended to encourage "a fatalistic acceptance of landlordism." With the arrival of famine, the organ of the Free Church and its clergy described the disaster as providential, as did many Irish priests, and they preached "spiritual introversion." There was a considerable unassisted emigration by middle-rank crofting families who raised the money for passage and resettlement. They were driven less by fear of starvation than by alarm at "serious and rapidly increasing threat to their economic and social position," as they perceived themselves "falling back in the world." The announcement of the Central Board's intention to wind up its activities in 1850, the strong likelihood that the cost of relief would then be transferred (as earlier in Ireland) to those who paid poor rates, and the passage of legislation to make loans available for assisted passages inspired landowners to introduce schemes. The intent was to rid the country of the poorest of the "redundant" crofters. Indeed, the crucial impact of the Scottish famine, no less than the Irish, was the impetus given to "emigration on a hitherto unknown scale." Aided by the Highland and Island Emigration Society, landlords exported the destitute in unprecedented numbers. In some parishes perhaps one-half of the inhabitants fled or were packed off, while in the region of the western mainland and western isles as a whole, one-third of the population disappeared. Often, the experience was brutal and disillusioning. The redundant poor were subjected to various forms of coercion – seizure of remaining live-stock, denial of fuel, refusal of relief – and on several of the islands reluctant emigrants were hunted down with dogs, bound like prison-ers, and thrown aboard waiting vessels. They had good reason to conclude that they had been forcibly banished by tyrannical land-lords, and their early poems and songs were of exile. It might have been written equally of the Scots, as of the Irish, that "not a year rolled by during which several thousands of [them], weary of a strug-gle against irremediable misery and interminable oppression, did not make up their minds to bid a last farewell to their dear [land], and to seek afar a better lot." Yet one witness to heart-rending departures noted that "the painfulness of the scene was greatly lessened by anyone who had witnessed the hopeless squalor, ignorance and sloth, which the emigrants were leaving behind." However deep their attachment to their homeland, their sense of nationhood, and their feelings of cultural and ethnic identity, many of the Scots on reaching British North America quickly concluded that their lives had taken a sharp turn for the better. Nor was this a sectarian conclusion. The Roman Catholics among them were led by clerics who were "profoundly conservative" and fully supportive of "the existing British political authorities." Consequently, they were speedily integrated into a tra-dition of loyalty which their priests propagated.[11]

The concept of loyalty underwent a subtle but significant change at least in Upper Canada, later Canada West, during the first half of the nineteenth century, and it was one that eased the absorption of immi-grants. The imperial relationship remained its core, but increasingly the connection was defined as one beneficial to the province. British con-stitutional models remained "sacred," and suspicion of the United States as an "aggressive and possibly expansionist neighbour" was another vital ingredient. However, loyalty no longer had to be earned by attachment to the tradition established by the Loyalist refugees from the American Revolution. Instead, with the growth of settlement, it "could be acquired through proper social values and good citizenship." Loyalty thus became "assimilative," embracing the concepts of a government responsible to the Assembly, the existence of political parties, and the legitimacy of political opposition. Here was a political society into which, or so it seemed, Catholic as well as Protestant Irishmen might easily fit.[12]

The Irish boasted a tradition of emigration, even an "emigration culture," the equal of that of any of their fellow natives of the British Isles. Perhaps a million braved the Atlantic between the end of the Napoleonic Wars and the beginning of the Great Famine. Initially, they journeyed to the United States, were heavily Protestant in religion, and were dominated by small farmers and artisans. But cheaper fares and land grants eventually succeeded in diverting this human flow to British North America, though many still travelled on to the republic soon after their arrival. Nor did the sectarian colouring remain the same. Assisted-passage schemes designed to remove from Ireland the lawless and the redundant, together with the remittances from earlier migrants, saw swelling numbers of Roman Catholic smallholders and cottiers boarding the boats. They tended on the eve of the Famine to be "generally poorer and less skilled" than their predecessors," more inclined to describe themselves as labourers, more literate, more "aggressively Catholic and nationalistic," and more deeply imbued with the culture of despair than that of hope.[13]

Famine suddenly bloated the ranks of Irish emigrants. In little more than a decade, the flight from hunger, disease, and despair took on the appearance of a stampede as two million people fled across the Atlantic, across the world, or across the Irish Sea. More of them were Roman Catholics than at any time since the seventeenth century. If less anglicized, less independent, and less skilled than those who had gone before, they were rarely the very poorest segment of Irish rural society. The discovery of a small treasure in gold on the bodies of the victims of one maritime disaster suggested that not all Irish emigrants were destitute. Remittances from North America continued to finance a vast number of the transatlantic passages, while small farmers continued to scrape together fares. Thousands were transported at the expense of their landlords and without the brutality associated with the expulsions from the Hebrides. Indeed, many Irish tenants petitioned for such assistance and subsequently wrote to express their gratitude for it. Ten large landowners, among them a future prime minister, Lord Palmerston, sent out nearly thirty thousand emigrants from their estates, and many smaller landlords aided smaller parties. Again the motive was to be rid of tenants who would otherwise have to be supported from the poor rates; landlords also hoped that large-scale emigration would counteract "growing agrarian violence." There were, however, great variations in the quality of these emigration schemes, and the medical officer at the Canadian reception centre on Grosse-Ile in the St Lawrence complained that in many instances those aided by landlords were the helpless, the infirm, the idle, and the lazy. An amendment attached to a relief bill in March 1847 by William Gregory, the author of the notorious quarter-acre test, permitted Poor Law guardians to provide partial funding of landlord-assisted schemes, but it was not until they were authorized to borrow for this purpose two years later that the numbers so assisted became significant. As for the calls for publicly funded schemes of mass emigration, they fell upon the deaf ears. Both government and taxpayers were frightened by the immense sums that would be required.[14]

The emigration commissioners concluded that 1847 marked the moment when this mass movement attained dimensions that made it "a matter of national importance." They estimated that over the next seven years Irish emigrants annually averaged well in excess of two hundred thousand and that approximately one million others had followed them by 1866. The commissioners duly reported the well-advertised dangers of the transatlantic crossing, putting the number of lives lost on vessels that foundered between 1847 and 1865 at fifty-three hundred. This was surely a severe underestimate given the two-score emigrant ships lost during a single decade. Moreover, to the deaths from drowning must be added the far heavier toll of disease. The long failure to require medical inspections of embarking passengers; the lack of sufficient officers to examine vessels or to ensure that regulations with respect to space, provisions, and clean water were being respected; the suspension and then repeal of the requirement that vessels transporting more than fifty passengers carry a surgeon – not until 1866 was this regulation successfully revived – these were all factors that contributed to repeated tragedies at sea. In response to mounting criticism of the numbers of emigrants being crammed into ships like sardines into a can, thereby greatly increasing the likelihood of epidemics, the emigration commissioners initially explained that additional restrictions would inevitably raise costs and thus render impossible the escape of the Irish to North America. Subsequently, they refined this argument. State restrictions on the number of passengers "would introduce uncertainty into the business and be therefore a detriment to the shipowner, and consequently must tend to discourage enterprise and improvement in the construction of ships and the conduct of emigration. The result would be fewer and inferior ships, and increased price with diminished accommodation." There were hopes that steam vessels would solve health and safety problems, for they offered faster passages, more space and light, and were generally more seaworthy than many of the small sailing ships. This optimism was misplaced. As late as 1863, perhaps a majority of the emigrants were still travelling aboard inferior vessels.[15]

If the transports engaged in the "emigrant business" varied greatly in size and seaworthiness, as did crews in competence, the conditions for steerage-class passengers were uniformly unpleasant. Legislation dealing with passenger health and space was all too easily evaded. Loopholes in the law with respect to infants and children permitted evasion of the minimum space allowance, while poor food and insufficient quantities of it, insufficient and weather-dependent means of preparing it, insufficient water, insufficient attention to personal hygiene, insufficient and primitive sanitary facilities, lengthy passages, and the continuing failure to screen out carriers of disease before casting off all contributed to nightmare experiences. Lice thrived and typhus swept through vessels. Cholera was another passenger. Infants and young children were most at risk, and women proved more vulnerable than men. Thus, while statistics indicate a surprisingly low death rate over the extended period of mass migration, there were more than enough "coffin ships" to leave another tragic imprint on the historic memory of the Irish. One in six of those who embarked for Quebec in the blackest year, 1847, died either at sea, at the colonial quarantine station on Grosse-Ile, or soon after their arrival in Canada. A similarly tragic tale was told of those who took passage for Saint John, New Brunswick, and one reason for it was the diversion to British North America of the poorest and least healthy emigrants. The American legislation limiting the passenger capacity of vessels, which drove up fares to the republic, together with capitation charges and local regulations in Massachusetts and New York, which obliged owners or masters to post large bonds against the danger of their passengers becoming public charges, ensured that the United States was for a time effectively reserved as a haven for the more affluent and robust immigrants. Shipsmasters compelled to leave Boston and New York with their sad and suffering human cargo still aboard had few options other than to make for British territory.[16]

The colonies had no desire to serve as the depository of the sick and needy. Recognizing this, the imperial government belatedly provided a modest measure of compensation for the expenses incurred ministering to the unfortunates. It also sought to plug the leaks in the Passenger Acts. Meanwhile, several colonies took a page from the Americans' book. They demanded bonds from masters, doubled the existing capitation tax, and imposed severe surtaxes on vessels arriving late in the season. As a result, British emigrants to British territories were soon paying a sum four times that charged at New York. This, together with a sharp reduction in the volume of traffic on the North Atlantic, as the timber trade collapsed, saw the movement of Irish to British North America slow and that to the United States surge. Moreover, as in the past, many if not most of those who safely reached British territory travelled on to the republic. The lure was economic rather than political. English, Scots, and European immigrants, as well as the Irish, were part of this southern flow. The republic's larger and more advanced economy, her vast areas of inexpensive arable land, offered far greater personal opportunities. An American official in his testimony to a parliamentary committee claimed that the vast majority of arriving Irishmen immediately found employment. Here was a powerful, if not irresistible, attraction for that disproportionately high number of Roman Catholic immigrants to British North America who described themselves as labourers. Harsh winters ensured that much labouring work there was seasonal. As late as 1866, less than one-quarter of the twenty-seven thousand steerage passengers who arrived in the St Lawrence settled in the colonies. The authorities found some consolation in the evidence that the "better class" of families who landed in Canada remained within the province. Moreover, the nine thousand immigrants entering from the republic included "a considerable number [of] persons of wealth and intelligence, driven from the States by the pressure of taxation, and the increased cost of living."[17]

Of the Irish who had by mid-century settled in British North America, the overwhelming majority arrived before the Famine, a substantial majority were Protestants, and a clear majority made their living from the land. They constituted the largest single body of foreign-born residents of Canada, New Brunswick, and Newfoundland, and challenged the Scots for that distinction on Prince Edward Island. They were "the principal English-speaking ethnic group in British North America." In Newfoundland, the Irish immigrants were overwhelmingly Roman Catholic and amounted to more than half of the population of the colony and its capital, St John's, by the 1830s, when the flow largely dried up. Many worked the land, if only on a small scale, others worked their way into the fishery, and still others prospered, however modestly, as traders and artisans.[18]

In Prince Edward Island they amounted to one-quarter of the total population by the century's midpoint. Although they were found in the professions and commerce as well as among the labourers, it was the availability of land that attracted most of the ten thousand predominantly Roman Catholic Irish who had entered the colony since the beginning of the century. Victims of evictions in Ireland or refugees from its tithe wars, they were soon prominent in the struggle against absentee English landlords whose control of the soil, arbitrary rent increases, and quick resort to evictions reminded them all too vividly of the island they had left. Enfranchised by 1830, they pursued land reform constitutionally only to discover that the local House of Assembly was powerless to create "a new agrarian order based on freehold and small scale production." Hence they resorted to tactics reminiscent of struggles in Ireland, for many of them had been drawn from those southeastern counties of the homeland where the tradition of rural protest and violence was long and strong. They formed a Tenant League and engaged in demonstrations, intimidation, and rent strikes, but rejected any resort to assassination. However, as the violence escalated, troops were brought in from Halifax to control the situation and the league was crushed.[19]

A garrison town, Halifax had long been home to an identifiably Irish community. The provisions trade with ports such as Waterford facilitated the emigration of several thousand Irish to Nova Scotia during the decade and a half following the defeat of Napoleon. By 1828 clergy estimated the colony's Catholic population at forty thousand. Some attempted to farm, but the colony's discontinuance of land grants for all but service pensioners saw many seek employment in Halifax and other coastal towns. But the vast majority of Irish immigrants to British North America made for New Brunswick and Canada.[20]

New Ireland had been suggested as the name for New Brunswick, and the colony's eventual ethnic composition would have made it a far from inappropriate choice. The thirty thousand immigrants who landed between 1818 and 1826 were almost exclusively Irish, and more than double that number arrived over the next eight years. Forming a quarter of the colony's population by 1830, the Irish quickly grew to one-third of the total. Again, the availability of land was the most powerful magnet, and farmers were a conspicuously large proportion of the early arrivals. Protestants enjoyed somewhat greater success than their Roman Catholic countrymen in establishing themselves on the land, and as Catholic labourers came to dominate the immigrant lists they concentrated in and around the port of Saint John, the capital city of Fredericton, and the region called the Miramichi. They were "urban workers to a much higher degree than the general population." The overwhelmingly Catholic Irish who poured in during the years of the Famine encountered even greater difficulty finding work, prompting a disillusioned arrival to report home that New Brunswick was a "good Country for them that is able to work and for nother [sic] person." Those unable to move on to the United States were either in the poor house, she added, or begging on the streets of Saint John.[21]

The story in Canada, or at least in the western division, was similar without being identical to that in New Brunswick. Attracted by land, two-thirds of the Irish who settled in British North America made it their home. By 1842 they already formed "by far the largest non-indigenous group." Unlike in New Brunswick, where the Irish were more or less evenly divided between Roman Catholics and Protestants, in Canada West those who belonged to the reformed faiths were a distinct majority. Roman Catholics hovered around one-third of the total, and their dispersal meant that they formed a solid, if not substantial, minority in several counties but a majority in none. The Irish farmed, worked farms, or engaged in lumbering and mining. To a greater extent than other immigrants, they needed to earn the capital to invest in land, and their late arrival in rural townships meant that Roman Catholics often, but not always, found themselves working smaller and less fertile holdings, and were thus somewhat less successful than their more established Protestant fellow countrymen in graduating from subsistence to commercial farming. In general, their climb up the ladder of agricultural success tended to be more laborious, perhaps because its rungs were more widely spaced.[22]

The disadvantaged situation of Irish Catholics extended to those who lingered whether by choice or necessity in the province's developing cities. Many of the Famine immigrants were obliged to retrace their steps from countryside to urban reception centres by farmers who refused them employment because they doubted their knowledge of "'the improved system of British agriculture'" and feared them as carriers of deadly diseases. As a result, although less than one-fifth of the province's population in 1851, the Irish provided more than two-thirds of the residents of its five largest cities. The growth of Toronto's Irish Catholic population was especially dramatic. By mid-century, they amounted to one-quarter of its residents and when combined with the more numerous Protestant Irish, they gave the city the right to claim to be "the most Irish ... in North America." Heavily concentrated in the poorer-paying jobs, these urban Catholics had peculiar difficulty escaping from the employment cellar. With the possible exception of French Canadians, they were more likely than other ethnic groups to be condemned to poverty and thus to "hunger, cold, sickness, and misery." Crowded into tenements and shanty towns, they led many contemporaries to the conclusion "that poverty and nationality were intimately associated." In Hamilton, for example, they were squeezed out of trades in which they had earlier established a foothold. Moreover, their children moved up in the world at a slower pace than did the offspring of Protestants. Yet by dint of hard labour they made sufficient progress to avoid surrendering either to despair or bitterness.[23]

The Irish population of Canada East was far smaller than that of the colony's western division, totalling some fifty thousand by 1861, yet they "were still more numerous than all the immigrants from Scotland, England, Wales, and the United States combined." As elsewhere in British North America, the great majority had settled before the Famine. Many of them were to be found farming the lands of the St Lawrence Valley, and a smaller number in the rural Eastern Townships. Nevertheless, they were also more concentrated than in Canada West. Close to half of them lived in the cities of Quebec and Montreal, where they worked in construction and on the docks, but the Montreal Irish, in particular, entered the ranks of the city's commercial and professional classes and gained some local political prominence. Nor was it surprising that in a colony with a heavily Roman Catholic population a majority of these immigrants were Catholics.[24]

The earliest Irish Catholic arrivals in British North America had encountered ethnic and sectarian opposition to their settlement by the authorities, but passage of the Quebec Act in 1774 was a harbinger of Catholic relief. Although the intent of the imperial authorities had

been to tolerate Catholicism only temporarily and eventually to establish English culture and the Anglican Church, these secret instructions
were "sensibly overlooked" by Governor Carleton and never
enforced. The outbreak of the American Revolution discouraged
restrictive policies sure to alienate the Crown's French Canadian subjects, thereby ensuring that "official anti-Catholicism was something
against which the Catholics of Upper Canada [later Canada West]
never had to contend." Religious liberty was officially extended to
Newfoundland's Catholics in 1779, but the suspicion that Irish
Catholics would, if the opportunity arose, support the Americans and
the French in the revolutionary war meant another five years would
pass before its implementation. Nova Scotia enacted its relief bill in
1783 and was the first of the Atlantic colonies to allow a Catholic to
take a seat in the legislature. Fifty years passed before Catholics on
Prince Edward Island and Newfoundland were entitled to vote, and in
the case of the former it was accompanied by franchise restrictions
that sought to exclude the "poorest landholders." Protestant Irishmen, on the other hand, received a friendlier welcome in colonies such
as New Brunswick and Canada West, whose citizens credited them
with cultural and ideological values similar to their own. More surprising was the hostility the Catholic Irish encountered in Lower
Canada (Canada East), with its overwhelmingly Roman Catholic
rural population that looked to its priests for leadership as well as
guidance and resented the power wielded by elements of the Protestant minority. The sources of the enduring ethnic tension were the
competition the Irish provided for jobs, the fact that they were English speakers, and their association with terrifying diseases. The
cholera outbreaks in the 1830s and the even more deadly epidemics
during the Famine era, which took a fearful human toll in Montreal,
galvanized the "nationalistic opposition" to them. They were identified by overexcited French Canadians as the " instruments of a conscious policy aimed at exterminating French Canada through epidemic
disease." As for the Catholic Irish, they regarded the preponderance
of French-Catholic clergy as evidence of a conspiracy to keep them in
an inferior position.[25]

The heart-rending plight of the Famine refugees did generate considerable sympathy within a colonial population that had already
donated generously to relief funds, and this sympathy frequently took
the form of sharp criticism of Irish landlords. They were accused of
shipping unwanted tenants to North America in no fit state to weather

the harsh winter, and of doing so disastrously late in the season following the callous extraction of a last summer's labour. Similarly pointed was the public censure of the imperial government. It was accused of pursuing a "barbarous policy" that disregarded not only "common humanity" but also the economic and political consequences of unrestricted mass migration – hence the Canadian Legislative Assembly's appeal for a halt to this human flow. Meanwhile, the colonial government's commissioning of a private contractor to ship the immigrants upriver from the quarantine station at Grosse-Ile, in order to relieve the pressure there and expedite their dispersal, was ill-considered and foolhardy. The primitive reception facilities that were provided for them, the belated establishment of health boards, and the resort to "improvised hospitals" failed to check the dispersal also of typhus, dysentery, and relapsing fever. Among the prominent victims was the Roman Catholic Bishop of Toronto. However, the relief measures "were criticized as much for their inadequacy in meeting the immigrants' needs as for their lack in protecting the local population." Inevitably, fear of contagion overwhelmed the initial optimism that Canada West could provide a haven for one hundred thousand refugees.[26]

The expectation had been that the immigrants would speedily be settled on the land, either with capital they had earned by working temporarily as farm labourers or as recipients of free land grants, which advocates of their rural dispersion, and prophets of their successful integration, pressed the government to revive. Sooner rather than later they would find themselves contentedly cultivating their own properties and thus undergo a conversion from "crushed peasantry" into "hardy and independent yeomanry." Instead, those despatched to the countryside as farm labourers, either at public expense or with the assistance of organizations such as the Emigrant Settlement Association, discovered that for a variety of reasons their supply exceeded the demand. A number managed to create rural "ethnic islands," but the many who returned to urban centres were greeted with popular hostility fostered by their number, poverty, and wretchedness. The government did begin the process of opening the southern Canadian Shield to settlement in 1847, but it was almost a decade before conditional and modest land grants were offered to settlers over the age of eighteen. Of those who took advantage of this scheme, and in some areas they were largely Roman Catholic Irishmen, many quickly discovered how unsuitable this region was to profitable agricultural pursuits. They

were able to eke out an existence only by securing employment repair-
ing the colonization roads during the summer months.[27]

The difficulties and hardships notwithstanding, several British visitors to North America noted the success of the Irish in building new
lives. Many of Toronto's Irish Catholics "had achieved a modest
prosperity" by 1860, but that achievement failed to erase entirely the
popular image of an indolent, feckless, disorderly, violent, and disloyal people. This reputation had been inadvertently reinforced by
the Famine-era immigrants. Irishmen who moved on to the United
States were frequently accused of leaving their families behind to sub-
sist on public relief. The inability of many who remained in Canada
to find agricultural work, together with their protective clustering in
the squalid urban areas to which their poverty condemned them,
excited complaints that they were "idlers who lacked the initiative to
seek out ready opportunities." Those who resorted to begging, either
to survive or to generate capital, were regarded with contempt. "The
principle on which they live is literally to care as little as possible for
the things of today, and to take no thought at all for tomorrow," one
observer commented disparagingly. The Roman Catholic chaplain of
the provincial penitentiary reported in 1853 that Irish Catholics
formed a disproportionately large segment of the Catholic convict
population, while a decade later the Bishop of Toronto lamented their
"disgraceful" criminal statistics. However, both he and the chaplain
were careful to identify poverty as the fundamental cause of a resort
to crime.[28]

Irish Catholics may well have been unfairly singled out for arrest and
incarceration by the justice system, but a spike in petty crimes in Saint
John, New Brunswick, followed so closely on the heels of a sudden
increase in the immigrant population that residents leapt to the obvious conclusion. Elsewhere, the Irish were all too conspicuous among
persons arrested. Two-thirds of the women committed to the Toronto
gaol as prostitutes in the early 1860s were Irish Catholics, whereas
their community provided barely one-quarter of the city's denizens. In
Montreal also, Irish Catholics were blamed, fairly or not, for the
growth of the vice trade. Catholic Irish women dominated the ranks of
females convicted of public order offences, and Irish men were similarly conspicuous among the male prison population. Little wonder,
then, that Canadians alarmed by a reported surge in arrests for drunkenness, prostitution, vagrancy, and violent street brawling identified
the Irish as the principal culprits. Organs of the temperance movement

singled them out as a "drunken and degenerate people" who under the influence of alcohol surrendered to their bestial instincts, engaged in family violence, sank into indolence, and drifted into crime. Hence the frustration when this "social people" resisted renewed efforts to transfer them from "overcrowded cities" to pastoral Canada with its reformative environment. As the Bishop of Toronto explained somewhat clumsily to one of his American episcopal colleagues, many preferred "pleasure in being amongst their neighbours and enjoying the comforts of city life with all its precariousness and temptations to the hardships and isolation and hard work for a while but in the end a homestead and independence."[29]

Indulgence in violence and an insatiable appetite for disloyalty were the two most damaging charges levelled against Irish Catholics. In the city of Quebec gangs of them invaded the French quarters in search of trouble. Irishmen desperate for work, in competition for jobs, or determined to improve their conditions of employment were at the centre of rioting in the Miramichi. They were identified as the instigators of the bloody conflicts among Canada's canal diggers, and damned as a "'turbulent and discontented people'" who would never work for long peaceably unless overawed by a force that commanded respect. Of course, they had much to be discontented, if not turbulent, about – insecure employment, low wages, contractors who delayed or defaulted on these payments, and company stores or country storekeepers who demanded usurious rates of interest on credit purchases. They were also held responsible for much of the electoral violence. In short, their behaviour excited fears that they had imported the violent culture of their homeland. A careful analysis of committals for crimes against the person in Canada West would not have supported their reputation for extraordinary violence, but the repeated disturbances by Catholic Irishmen digging canals, the long-running Shiners' War in the Ottawa Valley, the hounding of several magistrates out of the town of Brantford by an Irish Catholic mob, and extensive newspaper coverage of "atrocities committed by brutalized masses in Ireland" ensured that the popular image of the violent Irishman endured.[30]

Suspicions of Irish Catholic disloyalty to the imperial connection had long lurked in the minds of both officials and a Loyalist colonial public. There had been a number of disturbing incidents in the mid-eighteenth century, such as defections to or cooperation with the national enemy. The removal of the French from the region after 1763, at least as a significant presence, did induce greater Irish discretion, but the Newfoundland authorities had faced further crises first during the American Revolutionary War and then in 1798. Evidence provided by the Catholic bishop of extensive oath taking in support of the United Irishmen, even "a conspiracy to rebellion and mutiny" within the ranks of the Newfoundland Regiment, brought stern countermeasures. Several men were executed and the regiment transferred out of the colony. But Bishop O'Donel, an Irishman who was "staunchly loyal to the Crown" and abhorred "revolutionary tendencies," had earned the gratitude of the administration and strengthened the position of Roman Catholicism in the colony. A half-century later, the embarrassing denunciation by Halifax's Catholic Irish of colonial efforts to recruit in the United States for service with the British army in the Crimea excited a retaliatory storm of patriotic fury. Joseph Howe, a leading local politician deeply implicated in the recruitment folly, together with "the Liberal press, and the militant denominational journals[,] virtually declared open season on the Irish Catholics of the province." They characterized them "as a foreign element in the midst of the British community. " This was a charge seemingly confirmed by the emergence of "self-conscious" and "assertive" Irish Catholic communities, suggesting as they did an "urgent compulsion to proclaim Irish defiance of assimilation through visibility." This again distinguished them from their Protestant fellow countrymen, who by blending in with the host community did not draw attention to themselves as "a cohesive, identifiable ethnic group."[31]

How was it that immigrants whose lives had frequently been parochial in their homeland "interacted across the Atlantic and merged to form a new cultural identity" and ethnic community? A celebration of St Patrick's Day had taken place in Quebec in 1765, and in most colonies the Irish established benevolent, charitable, and national societies. These provided assistance to the fresh waves of arrivals and "acted as foci where immigrants from different parts of Ireland met, who previously would not have had that opportunity in the home country." They stimulated "Irish consciousness." The extent to which the Irish clustered, geographically and socially, was often a testament to the care with which emigration was undertaken by kith and kin. This facilitated the reproduction of the old world in the new. Moreover, Irish Catholics practised endogamy to an extraordinary degree, which allowed them to become "self-supporting demographically and self perpetuating." Here was another sharp distinction from their

Protestant countrymen, and one that ensured that a profound sense of Irishness extended into the second generation. Local institutions, such as the tavern – and by 1869 over half the tavern licences in Toronto were in Irish hands – together with an ethnic press, further promoted national consciousness and with it the growth of nationalist sentiment. Catholics were the single largest denomination of Irish even in Canada West, and those of them who either chose or were obliged to make their homes in urbanizing areas "naturally sought out the company and support of their compatriots and relatives" as they struggled to adjust to an environment so different from that of their homeland. These associations and the rivalries with other ethnic groups, such as the Americans and the Scots in the Miramichi and the French Canadians in Canada East, contributed to Irish Catholic "separateness." The hostility with which so many in the host communities regarded them erected another obstacle to assimilation, and the animus was usually rooted in denominationalism. Anti-Catholicism was an ideology that most Protestants affirmed, and it reflected the extent to which the Roman Church was recognized as "the main vehicle" of Catholic Irish ethnogenesis.[32]

Newfoundland's Catholics had received a bishop in 1796, and in little more than a generation, the same was to be true of their fellow religionists elsewhere in the Atlantic colonies. The Scots Catholics of Prince Edward Island and the heavily Irish Catholic population of New Brunswick were separated from the diocese of Quebec in 1829 and united in their own. Both Scottish and Irish priests accused the French Canadian bishop of neglecting the English-speaking Catholics. The difficulties of administering this episcopal territory, which were not eased by the suspicion with which Scottish priests regarded Irish clergy, whom they considered "unstable and unprincipled," and ethnic rivalry between Scots and Irish necessitated further diocesan reorganization. This saw the "northern portions" of the Nova Scotia diocese, which had earlier established its independence of Quebec, "sundered" from Halifax,while New Brunswick was detached from Charlottetown. Only eighteen years later, in 1860, another redrawing of episcopal boundaries saw New Brunswick divided into dioceses centred on Saint John and Chatham respectively. During this same period the increasingly Irish complexion of the faithful was matched by that of hierarchy and priesthood. The first Newfoundland bishop had been an Irishman, while the first six in New Brunswick were either of Irish birth or parentage. The Roman Catholics of Halifax had welcomed an Irish priest in 1785, and a succession of others followed. A similar pattern was subsequently followed in Charlottetown, home to many of Prince Edward Island's large Irish minority. Not that every Irish priest proved to be an unmixed blessing. Desperate need led bishops to accept the services of clergy of doubtful character and questionable credentials, and the increasing reliance on Irishmen put them at the centre of a series of sensational and unsavoury personal scandals. Nevertheless, religious institutions continued to provide "a cultural focus and source of cohesion" for newly arrived immigrants. In Newfoundland and the Maritimes, where it was increasingly regarded as "virtually synonymous with Irish Catholicism," the Catholic Church "stood as a focus and defence of a distinctive Irish identity." This "national defiance of assimilation" was viewed with deep suspicion by Protestants and was unwelcome even in heavily Catholic Lower Canada.[33]

French Canadians feared that the English speaking Irish Catholics would deny French Canada "a powerful and national church." Potentially, these fellow religionists seemed a far greater threat to the distinctive host community and its institutions than English Protestants. The francophone majority wished this anglophone Catholic minority to "acculturate," for French Canadians believed it was their vocation, not that of the Irish, "to promote true religion and civilization in North America." Furthermore, at a time when the Church was seeking an even closer understanding with the imperial authorities, having enjoyed a large measure of autonomy and liberty in return for professions of loyalty to the Crown, senior French Canadian clerics wished to distance themselves from a people they considered "disloyal and radically anti-British." One bishop, after complaining that these immigrants had not brought priests with them, had then gone on to charge that any who might have accompanied them would have been the dregs of the Irish clergy just as "they themselves [were] the scum of the population." Where islands of Irish Catholics did enjoy the spiritual care of fellow countrymen not only was their sense of ethnic and community identity sharpened but so also were tensions and conflict with the local French Canadian population. The Irish were quick to protest if parishes in which they were the majority failed to receive an Irish priest or if an Irish priest was replaced by a French Canadian. They did root themselves solidly in Montreal, with the paternal assistance of the Sulpicians, but progress was slower in the city of Quebec. Nevertheless, they had built their own churches and established their own schools and benevolent associations in both cities by the time of the

Famine influx. In 1853 the church of St Patrick was enlarged and formally recognized as "the Congregation of the Catholics of Quebec speaking the English language."[34]

The Canadian Constitution of 1791 had "allowed for two different geographical provinces, political governments, and religions in Upper and Lower Canada." In the latter there was a French government "based on Catholic politics," and in the former an English government founded on "Protestant politics." The Catholic Church developed slowly and cautiously in Upper Canada. Edmund Burke, an Irish-born priest, secured appointment as the province's first vicar-general in 1794, but difficulties with the ecclesiastical authorities in Quebec, under whose provincial jurisdiction the western branch was to remain for another seventy-five years, and his inability to provide spiritual care for a small and scattered population saw him depart soon after the turn of the nineteenth century. He reappeared in 1817 as vicar apostolic of Halifax. Alexander Macdonell had eventually replaced him in Upper Canada. In 1804 Macdonell had followed to Canada the veterans of a Highland regiment that he had helped raise, whom he had served as chaplain, and whose emigration he had sponsored. Three years later he was appointed vicar-general. At this time the Catholic population numbered only a few thousand and was composed essentially of the Scots and a French settlement. Macdonell's devotion to his fellow countrymen, his continued residence among them even after his consecration as a bishop in 1819, his decision to make Kingston the seat of the see created in 1826, and his reluctance to visit the Catholic Irish settling the central areas of the colony during the 1820s created tensions that led to problems. Macdonell was privately scornful of these "lukewarm, selfish and semi-barbarous Catholics" and profoundly suspicious of clergy trained at Maynooth. He wanted "neither political nor speculating nor fortune hunting priests." In his eyes, Irish and American priests were "unfit" to educate the young "because of their rank republican principles."[35]

Macdonell's conflict with one Irish priest undoubtedly deepened his ethnic prejudices. William O'Grady had acted as chaplain to a band of Irish mercenaries recruited to serve in the army of the Emperor of Brazil. When a number of them mutinied, disenchanted both with their duties and the climate, O'Grady persuaded a group of them to migrate to Canada along with their families. Following his own arrival at York in the summer of 1828, O'Grady so impressed Macdonell that the bishop substituted him for his own nephew as the resident priest in this expanding community. However, the two quickly fell out. O'Grady's support of the lower-class Irish element within his parish in their struggle against the dominant middle-class elite, his "democratical and demoralizing sermons," and his reform politics were anathema to his conservative superior. When O'Grady balked at a transfer, he was suspended, and he subsequently quit the priesthood for a second vocation. He became a member of the fourth estate. This episode highlighted Macdonell's deepening difficulties with an ever-swelling Irish majority of the Catholic population. His ardent loyalism, first evidenced in 1798 when he helped raise the Highland regiment to assist in the suppression of the Irish rebellion, for which he was rewarded with a government pension; his conviction that Catholics ought to be loyal because of the interlacing of their religious principles with a monarchical form of government and obedience to authority; his Tory politics and membership in the Legislative Council; his alliance with Orangemen against the Upper Canadian rebels of 1837 – all this did not endear him to the large Irish element within a church that by the time of Macdonell's death in 1840 numbered thirty-five priests and ninety thousand faithful. Plainly, there was a need to restructure an institution that had grown so dramatically in less than four decades. So, in 1841 the Diocese of Toronto was created. Six years later Bytown was separated from Kingston, and within another ten years Hamilton and London had been separated from Toronto.[36]

The first half of the nineteenth century saw a missionary church transformed into a far more complex and visible organization and the emergence of a hierarchy that increasingly reflected the national composition of the faithful. Remi Gaulin, a French Canadian, was Macdonell's successor at Kingston, for he was fluent in both English and Gaelic, and in his home province was seen as a means by which Quebec might "re-establish ecclesiastical hegemony" in Upper Canada, but he was soon involved in an unseemly struggle for control of the diocese with his Irish coadjutor, Patrick Phelan. Gaulin, whose mental health was fragile, initially retreated to French Canada, only to return to Kingston to torment his deputy. Although death removed the Frenchman in the spring of 1857, Phelan caught a cold at his funeral and survived as bishop for a mere month. Michael Power, born of Irish parents in Nova Scotia and trained in Lower Canada, "a loyal subject of the British Crown and a proud citizen of the British Empire," was elevated to the new see of Toronto. His successor was to be the French-born and educated Armand de Charbonnel. The francophone's command and comprehension of English was less than perfect, while his "inconstant and arbitrary plan of action," "peculiar temperament," and rigour in economic and monetary matters alienated many of his charges. But he demonstrated a special affinity for the Irish, having formerly been a member of the staff of the Sulpician seminary in Montreal. He secured the appointment of a native Irishman trained at Maynooth, John Joseph Lynch, as his auxiliary with the right of succession. Lynch became the first Irish-born Bishop of Toronto in 1860, and was elevated to archbishop a decade later. Although a French Canadian was appointed Bishop of London in 1856, in which year four of the six bishops were francophones, and he promptly invited trouble by replacing Irish priests with fellow French Canadians, the appointment of John Farrell as Bishop of Hamilton was more representative of the increasing Irish domination of "church administration and parochial work." The severe shortage of priests had eventually compelled Macdonell to accept a number from Ireland, several of whom had backgrounds that did not bear close scrutiny. They exhibited a tendency to defy episcopal authority, especially that of superiors who were not Irish. Their involvement in land speculation exposed them to the damaging charge of avarice, though most if not all of them were merely seeking to offset financial dependence on parishioners who had little to donate. Even more harmful to the image of the Catholic Church were the embarrassing scandals of priestly violence and drunkenness.[37]

The conspicuous presence of Irishmen in the priesthood and the national composition of the faithful ensured that in Canada West, as in the Atlantic colonies, Catholicism came to be regarded as synonymous with Irishness. The Irish Catholic Church in Canada may have been "largely a pre-Famine creation," but the diocese of Toronto was an exception to that rule. Nine out of every ten Catholics – they numbered ten thousand – who called the city home in the mid-1850s were Irish, and the bulk of them had arrived during the Famine. Michael Power, who sacrificed his life ministering to the refugees, and his French successor implemented policies designed to restore the reputation of the clergy, solidify the religious unity and loyalty of the immigrants, strengthen family ties, and improve the self-image and popular reputation of the Irish. By 1855, despite the hiatus of almost thirty months between Power's death and Charbonnel's arrival, forty-five churches had been built and another twelve were under construction, while the priesthood now exceeded one hundred. A local seminary was established, since recruitment even from Ireland was proving difficult. Episcopal authority was asserted, discipline enforced, financial abuses checked, and parish priests held accountable for the performance of their parochial duties. Priests were also ordered to dress in a manner that made them instantly recognizable, despite the unpleasantness and occasional danger to which they were thereby exposed in a heavily Protestant community. The clergy was being transformed into "a disciplined corps devoted to pastoral reform." Irish Catholic parishes were reorganized, and the faithful tied more securely to the Church through devotional, benevolent, and recreational associations. The Society of St Vincent de Paul sought to assist the poor materially as well as spiritually, and thus remove the temptation to accept aid from Protestant agencies. A temperance movement was launched to rescue the Irish from popular disrepute, though it quickly ran out of steam. The promotion of sobriety and respectability also promised to strengthen the Roman Catholic family. Mixed marriages were discouraged, and those that were sanctioned had to be performed by a priest and the partners had to make a commitment to raise and educate their children as Catholics.[38]

The Church sought to ensure that it was "the centre of the Catholic world," and it saw education as a vital buttress of its position. By building dykes against proselytism and plugging the holes that allowed "leakage," education would retain the Irish "as a practising Catholic laity and a distinct ethno-religious group." Both Macdonell and Power had sought public funding of Catholic schools without assailing or rejecting the common schools system established in the western province, but teaching orders, beginning with the Christian Brothers and the Sisters of Loretto, were invited to Toronto. The latter arrived on the very eve of Power's death. Bishop Charbonnel proved far more energetic than his predecessor in the establishment of charity schools and far more aggressive in his quest for state aid for Catholic institutions. He condemned mixed schools as "the ruin of religion, and a persecution" of his church. He demanded for the Catholics of Canada West minority rights equal to those granted to the Protestants of Canada East. Inevitably, this crusade became politicized.[39]

The property qualifications required of voters long kept many Irish Catholics off the electoral registers, but as in Ireland they had frequently been identified with "extra-legal political activity." Nevertheless, liberalization of the franchise resulted in their emergence as a significant political force in areas where they concentrated. Their politicization was actively encouraged by a church "determined to lead in political matters," its bishops having by mid-century asserted their authority in those colonies where lay trustees had sought to establish spiritual as well as temporal dominance. The dangers were illustrated in Newfoundland, where Bishop Michael Fleming, a Tipperary man, systematically built an Irish church organization following his appointment in 1830. "He was an impassioned defender of the Catholic religion," a "devoted follower" of Daniel O'Connell, and an aggressive and ardent champion of the colony's Irish poor. More than half of the island's population was now Catholic Irish, the majority of them recent immigrants, and from 1832 the Assembly was elected on "virtual adult male suffrage." But the governor still possessed "wide powers," the council was an appointive body, and the colony continued to be "administered as a Protestant state." The priests Fleming imported from Ireland were loyal to him and experienced in the use of churches as political pulpits, and following his lead they contributed mightily to the political radicalization of the Irish electorate. Priests harangued the faithful from the pulpit, one governor complained, and converted the chapel into "a political club house." Fleming ordered his flock to sever "social ties with Protestants" and imported Irish sisters to teach the young women of the capital and thus nurture them in "Catholic truth so that they could in turn nurture an educated Catholic middle class." More conservative and cautious Catholics, anxious to anger neither Protestants nor the imperial administration, and who on occasion attended Protestant services, were denounced, harassed, and attacked, even physically, by Fleming's allies. They were damned as "Orange Catholics" and "Mad Dogs," and during one of Fleming's absences his deputy denied the sacraments to twenty-eight "Liberal Catholics." Inevitably, the bishop's aggressive involvement in local politics heightened sectarian tensions, fed Protestant bigotry, and led both governor and Colonial Office to the conclusion that they were confronted by a Newfoundland version of MacHale. Fleming's successor, John Mullock, Irish by birth but a Newfoundlander by choice, published a manifesto for priests in politics and within a decade was arguably "the most important politician" in the colony. He advocated responsible government as a "diplomatic way to displace the Protestant Ascendancy," mobilized his priests to act as "'election managers of the Liberal Party,'" and instructed the laity on their political choices in the columns of the diocesan newspaper, the *Pilot*. Mullock's conduct and wild rhetoric fostered sectarian intimidation and violence before it led

to the erosion of his influence and an end to "widespread clerical intervention" in politics. By then, however, the anti-Catholic agitation of
the colony's Conservatives had seen electoral boundaries redrawn
along the lines of the sectarian divisions, thereby perpetuating sectarian
politics. Happily, most other members of the British North American
hierarchy proved to be more discreet.[40]

In the other colonies where Irish Catholics had settled in substantial
numbers, their politicization was also given impetus by a sectarian
press and a group of editor/politicians "whose careers were built exclusively on their ethnic affiliation." Timothy Anglin in New Brunswick,
Edward Whelan in Prince Edward Island, and Thomas D'Arcy McGee
in Canada fell into this category. McGee proved to be the most influential and controversial of them. Conflict with elements of the American hierarchy and disillusionment with American society prompted his
acceptance of an invitation from the Montreal Irish to found a newspaper in their city and provide them with political leadership. Their
sense of distinctive and separate identity had been sharpened there as
elsewhere by the educational and social services organized by priests
and by the hostility of organs such as the *Montreal Witness*. It railed
against the electoral dangers posed by "ignorant men who will not
learn and who are at the beck of a designing priesthood." McGee was
soon seeking to act as spokesman for a larger Irish Catholic community,
which embraced Canada West. He launched the *Canadian Freeman* in
July 1858 and won the backing of Charbonnel with assurances that it
would be family centred and responsive to the bishop's direction on all
religious matters, as well as patriotic, politically independent, and anti-
Orange. McGee identified state support of separate education as one
of the touchstones of Catholic political allegiance, and the two decades
following the union of the Canadas in 1841 saw passage of a succession of legislative measures dealing with education. They were intended to conciliate the Catholic Church. They failed in this, and in 1861,
at the urging of the hierarchy, the Catholic vote in the western division
was largely given to the Liberal Conservatives instead of the Reformers behind whom McGee had been seeking to organize it. He was
"forced to acknowledge the influence of the clergy, and followed the
Bishops into the Conservative ranks in 1863."[41]

The separate school system of Canada West was, with the exception
of the French-speaking areas, "an Irish Catholic institution." The costs
of this success included ethnic tensions within the Catholic Church and
sectarian hostility without. The dominant figure in the province's com-

mon school system was Egerton Ryerson, a Methodist. For a model he looked to Ireland's national schools, whose founding principles of mixed education but separate religious instruction he admired. The formation of a Christian character was in his mind "the only proper end" of education, and he considered Irish textbooks that promoted British as distinct from Irish values particularly suitable for a province where the majority of the Irish immigrants were Protestants and Loyalists. Ryerson deplored the denominationalism that had crept into the Irish national schools. A true believer in the benefits of the British Constitution and a devout opponent of republicanism, he envisaged common schools as instruments for inculcating loyalty and facilitating immigrant assimilation, and as safeguards against ignorance and crime. They would thus promote social stability. Hence his frustration, though he was no religious bigot, and that of such powerful figures as the publisher of the Toronto *Globe*, George Brown, for whom a similar denial would have been less credible, when the Roman Catholic Church in Canada West committed itself to separate schools and the preservation of a distinctive Irish Catholic identity. Its ambition was to provide "a cradle to grave culture separate from that of the Protestant majority," and the likelihood that this would heighten sectarian tensions was greatly increased by the Irish complexion of much of the Anglican clergy and community of the province. Moreover, societies that had aspired to be truly Irish began to divide along sectarian lines as the Roman Catholic population grew in number, confidence, and ambition. A similarly divisive pattern emerged in New Brunswick and Prince Edward Island, where even charities separated along sectarian lines.[42]

An aggressive ultramontane hierarchy, echoes of the "papal aggression" crisis in Britain following the Pope's re-establishment of a Catholic hierarchy for England and Wales, and the anti-Protestantism explicit and implicit in the episcopal denunciations of mixed education – Charbonnel issued a pastoral threatening to convict of a mortal sin any Catholic who failed to use his ballot to advance separate education – were all fillips to colonial anti-Catholicism. Many Protestants reacted hysterically to the rapid growth of the Roman Catholic Church. They feared the potential enhancement of its political influence as a result of the concentration of Irish Catholics in centres such as Toronto, where the "belligerently Irish" *Catholic Citizen* began publication in 1854. They suspected that an alliance was planned between the Catholic minority in Canada West and the predominantly francophone majority in Canada East, and saw in the passage of legislation under-mining common education evidence of this sectarian understanding. Of course, the four principal Protestant churches in Canada West were experiencing their own "staggering" growth, and the reduction of the Anglican Church from an establishment to a "voluntarist" institution opened the door to a broad Protestant alliance against both secularism and Roman Catholicism. Indeed, anti-Catholicism became "a persis-tent theme in the religious history of the nineteenth century in Cana-da."[43]

Protestants assailed the Catholic Church for withholding from its members the true word of God, the unedited Bible; they fulminated against the broad range of priestly intercessory powers; they regarded the confessional as another instrument of priestly power if not immorality; they deplored celibacy as unnatural and a denigration of marriage; they levelled accusations of idolatry and superstition; they charged the papacy with megalomania and centuries of persecution and tyranny; and they convicted it of obstructing liberalism and progress. The publication of the Syllabus of Errors in 1864 was seized upon as proof. In short, Catholicism was condemned as "errant in its theology, pernicious in its social impact and evil in its political tenden-cies." The cause of progress, whether industrial, civil, or intellectual, "belonged to Protestantism." A number of sensational incidents served only to harden attitudes. Popular attempts to prevent the delivery of a series of provocative lectures in Canada East by a former priest, an apostate to Catholicism, ended bloodily in Montreal with troops firing into the crowd and "killing almost a score." In Canada West, Protes-tants cited this tragic incident as additional proof of Catholic contempt for the freedoms of speech and conscience. That contempt seemed to be at the heart of the murder in Canada East of a Catholic convert to Protestantism, while the savagery of the crime and the acquittal of the accused killers were trumpeted as warnings of the consequences of "papist domination."[44]

One body dedicated to Protestant domination was the Orange Order. Following its founding in Ulster in 1795, the order spread rapidly to Britain and throughout the empire. In 1830 an Irish immi-grant to Upper Canada, Ogle Robert Gowan, provided the numerous local lodges in several colonies with a central organization in the shape of the Grand Lodge of British North America. Then, during the 1850s, membership exploded. From a total of twenty thousand in 1840, Orange ranks in Canada West grew fivefold in the space of twenty years. Many Irish Protestants saw in the order a means to parade loyalty to crown, empire, and the British connection, and thus differentiate themselves from their widely distrusted Catholic fellow countrymen. Even for non-Irish Protestants, the Orange Order provided a degree of reassuring unity at a time of growing Roman Catholic strength and influence. Thus in Prince Edward Island it was the "apparent aggressiveness" of Catholicism that fostered Orangeism "in a colony largely devoid of Protestant Irishmen." Similarly, New Brunswick's Protestant majority saw in the order a response to the increasing preponderance of Catholics among the Irish residents of Saint John and Fredericton and their formation of self-conscious and effective Catholic communities. In Toronto the order attracted members of the struggling working classes with its assistance to overcome the multitude of urban difficulties. There and elsewhere Orange lodges "served as social clubs, immigrant aid organizations, benevolent societies, and economic nexuses, as well as much publicized political lobbies." The Orange Order was a politico-religious organization whose influence was most evident at the municipal level of government and whose members "voiced their enmity and distrust of catholics perhaps more directly and loudly than other elements of Protestant Canadian society."[45]

The existence of the Orange Order and of a self-consciously Irish Catholic identity did not necessarily doom colonial society to chronic sectarian conflict. This was demonstrated in many of Canada West's local townships and by the residents of Prince Edward Island. Ogle Gowan, until 1846 the effective head of the Grand Lodge, also made a contribution to sectarian peace by his espousal of a moderate Orangeism. He cooperated effectively with Bishop Macdonell during the Canadian rebellion of 1837 and spoke of the need for Protestants and Catholics to work together in order to repel the threat of Yankee republicanism. Orange members of the Canadian legislature supported Catholic separate education, though not in a spirit of toleration. They were motivated by sympathy with High Anglicans, who wished to establish their own schools, or by the belief that the removal of Catholics from public schools would dismantle the principal barrier to the public schools' use of the Protestant Bible. However, the burgeoning influence of Roman Catholicism galvanized and armed the critics of Gowan's moderation, who dispossessed him of the order's leadership for several years. Similarly, the division of formerly Irish national societies into sectarian camps, the identification of St Patrick's Day

celebrations almost exclusively with Irish Catholics, and the provocative Orange celebrations of past victories over Roman Catholicism all
threatened to lead to violence. The Upper Canadian House of Assembly had unsuccessfully attempted to outlaw the order in 1823, and the
danger of sectarian disturbances loomed larger still with the union of
the Canadas. Canada East was even more Catholic than Canada West
was Protestant. A series of legislative measures in the early 1840s,
aimed "primarily at Orangeism" and dealing with processions,
emblems, the carrying of firearms, and electoral shenanigans, either
proved ineffectual or were not enforced. And while Gowan, following
his recapture of the order's leadership, sought to rein in his rambunc-
tious followers and create a sober and respectable image, by separating it from taverns and emphasizing benevolent and cultural activities,
Orange and Green came into collision on the streets of several
colonies.[46]

Rebellion in the Canadas and the violent rhetoric of a number of
colonial politicians suggested that British North America was no
stranger to arguments of physical force. Society was frequently turbulent, and social disorder "an everyday fact of life" in areas defi-
cient in local forces of order and where economic activity "encouraged ruthless and reckless pursuit of profit." Riots were sparked by
dissatisfaction over conditions of work and pay, political grievances,
and partisan enforcement of the law. Still, the colonies seemed far
removed from the culture of violence associated with Ireland and the
United States. Sectarian bullying and arson to enforce residential seg-
regation or the street brawls on Green and Orange banner days convinced some Canadians that the Irish had imported that culture into
North America. George Brown's Toronto *Globe* further inflamed the
situation, identifying Rome with tyranny and the subversion of civil,
as well as religious, liberties. Here was a mirror image of the intemperate denunciations of the United Kingdom by members of the Irish
hierarchy, and it was no less of an incitement to violence. Canada
West's most influential newspaper persistently depicted Irish
Catholics in the most unflattering of terms, at least until the publisher's political ambition and developing alliance with D'Arcy
McGee dictated a more moderate stance. For his part, the former
Young Irelander made the Orange Order his "primary target." Laying at its door responsibility for the political discrimination still suf-
fered by Catholics, he urged sectarian unity and an alliance of
Catholics with a powerful element in the western province. Brown's

Reformers were his first choice as allies, given the traditional association of Orangemen with the Conservatives.[47]

Responsibility for the violence was shared. Orangemen usually took the initiative on St Patrick's Days, and Catholics returned the favour on the anniversaries of the Battle of the Boyne and King Billy's birthday. In Toronto, soon dubbed the Belfast of North America, the clashes occurred with a depressing annual regularity, yet they were generally "controlled and not particularly violent" and usually "had direct political inspiration." Relatively few lives were lost, the four deaths in Hamilton in the summer of 1849 being the exception rather than the rule. That same summer saw heavier casualties in New Brunswick, perhaps a dozen victims. At least another ten deaths had resulted from a brawl two years earlier. Indeed, the two sides had been attacking one another in that colony since the summer of 1837, and virtually "all of the fatalities before 1845 had been Protestant; after 1845 they were largely Catholic." The Orange Order in New Brunswick has been described "as an institutionalized nativist response" to unwelcome Irish Catholic immigrants, who in times of economic hardship were viewed as a threat to employment and wages. But violence was often as much social as sectarian. Rioting around Christmas may have been the work of hungry men protesting a lack of fuel, liquor, and relief rather than an ethno-religious conflict sparked by the approach of a holy day. Nevertheless, the dramatic surge in the number of Catholics during the 1840s, rising to one-third of the population; their resistance to assimilation; and their maintenance of a distinctive national identity undoubtedly reinforced their Protestant hosts' crude stereotype of them. They were feared as a threat to the loyalism that was a cornerstone of the colony's political culture, to the Protestantism that had been the foundation stone of its civilization, and to a deepening Anglo-Saxonism. Thus in New Brunswick the order attracted descendants of the Loyalist refugees from the American Revolution—-now being accorded mythic status – Scots Presbyterians, English Methodists, and Irish Anglicans. In the volatile Saint John area, both "native-born and Protestant immigrants" joined Orange Lodges. Yet most New Brunswick communities escaped serious sectarian violence. Moreover, the economic recovery of the 1850s, together with the slowing of the pace of Irish Catholic immigration to an insignificant trickle and the decision of Catholics to avoid street confrontations with Orangemen, produced a relatively pacific social climate.[48]

The hostility, contempt, and occasional violence that Irish Catholics encountered in British North America encouraged them to look to one another for support. Treated "as a homogeneous pariah group constituting a very real threat to the health, employment and values" of those among whom they settled, they had every incentive to subsume native regional differences under the single banner of national identity. Not that this hostile reception fully explained a deepening commitment to a brand of Irish nationalism. Irish Catholics had brought with them to the new world as part of their mental baggage an identification of faith and fatherland. They "looked to the Church as a means of defining and preserving their identity." The canallers built shanty chapels and contributed to the construction of a new cathedral in St Catharines. They also demonstrated their support for the Irish nationalism of repeal. The Catholic Church promoted clustering and thus created an ideal climate in which nationalist sentiment, itself another means of offering individuals a sense of community, might thrive. More than this, elements within the hierarchy grasped nationalism as "a powerful and legitimizing ideology." Church leaders, no less than secular politicians, appreciated its value as a reinforcement of their authority and a means to mobilize "public support for them and their policies." Bishops Fleming and Mullock in Newfoundland provided examples of this strategy. Fleming harboured a "deep-seated fear and suspicion of the British-Protestant government" and hailed Daniel O'Connell as "the advocate of the oppressed throughout the world." In the middle of his sermon during the Mass to celebrate Catholic emancipation, he led the congregation in three cheers for the Liberator. Subsequently, he blamed all of Ireland's miseries and troubles on "the [English] system of misrule." Indeed, he called on all Irishmen everywhere to rise up and demand repeal of the Union. In Toronto, even Michael Power's priests "actively fused the spiritual and the nationalist." They frequently played prominent roles in St Patrick's Day festivities and sanctioned an "empathetic expression" of Irish nationalism while seeking to steer it towards Church identification.[49]

The separate schools that an ever-increasing proportion of Toronto's young Irish attended during the 1850s, staffed in part by Christian Brothers, perpetuated Irish identity. Children were taught that ceasing to be Irish was tantamount to apostasy, that the Protestant Irish were aliens "who had been planted in their homeland and, under the name of Orangeism, brought to the new city to persecute them." Textbooks were censored to ensure that there was no exposure to material considered immoral, anti-Irish, or anti-Catholic. The ethnic press censured the organizers of any public examination insufficiently redolent of "Irishness." Often that press was closely identified with the Church. This was true of the *Pilot* in St John's and of J. G. Moylan's *Canadian Freeman* in Toronto, the latter serving as "the semi-official diocesan weekly," while the Montreal *True Witness and Catholic Chronicle* was on occasion subsidized by the Church. The *Freeman* described a "prostrate, crushed, bleeding Ireland" whose people had to fight "persecution, tyranny and oppression" in both their native and adopted lands. The most successful of these early organs of transplanted Irish opinion was the *Toronto Mirror*, which began publication in 1837 and survived for almost three decades. Identified during the early 1840s as an "unofficial organ" of Bishop Power, it carried extensive reports on events in Ireland, regularly denounced British oppression of the Irish people, exploited the motif of involuntary Irish emigration, or exile, and linked the demand for repeal of the Union to the local agitation for ministerial responsibility in Canada. Prudently, it rejected any notion of armed resistance to British "tyranny" and interpreted the abject failure of the Young Ireland rebellion as proof that "moral force" had been a farce and "physical force" a tragedy.[50]

Both press and priests manipulated Irish history, the latter in sermon literature and pastorals, to generate pride in "unity of ethnic identity and religion." An "ostentatious Catholic clerical Hibernophilia" was frequently on display. The Toronto *Catholic*, which came to be regarded as Michael Power's "own weekly paper," darkly suggested that the United Kingdom would be inviting civil war if it continued to refuse to concede repeal. Significantly, a bishop who invariably exercised tight control over his priests granted them considerable latitude with respect to this particular agitation. Then came the tragedy of the Famine, to which Power was exposed both during a visit to Ireland and on his return to Canada. It shook his previously "unwavering loyalty to the British Empire." His successor, Charbonnel, adapted the temperance crusade to his purpose, claiming Father Mathew as the inspiration, and "elevated St Patrick's Day into a major religious and national festival." Clerical orations to celebrants in church and on the streets may initially have lacked the traditional passion of nationalist rhetoric, but together with the parades they still had a powerful impact. Listeners were provided with an understanding of a collective past and were provided with an historic memory that served as another foundation stone of nationalism. They were assured that they were a chosen people, one

divinely appointed to carry the message of St Patrick from Erin to distant parts of the world, while the extensive coverage of the ceremonies
in the ethnic press gave paraders in far-flung centres good reason to
believe that they "were participating in a genuinely national ethnic ritual." Thus were tribal memories revived, collective consciousness promoted, and national identity reinforced.[51]

Political dissidents in the Canadas – the *patriotes* in the Lower
province and the radical Reformers in the Upper – had looked to the
Irish Catholics for allies during the turmoil of the 1830s, which concluded in a pair of feeble rebellions. The approach was framed in terms
of common victimhood – French Canadians and Irish Catholics were
both sufferers at the hands of English Protestants, and British oppression of Ireland indicated the future course of imperial policy in Canada. There was also an emphasis on the O'Connellite character and
stature of the respective rebel leaders, Louis-Joseph Papineau and
William Lyon Mackenzie. Although the Irish editor of Montreal's *Irish
Vindicator* became a prominent *patriote* and the former priest and current publisher of the *Correspondent and Advocate*, William O'Grady,
initially supported Mackenzie, few members of the Irish community
followed their leads. Neither Papineau nor Mackenzie proved irresistible suitors. Several factors – the ethnic tensions between French
and Irish in Lower Canada, which in several elections saw the latter
respond more readily to linguistic rather than sectarian or national
appeals; the fact that the nationalist courting of Irish Catholics simultaneously estranged their Protestant fellow countrymen; occasional
anti-Catholic outbursts by Mackenzie; and the emergence in both
provinces of more moderate Irish groupings that claimed greater affinity with Daniel O'Connell and his commitment to constitutional
reform – ensured that when the rebellions were staged, the Irish were
conspicuous only by their virtual absence from rebel ranks. O'Grady
distanced himself from Mackenzie, while Bishop Macdonell entered
into his brief Loyalist alliance with the Orange leadership. Then, from
Britain, came word of O'Connell's condemnation of the risings, and a
legend was manufactured that Irish Catholic immigrants had stood
shoulder to shoulder with their Protestant neighbours in defence of the
state. Even the stridently nationalistic *Toronto Mirror* now drew a
sharp distinction between the condition of Catholics in Ireland and
that of those who had settled in the Canadas. The latter, it declared,
had no cause to rebel and every reason to remain loyal to the British
connection.[52]

The Catholic Church had won the gratitude of the state during the rebellions. Macdonell's conspicuous loyalty had been echoed, if somewhat more discreetly, by the influential hierarchy in Lower Canada. Bishop Jean-Jacques Lartigue of Montreal warned the *patriote* leaders against rebellion and in a pastoral letter reminded the faithful of their obligation to respect properly constituted authority. A "carefully worded *mandement* forbidding any revolutionary activity against the legitimate government of the province" divorced the Church from the rebel cause. With very few exceptions, the clergy disavowed a nationalism rooted in French Canadian "social, economic and political grievances" and nourished by resentment of a dominant English-speaking minority. Instead, the Church "was strongly identified with conservative, hierarchical, anti-revolutionary and anti-democratic forces," an identification reinforced by the reflexive anti-clericalism of the *patriotes*. That did not prevent the powerful Bishop of Montreal from seeking amnesty for the rebels and providing assistance to their families, thereby winning public admiration. He also supported the union of the Canadas in 1840, and the Church began to extend and consolidate its control over education and social institutions in what was now Canada East. At the same time, "clerical ideologists made religion integral to [French Canadian] nationalism and awarded the Church the central role in defence of the nation." In short, it was a nationalism whose "primary focus" was on the "Church rather than the state." French Canadians were educated in their "essentially religious" mission, which was to convert the faithless and extend the Kingdom of God "by the formation of a nationality that [was] above all Catholic." The similarity of French Canadian ethnoreligious nationalism with that of the Irish, their common but rival providential missions, their history of ethnic antagonism, and the desire of members of the French Canadian hierarchy to keep their distance from Catholics whose loyalty was widely questioned and for whom a number of them privately expressed a profound contempt, all ensured that the Catholic Church in the Canadas did not act as an institutional promoter of Irish nationalism.[53]

Among the other deterrents to the spread of Irish nationalism in British North America were the preponderance of Irish Protestants and the limited concentration of Catholics. In Canada West the latter remained a minority, and those settled in rural areas did not possess the numbers necessary for effective political agitation. Caution and discretion were further dictated by the strength of a colonial nationalism that had loyalty to the British connection at its heart. Nova Scotia's Protestants might talk of "bullying, boisterous, agitating Irish ecclesiastics," but in neighbouring New Brunswick the men of Irish birth or descent who led the Catholic Church gave little cause for Loyalist concern. They recognized the dangers of sectarian strife should Irish Catholics display radical nationalist sympathies. Even the Repeal Associations organized in the Atlantic colonies and Canada West to provide moral and financial support to O'Connell's constitutional campaign in Ireland stoked the suspicions of "imperial patriots and zealous Protestants ... about the loyalty of the Irish in their midst." Although some associations offered three cheers for the Queen at their meetings, this act of ritualized loyalty proved less eye-catching in New Brunswick than the controversial, qualified, and divisive editorial support of physical-force nationalism by a new Irish newspaper in Saint John, *The Mirror*. Loyalists surely agreed with a distinguished European visitor who concluded that many a Catholic Irishman harboured bitter memories that might not be "very historically founded but which [kept] alive in him an unshakeable ill-will for the British nation." How else were they to interpret the efforts of Halifax's Irish Catholics to celebrate with bonfires and "illuminations" mere rumours of British defeats in the Crimea?[54]

The late 1840s had seen Canada plunged into another extended political crisis, during which the governor general – James Bruce, the Earl of Elgin – kept a close eye on the Irish Catholics. He identified the source of his difficulties as a combination of apparent British indifference to the maintenance of the imperial connection, an impolitic public avowal of the assimilation of French Canadians as the principal objective of the earlier "forced union" of the Canadas, the recent loss of Canada's preferential trading position in British markets, incendiary political developments in France and Ireland, the attempts by the disaffected to fashion an alliance out of the French majority in Canada East and the significant Irish minority, and the egging on of the latter to rebellion by Irish American "fanatics on behalf of republicanism and repeal." The Irish were encouraged to believe, he noted, that England's behaviour in Ireland could only be compared with that of despotic Russia in Poland. Consequently, he took seriously the alarming reports of Irishmen taking secret oaths and readying for an "outbreak." By the summer of 1848, however, Elgin was more confident that emissaries from south of the border were making little headway in their efforts to galvanize the Irish Canadians into rebellion. The branch of the Irish Republican Union "planted" in the province had not "flourished," its organ, the Montreal *United Irishman,* was no more than a "miserable parody" of John Mitchel's Irish newspaper, while "[r]espectable repealers," without compromising their opinions on the justice of the Irish cause, were protesting "the introduction of Irish politics into Canada." Nevertheless, against the backdrop of street disturbances in Montreal in the spring of 1849 and a Tory manifesto issued during the summer in support of annexation to the United States, doubts of Irish Catholic loyalty persisted. The *Toronto Mirror* responded with a denunciation of the authors of the manifesto and a reaffirmation of the Irish Catholics' commitment to Canada's "British character."[55]

A decade later Montreal and Toronto remained two communities with Irish Catholic populations large enough to be organized politically with a realistic hope of making gains and where a more aggressive and radical Irish nationalism might be espoused with a degree of personal safety. The Church had created the ethnic environment in which this nationalism could germinate, and in Toronto it had been well nurtured by Bishop Charbonnel. Here Catholicism did qualify as an "ethnoreligion." Clergy spoke of justice for Ireland and attacked the Orange Order. Newspapers identified with the diocese – before the end of the decade the *Toronto Mirror* had joined the *Canadian Freeman* as an "authentic mouthpiece of the ecclesiastical hierarchy" – declared that "Ireland's rise to nationhood would be the salvation of the Irish at home and abroad." Charbonnel, given his national origins, viewed nationalism as a means to religious ends, and having lost his elder brother during the French Revolution of 1848, he was alive to the perils inherent in his strategy. So, in circular letters and pastorals, he was careful to damn secret societies and condemn the violence associated with Irish nationalism.[56]

The apprehension that the Irish nationalism fostered by the Toronto diocese was in danger of taking a more radical and unmanageable turn could only have been heightened by the founding in 1855 of the Young Men's Saint Patrick Association. The "first exclusively Catholic organization free from the church's control," it took over the organization of the St Patrick's Day celebrations the following year. "Ireland for the Irish" was the theme of a series of militantly nationalistic events. There was a new emphasis on cultural nationalism with the founding in London, Canada West, of a branch of the Ossianic Society. Inevitably, all of this led to heightened sectarian tension in

Toronto, a city that prided itself on being British, Protestant, and loyal to the Crown, and it resulted in a death during St Patrick's Day street brawls in 1858. This tragedy provided a justification of sorts for the establishment of the Hibernian Benevolent Association. Unlike the middle-class character of the Young Men's Association, which had dissolved as a result of internal partisan bickering, the Hibernians represented "a new social and ideological force in the Canadian political arena – lower class Irish Canadian nationalism." Professing to be protectors of Catholics, their homes, and their institutions, the Hibernians kept the sectarian pot simmering in the city. Yet the virtual absence of violence during the association's security patrols was a measure both of its restraint and discipline and the infrequency of organized Orange attacks. To recruit, however, the association required the sanction of the Church. At Charbonnel's request, it abandoned the oath of secrecy that members had been required to swear, and with that concession devout Catholics "could reasonably conclude" that Hibernians "now enjoyed the approbation of the clergy."[57]

A passionate opponent of the Hibernians more radical and provocative Irish nationalism was D'Arcy McGee. Physically unattractive but sociable, companionable, convivial, mawkish, and on occasion melancholic, McGee understood and exploited the charisma of the word both written and spoken. This former Young Irelander, former secretary of the Confederation, former agent of rebellion, former revolutionary, was now a former republican also. Not that he had forsaken opposition to the Union of Ireland and Great Britain, as he made clear in his *Popular history of Ireland*, published in 1863. But he had entered colonial politics soon after his arrival in Montreal to edit the *New Era*, and he understood the folly of embracing a species of Irish nationalism at odds with the dominant ethos of Canada. His message to his fellow countrymen was sweet music to the ears of those many colonials who regarded them with distrust and scorn. The Irish had every reason to be loyal in their new land because their civil, religious, and social beliefs were respected there. They had no grievances in Canada, he told a meeting of Montreal Irish in 1863. They were full citizens of British North America and ought to join hands with other hyphenates to forge a new Canadian nationality. Leading by example, he ignored Irish politics during his first seven years in the provincial assembly and advocated greater colonial unity. All of this came at a cost to his popularity within the Irish community and brought him into collision with the aspiring spokesman for New Brunswick's large population of Irish Catholics.[58]

Timothy Anglin, son of an affluent Irish family, had enjoyed the educational advantages wealth provides, only to discover that his career prospects had been blighted by the Famine. In the spring of 1849 he sailed for Saint John, where he soon began publication of a newspaper, another *Freeman*, which quickly "became the life-blood of the Catholic community in every nook and cranny of New Brunswick." Anglin's ambition to be the spokesman of that community was not harmed by stories of his involvement with the Young Ireland rebels and his declarations that Ireland suffered under the "British yoke." His reputation among Catholic Irishmen was further strengthened by his criticisms of the Crimean War, his ceaseless quest for evidence of institutional anti-Catholicism in the colony's government, his continuing interest in, and his newspaper's extensive coverage of, Irish issues, and his backing for ethnic associations. Although subsequently related by marriage to Ireland's most notorious revolutionary nationalist, O'Donovan Rossa, he carefully distanced himself from physical force and positioned himself as a constitutionalist in the O'Connell mould. Like McGee, he eventually championed a form of Irish Canadian assimilation and the retention of the British imperial connection as a source of strength and security in dealing with the United States. On the other hand, he rejected McGee's analysis of the cause of the American Civil War – "the weakness of the principle of authority in the republican institutions." Instead, Anglin laid the blame for that terrible conflict at Britain's door, arguing that she had passed a poisoned chalice to the United States in 1783 in the shape of a "fierce bitter intolerant fanaticism" in the Northern states and the institution of slavery in the Southern. Moreover, he rejected McGee's call for British North American union. He considered unity unrealistic in the context of the "disparate, detached colonies" and decried it as without obvious benefit to the citizens of New Brunswick.[59]

Anglin did accept another of McGee's claims, that Irishmen and Catholics were better off in British North America than they were in the United States. It was a position he shared with the most influential member of the Roman Catholic hierarchy in the Atlantic colonies. Thomas Connolly, appointed bishop in the province of New Brunswick in 1852, having spent a decade in Nova Scotia, returned seven years later to Halifax as archbishop. Born in Cork, "every inch an Irishman," an institutional ecclesiastic rather than a pastoral priest, and similarly Cullenite in his lack of grace in dealing with Protestant counterparts, he privately acknowledged a duty to sympathize with Ireland and "all her wrongs and grievances," but insisted that his first duty, and that of his clergy, was to take care of "our people" in the colonies. Moreover, he had long scorned politics and politicians. The time had come, he insisted, for the position of Roman Catholics to be defined and understood irrespective of Irish politics. After all, in Nova Scotia and New Brunswick, Roman Catholics had "all that the best government" could give them. Equally, it would be "absolutely destructive" to feed suspicions of their loyalty at a time when they were a minority, however significant, of the colonial population. Irish Catholics not content with the government of British North America should go elsewhere, though he was quick to dismiss as illusory any notion of an easier life in the United States. Labouring work was more plentiful there, he conceded, because of a much larger labour market and a less severe climate, but there was also more bigotry and more contempt "of everything Irish." Orangeism in Nova Scotia and New Brunswick was "no whit worse" than the anti-Catholic prejudice in the republic, while in the quality of life – "in wealth and social standing and in the esteem and respect of Protestants" – the position of Irish Americans could not stand comparison to that of the Catholics of British North America. Eventually he did overcome his aversion to politics and entered the lists on behalf of publicly supported denominational education and North American confederation, raised as he had been in the tradition of clerical leadership. However, he was careful to steer well clear of any association with Irish nationalism. Given the lead provided by Connolly and Anglin, it was not surprising that the Atlantic region's Irish Catholics failed to exhibit "revolutionary tendencies." Such discretion was scorned by the new Bishop of Toronto, who undermined McGee's efforts to dampen sectarian excitement and discourage radical nationalism.[60]

McGee drew for the bishop a generally optimistic picture of the situation of Roman Catholics. Clergy were now safer than they had been only a couple of years earlier from "ruffianism" on the streets of Toronto, the Orange Order had failed to secure the legal recognition it had sought, and favourable separate school legislation could not be long delayed. He detected a "weariness of bigotry & falsehood," which he attributed, at least in part, to the policy of "conciliation" and "moral courage" that he had advocated. None of this cut much ice with John Joseph Lynch. Born in County Fermanagh forty-four years earlier, educated in Ireland, prepared for the priesthood in Paris, and ordained at Maynooth, Lynch had served briefly in his homeland during the early months of the Famine. He then journeyed somewhat reluctantly to Texas, where he proved to be an energetic missionary. He subsequently distinguished himself as rector of a seminary in Missouri, served as advisor to the superior general of the Vicentians, with whom he travelled widely in North America and Europe, revisiting Ireland, and was selected to found a seminary near Niagara Falls. His solid reputation as missionary, educator, and administrator, together with his ethnicity, prompted Charbonnel to secure his appointment as coadjutor with right of succession in Toronto.[61]

An admirer later wrote of Lynch that he was a great churchman and a true Irishman whose love of his native land came second only to that of God and his church. In fact, for him they appear to have been inseparable if not indistinguishable. He had no time for McGee's vision of a new Canadian nationality. Catholic Irish Canadians in Lynch's mind owed a primary loyalty to Ireland. "An Irishman to be a good Canadian must also be a good Irishman," he believed. "It is a false sentiment, this exclusive Canadian nationality, and those who believe in it have narrow souls and still more narrow minds." As an Irishman and a churchman, Lynch considered his native land the victim of iniquitous laws and a tyrannical oppression. He claimed to have detected there a sectarian conspiracy to replace Catholic tenants with Protestants. This was a tyranny unknown in other parts of the civilized world, he announced, and the "English Government" relied on the pacific attitudes of the Roman Catholic Church and its ceaseless preaching of patience and forgiveness to Irishmen living under such intolerable oppression. Thus it was time for Ireland's bishops and clergy to unite to save their people. "The tyrant must yield to the united and well directed efforts of a whole people who have justice on their side and the aid and direction of competent and heaven-appointed guides," he wrote to the Archbishop of Cashel.[62]

Lynch was equally forceful and dogmatic on the subject of Irish emigration. The people had been driven into "exile" by tyranny and injustice, thereby risking Ireland's abandonment "to the pharasaical propagandists of error." He acknowledged the emigrants' mission to plant the faith in foreign lands and extend the territories of the Church, but gave an emphatic "NO" to the question, – did these gains match Ireland's losses? He painted a bleak picture of the lives of most of the Irish immigrants to North America and warned that many of the young

were in danger of being lost to the Church. In a letter to the Irish hierarchy, he deplored *The Evils of Wholesale and Improvident Emigration from Ireland*. Leaked to the press and widely republished, the letter immediately became the source of controversy. The critics of Irish
immigrants had inadvertently been provided with fresh ammunition,
for Lynch documented the disproportionate Irish contribution to crime
and the prison population, the immigrants' dependence on publicly
funded institutions for health services and relief, their prominence in
the vice trade, and the corruption of their young. "The social miseries
of the Irish" were filling jails, poor houses, hospitals, orphanages, and
the streets with "miserable creatures," he replied to one "good man"
who had written to him in defence of British policies in Ireland. The
British were responsible for this tragedy, he insisted, which explained
to his satisfaction why Irish associations in the United States and Canada were all "animated with the one wish, to see the miserable condition of the Irish improved, as they are ashamed of the taunts which the
people of other nations indulge in at their expense." Here was an
astute appeal to those North American Irish whose interest in their
native land might be weakening. The freeing of Ireland from tyranny
would win greater respect for them from their North American hosts.[63]

Lynch held "extreme nationalist views," one of his young priests
commented accusingly. In his widely read letter to Ireland's prelates, he
had proposed that Irish-American associations combine along the lines
of Daniel O'Connell's Catholic Association in order to "stretch a helping hand across the ocean to our persecuted and impoverished
brethren, in the well-grounded hope that England, in her wisdom, will
see the necessity of doing justice to Ireland, when her cause is backed
up by such a powerful combination." The Hibernian Benevolent Association was one such Canadian organization, and Lynch smiled upon
it far more broadly than had his predecessor. When moderate Catholics
questioned the wisdom of this, the bishop took refuge in the convenient excuse that to do otherwise would alienate a large proportion of
his flock. Following his lead, parish clergy began to cooperate far more
closely with Hibernians in the organization of social activities. Lynch
also sanctioned the revival of the annual St Patrick's Day parades,
which McGee in alliance with his predecessor had successfully halted
four years earlier. Michael Murphy, the Hibernians' leader, promptly
repaid the bishop with an impassioned denunciation of British tyranny
and a prediction that Ireland's liberation would soon be effected.
"Nothing could resist the Irish pike when grasped in the sinewy arm of

the Celt," he bombastically and belligerently declared to a very large audience. Here was a clear allusion to the Irish revolutionary nationalists of the Fenian Brotherhood in the United States, yet sitting beside him as he spoke was the bishop. By his very presence, let alone his own remarks on these occasions, Lynch appeared to be lending moral support to radical nationalism. As if to underline this, the St Patrick's Day sermon delivered in St Michael's Cathedral in 1864 by the Reverend W.J. White was no appeal for patience and forgiveness. "The work of spoliation goes on," White lectured the faithful, for "tyrannical oppression, unjust taxation, iniquitous ejectments and robbery, are draining Ireland of its bone and sinew."[64]

The American Fenians had appointed an envoy several years earlier to negotiate an understanding with the leadership of the Hibernians. He was Edward O'Meagher Condon, who eight years later was to be at the centre of a sensational Fenian incident and trial in Manchester, England. Nor could Lynch have pled ignorance of the close relationship between the Hibernians and the Irish American revolutionary nationalists. He was first advised of it by members of his clergy in 1862 and was warned by a trusted clerical confidant before the end of the following year that the Hibernians were "merely a Fenian Elementary School." The time had come, George Northgraves wrote, "to combat the evil, instead of remaining passive." The *Irish Canadian*, which the Hibernians had launched in January 1863, left little room for doubt about the association's attitudes and sympathies. It disparaged "[m]oral force" as a mere sham "to blind and deceive people" and an argument of the "weak and indecisive." Articles were reprinted from other organs of revolutionary nationalism calling for the liberation of Ireland by force, if necessary. The *Irish Canadian* boasted that the Fenian Brotherhood was eighty thousand strong in Ireland itself and constantly drilling. South of the border, the Union and Confederate armies swarmed with Fenians. Armed with military experience and skill, they would be ready at the civil war's end to strike a decisive blow for Irish freedom. Indeed, the constant lauding of the Fenians as the predestined liberators of Ireland appeared to contradict the newspaper's repeated denials that Hibernians and Fenians were one and the same. Only belatedly and following a denunciation of the association by Bishop Farrell of Hamilton, to which Michael Murphy made an insulting response, did Lynch follow his colleague's example. By that time, however, 1865, he had offered far too much encouragement to Toronto's revolutionary nationalists.

The local church had assisted both unintentionally and deliberately the growth of Irish nationalism, and Lynch had been unable to resist the temptation to assume a leadership role. In doing so, he was putting at risk the Church's painstakingly constructed relationship with the government. This may have contributed in turn to his strained relations with the French Canadian hierarchy. Further, Lynch had endangered the position of the Catholic Irish in Canada West by reviving and deepening suspicions of their loyalty. This was something Connolly sought to avoid in the Atlantic colonies with a very public assurance of Catholic loyalty to the constituted British authorities. He dismissed the American Fenians as "deluded knaves and fools."[65]

6

Emigration, Exile, and Nationalism:
The United States

Perhaps 1.5 million Irish arrived in the United States during the two decades beginning in 1840. They entered directly from their homeland, from Britain, from British North America, even from the British colonies of Australasia. With the exception of the Famine years, when the "overwhelming majority of the emigrants were drawn from the lowest classes of Irish society," the pull of hope was stronger than the push of despair. Only a minority carried much in the way of capital or possessed skills highly valued in an industrializing economy, but the great majority had youth and brawn, were accustomed to life's hardships, were more literate than their indigent appearance suggested, and in some cases may even have been reared for emigration by parents seeking old-age insurance. They were also overwhelmingly Catholic. They came "from a society where parish, church, and priesthood formed the very framework of life, and [were] also a product of a new nationalist ethos." Some left Ireland with great reluctance, and the pace of emigration tended to slacken whenever Irish living standards rose or there was news of a downturn in the American economy, but one of the features that distinguished the Irish from other European immigrants was their greater reluctance, or lack of ability, to return permanently to their native land. The Irish who under the "peculiar pressures" of their homeland flocked to the United States in the "greatest number" came "not to return and carry back the profits of casual speculations but to dedicate to the land of their hopes, their persons, their families, their posterity, their affections, their all," declared one Irish American organization. They were distinctive in another important respect – in their numbers was an unusually high proportion of females who travelled in the main with optimism. In

America, they saw the promise of a "status that they never could have at home." For them, it was indeed the land of opportunity.[1]

Newspaper reports, the promotional handbills of transportation companies, and the impressive remittances sent home by earlier emigrants all helped to burnish the image of a transatlantic promised land. On the other hand, immigrants did not want for warnings that the republic's streets were not paved with gold. Emigrant guides, the information circulated by agents posted at British ports by American emigration societies, and the cautions issued by senior clergy ought to have dampened unrealistic expectations that might lead to bitter disillusionment. The Bishop of Toronto's widely circulated account of the Irish immigrant experience described lives blighted by hard and exploitive labour, poverty, squalid housing, ill-health, crime, vice, and even apostasy. The fact that men and women still poured into the United States may have been a measure of their realism, not evidence of their delusions. By coming to America, the *Irish News* argued, the Irish masses among Victoria's subjects, few if any of whom could possibly hope to raise themselves in Ireland above "the verge of starvation," were raising the value of labour at home while greatly improving their own lot. "Each Irish emigrant cannot expect to become a millionaire," one American journal observed, "but he may be sure of getting everywhere in the United States a hearty meal of something more substantial than potatoes, and what seemed so greatly to surprise [Charles] Dickens, a whole coat to his back."[2]

The naive and the unwary were likely to be fleeced on arrival by wharf-wise fellow countrymen who regarded them as so many sheep to be led to the shearing shed, and the gross frauds to which they fell victim eventually brought imposition of a head tax with which the State of New York funded the Board of Commissioners of Emigration. Not only was the board tasked to protect immigrants from chicanery and provide assistance to those who quickly fell into the ranks of the destitute, but it also established a labour bureau to help them find work within the boundaries of New York City. Elsewhere, those tasks remained in the hands of emigrant aid societies.[3]

Attracted to the promise of work like bees to nectar, the Irish swarmed to a handful of industrializing states of the Northeast, and to a pair – Illinois and Ohio – in the Midwest. They congregated in large urban centres, such as the metropolis of New York, and in the multitude of much smaller "urban places," such as mill and mining towns. The rural character of Kingston, New York, for example, collapsed under the weight of a fivefold increase in its inhabitants in little more than a generation. The Irish came to dig the local canal and remained to work on the docks, while others arrived with the opening of quarries and industries. By 1855 they were one-third of the townspeople, who now numbered in excess of ten thousand. This proved to be an oft-repeated pattern. The population of Lawrence, Massachusetts, exceeded sixteen thousand within a decade of its founding in 1845, and the great majority of its large minority of foreign born were Irish. Of course, by no means all of the Irish remained urbanites. A number of those who followed the railroad to Northfield, Vermont, and helped the town grow into one of the largest in the state, eventually accumulated sufficient capital to turn to farming. Moreover, as urbanized as most Catholic Irish immigrants did necessarily become and remain, they were far from unique in this regard. The hordes of German immigrants flooding into the United States were similarly rural in their origins and similarly urban in their settlement of the United States.[4]

These urban pioneers, like their rural counterparts on the frontier, could look forward to hard if not bleak lives. The many Catholic Irish who found employment as unskilled labourers worked long hours in brutish and frequently very dangerous conditions. Employment was often seasonal and insecure, wages rarely adequate to support a family; thus children and wives entered the workforce. Housing was commonly overcrowded, squalid, verminous, and pestilential. The population density of Boston's inner core increased by 50 per cent in less than a generation, while block density in several of New York City's wards tripled in two decades. Terrifying and insidious diseases swept through rural "paddy camps" and city tenements alike, producing psychoses that were all too apparent in the mental illness and alcoholism to which the Irish of both sexes reportedly fell disproportionately prey. Interestingly, they were less prone than German immigrants to take their own lives.[5]

Their lack of material success in comparison to that of native-born Americans and other immigrants, their "destitution and degradation," and their greater dependence on public assistance may have cultivated in the Irish "paranoia, defeatism and feelings of inferiority planted by the past," and undoubtedly caused a number of them to surrender to demoralization. But were refugees from the terrors and horrors of the Famine likely to consider their hard lives in the

United States so bitter a disappointment that they looked back nos-
talgically on life in the homeland? Those who had lived in "dirty,
damp, crowded, dark, primitive dwellings" in Ireland, without fresh
water or sanitation facilities, were unlikely to be driven to despair by
the standard of housing in the United States. As one inexhaustibly
sympathetic clerical observer remarked, their homes in New York
were "not more deplorable nor more squalid than the Irish hovels
from which many of them have been exterminated." The many who
settled in New York City's notorious Five Points "may have perceived the tenements, at least initially, as somewhat pleasant" compared to their Irish cabins. Nor were they confined to ghettoes, being
too mobile and too dispersed to be genuinely segregated. Slums
gained a multicultural character with the arrival of Germans and
French Canadians, prompting the Irish to complain that the latter
lived like "mackerel packed in a barrel" and undercut wages. Equally,
the Irish in the United States may not have regarded good housing as
their highest priority, and pristine cleanliness may not have been a
fundamental cultural value. One priest denied that he had ever witnessed during his travels in Ireland the legendary "joint occupancy
of the poorest cabin, by the owner, and his pig or cow," but he did
admit that "cleanliness and health might oftentimes be more attended to."[6]

The notion that in the land of opportunity hard work ensured success may have seemed something of a hoax played upon vast numbers
of urban pioneers, yet there were reasons for them to cling to the hope
that progress towards respectability and a modest level of comfort
was possible. There is evidence that some of the immigrants who settled in Five Points "saved far more money than one would have imagined given their wretched surroundings and low-paying jobs." The
Irishmen, Catholic as well as Protestant, who settled in Paterson, New
Jersey, during the second and third decades of the nineteenth century
brought valuable skills and resources with them. This was especially
true of many of the Irish immigrants who had previously lived in
Britain. Certainly, Newark's craftsmen did not want for Irish members
by mid-century. Similarly, the "steady expansion of skilled occupations" among Irish males in Philadelphia meant that an "important
portion" of them "had begun a positive process of social advancement." Much the same held true of the Irish in the small Vermont
industrial town of Northfield. In short, many of the Irish made worthwhile gains in the United States. Owen Healy, who had been rescued

from starvation by Lord Palmerston's "massive emigration" of his surplus tenants, settled in one of New York's most notorious slums, and within a handful of years he was the proud owner of a saloon and a bank account.[7]

If the Catholic Irish in the United States, as in Canada, dominated the massed ranks of the "canallers," many of the craftsmen engaged in the vast construction projects were also Irish, and they enjoyed "higher pay and a degree of independent status." In some industries, such as the building trades, where Irish contractors rapidly acquired a dominant position, labourers received the "on-the-job training" that served as the "informal apprenticeship" to skilled positions. Second-generation Irish "gained access to the prestigious jobs" in Philadelphia's new metal industries and were a conspicuous element among Pittsburg's ironworkers and merchants. A strong Irish presence in New York's crafts and trades was evident from their prominence in the city's labour movement during the 1850s. Nor were wage differentials between the unskilled and the skilled often as great as might be supposed, and this was especially true for trades in decline. Labourers in Boston during the 1840s may have found in their pay some compensation for the slow pace of "upward occupational mobility." Even the exploited young Irish women who found employment in the mills of Lowell, helping to transform another Yankee village into an "immigrant industrial city," earned wages far higher and enjoyed a diet more varied and nourishing than those on offer at home. Although a disgruntled Irish immigrant complained to an English visitor that he "got 'three times the Irish wages'" but "did six times the Irish work," this may be one explanation of the extraordinary fact that between the Famine and the eve of the American Civil War Irish immigrants sent back to their native land "almost sixty million dollars."[8]

There was another measure of the gains made by Irish immigrants. They reached the republic during an era when politics appeared "to enter into everything," and the adult men discovered that they were peculiarly well equipped to take advantage of the situation. Many if not most of them had a command of English, and a large number were functionally literate. Even the "Eatanswill" carnival of American election days was reminiscent of home, while former members of Ireland's agrarian secret societies had received tutoring in the sinister arts of political persuasion and in the virtues of loyalty and obedience. The Irish had also received a solid grounding in the more conventional tactics of political organization and electoral manipulation. This had been one of O'Connell's bequests to his fellow countrymen. All this explains the welcome extended to them by American politicians seeking to "expand the base of party participation." New York's Democrats opened the Naturalization Bureau, and within twenty years naturalized voters in the city outnumbered the nativeborn. The Irish made up perhaps one-third of this electorate, for no other immigrant group could match their enthusiasm for naturalization and voter registration.[9]

The Catholic Irish soon became an essential cog in big-city political machines. They rented their strong-arm services to candidates, and one Irish gang leader, Mike Walsh, secured his own election to Congress for New York. Saloons, which served as the social clubs of the poor, became important centres of political activity. Saloonkeepers, an occupation in which Irishmen like Owen Healy had a conspicuous presence, organized their patrons and secured for themselves a dominant position in "the lower echelons of the urban Democratic party." Volunteer fire companies, frequently Irish in complexion and usually identified with particular saloons, functioned as the organizers' allies on the streets. In return for their votes, Irishmen secured a disproportionately large share of the multiplying minor positions in municipal administrations and steadily dominated the ranks of a number of city police forces. Irishmen wishing to enter the provisions trade and grocery business had no difficulty securing food market licences. Irish building contractors and their labourers benefited from public works contracts. The constant courting of the Irish vote in the seemingly ceaseless round of municipal, state, and federal elections, the evident and increasing Irish influence in the urban wing of the nation's dominant political party, and the many small rewards of their political loyalty could only have enhanced the immigrants' self-esteem and self-respect.[10]

Heavy concentration in and within a relatively small number of states, though the Irish were to be found almost everywhere in the United States, contributed to the growth of Irish political influence and power. "They huddle together as birds of a feather," one American complained in 1844. Whether in the shanty camps of the canallers, or the tenements of industrial centres – and the denizens of the former "were as much members of a proletariat as if they lived in a city slum" – the Irish practised a high degree of self-segregation. The paddy camps of Lowell; the "Patch" and "Tigertown" sections of

Paper City; the Dublin and Kerrytown areas of Stamford; "the hideous slums of Fort Hill and the North End" of Boston; the Fourth, Fifth and Sixth Wards of New York City; and the Moyamensing, Southwark, and Grays Ferry districts of Philadelphia were either predominantly Irish or had a distinctively green hue. Nor was this surprising, dependent as so many immigrants were on local emigrant aid societies for information on housing and work. Living among fellow nationals was one way to hold in check the psychopathology of emigration, and it was a strategy common to most immigrant groups. It eased the adjustment of "old patterns of life to the exigencies of new cultural, social, and economic circumstances." At the same time, it engendered "a feeling of detachment and alienation from the larger society." In the words of one critic, the Irish "avoid and keep aloof from Americans, and literally pronounce a curse of excommunication upon them."[11]

"Enclave consciousness" was exhibited by most immigrant groups, but ethnic identity in the case of the Irish was fortified by family emigration during the Famine and a strong commitment to endogamy made possible by the availability of young Irish women. The fact that they often outnumbered men may explain their greater willingness to look outside the ethnic group for spouses. Thus the pattern of Irish "clannishness" was followed as religiously in the United States as in the British territories to the north. Benevolent and Friendly Societies, Irish saloons and militia companies, and the building and loan associations that facilitated a substantial Irish ownership of properties in certain city districts were all additional manifestations of ethnic distinctiveness. Indeed, the continuity of their traditions and the strength of "social support" may go far to explain why so few of the "destitute and degraded" Irish succumbed to the ultimate despair of suicide. But at the heart of Irish "enclave consciousness" and at the centre of their "urban villages" was the Catholic Church.[12]

Much the same could be said of the Irish who reached the slave South. Again they were largely to be found, along with other immigrants, in the region's cities and were heavily represented within the ranks of unskilled labour. They took the servile, unpleasant, backbreaking, and dangerous jobs traditionally associated with free blacks and slaves. They also clung together for support and reassurance, created Irish sections and Irish streets, occupied primitive and unhealthy housing, and formed a voting bloc that delivered ballots and was rewarded with patronage positions and concessions. As in the North, a number prospered. In New Orleans, they secured entry to the professions, provided printers and journalists to the local publishing industry, formed a recognizable minority of commission merchants, agents, and traders, and set themselves up in the business of shop-keeping. They organized benevolent and social societies, staged St Patrick's Day parades, and regarded the Church as their "most important institution" and the parish as a principal focal point of their lives.[13]

Efforts were made to convince the Irish of New Orleans to take up good farming land in Texas and Louisiana, but neither liberal terms of purchase nor promises of substantial cash grants induced them to move. Far more ambitious were the Northern projects of western colonization. Daniel O'Connell was party to one elaborate Irish scheme, while many of the emigrant aid associations hoped to secure grants of public land on which to settle immigrants and thus facilitate their dispersal across the United States. With clerical encouragement, Irish communities were successfully established in Maine, Iowa, Arkansas, Wisconsin, Nebraska, and Minnesota. But the western movement was increasingly riddled with disagreements over the relationship of these "New Irelands" to society at large, and it encountered determined opposition from the most influential figure in the American Church.[14]

Some members of the hierarchy saw in the dispersal of the Irish the means to promote their fuller integration into American society, whereas others were committed to the creation of "segregated western villages," which the immensity of the country and its decentralized society seemed to invite. Critics of the Catholic Church welcomed dispersal as a means to dissipate Irish clannishness and check the influence of priests. Irish American politicians, on the other hand, opposed it for much the same reasons. They understood the relationship between heavy concentrations of the Irish, large voting blocs, and political influence. Similarly, a number of religious leaders, with John Hughes, Bishop and later Archbishop of New York, in the vanguard, considered the teeming eastern cities "bulwarks preserving not only the hard-won political and social privileges but safeguarding the immigrants' Faith through the instrumentality of the churches, schools, and charitable institutions already established or in process of erection." Hughes's opposition was also intensely personal. He disliked, even hated, several of the advocates of colonization and disputed their claims of urban degradation. The lot of the Irish in New York was "much better than it had been in Ireland," he countered. He dismissed colonization as impracticable, insisting that most Irishmen were ill-equipped to farm in the United States, and deplored the unsettling of urban Irish who had already established themselves successfully in the new land. He warned that "towns strictly Irish" would make the immigrants "as distinct as the Mormons" and thus more inviting targets for their critics. He rejected any suggestion that Catholic practices needed to be "Americanized," and regarded as a slur on Irish-born clergy calls for their replacement by a native priesthood trained in the traditions of the republic. Finally, he denounced a proposal that land-hungry Irish settle the vast empty spaces of British North America. This would place them, Hughes growled, within "the cold shadow of a government hardly to be pardoned on account of its hostility to their race and to their ancestors," leaving them as mere "catspaws" of the hated English. "No one but a mendacious and interested agent of Royalty," the *Irish News* chimed in, would dare suggest that the "material advantages" of the British North "American Siberia" equalled those of "the Western States."[15]

Hughes urged the Irish determined to head west to travel as individuals, not colonists, and this most of them did. They worked their passages in the familiar ways, digging canals, laying railroad tracks, and labouring on farms. Not a few of them then took up farming. A sizable proportion of the early waves reaching California from other regions of the nation, or from Australasia, became farmers. Irish and Germans made up more than one-quarter of the population of Iowa by 1850, and many "melted inconspicuously into the midwestern countryside." A number of Irish veterans of the Mexican War took their land grants in Wisconsin, while many of the men who went there to work in the lead mines later turned to agriculture. By 1860 a mere 20 per cent of the Irish population was resident in that state's five cities. Nevertheless, in that same year, the foreign born, of whom the Irish were everywhere a significant segment, provided approximately half the denizens of Chicago, St Louis, Milwaukee, and San Francisco, and in excess of 40 per cent of the residents of Buffalo, Detroit, Cleveland, and Cincinnati. In most of the western cities, the absence both of established elites and mature economies allowed for greater social mobility than in the East. The Irish entered the professions and were more conspicuous within the ranks of the entrepreneurial and mercantile middle classes. Still, the pattern of settlement and development was much like that followed in other regions of the Union. Progress and success were neither guaranteed nor uniform, and the real gains made by the Irish were frequently obscured by the constant stream of newcomers "entering at the bottom of the occupational structure." The bulk of the Irish remained heavily engaged in unskilled labour, were generally to be found in the least desirable urban residential districts, were politically active, tended to enrol in national associations and benevolent societies, practised endogamy, and formed enclaves without ever being completely segregated from natives or other immigrants. In the West, as in the East and the South, the "most important institution in maintaining a separate Irish identity" was the Catholic Church.[16]

That Church experienced dramatic growth during the first half of the nineteenth century. From a membership of some seventy thousand in 1807, it grew exponentially to more than 3.5 million by 1859. As "the largest religious denomination in the United States," Catholicism was suddenly far more visible. Within a single biblical lifespan, a missionary church of a single bishop and fifty-six churches had expanded into a vast institution of "six archdioceses, twenty-five dioceses, four vicariate apostolic, and nearly two thousand churches." Dioceses dotted a path across the breadth of the nation, from Buffalo to San Francisco, as well as its length from the border of British North America to the Gulf of Mexico. "Religion advances amidst difficulties. Conversions numerous, and the eagerness to hear Catholic truth is increasing," the Bishop of Philadelphia informed Paul Cullen in 1843. Three years later, his optimism undiminished, he reported the conversions of three Protestant ministers and pointed to the pace of cathedral and church construction as conclusive proof of the triumph of "Catholic truth." Much the same encouraging word had already arrived at the Irish College in Rome from New York. "Everything connected with Religion in this country is, on the whole, prosperous and consoling," John Hughes reported. Aware that such rapid progress was bound to alarm Protestants, senior clergy were at pains to offer public reassurances that Roman Catholicism was entirely consistent with the American republican principles of separation of church and state, civic equality, and religious freedom. Nevertheless, the Church remained vulnerable on the issue of religious freedom, for it saw no reason to compromise with "heresy." An effort was made to minimize the significance of the Pope's territorial sovereignty and emphasize his "distinctively spiritual character," only for Pius IX to undermine it with his spirited denunciation of Italian nationalism. His American episcopal defenders, like their Irish counterparts, argued that possession of territories ensured the Pope's political independence and thus his role as man's "moral guide," and they decried the Italian nationalists' resort to force. This they labelled a repudiation of those legitimate and constitutional means that alone "would produce authentic liberty."[17]

The American Catholic Church underwent a process of "Hibernization" that produced something approaching a "Hibernarchy" (a hierarchy dominated by Irish prelates). During the early years the highest offices had been held by French or Anglo-American clergy, but an ethnic transition was well underway during the 1830s. Priests of Irish birth or Irish origins progressively filled most of the multiplying dioceses, culminating at the century's midpoint with Francis Kenrick's elevation to the archiepiscopacy of Baltimore, the premier see. This was exactly what one of his Anglo-American predecessors had feared. The greater the number of Irishmen appointed to the episcopacy, the greater their ability to secure the appointment of still more of their fellow countrymen and to import an ever-larger corps of Irish clergy, Archbishop Whitfield had cautioned. The greening of the ordinary clergy did indeed take place, and Irish names soon dominated "the rosters of the clergy of New England, New York, Philadelphia, and Baltimore, as well as the other towns along the coast and also followed the Irish who went inland." Many of the priests were graduates of Maynooth or the lesser-known Irish seminaries. Others were products of All Hallows College on the northern outskirts of Dublin. It had been founded in 1842 for the express purpose of training missionary priests for service overseas. When the North American College finally opened its doors in Rome, its first rector was Irish-born.[18]

The Irish who eventually dominated the American Church introduced "a forwardness and aggression that it had lacked under the leadership of the Anglo-American-French hierarchy." This victory came at a price. The zealous and disciplined among the Irish priests flooding into the United States were accompanied, as in British North America, by a minority who did little to enhance the reputation of the priesthood. Bishops responded by seeking "to rule their dioceses with an iron rod." They strove to stamp American Catholicism "in an Irish-Catholic mold" that demanded "strict authoritarian obedience and discipline." They encouraged "social isolation from the surrounding Protestant society," together with "a militant feeling of ethnoreligious pride." An editorial in a Boston newspaper closely identified with the diocese was redolent of a spirit of triumphalism certain to infuriate American Protestants, alienate immigrant Irish Protestants, and even provoke non-Irish Catholics. The Puritans of New England were in decline, the *Pilot* trumpeted, whereas the Irish were on the rise because of their "great health, vigor, strength and purity." New Englanders were "marked by abortionism at every stage of uterine growth," it continued, employing a scandalous metaphor, while the "Catholicizing and Hibernicizing of the land and the disappearance of the Puritan" were proceeding swiftly.[19]

Religion and nationality were two of the fundamental referents of the "shared feeling of peoplehood," the "sense of belonging" that constitutes ethnicity. Religion as the "focal point" of so many immigrant lives constructed and reinforced those communal ties needed to confront "the disruptive forces of their new environment," such as discouragement and the "dissolvent power of assimilation." The Church was central to the organization of "allegiance around the ethnic group," but the monolithic character of the Catholic Church in the United States was more apparent than real. Irish domination of the hierarchy and the large and increasing Irish presence within the priesthood were resented by other Catholics. American Catholicism thus faced a peculiar challenge. Its membership was multi-ethnic. Although outnumbered by the Irish, Germans formed a substantial national minority. More than six hundred thousand of them arrived during the half-century following the end of the Napoleonic Wars, and they wanted fellow Germans as their priests. John Martin Henni, the first bishop of Milwaukee, was one member of the American hierarchy who successfully attracted German-speaking clergy from Europe. Considering themselves a cut above the Irish and better trained, these priests were unable to resist the temptation to duplicate those features of parish life with which they had been familiar in their native lands, and they strove "to keep German Catholic communities insulated from the majority Irish Church." Indeed, a papal investigator was moved to complain of their excess of religious nationalism, and Archbishop Kenrick made an unpleasant discovery: The German lay leadership was no less nationalistic.[20]

German resentment of Irish domination of the American Church was shared by French Canadians, Poles, and Italians, and was not entirely unwarranted. The Irish were rarely credited with bringing "peace into the Church." In New York, John Hughes governed a very large German community insensitively. Convinced that his fellow Irishmen were "the poorest and most wretched population that can be found in the world," he appeared to be less concerned with German poverty and deprivation, while the relatively small number of German priests complained that they were treated "with arrogance and even hate" by their Irish superiors. As a solution for the problems of mounting ethnic tension, bishops endorsed the expedient of national parishes. In effect, they sought to separate the different ethnic groups. William Quarter, appointed the first Bishop of Chicago in 1844, administered a diocese that was home to fellow Irishmen, Germans, and French Canadians. He approached German funding organizations for monies with which to build German churches and endeavoured to attract German priests to his diocese. Unfortunately, his lack of fluency in German told against him, and his conciliatory policy had been adjudged a failure before his sudden death in 1848. Moreover, there were accusations that some Irish bishops approached German and French funding societies for assistance and then used the grants for other projects. Quarter's successor was the multilingual James Van de Velde. A native Belgian but again trained in the United States, he quickly ran afoul of Irish priests and parishioners resentful of his "sometimes unhappy if not imprudent ... mode of governing." Following his departure for Natchez, Mississippi, in 1853, he was replaced by another Irishman. Antony O'Regan had been president of St Jarlath's Seminary, Tuam, an institution closely identified with John MacHale, but Rome hesitated over his appointment because of "the complaints made against the Irish." Although he was able to patch up relations with most Irish congregations, creating three additional national parishes for refugees from the Famine, O'Regan quickly alienated French-speaking Catholics. He ordered the relocation of their church to an inconvenient site, but one allegedly profitable for Irish realtors, and appointed as pastor a fellow Irishman who chose to preach his first sermon in Gaelic.[21]

The torments of Bishop Van de Velde were not unique. Louis de Goesbriand, the French-born bishop of Burlington, a diocese with a substantial French Canadian population, soon found himself the butt of Irish criticism. Another Frenchman, Amadeus Rappe, was appointed the first bishop of Cleveland. He opposed national parishes, fearing that they would create internal divisions and fritter away already inadequate financial resources on duplicate facilities. In short, he considered nationalism potentially fatal to the universal church. Soon butting heads with German Catholics over the use of their language, Rappe looked to the Irish as allies in a mistaken belief that they were less nationalistic than the Germans and thus more open to his assimilative policy of Americanization. On the other hand, he prejudiced hopes of a favourable working relationship by treating the Irish, whom he considered intemperate, "impoverished, improvident and ignorant," with barely concealed social contempt. He quickly discovered the strength of their "ethnic consciousness." They demanded Irish priests for Irish congregations, and Rappe's dismissal of a popular Irish priest even galvanized the city's mayor and council, all non-Catholics, into action. They appealed to the archbishop to reverse the decision, but it was not until an Irish priest carried the complaints of the Irish faithful to Rome that Rappe gave ground. He agreed to national parishes in order to restore and maintain internal peace.[22]

The "Hibernization" of the American Catholic Church was another source of pride and self-esteem for Irish immigrants and their offspring, and may have contributed to a weakening of the Irish hierarchy's opposition to emigration. After all, it was difficult to continue arguing that the emigrants, on arrival in the United States, were entering a spiritual wasteland. "In the number, wealth and influence of its followers, in the extent and perfection of its organization, and the splendour of its educational and ecclesiastical establishments," the *Cork Examiner* later proudly observed of the American Church, "it has surpassed every rival creed." The importance of ensuring a supply of priests to meet the staffing demands of the expanding church had long been obvious. Equally, the Irish immigrant faithful were regarded as peculiarly in need of spiritual and social guidance. "Many of our countrymen from this circumstance living far from any aid of religion become the disgrace of their religion and country," one clerical correspondent advised Paul Cullen in Rome. "Their excesses in drinking, party fighting among themselves etc. render them the objects of almost universal abhorrence which greatly operates against religion." Yet even their "greatest enemies," he went on, admitted "that *all, all* the great works, the canals, railroads, buildings, and finally the erecting of Catholic churches, the support of priests, the maintenance of religion is due to such." The Irish were "a perfect riddle."[23]

The natural anxieties of the immigrant Irish were undoubtedly quietened by "the presence of guides in the most basic internal forms of identity," for unlike other ethnic groups within the American Church they rarely had to contend "with a hostile pastor doggedly trying to impose an alien form of Catholicism." Irish priests, no less than German, played a "vital role" in the development of ethnic enclaves, and parishioners looked to them for general guidance. The parish priest of Newburyport was "the decisive factor in halting a disastrous run" on the local savings bank during the financial crisis of 1857. He counselled his congregation to leave their monies on deposit. "Recognized as "[c]ommunal diplomat and arbitrator," the Irish priest was committed to the spiritual reclamation of those immigrants who had been inactive members of the Church before leaving Ireland.[24]

Non-practising Catholics may well have formed a majority of Famine-era emigrants. Thus one New York priest estimated that fully one-half of the city's Irish population was Catholic "merely because Catholicity was the religion of the land of their birth." The creation of national parishes promised to check religious indifference, as did the immigrants' perception of churches as "tangibly representative of the culture they had left behind them, and havens of refuge in an utterly strange and alien landscape." But pew rents and charges for admission to services undoubtedly discouraged the attendance of the very poor. Another problem was the inability of construction to keep pace with the growth of membership. As late as the 1860s, New York City's churches could seat less than half the nominal Catholics. Parish missions therefore played an increasingly important role, reaching out to the unchurched. Worship and religious teaching were now standardized, "with the production and distribution of catechisms, reprinted sermons, and routinized parish functions." These were all aspects of a Catholic revival that further "strengthened the parish community," "awakened the piety of the people," "encouraged the formation of parish co-fraternities," and increased the influence of the priest as a source of "wisdom in all areas of life." Irish immigrants certainly exhibited a peculiar and remarkable willingness to scrimp and save in order to build and maintain their churches, for, unlike their French and the German fellow religionists, they arrived well trained in "voluntaryism." Their extraordinary support of the Church may provide a clue to the slower pace of their wealth accumulation when compared to that of the native-born and other ethnic groups.[25]

The binding of Irish Catholics more demonstratively to their church served to unite them. Brawls and disputes rooted in the regional differences of their native land had frequently erupted, whether bloody

battles over work on canals or an extended, foolish and bitter disagreement in some remote Iowa settlement over its name. Squabbling
Irish Catholics incurred the scorn of the host community. But the common celebration of their faith accustomed the Irish to working together and "provided local bases for wider community activity." St
Patrick's Church, Lowell, was carefully positioned equidistant
between two rival Irish enclaves, and both provided the financing and
much of the labour for its construction. The completed church quickly
became something of a "social club and, significantly, one which
included all of Lowell's Irish." Intragroup networks were further
"strengthened and deepened" by the Church's relentless discouragement of marriages to Protestants or even converts to Catholicism. The
certainty of immediate humiliation, in the form of public excommunication, or the terrifying threat of death without hope of salvation
dissuaded many Irish Catholics from unions outside their ethnic
group, let alone "outside the Church or its sacraments." As a result,
the Church could legitimately claim to be "the most important institution acting to maintain the homogeneous Irish community." Priests
who founded temperance societies were undoubtedly inspired by the
crusade of Father Mathew and evidently hoped to improve the social
reputation of the Irish, but the movement served the secondary purpose of binding the community together. By the same token, clerical
denunciations of drunkenness were an assertion of the Church's
"hegemonic claim to set and enforce standards of orderly, respectable
behavior."[26]

Members of the hierarchy intent on consolidating episcopal control
were equally determined to promote those agencies that ensured the
Church's "important physical and institutional presence in every
neighborhood" and solidified the position of the parish as the focus of
the residents' activities. That focus was peculiarly sharp in the case of
the Irish. In the absence of state aid, the local voluntary organizations
to which immigrants naturally turned for assistance and security acted
as cultural and social bonding agents. To a much greater extent than
most other immigrant communities, however, the Irish tended to shy
away from those "not associated in some degree of intimacy with the
Church." Officers of the thirty benevolent associations operating in
New York City submitted their constitutions to the bishop for his
approval and promised to delete any provisions to which he objected.
Hospitals, orphanages, Magdalen asylums, and St Vincent de Paul
societies were opened, and even Irish volunteer fire companies and

militia units were, in a city like Buffalo, "deeply affected by Catholic influence."[27]

The cultural and social gulf separating Irish Catholics from American Protestants and even from some fellow Catholic immigrants widened with the hierarchy's repeated exhortations to parents to secure a Catholic education for their children. As in Canada West, this resolve was at odds with the host community's faith in public schools, which were regarded as vital instruments in the work of uplifting all classes, but especially the lower, by correcting tendencies towards anti-social behaviour while assimilating immigrants into the majoritarian Protestant culture. This last objective alone guaranteed Catholic opposition. "The Public Schools are everywhere conducted in a way to leave the children without any religious impression, or to impress them with sectarian views," Bishop Kenrick of Philadelphia complained in 1843. "The Bible is the symbol and watchword of the sects," he maintained, and although he managed to exempt Catholic students from its use, Kenrick doubted that the arrangement would be honoured. "Justice and good faith are little regarded," he mordantly observed. Yet his criticisms were comparatively mild when set beside those of colleagues who assailed public schools as "[a]theistical, godless and pernicious – prolific hot beds of prostitution, indecency, blasphemy, naivery and crime." This excoriation of public education was fuelled by its perceived "Anglo-Saxon bias" and quasi-Protestant character. Protestants dominated supervisory boards, frequently held "a virtual monopoly of teaching positions; and the King James [Protestant] Bible was read in the classroom." There were claims that Catholic children were required to recite Protestant hymns and offer up Protestant prayers, while Bishop Hughes censured the textbooks in use within his jurisdiction as sectarian and "historically slanted." Public education, he fulminated, was "Socialism, Red Republicanism, Universalism, Infidelity, Deism, Atheism, and Pantheism – anything, everything except religionism and patriotism."[28]

Only a minority of Catholic children were able to attend parochial schools. The costs of construction and maintenance, together with a chronic shortage of teachers, meant that even in John Hughes's diocese places could be provided for less than half the potential enrolment. The significance of the deficiency was somewhat diminished by the apparent indifference of some parents to education. Then again, child labour was often essential for a family's survival. Others continued to send their children to public schools. This was a decision made easier for Catholics, as in Chicago, whenever local authorities made energetic efforts to attract immigrants into the public system by treating them with greater consideration. It was easier still for those living in New York's Sixth Ward, as it was for the denizens of Worcester, Massachusetts. Their public schools were so heavily Irish, and Irish teachers so numerous, that the education posed no threat to "the spiritual lives of Catholic children." Indeed, "Irish values" were instilled. Those values were naturally even more to the fore in the parochial schools, where pupils learned as much if not more of Ireland than of the United States. Hughes invited the Christian Brothers to New York and specified their readers for use in all parochial schools, which ensured that students were instructed in the religious values and "the special identity of the Irish." A similar curriculum was followed in the schools of other dioceses. History courses emphasized the Catholic experience of the Irish past and the fidelity and loyalty of a people who held to their faith throughout the oppression of the Penal Era. There was much emphasis on the Irish struggle against English tyranny, the stirring speeches of Irish martyrs, and the bitter memories of the Famine. Children so educated, members of the hierarchy such as Hughes believed, would "unconsciously acquire repellant strength against the insidious workings of Anglo-Saxonism, and all its soul-killing tendencies." If this education promoted a "separatist, ethnic Catholicism," that objective was furthered by a press that was frequently identified with the Church. The *Freeman's Journal* of New York, during its ownership by the bishop, counselled Catholics to be very cautious about socializing with non-Catholics, even on an individual basis, and reminded them of the Church's disapproval of societies whose membership included "unbelievers." Here was reason to suppress any lingering impulse to ethnic affinity with Protestant Irish-Americans. Newspapers were crucial to the definition and expression of "ethnic differences," and next "to the Church and school [were] the most influential social and educational force in the immigrant community."[29]

An American Irish press had long existed but had rarely flourished in the republic. That changed with mass immigration, the deepening "enclave consciousness," Irish domination of the American Catholic Church, and the establishment of national parishes. When the hierarchy assembled in Baltimore in 1866 for its second plenary council, the members formally "recognized the need for a Catholic press and lauded those dioceses that had official organs, while admitting that not everything published in such a paper should be attributed to the bishop." This denial of responsibility for the content of newspapers was not one many readers would have taken to heart. The Catholic press appeared, more often than not, to be the authoritative voice of a diocese, and usually it had a distinctly green tint. It was Irish as well as Catholic. The San Francisco *Catholic Guardian* announced in its first editorial, "[W]e cannot forget the land that gave us birth – the home of our childhood. Ireland is the mother country of the immense majority of American Catholics, and, as such, is dear to us all." The Boston *Pilot*, which developed into the most influential of these organs, was edited by a local priest for an entire decade, while Hughes's ownership of the *Freeman's Journal* lasted for several years, and even following its sale the new publisher announced that it would continue to reflect the bishop's views. Francis Kenrick, the Bishop of Philadelphia, personally assumed the editorship of the *Catholic Herald* because of its serious shortfall in funds and his conviction that much of its content had "often been wanting in a Catholic sense." Detroit's *Catholic Vindicator* claimed to be a diocesan spokesman for all Catholics, but "its editors and interests belonged to the Irish community." Wisconsin's *Catholic Citizen* wore its national sympathies on its sleeve and urged the teaching of Gaelic as well as Irish history in parochial schools. Writing in 1851, Thomas D'Arcy McGee noted that most of the journals were "in clerical hands" and that their "standing topic" was "the state and hopes of Ireland."[30]

Bishops were neither loath nor slow to attack newspapers of which they disapproved. A proposal in 1846 to revive the New York *Shamrock*, to advocate the rights of all immigrants but especially those of Irishmen, and to criticize nativist opposition to them was sternly discouraged by Hughes as "altogether inexpedient on public grounds." He feared a fanning of the flames of nativism. Subsequently, he drove McGee and his American *Nation* from the city following the former Young Irelander's criticism of the priests for their conduct during the rising of 1848. The secular *Irish American*, which quickly became "the most influential Irish newspaper" in New York following its establishment in 1849, benefited from McGee's exclusion and prudently avoided difficulties with the bishop by declaring as its objective the unity of "Irish American nationalism and Catholicity." As for McGee, he first set himself up in Boston, where he published the *American Celt and Catholic Citizen*, only quickly to be obliged to bend the knee to his distant relation in the episcopal palace. From there he moved on to Buffalo, at the invitation of Bishop Timon, only soon to find himself under renewed attack for proposing the settlement of Irish immigrants on the vacant lands of British North America. To encourage Irish Catholic immigrants to live under "the red flag of British tyranny" was apostasy. Readers of the "Catholic and Irish press" were as likely as the pupils attending parochial schools to conclude that love of Ireland required hatred of England. "The strongest and best hater of England is sure to prove the best American," the *Irish American* declared in 1852. In much the same hostile spirit, the Boston *Pilot* later embarked upon an extended campaign to prove the racial and moral superiority of Celts over Anglo-Saxons. It excoriated the latter as "the very dregs and offal of the white population of America" and as "essentially stupid ... false, cruel, treacherous, base and bloody."[31]

Glorification of the Irishman's "religious and racial distinctiveness," the emphasis placed upon the bond between immigrant and native land, the extensive coverage of Irish affairs, the publication of Irish short stories – these fostered a cult of Irishness that promised "to create a sense of unity and identity." This provided, in turn, fertile ground for Irish nationalism, for most editors agreed "on the need for an aggressive, uncompromising nationalism to which the immigrant was said to be duty-bound." There remained disagreements over means. The more closely a newspaper was identified with the Church, the more likely its support for repeal and its constitutional pursuit. Irish independence was so revolutionary an objective that physical force would need to be employed, and "most Catholic journals opposed armed revolution." Yet the position of the foremost Catholic newspaper on the morality of political violence was sufficiently ambivalent to confuse many a reader. Originally established by the Bishop of Boston, the *Pilot* had been sold in 1834, but after several uncertain years it prospered under the ownership of Patrick Donahoe. He capitalized on Boston's position as the American terminus for the Cunard Line's vessels to introduce more extensive and current coverage of Irish affairs. An ardent supporter of Daniel O'Connell, something he advertised by marching through the city's streets outfitted in a green coat and sporting a large repeal badge, he gave the newspaper a harder nationalist edge. His appointment in 1844 of McGee, during an earlier sojourn in the United States, as editor-in-chief, led the bishop to distance himself from this organ of Young Ireland radicalism. He terminated his subscription and sponsored a rival, the *Catholic*

Observer. But Donahoe subsequently patched up relations with the diocese by placing a priest in the editor's chair.[32]

Father John Roddan initially accepted the legitimacy of popular uprisings so long as they sought both to protect the people from oppression and secure "their social well-being." His belief in the workings of divine providence convinced him that revolutions were "divinely purposive," and he had briefly voiced acceptance of a republic in Rome. However, violence and the threat of violence closer to home transformed this clerical radical into a reactionary, and Roddan was soon dismissing Europeans, republicans, and Young Irelanders as socialists and communists. This could not alter the fact that, as editor of the newspaper dubbed the "Irishman's Bible" and widely regarded as an organ of the Church, he had provided Irish American revolutionary nationalists with a justification of physical force. Similarly ambivalent signals flashed from New York. The *Freeman's Journal* remained a champion of constitutional nationalism, but the most influential Catholic churchman in the nation, and the controller of that newspaper, avowed his support for Irish rebellion in almost the same breath that he castigated Italian nationalists for their failure to restrict themselves to constitutional means.[33]

A younger son of a poor Ulster farmer, John Hughes had been one link in the family's chain migration to the United States. There he worked as a day labourer and gardener before entering the Church under the influence of a priest, John Dubois, whom he succeeded in 1842 as bishop of New York. He rapidly emerged as the hierarchy's dominant figure and came to be regarded as "the chief spokesman of American Catholicism." Over his fellow Irish Catholics, especially those of New York City, the nation's largest Irish community and eventually "the center of Irish political, cultural and social activism," he wielded unprecedented and unequalled influence. "I had to stand up among these people as their bishop and chief," he declared in 1857, "to knead them up into one dough, to be leavened by the spirit of Catholic faith and Catholic union." He strove to form them into "an ethnically exclusive, militantly Catholic body" under clerical leadership. Raised to the rank of metropolitan in 1850, Hughes had much in common with the Archbishop of Tuam. He was another autocrat who brooked no opposition within his province, tended to personalize differences, and was an unforgiving enemy. Aggressive, arrogant, argumentative, adversarial, he excoriated Protestantism, public education, mixed marriages, and priests, such as the ecumenical

Father Mathew, who associated with heretics. He publicly predicted the approaching triumph of Roman Catholicism in the United States, an impulsive and indiscreet statement given the republic's large Protestant majority and its history of anti-Catholicism. Of course, this helped to make a hero of him in the eyes of Irish Catholic immigrants with their history of discrimination suffered at the hands of Protestants. But Hughes, no less than John MacHale, was an Irish nationalist and an anglophobe.[34]

They were martyrs, Hughes assured his countrymen, who had been "crushed by an apostate nation, which prospers withal." Had they been Protestants, like the Scots, they would have escaped conquest and confiscation, yet they had survived centuries of persecution and oppression. They had been denied a country until they reached the shores of the United States, and by their transatlantic transplantation they had proved that they were "the most *moral* of people." The tragedy of the Famine had resulted from bad government and "a defective and vicious system of social economy." Moreover, there had been no genuine famine. Ireland had continued to produce the food needed to sustain her people, he reminded Irish Americans, but the harsh doctrine of political economy left them too poor "to pay for the harvest of their own labour," which was then exported to the richer market of Britain, "leaving them to die of famine or to live on alms." Had such a calamity visited the Scots, English, French, or Americans, he added, they would not have submitted "to die rather than violate the rights of property." When these remarks were subsequently published, he entitled the pamphlet "The Tyrant and His Famine." An ardent supporter of O'Connell and repeal, he declared in 1848 that if ever there was a country in which emancipation by violent means was justified, it was Ireland. He then made a personal donation of $500 to a cause "in every way worthy [of] a patriot and a Christian." He later insisted that his contribution had been intended for those in need, but in effect he had invited the faithful to help finance a resort to the "*sword.*" When his remarks were reprinted in Boston's diocesan organ, the *Catholic Observer*, the Confederation of United Friends of Ireland quickly seized upon them as "implicit approval by the Church" of a resort to force and launched a successful fundraising campaign. The rising's ignominious failure saw Hughes flail Young Irelanders for "deception and poltroonery," but his enmity for them was sharpened by their embrace of the anti-clerical Hungarian nationalist Louis Kossuth. As for the former rebels who found refuge in the United States, Hughes was soon at war with those of them, such as McGee, who had the effrontery to blame the Irish clergy for their failure. Not that Hughes forsook nationalism. He sponsored, helped finance, and wrote for the *Metropolitan Record*, which began publication early in 1859 and by year's end was recognized as "the official organ of the New York Archdiocese." Its political content was selectively nationalist. On the one hand, the Italians were condemned for seeking to incorporate the papal territories into the new nation state, while on the other, the British were denounced for their rule of Ireland.[35]

An archbishop with such strong nationalist sympathies was bound to influence the behaviour of his priests, especially the majority who came from Ireland and "worked in admiration of his ability." Irish clergy in the United States had long exhibited anti-English sentiments. A number refused "to celebrate the English saints," and even more were careful to label as "English" the objectionable Protestant Bible, whose origins made it doubly objectionable. Priests recruited from Maynooth, All Hallows, and the provincial seminaries arrived heavily influenced by O'Connell's successful fusion of Catholicism and popular nationalism, and required little encouragement either to indulge in "filio-pietistic displays" or to thunder against centuries of English oppression. Celebrations of St Patrick's Day became annual exercises in national consciousness-raising, an intoxicating mixture of faith and motherland. Every true patriot observed this Catholic holiday. In the words of the Bishop of Brooklyn, "There was very little patriotism in that heart where there was very little religion, for where you found the highest patriotism, and the maximum of piety, there you found the greatest love of country and God." Following High Mass and a sermon that reasserted religion as "the primary identity of Irish immigrants" by identifying them as the people chosen by God to carry Catholicism throughout the world, there were parades, speeches, and banquets. The "single most important, annual, symbolic manifestation of the vigor, prosperity, and power of their ethnic community," this day was marked by bold, belligerent, and on occasion bathetic public expressions of Irish nationalism. British tyranny, Irish martyrdom, "the hagiography of the Irish revolutionary tradition," the unnecessary horrors of the Famine, and mass emigration recast as exile were recurring themes of speakers. Here was a version of the past, an historic memory designed to unite Irishmen in hatred of Britain.[36]

Fervid denunciations of Britain by refugee Young Irelanders were to be expected, but the rhetorical excesses of priests, most of whom were "extremely influential" within the Irish community, were more dangerous still. From New York to California, clergy gave vent to anti-English sentiment. Father Cahill spoke for two and a half hours to an overflow crowd at the end of one New York St Patrick's Day parade, dilating on British perfidy. He may have been the anonymous author of a published letter in which Prime Minister Palmerston was accused of condemning to death "more than one million and a half " Irish emigrants entrusted to the captains of unseaworthy vessels. Father P.E. Moriarty of Philadelphia similarly chronicled "seven centuries of tyrannical heresy and despotic intolerance," culminating in the wrong and death of the Famine and the exile of emigration. He subsequently explained the significance of the denunciation of the British government as a tyranny. A tyranny was not, properly speaking, a government, he declared in a pamphlet, while resistance was lawful and revolution "holy" whenever a "government becomes tyrannical." England's "whole end and purpose" in Ireland was "the torture and extermination of those whom she [had] unceasingly named aliens in blood, language and religion." Moriarty acknowledged that the promoter of any rebellion evidently doomed to failure was the worst enemy of his country, though not because rebellion was bad in itself. Rather, it was because unsuccessful rebellion produced "greater calamity than [was] found in the patient endurance of illegal dominion." On the other hand, he who rebelled with every hope of success performed "the strict duty of the citizen" to prevent "the triumph of iniquity."[37]

The American branch of the Catholic Church, like its Irish counterpart, and Bishop Lynch in Canada West were fostering a passionate nationalism in which hatred of England often appeared to outweigh love of Ireland. Clergy had strengthened the "sense of peoplehood" and "feelings of national identification" that so many immigrants brought with them to the United States. The average Irishman denied being English because he was a Catholic, one visiting priest later observed. Moreover, the Church in Ireland and the United States constantly assured the Irish that they were a chosen people whose religion and nationality were inextricably bound together. It had been built upon the foundations of their "urban villages," inculcating ethnic values through national parishes, parochial schools, an Irish press, and St Patrick's Day festivities – little wonder so many second-generation Irish Americans considered themselves "Irish all the time." The urban village had been transformed into something of a fortress within whose metaphorical walls "people had a social and cultural as well as a religious ethnic community." Members of this increasingly cohesive group were therefore peculiarly susceptible to the nationalism preached by many of their priests and their press. The "anglophobic" Bishop England of Charleston long advocated the formation of a national network of political associations, some of which then took the lead in organizing and staging the St Patrick's Day celebrations. Milwaukee's Total Abstinence Society marked its first anniversary on 17 March 1843, attracting some three thousand Catholics to a parade, and the day closed with the founding of a Repeal Association. Groups boosting nationalism in Detroit received the support of numerous priests who used their churches to promote the national cause, thereby earning the admiration of their communities. In Chicago, clergy permitted nationalist organizations "to meet on the same basis" as voluntary, charitable associations, "thereby channelling nationalist fervor and reinforcing Irish and Catholic identities." The danger in this, even though all but a few of the priests involved restricted their advocacy to constitutional nationalism, was that it "resulted in distortions of the Church's redemptive theology, sustaining the ideology, liturgy, and martyrology of physical-force republicanism."[38]

Ethnicity is not a synonym for nationalism, and modern ethnic movements may "function chiefly to protect or advance the economic, cultural, or religious interests of persons who, by reason of some combination of actual or supposed common origin, language, or faith, believe they constitute one people." Nevertheless, religion and ethnicity had become virtually indistinguishable in the minds of a great number of Irish Catholics, and in combination they defined the national identity of those who remained at home and those who emigrated. For the "uprooted," nationalism may have offered security and stability. The Irish had little difficulty either identifying the requisite oppressor, sustaining the "cultural distinctness" that facilitates popular mobilization, or finding elites "able to communicate and organize effectively across class lines." Bishops of the "Hibernarchy," priests of national parishes, educators in parochial schools, publishers and editors of ethnic newspapers, whether clerical or lay, willingly nominated themselves as spokesmen for the objectives of the entire community.[39]

The susceptibility of Irish immigrants to anglophobia, as distinct from "hibernophilia," may have been heightened by natural resentment and envy of the greater ease with which other former residents of the United Kingdom appeared to fit into American society. Britons seemingly enjoyed greater employment opportunities and material success. If a higher proportion of British as opposed to Irish immigrants made it onto the land as farmers and possessed the skills highly valued in an industrializing economy, labourers still "comprised a majority or large plurality of the English immigrant stream." They laboured to amass the capital needed to purchase land. Like the Irish, they responded to the problems of cultural and economic adjustment by seeking British wives and reassuring association with fellow countrymen. Unlike the Irish, they were slow to adopt American citizenship and throw themselves into politics. Their Protestantism aided assimilation, at least in rural areas, through membership of local churches. Industrial workers, on the other hand, were less likely to attend places of worship. In short, the British exhibited little in the way of ethnic nationalism. They had "no obvious ethnic leaders to interpret American society for them, no existing institutions they could join, and no strong consciousness of an English-American or Scottish-American identity." Only in the face of Irish Catholic revolutionary nationalism did they tend to pull together as a British-American community.[40]

The cause of Irish freedom had been promoted in the American colonies by small groups of immigrants whose demands for political autonomy made them natural allies of radical colonials. Following American independence, several thousand United Irishmen arrived and introduced into Irish American nationalist ranks "a fierce dedication to revolutionary republican principles." Those nationalists may all have shared the belief that "Britain was the primary source of evil in the world," but a common hatred could not entirely paper over their differences. They were cursed with personality conflicts, power struggles, competition for the patronage spoils resulting from their domestic political alliance with Jeffersonian Republicans, and disagreement over the inescapable problem of the future of slavery in the self-proclaimed land of liberty. A minority supported emancipation of the slaves, but the majority continued to indulge a fondness for victimhood. The suffering of no other people could be compared with the oppression of the Irish. If "slavery was an evil it was one that could be tolerated without too much difficulty." Americans seeking its abolition, especially any who spoke of "the right of resistance," were inviting the horrors of a servile insurrection. This same issue bedevilled O'Connell's relations with some American supporters of repeal, as did the residual effects of his earlier and successful agitation for Catholic emancipation. The struggle to achieve emancipation had gradually intensified the sectarian character of Irish nationalism, and Protestant Irish Americans began to drift away from repeal, eventually redefining themselves as "Scotch-Irish." This was something the Catholic Church welcomed and encouraged. Meanwhile, some former United Irishmen concluded "that revolutionary violence was counterproductive" and that peaceful reform had been vindicated by emancipation's triumph. Yet the political refugees of 1798 bequeathed an ominous legacy to future generations of nationalists. They had justifiably interpreted their emigration as exile; they had waged an unrelenting anti-British campaign through newspapers, memoirs, and patriotic societies that, in depicting the government of Ireland as a tyranny, legitimized a resort to physical force; and they had argued that the Irish of America should aid the cause at home by supplying nationalists there with means, muscle, and morale.[41]

Many middle-class immigrants and second-generation Irish Americans organized American auxiliaries of O'Connell's Repeal Association. The cause captured the imagination of a large element of the swiftly swelling ranks of Catholic Irish, and it enjoyed a broader and deeper measure of popular support than the earlier nationalist agitation. The Church and its clergy had helped ready them for involvement by binding them together in ethnic enclaves, strengthening their sense of national identity and of national injustice suffered at the hands of the British, and fomenting a national antipathy for the "villainous exploiter." More than this, as in Ireland and areas of British North America, priests provided nationalist leadership. Funds were raised and forwarded to Dublin in amounts that quickly dwarfed the total supplied to the Catholic Association little more than a decade earlier. A priest personally delivered the modest sum donated by the Mobile Association, and several thousand dollars was forwarded from the sparsely populated Wisconsin territory during the first six months of the local association's existence. The Boston Association remitted $10,000. Mass parades were staged, startling one English visitor to New York City, but as ever, tensions complicated relations within the nationalist movement and not least between members of the extended American family and its Irish head.[42]

Although O'Connell was a master of the implied threat of violence, those elements of the repeal leadership in the United States that looked back to the United Irishmen for their inspiration indulged a taste for forthright rhetorical violence with which he would have been distinctly uncomfortable. In the Southern states especially, "England's 'reign of terror'" was denounced and outright war threatened. Elsewhere, plans were set afoot to establish an arms fund, while a national convention in New York heard proposals to boycott British goods and seize Canada with the support of dissident French Canadians and the large Irish core of the imperial garrison there. Other Irish American nationalists urged the United States to hold firm to its territorial claim to "all" Oregon in the expectation that this would result in an Anglo-American war. They saw in such a conflict a means to free Ireland while enlarging the United States – hence the comment of a British Cabinet minister that the Irish were "too bad everywhere."[43]

Another issue disruptive of nationalist unity was the future of the institution of slavery. O'Connell had strongly supported West Indian emancipation a decade earlier and had more recently been highly critical, if not scornful, of the slave republic across the Atlantic. Courted by American abolitionists, he accepted as valid the analogy drawn by William Lloyd Garrison between the slaveholder's relationship to his human property and England's conduct towards Ireland. Indeed, the Liberator repeatedly stated "that he did not regard as Irish any man who condoned slavery." At other times he backed and filled on the issue, failing to establish clear guidelines on the acceptability of funds contributed by those American auxiliaries whose members supported the institution. Inevitably, his conduct attracted criticism. Bishop England in Charleston, Bishop Hughes in New York, the Boston *Pilot*, even Irish miners in Pennsylvania, entered the lists against O'Connell's meddling in domestic American affairs. England wrote a series of public letters asserting that the Catholic tradition was directed not against the institution of slavery but against the trade in human beings. For his part, Hughes exposed himself to the abolitionist counter-thrust that his concept of foreign intervention was a one-way street. He was happy to meddle in British affairs. But O'Connell's decision in the spring of 1843 no longer to accept "blood-stained" money prompted all of the Southern associations save that in Savannah to dissolve, caused schism in Philadelphia, and saw donations dwindle even before the Liberator's personal humiliation at Clontarf.[44]

News of the Great Famine saw Irish Americans overcome their dif-

ferences to pull together in campaigns to aid their suffering homeland. Thus, in Wisconsin, repeal "became a movement for Irish
relief," but the cause was not confined to the Irish American community. Other nationalities and native-born Americans participated
in the special relief committees established across the nation, such as
the one in Milwaukee that "gave most generously to support the famishing." Inevitably, cities with huge Irish populations made the
largest contributions. New York and Boston forwarded substantial
sums of money, while the Philadelphia committee raised $48,000 in
cash and shipped another $20,000 worth of supplies to Ireland.
Opinion leaders, such as Bishop Hughes, were quick to point the fin-
ger of blame at Britain and her "crushing tyranny." The Bishop of
Boston, in an emotional appeal for aid delivered from the pulpit of
his cathedral, did not overlook the "galling fetter" that bound Ireland
to the United Kingdom.[45]

Against this background, and with the formation of the Confederation by the Young Irelanders following their break with O'Connell,
the emergence of a truly radical nationalist faction for whom John
Mitchel spoke and Fintan Lalor served as an ideologist, and then the
revolution in France, a powerful current of excitement pulsated
through Irish America. Local "Directories" were established, much as
repeal auxiliaries had been earlier, to fund agitation and action in Ireland. Bishop Hughes gave explicit support to this effort in New York,
and in Boston it received the implicit approval of the diocese. The
New York Directory reputedly raised $40,000 in just a few weeks,
while more modest sums were forwarded from smaller Irish centres,
such as New Orleans. Ambitious plans were set afoot to organize an
"Irish Brigade" expeditionary force to assist in the liberation of the
homeland. The hope that republican France would agree to act as a
munitions entrepôt was quickly dashed by a government that placed
realism ahead of idealism. Other projects included the rescue of
Mitchel from the Antipodes and an invasion of the Canadian
provinces to coincide with rebellion in Ireland. Both fell through. The
naive assumption of those looking north was that "hundreds of thousands of patriotic Irishmen" resident there, as well as a great many
Canadians, desired annexation to the "great and glorious republic."
The prize of the Irish vote in an election year that saw the presidency,
one-third of the Senate, and the entire House of Representatives
at stake tempted a number of American politicians into rash expansionist comments. The governor general of British North America

recognized the electoral stimulus to the rhetoric, but he did not doubt that covetous Americans had designs on the British territories. But the demoralizing news from Ireland of the "cabbage patch" rebellion sapped the Irish Americans' will to fight and exposed fresh divisions within their ranks.[46]

The revolutionary year had produced, however, a far more passionate Irish American marriage of "republican separatism and physical force," and this was one union the Young Ireland exiles were determined should endure. They realized that they might "exercise an immense influence" over their fellow countrymen in the United States, while the few who escaped or were released from the Van Dieman's Island penal colony were hailed as heroes on arrival in the republic. Exiles and martyrs, they travelled the Union giving stirring lectures, wrote memoirs or histories – McGee's *History of the Irish Settlers in North America* went through six editions within four years of publication in 1851 – and founded newspapers. They were seeking to arouse and sustain a revolutionary nationalism rooted ever more deeply in hatred of England, and John Mitchel quickly emerged as the most powerful propagator of this message.[47]

Mitchel reached the United States in 1853 and early the following year launched the *Citizen* in New York. His co-publisher was Thomas Francis Meagher, whose earlier escape from the penal colony had been shrouded in controversy following accusations that he had dishonourably violated his parole. Mitchel concluded, without apparently intending the irony, that the issue would be resolved in Meagher's favour by his friends and those of the cause. But Meagher took little interest in the running of the *Citizen*, or even of the *Irish News*, which he later founded. He continued with his rewarding lecture tours, secured admission to the New York bar, acquired American citizenship, and pursued alternative paths of personal advancement. In the prospectus for their newspaper, the two men had emphasized their years of "penal exile at the hands of the British Government," their resolute commitment to the cause of Irish independence, their conviction that western and southern nations were moving towards republicanism, their refusal to believe that Irishmen at home or in the United States were willing to abandon the drive for Irish freedom, and the necessity to exploit favourable international developments to advance the cause. Thus Mitchel personally approached the Russians in 1854, as the likelihood of war between that empire and Britain and France increased, urging them to equip a diversionary Irish rising. They were too sceptical of the logistics of such an enterprise to endorse it. Meanwhile, Mitchel sought to spell out for naturalized Irish-Americans "*what* their rights [were] as American citizens, and what they [might] lawfully and conscientiously do in the direction of liberating their native country from British dominion." He believed that a hundred thousand of them only awaited the opportunity to get to grips with the "tyrants who oppressed their kinsmen at home," and week in week out the *Citizen* laid before them "the true nature" of Britain's "atrocious policy" in Europe, in America, and in Ireland. This "clear understanding" would ensure that Irish Americans were ready "to act more zealously when the day of action came." The *Citizen* was an organ of physical force propaganda.[48]

Mitchel's anglophobia seemingly knew no bounds, for, as he proudly declared, hatred was the thing he "chiefly cherished and cultivated." Or as he informed the Russian minister to the United States, "England (that is the English Empire, English Government, English *thing*, as Cobbett called it) is the enemy of the human race; and the most authentic agent and viceregent of the Fiend upon the earth." The British government could never be on the same side as justice, he declared to one friend, until the whole structure of British society had been destroyed by revolution. Was this hatred the product of a philosophical commitment to individual liberty that British rule in Ireland violated? If so, it was not without contradictions and ironies. Black slaves were not embraced by it, for even as an exile in the Antipodes Mitchel had denied any "virtuous indignation" over the "peculiar institution." Instead, he recalled that "the grandest states and greatest and best nations have been slaveholding states and nations." He was another defender of a "benevolent" institution that in his opinion stood in stark humanitarian relief to the "wage slavery" of Britain and the industrializing states of the American Union. Liberty was reserved in his mind for peoples equipped to exercise its responsibilities, and this level of civilization had yet to be achieved by African Americans. The irony here was the employment by many Britons of the very same argument to dismiss Irish demands for greater political autonomy.[49]

Mitchel's hatred was always more pathological than ideological, and at times it appeared to be virtually all-embracing. At its core, eating away at his reason like some insidious and terminal disease, was perfidious Albion. He assailed American abolitionists as dupes of a British conspiracy to disrupt the United States and promoters of the nativist hostility to Irish immigrants, which he again traced to a British source. Anti-Catholicism was another English import, and his position on the freer trade in goods was determined by the hope that a tariff wall around American industries would damage British commerce. His *Jail Journal*, first published in serialized form in the *Citizen*, sought not only to vindicate his claim to have suffered a martyrdom for Ireland but also to foment a fresh outburst of Irish American anger against British injustice. While still a prisoner, he had bitterly resented press descriptions of his gentlemanly penal exile, joined as he had been by his family on a modest farm. "The truth is this state is a living death," he protested to one correspondent, "and is only not utter misery because it is not embittered by remorse and disgrace." He had been condemned to live among "de-civilized savages" who united "more than the brutality of Timbuctoo with all the loathsome corruptions of London." Yet even he was unable entirely to conceal the extraordinary nature of his imprisonment in "Demon's Land," where he had enjoyed considerable freedom of movement and "the glorious health" that the matchless climate allowed, had mingled in the society of "the good quite [free] colonists," and had been able to associate covertly with his fellow political prisoners, one of whom was permitted to establish a newspaper.[50]

The main thrust of the *Jail Journal* was to be found in its lengthy introduction and first few pages. They catalogued English crimes and British tyrannies in Ireland: the rebellion of 1798 had been deliberately provoked to frighten the gentry into the Union, only for the provocateurs to lose control of it; Ireland's industry and produce had been placed entirely in Britain's power; the Irish had been deliberately and permanently under-represented in Parliament; and chronic suffering had become a feature of Irish life as food was exported to Britain, the full extent of the trade being cunningly concealed, with the result that "the exact complement of a comfortable family dinner in England, is a coroner's inquest in Ireland: verdict, Starvation." Every Parliament enacted an arms bill with the intent "to deprive all mere Celts of necessary weapons for defence, and to kill in them the spirit of men." Daniel O'Connell's successful campaign for Catholic emancipation had been the ruin of him and his nation, for it had led many to the false conclusion that by "mere *agitation*, by harmless exhibition of numerical force, by imposing demonstrations (which are fatal nonsense), and by eternally half-unsheathing a visionary sword, which friends and foes alike knew to be a phantom," he had compelled the Wellington administration to admit Catholics to Parliament and some offices. Instead, the Relief Bill had been passed to attract educated Catholics to the British interest. Mitchel claimed for himself the distinction of demonstrating that there was no alternative to violence in Ireland. His prosecution before a packed jury by a supposedly enlightened Whig government had proved that there was no true law for the Irish, and this knowledge ought to end all thought of constitutional agitation. He had "shamed the country out of 'moral force'" by revealing to it that there was "but one and all-sufficient remedy, *the edge of the sword*." Further, Mitchel provided his countrymen with the most profound justification for a resort to violence – the Famine had been an act of Irish extermination by a "diabolical" British government.[51]

In a series of letters published in 1858 and three years later distributed in book form under the title of *The Last Conquest of Ireland (Perhaps)*, Mitchel expanded on the *Jail Journal*'s introduction and indictment. He, more than anyone else, successfully imprinted the terrible charge of genocide on the Irish historic memory. Assertions that two million Irish had been killed by the British and another million driven into exile; that mothers driven insane by anxiety and hunger had resorted to cannibalism, eating their young; and that dogs had dined on human carcasses were calculated to horrify and inflame readers. Victims of the Famine were recast as martyrs and placed alongside the Catholics executed by Cromwell and those who suffered under the Penal Laws. Yet popular acceptance of his declaration that "God sent the blight but the English created the Famine" may have been eased by his readers' recollections of the charges of murder brought against the British by respected opinion leaders during the darkest days of the Famine. Bishop Hughes along with members of the Irish hierarchy had held the government in London entirely responsible for the Famine, labelling its policy "extermination." More recently, D'Arcy McGee, in his immensely popular *History*, had repeated the less emotive but bitter claim that there had been food enough in Ireland to feed the starving before its shipment to Britain. In short, Mitchel's interpretation of the Famine appeared to be consistent with that of other observers. Moreover, it provided many of the survivors of the tragedy with an escape from the feelings of guilt they harboured as a result of their own conduct, or inaction, when confronted with human suffering on a terrifying scale. Responsibility for the disaster was allowed to rest entirely with the British government.[52]

Mitchel's influence had its limits. He urged Irish Americans to enrol in state militias, and thus gain training and a basic education in tactics. But the enthusiasm with which such companies were formed, some of them bearing Mitchel's name, undoubtedly owed as much to the attractions of fellowship and a sense of power within the broader society as it did to a desire to prepare for the liberation of the homeland. Mitchel also engaged John Hughes in a bitter and costly personal exchange. The archbishop sought to tarnish this Protestant's reputation among Catholics first by implying that he was another Orangeman and then by ridiculing his fondness for slavery. However ironic this line of attack from a cleric who had gone to such pains to distance himself from O'Connell on the slavery question, Mitchel was aware of the embarrassment his own stand caused other advocates of Irish emancipation. He declared that he would respond "Yes" to those who asked sardonically whether he would like an Irish republic with slave plantations. Not surprisingly, he decided to leave New York. Lacking the means to carry off his family to Paris and its pleasures, he initially opted for the Tennessee "backwoods." He found a spot he described as one of the most beautiful and most barbarous in the United States, but his passion for the wilderness quickly cooled. He moved to the city of Knoxville, where he launched the *Southern Citizen*. Irish as well as Southern, the newspaper helped to make Mitchel the most influential Irish nationalist in the slave states.[53]

Mitchel never tired of informing his fellow countrymen that they and he were exiles from their native land. "*Here we are*, exiles from an island home that but for alien laws and rank misrule thousands of us might now cling to, and which, notwithstanding her misfortunes and unhappiness, we cherish as the apple of our eye." But why did so many immigrants respond to an assertion so at odds with their personal decision to seek a better life in a new land? Was it the result of a cultural definition of emigration as exile, an overpowering homesickness originating in a uniquely mystical attachment to the homeland? The attachment was equally as strong for the Welsh and the Scots, and many of the latter had every reason to regard emigration as banishment by tyrannical landlords. As for the Irish "assessment of 'forced-exile-by-cruel-landlords,'" that appears "mainly to have been made by those left behind" during the massive migration of the Famine years. Furthermore, many of those who emigrated were aware that successful, middle-class Catholic farmers were often no less responsible than Protestant landlords for a situation that made departure advisable if not essential. Equally, some emigrants welcomed their "escape from a stifling and profoundly resented social and familial order" and thus suffered "few sentimental reverberations." The chances of acquiring land and a spouse were more limited in Ireland after the Famine than before and were at best likely to be long postponed. Perhaps an even stronger indication of how few in number were the emigrants who initially considered themselves exiles and regarded America only as a temporary refuge was their conspicuous failure to return home to live. Irish returnees never matched those of other immigrant groups. The astonishing sums sent back to Ireland as remittances, either to strengthen the links of chain migration or make more comfortable the lives of those family members who had remained there, and the letters sent home encouraging others to follow the writers across the Atlantic suggested that lack of material success was a far from complete explanation of this anomaly. Most of the Catholic Irish had simply made better lives for themselves in the United States and British North America. As one pre-Famine era immigrant reported home, disappointment and loneliness were predictable during the first six months of residence but the United States remained "a fine country and a much better place for a poor man than Ireland." Yet the status of exile proved to be a fluid one, allowing for the transformation of the emigrant as circumstances changed in the homeland or acceptance was resisted by the host community. Those who fled from the Famine had for the latter reason greater cause to consider themselves exiles.[54]

The structure of Irish American society virtually assured wide acceptance of the dubious claim that emigration had in fact been exile. Members of a church increasingly Irish in character, from "Hibernarchy" to national parish priest, a priest regarded as father, magistrate, and monarch; readers of an ethnic press; graduates of a parochial school – Irish immigrants and their children were constantly exposed to nationalism's proselytizers and propagandists. They acquired the exile's profound interest in his homeland. They were taught that Ireland was the victim of a tyranny of unparalleled severity, that Britain was responsible for all of Ireland's ills, and that she was answerable for the problems of the Irish in America. Foremost among these was the almost singular hostility with which native-born Americans regarded them. Moreover, their American victimizers, Anglo-Saxon and Protestant, bore a remarkable resemblance in race and religion to the Irishmen at whose hands they had historically suffered. Rejection inevitably deepened the depression and heightened the paranoia to which all immigrants were susceptible. A sense of exclusion gave additional stimulus to the "formation of an autonomous, separatist subculture," yet there was a chicken and egg conundrum here. The enclave consciousness and ethnoreligious behaviour of Catholic Irish immigrants, their nationalism, their apparent rejection of assimilation helped excite the nativist enmity to which they fell victim.[55]

7

American Nativism
and Irish Nationalism

The Catholic Irish who emigrated to the United States excited the
enmity of their hosts "by disorderly conduct, absurd prejudices, [and
a] half-civilized and intemperate mode of life." So wrote an Irish priest,
who went on: they injured themselves by a want of that "sober reflection and steady perseverance" that enabled Germans to overcome
"greater disadvantages" and get ahead in their adopted land. Indeed,
they compounded their problems by a seemingly exclusive love of their
native land and a relentless harping on its wretchedness and misery in
order "to exaggerate the highly wrought pictures of political discontent
at home, or to flatter the pride of free born Americans." By blaming all
of Ireland's troubles on Britain and the existing system of government,
thereby exculpating her people and themselves "from being instru-
mental to some extent in the continuance" of evils, they confirmed
many Americans in their "unfavourable and frequently unjust impressions" of that country and its inhabitants.[1]

Americans were similarly irritated and disturbed by the immense
number and "clannishness" of the Catholic immigrants, Irish and German. They accused them of creating alien communities "almost as
impervious to American sentiments and influences as the inhabitants of
Dublin and Hamburg." Cheap and ethnically distinct immigrant
labour was a particular grievance of American working people, especially during the cyclical hard times of an industrializing economy,
when they viewed the Irish as "symbols of [their] deteriorating status
within American industrialism." The heavy criticism of the Catholic
Irish for their dependence on charity and residence in almshouses had
much to do with the mounting "nativist" hostility to these "foreign"
beneficiaries of public relief. It found expression in the reluctance of
many Americans to contribute to relief funds during the recession of

the late 1850s, in the stinginess of public relief, in the abandonment of the traditional efforts to reform and rehabilitate paupers, and in the progressively more draconian regimes established in poorhouses.[2]

Irish pauperism was frequently traced to the bottle, and temperance crusaders, such as those in Northfield, Vermont, indicted the Catholic Irish for the epidemic of "'beastly drunkenness.'" Nor was this a gender evil. Irish women were reputed to be as addicted to strong drink as their menfolk, and drunken immigrants were a peculiar affront to the swelling number of Americans who considered abstinence a stepping stone to personal success and respectability. Of course, native-born Americans drank heavily and abstinence was by no means a purely Protestant crusade. Catholic societies were at work in several cities by 1840, the year that saw the American hierarchy give hesitant support to a movement that several of their number associated with fanaticism. Father Mathew arrived in the summer of 1849, having been sent off from Ireland with a nationalist flea in his ear. He ought to be visiting the United States as the "'Ambassador of Temperance'" and in "'nowise as the secret ambassador of the British Ministry,'" the *Freeman's Journal* cruelly remarked. In fact, he was seeking to recover his health and raise enough money to pay off his personal debts and complete his church in Cork. Over the course of the next two years he travelled thirty-seven thousand miles, visited twenty-five states, administered the pledge in more than three hundred urban centres, and added more than half a million names to temperance rolls. Many who took the pledge were Irish Americans. However, the nationalists' attack, the suspicion that Mathew's "ecumenical attitudes" aroused within the ranks of the hierarchy, the severe criticism he suffered at the hands of the nation's most ardent abolitionist for his refusal to align himself publicly with that cause, his difficulties with Southern temperance advocates because of his earlier identification with O'Connell's opposition to slavery, and his denunciation by two of the most influential slave states' senators, John Calhoun and Jefferson Davis, militated against a decisive victory. The fundraising had been a failure, and he departed the United States broken in health and virtually bankrupt. He subsequently appealed to Paul Cullen for aid in securing from the Pope an episcopal appointment in the Caribbean, but the archbishop was not about to recommend for a bishopric a priest who had been awarded a modest pension by the British government for his earlier good works. Father Mathew died in 1856. Meanwhile, neither limited Catholic Irish involvement in the anti-liquor movement, which nevertheless distinguished them from German immigrants, nor the culture of drinking that American Protestant working people shared had shaken the popular reputation of the Irish as the nation's principal drunken brawlers. Irish ownership or management of the multiplying grog shops, bars, and saloons of Atlantic coast cities, the statistical evidence that the Catholic Irish accounted for a very large proportion of persons arrested for drunkenness, and their prominence in a series of bloody popular protests against the more rigorous enforcement of liquor laws served to strengthen this unsavoury reputation.[3]

That the drinking of alcohol led to crime, insanity, and disease seemed obvious to many contemporaries. The extent of foreign-born, but especially Irish, confinement in prisons and lunatic asylums may well have been distorted and exaggerated by inaccuracies in the published data, but its interpreters found a ready explanation of the ethnic colouring. "The want of forethought in them to save their earnings for the day of sickness, the indulgence of their appetites for stimulating drinks," together with "their strong love for their native land," were identified by the administrator of one state institution as "the fruitful sources of insanity among them." As in the case of the poorhouses, the large presence of the foreign born in prisons and asylums contributed to a loss of popular faith and interest in their reformative and rehabilitative possibilities. Instead, punishment became the norm of such institutions. Irish intemperance and lack of personal cleanliness, their reputation as carriers of disease, also provided their hosts with a convenient explanation of the epidemics that swept through large cities. Most were traced, accurately or not, to an Irish enclave. The "ignorant and filthy thousands" had come among them "like the frogs of Egypt," and around their homes gathered "the filth and stench that invited pestilence," one newspaper complained. Thus was disease "socially constructed by nativists to stigmatize Irish immigrants."[4]

Irish youths were similarly conspicuous among the ever-swelling ranks of juvenile offenders, prompting reformatories and refuges to emulate adult prisons and abandon reformation. The alarming increase in juvenile crime served to remind many Americans of yet another long-standing grievance against the Catholic Irish. Public school and Protestant Bible were widely held to be the essential means for the successful transformation of the "impressionable and pliable child into a morally mature Christian adult." This was considered particularly important for Catholic children if they were to learn to think for themselves and thus escape "the shackles of Roman Despotism." Members of the hierarchy complained with some justice of "the printed slanders of the Catholic Church" found in public school texts and their eulogizing of "Protestant divines and martyrs." There was, however, an ironic aspect to their protest that schoolchildren could scarcely open a book that did not portray one or more Catholic institutions and practices in a manner greatly to the Church's disadvantage and that "'the entire system of education'" was "'tinged throughout its whole course.'" Much the same charge had been levelled by Irish Anglicans against the texts produced by the Christian Brothers. Some Catholic leaders took condemnation even further, provocatively denouncing public schools as prolific hotbeds of crime and sin. Then, adding injury to such insults, Catholic bishops applied for public monies to finance parochial institutions. By so doing, they stirred up a nest of Protestant hornets.[5]

Damned as indigent, intemperate, irresponsible, infected, and ignorant, Catholic Irish immigrants were also cursed with a reputation for violence. This was not entirely a figment of overwrought middle-class imaginations. The "wild" Irish appeared to stand in sharp contrast to stolid Germans and the "right thinking" English and Welsh. Sensational accounts of ethnic brawls aboard emigrant vessels, in which the Irish were invariably depicted as the aggressors, brawls that on occasion spilled over onto the docks when Irish stevedores took up the cudgels in aid of their battered countrymen, were cited as evidence of the importation of the well-developed and insatiable Irish appetite for violence. Terrorism was a feature of a number of labour disputes, such as those on canal construction sites and in the Pennsylvania coalfields, and it drew upon the "Irish peasant tradition of secret societies" and "collective violence." Locked in desperate struggles with industrial employers over regular employment, control of the labour market, wages, and conditions of work, the Irish "understood not only how violence in contexts of their own choosing was an equalizer against a powerful enemy, but also how potent and strategic was the *threat* of violence, which gave one some of the same benefits at much reduced cost." At times the violence was intra-ethnic, but the Catholic Church worked hard to stamp it out. More commonly it was inter-ethnic and directed against competitors for work, reluctant strikers, strikebreakers, managers, and employers. The involvement of "Paddyesses" in strong-arm industrial actions and street fights was merely the additional evidence that helped to satisfy a jury of native-born Americans that the Irish personality "tended towards violence because Irish society stressed fighting, aggressiveness, and combativeness."[6]

Extraordinary incidents, such as the Irish stoning of the dignitaries attending the ceremonial opening of the Illinois and Michigan Canal and the frequent and bloody collisions of Irish "canallers" with the residents of the areas through which they were digging, inevitably antagonized the host society. So did the street brawling in Irish urban enclaves. In these, the Irish were often responding to insults to their nationality, resisting territorial encroachments by other immigrant groups, opposing efforts to regulate more strictly the liquor business, 'influencing' the outcome of elections, conducting warfare against rival gangs, as well as engaging in drunken fights and domestic abuse. Whatever the cause or provocation, many contemporaries found in the violent Irishman a convenient explanation of an increasingly and alarmingly disorderly urban environment. Nor did the professional police forces established in cities such as Boston and New York quickly inspire a great deal of confidence, given their Irish complexion. Men of Irish birth made up more than one-quarter of the total force in New York City, and that proportion was higher still in some heavily Irish wards, but arrest records did not suggest any ethnic favouritism. Furthermore, the deadly rioting in the summer of 1857 was precipitated by a partisan attempt by Republican state legislators to weaken Irish influence and to restructure the New York City force in an effort to make it a less effective instrument of the rival Democratic Party and a more effective agency for the enforcement of temperance.[7]

Some Americans were at pains to distinguish the Irish who had arrived before the Famine, a substantial proportion of whom were Protestants, from the Catholic multitude who followed them to the republic. In Lowell the former won favourable comment for educating their children in public schools and for "appreciating order, cleanliness, and respectability on a Yankee scale." There had also been general acceptance of other British and British North American immigrants, none of whom sought to establish a separate "communal religious life." On the contrary, they affiliated "with churches composed largely of Americans." Nor were the Germans, their language notwithstanding, "nearly as separated socially and culturally from Americans as the Irish." The German press was only too willing to join American newspapers in a campaign to identify violence, crime, drunkenness, and electoral intimidation and corruption exclusively with the Catholic Irish community. The Irish served as "a perfect foil" for the "efforts to draw boundaries around ethnic standards of proper behavior," but they did earn a measure of public sympathy. The harsh exploitation of Irish labour attracted editorial comment and criticism, while members of New England's intellectual and literary circles, including Margaret Fuller, John Greenleaf Whittier, and Walt Whitman, championed them. Conversely, Henry Thoreau and Ralph Waldo Emerson dealt in stereotypes. The Catholic Irish were never destined "to occupy any very high place in the human family," they remarked, and then described the identification of the Irishman with the family pig as unfair to the animal, since it was "comparatively clean about [its] lodgings."[8]

During their own long pre-revolutionary struggle with imperial authority, American radicals had looked to Ireland's Protestant patriots and incipient nationalists as potential allies. Benjamin Franklin visited Dublin in the autumn of 1771 in search of allies against the rigid exercise of imperial authority. He failed to find them, but the Irish exploited the subsequent revolutionary war to secure a greater measure of legislative independence for themselves. Ireland continued to be regarded sympathetically in the newly independent United States, but before long the more conservative elements in American society became far more critical of the Irish. The arrival in the temporary national capital of Philadelphia of "new Irish" immigrants after 1790, the founding of the Hibernian Society in 1791, the activities there of the American Society of United Irishmen from 1796, Irish denunciations of Jay's Treaty, signed with Britain, their accusation that the Washington administration was under "'a very strong British influence,'" and their rallying to the emergent Jeffersonian opposition to the ruling Federalists all prompted the latter to charge that the infant republic's independence and security were being threatened by "Irish ways." They assailed these immigrant voters as "violent, corrupt and easily bought by alcohol," setting the pattern for future generations of detractors. The alliance of the United Irishmen and French revolutionaries saw the Irish immigrants, many of them Protestants, convicted of guilt by association with "international conspiracy and political agitation." Their nation was becoming "a receptacle of malevolence and turbulence, for the outcasts of the universe," Federalists charged. Their political heirs, the Whigs, were far more persistent in their overtures to the increasingly significant Irish voters, not least during the excitement of the repeal years and the revolutions of 1848, only to be rebuffed. This rejection "tended both to drive the Whigs into the arms of nativism and to enhance the Whig thirst for political power which control of the Irish vote might bring."[9]

The "half-contemptuous" American opinion of the Catholic Irish slowly evolved into one that was far more critical. A good-natured, warm-hearted, earthy and courageous, if wild and pugnacious, Catholic Irishman – only somewhat troublesome in a well-ordered society – was transformed into a buffoon capable of wit, a trickster wearing the "mask of the fool," an amoral violator of the law, an unrepentant criminal, and an unregenerate brawler. If dramatists increasingly cast the Irish bumpkin as comic relief, confident that he would draw a response from the most difficult of audiences, Americans in general considered the Irish less rational and less civilized than themselves, a people whose many deplorable traits had finally overwhelmed their fewer virtues. Even so, there was a lingering willingness to regard the Irishman as an unfortunate product of his environment. British misgovernment was partially responsible for Paddy's retarded development, but other Americans embraced a sinister, pseudo-scientific explanation of his shortcomings, one that eventually united them and Britons in a "racial nativism."[10]

Nativism was one of nationalism's uglier faces. Native-born Americans, their nation still in its infancy, striving for a clear definition of national identity and increasingly aware of the threat that slavery posed to national unity, rounded on the alien and seemingly unassimilable elements within their society. There was a sense that assimilation required a degree of cultural integration that would leave newcomers indistinguishable from their hosts. Immigrants who arrived en masse only to parade a separate ethnic and religious identity presented an inviting and easy target for sceptics who doubted that "Old World subjects" could be speedily transformed into "New World citizens." No group was more conspicuous in this regard than the Catholic Irish. Their rejection of public schools was interpreted as a rejection of the system that "Americanized" the foreign population. Hence the decision by some other immigrants to join "anti-foreign associations" in an effort to win acceptance by Americans. Nativist hate was more fiercely directed against naturalized citizens of Irish descent than it was against naturalized citizens of any other foreign extraction, one ethnic newspaper acknowledged. Turnabout being fair play, expressions of nativist contempt for German immigrants received the "qualified approval" of several influential Irish Catholic spokesmen. The Boston *Pilot* was surely indulging a taste for irony when it suggested that denial of political power to the German community might cause posterity to regard nativism more charitably, its ignorance and bigotry notwithstanding. However, it remained the conviction of nativists that the Irish were peculiarly unqualified for the responsibilities of American citizenship. Their preservation of a "'distinctive nationality'" was one of the reasons given. Another was their long subservience to British rule; they had thereby developed habits of servility and dependence that in the United States would see them "all too easily become a tool of unethical and overcompetitive native politicians and their supporters."[11]

Dislike of all foreigners was "one of the strongest of the national prejudices of the mass of the people of America," English visitors to the republic concluded, but noted its peculiar intensity in those areas of the Union where the Irish were most heavily concentrated. Again, the reasons appeared plain enough. Americans resented Irish clannishness, their heavy involvement in the liquor trade and heavy drinking, the additional financial burdens resulting from their especially heavy resort to poorhouses and hospitals for the indigent sick, their "ruffianism" at work and at play, and their enthusiastic participation in politics. Their growing political influence was regarded as an extension of their unwelcome clannishness, creating as this did an Irish bloc vote in a number of urban centres. Additionally, they were charged with a willingness to direct their violence to electoral ends and to be agents of political corruption. Stories were legion of Catholic Irish immigrants stepping ashore in the morning and voting illegally in the afternoon. The indictment embraced their priests, who were accused of acting as political organizers. John Hughes's organization of a slate of Catholic candidates in New York committed to public support of parochial schools was cited as a case in point.[12]

From the republic's earliest days the curtailment of the political rights of immigrants was a fundamental objective of embryonic nativists. The Alien and Sedition Acts of 1798 prompted one Irish-born newspaper editor to describe them as an attempt to cut Irish immigrants off from the prospect of freedom that had induced them to enter the United States. The Federalists who gathered in Hartford, Connecticut, in December of 1814, to seek revisions to the Constitution, demanded the legal exclusion of naturalized citizens from federal civil offices. This was not an objective likely to be realized in a society where some jurisdictions permitted adult aliens to vote after only a brief residence. Just such a liberal provision, written into the Illinois Constitution, allowed ten thousand foreigners onto the state's electoral rolls within two decades. The fact that so many immigrant voters supported the Democratic Party did not sit well with other members of that party, let alone their opponents. "I claim to be a Democrat myself," one grumbled, "but I do not go for electing Irish Democrats all the way from Ireland to legislate and to execute the laws, as though no one among ourselves is fit for such offices." Similar complaints were heard in New York, where these "strangers" without "a feeling of patriotism or affection in common with American citizens" were believed to have decided the most important elections. In truth, in Paterson, New Jersey, as in Chicago, Illinois, the Irish attracted attention to themselves not only by voting heavily, disrupting opposition meetings, and assailing the Whigs as lackeys of the British, but also by running for and winning office. Even in cities such as New Orleans, where their political influence was always more potential than actual, they alarmed Americans who worried that they might, should they so choose, determine the result of electoral battles. Hence the organization there, and elsewhere, of Native American Associations committed to lengthening the period of an immigrant's residence before he became eligible to vote and to excluding the foreign born from public office. Newcomers should at least wait the twenty-one years served by native-born males between birth and majority, nativists argued. These demands became the platform of the American Republican Party, which sprang up in major Southern, Western and Northern cities, though it was equally committed to Bible reading in public schools. Thus, as Irish immigration became ever more heavily Catholic, so did nativism become ever more deeply stained by sectarian enmity.[13]

The earliest settlers of colonial America arrived deeply infected with the virus of sectarianism, but fragmented Protestants could all rally to the standard of anti-Catholicism. In one colony after another, this form of religious discrimination acquired legislative force. Even Maryland, which had been intended as something of a Catholic haven, eventually resolved to "Prevent the Growth of Popery." Protestant colonists deplored the centralized structure of the Roman Church, with the ultimate source of authority located in a distant and foreign land, and they rejected the sovereignty of the priest in his parish. Inspired by the dramatic and widespread Protestant revival of the Great Awakening, they were forming a self-image that was both Anglo-American and Protestant. After all, on the eve of the revolution, the free population was largely English, heavily British, and almost totally Protestant. That revolution secularized the Puritan sense of mission and election, converting the new Jerusalem into the beacon of liberty, but the light that shone forth still did so with Protestant intensity. The new American republic was identified "with the advent of the millennial period, which was to usher in the final salvation of mankind and the end of history," and neither the invaluable assistance of a Catholic power in the achievement of independence nor the later adoption of a federal constitution that omitted any religious test for office-holding extinguished religious intolerance. Instead, Roman Catholicism continued to be regarded as incompatible with "the Enlightenment values and republican ideology that [now] underlay American political institutions."[14]

The republic's millennial identity was sealed by a fresh awakening of Protestant revivalism and by the deepening nationalism following a second war, that of 1812, against the former mother country. Inspired yet again to identify those who threatened American institutions, evangelicals fixed a fearful eye on the ever-swelling numbers of Catholic immigrants. Was popery compatible with civil liberty? The evangelicals' answer was a decisive no. They disparaged the Catholic Church as an enemy of republicanism, democracy, and progress and an ally of corruption, despotism, and tyranny. Samuel Morse, one of the nation's most respected men of practical science, published his *Foreign Conspiracy against the Liberties of the United States*. Roman Catholicism was indicted for placing priest between man and his maker by denying the former free access to the word of God, and was convicted of suppressing "the liberty of individual judgment and conscience on which republican government depended." Crusading evangelical societies professed to distinguish between Catholic clergy and laity, and declared a desire to convert the latter to Protestant truth, but their denunciations of Romanism and papal tyranny, their labelling of Jesuits as the "emissaries of Satan," inevitably aroused passions and licensed bigotry. These were always likely to spill over into hatred of the individual as well as the institution. Indeed, the lack of proselytizing success, confirmed as it was by a trebling of Catholic dioceses and churches in little more than a decade and the missionary activities of the multiplying Catholic revivals in which Jesuits were conspicuous, ensured that the likelihood became a certainty. The newly appointed Bishop of St Louis summarized an increasingly unpleasant state of affairs. Ignorance of the principles of Catholicism were to be found everywhere, together with a hatred of Catholics and an unwillingness to employ them. It was "quite notorious," he reported to Rome, that being a Catholic was generally sufficient to exclude a man from office except in those place where Catholics were "sufficiently numerous to carry the election." Increasingly, anti-Catholics concentrated their fire on the most conspicuous immigrant members of the faith, the Irish. Bishop Hughes deserved a cardinal's hat for what he had done "in placing Irish Catholics upon the necks of native New Yorkers," one sarcastic critic remarked.[15]

A prominent American convert to Catholicism identified Catholic Irish "separateness" as the source of much of the Protestant suspicion of the Catholic Church. The bitter controversies over public funding of parochial education and the use of the Bible in public schools added fuel to the sectarian flames. Organs of militant Protestantism construed these as proof of a Catholic conspiracy to subvert the nation's cultural identity. Catholics stood condemned of giving political as well as religious allegiance to a "foreign spiritual despotism," but the fears that nourished anti-alien, anti-Catholic, and anti-Irish sentiment intensified and became even more politicized during the 1850s. The Pope inadvertently played his part with a succession of jubilees that he used to summon the faithful to come to his aid as he struggled to fend off enemies of his temporal privileges and power. More frightening still for American Protestants was the gathering momentum of a domestic Catholic revival. Bishops, priests, and journalists indulged in aggressive, messianic, and triumphalist rhetoric. John Hughes, who had some two decades earlier founded the Catholic Tract Society to defend his faith and attack Protestantism, delivered a widely reported lecture in the late autumn of 1850 entitled *Decline of Protestantism, and Its Cause*. The millenarianist followers of William Miller, who accepted his imminent dating of the Day of Judgment, were held up to ridicule. They were "crazy with the idea that the last day has come." The Mormons served as another illustration of Protestantism's inability "to prevent such impostors from sweeping away thousands of souls." Catholics alone had received the "*command*" of God "to go and teach all nations," Hughes proclaimed, and in the United States that divine duty embraced the people, the officers of the armed forces, and the political leadership.[16]

Orestes Brownson, who aspired to the intellectual leadership of American Catholicism and whose *Review* was its only quarterly, had long bemoaned the American tendency to identify "Catholicity with Irish hoodlumism, drunkenness and poverty." And while he doubted the honesty, truthfulness, and reliability of Irish immigrants, he considered them "far less unAmerican than their clergy." They were a "noble people when not misled," and it was a clergy who had "the characteristics of an old national clergy, but of a nation not ours," he wrote, who were the "great difficulty in getting [the Catholic] religion fairly represented to the American mind." The Boston *Pilot*, organ of a diocese that in the judgment of the prolific and respected Brownson was "becoming more and more Irish," repeatedly boasted that Catholics would soon form a majority of the population. "Contraceptives have weakened their women," it indelicately remarked of Protestants, "and many of their men do not contemplate marriage until their constitutions have been essentially impaired by debauchery."[17]

Religious tension heightened as the fractious decade of the 1850s wore on. The dramatic surge in Catholic Irish immigration during the Famine, the visit by the Hungarian patriot Louis Kossuth – hailed as a noble symbol by American Protestants but anathematized by Catholics – and the arrival of the defrocked Italian priest Alessandro Gavazzi, who fed nativist paranoia, all contributed to a deepening sectarianism. Gavazzi drew large audiences, to whom he spoke of the "anti-republican character of the Romish Church," a sinister Jesuit conspiracy, and the Irish papal fifth columnists sent to undermine his listeners' freedoms. The *Irish-American* saw in all of this a dastardly plot to inflame Protestant hatred of Roman Catholics in order to destroy them "root and branch." The situation deteriorated with the arrival of a papal nuncio. The diplomatic courtesies extended to the Pope's representative by the federal government, which included dinner with the president and the secretary of state, moved a number of Protestants to fury. Their denunciation of him as a butcher of Italian patriots and wild charges that he was the advance guard of a papal invasion provided demagogic street preachers with a wealth of incendiary material. Protestant propagandists gleefully republished Brownson's criticism of immigrant Catholic Irish agitators for treating the United States as if it were a province of Ireland and his dismissal of the Catholic press as mere Irish newspapers. American society appeared to be dangerously unstable, and the likelihood of its violent disruption grew as the strains between slave states and free became ever more difficult to manage. Inevitably, under these stressful and febrile circumstances, the political implications of Catholic immigration again came to the fore. A popular belief, shared by the current occupant of the Executive Mansion, that the Catholic Irish were mere political pawns of their church, was strengthened by the renewed agitation, led by priests and allies in the Democratic Party, for a ban on the reading of the Bible in public schools and the transfer of taxes paid by Catholics to the support of parochial education. Foreign-born Catholics were credited with Franklin Pierce's election as president in 1852, and his subsequent appointment of a Catholic to his cabinet and that of several others to senior diplomatic posts were cited as the proof. This was, after all, an important moment in the evolution of American democracy. The progressive commitment to universal, White adult male suffrage, the direct election of officeholders, and the development of mass political parties "raised new questions about the responsibilities of the voting public." And it was a public swollen by the unprecedented number of immigrants who, having arrived in the late 1840s, had completed the five years of residence required for naturalization.[18]

The Catholic Irish were also assailed as obstacles to social reforms. Their resistance to temperance and reputed domestication of swine were spitefully captured in a popular saying: "It's as natural for a Hibernian to tipple as it is for a pig to grunt." Perhaps alienated by the Protestant leadership of reform movements, certainly sceptical of man's ability to overcome his original sin, or simply resentful of patronizing middle-class plans to redesign society and modify their traditional lifestyle, the Irish "rejected and derided the ethos and ends of Reform." Of all reforms, the effort to check the growth of slavery, if not abolish it, posed the greatest threat to the Union's survival. Nativists and campaigners against slavery did subscribe to the belief that conspirators were at work sabotaging the republic, the former fixing on the Roman Church and the latter on the "slaveocracy." Some nativists happily combined the two, accusing the Catholic Irish and their church of being friends of the institution, but opponents of slavery and nativists were not one and the same. Many abolitionists were highly critical of the Catholic Irish but steered well clear of political nativism. Moreover, the ambivalence and complexity of Irish Americans' attitudes towards African Americans were conveniently overlooked by their nativist detractors. Charles Redmond, one of the earliest of the Black abolitionists, received an enthusiastic popular reception during a tour of Ireland in 1841, and O'Connell gave the cause of slave emancipation sterling support. Yet the image of Blacks that many Irish emigrants may have carried in their minds was probably shaped by the popular touring minstrel shows, which tended to reinforce notions of racial inferiority. Once they reached the United States, the Catholic Irish undoubtedly viewed Blacks as competitors for unskilled labour and service occupations. On occasion they had reason to despise them as strikebreakers, and they displayed "an antipathy to Negro voting" in the New York State referendum in 1846. The fact that several years later an Irish militia unit assisted in the most notorious return of a fugitive slave to the South, even though his plight attracted widespread public sympathy, was seized upon by some reformers as evidence of Irish support for the despised fugitive slave legislation. The publisher and proprietor of the *American Celt* served only to strengthen this unfortunate impression with a public declaration that the law had been "openly and violently resisted" in Boston by the descendants of Puritans only. Citizens of Irish birth, on the other hand, intended to honour their oath to sustain the Constitution and the laws of the union. Similarly, the Irish acquired a reputation for racial violence and it was this that earned them a rebuke from Daniel O'Connell and convinced Frederick Douglass, the most famous Black abolitionist, that they were oppressors of his race. Nor did the Boston *Pilot* rescue their reputation with its racist diatribes, in which all abolitionists were represented as "Nigger-worshippers" and abolitionism dubbed "Niggerology." On the other hand, some Catholic Irish women evinced a willingness to "intermarry" with Black men, while the ability of the Irish often to coexist relatively harmoniously with Blacks did not go unnoticed in areas of the slave South. Hence the suspicion of a paranoid planter class that they were abolitionists at heart, though this was contradicted by their loyalty to the Democratic Party and the position of their church.[19]

The rebuke issued by the Boston *Pilot* to the three thousand New England Protestant clergymen who petitioned Congress against passage of legislation to reopen to slavery territory from which it had long been excluded, served merely to harden the opinion that the Irish-dominated Catholic Church was no friend of slave freedom. Subsequently, the same diocesan organ, and arguably the most influential Irish American newspaper, insisted that slaves would reject emancipation because "they love their masters, as dogs do, and servile plantation life is the life nature intended for them." According to Catholic doctrine, slavery "was not opposed to the divine or natural law." Archbishop Hughes argued that at worst it was a comparative evil and one much to be preferred to the condition under which Negroes would have lived had they remained in Africa. He likened slavery to a parental relationship and urged slave-holders to practise paternalism. He rejected abolitionism, echoing the pro-slavery argument that it was English inspired, perhaps with the intent to destabilize American society, and lumped it in with the other reform movements that he associated with European "Red Republicanism." Indeed, Black Catholics in Hughes's archdiocese inferred from the systematic racial discrimination to which they were subjected that he did not regard them as part of his flock. They eventually left the Catholic Church.[20]

The Irish themselves fell victim to similarly crude racial stereotyping, as Hinton Rowan Helper, a Southern abolitionist concerned exclusively with the damage slavery inflicted on poor White farmers, demonstrated. His book *The Impending Crisis* (1857) was widely distributed by Northern political opponents of the institution but revealed not a shred of sympathy for African Americans. Delivering what in his mind was a supreme insult, he placed the Irish even lower on his scale of civilization than Blacks and suggested the former might improve their character through interracial unions. It was the misfortune of the Catholic Irish to settle the United States in huge numbers at a time when much of the American intellectual world was developing the new science of ethnology and a number of associated pseudo-sciences, such as phrenology. Much of this investigation of race was directed to the task of establishing "scientifically" the superiority of Whites over Indians, Mexicans, and "Coloureds." There was a delicate religious problem to be finessed, the literal inerrancy of the Book of Genesis. By the middle of the century, most leading ethnologists discreetly accepted polygenesis, and few of them disputed the existence of a hierarchy of races at the peak of which stood Anglo-Saxons. The widely read novels of Sir Walter Scott and an American edition in 1841 of Sharon Turner's *History of Anglo-Saxons*, which had first been published in England at the beginning of the millennium, helped to popularize the notion that those virtues of which Americans considered their nation the exemplar – the perfection of governmental institutions and love of liberty – were among the innate endowments of the Anglo-Saxon race. Robert Knox's *Races of Man*, published in Britain in 1850, quickly had an impact on American thinking, especially in the slave South, but it also gave a fillip to efforts to distinguish between, and to classify, different ranks of White men. Irish adherence to Catholicism had long been regarded by Protestants as conclusive evidence of "Celtic racial inferiority." Now a distinctive Celtic physiognomy was constructed – coarse red hair, dark eyes, florid complexion, stocky build, and simianized features. On the stage it was the Irishman's physical appearance that was most often featured in melodrama. Writers and politicians, not least those of Irish origin, responded by seeking to identify a "Celtic-Anglo-Saxon division" of the Caucasian race. Irish-American novelists, many of them priests, refuted Protestant and nativist myths that the Pope was a despot, that Catholics were forbidden to read the Bible, that convents were "havens for prostitutes and baby killers," and that the Irish were uncivilized. Instead, readers were reminded of Ireland's glorious golden age and assured of the superiority of "the Celtic 'race' to the Saxon." They also depicted the Saxon as a tyrant and the Celt as a victim, but in so doing, as Brownson warned, the authors were in danger of "alienating the very Saxons who held the keys to Irish acceptance as whites in America." Thus, the argument that Irish humanity separated them from, and elevated them above, Africans and Asians remained very much a minority position. Far more prevalent was the increasingly negative Irish stereotype, which emphasized "quarrelsomeness, ferocity, and lawlessness." The Catholic Irishman was considered beyond the pale of true Americanism, because of his "innate, inheritable and ineradicable" affection for "political and religious 'despotism.'" The conviction that these traits were inheritable helps explain the alarm with which nativists responded to census returns suggesting that the foreign born were outbreeding the native born. It was further heightened by the growing acceptance of birth rates as "all-important indices to national vigor and thus social health."[21]

Nativist concern was also prompted by evidence that Irish progeny were a disproportionately large segment of the children born in Massachusetts, that by the mid-1850s they "accounted for almost half of the total increase in the state's population," and that the principal port cities along the Atlantic coast, from Boston to Baltimore, had all witnessed an exponential growth in their "alien" populations, with a correspondingly dramatic expansion of the foreign-born electorate. In New York City immigrants constituted approximately half of the voters. Efforts in Massachusetts to reapportion seats in the state legislature, to reduce Boston's influence and increase that of outlying small towns, foundered by all accounts on the Irish bloc vote. Incessant complaints that Irish Americans secured too many patronage positions, that they were a drain on the public purse, an obstacle to reform, and enemies of public education, yet had been "scientifically" shown to be an inferior breed to native-stock Anglo-Saxons, now contributed in mid-decade to the eruption of an especially virulent species of political nativism dubbed "Know Nothingism." Other factors were involved, such as the "traumatic" changes wrought by a modernizing economy and a harsh winter in the Northeast that obliged a great many workers already fretting over a loss of "personal autonomy" to resort humiliatingly to public charity. Small property owners and independent producers, on the other hand, were increasingly fearful of the ever-expanding class of propertyless wage earners. Nativists successfully focused much of the mounting anxiety on the foreign born in general and the Catholic Irish in particular, with the result that the Know Nothing Party briefly enjoyed dramatic electoral success in several states. Its members declared the Protestant character of American civilization to be in peril, characterized Catholicism as utterly incompatible with American values, and accused Catholics of wielding too much political influence and of corrupting American democracy. In the Northern states they tended to support restrictions both on the consumption of liquor and the further expansion of slavery. By way of a general program of action, they revived the traditional nativist demands – twenty-one years of residence before naturalization, Bible reading in schools, the deportation of foreign-born paupers and criminals, and the removal of Catholics from government office. The startling discovery that two-thirds of New York City's volunteer militia were immigrants brought a demand for their disarming there and elsewhere, and it was one to which several Know Nothing administrations made a prompt and positive response. All of this lends weight to the conclusion of one distinguished modern historian that Irish immigrants to the United States "encountered in the nineteenth century the most racist country in the English speaking world and the one in which anti-Catholic discrimination was greatest."[22]

However bright the flame, the candle of Know Nothingism had a very short wick and quickly flickered out. Sectional and regional differences undermined the ambitious attempt to construct a cohesive national movement. The Catholic Creoles who rallied to the local organization in New Orleans, largely out of repugnance for Irish immigrants, discovered how unwelcome they were at national conventions. In Georgia the national party was seen as an instrument with which to protect the South and its peculiar institution within the Union; hence the disillusionment when Northern Know Nothings made plain their opposition to slavery's expansion. Yet, in the North, recognizing the threat the nativist party posed to their more radical anti-slavery goals, prominent abolitionists denounced it and its principal objective. William Lloyd Garrison upheld the right of all men to worship God in their own way and "defended the right of Roman Catholics to use their

version of the Bible and prayer books in common schools." This argument resonated with those elements within the Protestant elites whose
lack of success in proselytizing Catholic immigrants belatedly stirred in
them a discreet and "deeper appreciation of Catholic charity, the
Catholic clergy, and the Church itself." Many evangelicals, whose
revivals had done so much to inspire anti-Catholicism, grew to distrust
a nativist party that adopted much of the Masonic paraphernalia –
secrecy, passwords, ceremonies, and pledges – at odds with Christianity's aversion to "the unfruitful works of darkness." Moreover, the
Know Nothings' willingness to employ the power of the state to
advance sectarian ends appeared both to violate the American belief in
separation of church and state and to disregard the principle of volun-
tarism to which evangelicals adhered almost as an article of faith. Others simply shunned association with xenophobia. Finally, the evangelical revival to which the economic difficulties of 1857 and 1858 gave
fresh fillip manifested itself as a desire to apply emollients, not irritants, to the bitter sectional disputes that divided churches, political
parties, and regions.[23]

   The Know Nothings also had some of their popular articles of clothing stolen by another new political party, one that nevertheless managed to dress itself up in a manner less open to principled objection.
Republicans were united in their determination to confine slavery to
those areas where it was already established, and they placed this fundamental commitment ahead of anything smacking of nativism. Abraham Lincoln, a prominent Illinois Republican, did not see how anyone
professing to be sensitive to the wrongs of the "Negro" could join in
"a league to degrade a class of White men." He considered the
nativists' principles "little better" than those of the advocates of slavery's expansion. Yet many of his old "political and personal friends"
had rallied to the nativist cause, which he believed would prove
"ephemeral," and he hoped to "get the elements" of the "American
organization" into the new political party. The accusation of Know
Nothingism cost Republican candidates vital "English" votes in close
elections, and Illinois Democrats were among those who denounced
the alleged coalition of "Whigs, Abolitionists, Know Nothings, and
renegade Democrats." Although in the state of Ohio a fusion with
Know Nothings was deliberately and successfully pursued, even there
Republicans still managed to avoid committing themselves formally to
an anti-Catholic and anti-foreign platform. Leading figures, such as
Lincoln, continued to denounce and distance themselves from crude

nativism. Were the Know Nothings to gain control of the nation, he mordantly remarked, instead of announcing as it currently and sadly did that all men were created equal except Negroes, the United States would quickly add foreigners and Catholics to the excluded. However, in the presidential and congressional elections of 1856, Republicans did appeal to popular anti-Catholicism in an effort to attract Know Nothings without alienating the entire foreign-born vote. They conceded the Catholic vote to the Democrats, denouncing the latter in Pennsylvania's mining districts as "swindling Irish-toadying Demagogues," they blamed their presidential candidate's narrow defeat on "Irish bog-trotters, with necks yet raw with a foreign priestly yoke." But the Republicans had emerged as formidable contenders for national power, and looking down the road that would lead in 1860 to the Executive Mansion, they continued to solicit Know Nothing support in several states with a tepid anti-Catholicism and mildly nativist proposals. In response, a Southern Democrat issued the ominous warning that, in the event of the Republicans' capturing control of the federal government, "the condition of the Southern States in the Union would be like that of Ireland toward Great Britain – a conquered province." Fear that a Republican victory would bring disunion and even civil war led many Know Nothings and some Irish Americans to vote in 1860 for "the patriotic Americanism of the Constitutional Union party." The Irish support given to the successful Republican candidate, Abraham Lincoln, at least in the Midwest, may have come exclusively from Protestants.[24]

However repellent the nativist face of American nationalism, there were Catholics who continued to concede that a militant priesthood had invited the hostility with its "hatred of heretics" and brutal denunciations of public schools. Those self-assured enough to argue this case, such as Orestes Brownson, were publicly censured by the Archbishop of New York. Nevertheless, Brownson privately held fast to his controversial position that the "few acts of violence" of the Know Nothings were as nothing compared to what was "constantly occurring in countries governed nominally by Catholic princes." He continued to insist that in "no Catholic country in the world" were the laws so favourable to "Catholicity" as in the United States, and doggedly asserted that the difficulties experienced by American Catholics resulted from the hierarchy's neglect to study and take advantage of those laws. Another spur to nativism had been an anglophobic Irish American nationalism peculiarly unwelcome to those conservative Americans who were looking ever more favourably on Britain as their "cultural homeland." In the words of one diarist, Irish Americans ought not to be endorsing efforts to subvert the United Kingdom, nor should they encourage rebellion in a country with which Americans had "just been kissing and making friends." There was a sectarian edge to such criticism, for in cities such as Philadelphia the diocesan newspaper made no secret of its O'Connellite sympathies, pulpits were used for fundraising, and priests appeared on platforms at repeal rallies. From the other side of the sectarian divide, the *Christian Advocate* restated the argument that the Catholics of Ireland had brought "evil disabilities" and British "oppressions" upon themselves with their "intolerant persecuting spirit." Irish Americans stood accused of the same folly. By maintaining "their distinctiveness of race and religion in a manner antagonistic to the great mass of the American people" and by "their societies, their newspapers, and their foreign politics," wrote one British student of their transatlantic experience, they had made themselves "distasteful to the undemonstrative or more Puritanic or native American." The "first large, self-conscious ethnic minority" to engage in "transatlantic politicking," they rubbed raw the suspicion that they were "a perpetually unassimilable community of foreigners." The *Irish American* applied an abrasive to such sores, bellowing: "There is no cant more in vogue than that the Irish ought to lose their identity in the American people. Forget your past and become Americanized, is the common cry. It is, nevertheless, a false, foolish, and absurd cry."[25]

From his Toronto vantage point and calling upon his personal knowledge of Irish America, Bishop Lynch endeavoured to explain Irish American nationalism. The freedom the people of the republic enjoyed, the laws protecting poor tenant as well as wealthy landlord, and the absence of a state church and thus of taxes to support an institution they detested excited in Irish Americans an exasperation against their former rulers that knew no bounds and caused them to "take an oath of allegiance to the United States almost immediately upon their arrival and renounce their former allegiance 'with a vengeance.'" In other words, swift naturalization was less a manifestation of the sinking of "their original nationality in the newly-adopted character" and more a repudiation at the earliest opportunity of British identity. Lynch also linked the far less attractive side of the immigrants' experience to their "foreign politics." Their many associations were all "animated with one wish," he insisted, "to see the miserable condition of the Irish improved, as they are ashamed of the taunts which the people of other nations indulge in at their expense." Undoubtedly, their nationalist sentiment was reinforced by nativist rejection. "[S]lighted as a man, and his people despised as a race," the Catholic Irish immigrant may have been attracted by the "sense of autonomy" and the "natural community" found in nationalism. That is not to say that nativism's deeply resented insults created his nationalism or that Celtic pride developed as a reaction to its Anglo-Saxonism. Ethnic consciousness and ethnic nationalism had long been promoted by Irish nationalists, clerical as well as lay, and then transported across the Atlantic. Nor is the argument entirely convincing that Famine refugees experienced an overwhelming desire to be rid of Britishness because of the hatred of England they carried in their hearts. Speedy acquisition of American citizenship might just as plausibly be attributed to a natural desire for political empowerment.[26]

Writing in the early 1880s, having visited Irish centres in the United States, Philip Bagenal described "a people numerous, comfortable and influential, animated by a spirit of nationality beyond all belief, and impelled to action by a deep-seated hostility to the English Government." Startled by "the amount of Irish feeling" he encountered, Bagenal was equally struck by the fact that the sons of Irish parents were "in reality often more Irish in sentiment than their own fathers and mothers." He traced this extraordinary situation to the combination of the Famine exodus, the Young Ireland movement, and the radical ideas of John Mitchel. In so doing, he anticipated much of the modern interpretation of Irish American nationalism. The emigrants left with the "thrilling writings" of Young Ireland ringing in their ears, he wrote, and in the United States were soon exposed to the propagandist journalism of talented Young Ireland refugees. Thus was created a new Irish nation "whose principal literature was hostile to England, whose heroes and martyrs were either political prisoners or executed felons, and whose every aspiration and hope was at variance with the established order of things in the land which they had left." He credited Thierry's *Conquest of England by the Normans* with the racial colouring of this nationalism, the notion of "Celt *versus* Saxon." The dream of Thomas Davis, Bagenal went on, was "to educate the people of Ireland into an acknowledgment of this race characteristic" and thus "fire the spark of nationality in the breast of every Irishman." But he credited Mitchel and his followers with having convinced so many of the emigrant Irish that their dispersion was nothing short of exile, and argued that exposure to the principles of American republicanism deepened their abhorrence and hatred of the British system of government, "which they were sedulously taught to believe was the fountain of all their woes, real and imaginary." They also blamed England for the contempt with which the Irish were everywhere regarded, "but particularly in America." They asked themselves, "What might not Irishmen have been under proper treatment and good government, instead of the despised and rejected of nations?"[27]

Were the Irish conditioned by their cultural traditions to regard "*all* Irish Catholic emigration negatively as involuntary and sorrowful exile"? Were Famine-era emigrants peculiarly susceptible to nationalism as a result of their "impoverished and embittering" experience in the United States? Did this experience "engender bitter disillusion and profound homesickness" that prepared them for conversion to nationalism? Did Irish American nationalism have its origins not only in "loneliness, poverty and prejudice" but also in a "yearning for respectability"? The picnics and parades sponsored by national societies undoubtedly served as "an important center of social activity" and an expression of a desire for self-improvement as well as for a free Ireland. There was, of course, considerable contemporary support for many of these modern theories. Thomas Larcom, undersecretary in the Irish administration, subsequently observed of Irish revolutionary nationalism: "The root is in America and the manure is the discontent of a million and a half people mourning and brooding over a grievance – expatriation – which though past yet lives – as a sentiment – intangible – not to be reasoned with." Of course, the Executive that Larcom served so loyally had a self-serving reason to locate the source of its political difficulties in a foreign land. But a modern study of Irish American popular culture in the form of sheet music uncovered surprisingly few references to exile. Irish immigrants who were modestly successful, or at least made better lives for themselves in the United States, were surely thankful for transplantation, while in areas of the American West material success and social mobility came far more rapidly. Evidently, the vigorous nationalist movement there was far more than the product of bitter disillusionment.[28]

The Irish differed little from other emigrants in their homesickness. Indeed, their suffering in this respect appears to have been no more severe than that of other Celts, whose attachment to their native land was just as strong and no less mystical. The Catholic Irish were certainly singled out as targets by American nativists, an unpleasant fate that surely intensified for many individuals the psychopathology of emigration. The resultant depression, paranoia, and confusion may explain the disproportionate numbers of them who were confined in state asylums or drank heavily, but there were centres, such as San Francisco, that experienced "only slight discomfort" from Know Nothingism. The fact that the initial nativist candidate for the office of mayor was a Roman Catholic merchant indicated that "anti-foreigner or anti-Catholic attitudes" were not the "overriding reasons" for the movement's political organization." Yet an energetic nationalism characterized the local Irish community, even though its appeal there and elsewhere was far from universal. One British agent estimated that perhaps 60 per cent of Catholic Irish Americans sympathized with the cause of Irish independence, but he concluded that no more than 10 per cent were wholeheartedly committed to it.[29]

Many of the Irish who reached the United States had already received a primary education in nationalism. They had been taught that they and their church were the victims of tyranny, that they were an ethnically distinct people misgoverned by aliens, that the constitutional structure of the United Kingdom was invalid, discriminatory, and unresponsive to peaceful demands for fundamental reform, that the Famine would have been avoided had food not been taken from Ireland to fill already well-stocked English larders, that Famine deaths amounted to murder, and that flight across the Atlantic had been involuntary. Those immigrants who accepted this interpretation of their individual decisions to leave the homeland would surely have experienced great difficulty integrating into American society. But enclave consciousness and self-segregation were encouraged by an American Catholic Church that increasingly spoke with an Irish accent, and in their "urban villages" immigrants received a secondary education in nationalism. The creation of national parishes, the appointment of Irish priests, many of them nationalists, the establishment of parochial schools that ensured that the young were familiar with Ireland's sad history, the organization of associations and national societies, the staging of ethnic parades, and the founding of ethnic newspapers had all been either the work of the Church or activities in which it was deeply involved. An environment had been created that smoothed over the regional and cultural differences of Catholic immigrants. They now thought of themselves as Irishmen, something the generalized hostility of nativists reinforced. Here was a hothouse in which a nationalism rooted in hatred of England or Britain could flourish. Here residents were reminded that the English had oppressed them, that the English were responsible for Ireland's chronic poverty, that the English were responsible for the calamity of the Famine, that the English were responsible both for their exile and their rejection by native-born Americans. Hate incites violence, and while the Church certainly shunned identification with physical force, there was in the United States, as in Ireland, an ambivalence in the conduct of a number of clergy that allowed the faithful to persuade themselves that the use of physical force as the instrument of Ireland's freedom was not contrary to Catholic doctrine. John Hughes had foolishly, if briefly, offered a personal endorsement of the rebels of 1848, while other priests not only spoke wildly at St Patrick's Day parades but justified in print the forcible overthrow of British "tyranny." The Young Ireland refugees, led by John Mitchel, with his accusations of genocide and appeals for revolution, were even more forthright and adamant. But their criticism of the Irish clergy for a lack of revolutionary mettle in 1848 alienated and alarmed powerful figures in the American hierarchy. John Hughes, for one, sought to keep the nationalist movement firmly under the Church's control and within the bounds it set. However, the appeal of physical force as the only viable means with which to effect Ireland's liberation and create a republican nation drew strength not only from the culture of violence that many immigrants brought with them to the United States, but also from that of the society and nation in which they had chosen to live. The unlimited liberty in the United States had an intoxicating effect on "the lower orders of the Celts," one English newspaper remarked. Freedom flew to their heads and they became revolutionary nationalists – Fenians – "ready to go about doing evil; republicans in politics, roughs in conduct, and only Irish in aim and name."[30]

Britain, the cultural homeland of so many Americans, had a long his-tory of violence. Civil war, revolution, and rebellion had left scars on England and Scotland during the seventeenth and eighteenth centuries. Nor had Great Britain been a stranger to urban disturbances, most notably the savagely sectarian Gordon Riots, which brought four days of terror to London's streets in 1780. School riots, food riots, political riots, sectarian riots, riots to protest the dislocations resulting from economic modernization, and serious agricultural disturbances extend-ed deep into the nineteenth century. The establishment of professional police forces checked, without eradicating, popular disturbances. Never-theless, by mid-century, the British had concluded that American society was exceptionally violent and that the polyglot populations of the republic's booming cities had grown too rapidly to be controlled effectively by the forces of law and order. Vigilantes stepped forward in some locations to fill the void, while a people accustomed to "individual recklessness" were arming themselves with weapons and using them with a readiness entirely unknown in Britain.[31]

The Britons and the Irish who settled colonial America had helped to establish a tradition of violence. The early colonists who arrived in the wilderness seeking "to regenerate their fortunes, their spirits, and the power of their church and nation" quickly resorted to force as the essential instrument. Initially the targets were the various Aboriginal tribes, and later the Africans imported as slaves. Uprisings and suspected rebellions brought retaliatory bloodlettings. Then, in the 1760s, an eruption of vigilantism in the Carolinas saw self-appointed "Regulators" maim or kill suspected lawbreakers before broadening their definition of undesirables in need of greater social discipline. Although they disbanded soon after the colonial administration strengthened the forces of law and order in the back country, the vigilantes had seemingly justified private gun ownership in districts where the legal system was failing the citizenry. Meanwhile, the principal colonial cities had become familiar with a mob violence that found a patriotic outlet in resistance to Britain's attempt to tighten imperial control in the aftermath of the French and Indian War. The "myth of regeneration through violence," which emerged as "the structuring metaphor of the American experience," was one to which mid-eighteenth century Americans successfully appealed in their dealings with the mother country.[32]

The violence of the American Revolutionary War took both the traditional form of formal military engagements and the peculiarly tragic brutality of civil war. The "meanest and most squalid sort of violence was from the very beginning to the very last put to the service of revolutionary ideals and objectives," and it did not end with the treaty of peace. The young nation was soon confronted by rebellion and Indian wars, while the emergent doctrine of "popular sovereignty" eventually lent ideological justification to a new generation of vigilantes. Equally disturbing was the continuing increase in personal violence that invaded schools, universities, legislatures, public transportation, and dining rooms. Americans mutilated one another over the most trivial of incidents, tearing off ears, biting noses, and gouging eyes. More sinister still was the "practice of carrying murderous weapons," which

continually resulted in "the most bloody and repulsive scenes." The
knife was long the weapon of choice, but Samuel Colt's revolution in
the manufacture of handguns soon placed an inexpensive and deadlier
weapon at the disposal of private citizens. Convinced that crime was rising sharply in the rapidly swelling cities, Americans identified the
revolver with self-defence. In a heavy-drinking society, one in which
notions of personal honour or manliness often sought a display, the
combination was highly dangerous. And while the ritualized confrontation of duelling had declined in the North following the killing of
Alexander Hamilton in 1804, it continued in the Southern states. There
seemed more than a touch of lunacy in challenges to settle questions of
honour with rifles at pistol distances. Violence was also essential to the
maintenance of slave control. "The South has the unenviable distinction
of having slain a greater number of their fellow men with murderous
hands, than all the other States, including California, put together," a
Southern clergyman mordantly observed in 1855. Long before this
date, Americans had begun to construct "an image of themselves as a
violent people and to act on that self-perception." There was a shift
towards "ever-accelerating passion and violence," which was alarmingly collective as well as personal, Northern and Western as well as Southern. Immigration had given it fresh impetus by introducing fresh supplies of the young, single men traditionally more "prone to violence and
disorder" than their elders and whose presence also exacerbated ethnic
tensions.[33]

Men fought for control of land and local power, and New York was
the scene of a succession of rent rebellions and wars. The Mormons were
drawn into a lengthy and bloody struggle in Missouri, which was only
partly sectarian. They retreated from there to Illinois, only to be met
with fresh violence that ended in the lynching of their prophet, Joseph
Smith, and another lengthier withdrawal westwards. They in turn murdered more than one hundred members of a party crossing their lands in
Utah en route to California in 1857. Meanwhile, a murderous struggle
had erupted in Kansas for local dominance and territorial control
between individuals who killed in the name of slavery and those who did
so in the name of free soil. The most notorious of the abolitionist vigilantes was John Brown, who went on to stage a raid on the federal arse-
nal at Harper's Ferry in 1859, intending it as the first stroke of a master
plan to liberate the slaves of the South. His finding a martyr's death on
a Virginia gallows lent, at least in the minds of a minority of Northern-
ers, a certain respectability to his extraordinary resort to physical force.[34]

The disturbances that seemed endemic on the urban frontier were similarly deadly, far exceeding, even proportionately, in number and horror those that took place in British North America. In excess of twelve hundred riots occurred in the thirty-three years that separated Andrew Jackson's election as president in 1828 and Abraham Lincoln's taking of office in 1861. They rarely had a single cause. Disputes of class and labour, political contests and social struggles, racial and ethnic enmities, sectarian and sectional animosities, interacted to produce violence and bloodshed. The street brawls between rival gangs and between rival volunteer fire companies were often political as well as ethnic and sectarian. The mob that destroyed the Ursuline Convent in Charlestown, Boston, in 1834 was heavily Protestant and drawn from the labouring classes who feared job competition from Catholic Irish immigrants. The handful of race riots that divided the less than fraternal city of Philadelphia between 1829 and 1849 were also driven by White resentment of the success of Blacks in securing employment and achieving a modest measure of affluence best illustrated by their growing number of institutions. Jobless Whites were all too easily aroused against Blacks who lived comfortably. The "chiefly Irish" mob that attacked a Black temperance parade in 1842 and then set about the destruction of a Black area, looting houses, burning down meeting halls and churches, and generally terrorizing residents, was evidently motivated by something in addition to crude racial antipathy. The twin riots of May and July 1844 that caused at least twenty deaths and left another hundred persons seriously injured were clashes between the Irish and nativists. The origins were not simply sectarian – the dispute over the use of the Bible in public schools – but ethnic, economic, political, and social. A depression that had deepened sectarian differences between workers infused temperance advocates with fresh energy. "Yet the triggering event was political," the decision of nativists to stage a rally in an Irish-dominated area of the city and the action of locals in firing into their provocative parade.[35]

Theatre riots occurred, often with casts of thousands. The targets were occasionally Black actors but more frequently visiting thespians from Britain who were accused of insulting the American people. In some instances these incidents were an extension of urban mob attacks on abolitionists, given the identification of the anti-slavery movement with the United Kingdom. But the mobs were also responding to class, ethnic, and racial concerns, and to the fear that radical opponents of the institution were undermining national unity. The bloodiest episode occurred in New York in May of 1849, when a feud between two prominent actors – one British, the other American – eventually spilled out onto the streets. Men "of wealth and standing" rallied to the support of the Briton, only for the "Bowery B'hoys" to accept this as a challenge. Twenty-five persons were killed and another forty-eight were wounded when troops summoned to maintain order fired into the attacking mob. The majority of the dead and the arrested were Irish. Similarly complex combinations of motives and concerns continued to shape vigilantism, most dramatically in California. There, more than two hundred unfortunates were subjected to lynch law between 1849 and 1853, almost half of whom were indeed hanged. The merchants who controlled the most highly publicized of the vigilance committees, that which operated in San Francisco from 1856, were plainly responding to class, political, and ethnic considerations. Their primary purpose was less the punishment of the lawless than the ousting of Democrats from city government. They sought a business-oriented administration that would reduce expenditures, lower taxes, and inaugurate a "new order." The committee denied that the new order would exclude the Catholic Irish, but the fact that "Irish Catholic lower class laborers" had been the essential prop of the Democratic regime and that applicants for membership of the vigilance committee were required to state their places of birth cast considerable doubt on the worth of that denial.[36]

Speaking to an audience in the Young Men's Lyceum of Springfield, Illinois, early in 1838, a young, ambitious lawyer warned that a "Mobocratic spirit" was abroad in the nation. "Accounts of outrages committed by mobs form the every-day news of the times ... from New England to Louisiana," Abraham Lincoln observed. The vicious portion of the population had been permitted to gather in bands of hundreds, at times in their thousands, to "burn churches, ravage and rob provisions stores, throw printing presses into rivers, shoot editors, and hang and burn obnoxious persons at pleasure, and with impunity." The hate and revenge that had long been directed outwards, against the British nation, was now being turned inwards by Americans against one another. Here was a source of well-placed pessimism about the future. Of course, for one group of American citizens and residents, the Catholic Irish, the hostility continued to be directed also against the British state. They had arrived in the United States in unprecedented numbers just as personal, collective, and national violence was approaching a peak there. The war declared on Mexico in 1846 was one of territorial expansion and revealed a national readiness to resort promptly to physical means to achieve imperialist ends. The barbaric conduct of some American volunteers towards Mexican non-belligerents – "Murder, robbery and rape of mothers and daughters in the presence of tied-up males of the families" – appalled their commander and confirmed a taste for personal violence that was unlikely to be sated by war's end. Few contemporaries doubted that, of the immigrant populations, the Catholic Irish were the most ready to embrace the culture of violence. An Irish editor regretfully admitted that "the boys readily acquire the savage practices so common here, and become as bloodthirsty as the natives." As well as retaliatory, their violence was on occasion pre-emptive. The Irish took the initiative in many instances, whether to discourage competitors for work or to punish perceived national insults, as in the case of the family of Irish bartenders who beat to death a German patron for calling them "bloody transports." They terrorized Blacks, disrupted Protestant parades, especially those on the anniversary of the Boyne, and brutally influenced election results. In New York, in 1854, an Irish mob beat to death an election official who sought to challenge citizenship papers, and then drove off the group of deputies sent to protect the polls, killing one of them in the process. Significantly, "the Irish participated in riots much more often in New York and Philadelphia where they were quickly welcomed into the political system than they did in Boston where they were given no political jobs prior to the Civil War."[37]

The immigrants had long been familiar with violence in their homeland, verbal and physical. They had been taught that the political system was alien and oppressive and law enforcement sectarian and partisan. Many of them had been raised to regard with suspicion if not hostility, persons in positions of authority. They now found themselves in a society where violence seemed pervasive and lawlessness endemic. Andrew Jackson, a president with a well-earned reputation for deadly personal violence, had exhibited a stunning lack of respect for law when he declined to enforce a decision of the Supreme Court. In 1857 another holder of the nation's highest office, James Buchanan, placed a detachment of marines at the disposal of the mayor of Washington, D.C., to assist this fellow Democrat beat back the electoral challenge of a nativist candidate. The troops fired into a group of voters, killing ten and wounding more than double that number. The same president was soon endeavouring to persuade Congress to accept a pro-slavery constitution for Kansas that had been the work of a convention noto-riously elected with the assistance of massive fraud and intimidation. This was also a decade of filibustering raids against Latin American countries, and one of the raiders, William Walker, briefly established his own regime in Nicaragua. John Brown then devised a form of domestic filibustering. The ability of Irish immigrants to adapt their own tradition of violence to their new situation was displayed in the anthracite mining districts of Pennsylvania. The fact that supervisory and the more highly rewarded skilled positions were frequently held by British immigrants, while the Catholic Irish dominated the ranks of poorly paid labourers, added an ethnic colouring to the economic grievances that erupted into gang warfare and murder. A conflict between the labourers and skilled Kilkenny miners simply substituted sectarian for ethnic prejudices, for many of the latter were Protestants and all were traduced by Catholics as "soupers." The crimes were promptly attributed to a transplanted secret society, the Molly Maguires, whose members had first acquired notoriety and a reputa-tion for murderous violence more than a decade earlier in Roscom-mon. Given the immigrants' own culture of violence and that of the nation in which they had come to live, given the hate they had been encouraged to harbour against Britain, given the resort to force every-where around them to advance political interests and resolve political problems, was it any wonder that a number of Irish Americans responded positively to those radical nationalists who asserted that a resort to physical force was the legitimate and necessary means of Irish liberation?[38]

8

The Irish Revolutionary
Brotherhood

"Fenianism was the natural, or at least a natural, outcome of Young Irelandism," wrote one of its leading lights in his *Recollections*, and "the
immediate origin of the movement [was] undoubtedly to be found
among the '48 refugees in America." John Mitchel, Thomas Francis
Meagher, Thomas D'Arcy McGee, Michael Doheny, and John O'Mahony were among those who found their way to the republic and then
sought to demonstrate "what a powerful factor in Irish politics the Irish
in America had become." In 1848 the Young Ireland revolutionaries
had lacked a coherent ideology, a clear and fixed objective, a settled
strategy, and close contact with the mass of the people. Those of them
who fled first to Paris following the disastrously mismanaged rebellion
found themselves at the intellectual centre of revolutionary nationalism
and were reminded of the "link between journalism and revolution."
The press was an essential instrument of mass mobilization. The "smell
of the printer's ink [was] the incense of modern revolutionary organization," and the "people" were "the source of legitimacy for the exercise of sovereign power." That connection could be made simply and
graphically on a newspaper's masthead, as was to be the case with the
appearance of the *Irish People*. The Irish refugees also received instruction in the techniques of conspiracy, which included not only the obvious commitment to secrecy but also the enforcement of hierarchical discipline rooted in absolute obedience to superiors. Further, members of
a revolutionary organization should be enrolled in a brotherhood that
would symbolically embrace them in a fraternity, and its strategy ought
to accept the necessity of violence as the instrument of freedom. The
Poles, with their advocacy of "'salutary' terrorism and mobilization of
the peasantry for acts of violence" and their concept of a "people's war"
in which "national revolution was inseparable from social revolution,"
provided one possible model for Irish revolutionary nationalists.[1]

In December 1853 John O'Mahony quit Paris for the United States. He was a gentleman by birth, and his bearing, manners, tastes, and interests were those of his class. He possessed a fine physique, and his dark complexion, gaunt features, hooded eyes, prominent cheekbones, and full and drooping moustache gave him a forbidding, even sardonic, appearance that was at odds with his personality. His "mental capacity" was of "the highest order," his fellow refugee in Paris, James Stephens, later attested, while hatred of English rule in Ireland "became an element of his being." Raised in a nationalist family, his father and his uncle having turned out in 1798, he had supported repeal before siding with the Young Irelanders when O'Connell purged them from the Repeal Association. His study of language and fascination with philology marked him as a cultural as well as a political nationalist. "For in loving Ireland," Stephens wrote, "he loves more than the principles of justice: intensely, passionately he loves the Irish race, the memories of times gone by and hallowed by the deeds of men of his blood, the language, the literature, the monuments ... speak to him as to no other." Hence O'Mahoney's quixotic decision following Ballingarry to launch his own doomed campaign in an effort to "keep the kettle of public excitement boiling." The price he paid for this romantic gesture was exile, having had the foresight to transfer his property to his family in order to save it from confiscation. He supported himself in the French capital with pen and tongue, giving lessons in Irish to the students of the Irish College, and he received the occasional remittance from home. Residence in Paris strengthened his "ultra-democratic" views and excited his admiration of "the stern front and untiring constancy of the continental apostles of liberty and the ceaseless preparation of their disciples." Indeed, he and Stephens may have participated in the republican resistance to Louis Napoleon's *coup d'état* in 1851.[2]

O'Mahony's first impressions of Irish American nationalism were surely encouraging. The diaspora exhibited a reassuring degree of internal cohesion and maintained its links with Ireland. The fresh waves of immigrants – the ethnic and cultural reinforcement provided by national parishes, Irish priests, separate schools, and a national press – promised to facilitate the nationalist mobilization of the Irish community. The Catholic Irish of the United States appeared to have taken to heart the caution that "[t]o forget your country is to be ashamed of your creed, and next to lose your faith." An eagerness to contribute to the liberation of Ireland had survived the disappointments of 1848. Young men whose traditional culture embraced secret societies and faction fighting, and whose American working-class culture found one expression in street brawls, provided recruits for military clubs that often melded into state militias. They enrolled, if in fewer numbers, in conspiratorial associations dedicated to the training of an expeditionary force of liberators. But the negotiations that O'Mahony and Doheny conducted with the Russian consul in New York during the Crimean War, seeking support and aid from the Tsar, had no greater success than Mitchel's earlier endeavour. There was, after all, a large element of fantasy in their talk of launching an invasion of Ireland. Little wonder such schemes attracted ridicule, while additional cold water was thrown on them by the action of a United States marshal in Cincinnati. In January 1856, at the instigation of the British consul, the marshal arrested a group of Irishmen on a charge of violating the neutrality laws by conspiring to invade Ireland. From the bench, the accused were criticized, not for sympathizing with their native land, but for indulging such feelings "at the hazard of the interests and peace of the country of [their] adoption." Divided allegiance, the judge made clear, was unacceptable. One of those arrested quickly took sweet revenge by charging the consul with the illegal enlistment of men to serve with the British Army in the Crimea. The British were obliged to recall him. Meanwhile, O'Mahony had decided to withdraw from conspiracy and concentrate on one of his literary projects. He was tired of "Irish tinsel patriots," weary of the superficiality of many of his fellow former Young Irelanders, disheartened by the schism within Irish Catholic ranks, and scornful of "Yankee-doodle twaddle." However, by this time, 1856, contact had been established with revolutionary nationalists at home.[3]

An emissary despatched to Ireland the previous year had met with O'Mahony's fellow refugee and former companion in Paris, James Stephens. Born into a petty bourgeois Catholic family, Stephens briefly attended a seminary before pursuing a career as a civil engineer. Nationalism was as much a part of his birthright as it was of O'Mahony's, linked as Stephens was on his mother's side to the United Irishmen. He later claimed that the "patriotic sentiments ... instilled into him from childhood" had been further "excited and stimulated" by his reading of the Nation. As a member of the supporting cast in the Ballingarry farce, he had earned O'Mahony's admiration as "the coolest and most stoically brave in danger, the most light-hearted in adversity, and the most indifferent in physical suffering." An aide to Smith O'Brien, Stephens had received a hard lesson in the folly of launching rebellion without the most careful preparation, and it was reinforced during his seven years in Paris. Still a relatively young man of thirty-one when he set out for Ireland in 1855, he spent some time in England, perhaps re-establishing contact with the extra-parliamentary radicals there. Once back in Ireland, his extended rambles throughout his homeland allegedly persuaded him of the possibility of organizing "a proper movement for the independence" of his native land.[4]

Although he experienced a severe bout of ill-health shortly after his arrival in Dublin, Stephens possessed the physique and temperament suitable for physical and organizational exertion. He was short and seemingly sturdy, and his fast-receding hairline exaggerated a dome-like forehead that, together with a full and luxuriant beard and "small aris-tocratic white hands," prompted one journalist to liken him more to a "German theorist than a plotter of plots." His intellectual appearance, his "self-contained and dignified bearing," his attractive musical voice, his "luxurious habits and refined delicate tastes," his "dogged patience," and his "immense faith in himself" endowed him with "a wondrous gift of winning over young men." Unfortunately, overween-ing self-confidence is frequently indistinguishable from conceit. He had "grasped more of the truth than almost any other man," Stephens liked to boast. Thus, when approached by a second Irish American emissary in 1857, this one bearing promises of money and men to support a new Irish revolutionary movement, he demanded a regular, assured, and adequate supply of funds and absolute control of the organization. He insisted on being "perfectly unshackled – in other words a provisional dictator." Only unfettered power could guarantee his freedom as leader from "the wavering or the imbecile." Ever the braggart, he informed his "transatlantic brothers" that if these conditions were met, he would have ten thousand men enrolled within three months, with fifteen hun-dred of them armed and ready to take to the field on a single day's notice, while his organization would embrace "the *whole* body of Irish nationalists." Even the "*indifferent*" would be drawn in once the "start" had been given, he promised.[5]

The Irish Revolutionary Brotherhood was launched on 17 March 1858 with a small group of men swearing an oath of secrecy and of obe-dience to superior officers. Significantly, a number of fellow former Young Irelanders, to whom Stephens extended invitations, elected to keep their distance from an organization whose chief aspired to dicta-torial authority. Nevertheless, over time, he succeeded in attracting intelligent and energetic associates from backgrounds similar to his own. One of the youngest was John Devoy. He came from small farmer

stock that claimed a remote service connection to the intended aristocratic leader of the United Irish rebellion. Several family members were
reputed to have participated in that bloody rising, and Devoy "grew up
on tales" of it. His father was both a supporter of O'Connell's agitations and associations and a subscriber to the Nation, which he read to
his neighbours within the hearing of his children. Although on occasion
reduced to labouring, William Devoy eventually raised himself to the
position of managing clerk of a Dublin brewery. Son John joined the
Brotherhood in 1861, though fear of arrest induced him briefly to pursue military training in the French Foreign Legion before returning to
Ireland. At the age of twenty he was ordered to his birthplace, Naas, to
supervise recruitment and training in that area. Two other important
recruits were John O'Leary and Charles Kickham. Both were children
of well-to-do Tipperary shopkeepers, both were introduced to nationalist politics by their fathers, both were captivated as very young men by
Young Ireland and the Nation, both played minor roles in 1848, and
both subsequently entered the Irish Revolutionary Brotherhood only
after some hesitation. Thomas Clarke Luby, on the other hand, was a
founding member. Already entering his late thirties by 1858, he also differed markedly in another particular from many of his colleagues in the
organization's senior ranks. He was a child of the Establishment. His
father was an Anglican clergyman and his uncle a distinguished member of the faculty of Trinity College, though his mother was Catholic.
Heavily influenced by the Nation, for which he wrote occasionally in
1844, he was active in planning revolt in 1848 and even more deeply
involved with Fintan Lalor in the conspiracy that fizzled the following
year. Prevented by a temporary suspension of recruitment from joining
the French Foreign Legion to learn infantry tactics, he spent a year in
Australia before returning to Ireland, where in 1855 he was appointed
editor of a nationalist newspaper. He was among those who met with
the first emissary from Irish America and was one of the handful present on 17 March 1858. Indeed, he drafted the oath they took and was
second only to Stephens in swearing it.[6]

The Brotherhood's objective was the violent overthrow of "English
rule" and the establishment of an independent Irish republic. To that
end, Stephens sought to create a large force of well-drilled, armed men.
The necessity for secrecy was obvious. The Italian Carbonari, the first
movement of the early nineteenth century "to mobilize the masses for a
national cause through a secret organization," provided one organizational model. Stephens also appears to have been influenced by Auguste

Blanqui, who had been a member of the French version of the Carbonari, and though a social revolutionary, argued for exclusive concentration, in the first instance, on the overthrow of an illegitimate government. Blanqui was equally insistent that "[l]abor is the people; intelligence is the men of devotion who lead them." He advocated a revolutionary elitism that sat well with Stephens and the other former Young Irelanders surrounding him. The revolutionary movement would be the means of educating the masses. Although Stephens was preparing for a full-scale insurgency, the door leading to terrorism was left ajar by the Brotherhood's unreserved commitment to violence, Stephen's failure to draw distinctions between its possible varieties, Ireland's history of brutal agrarian outrages, and the ceaseless depiction of the existing government as a tyranny. The Brotherhood had a cellular structure, with units called "circles," each composed theoretically of eight hundred members, but within this large circumference were ever-tighter and supposedly virtually hermetically sealed smaller circles, the smallest containing fewer than a dozen men. This structure was not only ill-adapted to the rapid and mass absorption of recruits, but also far from secure, since members often knew of others outside their own circles. However, the comradely group of the small cell was well suited to terrorist activities. Armed robberies were planned and staged to acquire weapons, and a policy of selective assassinations, first recommended by Irish Americans and seriously entertained by the organization's leadership in 1859, was eventually adopted and implemented by a special "shooting circle." Initially, its targets were informers and suspected informers, but almost inevitably policemen and senior political figures were added to the list.[7]

Stephens founded the Irish Revolutionary Brotherhood against a backdrop of imperial crisis and European tensions. Britain appeared to be experiencing those international difficulties long regarded as the nationalists' opportunity. The Indian Mutiny was quickly followed by France's leap forward in naval technology, with the construction of ironclad warships that presented a bold and serious challenge to Britain's wooden-hulled naval supremacy. The creation in Britain of a volunteer movement to serve as a home guard in the event of a French invasion, the hatching in England of the plot to assassinate Napoleon III, which came perilously close to success, and the collapse of the first Palmerston administration when it sought to appease the angry French could only have infused Stephens with fresh confidence that he would soon have an opportunity to strike. He was thus intent on receiving reliable funding from the United States that would allow him to finance recruitment drives and then equip and drill his men. The disappointing sum collected by the first fundraiser despatched across the Atlantic, a mere £40 in his begging bowl on his return, led Stephens to visit the republic himself in the fall of 1858.[8]

Although he raised £600, the expedition was not a success. Stephens formed a poor opinion of the United States, in which he saw a "false notion of equality and spirit of insubordination." As leader of a secret conspiracy, he deplored the fact that everything got into the American press. He dismissed Washington, D.C., with its incomplete capitol, as a "city of magnificent distances and shabby foregrounds" and bemoaned "the absence of a creative mind in art," which he deduced from its architecture. Apart from the Office of Stamps, which he considered a mere facsimile of the Parthenon, he lamented the "monstrous agglomerations of stone and mortar [that] ... elsewhere smite you with their ugliness." Introduced at a public reception to President Buchanan, a former American minister to the United Kingdom, who politely enquired about Ireland, Stephens privately belittled him as "a Yankee development of the Artful Dodger." Nor did he hold in higher esteem the Irish American nationalists with whom he mixed. Mitchel lacked a "profound knowledge" of the Irish people, while not even Meagher's obesity could make him an imposing figure in Stephens's eyes. Both men, in his opinion, were too self-centred to be genuine patriots. His equally poor opinion of Doheny was undoubtedly influenced by the latter's obvious lack of admiration for Stephens and his revolutionary work in Ireland. Indeed, the "provisional dictator" suspected that his hosts considered him a megalomaniac. Consequently, he felt obliged to deny any lust for power and promised to retire from the scene as soon as a free Irish republic had been established. He protested that his insistence on temporary supreme authority resulted from the knowledge that he stood alone as a man who was both practical and devoted to the people. Of the Irish Americans, only his former companion and constant admirer John O'Mahony commanded his "implicit trust." He had been the only senior figure to inquire whether Stephens had sufficient funds for his personal use, and despite his own straitened circumstances had provided him with shelter and food at the cost of debts that made his life "a torture." O'Mahony was therefore judged "far and away the first patriot of the Irish race," having successfully resisted the "debasing influences" of American residence. So Stephens, having extracted from the Irish Americans an acknowledgment of his "supreme authority and absolute control" over the entire organization, appointed O'Mahony the leader of the American wing of the conspiracy, assuming he would serve as a willing and loyal subordinate and provide the direction that would see the Irish in America do much for Ireland. O'Mahony quickly renamed the American branch of the revolutionary movement. This might have been viewed as a symbolic assertion of its independence, but his choice – the Fenian Brotherhood – satisfied Stephens that the intent was merely to symbolize the movement's twin fundamental principles. They were Ireland's natural right to independence, and the necessity of armed revolution. The name, Fenian, attached as it subsequently was to revolutionary nationalists on both sides of the Atlantic, quickly excited an academic debate. Those scholars who traced the name to the legendary hero Finn Mac Cumhal were contradicted by others who found its origin in the *Fene*, "the old Irish militia who were embodied in defence of the crown and nobility of Ireland in the third century." This interpretation could claim the support of one of the Ossianic Society's publications, the *Battle of Gabhra*, with which O'Mahony as a Gaelic scholar was surely familiar. The editor of that text "had described the Fianna as a large army which defended Ireland from invasions," thereby implying that ancient Ireland had been "an independent, militarily strong nation."[9]

Stephens recrossed the Atlantic early in 1859 but made straight for the French capital, which was to be his base for the better part of the next two years. No doubt he wished to be readily available to the French government should Anglo-French relations worsen, a far from unlikely prospect well into 1860. Napoleon's annexation that year of Savoy and Nice in the aftermath of his short but bloody war with Austria, ostensibly in support of Italian unification, kept popular francophobia on the boil in Britain. But the signing of the Cobden Treaty and the growth of freer trade between the two nations eventually worked the calming international effect in which Cobdenites trusted. Similarly, the imperial strains on Britain had eased with the harsh and successful suppression of the Indian Mutiny.[10]

Disappointed but undismayed, Stephens continued to plot. He had undertaken a series of membership drives in Ireland before his visit to the United States, earning the admiration of one companion for the perseverance and persuasiveness with which he approached prospective recruits. It would have been surprising had he failed to make overtures to Ribbonmen. Not only were they active at this time, at least in several Midlands' counties, but they also had much in common with the Revolutionary Brotherhood. Both were committed to secrecy, to a nationalism that drew strength from hatred of England, and to violence, and they attracted recruits with similar social profiles. Moreover, men who had shown a willingness and ability to enforce "their will on local land politics through assassination, were clearly ideal candidates for recruitment for more ambitious enterprises." But many Ribbonmen resisted quick induction into the Brotherhood. More responsive were a number of other local associations of nationalists, such as the artisans and small traders enrolled in the St Patrick's Society of Kingstown and the remnants of Fintan Lalor's secret society in Dublin. A small group in Belfast had already dedicated itself, in imitation of the United Irishmen, "to organize and fight for the establishment of the Irish Republic." The leading light was the very young Frank Roney, grandson of a Protestant rebel in 1798 but a child of Catholic parents and son of a carpenter, union organizer, and repealer. Roney, who had at home and in school been fed a steady diet of bitter hatred "of everything English," received his commission personally from Stephens. His assigned task was to organize five thousand men within three years and make what provision he could for their arming. He and his closest associate enlisted the service of the colour sergeant of the Antrim Militia, who had charge of the regimental armoury. Thus they secured a skilled military instructor and were well placed to lay their hands on a thousand rifles and ammunition when the time came. Elsewhere, Stephens made contact with the various Phoenix Societies, a self-explanatory symbol, which while not closely allied were thought to be loosely connected to a parent society in the United States and were identified by the police as a new form of Ribbonism.[11]

The Phoenix National and Literary Society of Skibbereen was a revolutionary organization, but not an oath-bound one, of some one hundred members when James Stephens arrived in the town in the early summer of 1858. Most were young artisans and shop-boys, but the dominant figure was Jeremiah O'Donovan Rossa. Likened by one journalist to an Irish wolfhound, "gentle when stroked, fierce when provoked," he claimed to be a descendant of a family of Catholic landowners who had lost their large property during the confiscations. His father had been reduced to the rank of small farmer following the collapse of the local linen industry, but the young Rossa opened a hardware store. With two friends, Mortimer Moynahan, owner of a pub, and Daniel MacCartie, he had joined the Ossianic Society, and all three were at the heart of the local Phoenix Society. Appropriately enough, Stephens and Rossa met in the society's reading room, another of the

"'Academies of Nationality,'" and within a month 90 per cent of its members had enrolled as Fenians. They swore themselves to secrecy, renounced all allegiance to "the Queen of England," solemnly promised to do their utmost to make Ireland an independent democratic republic, and undertook to obey the commands of superiors and to take up arms at a moment's notice. But assiduous and successful recruiting in the towns of southwest Cork and south Kerry, in which Rossa took a prominent part, came at a price. The swelling membership, estimated by some to approach four thousand, attracted the attention of the authorities. The Phoenix men were less than discreet. Their circulation of a drill manual, the arrival from Dublin of a drill master trained in the United States, and the drilling of some members bearing rifles and others carrying pikes caused alarm. Local priests condemned this secret, oath-bound conspiracy, while the Bishop of Kerry, David Moriarty, urged the publisher of the *Nation*, A.M. Sullivan, to direct its fire at secret societies. Friendly warnings, the bishop hoped, would induce some young men to quit the society and discourage others from joining it. The *Nation* also published a letter from Smith O'Brien, recently returned from transportation, lending his support to this cautionary campaign. Other constitutional nationalists were far more reluctant to take a public stand. It "does not surely lie in *our* mouths to condemn or in the least discountenance the alleged *intentions* of men whose real crime in the eyes of the enemy is their desire to free their country from a foreign yoke," one of them wrote to O'Brien.[12]

The Irish Executive responded early in September 1858 to the worrying reports, some coming from Catholic clergy, of the Phoenix Society's activities. Recalling the *Nation*'s "virulent" sepoy articles during the Indian Mutiny, officials initially and mistakenly suspected the nationalist organ of being behind the conspiracy. Apart from placing the newspaper's office under surveillance, they took no further action out of fear that Sullivan was inviting prosecution in an effort to revive a faltering circulation. However, an energetic stipendiary magistrate experienced in hunting down Ribbonmen was transferred to the area of Cork and Kerry, and he was followed by detectives on loan from the Dublin Metropolitan Police. James Stephens's involvement was quickly uncovered and the disquieting rumour picked up that a regiment of Irish Americans was coming over to the "old country" on an "excursion." The discovery of correspondence traced to Rossa, the willingness of one of the men he had recruited to turn informer, the forwarding of the Phoenix Society's oaths by a local priest, the fact that the Roman

Catholic clergy had "with one accord pronounced against [it] – even from the altar," and fresh reports in mid-November of the society's continuing success recruiting members galvanized the Irish Executive into action. A proclamation reminded the public that oath-bound secret societies were unlawful and that persons involved in their promotion were guilty of a felony, and several known members of the society were detained. They were formally charged with "combining, conspiring and confederating with others to levy insurrection" against the Queen; conspiring "to move the citizens of the United States of America with force to invade Ireland"; establishing an oath-bound secret society "to make Ireland an independent democratic republic;" and "being trained and drilled to the use of arms, and to the practice of military movements and evolutions, in order to fight the soldiers and subjects of the Queen."[13]

Suppression created its own difficulties. Bishop Moriarty and several parish priests, moved by compassion, sought clemency for the "foolish boys" who had been arrested. The *Cork Examiner* and the *Nation* established a "Fair Trial" fund, which the Cork newspaper backed with an emotive campaign alleging physical abuse of the detainees. They had been transported in irons and open carts over long distances in foul weather, it claimed, and then thrown in their sodden clothes into cells and held for days without either accusers or accusations being revealed to them. Smith O'Brien, in contributing to the fund, drew a sharp distinction between his opposition to secret societies and his sympathy for the prisoners, but Archbishop MacHale was characteristically provocative. The Church was "no less opposed to those unhallowed combinations of bigoted might by which truth and innocence are so frequently overcome" than to illegal associations, he announced. The first trial, held at the Kerry Spring Assizes in 1859, resulted in a hung jury following the refusal of two witnesses to testify – they were sentenced to six months' imprisonment for contempt – and a brilliant forensic performance by the defence counsel, Thomas O'Hagan. His summation took almost thirteen hours to deliver. When the case was retried, the Crown took the precaution of excluding Roman Catholics from the "peers" who weighed the evidence. Daniel Sullivan, master at a national school, was convicted and sentenced to ten years' penal servitude. The strong odour of jury packing brought an embarrassing question in the House of Commons and a vehement public protest from the moderate Bishop of Kerry, David Moriarty. He had loudly decried any attempt to "canonize as patriots" the members of this "so-called conspiracy" or to claim that "the nationality of Ireland" was represented "by a company the only avowed and self-confessed members of which are certainly no credit to the old Milesian stock," but now denounced the setting aside of jurors solely on account of their religion. This action he labelled a grievous insult to the entire Catholic community. Alive to the perils of pressing on with tarnished prosecutions, the Irish Executive quickly accepted a proposal devised by the solicitors of the remaining prisoners and brokered by John Pope Hennessy, an intensely ambitious Conservative parliamentary candidate keen to establish his credentials as "an Irishman and a thoroughgoing nationalist." Rossa and five of his associates, on entering a "plea of legal guilt," were discharged on a form of probation, each on his own recognizance of £200. Six months later Sullivan was released on licence, and subsequently his sentence was commuted.[14]

The evidence that several schoolmasters were active in the conspiracy saw the Executive recommend to the commissioners of national education that all future appointees to teaching posts, perhaps the entire current staff, be required to declare on oath that during their employment they would not "join, subscribe or belong to any secret society whatsoever, unless to the Society of Freemasons." Similarly troubling was the knowledge that effective cooperation with the prelates and priests whose opposition might check the progress of such societies was likely to be difficult. David Moriarty, perhaps the strongest unionist within the hierarchy, had balanced his condemnation of the conspiracy with calls for clemency for the conspirators. Clearly, any resort to exemplary punishment was unlikely to win clerical support. Moreover, the constitutional nationalists, for whom the *Nation* and the *Cork Examiner* spoke, had demonstrated how easily a passively alienated citizenry could be aroused with accusations of harsh treatment of "foolish boys." As for the manipulation of jury selection to increase the chances of conviction, that simply exposed the Irish administration to the charge of enforcing sectarian justice. No less important, the release of the indicted men after eight months of detention suggests that the government had failed to detect the entirely new revolutionary organization into which they and many others had been sworn, this despite the fact that agents had identified James Stephens as a central figure. For his part, although embarrassed by the unwelcome publicity the entire affair had brought to his covert organizational activities, Stephens adeptly made the best of the situation. The realization that he had been identified undoubtedly influenced his decision to direct operations from Paris, while the conduct of the Catholic clergy in Cork and Kerry led him to amend the Brotherhood's oath. The formal commitment to secrecy was deleted. Beyond that, and as a former Young Irelander who held the clergy largely responsible for the humiliating events of 1848, Stephens silently and pragmatically accepted the aid of several clerical sympathizers, while his organization stood on the principle that priests should not meddle in politics.[15]

Stephens found other ways to turn the Phoenix episode to his advantage. Constitutional nationalists, working heroically to intensify national consciousness, struck a committee in the spring of 1859 to launch a national subscription campaign so that they might present a ceremonial sword to Napoleon's victorious general in the war with Austria, who happened to be of Irish descent. The presentation was duly made at Chalons in September of the following year. Meanwhile, led by A.M. Sullivan among others, the national petition campaign in support of a referendum on self-determination – effectively repeal – collected more than four hundred thousand signatures in 1860. A number of these activists were soon drawn into the Fenian movement, but as useful as the constitutionalists remained in creating a climate of opinion favourable to Fenian recruitment, Stephens scorned their strategy and viewed them as rivals for popular support. The Phoenix arrests and prosecutions provided him with a convenient scapegoat for his own organizational mistakes and thus an opportunity to discredit the leadership of the constitutional nationalists. He seized on the warnings published in the *Nation* against secret societies to accuse the publisher repeatedly and falsely of being an informer and "felon-setter." The vilified A.M. Sullivan, O'Connell-like in his calculated ambivalence with respect to physical force as a means of exerting greater pressure on the government to make concessions to Irish nationalism, played a large role in the founding of the National Brotherhood of St Patrick. Announced at a St Patrick's Day banquet in 1861, it initially represented another attempt to unite nationalists within "legal and constitutional lines." Local branches were to be loosely allied with a central office in Dublin, and all were dedicated to celebrations of the national day and the establishment of reading rooms. From the outset there may have been an intent, of which the likes of Sullivan were unaware, to look "to revolution, foreign aid and more or less directly preparing for that, though for the moment within the forms of law." Certainly, the National Brotherhood was speedily infiltrated by Fenians and thus widely regarded as no more than a front for revolutionary nationalism. Ireland's most notoriously nationalistic priest, Patrick Lavelle, accepted the vice-presidency.[16]

Branches of the Catholic Young Men's Society, founded by Father Richard O'Brien, were also Fenian targets. A devoted young follower of O'Connell in the struggle to secure Catholic emancipation, O'Brien's first parish following ordination had been in Nova Scotia. He promptly set about the task of organizing North American support for repeal and contributed patriotic poems to the *Nation*. Returning to Ireland on the eve of the Famine, which affected him deeply, he briefly served on the faculty of the "great Missionary College" of All Hallows, which sent forth young priests imbued with "love of faith and fatherland." O'Brien was next despatched to St Mary's, Limerick, as curate. The spring of 1848 found him working energetically to effect a reconciliation between repealers and Young Irelanders, only for his opposition to John Mitchel to earn him the enmity of the more radical nationalist elements. He launched the Young Men's Society in 1849, whose members were expected to make confession and take Holy Communion monthly and steer clear of party politics. Over the course of the next fifteen years, the society's branches multiplied, only for O'Brien, who was appointed parish priest of Newcastle West in 1861 and dean of Limerick four years later, suddenly to resign as its president general. He appears to have made the disheartening discovery that not only were its "brothers [being] sworn as members of the Fenian conspiracy, but collections were [being] made amongst them to buy firearms, which they designated fire-irons."[17]

Even as Stephens attracted recruits and effectively co-opted elements of constitutionalist organizations, claiming in the spring of 1860 to have thirty-two "centres" already at their posts, he continued to complain that additional local commanders could not be appointed, nor the scattered Fenian forces brought into "complete order," without the reliable funding that Irish America had promised him. It was entirely "the fault of the American branch that brother is not within call of brother from one end of Ireland to the other by this time," he charged. To stimulate giving, perhaps to loosen the purse strings of the large fund that had reportedly been amassed in the United States in aid of the Phoenix Society prisoners, Stephens decided to send those released patriots on transatlantic tours of Irish American communities. He had earlier despatched John O'Leary on much the same mission, only to compromise his mission by privately informing O'Mahony that the young agent lacked republican commitment, absolute faith in the success of the movement, and complete confidence in Stephens's abilities. O'Leary returned to France in the autumn of 1859 "with no stronger faith in Fenianism" and harbouring an unflattering opinion of Irish Americans. He was convinced that emigration had changed them essentially for the worse and that in intelligence they did not compare with Dublin men of the same class. There was one change of which he did approve, because it operated "powerfully for the good." That was the freedom an Irish American enjoyed "to say what he thinks and to do what he wishes; and the first wish of the natural man is ... to do something against England."[18]

O'Leary succeeded in promoting at least one of Stephens's projects. He secured the services of Irish Americans with military experience to act as drill-masters of Irish Fenians. Thomas Clarke Luby prophetically but unavailingly cautioned that damaging consequences would follow if these men arrived in Ireland without the means to support themselves and discovered that the local organizations were unable to maintain them. This proved to be the experience of several of the instructors, while others were disappointed by the absence of "circles" in their birthplaces. Inevitably, they grew discouraged and returned to the United States, disillusioned. There they voiced serious doubts of the extent of the Fenian organization in Ireland. O'Mahony, having long suffered Stephens's bitter reproaches, responded by sending a pair of his own agents to the homeland to obtain "a peep behind the scenes so that they may form their own judgment of the progress made and our prospects in general." Then, towards the end of 1860, he undertook a personal investigation.[19]

O'Mahony called on Stephens in Paris before travelling on to Ireland, where Luby was in temporary charge of organizational matters. He was enjoying some success in Dublin, especially among drapers' assistants, who had been radicalized by a long struggle with their employers to limit working hours. Bakers were another group whose employment griev-ances might be channelled to political ends. They were seeking an end to night work and Sunday work. When Stephens finally returned to Dublin, he and O'Mahony agreed to a series of meetings. The omens were not good. Stephens may have delayed his departure from Paris not simply out of fear of arrest but also to signal profound irritation with the "inquisitorial tendency" of a man he considered a subordinate. For his part, O'Mahony surely sensed and resented the contempt with which Stephens and a number of his colleagues, such as O'Leary, regarded Irish America. Equally unwelcome were the incessant complaints about the sums of money forwarded from the United States, suggesting as they did either ignorance of, or indifference to, the difficulties with which O'Ma-hony had to contend. In 1857 a sharp recession had "closed down over the country like a chill mist, filling the next two years with slowly diminishing misery and discontent." It complicated fundraising within an Irish community still heavily weighted at the lower end of the employment scale. Even as the economy warmed up, so did the political crisis over the future of slavery, further intensifying anxiety about the republic's future and concentrating minds on domestic concerns. And to the extent that Americans were willing to give thought to their nation's foreign relations, there was evidence by 1860 that the long contradiction within their nationalism, "between those who believed that the essence of American identity lay in being 'not English' and those who believed that American interests demanded the cultivation of past and present associations," was being resolved in a way favourable to the latter. In Buffalo, anxiety that Americans find a national sport saw some locals give thought to cricket as a possibility. The visit of the Prince of Wales to the United States was highly successful, with the nation's most influential woman, the author of *Uncle Tom's Cabin*, Harriet Beecher Stowe, publicly lauding the diminutive heir to the throne as "an embodiment, in boy's form, of a glorious related nation." A New York Irish militia regiment did seize its opportunity to deliver an embarrassing snub to the prince, but it was quickly forgotten. Instead, leading newspapers on both sides of the Atlantic waxed enthusiastically on the "common origin," "common language," "common principles," common Anglo-Saxonism of the two peoples, and "common bond of sympathy between two liberal governments." This was not an ideal climate for the flowering of Irish American anglophobia.[20]

When Stephens met with O'Mahony, he subjected him to a brutal verbal attack, dwelling upon "his shortcomings, feebleness and insincerity and wound up reminding him how he, Stephens, had dragged him out of obscurity and put him in a position he never dreamed of." Nevertheless, even in the absence of any realistic hope of an imminent Anglo-French conflict, they agreed that a rebellion should be launched. Irish America was to provide five thousand competent officers and trained men, and ten times that number of rifles and muskets. Armed with these promises and talking of imminent revolution, Stephens and his lieutenants attracted a fresh wave of Fenian recruits. But O'Mahony returned home deeply humiliated by his treatment at the hands of his former friend, and Luby later concluded that from "this date onwards, feelings of jealousy" between the two "grew daily more intense and bitter." Moreover, by the time O'Mahony disembarked in New York, the American Civil War had broken out. It dashed any hope of the promised men and materiel soon being shipped across the Atlantic. Instead, young American Fenians found themselves fighting to decide the future of the American Union. Some fifty "circles" simply dissolved with the enlistment of their members in the Union and Confederate armies.[21]

However disruptive of Fenian plans and costly in Irish American lives, the civil war ultimately aided the cause. The desire to attract men of Irish birth to the defence of the United States saw Unionists talk less of Anglo-Saxonism and more of a "'Celtic-American' ethnicity." They now avowed a racial kinship with Irish Americans. Not that the unflattering stereotype of Paddy was completely discarded. The publicity given to Irish desertions and to Irish resistance to the draft, which in the anthracite regions of Pennsylvania was a factor in the assassination of an unpopular mine owner and led to disturbances elsewhere, most tragically in New York City during the summer of 1863, ensured that the Irishman's reputation for violence endured. But hostility towards the Irish paled beside a resurgent anglophobia. Anglo-American relations deteriorated dramatically. Britain's Proclamation of Neutrality in May1861, recognizing as it did the Confederacy as a belligerent, was deeply resented by Unionists. Hatred of Britain was now back in vogue as a popular and patriotic sentiment. A tense diplomatic crisis following the removal on the high seas of two Confederate diplomats from the deck of a British mail steamer, the *Trent*, was only brought to an end by Lincoln's decision to surrender both men. American minds were further poisoned by the injudicious public comments of William Gladstone, chancellor of the Exchequer, which appeared to betray a desire in the highest circles of the British government to see the Confederacy successfully established; the construction of Confederate commerce raiders in British yards, one of which wrought havoc among the American mercantile marine; British running of what was for long merely a paper blockade of Confederate ports; British contempt for Lincoln's preliminary proclamation announcing his intention to free the slaves of rebels, which *Punch* captured in a cartoon depicting the president playing his last card, the ace of spades; and the evident public admiration in Britain of the Confederate struggle. In the opinion of one Irishman serving in the Union army, Britain's "whole course has been in aid of the rebels just as far as she could without comiting [sic] herself to a war with this government." He was far from alone in this belief, and Fenians smartly exploited it. In Philadelphia, for example, they took the lead in organizing a mass meeting to protest Britain's conduct during the *Trent* crisis and to voice their own grievances against her.[22]

The civil war also assisted Fenianism to the extent that it legitimized violence as a solution to political problems and reinforced its utility "in crafting a national identity." Close to two hundred thousand men of Irish birth served in the contending armies, three-quarters of them under the flag of the United States. The sense of Irish identity among these young men, concentrated as never before, often in Irish regiments, several of which formed the Irish Brigade commanded by the former Young Irelander Thomas Meagher, was greatly strengthened, as was their nationalism. In Wisconsin a dispersed Irish population developed greater group consciousness with the formation of an Irish regiment. Members of such regiments celebrated St Patrick's Day and were reminded of Ireland's sad history. Several lessons were driven home – the Famine had resulted not from a failure of the potato but from tyrannical laws and damnable oppression, and on "no other spot on the face of the earth was such tyranny and treachery practised as in Irland [sic] by its vilianous [sic] rulers." Peter Welsh, a color sergeant in a regiment of Massachusetts volunteers, advised his father-in-law in Ireland that "[w]hen we are fighting for America we are fighting in the interests of Irland [sic] striking a double blow cutting with a two edged sword[.] For while we strike in defence of the rights of Irishmen here we are striking a blow at Irlands [sic] enemy and opressor [sic]." This war, he added, was "a school of instruction for Irishmen" who hoped one day to have an opportunity "to strike a blow for the rights and liberty" of their homeland. The recruitment of such men by the Fenian Brotherhood was facilitated by the War Department, which permitted organizers, among them Luby in 1863 and Stephens the following year, to move freely through the ranks. This Irish American nucleus of an Irish army of liberation promised to be not only well drilled and well trained but also battle hardened. Furthermore, those Fenians who supported emancipation of the slaves were effectively distancing themselves from the traditional Irish allegiance to the Democratic Party and making friends of influential members of the ruling Republicans.[23]

The war years also saw a restructuring of the American Fenian Brotherhood, and one that enhanced its organizational efficiency. Under pressure from dissidents, O'Mahony agreed to summon a Fenian convention to settle differences, and he grasped the opportunity to assert his independence of Stephens. Resentful of the latter's "dictatorial arrogance," of being used as a scapegoat, and suspecting Stephens of being in league with the American critics of his leadership, O'Mahony initiated a "radical change" in the Brotherhood's "constitution and working machinery." No longer was the American organization to be subordinate to Stephens. Instead, it declared itself separate, equal, fixed, and permanent, one of two "closely allied but independent powers." Consistent with his own democratic views and the liberal traditions of the United States, O'Mahony successfully proposed that its chief executive be elected for a fixed term, be accountable to annual conventions, and be advised by a small, elected council. Also, a financial department was created, directed by an elected central treasurer who would disburse all monies. To re-emphasize their commitment to the goal of the Irish Revolutionary Brotherhood, the delegates who assembled in Chicago early in November 1863, having unanimously re-elected O'Mahony as head centre (commander), avowed "intense and undying hatred" of the monarchy and ruling elite of Britain, and proclaimed their determination to seek Ireland's freedom. Further, O'Mahony assured Stephens that he would be provided with "a certain and definite amount monthly as a subsidy, said sum being sufficient for the proper working of the I.R.B." As he argued in an explanatory letter to Charles Kickham, then in the United States fundraising but about to return home, the Fenian Brotherhood had no need to resort to secrecy. It was able to operate legally and openly, and was therefore "beyond the reach of hostile *churchmen*" whom he recognized as its "most formidable enemies." These were as yet individual enemies only, since the American hierarchy had up to this time officially ignored the Brotherhood.[24]

If the civil war years held American disappointments for Stephens, they witnessed his movement's advance across the domestic terrain. The conflict placed many Irish nationalists in something of a quandary. Could they in good conscience support a war to preserve the American Union even as they sought to secede from the United Kingdom? On the other hand, a strong and united America would be an invaluable ally in the struggle to secure self-determination. William Smith O'Brien and John Martin, two leading constitutional nationalists, urged the amicable separation of the Southern states from the Union. Martin's sympathies may have been influenced by those of his brother-in-law, John Mitchel, who nobly gave up the pleasures of Paris to return to the South. He edited the Richmond *Enquirer* in the Confederate capital and dashed off letters to the *Cork Examiner* proclaiming Confederate repudiation of "Anglo-Saxonism" and avowing Southern kinship with Celts. Elements of the Irish nationalist press also advocated recognition of the Confederacy and criticized England for failing to respond to French proposals for a joint diplomatic intervention. The slaughter of the Irish Brigade at Fredericksburg in December 1862, another sacrifice to Union military incompetence, the bloody Draft Riots of the following summer, in which the Irish were so prominent, and stories of Federal recruiters at work in Ireland served to alienate "a majority of the Irish from the Union cause." A succession of Confederate agents, several of them priests, arrived to counter Union activities. They had some success, both in stimulating "closer British scrutiny of Federal activity and [winning] increased support from the Church and Irish nationalist leaders." Led by Paul Cullen, most members of the hierarchy appear to have sympathized with the Confederacy. They identified the Union with anti-clerical liberalism, "the debasement of religious liberty," and radical Young Irelanders of the Meagher stamp, and loudly deplored the tempting of brave young Irishmen to sacrifice their lives for an American cause.[25]

Cullen accused the Fenians of being the domestic agents of the Northern states, but the conduct of the extreme nationalists was far less consistent and straightforward than this criticism implied. O'Donovan Rossa publicly supported the American Union, as did the *United Irishman and Galway American.* Edited by the former joint editor of an American Fenian newspaper, the New York *Phoenix,* the Galway paper was closely identified with Father Lavelle and widely regarded as the organ of the National Brotherhood of St Patrick. The *Irishman,* on the other hand, allowed the British government to determine its position. "England having taken one side of the question, we must be right in taking the opposite," it declared. Thus, once the government was identified as sympathetic to the South, it did an about-face and called for the preservation of the United States, both to humiliate England and advance the cause of Irish freedom. Similarly, British condemnation of Lincoln's Emancipation Proclamation as an incitement to servile rebellion saw the *Irishman,* formerly no friend of abolition, again urge Irishmen to rally to the Union cause. However, this pro-Fenian organ remained anything but consistent. Initially supportive for obvious reasons of Irish American military service, it subsequently rounded on those in Ireland who encouraged emigration and Irish enlistments. This was a conflict in which Irishmen had no concern, it declared. After all, the longer the war dragged on, the more Irish American resources, physical and fiscal, it would absorb. These were needed for the forthcoming struggle in Ireland. But Fenians consoled themselves with the thought that at the civil war's end many soldiers of Irish birth or parentage would be trained and willing to make another sacrifice, and this one for Ireland.[26]

Cullen's attempt to damage the Fenians by tarring them with the brush of Federal recruitment was an acknowledgment of their increasing strength, for Stephens engineered a series of public relations coups. A modest proposal of a group of nationalists in San Francisco, to raise a monument there to Terence Bellew McManus, the former Young Ireland rebel who had escaped from Van Diemen's Island to the city in 1851 and died a forlorn if not entirely forgotten figure a decade later, was transformed by local Fenians into a far more ambitious enterprise. McManus's attraction as a symbol was his commitment to physical force. He had publicly refused in the late 1850s to be embraced by the amnesty that activists in Ireland were urging the British to extend to the three transported rebels who had escaped to the United States. The remaining prisoners, among them Smith O'Brien, had been permitted to return home. McManus had bombastically announced his refusal ever to place himself under an obligation to a government "foreign to the *genius*, to the *religion*, and to the *liberty*" of Ireland, so the San Francisco Fenians decided to disinter his remains and return them to Ireland for reburial. This elaborate exercise in funeral propaganda was launched with full clerical cooperation, even though McManus had been identified as one of those Young Irelanders "who not content with emancipating themselves from British bondage [had] shaken off the sweet yoke of their Divine Master in a great measure ignoring Priests & Confession & Church." Exhumation was followed by a Mass in the cathedral, presided over by the archbishop, and the delivery of a nationalistic sermon by an Irish priest. There followed an impressive procession through the city's streets to the docks, where the casket was placed aboard a vessel for a journey to New York via the overland route across the Isthmus of Panama. In New York, O'Mahony took charge of the arrangements. The highlights included a Solemn High Requiem Mass in the cathedral, a fiercely nationalistic address delivered by Archbishop Hughes, and another impressive procession to the docks for the beginning of the transatlantic crossing. "Designed to create both an awe-inspiring occasion and to garner as much publicity as possible for the Fenians and the Irish separatist cause against England, the McManus funeral in New York succeeded in all respects."[27]

The architects of this extravaganza encountered a less uniformly helpful hierarchy in Ireland. Stephens was initially wary of a demonstration. He feared it might be interpreted as the signal for a rising that would be folly in November 1861. However, the propaganda value of an elaborate funeral could not be ignored. This had been demonstrated a quarter-century earlier by British trade unionists and Chartists. So Stephens ensured that his men controlled the committees organizing receptions for McManus's remains as they were ceremonially transported from Cork to Dublin, and that Fenians were in control of events when they arrived. The moderate nationalists involved were adeptly marginalized. The final procession through Dublin's streets to Glasnevin Cemetery was a truly impressive event, meeting Stephens's requirement that the crowds present outnumber those who had greeted Queen Victoria on her private visit only three months earlier. Mourners at the gravesite heard one of the accompanying Californians deliver a "perfervid exhortation," which Stephens had written, and witnessed Father Lavelle conduct the interment ceremony that Archbishop Cullen had forbidden. This grave held "the symbol of resurrection," Lavelle declared, which may explain why the Fenians long failed to mark the spot with a headstone. Never one to withhold praise from his own handiwork, Stephens claimed that a hundred and fifty thousand Dubliners had lined the streets and that every man among the thirty thousand marchers had uncovered his head as he passed the spot where Robert Emmet had been executed a lifetime earlier. Summarizing the episode for O'Mahony, he described it as "an act of scorn and defiance of British rule almost tantamount to an act of open rebellion." Here was proof that had they been "fairly supported" by their "transatlantic brothers," the Fenians of Ireland would have "wrought great results out of the feeling awakened." Only those areas of the country already organized by the Brotherhood had sent delegates to march in the procession, he informed the American, which proved to his satisfaction that outside of its ranks there was "no national life in Ireland." If the carefully staged funeral "gave a strong impetus to the Fenian Movement and made recruiting easy," it represented another outmanoeuvring of the constitutionalists.[28]

Within a month Stephens had repeated this success. Moderate nationalists such as A.M. Sullivan and The O'Donoghue, although the latter impressed at least one radical with his discreet personal belief in physical force, took the lead in organizing a public meeting during the *Trent* crisis to express support of the United States and lay the foundation of a new national organization that "would embrace all shades of Irish politics." But it was a fundamental Stephens maxim that "legal agitation" had always been "debasing and delusive." Similarly, he deluded himself that he had found "the cause of Ireland *dead*" and had single-handedly "awakened the dead and gave it action and power." In his opinion, "*[n]ò* man of brain could conscientiously question this after such a manifestation of life and power as was given at the McManus Funeral." Convinced that he alone had both earned the right and was qualified to lead the Irish cause, Stephens contemptuously dismissed the proposed new organization as another "of the driftlessly peaceable and legal kind." Scornful alike of The O'Donoghue's musings on the worthlessness of Irish representation in a British parliament and of the *Nation*'s adherence to the old Young Ireland refusal to exclude on principle any resort to physical force, he ordered Fenians to disrupt the gathering. They were numerous enough to intimidate the platform and control from the floor nominations to the committee struck to report on the advisability of the new organization. Once again he had put the "clique" of moderates to rout, Stephens privately boasted.[29]

A "growing popular belief in [Fenian] power and audacity" was further strengthened by Archbishop Hughes. He briefly visited his homeland in November 1861 on an informal diplomatic mission on behalf of the Union, and returned the following summer on his way back to the United States from Europe. He was scheduled "to deliver a discourse on Catholic education in connection with the new [Catholic] University." Among the delegations who sought and secured a meeting with him was one from the National Brotherhood of St Patrick, headed by The O'Donoghue. Hughes was characteristically indiscreet, repeating to this party much of what he had said in his address following the Solemn High Mass for McManus in New York. He denigrated bishops who were "regular government" men, voiced respect for activists like McManus, who "struggle for a righteous cause, though they may act rashly and imprudently," and attributed the failure of the rebellion in 1848 to the fact that "the means were not equal to the object proposed." He then reiterated the three grounds on which Catholic doctrine justified rebellion – tyranny, a popular conviction of "intolerable oppression," and a reasonable prospect of success. And while he recommended to the representatives of the National Brotherhood that they remain patient, steady, and resolute of purpose, he suggested, in an apparent allusion to the rapidly worsening Anglo-American relationship, that "events [were] occurring calculated to bring the wrongs, the miseries, the sufferings of the Irish people under consideration elsewhere."[30]

Within a fortnight Hughes was scrambling to extricate himself from the embarrassment caused by the publication in the *Freeman's Journal* of a verbatim account of his remarks. In letters to the *Cork Examiner* he claimed to have been duped into granting the interview by Peter Gill of the *Tipperary Advocate* and to have been unaware that the deputation was from the National Brotherhood, that it was a secret society and thus "condemned by the laws of God," and that "a skilled short-hand writer of many years practice" was present. Here was another error, for this Brotherhood was not a secret society. Before year's end Cullen offered Hughes the politic reassurance that his explanations had corrected the unfortunate impression created by his meeting with a Fenian front organization and that "all good Catholics" condemned the men "who attempted to practice a cheat upon [him]." But many newspaper readers, and surely Fenian recruiters, had undoubtedly by then interpreted the Archbishop of New York's comments as evidence of his sympathy for Irish rebels and support of a rebellion that had a good chance of success. Moreover, popular nationalism was given another archiepiscopal fillip when a group of Dublin liberals and Catholic clergy founded a committee in October 1862 to raise the funds with which to erect a monument to Daniel O'Connell. Their intention to honour him as the emancipator of Catholics allowed John MacHale to inject some spice into the movement by refusing to contribute on the ground that O'Connell's work as a repealer was being ignored.[31]

Growing Fenian confidence may explain the publication in 1862 of a model constitution for an independent Irish republic. The document reflected an eclectic mix of ideas – a bicameral legislature elected on the basis of universal suffrage, an indirectly elected president for life, the separation of powers, separation of church and state but considerable church influence over education, the abolition of the historic provinces, the transfer of the capital from Dublin to a more central location, and a naval and military establishment of some considerable size. But the following year opened with the Irish Revolutionary Brotherhood facing the reality of virtually empty coffers. Stephens postponed his own planned trip to the United States, complaining to O'Mahony that the "want of money has been a far greater injury than all our enemies could have done us, and the longer the want continues the greater the injury will be." Although Luby was despatched to "stir up" the American head centre, he returned in July with a mere £100. To generate an alternative source of income, Stephens turned to newspaper publishing. He harboured the fanciful belief that the *Irish People*, which appeared in the late autumn of 1863, would quickly establish a circulation of fifteen thousand in Ireland, five thousand in Great Britain, and a similar number in the United States. Even when the American circulation failed to materialize and that in Britain grew to a mere two thousand, he still expected to be able to turn a substantial annual operating profit, which he estimated would bring in "over ten times more" than the sums currently arriving from the United States. To promote the newspaper's circulation throughout Ireland, he despatched agents "to all parts." In some areas, however, they were successfully discouraged by priests hostile to the newspaper, while a number of newsagents declined to offer it for sale lest they lose the patronage of wealthy customers. Elsewhere, the conduct of the newspaper's manager, O'Donovan Rossa, who on occasion subsidized it out of his own pocket, severely reduced revenues. John Devoy as a Fenian agent received twenty-five copies each week, later increased to fifty. He distributed them free of charge. Similarly, Rossa restored to the list of subscribers a pair of schoolteachers in Devoy's area who had been stricken from it for failure to pay their bills. "The [Fenian] organization can't be run on business principles," the manager of the *Irish People* explained, "and we must push it every way we can." In short, the generation of income had quickly become secondary to the dissemination of the Fenian message.[32]

The circulation of the weekly appears never to have climbed above ten thousand, though the readership was undoubtedly far larger. This disappointing figure was partly attributable to the newspaper's primary function as an organ of propaganda. Its subscribers were unlikely to find any discussion of the "trivia of everyday living." The *Irish People* was founded "to propagate thoroughly national ideas," and the first of these was the necessity of violence for the achievement of genuine national independence. The Fenian program, from which no deviation could be made by the truly committed, called for "armed revolution on Irish soil for Irish independence." Constitutional agitation was ceaselessly ridiculed by the *Irish People*, and all of Ireland's ills traced with the same consistency and regularity to British misgovernment. The coverage of international affairs was similarly selective and narrow, being invariably restricted to those developments that might embroil Britain in foreign difficulties. A second of the national ideas propogated by the newspaper was the withdrawal of priests from politics. This seemed all the more urgent given clerical denunciations of the National Brotherhood of St Patrick. A related necessity was the severing of the exclusive identification of nationality with Catholicism. The task of delivering this message was given to Charles Kickham, who as a practising Catholic on the editorial staff was considered by his colleagues the best-equipped member to handle this sensitive issue. Beyond the constant repetition of such "national ideas," the Fenian organ did serve a defensive purpose. It answered the "scandal-mongers and calumniators" who in Stephens's opinion sought to blacken the characters of members of the Brotherhood and misrepresent their principles. And while it may not have achieved another of the objectives he set for it, that of rallying to Fenianism "the talent of the land," it did help to solidify and expand support. "The proposal and effort to bring it out kept us alive for months," he later claimed, and the exercise had facilitated his disciplining of "the organization in the south." The "regular weekly arrival of their own 'in-house' journal gave fenians an enhanced sense of solidarity; it was taken as visible evidence of an extensive movement under able leadership." In Stephens's opinion, the newspaper gave "a new life and color to the organization." It certainly proved to be an effective instrument with which to penetrate the large Irish community in Britain. A.M. Sullivan later acknowledged that the *Irish People* "swept all before it among the Irish in England and Scotland" and almost "annihilated" the circulation of his own newspaper. Together with organizers of the National Brotherhood of St Patrick and Fenian recruiters, such as Rossa, the *Irish People* could claim credit for the "immense organization" in England that so impressed an investigator from the American Brotherhood in 1865.[33]

In Ireland, Fenianism needed to expand its rural base. Approximately half of the membership of the Irish Revolutionary Brotherhood was drawn from the ranks of artisans, while shop assistants and clerks formed a separate and significant minority in Dublin and provincial towns. Many of them were undoubtedly younger sons of farmers, but farmers and their farm-labouring sons were a mere 10 per cent of the rank and file. Making a virtue of necessity, the *Irish People* identified young working men as the only reliable fighters against tyranny. The middle classes, commercial and agricultural, were dismissed as too selfish to put at risk their wealth or chances of social advancement. The large farmers, in particular, were scorned. They were devoid of sympathy for the people, Kickham charged, and had "no more souls than the brutes which they fatten for the tables of our English masters." Stephens held to the conviction that anything short of "a thoroughgoing *social* revolution can effect but small good for the people," but keen to avoid making unnecessary enemies, both clerical and lay, or providing those who already existed with additional ammunition, he denied being either a socialist or a communist. Later, having fled to the United States, he was to join the International Workingmen's Association but never impressed Karl Marx. Stephens understood that any plan for an Irish social revolution had to address the land problem. This meant an appeal to small farmers and peasantry. They were assured by the *Irish People* that they were the rightful owners of the soil. Further, the newspaper insisted that the only sure means of ridding the land of "territorial landlordism" was with "a *force* more deadly and destructive" than that by which landlords had "hitherto been maintained and preserved." By no other means would the land of Ireland be restored to its people, the Fenian organ declared. In short, support of the Fenians and adoption of Fenian means would rid the land of robbers and produce a nation of peasant proprietors, where every cultivator of the soil would be his own landlord, "the proprietor, in fee simple, of the house and land of his father." If this campaign did eventually swell Fenian ranks in the western counties of Ulster and Connacht, most of the gains were only made after the Brotherhood's local leaders focused on agitation of the land question. But Stephens's insistence on his absolute authority and his inflexible commitment to physical force meant that the struggle for land reform had to be fought on his terms and in accordance with his priorities. National independence was the priority, and his refusal to countenance constitutional agitation of the land issue ensured that there was no mass enlistment in the Revolutionary Brotherhood by small farmers and peasants.[34]

By 1863 there were reports of the Irish in Britain joining the Brotherhood in large numbers. Patrick Lavelle, following a tour of English and Scottish industrial cities, announced that the Irish in those two countries were more advanced in their nationalism than their brothers at home. Moderate Irish nationalists repeatedly asserted in the aftermath of the Chicago convention that Fenianism was an entirely American movement and that it would be the "height of imprudence" to seek to plant it in Ireland. Yet estimates of the size of the Irish Revolutionary Brotherhood put its strength at eighty thousand. Moreover, members were believed to be drilling regularly and holding midnight meetings. Nevertheless, John Martin, in another of his epistles to the *Nation*, sought to draw a sharp distinction between the American "military organization" and the National Brotherhood of St Patrick. The latter, he argued, was non-military and committed to the peaceful promotion of national independence. However, he continued to recite his own nationalist mantra – "We cannot obtain justice under English rule, we cannot obtain good legislation from the English Parliament" – while the *Nation* expressed sympathy for those "exiles" in the United States who

banded together "to strike some day for the liberation of their country."
This continued stoking of nationalist fires by moderates clearly aided
Fenian recruitment, yet Stephens continued to pour scorn on constitu-
tionalism.[35]

Early in 1864 Martin took the lead in founding the Irish National
League. He envisaged it as the kind of nationalist umbrella beneath
which much of the nation might cluster. Lecturers despatched the length
and breadth of the country would instruct the people in their rights,
"awaken them to their glorious past," reassure them that Ireland had
not always been "the Niobe of nations, the vassal of the fair-haired
Saxon churl," and remind them that they had once "enjoyed the price-
less blessing of native and legitimate legislation." But Fenians were soon
in evidence at National League meetings, either disrupting or compromising them with demands for physical force as the only sure instrument of national independence. The *Irish People* kept up the assault,
dismissing as worthless resolutions and petitions, monster meetings and
eloquent denunciations of the Saxon, legal leagues and penny pamphlets. Martin argued in vain that were all nationalists to unite in a new
repeal movement, "England would before long find it her best policy to
yield to our just demand." Peaceful protest, a peaceful demand made by
the great majority of the Irish people backed by the diaspora, would not
fail this time, he insisted. By year's end he was obliged to admit that the
popular response to the league had been disappointing.[36]

There were other fillips to nationalism in 1864 that, together with
outbursts of anti-English rhetoric by opinion leaders, worked to the
Fenians' advantage. A meeting held at the Rotundo, Dublin, in February, to condemn a decision of the corporation to reserve a portion of
College Green for a statue of Prince Albert (it was subsequently erected
on a more peripheral site) was broken up by a Fenian raiding party led
by Rossa just as A.M. Sullivan was about to speak. A second meeting
was called, at which a second Fenian attack was beaten back, allowing
Peter Gill of the *Tipperary Advocate* to predict that Ireland would yet
rise from her grave "to clutch the tyrant by the throat." A few months
later Smith O'Brien died, and in making his contribution to a monument fund the Bishop of Limerick expressed sentiments that he insisted
were shared by most members of the hierarchy and the great majority
of priests. Smith O'Brien had been convinced, and millions of Irishmen
shared the conviction, the bishop reportedly remarked, that Ireland was
"not only robbed and ruined, but also enslaved – debased to very serfdom – by its subjection to England." Shortly afterwards, the ceremonial

laying of the foundation stone of the O'Connell monument was staged, and the event was marked by an impressive nationalist demonstration. A procession numbering perhaps sixty thousand strong, in which several members of the hierarchy participated, marched through streets lined with spectators who numbered in excess of one hundred and fifty thousand. Everywhere the national colour, green, was on display. Moderate nationalists had resolved to adorn Dublin and other cities with monuments to heroes of the past, and they were careful to place them in the most prominent locations. Sullivan opened a campaign in 1864 for a statue of Henry Grattan, which was to be unveiled in 1876.[37]

Cullen, among others, saw in the iconic Daniel O'Connell a "weapon with which to beat the Fenians." Indeed, he had staged an impressive public demonstration in support of a Catholic university the previous summer partly as a response to the McManus extravaganza. Meanwhile, Charles Kickham was using the Bishop of Toronto's controversial and widely circulated letter to the Irish clergy as a stick with which to beat both clerical critics of Fenianism and the Fenian drum. Writing in the *Irish People*, he characterized Bishop Lynch's account of the "misery and degradation of the outcast children of Erin" as proof that their suffering had been unprecedented in the history of man and remained a standing rebuke to priests who regarded the Famine as providential in that it drove "the Irish abroad to spread the Catholic faith." Lynch's assertion that Fenianism was spreading rapidly in North America because the young Irish there were less obedient to their priests provided Kickham with an opening to develop the Fenian case against clerical politicians. In no country of the world had the clergy proved themselves such bad politicians as in Ireland, he charged. Further, if "the people were submissive to the clergy in politics there would be no Fenian Brotherhood. Ireland would be allowed to perish without a hand being raised to help her." What made this indictment so apposite was the announcement in December 1864 of the founding of the National Association, widely viewed as a Cullen-inspired and -controlled alternative to the Irish Revolutionary Brotherhood.[38]

The National Association was first bruited shortly after Stephens's return from yet another tour of Irish America. A Fenian fair had been organized in Chicago by a group seeking more active leadership of the Fenian Brotherhood, and Stephens hoped to lay his hands on the revenue it generated. As ever, he quickly found much to complain about – the funds provided to him were insufficient, his personal reception had

on occasion lacked courtesy, the strength of the Fenian Brotherhood was a mere fraction of what he had been led to expect, while
O'Mahony was personally unwilling to throw himself energetically into
fundraising. In short, perhaps in revenge for O'Mahony's declaration of
independence, Stephens compounded the head centre's problems by
allying with his critics. At the same time, his language of urgency and
immediacy, his unqualified commitment to launch a revolt in 1865,
made for a very successful recruiting drive through the ranks of the
Union army. A weakened O'Mahony had little option but to agree to a
further restructuring of his organization. He accepted the appointment
of a full-time organizer as his deputy at the national level and of similar deputies in each state organization. He even sanctioned direct communication between his local branches and the Irish Revolutionary
Brotherhood "in the matter of finances," only to retract this last, humiliating concession once Stephens was safely out of the country.[39]

Two months after Stephens's return to Ireland in August 1864, the
hierarchy resolved to engage even more actively in politics. The spread
of Fenianism alarmed the bishops, as did the surge in emigration. John
Blake Dillon, the former Young Irelander, took the initiative in the formal launch of the National Association, having persuaded a reluctant
Cullen to take a leading role. The decision taken, the archbishop dominated the aggregate meeting held in the Rotundo on 29 December
1864. On his feet for well over an hour, he dwelt on Ireland's miseries
and grievances before sketching the association's reform agenda. It
sought compensation of tenants for improvements made to their holdings. However, apparently in response to a letter from John Bright and
conceivably with a wary eye on the Fenians' radical land policy as outlined in the *Irish People*, he advocated peasant proprietaries as the ultimate solution of the question. The other two principal demands of the
association were disestablishment of the Church of Ireland and denominational education. From the outset, however, it was plagued by clerical disunity despite the presence of Cullen, Archbishop Leahy of Cashel,
and five bishops at the inaugural meeting. MacHale publicly dissociated
himself, declaring repeal the only remedy for Ireland's grievances. Other
clergy, especially those who had been prominent in the now defunct
Tenant League, initially held back because of the failure to place the
land issue at the top of the agenda immediately. Hence the association's
subsequent avowal of the priorities and strategies of the previous
decade. Members of Parliament elected under its standard were to provide independent opposition to any government that failed to adopt the

association's entire program, the first item of which was now land reform. Not that these decisions were welcomed by every lay nationalist. John Martin, sounding all the world like a MacHale echo, had already declared that he did not seek "good legislation ... from the English Parliament, but the renunciation of their usurped right to legislate at all for Ireland."[40]

The *Irish People* was the most persistent and strident critic of the National Association, ridiculing such "piecemeal" reforms as disestablishment. The Irish had to focus on the cause of all their ills, which it identified as the constitutional connection to Britain. Tenant rights, or any rights, would never be secured until Ireland was free, and to achieve this, the Irish had to fight. The lesson of history was that subject nations could only escape an oppressor's yoke through a resort to arms. Nor was the newspaper afraid, in this belligerent mood, to confront the challenge of O'Connell's memory. His incremental strategy had proven disastrous for Ireland, the Fenian organ charged, so it was certain to be ruinous in the hands of his less able successors. Small farmers were reminded that the rank and file of the emancipation struggle, the forty-shilling freeholders, had been destroyed in that "so-called victory." So what could they expect from the National Association, apart from a mere nibbling at the edges of aristocratic privilege that would merely further inflame the influential aristocracy against the "working classes."[41]

By the beginning of Stephens's promised year of action, 1865, the Fenians were boldly, if somewhat foolishly, attracting the attention of two formidable enemies – the Catholic Church and the Protestant state. Clerical warnings against secret societies were increasing in number, though many of them were framed in language that tended to minimize the negative impact on the Irish Revolutionary Brotherhood. Thus the Bishop of Limerick and his then archdeacon, Richard O'Brien, were at pains to deny that their opposition had anything to do with the hostility of such societies to the "English government." Bishop Butler admitted to no astonishment "that people who have lost all hope betake themselves to the ranks of violence – or even imprudent or rash endeavour." It was unfortunate statements such as these that led an otherwise thoughtful analyst of "The New Irish Difficulty" to the disturbing conclusion that there was "not a single Fenian outburst against 'English rule' that could not be paralleled from past pastorals of Irish Catholic bishops, and past speeches of Irish parish priests."[42]

The *Irish People* was evidently a Fenian propaganda asset, assiduously cultivating that sense of injustice, deprivation, and frustration that promised to generate widespread popular support for a resort to violence. On the other hand, it remained a fiscal and security liability. Stephens had invested too much prestige in the newspaper's survival, however, to block this drain on the Brotherhood's meagre resources. He would not close down the *Irish People*. "The moral defeat would be so great that we could no longer raise our heads here," he explained to an American correspondent. "There would be a yell of triumph on the part of our enemies, apparently well enough justified to drive away many from our ranks." He might have given more careful thought to another danger. As the newspaper's editor conceded, "it was soon inferentially evident [to the reading public] that a secret body was spread over the country, having for its object the overthrow of English rule in Ireland." He assumed that the Executive was well aware of this from its own intelligence sources. The attention of the authorities was evidently being drawn to the office of the *Irish People,* "the seat and center of Irish revolution in Parliament Street," and not least by the bully-boy tactics that Stephens authorized to break up constitutionalist gatherings. These skirmishes, in which the newspaper's business manager, Rossa, invariably played a leading role, were in the opinion of one nationalist a "suicidal and calamitous check to secret propaganda for national liberty." Equally imprudent was Patrick "Pagan" O'Leary. It was foolish and irresponsible of the Pagan, being the Fenian agent charged with the implementation of the strategy of subverting the large Irish element of the military garrison, to appear so frequently at a newspaper office under police surveillance. His arrest at Athlone in mid-November 1864 provided the authorities with clear evidence of Fenian subversion. He was unwisely carrying a letter from Stephens as well as a bundle of copies of the *Irish People*. Could it be long before the Executive took direct aim at the Fenians? As one observer remarked, "Silent, practical, unpoetical, unsectarian, democratic, and Socialistic" – the last an allusion to the promise of peasant proprietorships – Fenianism possessed "unexpected characteristics" that entitled it to "more consideration" than earlier "frothy agitations."[43]

9

The Roman Catholic Church and Fenianism

Fenian delegates attending the convention held in Cincinnati early in 1865 heard O'Mahony declare their Brotherhood "virtually at war with the oligarchy of Great Britain." Having unanimously re-elected him head centre, they doubled the size of his central council, from five to ten members, and adopted a series of measures intended to swell the treasury as rapidly as fresh members were sworn. To hasten that process, paid organizers were appointed and a closer eye kept on the Brotherhood's accounts. One promising area of expansion was British North America, with its large Irish Catholic population. Eight Canadian delegates from five separate cities had attended the first convention in Chicago, others had put in an appearance at the Fenian Fair held in the same city, and several were present in Cincinnati. Moreover, the British territories made a tempting military target. The ease with which the border could be reached by rail from most centres of Fenian strength, the knowledge that it was sparsely defended and that British naval power could not easily be employed in its defence, the confidence that enough territory could be occupied to allow the flag of an Irish republic to be raised and a request then made to the United States for recognition of its belligerent status, and the belief that such a dramatic turn of events would bolster Fenian morale and generate greater financial support from Irish America caused many an eye to turn northwards. The apparent aversion of some Catholic Irish Canadians to loyalism, if not receptivity to Fenianism, had been displayed during the *Trent* crisis. A meeting called in Montreal by D'Arcy McGee, to form an Irish battalion for the defence of Canada in the event of an Anglo-American conflict, had been broken up by elements he identified as local Fenians. The episode dissuaded the wary authorities from seeking to raise Irish battalions in either Montreal or Toronto, though many Irishmen did join other regiments.[1]

Fenianism in the guise of the Hibernian Benevolent Society had enjoyed modest growth during the civil war years. Branches were established in Quebec and Montreal, and while fewer than fifteen regulars initially attended meetings in the latter city, several prominent members of the local community did put in an appearance at St Patrick's Day dinners, where they heard Fenian speeches and renditions of republican songs. Even "the very loyal and respectable St. Patrick's Day Society" was successfully infiltrated by a nucleus of Fenians. Meanwhile, the Hibernians were active in Toronto, where Michael Murphy had become Fenian head centre in 1860. The parades celebrating the national day in 1863 and 1864 were of unprecedented size, the Fenian sunburst banner much in evidence, and Murphy's speeches provocative and belligerent. He invariably boasted that he led twenty thousand Irish Canadians ready to die for a homeland "whose liberty could be obtained only by blood," his influence in the community enhanced by the presence of Bishop Lynch beside him on the platform. Meanwhile, the Hibernians' organ faithfully preached from a Fenian text. Ireland had "never yet got a single request from England unless that request was backed by a show of physical force," the *Irish Canadian* maintained. The destiny of Ireland was in the hands of her children on the North American continent, and they would answer her cries of distress "in the only possible way to bring about permanent succour, namely through revolution aye, to a revolution of blood, if needs be."[2]

Hibernians, "armed to the teeth with guns and pikes," even briefly took control of several Toronto streets on the night of 5 November 1864, ostensibly to confront the Orangemen rumoured to be planning to burn effigies not only of Guy Fawkes but also of O'Connell and the Pope. The incident sparked a Fenian panic, which the province's leading newspaper happily fed. A Catholic Fenian network had been established across "the whole of Canada" and was plotting a mass slaughter of Protestant innocents, the Toronto *Globe* hysterically warned. The announcement by Toronto's chief constable that three thousand rifles had been shipped from the United States and buried in an Ottawa cemetery, the discovery of a cache of pikes in an Irish-owned tavern, and the report that Murphy had been detained in Buffalo while on an arms-buying mission, only to be released following the intervention of a Toronto policeman, lent credibility in excited minds to the hysterical talk of a second St Bartholomew's Day Massacre. Protestant farmers fortified their homes and barricaded their communities, but the sectarian paranoia slowly subsided as it became clear that bands of Irish Catholic assassins were not prowling the countryside. However, an undercover police force that the provincial government had formed recently to bring a halt to embarrassing Confederate conspiracies hatched on British territory against the border states of the Union, as well as to Union recruitment, which had allegedly drawn tens of thousands of Canadians into the American conflict, soon got wind of Fenian activities. They detected Fenian circles in several cities and, with the end of hostilities in the United States, gave their full attention to the subversive organization. Reports that there were six hundred and fifty sworn Fenians in Toronto excited concern for the security of the weapons stored in the city's armouries, and it was estimated that double that number were active elsewhere in the province. The Toronto Hibernians further heightened the tension by inviting one of O'Mahony's intimates to be the guest speaker at their St Patrick's Day celebration in 1865. Red Jim McDermott, later to be exposed as a British informer, boasted on his return to New York that while in Toronto he had spoken treason for three hours without fear of arrest. Were a force of five thousand Fenians to invade Canada, the Catholic Irish population there would rise in their support, he predicted.[3]

He was talking nonsense. Some leading figures in the Irish community of British North America, such as Timothy Anglin in New Brunswick, were admittedly studies in ambivalence. Anglin dismissed the Fenian threat as "grossly exaggerated," but his conviction that the government of his native land was "one of the worst in Europe" led him to voice sympathy for the Fenians' ultimate objective while questioning the wisdom of their chosen means. Many other middle-class Irish immigrants, however, were keener to win "the confidence of the host society." This they did by "quickly discarding those aspects of their traditional culture which were found objectionable, and by working through the political system to redress outstanding grievances." A forthright commitment to constitutionalism shaped their response to Ireland's problems. D'Arcy McGee, who spoke to and for this ambitious sector of society, was the sternest and most influential Irish Canadian critic of Fenianism. He had long insisted that the Irish had no right to bring their patriotism to the soil of Canada. Their first duty, he constantly reminded his fellow countrymen, was to their new land. Promoted to ministerial rank, first as a

Reformer in the administration of Sandfield Macdonald and then, in 1864, as a Conservative minister of agriculture in the government formed around George-Etienne Cartier and John A. Macdonald, McGee waged an unrelenting campaign against the Brotherhood. He warned Irish Canadians that association with this subversive society would revive doubts of their loyalty and place in jeopardy all the economic and social gains they had made in British North America. Perhaps galvanized by evidence of the expanding Fenian organization in Montreal, he stepped up his rhetorical attacks on this "foreign disease," dubbing it "political leprosy," and turned to the Church for assistance in preventing its further transmission. There was little danger of the "malady spreading far, if at all," he reasoned, so long as the Catholic laity was "advised & directed in matters of faith & morals (including, of course, all secret societies, most especially secret seditious societies), by their law-abiding & law-enforcing clergy."[4]

News that individual members of the American hierarchy had publicly condemned Fenianism saw the *Irish Canadian* struggle to limit any collateral damage to the Canadian branch of the movement. The churchmen involved would quickly reconsider their actions, it confidently predicted. After all, O'Mahony had denied that his was a secret organization and had demanded to know how the Brotherhood differed from those Polish societies whose activities the Church had declared praiseworthy. More helpful, still, was John MacHale's forwarding of three autographed prints of himself to be sold at the Chicago Fenian Fair. Here was proof of the favour with which one of the greatest figures of the Irish hierarchy regarded the Fenians, the *Irish Canadian* reported, before further stretching the truth with the claim that the archbishop's stand was supported by the laity and clergy of Ireland. This defensive campaign served to strengthen the Protestant conviction, which Bishop Lynch and the Hibernians had either inadvertently or thoughtlessly fostered, that Catholicism and Irish nationalism were one and the same. From here it was but a short step, and one promptly taken by the Toronto *Globe*, to identify Fenianism with Catholicism.[5]

The Hibernians fanned sectarian flames by wrecking "an Orange hall in Toronto, desecrating the Bible, the flag, and the Queen's portrait to boot." Inevitably, Lynch's close association with them threatened acute personal and institutional embarrassment. He had sponsored the society and defended it against those "respectable" Catholic critics who urged him to condemn it as an "unlawful society" connected to American Fenians. Indeed, several of those who signed an address requesting episcopal action subsequently accused the bishop of revealing their identities to the Hibernians. Despite repeated warnings from his own priests of the society's association with Fenianism, Lynch denied that there was a Fenian organization in Canada West and insisted that the Hibernians were committed to good and benevolent purposes. He continued to grace the platform from which Michael Murphy delivered his bellicose threats during St Patrick's Day festivities and made no effort to dissociate himself from the Hibernian's remarks. On the contrary, he presented his own indictment of British rule of Ireland. Had the subjects of the papal states fled in rags and misery from their fertile land to a country engaged in a cruel civil war, he declared, the Pope and his government "would be held up especially by the Protestant press to the execration of the whole world." Three months later he did issue a formal condemnation of Fenianism, only to minimize its effect in Canada by insisting that the movement was exclusively American. Similarly, his criticism of the armed demonstration by Hibernians on Guy Fawkes Night was virtually lost in an accompanying excoriation of Orangeism that to some minds smacked of an implied justification of Fenianism. The basic error of this apologia was privately pointed out to Lynch by McGee. Orangeism was a great evil, though not seditious, and it could never justify Fenianism. Those who selected that ground of defence chose "a low & false ground, for a bad and indefensible cause," McGee remarked. Nor was the bishop's reputation in the wider community enhanced by the sectarian belligerence and anti-English sallies of a newspaper widely regarded as his organ, although few knew that the *Canadian Freeman* owed its survival to financial aid advanced by the Conservative government at Lynch's request. Undoubtedly, his strident Irish nationalism and association with the Hibernians lent a measure of credibility to the bizarre accusation levelled by a Montreal Catholic newspaper in the spring of 1865 that he had met with Red Jim MacDermott during the latter's recent visit to Toronto and had spoken to him favourably of Fenianism. The *Irish Canadian* doubted that any such meeting had taken place or that Lynch would ever have made such an indiscreet remark, but it also disputed the Montreal paper's claim that no Catholic could be a Fenian. "There are many thousands of earnest and devoted Catholics, as earnest and devoted Fenians," it declared. "They hold their religion first, their country next."[6]

Toronto remained the centre of Fenian activity in Canada. All Hibernians were not Fenians but most Fenians were also Hibernians. As such, they enjoyed "the support of the clergy and the vast majority of Irish Catholics" in Canada West. Bishop Farrell of Hamilton did denounce the Hibernian Society in May 1864, only for Murphy to respond with a hymn of praise to the Bishop of Toronto's Irish nationalism. When Farrell repeated the condemnation fourteen months later, echoing a vigorous condemnation of Fenianism in Canada East by Bishop Bourget, the Hibernian president was tempted into a greater indiscretion. He launched a verbal assault on Farrell for meddling in temporal affairs, clumsily implying that he was a renegade and traitor to the Irish cause. The bishop promptly excommunicated the local Hibernians, leaving Lynch with little choice other than to rally to the defence of episcopal dignity and authority. He finally put some distance between himself and the society, apologizing to his brother bishop for Murphy's taunts and insults. He described the Hibernian's remarks as "highly offensive" and acknowledged a "sacred duty to entreat all good Catholics to quit a society that has fallen away from Catholic principles, and in as much as it is governed by imprudent men." Significantly, there was still no formal ban on the Hibernians in Toronto. Instead, Lynch argued that if Fenians were defined as persons who objected to the oppression of Ireland and hated England, then they were to be found everywhere. None of this prevented the disappointed *Irish Canadian* from expressing disbelief that an Irish bishop would hound Hibernians simply because a fellow prelate "conceived a certain hostile and unaccountable hatred towards them."[7]

That Lynch remained a devout nationalist was evident from his subsequent exchange with Archbishop Connolly of Halifax. Declaring the material and social condition of Roman Catholics in British North America far superior to that of their fellow religionists in the United States, Connelly publicly expressed the opinion that Catholics had nothing to expect from the success of the Fenians "but bloodshed, rapine and anarchy, and the overthrow of God's religion." He suspected these militant nationalists of being agents of American annexationism. Lynch disagreed. He disputed Connolly's comments with respect to individual wealth and access to public office, insisting that in Canada West the Irish had long been the victims of Orangeism and bigotry. He dwelt on the plight of "a downtrodden and oppressed race ... banished from their country, in poverty and destitution," which explained to his satisfaction both their sad contribution to criminal statistics and their membership in the Fenian Brotherhood. He professed to deplore not only Fenianism but also "the causes which give rise to this vast organization." The first of these was "the suppuration of a deep chronic wound inflicted on Ireland" by the British. He pointedly warned Connolly of the danger that clergy ran of alienating Irish Catholics when they denounced the Fenians but uttered "scarcely a word of reproof for the exterminators of the poor," and argued that the British had schooled the Irish in revolutionary nationalism by their admiration for Garibaldi.[8]

Connolly opened his reply diplomatically, declaring his hearty concurrence in almost all of Lynch's statements, but he went on to deliver several well-aimed counter-jabs. Irish priests in North America could sympathize with Ireland and "all her wrongs and grievances" so long as they understood that their "first duty" was to take care of their own people. The time had come, he insisted, hewing to the McGee line, for the position of the Catholics of British North America to be defined and understood irrespective of Irish politics. In Nova Scotia and New Brunswick they had all that the best government could give them, while their minority status everywhere meant that suspicion of their loyalty would be "absolutely destructive." There was Orangeism in the Atlantic colonies, he conceded, but it paled beside American nativism. He had never in his whole life seen "more bigotry and more contempt for everything Irish" than that on display in the republic. As for Lynch's challenge to his assessment of the comparative success of the Catholic Irish populations of the two lands, he tartly remarked that it would be difficult to find five individuals out of Boston's seventy thousand Irish with whom the Bishop of Toronto "could decently sit down to dinner." Those Irish unhappy with the government of British North America could take themselves off to the republic. Connolly did not dispute that Ireland's grievances would have made rebellion there lawful at any time over the last six hundred years, but he insisted that there had never been a day when the Irish could have risen successfully and never had there been so little chance of success than at the present. He did not approve of attempting the impossible, and he felt nothing but contempt for those who whined, screeched, and brandished foolish threats against the "Bloody Saxon." Unfortunately, this was the very essence of Irish American politics, he concluded, as venal knaves and demagogues exploited honest and patriotic fools for their own monetary benefit.[9]

A belated realization that he needed to convince the province's public that he did not endorse the Fenian remedy for Ireland's evils prompted Lynch's sponsorship of "a humble petition and remonstrance" founded on the proposition that the imperial parliament could cure Ireland's ills "in one session by repealing unjust laws." Catholics should be freed from the obligation to support the Protestant Church, tenants should be protected from landlords who were currently able under the law to rob them of "the fruits of their honest labour & outlay," and the system of mixed education should be dismantled. Indeed, what Ireland required were the laws that accounted for the absence of such evils in Canada, but foremost among British North America's blessings was local representative government. Canadians enjoyed the privileges of the British Constitution, not least home rule. Only fundamental constitutional reform in Ireland could halt the spread of "disaffection and hatred against England throughout the length and breadth of the American Continent" by "a huge organization, which [was] insanely preparing to attempt to right the wrongs of Ireland with the sword." This implied acceptance of his position saw Archbishop Connolly agree to sign a carefully worded petition. For his part, as an ally of Lynch's in the petition endeavour, McGee cautioned that no address would have "any serious effect for good, unless accompanied by a simultaneous demonstration *against* Fenianism." Lynch subsequently issued a second condemnation of the Brotherhood, but again appended a statement in which he deplored "sincerely the causes which give rise to this vast organization." Obliged to denounce the Fenians, he refused to "pass over the iniquity of the oppressors of the poor, which will bring sooner or later the vengeance of Heaven on their heads." Moreover, he selected an Irish nationalist with a somewhat suspect commitment to constitutionalism, The O'Donoghue, to present the petition to Parliament.[10]

In Canada, Toronto remained the only centre where the strength of the Fenian Brotherhood gave the provincial government cause for concern. The relatively few cities of any size where concentrations of Irish might have provided organizers with opportunities for significant recruitment; the tradition of loyalty that the Fenian threat served merely to strengthen, thus reinvigorating Orangeism; the minority position of the Roman Catholic population, which dictated discretion rather than nationalist valour; the absence of intensely nationalist refugees in sufficient numbers to provide a substantial nucleus of an extremist movement; the lack of a widespread, vehemently nationalist press; the refusal of the Catholic hierarchy, with the notable exception of the Bishop of Toronto, to take a vanguard position on Irish nationalism; the insistence of religious leaders that the solution to Ireland's problems was the establishment there of a regime similar to that under which Irish Canadians lived; and the consistency with which clerical and lay spokesmen urged Irish Canadians to count their blessings and concentrate on the development of their adopted land, all helped to limit the appeal of Fenianism to the Catholic Irish population of British North America. This rendered highly unlikely, in turn, its cooperation with a Fenian invasion. "To attempt to enslave four millions of us in order to effect the mock liberation of 4,000,000 in Ireland is a farce[,] a mere comedy, I hope," Connolly had observed in his exchange with Lynch. Still, Irish nationalism did not simply fade away. During Canada's long winter nights, Lynch noted approvingly, children were still being instructed by their parents in Irish history and Irish wrongs. "Irish tales, songs, Irish newspapers reproduced here, Irish patriotic speeches at school exhibitions, keep up the spirit of Irish nationality not to speak of the processions on St Patrick's day." D'Arcy McGee eventually made this discovery for himself. His militant anti-Fenianism proved unacceptable to many of his former supporters in Montreal.[11]

Bishop Wood of Philadelphia was the first member of the American hierarchy to denounce the Fenians. The violence of the Molly Maguires in the anthracite regions of Pennsylvania may have been the trigger for his condemnation of secret societies in January of 1864, but he was careful to take aim publicly at the Fenian Brotherhood. He could count on the backing of the *Catholic Herald*, the official organ of the diocese, and he despatched Catholic revivalists to the mining towns to continue the struggle. They arrived armed with the right to deny confessional absolution to any member of the Brotherhood who failed to resign from it "by a written oath of renunciation." The bishop was confident that his decisive action had been worthwhile. "It had the effect of preventing in a great degree their institution in our mining districts where they would do incalculable harm," he wrote to Paul Cullen. Bishop Duggan of Chicago followed suit with a condemnation of the Brotherhood even though he privately excoriated the "villainous Government" that had driven the Irish "from their own soil." At their Chicago convention only three months earlier, the Fenians had loudly denied that theirs was an oath-bound secret society, yet this was the very basis of Duggan's action. He instructed his priests to refuse the sacraments to all who continued as members or who "aided and encouraged" the Brotherhood. Both bishops had as authority for their actions Vatican decrees of 1846 and 1850, the latter making it clear that secrecy alone justified a society's condemnation. Proof that it was plotting against church or state was not required. O'Mahony's response to this threatening turn of events was twofold. He repeated his denial that the Brotherhood was a secret society, and vigorously disputed Duggan's claim that the Irish hierarchy had already condemned the organization. The bishop had confused the National Brotherhood of St Patrick with the Irish Fenian movement, the head centre correctly pointed out, before going on somewhat more speciously to disavow any connection between the two. Furthermore, since the Fenian Brotherhood was exclusively American, it was not subject to the authority of Irish bishops. Although O'Mahony subsequently acknowledged that "certain Catholic clergymen" were the Fenians' most formidable adversaries, he assured the delegates attending the Cincinnati convention in January of 1865 that the organization had not suffered "much material damage" as a result. Instead, he sarcastically thanked "the Reverend opponents" for the publicity they had given it.[12]

Archbishop Purcell of Cincinnati added his voice to those of Wood and Duggan, having long since published in the *Catholic Telegraph* the constitution, bylaws, and oath of the Brotherhood. In February of 1865 he lashed out "strongly and pointedly" against the Fenians, insisting that, the denials notwithstanding, theirs was an oath-bound society in which "monstrous arbitrary power" was wielded by the leader. His brother, the vicar-general, joined the attack, taking the Fenians to task following the announcement of their intention to disregard a papal condemnation. But the Fenians did not want for allies, clerical and lay. Significantly, even Archbishop Purcell had concluded his denunciation of Fenianism with an affirmation of his love for Ireland, his desire for her independence, and his recognition of "England's injustice, inhumanity and tyranny." Privately, he chided the editor in chief of the *Telegraph* for the newspaper's lenient treatment of the Fenians, but they continued to receive "sympathetic coverage" in the *Boston Pilot* and other newspapers connected to the Church. There could be no conflict between "the Irish national party and the Church to which the majority of the Irish people belong, and which has been so intimately identified with them in their trials and persecutions," the *Irish American* protested. James McMaster, editor of the New York *Freeman's Journal*, which was widely regarded as an organ of the archbishop, had first welcomed the Fenians' denial of secrecy, only then to argue that the secrecy essential to prevent any political organization's deliberations becoming public knowledge had never been objected to by the Church. Nor did he waver from this sympathetic line following the condemnations issued by Wood and Duggan, impressed as he remained with the Brotherhood's popular support in the local community. He simply urged it to do what was necessary to escape general clerical criticism. In truth, the American hierarchy's response to Fenianism was complicated and compromised by the conduct of sympathetic clergy. John Hughes had denounced secret societies, but his target had been the violent Irish gangs seeking to control employment on large public works projects. His imprudent response to the Young Ireland rebellion and his provocative "address on the nature of lawful resistance to the state within the context of Catholic doctrine," first delivered before those attending the Solemn High Requiem Mass for McManus but reiterated in Dublin to a group of nationalists, were unlikely to convince Irish Americans that the dominant figure in the American Church entirely repudiated physical force. On the contrary, Hughes appeared to be providing them with "instructions for harmonizing rebellion with the laws of the Papal Church." By the civil war's end, there existed in New York "a small but influential group of priests" openly sympathetic to the Fenians, while Hughes's successor, John McCloskey, complained that *"most"* of the clergymen arriving from Ireland on fundraising missions allowed themselves to be caught in the Fenian trap. Their attendance and remarks at Brotherhood meetings permitted the Fenians "to boast of their countenance and support." In Philadelphia, Father Moriarty made a mockery of his bishop's denunciation of the Brotherhood with a lecture on the Irish right of rebellion against Britain. Although obliged to make a public apology for these controversial remarks, he immediately vitiated its effect by publishing them in pamphlet form. Elsewhere, the superior of the Jesuits led a Fenian procession in the national capital, and a priest was the dominant figure in Indiana's powerful Fenian organization. As McMaster acknowledged in the *Freeman's Journal*, "So long as Catholic priests, unrebuked, belong to the Fenian Brotherhood, and no *general* law of the Catholic Church is brought to bear in its condemnation, the condemnation of individual Bishops, seems, in our best judgment, only to complicate the matter."[13]

The embarrassing clerical divisions that surely confused many of the faithful, the evidence that the Fenian leadership regarded the Catholic Church as its most formidable potential adversary, and the recognition by members of the hierarchy "that the Society was immoral in its object, the exciting of rebellion in Ireland, and unlawful and illegal in its means, a quasi military organization here to be rendered effective in the contingency of a war with England," clearly established the necessity for a coherent episcopal policy and the disciplining of priests who ignored it. Sadly, both the American hierarchy and the Vatican shirked this responsibility. Cullen did gently but persistently press the American bishops for decisive action, convinced as he was that the American Fenians were subsidizing not only the *Irish People* and the Irish branch of the Brotherhood, but also the infuriatingly insolent Patrick Lavelle. He feared that with American encouragement the more "foolish Irish" would resort to physical force "and get their necks into the halter." But his American ally Duggan noted the embarrassing fact that Poland was a favourite topic of American Fenians. They were able to point to the support that the Pope, the Polish clergy, and Cullen himself had given to the Poles' struggle against Russian despotism. This had been the source of some amusement to Lord John Russell, given the attacks upon him for his support of Italian nationalism. Of course, his rejection of Irish nationalism attested to his own selectivity. Meanwhile, Bishop Duggan clung to the hope that many of his currently mute colleagues would "soon be forced to speak" against Fenianism. As the months passed without a definitive statement from the American hierarchy, Cullen wrote to its nominal leader, Martin Spalding, Archbishop of Baltimore, in August 1865, to re-emphasize the importance of timely action. He was already too late. At a meeting a month earlier of the senior clergy of the province of Cincinnati, general agreement on the dangerous nature of Fenianism had failed to persuade those present to denounce it. A frustrated and resentful Duggan remained isolated in Chicago. Then, New York's bishops met and held to much the same line as their brethren in Cincinnati. They opposed any public denunciation of the Fenians, recommending instead that clergy discreetly discourage membership in the Brotherhood and that Spalding seek from Rome "some more formal or satisfactory solution of its difficulties than has as yet been given."[14]

The American bishops' reluctance to confront an organization that many of them considered extremely dangerous was another example of hope vanquishing experience. A number preferred to believe that

Fenianism was a "temporary evil," a "humbug" that if left alone would eventually explode through the escape of its own "exuberant gas." Others were intimidated by the vicious abuse to which Wood and Duggan were being subjected. The former's English antecedents inspired nasty *ad hominem* assaults, while Duggan, an Irish nationalist, found himself accused of being a lackey of the British government. A plan by a group of his supporters to stage a St Patrick's Day parade in 1864 from which Fenians would be excluded never got off the ground, and the streets were left to a triumphant Brotherhood and its allies. All of this certainly impressed and influenced Peter Kenrick, Archbishop of St Louis. Any public condemnation would prompt "misguided men" to respond everywhere as they had in Chicago and array themselves against episcopal authority, he feared. "These men will support authority when exercised against Protestants," he cautioned Martin Spalding, "but will resist it, if exercised against themselves." Memories of 1848 and the bitter complaint of Young Irelanders that clergy had betrayed their cause were other factors influencing the conduct of several members of the hierarchy. Spalding was certainly keen to ensure that the inevitable failure of Fenianism not be laid at the bishops' door, for that would surely prompt "crazy headed young Irish" again to charge priests with being enemies of progress and liberty. Nor were he and his colleagues unmindful of political and diplomatic considerations. The Brotherhood's growth during the civil war, under "government influence or encouragement," had not escaped their notice. Fenian leaders and recruiters had been permitted to move freely through Irish regiments. With the war's end, the bishops expected the administration to tolerate and even foster the Brotherhood "as a sort of standing menace to England," from whom it was seeking compensation for her less than perfect neutrality. Why irritate the American government by indirectly undermining this diplomatic strategy? Further, "open & public denunciation" at a time when "the current of government influence [was] setting so strongly in [the Fenians'] favor, would have rather aided than injured their cause, and as such was the feeling, would perhaps have reared up an abundant harvest of what is so unusual, Irish infidels." Or as one visiting nationalist Irish priest later summarized the position of the American bishops, their refusal to speak out had been governed by the discovery that it "would not pay, that it drew on them the wrath of the Irish population and even prevented numbers from going to their Churches or minding religion at all."[15]

Spalding forwarded his request for Vatican guidance in the late autumn of 1864. As an admiring Kenrick noted, it was artfully framed and phrased to secure a papal endorsement of the current policy of public inaction. "Indeed I think it will puzzle their Eminences to determine what course to pursue," he congratulated Spalding, "nor should I regret this circumstance, as I trust more to time and reflexion than to prohibition or condemnation in the matter." Thus Spalding carefully emphasized the episcopal confusion on how to proceed and the reluctance of a majority of his colleagues to condemn the Brotherhood. They feared alienating Irish Americans "whose patriotic ardor was sometimes stronger than their faith," he explained a little disingenuously. Yet even Wood approved his presentation of the problem, while Duggan had already advised the Vatican that in Chicago the Fenians were "dead and give us no trouble whatever." All of this strengthened the Holy See's traditional disinclination to act boldly or speedily. A "tardy course" had become especially ingrained with respect to American affairs as a result of past embarrassments arising out of "conflicting and frequently challenging representations from members of the Hierarchy." Caution in this particular instance was further dictated by the fact that the Brotherhood had sometimes been viewed by Irish bishops in "a very different light." Rome did specifically contradict a claim, which had first appeared in the *Connaught Patriot*, that it had issued instructions not to "disturb" the Fenians. However, the Brotherhood had already exploited the almost identical instruction issued by Spalding while still bishop of Louisville to reassure the devout that membership did not conflict with faith. Nevertheless, the spring of 1865 found several bishops impatiently awaiting word from Rome. "If to be checked at all, it must be done soon, [the Fenians] are growing rapidly," Timon wrote to Spalding from Buffalo. The Bishop of Newark suggested that the archbishop give the Vatican "a hint, that we need a 'Roman knife' to cut out the cancer, before it gets too deep." But there was scant prospect of radical surgery. The document the Propaganda forwarded to select members of the hierarchy in mid-July 1865 was simply a reiteration of the 1846 decree. Even this was not to be published or publicized, but merely to form the basis of instructions given to confessors.[16]

The Fenians "are rampant everywhere just now, where they are not opposed by clergy," yet Rome insists on treating them "gingerly, tenderly, paternally," a disappointed Purcell wrote to Spalding in August. Of course, the caution of the Holy See reflected the advice received from the United States and the ambivalence of members of Ireland's hierarchy. Understandable as it was in the circumstances, the refusal to provide clear instructions from Rome was unfortunate. The ambiguous directive, which did not refer to the Fenians by name, guaranteed that interpretations of it would vary widely, while its restricted circulation ensured that many clergy remained in ignorance of it. Spalding and Purcell issued instructions to their clergy to refrain from public denunciations of Fenianism but seek to discourage it through the confessional. Kenrick, a former enthusiast of public non-intervention, was so enraged by the attempt of the Fenians of St Louis to stage a funeral demonstration along the lines of the McManus extravaganza that he denounced the entire affair, forbade any religious ceremony, ordered the exclusion of anyone sporting Fenian insignia from the cemetery, and declared "all persons associated with the Brotherhood inadmissible to the sacraments." In Brooklyn, on the other hand, the bishop instructed his clergy not to meddle with Irish political sympathies and to give absolution to all, whatever their political creed. Purcell, for one, was not surprised to discover in mid-October that "immense numbers" of Irish Catholics continued as members of the Brotherhood and that "immense sums" were still being contributed to its treasury. Nor had all priests been discouraged from direct involvement in Fenian activities. Purcell informed Cullen that he had been obliged to suspend another "young and rash Irish priest" following his delivery of a sermon in support of the organization. Well over a year later, the diocesan priest of Wheeling, West Virginia, was writing to the Propaganda to describe his activities as a Fenian representative and to plead their cause.[17]

A surprisingly sanguine Archbishop Spalding predicted in mid-November 1865 that the Fenian bubble would soon burst. One month later, following the division of the Brotherhood into two warring factions, he assured Paul Cullen that "Fenianism has exploded in this country ... though its death throes may be yet protracted through some weeks and months." The Bishop of Philadelphia was less optimistic. Wood had initially welcomed the Vatican directive as "prudent," loyally accepting that a formal condemnation of the Brotherhood would be inexpedient "and probably after a time entirely unnecessary." Within a few months, however, he was singing from a different hymnal. "I am quite convinced that if some of our Archbishops had moved in this matter, the organization would have been much crippled, and would never have succeeded in swindling our poor people to the extent it has," he complained. "But of course it is not in my province to criticize my Seniors and superiors." By the following spring, even Spalding was prepared to admit that he had been "partially mistaken" and had "rather anticipated a little" the disintegration of the Fenians. They have survived, he argued, because of the secret influences and promises of the American government and "especially of the evil Secretary Seward," who he believed had utilized them as threatened retaliation for the damage inflicted on Union commerce during the civil war by British-built Confederate raiders. However, now that the Fenians' plans to invade British North America threatened to drag the secretary into a collision with the United Kingdom, he had finally "cast them off and disowned them." Hence Spalding continued to cling to the hope that the Fenians would "soon cease operations, at least wane day to day." Not that their survival prodded him to re-evaluate the policy of procrastination, something he made clear when the desirability of collective action brought requests from several bishops for a national council. The second plenary council met in Baltimore in October 1866, only for Spalding to use his control of the agenda to ensure that no notice was taken of the Fenians in either the council's acts or decrees. The references that were made to secret societies specified that prelates should not condemn a society by name. Revealingly, when he wrote to Cullen in December to congratulate him on receiving the purple, Spalding made no mention of Fenianism.[18]

When Archbishop Cullen first approached Spalding about the Fenians in August 1864, he had been somewhat contemptuous of the Irish branch of the revolutionary organization. They had no chance of success, he observed. They lacked arms, discipline, and money, while the great body of the population was averse to revolution. Therefore, they were unlikely to make any progress but were capable of bringing greater ruin on the country. In fact, even as Cullen wrote, the weaknesses he identified were being addressed. Although Stephens was forever complaining of niggardly American support – "Only think of it: a house that can show assets of *over* 90,000 pounds [a figure he was soon to raise to 112,000] to be on the brink of bankruptcy for want of a most beggarly sum" – cash was finally beginning to flow across the Atlantic in unprecedented amounts. His claim of a very large membership may have seemed excessively optimistic, but another "intensive organizing tour" of the country had undoubtedly been a success. Furthermore, if the stockpile of weapons remained comparatively small, it was growing. Pikes were being manufactured, and guns, including rifles, legally but discreetly purchased in English cities and then shipped to Ireland in boxes labelled with the names of an assortment of heavy equipment. On arrival, they were distributed to Fenian circles for drilling and safe storage. The effective end of the American Civil War in April created an even more favourable purchaser's market, and by summer of 1865 the Irish Fenians had perhaps six thousand stands of arms of varying quality on hand. Scores of Irish American veterans were also arriving in Ireland to provide the domestic revolutionaries with training and leadership. Meanwhile, the campaign to subvert Irish elements of the British military force stationed in Ireland had quickly recovered from the setback of Pagan O'Leary's arrest the previous November.[19]

The British soldier's lot was not a happy one. Reform had been given impetus first by the disastrous campaign in the Crimea, then by the performance of the American soldiery in the civil war, and finally by the re-emergence of Prussia as a formidable military power – hence the effort to improve discipline, educational standards, medical services, and recruitment. Instead of attracting the dregs of society with drink and bounties, military planners hoped to boost the reputation of soldiering as a profession and make it a serious competitor of alternative forms of civilian employment. A pair of royal commissions produced a number of cautious recommendations with respect to recruiting. The "stoppages" that virtually halved the infantryman's already thin pay packet were reduced and then his pay modestly increased, but such half-hearted measures brought little real improvement in society's perception of the rank and file. The lower ranks continued to occupy one of the lowest rungs on the occupational ladder and to be generally considered social lepers. The discontent this bred and fed threatened to be peculiarly dangerous in Ireland, where men of Irish birth or descent constituted in 1865 at least one-third of the force of more than seventeen thousand regulars. The correspondence found on Pagan O'Leary pointed clearly to a Fenian policy of subverting the military. The loyalty of the Irish militia excited even greater concern. That of North Cork was reported to have sung a chorus of "Out and make way for the Fenian Men" as it marched through the streets of Mallow to the parade ground. Its arms and those of other militia regiments were removed and stored at four depots, and annual training exercises were suspended indefinitely. The authorities, no less than the Fenian leadership, understood that the "likelihood of conspiracy varies inversely with the loyalty of the coercive forces of the regime." Put another way, any subversion of the military would increase the Fenians' "coercive capacity" and greatly strengthen their ability and determination to take to the field.[20]

Fenian recruiters frequented the public houses ever adjacent to military barracks, for apart from satisfying the notorious fondness of servicemen for drink they provided a convivial as well as convenient setting. They were places of "comfort and camaraderie," their rooms used by trade unions and young men's societies, and the politics of many a publican had a distinctly green hue. William Roantree, a former assistant to O'Leary, had succeeded the Pagan as chief Fenian organizer. He boasted a service record, having served in the United States Navy, and had proven his skill as a recruiter by establishing, following his return home to Leixlip, one of the Brotherhood's largest formations. His arrest along with several of his assistants in September 1865 saw a former aide, John Devoy, assume command. The young organizer and his staff of eight elected to concentrate on the Dublin area, where the "critical blow" seemed likely to be struck, and they increasingly focused on the task of organizing those men already recruited. Several non-commissioned officers, a very important element in any regiment, joined the Brotherhood, but Devoy's later claim to have subverted a third of the entire military establishment was a gross exaggeration. Moreover, he failed to establish either a solid organization within the army or an effective means of communication with and between soldier Fenians. This did not augur well for their decisive employment in a rising.[21]

The state of Irish Fenian readiness was not a matter on which Stephens, the "provisional dictator," felt compelled to keep those he regarded as American subordinates fully informed. This merely sharpened their irritation with him, tired as they were of his incessant complaints. "Now that the means for sending over a special messenger are no longer beyond your reach," O'Mahony wrote in mid-April 1865, "it is no longer unreasonable for us to expect that ample information would be sent to us by such means." To secure the "full and clear light" they needed in order to work "conscientiously" and "well," hostile to the autocratic model of the Irish Revolutionary Brotherhood to which Stephens continued to cling in the face of demands for a more collective leadership, and sceptical of its readiness in this the promised year of action, O'Mahony and his council despatched a succession of special investigators to Ireland. Philip Coyne had followed Stephens home in 1864, and despite his favourable report to the Cincinnati convention, the central council ordered Captain Thomas J. Kelly to Ireland in March 1865. Born in County Galway in 1833, Kelly had emigrated to the United States at age eighteen. His prior apprenticeship in the printing industry stood him in good stead, and he quickly found work in New York. Moving to Nashville in 1857, where he founded his own newspaper, he enlisted in the Union army on the outbreak of the civil war. He rose to the rank of captain, serving as chief signal officer in the Army of the Cumberland, before being seriously wounded and invalided out of the service. He was followed to Ireland in turn by General Francis F. Millen, who "claimed to have earned his spurs under Juarez in Mexico," and General William G. Halpin. The latter had first come to public notice when he was named in the British-inspired prosecution in Cincinnati almost a decade earlier, and he arrived in Ireland carrying a commission as "the official representative of the American Fenians" at the headquarters of the Irish Revolutionary Brotherhood. Finally, a pair of central councillors were despatched across the Atlantic. They and the investigators who had preceded them all submitted positive reports, hence the Fenian Brotherhood's decision to issue the "final call" on 5 August 1865.[22]

That the Roman Catholic Church wielded sufficient popular influence in Ireland to cause the revolutionary nationalist conspirators much grief was implicitly acknowledged by Stephens when he struck the secrecy clause from the Fenian oath. The *Irish People*, meanwhile, took the more aggressive tack of criticizing clerical meddling in politics – not that it held fast to this principle when the meddlers were friendly. Yet the Irish Church, no less than its American counterpart, was poorly positioned to confront an organization that many of its clergy, like their American counterparts, regarded as extremely dangerous. The tradition of constitutional nationalism had not prevented "many priests" from speaking out "in ominously revolutionary tones" during the months leading up to the rising in 1848, while the following decade echoed with a "fiercely Anglophobic form of religious nationalism." The rhetorical excesses of some clergy during the early 1860s, their talk of a conspiracy "to exterminate the Irish as a people" by driving them to emigrate, could all too easily be interpreted as an implied endorsement of the Fenian solution for Ireland's plight and problems. Certainly, the understandably bitter criticism of the "English government" for its failure to alleviate Ireland's misery and destitution was likely to bring many of her people to the conclusion "that there was really little effective remedy for their grievances in a political system of which they were only nominally a part." Nor did the emergence and growth of Fenianism prompt a prudent tempering of clerical nationalism. Instead, a number of priests made plain their Fenian sympathies.[23]

Paul Cullen's nationalism had not lost any of its intensity. The Irish would deserve to be branded as slaves, the archbishop declared on one occasion, were they to accept silently their "degrading inferiority" in their own land. His hatred of England remained as virulent and manifest as ever. He accused her of seeking "to centralize the wealth of the world in her factories and trading establishments," identified "Mammon" as her ruling power, and declared that the "safety and rights of the people" were being " immolated to that idol." Ireland and the Irish, in particular, were being "sacrificed to promote that unholy project." In the state's tolerance of the *Irish People*, despite its support of revolution, he again found a sinister British motive. With the people of Ireland divided on the issue of physical force, all the Protestants and a great body of the Catholics being opposed to its use, he believed that a Machiavellian British government committed to the maxim of divide and rule saw in Fenianism a useful instrument. Nor had he altered his opinion that the British hated the "old religion of Ireland." They therefore welcomed the Fenians' criticism of the clergy and espousal of revolutionary ideas, seeing them as instruments with which to weaken and discredit the Catholic Church. Cullen's reading of R.R. Madden's sympathetic *Lives of the United Irishmen* (1842–46) prompted him to stigmatize contemporary revolutionary writers as paid agents of the British government. Nothing would be more pleasing to the "savages of England," he remarked, than to engage Ireland in a "trial of brute force." She would then be able to repeat the massacres of Cromwell, inflict on the Irish the brutal punishment meted out to Indian sepoys, or imitate the Russians' treatment of the Polish rebels. The English would have an excuse "to oppress the country" and deprive the Irish of those rights they did possess. All that religion had gained during the present century was in danger of being swiftly lost, he suggested.[24]

Cullen's repudiation of revolution was increasingly framed in pragmatic terms. He did not consider resistance to established authority "inherently wicked," but remained convinced that rebellion would result in disaster. The Fenians were engaged in "a most foolish and ruinous project," given their lack of arms, money, and influence and the strength of British forces. He noted their failure to explain how a rising would be managed. Indeed, for some considerable time, he was satisfied that they had no intention of putting their own necks in the noose by actually coming to blows with the authorities, and he expressed contempt for Irish Americans whom he considered mere braggarts. They knew that it was "impossible for any one to send them to proposed battlefields across the Atlantic." Indeed, he suspected that the American movement was a mere fraud designed by its leadership to dupe the poor out of their hard-earned monies. He estimated the cost of the McManus funeral at more than £5,000 and recalled the lavish personal expenditures of the accompanying American delegation. His reading of the proceedings of the Chicago convention persuaded him that there was a double deception in play. The Fenians' objective during the civil war was not the liberation of Ireland "but to get poor Irish fools to fight for America." And when he did give thought to the unlikely possibility of a successful revolution, he feared it would bring "the liberty of Mazzini." Cullen was "firmly convinced" that the revolutionary leadership was "hostile to the Catholic Church," although he regarded with a degree of *schadenfreude* Fenian abuse of Tipperary priests, who in his opinion had been "rather bitter with Young Irelandism." In short, the Fenians' principles were "bad," their designs "wicked," and they promised "to do a great deal of mischief." A patriotism that rushes into "wild and improbable projects," or propagates "maxims dangerous to religion and society" "forgets the dictates of prudence and commonsense," he warned in one pastoral, and was doomed to degenerate into folly and become "a degenerate fanaticism." Revolutionary movements, he cautioned the citizens of Dublin in December 1864, were the "worst enemies of Ireland" and her ancient faith. "It would be wicked and foolish to have recourse to force or violence" at this time because they "would only be the cause of greater misery and ruin." What was equally to be deplored, Cullen declared, was the certainty that "[m]isguided efforts of false patriotism" would prevent the attainment of real reforms. The people would be distracted from important issues, such as denominational education and the conditions of the poor, while their enemies would be presented with "a pretext to refuse the redress of every grievance."[25]

Predictably, Cullen blamed the British for his difficulties in convincing "the Irish people that the Fenians deserved the censures of the Church." Poor Catholics could be forgiven for thinking that "secret societies [were] not so bad" when the government publicly patronized them and gave "the greatest honors to their supporters and defenders." He was alluding to the Freemasons, whose membership included "the greatest gentlemen, and the employees of the government," and to British support of Mazzini and popular idolization of Garibaldi. Yet Cullen contributed to the confusion in the minds of the faithful by concentrating so much of his fire on the National Brotherhood of St Patrick. He considered it a Fenian organization, but the leadership was able to make a credible denial of secrecy. Of course, any move to condemn Fenianism by name was compromised by the obvious divisions within the ranks of the Church he led.[26]

MacHale remained Cullen's most persistent and formidable adversary, given his rank and popularity. In his reply to an American priest who wrote to him in 1862 seeking advice and guidance on Fenianism, the Archbishop of Tuam pretended that there were neither Fenians nor members of the National Brotherhood in his province. He observed that the latter repudiated secret oaths, and urged his correspondent to make careful inquiry into organizations before confounding them with unlawful societies. Clearly, he had no intention of any taking action and was encouraging others to err on the side of caution. The following year he sought to subvert Cullen's campaign against the National Brotherhood of St Patrick by announcing his personal subscription to the *Irishman*, which was generally regarded as its "great Organ." That such a newspaper attracted the support of an archbishop was a "fearful portent," one alarmed archdeacon commented. Then when American Fenians forwarded funds to help relieve poverty in his province, MacHale publicly thanked the "benevolent Brotherhood" and forwarded three autographed likenesses of himself to their Chicago Fair even though the local bishop had already condemned the organization. Simultaneously, he was unrelenting in his public assaults on "oppressive and bigoted" landlords and the mixed system of national education, and he continued to tie landlord inhumanity, "commercial fraud and immorality" to the "malignant influence" of the Established Church. Speaking at the dedication of a church in Ballinrobe in the summer of 1863, he thundered: "The misgovernment now existing in Ireland is as great, if not greater than ever was witnessed in the days of the darkest persecution, and it was time for the clergy now again to come to the aid of the poor." His pastorals were no less inflammatory. In one marking the Feast of St John Chrysostom, he dwelt upon the "tyrannical lengths" to which English "hatred" of the Irish and their language was carried. English was the language of the national schools in which "anti-Catholic schemes" were promoted, and it was the only language of the courts despite the fact that many witnesses did not understand it. "There will be no pause in this work of extermination of our people and the persecution of their faith," he concluded, "until the huge injustice done to Ireland in the first year of this century by violence and treachery is repaired." The Union had to be repealed. In the words of one young Fenian organizer, "His pastoral we construed as an approval of our plans and actions."[27]

Cullen's problems within the hierarchy were not confined to MacHale. He sponsored an address to the Prince of Wales on the occasion of the royal marriage in March 1863, arguing that it was "desirable to conciliate one who will soon have so much power." Hostility "in other quarters" quickly obliged him to abandon it. Of his fellow metropolitans, Leahy joined MacHale in opposing the proposal, as did a clutch of bishops. If this was a comparatively harmless expression of episcopal nationalism, differences of opinion threatened to be more damaging when minds turned to the issue of Fenianism. Some bishops, like their American colleagues, preferred to believe the problem would soon fade away. "It is a piece of American mountebankism," the Bishop of Ferns judged at the time of the McManus funeral, "which will serve for a nine days wonder and then be forgotten." Gillooly of Elphin was far less sanguine, afraid as he was that Cullen was losing the battle for public opinion. The archbishop's banning of the McManus funeral rites had been "a subject of surprise and regret [to] very many good people," he warned. Equally, a claim by episcopal colleagues that it had been the withdrawal of the "steadying influence" of priests from politics that permitted the rise of Fenianism amounted to implied criticism of Cullen. Of course, he had never sought to exclude priests from politics, nor had they ceased their political activities. His principal concern was to exert greater discipline on clerical activists. This did not prevent the Bishop of Down and Connor from continuing to assert that the lack of clerical leadership had driven the people in despair "to combine illegally when they saw that nothing was to be done but sell them for sops to place hunters."[28]

Cullen and Archbishop Dixon of Armagh, together with several bishops, did issue condemnations of secret societies in their Lenten pastorals of 1862, and at the urging of John MacEvilly, his episcopal ally within MacHale's fiefdom, Cullen placed the brotherhoods on the agenda of the bishops' meeting set for early May. They passed a resolution warning Catholics against secret associations, "whether bound by oath or otherwise, and especially against those that have for their object to spread a spirit of revolution, which, in other hands, is now producing such disastrous results." The impact of this admonition was again diminished, however, by an accompanying statement. This acknowledged the "many injustices" the Irish suffered, and dwelt upon their "manifest inequality before the law." Individuals were therefore infused with a deplorable "spirit of alienation from authority and of resistance to public order leading in some cases to crimes." Then, at their meeting in August 1863, the bishops "unanimously condemned" the National Brotherhood of St Patrick on a charge of "having for its object the support and defence by arms of what is called in the oath of membership the Irish republic." The effect was less telling than may have been expected, for as the *Irish People* immediately pointed out and O'Mahony subsequently emphasized in his confrontation with the Bishop of Chicago, the hierarchy had not condemned Fenianism. Instead, in repudiating a resort to the sword, the bishops were running the danger of sustaining "the act negatively" by dwelling so heavily on the plight of their "oppressed" countrymen and denouncing the English government and legislature. This argument had been made twenty years earlier during the Rebecca disturbances in Wales. A Tory commentator had then assailed the dissenting minister who published "an inflammatory magazine" entitled *Y Diwygiwr* (the Reformer), describing him revealingly as the "little pope, within his own circle of the 'great unwashed,'" whose "infallibility" was a "dogma with his followers and readers." Clergy who "[i]nflame, enrage, and then gather 'thousands' of the most ignorant of mankind, pointing to a body, or a class, or a government, as the sole cause of whatever they suffer or dislike, and then – *tell* them to be moral, peaceable," he added, were employing a favourite "stalking horse of incendiary politics" as "the secret hiding-place of retreat from the 'force of the government.'"[29]

Despite the unanimous episcopal condemnation of the National Brotherhood, the hierarchy's unity remained an illusion. David Moriarty fretted over its divisions and the ambiguous advice given to the people. A scholar and administrator, he had served as vice-rector of the college in Paris before joining the faculty of All Hallows and subsequently rising to its presidency. Moriarty had been Cullen's first choice as Bishop of Kerry, despite his former close association with leading Young Irelanders, although the archbishop belatedly had second thoughts. The abject failure of the rising in 1848 appears to have persuaded Moriarty long before his promotion to the episcopacy that Ireland's future and her prosperity lay within the Union. He had issued a forthright condemnation of the Phoenix Society and avowed that he could not sanction rebellion except where the tyranny was excessive. He denied that this was the situation in Ireland. Jeered by young men who were probably Fenians at a meeting he called in 1862 to raise funds for the suffering operatives of cotton-starved Lancashire, he disbanded the Tralee branch of O'Brien's Young Men's Society the following year because of its infiltration by members of the National Brotherhood of St Patrick. He declared membership of any oath-bound secret society a "reserved sin" and instructed priests to deny absolution to members until they renounced the society in writing before witnesses. But the papal decree of 1846 on which he and others relied to justify their actions was less than crystal clear. Other clergy insisted that only societies that were secret *and* opposed to church and state warranted condemnation, though this position appeared at odds with the decree issued in 1850. Nevertheless, this strained interpretation was particularly helpful to the National Brotherhood, against which it was difficult to make a convincing case of hostility to the Church. Given the confusion over Church policy, it was not surprising, Moriarty mordantly remarked, that people educated to reason logically rather than canonically were driven by bitter clerical criticism of the government "into disaffection and a spirit of rebellion."[30]

That a hierarchy of fewer than thirty bishops could not agree on a common policy towards the Fenians ensured that the legions of priests under their command did not march in step. Nor was it surprising that many showed a certain sympathy towards Fenianism. Maynooth, St Colman's, Fermoy, St Jarlath's, Tuam, All Hallows, and the Irish College in Paris, all had reputations as nurseries of nationalism. Cullen privately expressed the belief in March 1863 that "many young priests are open revolutionaries, especially in Meath." Indeed, one of them was soon to acquire notoriety and suffer episcopal censure for urging members of the National Brotherhood to become Fenians. Writing towards the end of the year, one of Cullen's regular clerical correspondents expressed his shock "at hearing but too many young Priests gloating over anticipated rebellion and Revolution through American intervention." And while the number of priests openly supportive of the Fenians was always very small, even in Meath, there were others in that diocese, like Anthony Cogan, "who longed for a free and better Ireland but were confused as to how best this could be accomplished" and despaired of "finding a political solution for Ireland's ills." Archdeacon O'Brien of Limerick,

whose alarm over the infiltration of his Young Men's Societies had
seen him first appeal to Cullen and Dixon for help and then resign as
their president-general to fight Fenianism politically through the
National Association, mounted a public platform in his parish of
Newcastle West in 1864 to declare that Ireland had never been so
disaffected, never so disloyal, and to admit that this was as true of clergy
as of the people. The Irish had liberty in every way bar one, he
declared, and that was "the power of exercising liberty." They could
never be loyal until they had the power to make their own laws, and
he condemned the Fenians, not because of their opposition to the
"English Government" or their objective of Irish independence, but
solely on account of the manner in which they sought to achieve it.
Agitation by the clergy "has led to Fenianism in the people," one
worried lifelong Catholic activist wrote to Cullen.[31]

Episcopal censures of secret societies were frequently interpreted by
parish priests in a way that permitted Fenians to reconcile their membership in the organization with their religious beliefs. Within Cullen's
own diocese, Fenians were admitted to the sacraments by the Jesuits of
Dublin. They found additional clerical reassurance in the press, where
letters signed by persons claiming to be priests, but unwilling to give
their names, restated the pragmatic Catholic doctrine of lawful revolution. One priest who scorned anonymity and revelled in notoriety
was Patrick Lavelle. Another product of middle-class farming stock,
his education financed by a wealthy uncle, he attended St Jarlath's College, Tuam, before going on to a brilliant career at Maynooth.
Ordained in 1853, he was appointed to the faculty of the Irish College
in Paris the following year, where he eventually led a revolt against the
rigidly Cullenite rector. Lavelle had been temperamentally and politically at odds with Cullen's ultramontanism even before his ordination.
Recalled by MacHale to Tuam in 1858, he was eventually appointed
administrator of the remote Mayo parish of Partry and was quickly
at war with the local Anglican bishop, whose behaviour as a landlord
invited condemnation, as did his his crude proselytizing. Lavelle's campaign won him "enormous" newspaper coverage and saw him hailed
both in Ireland and Irish America as the defender of poor tenants and
as the saviour of "poor children from the doom of proselytism."
MacHale gave him every support. The archbishop had only to glance
across the street from the windows of his own "plain house" to the
palace and demesne of his Anglican counterpart, which generated an
income ten times his own, to be filled with resentment. Religious fric-

tion overlaid by agrarian grievances predictably led to violence and retaliatory evictions by the bishop, which merely strengthened Lavelle's nationalism and intensified his hostility. The financial assistance he received from "advanced nationalists" in Britain and the United States had much the same effect. Indeed, Lavelle appears to have asked himself essentially the same question that John Kenyon, the Young Ireland priest, had posed a decade earlier: "What is there in political rights more than any other rights that they should be attainable by moral force alone?" Kenyon's answer was one with which Lavelle evidently agreed: "Moral force may obtain some rights ... but it cannot obtain all rights, personal or political." The final collapse of the Independent Irish Party, the conviction that Parliament was unlikely to redress the grievances of Irish tenants, which the Land Bill of 1860 seemingly confirmed, eroded whatever remained of Lavelle's faith in constitutionalism. He concluded that only a "free Ireland" could or would remove tenant grievances. Thus his position was close to that of the Fenians.[32]

Lavelle quickly made a career of cocking a clerical snoot at Cullen. He ostentatiously contributed to the McManus funeral expenses and spoke at the gravesite. He published letters highly critical of the archbishop, accusing him on one occasion of gouging the poor to fund the Catholic University of Ireland, which Lavelle characterized as "West British" and anti-Irish. He accepted the vice-presidency of the National Brotherhood of St Patrick and publicly challenged Cullen's condemnation of it. He returned to Dublin in February 1862 to lecture on the Catholic doctrine of the right of revolution. His themes were the familiar ones: subjects had an indisputable right to oust tyrannical rulers; no subjects in the world were more oppressed than the Irish; and while immediate revolution would be madness and wicked, the people were duty bound to prepare for the day of liberation. Little wonder the Archbishop of Armagh remarked with grudging admiration, "He is becoming a very remarkable person. The times are certainly very dangerous." Ambitious, aggressive, abrasive, Lavelle developed and popularized his radical argument on public platforms and in a spate of letters to the press. A people whose condition was "worse than that of the negro" had to insist on their freedom and independence. He was assured of unrestricted access to the *Connaught Patriot,* published in Tuam. It had been saved from bankruptcy by MacHale, who made a personal donation and publicly recommended it as "the true organ of Catholicity in this part of the country." In short, it became the "nationalist propaganda sheet" of MacHale and Lavelle, and its editor accompanied the agitating priest on his recruiting tours of Ireland and Britain on behalf of the National Brotherhood. In the columns of the *Patriot* and other newspapers, domestic and foreign, including the *Irish American* and the *Irish Canadian*, Lavelle defended the Brotherhood as the "only political organization having in view the ransom of Ireland from alien rule" and one whose "principles [were] genuine, legal and not opposed to tenets of any body of Christians." He urged fellow priests to "despise the diocesan reservations" against both brotherhoods, and heaped praise on the Fenians for their noble, "well known, openly avowed object ... the redemption of an enslaved people." He assured young men that Fenian membership was not a mortal sin, for no pope had ever condemned or would condemn "any organization of an enslaved and plundered and exterminated people, whose only aim was the subversion of the tyrant's sway and the restoration of the people's freedom." Only secret societies that sought to overthrow church as well as state were under a papal ban, he continued to declare. Thus the Fenians as well as the National Brotherhood were exempt from censure because they were "only anxious to overthrow a wicked tyranny." This was the rhetoric and contention that won for Lavelle the support and admiration of other nationalist provincial newspapers, such as the *Tipperary Advocate*. "This encouragement given by Lavelle to the Fenians has given them great courage," Cullen wrote to Kirby in Rome. Even more galling was the knowledge that it had been given after the priest's return from the Vatican, where he had been obliged to make an apology to the Pope for his earlier conduct.[33]

Cullen's obsession with Lavelle was partly a product of affronted dignity. This publicity hound of a priest was a study in insubordination. He was also incurably and infuriatingly insolent. Yet Cullen recognized Lavelle's usefulness as a weapon in his long-running institutional battle against MacHale, with whom the priest was closely identified and for whom Lavelle was always careful to express profound admiration and respect. Within the hierarchy, where Tuam was his shield against effective domestic discipline, Lavelle unintentionally aided Cullen in his struggle to isolate MacHale and hold in check any revival of his influence. No less important, the firebrand acted as a guarantee that his patron would continue to excite deep suspicion in Rome. The Vatican understood that its disciplinary measures against Lavelle had little impact on his conduct largely because of MacHale's inaction. Of course, having itself suffered at the hands of ardent Italian nationalists, the papacy was reluctant to resort to stern disciplinary measures for fear of provoking a damaging confrontation with Ireland's clerical extremists.[34]

Frustrated at practically every turn in his efforts to silence Lavelle, Cullen sought from Rome in 1864 a definitive opinion on whether the Fenians were censurable as a secret society. He received in June, by way of reply, as did the Americans one year later, a copy of the ambiguous decree issued in 1846. Undoubtedly contributing to the Vatican's caution were the evident divisions within both the Irish and American hierarchies; perhaps the fear that a clear and firm stand would alienate a good proportion of the faithful from their clergy, given the reports of a surging Fenian membership; the traditional reluctance to issue specific censures; and the serious doubts raised by Lavelle and his supporters about which societies were censurable. Cullen was instructed to refer the matter back to Rome should the decree fail to have the desired effect, but this provision could not mask how "disastrous" the reply was for him or its "very serious implications for the Irish Church." He was subjected to the triumphal abuse of Lavelle, while whatever slight chance there had been of the Irish hierarchy acting collectively against Fenianism now vanished. MacHale and the Bishop of Cloyne declined to instruct their priests to deny absolution to Fenians, for the revolutionary nationalists and their clerical friends and sympathizers could continue credibly to claim that the Fenian Brotherhood had not been banned by the Church. Catholic Fenians insisted that they were devoutly attached to their church and fully accepted the Catholic doctrine on the right of revolution. They simply contended that British tyranny was intolerable and that a rebellion could be launched with a real prospect of success. They took additional encouragement from the disappointing electoral performance of the Cullen-controlled constitutional alternative to revolutionary nationalism. There had been a conspicuous lack of popular and clerical enthusiasm for the National Association's successful candidate in a Tipperary by-election in February 1865. The general election five months later saw the National Association return barely one dozen of the island's 105 members of parliament. Again, there could be no disguising the apathy with which the clergy viewed the association. Many of them still considered repeal the only remedy for Ireland's grievances. The "[p]eople have lost hope, and have no confidence in the bishops, except a few, nor in the Association," one clerical nationalist concluded. "They cannot and will not understand the condemnation of societies opposed to the state, secret or otherwise."[35]

By 1865 it was clear that the Roman Catholic Church had failed in both Ireland and the United States to act as an effective brake on the accelerating growth of Fenianism. By that year also, it was evident that the United Kingdom was failing to gather strength by winning genuine Irish popular acceptance. Ireland remained its "only real nationalist problem." Why was this the case? After all, two other Celtic peoples had been incorporated into the multi-ethnic state. Did not "all nations and reasonable men prefer to be governed by men of their own country and nation – who know their habits, laws and customs and share the same language and life-style as them – rather than by strangers"? In the case of Wales, there was an unwillingness to recognize her as a nation. She was regarded as no more than "part of greater England." The principality had seemingly provided the English with the model for their Irish policy, though it was not an attractive one. The Welsh had been subjected to "rigorous laws," an observer remarked, designed to keep them poor, "deprive them of good education," and make them "uncivil and brutish." Like the Irish, they were disparaged by the English as unfit for self-rule and also dismissed as "stupid," poor, and illiterate. The "people in general are so different from the English one is amazed to think they are subjects to the same monarchy," commented a romantic visitor attracted by the country's wild and rugged beauty. The Welsh no less than the Irish were regarded as the "antithesis of Britishness," if not racially inferior as Celts to Anglo-Saxons. "The main evil that the Welsh have to contend against is one that belongs to their blood as a Celtic nation," wrote a Tory commentator on the "Moral and Social Condition of Wales." The purity of their blood was their principal handicap, he explained, for like all "Celtic tribes" they exhibited a "national indolence and want of perseverance" and lacked the "indomitable energy and spirit of improvement which has raised the Anglo-Saxon race, crossed as it has been with so many other tribes, to such a mighty position in the dominion of the world." The Welsh, perhaps more so than the Irish, were credited with "many excellent qualifications" that tended to "counteract their innate weaknesses." "Intellectual acuteness," "natural kindliness of heart," "constitutional poetry," "religious enthusiasm," "passionate sense of honour," and "indomitable love of country" were the counterbalances to their failings. Indeed, the English constructed a hierarchy of Celts that found St David sitting beneath St Andrew but above St Patrick.[36]

The structure of Welsh agriculture and agrarian society, at least in the western counties, was not unlike that of western Ireland. There were large and small farms and a host of cottagers. An "impoverished and underdeveloped peasant country" in the mid-eighteenth century, Wales, like Ireland, underwent a rapid population growth that saw the total more than double over the first half of the nineteenth century. Yet two-thirds of the more than one million Welsh remained in the countryside. The increasing pressure on land saw a reduction in the size of many farms and an expansion of the class of landless labourers. Many tenants found themselves confronted with the problems popularly associated with Ireland – insecurity of tenure, rack-renting, and poverty. The impoverishment of the landless was evident in their primitive housing and susceptibility to disease, such as tuberculosis, which appeared endemic in several areas of the principality. Such conditions bred in Wales disturbances of a kind identified again with Ireland. Food and enclosure riots were eventually dwarfed by something approaching revolt, with "the emergence of the rural guerilla bands known as Rebecca." They protested road tolls, tithes, tenure insecurity, and high rents. Also present was an element of national feeling and more than a hint of anti-English sentiment, for "English toll farmers and land stewards" were two of their targets. But the violence was never "separatist," and the labelling of aristocratic landlords as aliens, as well as tyrants, was less than convincing. Landlords were becoming separated from the life of the community, but more often than not were Welsh born, if anglicized, more likely than their Irish counterparts to be residents, and sought, by and large, to maintain good relations with their tenantry. The Welsh peasants also differed from those of Ireland in that they were less dependent on the potato. They escaped famine, while the rapid industrialization of South Wales offered a means of support off the land that the Irish lacked.[37]

Wales benefited, as Ireland had not, from a surge of English capital investment. Metal smelting and iron production (by mid-century the principality had "the largest iron industry in the world"), coal mining, and the construction of a network of railway lines made southeast Wales a heavily industrialized region and an integral part of the British economy. Industrialization encouraged a "phenomenal internal migration" that prevented the emigration of biblical proportions associated with Ireland. But the deplorable conditions of work and living in the developing industrial towns bred disease, discontent, and working-class consciousness. Ethnic tensions surfaced within the workforce, between the Welsh and immigrants from England and Ireland, though the animus towards the latter was especially intense. Such tensions also complicated the relationship between Welsh workers and their largely English masters. The result was a succession of violent strikes. That in Merthyr Tydvil in 1831 "metamorphosed from strike into riot, and briefly, into open rebellion." Working men resisted wage cuts and dismissals, and fought for parliamentary reform. The secret "Scotch Cattle" movement sought "to 'scotch' those who undermined the solidarity of the working class community," and its resort to terror was briefly reminiscent of Irish agrarian secret societies. It was in Wales that the only serious Chartist rising took place, at Newport in 1839. To some nervous English observers it appeared that misrule had rendered Wales "as *volcanic* as Ireland," but there was a marked absence of separatist sentiment. Welsh Chartists were part of a larger British movement and were motivated by "the severity of the conditions of labour" and the cause of radical parliamentary reform. Political nationalism, had it been present, might have papered over the differences within the Welsh working classes.[38]

A powerful cultural nationalism did emerge in Wales. Even in the seventeenth century "ethnic identity and loyalty were most clearly expressed in cultural matters," while the following century saw the Welsh evince the same interest as other members of England's "Celtic periphery" in "history, antiquities, language and folk custom." Historical memory and mythology were essential to the "identity and ethnic homogeneity of a people," something the Welsh expressed in their name for themselves, Cymry. As in Ireland, discovery of a glorious past was one way to generate self-respect in a present blighted by English ridicule. Welsh expatriates in London took the lead in the founding of those antiquarian societies that exalted traditional cultural distinctiveness. They formed in 1751 the first Cymmrodorion Society and gave generous support to a wide range of publications in Welsh that sparked renewed interest in language and literature. These flourished with the revival and dramatic growth of 'Eisteddfodau,' bardic festivals of poetry and song. The red dragon reappeared, after long neglect, as a patriotic symbol on the banners and badges of clubs and societies, St David's Day was celebrated, and 1856 saw the composition of *Hen Wlad Fy Nhadau*, which quickly gained acceptance as a national anthem. The growth of Welsh literacy had been stimulated in the eighteenth century by circulating schools, though by the beginning of the new millennium they were in sad decline. British and national schools, the first mainly for Dissenters and the second for Anglicans, sought to fill the void and did begin to spread rapidly during the 1840s, but that did not prevent the three commissioners appointed by the government to investigate "the state of education and the moral condition of the common people of Wales" from delivering a savagely critical report. In their infamous Blue Books, published in 1847, they damned the Welsh as "ill-educated, poor, dirty, unchaste, in danger of being led into sedition and even revolution." The women were unchaste, the men congenital liars and cheats, and the community lamentably backward. The commissioners identified the causes of this sorry state of affairs as "the prevalence of the Welsh language and the adherence of the mass of the people to nonconformity." By way of a solution, they argued the necessity for English to become the language of the people if Wales "was to take part in the progress of Britain." The bitterness with which the Welsh responded to such comments masked a sense of "inadequacy and inferiority" that increasingly diverted them from history and poetry to "more practical knowledge" and laid the groundwork of their subsequent acceptance of both a state system of education and the need to learn English.[39]

If the Blue Books ultimately helped to check the contribution of the Welsh language to ethnic mobilization, that language had long bonded the people – hence the suspicion that it had been the means by which the Newport rising was organized with "so little interruption." This was one area of the United Kingdom "where the lower orders [spoke] almost universally a language unknown to the educated classes." Further, the linguistic gulf was identified as "one of the principal, though not the main, nor the only, cause of unpleasantness" between Saxon and Celt. Perhaps 70 per cent of the population spoke it, and fully half of them were monoglots. There were complaints, as the midpoint of the nineteenth century neared, "that double the number of people now [spoke] Welsh who spoke that language in the reign of Elizabeth." The alarmists overlooked the recent doubling of the principality's population, but there could be no mistaking "an efflorescence of Welshness that was astonishingly prolific and varied in its expression" and that fed English concerns. There was a proliferation of Welsh periodicals and newspapers, and this era saw the coining of Welsh words for nationalism, nationalist, and nationality. English commentators who avowed an understanding of the attachment to Welsh as a medium of intercourse nevertheless were moved to declare linguistic unity indispensable to that freedom of intercourse essential "for the generation and maintenance of a friendly feeling among diverse races." Thus calls for bilingualism were frequently drowned out by the demands for the "extirpation of Welsh, as a spoken language." The Welsh language excluded the Welsh people from progress and civilization, the *Times* bellowed, echoing the Blue Books. Even Matthew Arnold in his defence of the principality against this particular attack – *On the Study of Celtic Literature* (1867) – insisted that the successful uniting of Britons and the integration of provincial nationalities in furtherance of modern civilization required the disappearance of Welsh and the establishment of an "English-speaking whole." He was simply returning to the assumptions that had dictated the terms of union in 1536, and the strong survival of the language may go far to explain the state's refusal "to endorse Welsh local habits and customs."[40]

The strength of that survival owed much to religion. Unlike the Irish, the Welsh wholeheartedly accepted the English Reformation, led as it was by monarchs whose roots lay in the principality. In their eyes, the Tudors had restored the ancient British monarchy. The confiscation of monastic properties and the redistribution of ecclesiastical benefices were additional incentives for the gentry to embrace Protestantism. Steps were quickly taken to ensure that the people understood the reformed faith. Although Welsh had been proscribed for official purposes in the Act of Union, the printing of books in the vernacular had not been prohibited. A Welsh prayer book was published in 1546, the New Testament in 1567, the entire Bible in 1588, and to these were added before the end of the following century psalms, catechisms, hymns, sermons, and a broad range of works of divinity. Welsh as a literary language not only survived but prospered as ever-greater numbers of religious books were subsidized and distributed either free or at reduced prices by charitable societies and organizations such as the Society for the Propagation of Christian Knowledge (SPCK). Biblical literacy was the basis of the curriculum of the circulating schools, for which the SPCK produced fifteen thousand Welsh Bibles in 1746. By 1820 Wales, with a population only one-tenth that of Ireland, had fifteen times as many works in print in the vernacular. Wales emerged as "the most biblically minded nation in the world," and the fact that this development coincided with a Methodist revival led Anglican clergy to blame their evangelical colleague who founded the circulating schools for the rise of Dissent. But the Established Church created many of its own difficulties. Unilingual anglophone clergy dominated its ranks, including the episcopacy. The "reasonableness" of the Welsh demand for a bishop "able to preach and minister to them in a tongue 'understanded of the people'" was acknowledged in 1859 by a Tory prime minister, Lord Derby, but he was either unwilling or unable to force the issue. Not until 1870 was a Welsh-speaking bishop appointed. The alienation of more than half the income intended for parochial purposes and the prevalence of pluralities and non-residence simply added to the woes of the Church of Wales. The wonder was that it "should have continued to exist at all," *Blackwood's* remarked.[41]

Since Welsh was "the ordinary language of public worship, and the common medium of conversation," the Anglican Church effectively conceded to the Dissenters "a monopoly over the development of Welsh as the language of popular religion." Nonconformity triumphed in the nineteenth century, its ministers assuring the people that they and their language "were objects of special concern on the part of the Deity." The secession of the Calvinistic Methodists in 1811, forming "the only church of Welsh origin," and the growing strength of the Baptists, Congregationalists/Independents, and Unitarians marked a dramatic shift in religious allegiances. Nonconformity also benefited from its energetic response to the industrialization of South Wales. An evangelical message, itinerant preachers, prudent measures to retain the allegiance of migrants from countryside to town, and the fellowship provided by chapel to those who now found themselves in an alien industrial environment, all contributed to its appeal and remarkable success. Nonconformist ministers artfully exploited the English and Anglican authorship of the Blue Books, depicting the deeply resented criticisms as an attempt to besmirch the reputation of Welsh nonconformity. The extent of the Dissenters' dominance was documented by the Religious Census of 1851, which indicated that they formed an even larger proportion of the principality's population than did Roman Catholics that of Ireland. Of course, they were not a monolith. The separate and competing elements of this overwhelming majority were united only in opposition to the Established Church and in hostility to "Popery."[42]

Welsh nonconformist ministers were men of considerable influence and power within their communities, and Conservatives accused them of engaging in a form of "spiritual terrorism" more commonly associated with Irish priests. A Calvinistic Methodist minister did publish "the first Welsh political newspaper," and it was a Congregationalist minister who drew English criticism for his promotion of radical causes in his monthly, Y *Diwygiwr*. The nonconformist community did petition for the repeal of the Test and Corporation Acts and against both Catholic emancipation and the re-establishment of a Catholic hierarchy for England and Wales. They objected to tithes, and the tenantry seized upon an anglicized landlordry's identification with the Established Church to denounce them as exploitive if not alien. Thus "the Nonconformist faith became the ideological basis of resistance to landlord hegemony." Politically, the commitment of Whig-Liberals to religious equality saw many ministers instruct their congregations during election campaigns in the "moral aspects of politics," which they reduced to a choice between good and evil. Welsh-language newspapers threatened to publish the names of electors who failed to vote for Liberal candidates, who they warned "would be regarded as traitors to their faith." However, the great majority of nonconformists found in their chapels "an outlet, elsewhere provided by politics or conspiracy or riot, to the craving for self-expression and the search for justice." They were committed to civil and religious liberty, but were taught to obey the civil power and be loyal to the monarch. M.D. Jones, born in Wales, educated there and in London, ordained in the United States, promoter of the attempt to establish a self-governing Welsh community in Patagonia, and principal of the Congregational College in Bala, North Wales, was a rare example of a minister whose cultural nationalism evolved into something far more political. Most of his colleagues used their "all-pervasive" influence to maintain the tranquility of Welsh society, and the most prominent Welsh Radical, Henry Richard, described them as the country's "unpaid policemen." They kept Wales "relatively free of crime" and helped "check the passions of the people." In this latter respect, they differed from many Irish priests.[43]

If the Welsh clearly possessed a national awareness and if in some sense this qualified as a form of "collectivist culturalist nationalism," neither repeal of the Union nor revolutionary nationalism had any appeal for them. They had, of course, been long integrated into the English state, and they lacked national institutions, a capital city, even a university. They were conscious of the geographic division of their land, between the North and the South, both with distinctive versions of their common language. Wales was physically joined to England, the Welsh were comparatively few in number, and they were alive to the economic benefits of the existing relationship. Their reading of the distant past had informed the attack on "The Treason of the Blue Books," but they had failed to produce a history that was truly usable politically. The very evangelical enthusiasm that contributed to their reinvention of tradition also brought them more firmly within the embrace of a British Protestant nationalism shaped from "anti-Catholicism, imperialism and constitutional chauvinism." From the time of the Tudors, Welsh patriotism was regarded as "fully compatible with loyalty to, indeed enthusiasm for, the British Constitution." Similarly, the image of the preacher in this deeply religious land expressed national pride "without threatening a broader British loyalty." Radicals did begin to assert from mid-century that Wales was a nation with the ambition for equal representation with the other nations of the United Kingdom. This new national consciousness was disseminated by a Welsh-language press. The *Baner ac Amserau Cymru* sponsored a campaign for the erection of national monuments to Welsh heroes. Yet even these radicals believed that Wales "should express her nationality in religious terms." That included cooperation with the Liberation Society, and thus indirectly with Irish Roman Catholics, in the campaign for disestablishment of the Anglican Church. But Welsh leaders during the 1860s were keen to convince their mighty neighbours that the people of Wales had been transformed "into an outward-looking, progressive people." Little wonder the former radical Congregationalist minister who published *Y Diwygiwr* had become "defeatist" about the future of the Welsh language and "scornful of the Irish for resisting things British." And it was a Welsh member of Parliament who urged the crowds attending the Swansea Eisteddfod in 1863 to remember that they were all "Englishmen" as well as Welsh. Perhaps Engels was right when he observed that, as tenaciously as they had struggled to defend their language and culture, the Welsh were "entirely reconciled with the British Empire."[44]

Scotland rather than Wales served as the national counterpoint for those Britons convinced, or hopeful, that Ireland could yet be brought into harmony with the rest of the United Kingdom. The historic memory did not need to be especially long, just two biblical lifespans, to recall an independent Scottish legislature. Scotland had a far more extensive history of rebellion than the principality, the most dramatic rising having been put down only with considerable difficulty a century earlier. Indeed, she far more than Wales appeared to be a potentially viable entity as a separate state, given a territory four times as large, a population approaching three million by 1851, a larger and more

developed economy, and greater distance from the political and economic centres of English power. Moreover, the Scots had retained "the
Scottish crown and regalia," together with an institutional distinctiveness of which the Welsh, and to a lesser extent the Irish, had been
robbed. They possessed their own Presbyterian Established Church,
their own separate legal and educational institutions, and their own
ancient capital. Here was an obvious "focus for national identity and
national pride." But like Wales, Scotland was divided. The division of
Highlands and Lowlands was not simply geographical but cultural,
social, economic, and religious. The "slow de-Gaelicization" of the
Lowlands, the abandonment of the language and culture, aroused
strong Gaelic resentment, which by the end of the sixteenth century
found expression in denunciations of "foreigners" and traitors. For
their part, English-speaking Lowlanders held Gaelic-speaking Highlanders in contempt as impoverished and violent savages. They also
served as convenient scapegoats for the Jacobite rebellions, whereas
Charles Edward Stuart had in 1745 raised thousands of troops in the
Lowlands. The Highlands and Islands also remained rural, featuring
large estates, the grinding poverty of crofters (whose plight was not
unlike that of Irish cottiers), massive evictions, occasional disturbances, and a culture of emigration. As in the case of the Welsh, some
displaced Highlanders were able to migrate south to rapidly industrializing centres. The coal and iron resources of central Scotland were
being rapidly exploited and developed in the nineteenth century, and
marine engineering was emerging as an important industry along with
a broad range of textiles. By mid-century, more than half of all Scots
lived in towns and cities.[45]

Roman Catholic Highlanders were damned as doubly disloyal by
the Calvinist Lowlanders, although the last Jacobite army had been
stocked by far greater numbers of Episcopalians. The early nineteenth
century found many if not most Highlanders successfully proselytized
by evangelical missionaries of the Church of Scotland. Thus it could
claim to be even more of a national institution than before, and it exercised extensive influence over education, poor relief, and the code of
social behaviour. The proselytizers used the vernacular with the result
that Gaelic oral culture "gave way to a biblically-oriented literacy, also
in Gaelic." Evangelicals then took the lead in the mass defection from
the Established Church, founding the Free Church in 1843. Ironically,
the disruption of this the most national of Scottish institutions was
achieved with appeals to national sentiment. The traditional theme of

English perfidy was fully exploited, and the Free Church *Witness* served as a vehicle for advertising national grievances against the old enemy, which fostered the argument that the disruption was "partly fuelled by something very close to nationalism." If Free Church Scots, like the Catholic Irish, were damned in England as "priest-ridden and bigoted," they were also regarded as "hopelessly ignorant of the opinions and rights of others" and therefore only "unconsciously under clerical influence." Moreover, many of the migrants who moved out of the Highlands in search of work encountered in the Lowlands an integrationist spirit with respect to the Union that was further reinforced, as in the principality, by the assimilatory consequences of industrial development.[46]

Historians of the Scottish Enlightenment were vanguard "North Britons," advocating "an Anglo-British institutional identity." England's "liberties and mixed constitution" were contrasted with the pre-Union "backwardness" of Scotland's native institutions, and English society accepted as "a higher norm to which Scotland should aspire." Union would eventually be the means of remedying the Scots' defects and creating a "civility" that resembled England's. In this way Scots would be raised to the level of truly equal partners of the English. Not surprisingly, there was an accompanying claim to racial similarity if not equality. North Britons began to argue that they were close relatives of the Anglo-Saxons to the south who traced their liberties to the Germanic tribes. Scotland was another home of Saxon democracy, David Hume claimed. He lauded England for her restrained employment of violence and injustice in her pursuit of power, and excused her imposition of "'just terror'" on the "'deluded,'" "'savage,'" "'untractable,'" and ignorant Irish. In short, Scots were "an integral part of the dominant British Saxon core of the burgeoning multi-ethnic empire." George Combe, the phrenologist, added his influential "scientific" voice to this chorus, asserting that Lowlanders had been responsible for "everything by which Scotland [was] distinguished." The success with which many anglophone Scots "adapted themselves to life and opportunities in England," their greater acceptance there than either the Welsh or the Irish, appeared to substantiate their professions of racial affinity. Similarly, privileged Scots believed that the Union would "support them in their privilege" even as it permitted the parading of a non-threatening difference from the English under the banner of "pedantic antiquarianism." Not that the common people of Scotland, including those of the Lowlands, escaped the sting of English contempt. "All the stories that are propagated of the filth and habitual dirtiness of this people are surpassed by reality," one English visitor wrote towards the end of the eighteenth century. "Their manners are equally unpleasant, being uncommunicative and forbidding in the extreme."[47]

Urban life and the harsh conditions of industrial work bred unrest, but in Scotland as in Wales the agitation was usually kept "within the bounds of the existing political system." The United Scotsmen of the 1790s were radical republicans with ties across the Irish Sea, and they urged support of Wolfe Tone, but if they were evidence of "a surviving strain of anti-union feeling" they never posed a "credible threat to the state." They were simply too few in number, while Scots regiments played a large and often brutal role in the suppression of the Irish rebellion of 1798. Then, in the face of a threatened invasion by Napoleonic France, tens of thousands of Scots enrolled as volunteers to defend the nation, and they formed a similarly conspicuous element of the armed forces throughout the French Wars. The difficult postwar era did bring strikes, the organization of secret societies, and fresh eruptions of radical activity, even a brief Radical War in 1820, which was "arguably the most serious radical challenge faced by the government in mainland Britain." An undercurrent of nationalism was present in street literature, but rarely if ever did it manifest itself in a clear demand for Scottish independence. Instead, there was greater radical devotion to reform than to the concept of the nation. The Scottish Reform Act that followed the Great Reform Bill of 1832 increased a minuscule electorate fourteenfold, though a lower standard of living in Scotland resulted in the enfranchisement of a significantly smaller proportion of the population. The number of constituencies was also increased, the eight additional seats going to urban centres, but these changes fell far short of popular demands. If disappointment contributed to the founding of a distinctively Scottish Chartist movement, it was in no sense a truly nationalist movement. The same was true of the Reform League established two decades later to agitate for democratization. It was affiliated with that in London.[48]

Even that remote region of the country long associated with resistance to Britishness underwent a metamorphosis. The Highlands and Islands, regarded by outsiders as " a barren and sterile wilderness, inhabited by a barbarous population" speaking the "Irish language," practising Roman Catholicism, organized in feudal and "tyrannical" clans, and naturally lawless and violent, evidently needed to be brought within the pale of civilization. An improvement in communications – roads, bridges, and canals – served, as in Ireland, to facilitate the deployment of troops and open a formerly enclosed world, while the clan system began to decline. The Highlanders' conversion to Presbyterianism had been considered equally essential, because "catholicism and episcopalianism were the twin ideological sources of Jacobitism." This success seemed at first glance to have been purchased at the expense of another objective, for it was rooted in biblical literacy in Gaelic. If this nourished the vernacular that many educators were struggling to supplant, Gaelic literacy paradoxically proved to be a first step towards knowledge of English and the steady advance of bilingualism. Gaelic-speaking Highlanders, no less than Irish speakers, recognized the doors the English language opened to opportunity and progress. Those of them who migrated south temporarily to work in the booming industries brought the language and this conviction back home with them. Moreover, acceptance of Presbyterianism and a Scottish version of English appeared to inaugurate a Highland society virtually free of serious crime. Even the protests against the infamous clearances were short-lived and relatively subdued, at least "compared to the chronic discontent of parts of the Irish countryside." This prompted contemporaries to ask themselves why a people "of the same origin and the same race as the Irish Catholics" behaved so differently, even though "Highland Presbyterians [were] almost as poor as the Irish Papists"? The predictable answer was Protestantism, which had removed "the stain of Celtic origin." Nevertheless, as Scottish Catholics were reduced to an insignificant minority and demonstrated their loyalty by raising the Glengarry Fencibles following the outbreak of war with revolutionary France, the government applied to Scotland the policy already implemented in Ireland. A grant to assist the training of young Scots for the priesthood was followed by another in aid of the proposed Highland seminary.[49]

In Scotland, as in Ireland and Wales, antiquarianism promoted respect for Celtic culture, which led in turn to the rehabilitation of Gaeldom. James MacPherson was a pivotal figure, publishing in the early 1760s his alleged reconstructions of the works of Ossian. Although their authenticity was quickly challenged, with some critics accusing him of stealing Fenian legends from Ireland, MacPherson "brought the Gaelic literary tradition into the public eye." The Ossian poems persuaded some Lowlanders that "the Celtic languages were true vehicles of culture, religion and education," for MacPherson established "the importance and centrality of the Celtic contribution to British society in a manner which rendered it devoid of all threat." He also sought to prove that the "Celtic peoples of ancient Britain had been just as freedom-loving as the other peoples of northern Europe," that they had developed "representative estates," and that the clans had been autocratically governed only in the most exceptional of circumstances. This was the favourable environment in which the London Highland Society was founded by expatriates, perhaps inspired by the example of the Welsh. Six years later, in 1784, the Highland Society of Scotland was established in Edinburgh. Little wonder there was mounting English and Lowland interest in visiting the Highlands, journeys made far less uncomfortable by the improvement in communications. Not only was a Scottish tour much cheaper than the Grand Tour of Europe, but with the opening of the French Wars, the Highlands were one of the few places of mystery, romance, hospitality, and wild beauty that English tourists could visit safely. Although struck by the poverty and wretchedness of the peasants, their shabby clothing and "stone huts," visitors formed the impression that these "men-sties" were not inhabited, as they were in Ireland, "by a race of ignorant and ferocious barbarians" who could never be civilized until they had been "regenerated." The folk they encountered, they were assured, were "quiet, thoughtful, contented, religious people, susceptible to improvement."[50]

The dramatic transformation of the Gaelic Highlander from disloyal savage into a "loyal and courageous defender of British interests" was completed by his military service. Highlanders enlisted because they hoped to be rewarded with a tenantry and because soldiering was an acceptable form of employment, preferable to the physical drudgery that was frequently the only alternative, and "bestowed prestige in a personal and social sense." The Scots distinguished themselves in the Seven Years War and in the Irish rebellion, and they made a remarkable contribution to the victory over the French. Greater proportionately than that of the English or even the Irish, their contribution justified their being singled out for praise following the final victory at Waterloo. To a greater degree than the Irish, they were embodied as distinctively Scottish units that continued to form an admired element of the Victorian army. Indeed, regiments that were heavily Irish often lacked Irish officers and had "only casual connections with Ireland." They tended to be moved quickly out of their native land, whereas Scotland was garrisoned by Scottish troops. Military service had finally

purged the Highlanders of their cultural associations with Ireland and
Jacobitism, and promoted their anglicization. Lowlanders began to
parade the Highland soldier as a proud symbol of "Scotland's ancient
nationhood and her equal partnership with England in the British
empire." Indeed, as the clearances and emigration reduced the population of the Highlands, so recruits were necessarily drawn from the
Lowlands and its urban centres. The men came increasingly "from the
lower working classes, in contrast to the rural, clan-based, Highland-
born warriors of popular legend." In short, the Highland regiments
generated Britishness even as they were serving Scottish purposes.
Being British, in other words, neither conflicted with nor undermined
"an individual's sense of Scottishness."[51]

The Highlander was further romanticized and popularized by Sir
Walter Scott, who naturally endowed him with the martial virtues –
fearlessness, fortitude, and fidelity. In *Waverley*, which Scott wrote on
and off between the year of Nelson's victory at Trafalgar and that of
Napoleon's exile to Elba, he presented the rebels of 1745 as sympathetic figures whose principal failing had been "a misplaced loyalty to
a deserving albeit hopeless cause." His purpose in the Waverley novels
was "to complete the union by educating the English in Scottish history" and to further the reconciliation of Lowland and Highland
Scots. Thus he balanced his own rejection of the authenticity of Ossian with the legend that fifteen hundred years earlier the Caledonians
had worn the tartan kilt. There is evidence of "tartan and the kilt
being used as a sign of traditional, authentic Scottishness from at least
1596," but clan tartans do not appear to have existed at the time of
the rebellion in 1745. The reversal of the ban on Highland dress
imposed following the rebellion was an early objective of the Highland
Society, and with its success the kilt became an item of fashion. Its
adoption by Highland regiments, both because of its greater conve-
nience as an article of clothing than the traditional belted plaid and
because of the resort to tartans to distinguish regiments, probably
inspired the innovation of clan tartans. Certainly, the visit of George
IV to Edinburgh in 1822, stage-managed by Scott, saw the costume
receive royal patronage. In Highland dress and associations, canny
Scots had found another way to assert "a distinctive Scottish identity
without in any way compromising the union."[52]

The cult of the Highland hero was one to which Queen Victoria subscribed, perhaps a little too intimately in the opinion of scandalmon-
gers. She considered Highlanders "the finest race in the world." Here

was an "ethnic identity" with which MacPherson, Scott, and Robert Burns, among others, appeared to be laying the foundations of Scottish nationalism. Here was the evidence that Scotland differed profoundly from England. Cultural nationalists were projecting a new historical consciousness, one that linked past to present, and in the person of Burns they popularized Scots, as distinct from Gaelic, as a literary language. Yet a Scottish ethnic identity remained something of an illusion. The "cult of tartanry," the enlistment of Lowlanders in Highland regiments, did not suppress their "Teutonic racialism," not least because "Scottish thinkers and academic institutions were directly involved in the rise of nineteenth-century racial determinism." Even Scott was not immune to it, as he revealed in *Ivanhoe*. Lowlanders found in "Teutonist ethnology" the assurance that they belonged to the dominant race, and that conviction deepened with the success of Scots in British politics and their free access to the British Empire and large involvement in its exploitation and administration. The hidden danger here was that the sense of Britishness was excessively dependent on the existence of the empire. For the time being, however, the British state continued to sit "lightly upon civil society." Consequently, it was far less vulnerable to the charges of oppression and tyranny levelled so loudly and persistently in Ireland. The daily life of Scots remained in the hands of "essentially self-governing localities," and this high degree of practical autonomy was reflected in the British Parliament's rare interventions in Scottish affairs and the control retained by the Lord Advocate over law enforcement and policing.[53]

The steady progress in communications with the arrival of the railway age and the telegraph, which promoted industrialization, economic integration, and anglicization, alarmed some Scots that the state was becoming more centralized, and made them more speedily aware of English slights and lack of respect for Scottish interests that betrayed less than full acceptance of them as equal partners in the Union. The extraordinary popular excitement generated in 1826 by the announcement in London of the government's intention to abolish paper currency of less than five pounds and to extend the ban to Scotland signalled the first of a series of irritants. These small notes made up the bulk of the money in circulation in Scotland, and beyond their abolition there lurked the threat to grant a monopoly to the Bank of England and to terminate the power of Scottish banks to issue notes. Perhaps influenced by his own severe losses in the collapse of the London money market, Scott took the lead in urging his countrymen to protect Scotland's rights "while preserving 'every feeling of amity and respect towards England.'" He was arousing nationalist emotions in order to check excessive assimilation, but directing them at the symbolic target of the banknote. The government eventually abandoned the proposal, though Scottish affairs were formally moved to the Home Office. Englishmen, Irishmen, and Scotsmen should remain as nature had made them, Scott asserted in a series of public letters, "with something like the impress of [their] several countries upon each." Plainly, there was neither wish nor intent to put at risk the political stability and prosperity that the Union had delivered to Scotland.[54]

Scottish sensitivity was soon on display again. The inability of Scotland's small band of representatives to obtain sufficient parliamentary time to enact legislation they deemed important; the lack of a Scottish minister, comparable to Ireland's chief secretary, to shape policy at the highest level of government and steer bills through the Commons; a belief that England was deriving greater benefit from union than Scotland because its terms were not being respected nor promises honoured; evidence that Ireland contributed less to the Treasury but received more from the state and had been a greater beneficiary of famine relief; the use of "English" instead of "British" by senior figures when referring to the citizens of the United Kingdom; the incorrect positioning of the Scottish heraldic symbol on the royal standard; the failure of branches of the armed forces to fly the Union flag; and disparaging references to Scots in English newspapers, all helped to produce popular support for the National Association for the Vindication of Scottish Rights, founded in 1853. The association's agenda has encouraged modern historians to characterize its dominant sentiment as "unionist-nationalism." The most radical dissident, James Begg, a Free Church minister, did resort to the threat of home rule to reinforce demands for greater Scottish representation in Parliament, "fairer treatment ... from the Exchequer," and the restoration of a secretary of state for Scotland, but there was scant support for repeal of the Union. The aristocratic chairman of the association's first public meeting declared: "'I am not wrong-headed enough to wish that the Union, which has been established so happily for the peace and tranquillity of both, should be interfered with.'" He went on: "'We love our English brethren, and we are proud to be associated with them in an empire on which the sun never sets – but we are Scotchmen still.'" In the words of the *North British Review*, the journal of the Free Church, "Increased quiet, increased commerce and wealth, increased liberty, increased civilization, these have been the consequences to Scotland of the once detested Union." Nor did the erection of imposing monuments to the medieval warrior William Wallace, which both preceded and followed the short-lived National Association, represent a national craving for Scottish independence. Instead, Wallace was commemorated as a national hero who, by his defence of Scotland from Norman invaders, had made it possible for modern Scots to enter the Union as partners of the English.[55]

Nor did the erection of an imposing monument to another hero, Sir Walter Scott, amount to an expression of Scottish nationalism, since he was regarded as the dominant British literary figure of his age whose "nationality was partially subsumed within his British identity." In this sense it was appropriate that a shortfall in funding was covered with the aid of a Waverley Ball in London, for which the great and the eminent acted as stewards. The centennial celebrations in 1859 of the birth of Robert Burns did represent another affirmation of the Scots' sense of being a nation independent in spirit. At the most impressive of the many celebrations, that in Edinburgh attended by seven hundred dinner guests, there was a particularly enthusiastic response to a toast to Scottish military veterans. "The Scottish regiments were a proud symbol of Scotland who maintained their own identity, through their own clothing, within the British army." This determination to maintain a distinctive national identity, to exhibit pride in their history and culture, did not imperil the Union. As in Wales, cultural nationalism failed to plant and nourish a popular movement for national independence. The material benefits of the existing arrangement, especially for the burgeoning middle classes, and the success of professionals and the intelligentsia within the British state ensured that the Scots provided few advocates of, or agitators for, political nationalism. If a "genuinely pan-Britannic national identity" had not been constructed, a popular Britishness had developed and anti-Catholicism remained an important ingredient. Scotland's Presbyterians assailed the "terrorism, clothed in a British Constitution," with which Irish Catholics browbeat the government and extorted "'concessions, revenues, and patronage, and repaid them with scorn, disaffection, and insolent defiance.'" This sectarian hostility was dramatically reinvigorated by the arrival in Britain of a tidal wave of Irish Catholic immigrants. If religion heightened national consciousness in Ireland, Wales, and Scotland, Protestantism had long provided a countervailing British unity against the Catholic "other." Nevertheless, by the 1860s there was a recognition in England that for Ireland to be reconciled to the Union she needed to be treated with as much fairness and consideration as Scotland. The argument that Scotland while not Anglican was at least Protestant, whereas the Catholic Irish were the subjects of a foreign power and thus not to be trusted with full equality, was ridiculed as a varnish lightly covering "bigotry of race and creed."[56]

The *Daily Telegraph*, which could claim to be England's most popular newspaper, reminded its readers that the British state had by implication admitted that instruction in Catholicism was a benefit to society. Catholic chaplains were tolerated in prisons, workhouses, and the armed forces, and in some instances paid out of public funds. Roman Catholics paid taxes, served on juries, and were embraced by the doctrine of indefeasible allegiance. They owed the Pope spiritual allegiance only. Moreover, full rights had been extended to the Roman Catholics of Canada at a time when the monarch's conscience would not allow him to accept Catholic emancipation in Ireland. The reason was expediency. "Popish Canada, discontented, would have joined the new United States: Popish Ireland, discontented, was within easy reach of the Protestant swords of Protestant dragoons." A similar pragmatism had seen the English accept in 1707 the legal endowment and status of the Presbyterian Church, which commanded the spiritual allegiance of the majority of Scots. In Ireland, on the other hand, the church of the Anglican minority had been imposed on the vast majority of Irish Catholics as the Established Church. The church of the majority had no legal standing and its priests were even subjected to insults by representatives of the Crown. Little wonder that the clergy of the Church of Scotland were recognized as friends of the state and that the hierarchy of the Catholic Church of Ireland were its adversaries. In Scotland, local education was partially controlled by the clergy of the majority and their catechism was taught in schools. In Ireland, the national schools were "anti-clerical in their primary idea." In Ireland, landownership was in the hands of men who professed the creed of the minority and were either English or of English descent. In Scotland, the soil was owned by Scots, or persons of Scottish descent, who subscribed to the creed of the majority. Finally, in Scotland "national feeling" was encouraged by everyone in authority from the Queen down. Scottish regiments wore a national costume, thereby demonstrating the ability of loyalty and nationality to flourish side by side. This was all in sharp contrast to Ireland, the *Daily Telegraph* remarked, where no Irish regiment had green facings on its uniforms and no national emblem or colour was permitted. Indeed, there was no purely native institution that the loyal Irish were allowed to support or cherish. All of this tended to contradict Engels's assertion that "[t]he English know how to reconcile people of the most diverse races with their rule." After more than fifty years, it was obvious that the Irish had yet to be reconciled to the Union. Equally, there was no likelihood of the British agreeing to Irish demands for political autonomy, let alone independence. Britons continued to cling to the belief that "Ireland is too great to be unconnected with us ... too near us to be dependent on a foreign state, and too little to be independent."[57]

Notes

CHAPTER ONE

1 *Edinburgh Review* 84 (1846): 267; Jenny Wormald, "The Creation of Britain: Multiple Kingdoms or Core and Colonies?" *Transactions of the Royal Historical Society,* 6th ser., 2 (1992): 175–94; see also Bruce Galloway, *The Union of England and Scotland 1603–1608* (Edinburgh, 1986); Niall Ferguson, *Empire: The Rise and Demise of the British World Order and the Lessons for Global Power* (London, 2002), 25; Jane Ohlmeyer, "Seventeenth Century Ireland and the New British and Atlantic Histories," *American Historical Review* 104 (1999): 450; P.J. Cain and A.G. Hopkins, *British Imperialism: Innovation and Expansion 1688–1914* (London, 1993), 90; T.C. Barnard, *Cromwellian Ireland: English Government and Reform in Ireland 1649–1660,* new ed. (Oxford, 2000), 26, 71; *Bristol Gazette,* 29 January 1801.
2 James Kelly, "The Origins of the Act of Union: An examination of Unionist Opinion in Britain and Ireland, 1650–1800," *Irish Historical Studies* 30 (1987): 237, 239; J.G.A. Pocock, "The Union in British History," *Transactions of the Royal Historical Society* (TRHS), 6th ser., 10 (2000): 183; R.R. Davies, "The Peoples of Britain and Ireland, 1100–1400: iv Language and Historical Mythology," *TRHS,* 6th ser., 7 (1997): 12–13; Nicholas Canny, *Kingdom and Colony: Ireland in the Atlantic World 1560–1800* (Baltimore, 1988), 19, 34; Arthur Herman, *How the Scots Invented the Modern World* (New York, 2001), 114–15; Michael Brown, Patrick M. Geoghegan, and James Kelly, eds., *The Irish Act of Union, 1800: Bicentennial Essays* (Dublin, 2003), 90, 61; Kathleen M. Noonan, "'The Cruel Pressure of an Enraged, Barbarous People': Irish and English Identity in Seventeenth-Century

Policy and Propaganda," *Historical Journal* 4 (1998): 151–77; Moustafa Bayoumi and Andrew Rubin, *The Edward Said Reader* (New York, 2000), 295; Andrew Hadfield and John McVeagh, eds., *Strangers to the Land: British Perceptions of Ireland from the Reformation to the Famine* (Gerrards Cross, 1994), 17; Ohlmeyer, *American Historical Review* 104: 460–1; Thomas Bartlett, "Review Article: A New History of Ireland," *Past and Present* 116 (1987): 214–15; *The Speeches of the Right Honourable Henry Grattan in the Irish and in the Imperial Parliament*, 4 vols. (London, 1822), 2: 368; Barnard, *Cromwellian Ireland*, 5.

3 Marianne Elliott, *The Catholics of Ulster* (London, 2000), 99–102, 115; Barnard, *Cromwellian Ireland*, 5; David Hayton, "From Barbarian to Burlesque: English Images of the Irish c. 1660–1750*," *Irish Economic and Social History* 15 (1988): 5–31; Niall O Ciosain, *Print and Popular Culture in Ireland 1750–1850* (New York, 1997), 89; Clare O'Halloran, "Irish Re-creations of the Gaelic Past: The Challenge of Macpherson's Ossian," *Past and Present* 124 (1989): 72–3; Thomas McLoughlin, *Contesting Ireland: Irish Voices against England in the Eighteenth Century* (Dublin, 1999), 146–8; Bernadette Cunningham, *The World of Geoffrey Keating: History, Myth and Religion in Seventeenth-Century Ireland* (Dublin, 2000), 218, 59, 7, 12, 114, 116; Hadfield and MacVeagh, *Strangers to That Land*, 19–20, 148.

4 Kelly, *Irish Historical Studies* 30:238; William Doyle, "The Union in a European Context," TRHS, 6th ser., 10: 170; Thomas Bartlett, *The Fall and Rise of the Irish Nation: The Catholic Question 1690–1830* (Savage, Md, 1992), 212; McLoughlin, *Contesting Ireland*, 20, 39, 66, 68, 107; D. George Boyce and Alan O'Day, eds., *Defenders of the Union: A Survey of British and Irish Unionism since 1801* (London, 2001), 19; Hugh Gough and David Dickson, eds., *Ireland and the French Revolution* (Dublin, 1990), 110; Stephen Small, "The Twisted Roots of Irish Patriotism: Anglo-Irish Political Thought in the Late-Eighteenth Century," *Eire/Ireland* 35 (2000): 191–3, 195; Elliott, *Catholics of Ulster*, 220, 241.

5 Ian B. Cowan, "Anglo-Scottish Relations," *Historical Journal* 32 (1989):229–35; T.M Devine, *The Scottish Nation 1700–2000*, pb. ed. (London, 1999), 16, 23, 213; see Keith Robbins, *Nineteenth-Century Britain: Integration and Diversity* (Oxford, 1988); also Hugh Kearney, *The British Isles: A History of Four Nations* (Cambridge, 1989), 153; Graeme Morton, *Unionist-Nationalism:*

Governing Urban Scotland, 1830–1860 (Edinburgh, 1999), 47,
30–3; K. Theodore Hoppen, *Mid-Victorian Generation 1846–
1886* (Oxford, 1998), 576; Herman, *How the Scots Invented*,
86–7; Victor Edward Durkacz, *The Decline of the Celtic Languages: A Study of Linguistic and Cultural Conflict in Scotland,
Wales and Ireland from the Reformation to the Twentieth Century*
(Edinburgh, 1983), 3; T.C. Barnard, "Protestants and the Irish
Language, c. 1675–1725," *Journal of Ecclesiastical History* 44
(1993): 245; Barnard, *Cromwellian Ireland*, 173, 175.

6 *Times*, 6 November 1866; Brian P. Levack, *The Formation of the
British State: England, Scotland and the Union 1603–1707*
(Oxford, 1987), vi, 13, 65–6, 103, 113, 172; R.R. Davies, "The
Peoples of Britain and Ireland 1100–1400: iii Laws and Cus-
toms," TRHS, 6th ser., 6 (1996): 18; Linda Colley, *Britons: Forging
the Nation 1707–1837* (New Haven, 1992), 6; Morton, *Unionist-
Nationalism*, 14–15; *Fortnightly Review*, n.s. 3 (1868): 319;
Wormald, TRHS, 6th ser., 2:188; James D. Young, *The Rousing of
the Scottish Working Class* (London, 1979), 16, 79; *Fortnightly
Review* 4 (1866): 299–300; Devine, *Scottish Nation*, 55, 61–2;
McLoughlin, *Contesting Ireland*, 18; Elliott, *Catholics of Ulster*,
163–4.

7 J.C.D. Clark, "Protestantism, Nationalism and National Identity,
1660–1832," *Historical Journal* 43 (2000): 249–76; Paul Lang-
ford, *A Polite and Commercial People: England 1727–1783*
(Oxford, 1983), 700–2; Daniel Statt, *Foreigners and Englishmen:
The Controversy over Immigration and Population, 1660–1760*
(London, 1995), 188: T.H. Breen, "Ideology and Nationalism on
the Eve of the American Revolution: Revisions *Once More* in
Need of Revising," *Journal of American History* 84 (1997): 21–2.

8 Anthony D. Smith, *Nationalism and Modernism* (London, 1998),
172; Benedict Anderson, *Imagined Communities Reflections on
the Origin and Spread of Nationalism*, revised edition (London,
1991), 110; Elliott, *Catholics of Ulster*, 213, 232; *Parliamentary
Debates*, 1st ser., 36:412; Brian Jenkins, *Era of Emancipation
British Government of Ireland 1812–1830* (Montreal, 1988),
54–5; Hoppen, *Mid-Victorian Generation*, 575; Levack, *Formation of the British State*, 22; Privy Council (PC) 2/260, Public
Record Office (PRO), Kew.

9 Leon Litvack and Glenn Hooper, eds., *Ireland in the Nineteenth
Century: 'Regional Identity'* (Dublin, 2000), 229–30, 232;
Edward Wakefield, *An Account of Ireland Statistical and
Political*, 2 vols. (London, 1813), 2:325–7; Pocock, TRHS, 6th ser.,
10:190; James Kelly, *Prelude to Union: Anglo-Irish Politics in the*

1780s (Cork, 1992), 14, 5; Cain and Hopkins, *British Imperialism*, 90; *Parl. Deb.*, 2nd ser., 9:1283; *Daily Telegraph*, 21 November 1867.

10 Statt, *Foreigners and Englishmen*, 167; Clark, *Historical Journal* 43:272; Barnard, *Journal of Ecclesiastical History* 44:266–7; Colley, *Britons*, 23, 54; Elliott, *Catholics of Ulster*, 59, 69, 79; E.W. MacFarland, *Ireland and Scotland in the Age of Revolution: Planting the Green Bough* (Edinburgh, 1994), 37; *Parl. Deb.*, 1st ser., 36: 650–1; Kevin Whelan, *The Tree of Liberty: Radicalism, Catholicism and the Construction of Irish Identity 1760–1830* (Notre Dame, 1996), 33, 3.

11 Jim Smyth, *Men of No Property: Irish Radicals and Popular Politics in the Late Eighteenth Century*, pb. ed. (London, 1998), 33; *Parl. Deb.*, 2nd ser., 6:12–13; Neil Graham, "How Violent Was Eighteenth-Century Ireland?" *Irish Historical Studies* 30 (1997): 377–92; *Edinburgh Review* 37 (1822): 62; T.A. Critchley, *The Conquest of Violence: Order and Liberty in Britain* (New York, 1970), 5.

12 J.E. Cookson, *The British Armed Nation 1793–1815* (Oxford, 1997), 52; Thomas Bartlett, "From Irish State to British Empire: Reflections on State-Building in Ireland, 1690–1830," *Etudes Irlandaises*, n.s., 20 (1995): 25; Kelly, *Irish Historical Studies*, 30:249; John Hutchinson, *The Dynamics of Cultural Nationalism: The Gaelic Revival and the Creation of the Nation State* (London, 1987), 63; *The Speeches of the Right Honourable William Pitt, in the House of Commons*, 4 vols. (London, 1806), 3:363; 4:369; 3:354–61, 382, 396; 4:71; McLoughlin, *Contesting Ireland*, 21; Peter Jupp, "Britain and the Union, 1797–1801," TRHS, 6th ser., 10:208.

13 Brown, Geoghegan, Kelly, *Irish Act of Union*, 112–13, 125, 49; Daire Keogh and Kevin Whelan, eds., *Acts of Union: The Causes, Contexts and Consequences of the Act of Union* (Dublin, 2001), 129–35, 159–60, 166–9; Jacqueline Hill, *From Patriots to Unionists: Dublin Civic Politics and Irish Protestant Patriotism 1660–1840* (Oxford, 1997), 258–60; *Speeches of Pitt*, 3:354, 379–81; John Ehrman, *The Younger Pitt: The Consuming Struggle* (Stanford, 1996), 175ff.; Patrick M. Geoghegan, *The Irish Act of Union: A Study in High Politics 1798–1801* (New York, 1999), 3; *Speeches of Grattan*, 3:362; Patrick Geoghegan, "The Catholics and the Union," TRHS, 6th ser., 10:253–4; Richard Willis, "William Pitt's Resignation in 1801: Re-examination and Document,"*Bulletin of Historical Research* 44 (1971): 245.

14 Jenkins, *Era of Emancipation*, 22–6; Hill, *From Patriots to*

Unionists, 265–9; *Dublin Evening Post*, 13 September 1810;
Wormald, TRHS., 6th ser., 2:193.

15 Cormac O Grada, *Ireland: A New Economic History 1780–1939*
(Oxford, 1994), 44; *Edinburgh Review* 43 (1826): 489; L.M.
Cullen, *An Economic History of Ireland since 1660* (London,
1972), 101, 103; James H. Murphy, *Ireland: A Social, Cultural
and Literary History, 1791–1891* (Dublin, 2003), 93; Whelan,
Tree of Liberty, 52; D. George Boyce and Alan O'Day, *The Making of Modern Irish History: Revisionism and the Revisionist
Controversy* (London, 1996), 22; *Dublin Evening Post*, 3, 7, 10,
14, 31 July, 25 August 1810.

16 Hill, *From Patriots to Unionists*, 269, 275–9; O Grada, *Ireland*,
45; Boyce and O'Day, *Making of Modern Irish History*, 43–4;
Ferguson, *Empire*, 43; Brendan Clifford, ed., *Selections from
Walter Cox's 'Irish Magazine': 1807–1815* (Belfast, 1992), 120;
MacFarland, *Ireland and Scotland*, 242.

17 Peel to Gregory, 20 July 1814, British Library (BL) Add. MSS
40287; O Grada, *Ireland*, 159; Peel to Whitworth, 23 February
1815, Whitworth Papers, U269/0225/11, Centre for Kentish
Studies, Maidstone; *Speeches of Grattan*, 4:369; *Parl. Deb.*, 1st
ser., 27:740–1; Boyce and O'Day, *Making of Modern Irish History*, 38, 44, 39; O Grada, *Ireland*, 120; Cullen, *Economic History
of Ireland*, 109.

18 Jenkins, *Era of Emancipation*, 126–7; Brian Jenkins, *Henry
Goulburn 1784–1856: A Political Biography* (Montreal and Liverpool, 1996), 128; *Cambrian*, 24 May, 7, 14 June 1822; Wellesley-Pole to Ryder, 10 July 1810, Home Office (HO), 100/158,
PRO.

19 K. Theodore Hoppen, *Elections, Politics, and Society in Ireland
1832–1885* (Oxford, 1984), 378; Charles Stuart Parker, ed., *Sir
Robert Peel from his Private Papers*, reprint edition, 3 vols. (New
York, 1970), 1:235; Jenkins, *Goulburn*, 150; Goulburn to Wellesley, 15 June 1822, BL Add Ms. 37299; *Parl. Deb.*, 2nd ser., 7:
148; Peel to Sidmouth, 21 July 1817, HO 100/192; Peel to Whitworth, 9, 13 June 1817, BL Add Ms. 40293; Peel to Whitworth,
n.d. [March 1817], 8 March 1817, BL, Add Ms. 40292; Goulburn to Wellesley, 2, 15, 16 April, 19 June 1822, BL Add MSS
37299; O Grada, *Ireland*, 189.

20 Goulburn to Gregory, 18 June 1822, William Gregory Papers,
Emory University, Atlanta; Cullen, *Economic History of Ireland*,
110; *Cambrian*, 8 November 1823.

21 Oliver MacDonagh, *States of Mind: A Study of Anglo-Irish Conflict 1780–1980* (London, 1983), 71–2; W.E. Vaughan, ed., *A*

New History of Ireland, vol. 5: *Ireland under the Union, 1: 1801–1870* (Oxford, 1989), 81–2; Michael Beames, "Peasant Disturbances, Popular Conspiracies and Their Control: Ireland, 1798–1852," Ph. D. thesis, University of Manchester (1975), 16; Virginia Crossman, *Politics, Law and Order in Nineteenth Century Ireland* (New York, 1996), 12, 3; Patrick Ward, *Exile, Emigration and Irish Writing* (Dublin, 2002), 46; MacFarland, *Ireland and Scotland*, 40; *Fortnightly Review* 1 (1865): 328; *Blackwood's Magazine* 54 (1843): 767.

22 Peel to Sidmouth, 1 November 1816, HO 100/191; Peel to Whitworth, 28 February 1816, BL, Add. MSS 40290; Keogh and Whelan, *Acts of Union*, 25; *Parl. Deb.*, 2nd ser., 9:1283; Liverpool to Peel, 28 January 1816, BL, Add. MSS 40181; *Daily Telegraph*, 13 December, 21 November 1867; Peel to Goulburn, 6 November [1822], Henry Goulburn Papers, Acc. 304/36, Surrey Record Office; Goulburn to Wellesley, 28 February 1822, BL, Add. MSS 37298.

23 Crossman, *Politics, Law and Order*, 17, 25; Cookson, *British Armed Nation*, 257; Galen Broeker, *Rural Disorder and Police Reform in Ireland, 1812–36* (London, 1970), 128–59; Stanley Palmer, *Police and Protest in England and Ireland 1780–1850* (Cambridge, 1988), 243–4.

24 Daire Keogh, *The French Disease: The Catholic Church and Irish Radicalism, 1790–1800* (Dublin, 1993), 120; O Ciosain, *Print and Popular Culture*, 28; *Dublin Evening Post*, 15 April 1809, 19 June 1810; Wellesley-Pole to Ryder, 14 July 1810, Harrowby MSS, XCV, Sandon; Wellesley-Pole to Ryder, 23 July 1810, HO, 100/158; Peel to Sidmouth, 21 October 1813, HO, 100/173; Peel to William Gregory, 29 March 1816, BL, Add. MSS 40290; Jenkins, *Era of Emancipation*, 94, 206; Oliver MacDonagh, *The Hereditary Bondsman: Daniel O'Connell 1775–1829* (London, 1988), 117–24.

25 Peel to Whitworth, 13 June 1817, BL, Add MSS 40293; Parker, *Peel*, 1:89–90; *Parl. Deb.*, 1st ser., 9:1283; Donal A. Kerr, ed., *Religion, State and Ethnic Groups* (New York, 1992), 13; R.V. Comerford, Mary Cullen, Jacqueline R. Hill, and Colm Lennon, eds., *Religion, Conflict and Coexistence in Ireland* (Dublin, 1980), 207; O Ciosain, *Print and Popular Culture*, 42; H. Goulburn to J. Goulburn, 31 March, 1824, Henry Goulburn Papers, Acc. 304/67.

26 Jenkins, *Era of Emancipation*, 123, 185, 201–4; Hoppen, *Elections, Politics, and Society*, 262; Jenkins, *Goulburn*, 158–9; Crossman, *Politics, Law and Order*, 35; Douglas Hay and Fran-

cis Snyder, eds., *Policing and Prosecution in Britain 1750–1850* (Oxford, 1989), 427–56.

27 *Edinburgh Review*, 43 (1826): 478, 493; James E. O'Neill, "The British Quarterlies and the Religious Question, 1802–1829," *Catholic Historical Review* 52 (1966–67): 358.

28 A.T.Q. Stewart, *A Deeper Silence: The Hidden Origins of the United Irish Movement* (London, 1993), 23, 27–9; Canny, *Kingdom and Colony*, 121; John Hickey, *Urban Catholics: Urban Catholicism in England and Wales from 1829 to the Present Day* (London, 1967), 15; C.D.A. Leighton, *Catholicism in a Protestant Kingdom: A Study of the Irish Ancien Regime* (London, 1994), 6–7, 9–11, 15, 90–3; Gough and Dickson, *Ireland and the French Revolution*, 54.

29 Bartlett, *Past and Present* 116:213, 217; *Quarterly Review* 83 (1843); Liam Kennedy, *Colonialism, Religion and Nationalism in Ireland* (Belfast, 1996), 14, 16; Keogh and Whelan, *Acts of Union*, 163; Smyth, *Men of No Property*, 83; Neil Longley York, *Neither Kingdom nor Nation: The Irish Quest for Constitutional Rights, 1698–1800* (Washington, D.C., 1994), 20; T.C. Barnard, "The Uses of 23 October 1641 and Irish Protestant Celebrations," *English Historical Review* 106 (1991): 911; Elliott, *Catholics of Ulster*, 159; Cookson, *British Armed Nation*, 18, 13.

30 Hill, *From Patriots to Unionists*, 134–5, 213; Donald MacCartney, "The Writing of History in Ireland 1800–30," *Irish Historical Studies* 10 (1957): 353; Jim Smyth, "Anti-Catholicism, Conservatism, and Conspiracy: Sir Richard Musgrave's *Memoirs of Different Rebellions in Ireland*," *Eighteenth Century Life*, n.s. 22 (1998): 65, 71; Brown, Geoghegan, and Kelly, *Irish Act of Union*, 63–4; Jacqueline R. Hill, "Popery and Protestantism, Civil and Religious Liberty: The Disputed Lessons of Irish History 1690–1812," *Past and Present* 118 (1988): 127; Keogh, *French Disease*, 204, 199; David Dickson, Daire Keogh, and Kevin Whelan, *The United Irishmen: Republicanism, Radicalism and Rebellion* (Dublin, 1993), 124, 134; Bartlett, *Fall and Rise of the Irish Nation*, 270, 228, 235, 277.

31 Keogh and Whelan, *Acts of Union*, 24; Bartlett, *Fall and Rise of the Irish Nation*, 270, 294; *Edinburgh Review* 27 (1816): 324–5, 311; *Saunders's Newsletter*, 23 January 1810.

32 Louis J. Jennings, *The Croker Papers*, 3 vols. (London, 1885), 1:89; *Chester Chronicle*, 23 May 1813; Edward Norman, *The English Catholic Church in the Nineteenth Century* (Oxford, 1984), 30; Peel to Richmond, 21 May 1813, BL, Add. MSS 40282; *Edinburgh Review*, 27:314; *Parl. Deb.*, 1st ser., 31:682,

36:650–1; Goulburn to Peel, 13 September 1826, BL, Add. MSS 40332; Wellesley-Pole to Ryder, 31 December 1811, HO, 100/165; Wellesley-Pole to Ryder, 23 July 1810, Harrowby MSS, XCV; Wellesley-Pole to Ryder, 20 July 1811, Harrowby MSS, XCVIII; Wellesley-Pole to Ryder, 6 September 1811, HO, 100/164.

33 *Dublin Evening Post*, 8 November 1810; Wellesley-Pole to Ryder, 16, 23 July 1810, Harrowby MSS, XCV; Richmond to Peel, 6 May 1813, Richmond Papers, 69, National Library of Ireland (NLI); Whitworth to Sidmouth, 5 May 1814, HO, 100/178; *Parl. Deb.*, 1st ser., 36:416–17.

34 Maurice O'Connell, ed., *The Correspondence of Daniel O'Connell*, 8 vols. (Dublin, 1972–81), 2:347; MacDonagh, *Hereditary Bondsman*, 206–10; *Chester Chronicle*, 23 May 1813.

35 Goulburn to Peel, 27 October 1824, Acc. 304/35; Goulburn to Peel, 10 October 1826, HO 100/216.

36 Cunningham, *World of Geoffrey Keating*, 110, 116; Laurence M. Geary, *Rebellion and Remembrance in Modern Ireland* (Dublin, 2004), 34, 16–31; Rosalind Mitchison, ed., *The Roots of Nationalism: Studies in Northern Europe* (Edinburgh, 1980), 102; Clifford, *Irish Magazine*, 38, 121, 65, 76, 82, 103–4.

37 Clifford, *Irish Magazine*, 38, 78, 80, 60, 75, 79, 126, 53, 110–12, 123–5.

38 Samuel Clark and James S. Donnelly, Jr, eds., *Irish Peasants Violence and Political Unrest 1780–1914* (Manchester, 1983), 107–8, 110–15, 120, 122, 125; Geary, *Rebellion and Remembrance*, 74, 82–3, 95–7, 99, 126, 121.

39 Clark and Donnelly, *Irish Peasants*, 135; Geary, *Rebellion and Remembrance*, 98; MacDonagh, *Hereditary Bondsman*, 218, 225; Fergus O'Ferrall, *Catholic Emancipation: Daniel O'Connell and the Birth of Irish Democracy 1820–30* (Dublin, 1985), 176–7, 180; Norman, *English Catholic Church*, 63; Cookson, *British Armed Nation*, 181.

40 *Edinburgh Review* 49 (1829): 218; Colley, *Britons*, 368, 328–31; J.H. Hexter, "The Protestant Revival and the Catholic Question, 1778–1829," *Journal of Modern History* 8 (1938): 297–319; O'Ferrall, *Catholic Emancipation*, 155; R.W. Linker, "The English Roman Catholics and Emancipation: The Politics of Persuasion," *Journal of Ecclesiastical History* 27 (1976): 151–80; Norman, *English Catholic Church*, 38–9; J. Derek Holmes, *More Roman than Rome: English Catholicism in the Nineteenth Century* (London, 1978), 28; O'Neill, *Catholic Historical Review* 52:355.

41 *Quarterly Review* 37 (1828): 459; 82 (1848): 282; O'Ferrall,

Catholic Emancipation, 197; Holmes, *More Roan than Rome,*
39; Gary Owens, "'A Moral Insurrection': Faction Fighters, Public Demonstrations and the O'Connellite Campaign, 1828," *Irish
Historical Studies* 30 (1997): 513–39.

42 Cunningham, *World of Geoffrey Keating*, 110, 116; Murphy, *Ireland*, 25; Parl. *Deb.*, 1st ser., 36:418–19.

43 *Edinburgh Review* 43 (1826): 462; Hilary Andrews, *The Lion of
the West: A Biography of John MacHale* (Dublin, 2001), 46–7;
A.D. Kriegel, "The Irish Policy of Lord Grey's Government,"
English Historical Review 86 (1971): 22; *Edinburgh Review* 41
(1825): 356–7, 366; Ian Newbould, *Whiggery and Reform
1830–1841: The Politics of Government* (Stanford, 1990), 283.

44 Crossman, *Politics, Law and Order*, 49–50, 71; Elizabeth Mal-
colm, "'The Reign of Terror in Carlow': The Politics of Policing
Ireland in the Late 1830s," *Irish Historical Studies* 32 (2000):
59–74; Kriegel, *English Historical Review* 86:24–5; Newbould,
Whiggery and Reform, 296–7; D. George Boyce, *Nineteenth-
Century Ireland: The Search for Stability* (Dublin, 1990), 72–3.

45 Kriegel, *English Historical Review* 86:34–9; Newbould, *Whiggery
and Reform*, 284–7.

46 W.J. O'Neill Daunt to Leahy, 13 November 1865, Leahy Papers,
microfilm, reel 6008, NLI; Thomas MacNevin, ed., *Speeches of
the Right Honourable Richard Lalor Sheil* (Dublin, 1865), 92.

47 Crossman, *Politics, Law and Order*, 69–72; Broeker, *Rural
Disorder and Police Reform*, 224–7; Boyce, *Nineteenth-Century
Ireland*, 66–74; Nuala Costello, *John MacHale Archbishop of
Tuam* (Dublin, 1939), 47.

48 Boyce, *Nineteenth-Century Ireland*, 66–74; *Quarterly Review* 43
(1830): 244–6; Newbould, *Whiggery and Reform*, 291–3.

49 Crossman, *Politics, Law and Order*, 76; E.R. Norman, *Church
and Society in England 1770–1970* (Oxford, 1976), 64; Helen F.
Mulvey, *Thomas Davis and Ireland: A Biographical Study* (Washington, D.C., 2003), 93–5; Boyce, *Nineteenth-Century Ireland*,
61,70; Patrick Maume, "Young Ireland, Arthur Griffith, and
Republican Ideology: The Question of Continuity," *Eire/Ireland*
34 (1999): 158.

50 Mulvey, *Thomas Davis*, 146; Boyce, *Nineteenth-Century Ireland*,
72; K. Theodore Hoppen, *Ireland since 1800* (London, 1989),
62–3; Oliver P. Rafferty, *The Church, the State and the Fenian
Threat 1861–75* (London, 1999), xi.

51 Joel Mokyr, *Why Ireland Starved* (London, 1985), 291, 116, 124,
132, 144; Hoppen, *Ireland since 1800*, 50; Boyce, *Nineteenth-
Century Ireland*, 64; Ted Robert Gurr, *Why Men Rebel* (Prince-

ton, 1970), 196; P.J. Waller, ed., *Politics and Social Change in Modern Britain* (New York, 1987), 34; Monica D. Blumenthal, Letha B. Chadiha, Gerald A. Cole, and Toby Epstein Jayanatne, eds., *More about Justifying Violence: Methodological Studies of Attitudes and Behaviour* (Ann Arbor, 1975), 181.

52 Boyce, *Nineteenth-Century Ireland*, 85; *Daily Telegraph*, 30 December 1867; Dermot Quinn, *Patronage and Piety: The Politics of English Roman Catholicism, 1850-1900* (London, 1993), 38.

CHAPTER TWO

1 Maurice O'Connell, ed., *The Correspondence of Daniel O'Connell*, 8 vols. (Dublin 1972-81), 7:155-60; James H. Murphy, *Abject Loyalty: Nationalism and Monarchy in Ireland during the Reign of Queen Victoria* (Washington, D.C., 2001), 32, 55-7.

2 Murphy, *Abject Loyalty*, xix; Helen F. Mulvey, *Thomas Davis and Ireland: A Biographical Study* (Washington, D.C., 2003), 122-3; Michael Brown, Patrick M. Geoghegan, and James Kelly, eds., *The Irish Act of Union Bicentennial Essays* (Dublin, 2003), 14; John F. Quinn, *Father Mathew's Crusade: Temperance in Nineteenth-Century Ireland and Irish America* (Amherst, 2002), 17; O'Connell, *Correspondence of O'Connell*, 7:155-60; Jacqueline R. Hill, "The Intelligentsia and Irish Nationalism in the 1840s," *Studia Hibernica* 20 (1980): 76.

3 O'Connell, *Correspondence of O'Connell*, 7:234-7; Kevin B. Nowlan, *The Politics of Repeal: A Study of the Relations between Great Britain and Ireland, 1841-50* (London, 1965), 38; Thomas MacNevin, ed., *Speeches of the Right Honourable Richard Lalor Sheil* (Dublin, 1865), 356-9.

4 O'Connell, *Correspondence of O'Connell*, 7:256-7; John Kendle, *Ireland and the Federal Solution: The Debate over the United Kingdom Constitution, 1870-1921* (Montreal and Kingston, 1989), 9-10; Robert Sloan, *William Smith O'Brien and the Young Ireland Rebellion of 1848* (Dublin, 2000), 118-20; Ambrose Macaulay, *Dr. Russell of Maynooth* (London, 1983), 31; Richard Davis, *Revolutionary Imperialist: William Smith O'Brien* (Dublin, 1998), 140; John Breuilly, *Nationalism and the State*, 2nd ed. (Manchester, 1993), 19.

5 Walker Connor, *Ethnonationalism: The Quest for Understanding* (Princeton, 1994), 56; Ryan Dye, "Catholic Protectionism or Irish Nationalism? Religion and Politics in Liverpool, 1829-1845," *Journal of British Studies* 40 (2001): 367-9; Joseph

Rothschild, *Ethnopolitics: A Conceptual Framework* (New York, 1981), 7; Rosalind Mitchison, ed., *The Roots of Nationalism Studies in Northern Europe* (Edinburgh, 1980), 93–5; Tadhg Foley and Sean Ryder, eds., *Ideology and Ireland in the Nineteenth Century* (Dublin, 1998), 213, 155; Jim Mac Laughlin, *Reimagining the Nation-State: The Contested Terrains of Nationbuilding* (London, 2001), 107.

6 Daire Keogh and Kevin Whelan, eds., *Acts of Union: The Causes, Contexts and Consequences of the Act of Union* (Dublin, 2001), 30; J.E. Cookson, *The British Armed Nation 1793–1815* (Oxford, 1997),18; Allan Blackstock, "The Union and the Military, 1801–c1830," TRHS, 6th ser., 10:349; Virginia Crossman, *Politics, Law and Order in Nineteenth Century Ireland* (New York, 1996), 90; Keith Jeffery, ed., *An Irish Empire? Aspects of Ireland and the British Empire* (Manchester, 1996), 94–5; Christopher Morash, *Writing the Irish Famine* (Oxford, 1995), 55; Margaret Canovan, *Nationhood and Political Theory* (Cheltenham, 1996), 77; Adrian Hastings, *The Construction of Nationhood: Ethnicity, Religion and Nationalism* (Cambridge, 1997), 2–3; John Stuart Mill, *Considerations on Representative Government* (London, 1904), 291–3; John Acton, *The History of Freedom and Other Essays* (Freeport, N.Y., 1967), 290.

7 Gopal Balakrishnan, ed., *Mapping the Nation* (New York, 1996), 179; Acton, *History of Freedom*, 298; Peter Alter, *Nationalism* (London, 1985), 30; Canovan, *Nationhood and Political Theory*, 8; Rothschild, *Ethnopolitics*, 21; Mill, *Considerations on Representative Government*, 291–3; Mulvey, *Thomas Davis*, 77.

8 Per Bauhn, *Nationalism and Morality* (Lund, 1995), 27; Barry C.J. Singer, "Contractual versus Cultural Nations: Rethinking Their Opposition," *History and Theory* 35 (1996): 311; Stuart Woolf, ed., *Nationalism in Europe 1815 to the Present: A Reader* (London, 1996), 27; Anthony D. Smith, *The Ethnic Origins of Nations* (Oxford, 1986), 136; Laurence Brockliss and David Eastwood, eds., *A Union of Multiple Identities: The British Isles c1750–c1850* (Manchester, 1997), 9–24; Mary Poovey, *Making a Social Body: British Cultural Formation 1830–1864* (Chicago, 1995), 4; Connor, *Ethnonationalism*, 21; see also Liah Greenfeld, *Nationalism: Five Roads to Modernity* (Cambridge, Mass., 1992); Hastings, *Construction of Nationhood*, 4, 64; Gerald Newman, *The Rise of English Nationalism: A Cultural History 1740–1830* (New York, 1987), 133, 126; J.C.D. Clark, "Protestantism, Nationalism and National Identity, 1660–1832," *Historical Journal* 43 (2000): 267; Daniel Statt, *Foreigners and English-*

men: The Controversy over Immigration and Population,
1660–1760 (London, 1995),193; Margot C. Finn, *After Char-*
tism: Class and Nation in English Radical Politics, 1848–1874
(Cambridge, 1993), 18; David Eastwood, "Robert Southey and
the Meanings of Patriot or Briton," *Journal of British Studies* 31
(1992): 265–87.

9 Jerome Blum, *In the Beginning: The Advent of the Modern Age,*
Europe in the 1840s (New York, 1994), 88–9; *Irish Catholic*
Banner, 14 March 1868; John Stevenson, "William Cobbett:
Patriot or Briton," *TRHS* 6th ser., 6 (1996): 134; Statt, *Foreigners*
and Englishmen, 193, 30; Tony Claydon, "Problems with the
British Problem," *Parliamentary History* 16 (1997): 222; *Parlia-*
mentary Debates, 3rd ser., 87:1013; Roger Swift and Sheridan
Gilley, eds., *The Irish in Victorian Britain: The Local Dimension*
(Dublin, 1999), 244–5; Linda Colley, "British and Otherness: An
Argument," *Journal of British Studies* 31 (1992): 314; see also
Keith Robbins, *Nineteenth-Century Britain: Integration and*
Diversity (Oxford, 1988); Newman, *Rise of English Nationalism,*
77; Poovey, *Making a Social Body,* 54; "The Irish Question"
(Paris, 1860), Pamphlet 944, American Catholic Historical Soci-
ety, Philadelphia; E.J. Hobsbawm, *Nations and Nationalism since*
1780: Programme, Myth, Reality (Cambridge, 1990), 75; *Speech-*
es of Sheil, 269; *Edinburgh Review* 41 (1825): 357, 363; Greenfeld, *Nationalism,* 14.

10 Mill, *Considerations on Representative Government,* 285–91;
Acton, *History of Freedom,* 270–99; Harold J. Abramson, *Ethnic*
Diversity in Catholic America (New York, 1973), 9; Hugh A.
MacDougall, *Racial Myth in English History: Trojans, Teutons,*
and Anglo-Saxons (Montreal, 1982), 112.

11 Sukimar Periwal, ed., *Notions of Nationalism* (Budapest, 1995),
37; Ernest Gellner, *Thought and Change* (Chicago, 1964), 176;
Robert Miles, "Recent Marxist Theories of Nationalism and the
Issue of Racism," *British Journal of Sociology* 38 (1987): 30;
Peter S. Li, ed., *Race and Ethnic Relations in Canada,* 2nd ed.
(Don Mills, 1999), 4; Acton, *History of Freedom,* 292–3; Con-
nor, *Ethnonationalism,* 215; Rodolfo Stavenhagen, *The Ethnic*
Question: Conflicts, Development and Human Rights (Tokyo,
1990), 3: Colin Graham and Richard Kirkland, eds., *Ireland and*
Cultural Theory: The Mechanics of Authenticity (London, 1999),
50–2.

12 Wilson McLeod, *Divided Gaels: Gaelic Cultural Identities in*
Scotland and Ireland c. 1200–c. 1650 (Oxford, 2004), 142, 147,
112; Bernadette Cunningham, *World of Geoffrey Keating: History,*

Myth and Religion in Seventeenth-Century Ireland (Dublin, 2000), 131, 106; David Cairns and Shaun Richards, *Writing Ireland: Colonialism, Nationalism and Culture* (Manchester, 1988), 18, 20.

13 Cunningham, *World of Geoffrey Keating*, 218; Thomas E. Hachey and Lawrence J. McCaffrey, eds., *Perspectives on Irish Nationalism* (Lexington, 1989), 61–4; Kevin Collins, *Catholic Churchmen and the Celtic Revival in Ireland, 1848–1916* (Dublin, 2002), 28–9, 47, 60–1, 70–1.

14 Anthony D. Smith, *Nationalism and Modernism* (London, 1998), 23, 35, 45, 56, 136, 186; Benedict Anderson, *Imagined Communities: Reflections on the Origins and Spread of Nationalism* (London, 1983), 18, 77; John Hutchinson, *Modern Nationalism* (London, 1994), 48; Leonard W. Doob, *Patriotism and Nationalism: Their Psychological Foundations* (New Haven, 1964), 38, 253; James G. Kellas, *The Politics of Nationalism and Ethnicity* (London, 1991), 12; Terry Eagleton, *Scholars and Rebels in Nineteenth Century Ireland* (Oxford, 1999), 18; Periwal, *Notions of Nationalism*, 37; Smith, *Ethnic Origins of Nations*, 157–8; Hobsbawm, *Nations and Nationalism*, 68; Guenter Lewy, *Religion and Revolution* (New York, 1974), 565; Donald Eugene Smith, *Religion and Political Development* (Boston, 1970), 274–5; Daire Keogh, *The French Disease: The Catholic Church and Radicalism in Ireland 1790–1800* (Dublin, 1993), 66; Collins, *Catholic Churchmen and the Celtic Revival*, 28.

15 Smith, *Nationalism and Modernism*, 110, 113, 15, 132, 141; Breuilly, *Nationalism and the State*, 29; Anderson, *Imagined Communities*, 18; Salo Wittmayer Baron, *Modern Nationalism and Religion* (New York, 1960), 45, 15, 46, 49, 127; Mac Laughlin, *Reimagining the Nation-State*, 31; Donald A. Kerr, ed., *Religion, State and Ethnic Groups* (New York, 1992), 19; Hastings, *Construction of Nationhood*, 12, 18, 51; Conor Cruise O'Brien, *God Land: Reflections on Religion and Nationalism* (Cambridge, Mass., 1988), 40–1; David Vincent, "The Origins of Public Secrecy in Britain," *TRHS*, 6th ser., 1 (1991): 229; Sydney E. Ahlstrom, "Religion, Revolution and the Rise of Modern Nationalism: Reflections on the American Experience," *Church History* 44 (1975): 496–8; Alter, *Nationalism*, 10; Eric R. Wolf, ed., *Religious Regimes and State-Formation: Perspectives from European Ethnology* (Albany, N.Y., 1991), 10; Keogh, *The French Disease*, 125; Doob, *Patriotism and Nationalism*, 253; Harold J. Abramson, "Ethnic Diversity within Catholicism: A Comparative Analysis of Contemporary and Historical Religion,"

Journal of Social History 4 (1970–71): 366–7; Eugene O'Brien, *Examining Irish Nationalism in the Context of Literature, Culture and Religion: A Study of the Epistemological Structure of Nationalism* (Lewiston, 2002), 19, 96–7; Patrick O'Farrell, *Ireland's English Question: Anglo-Irish Relations 1534–1970* (London, 1971), 10.

16 *Edinburgh Review* 41 (1825): 356–7, 361; Woolf, *Nationalism in Europe*, 35; Gellner, *Thought and Change*, 172; *Parl. Papers, 1825* [8]:98; *Speeches of Sheil*, 165, 189–90, 192, 285; Robert Sloan, "O'Connell's Liberal Rivals in 1843," *Irish Historical Studies* 30 (1996): 47–65.

17 See D.W. Cunnane, "Catastrophic Dimensions: The Rupture of English and Irish Identities in Early Modern Ireland, 1534–1615," *Essays in History* (Internet journal) 41 (1999): 1–19; Jane Ohlmeyer, "Seventeenth Century Ireland and the New British and Atlantic Histories," *American Historical Review* 104 (1999): 446–62; Sean Cronin, *Irish Nationalism: A History of Its Roots and Ideology* (New York, 1981), 2, 23; J.R. Archer, "Necessary Ambiguity: Nationalism and Myth in Ireland, *Eire/Ireland* 19 (1984): 24–6; Tom Garvin, *The Evolution of Irish Nationalist Politics* (Dublin, 1981), 14–19; S.J. Connolly, R.A. Houston, and R.J. Morris, eds., *Conflict, Identity and Economic Development: Ireland and Scotland, 1600–1939* (Preston, 1995), 2; Francis Plowden, *The History of Ireland from Its Union with Great Britain in January 1801 to October 1810*, 3 vols. (Dublin, 1811), 1:90; *Irish Catholic Banner*, 14 March 1868; Abramson, *Journal of Social History* 4:367; Desmond J. Keenan, *The Catholic Church in Nineteenth Century Ireland: A Sociological Study* (Dublin, 1983), 32; Farrell to O'Donoghue, 7 March 1862, Cullen Correspondence, Secular Clergy 340/4/I, Dublin Diocesan Archive (DDA), Archbishop's House, Drumcondra, Dublin.

18 Fergus O'Ferrall, *Catholic Emancipation: Daniel O'Connell and the Birth of Irish Democracy, 1820–30* (Dublin, 1985), 280; Brian Jenkins, *Era of Emancipation: British Government of Ireland 1812–30* (Montreal, 1988), 222; James A. Reynolds, *The Catholic Emancipation Crisis in Ireland, 1823–1829*, reprint ed. (Westport, Conn., 1970), 15–54; Cronin, *Irish Nationalism*, 27; K. Theodore Hoppen, "Politics, the Law, and the Nature of the Irish Electorate 1832–1850," *English Historical Review* 92 (1977): 774; J.H. Whyte, "Daniel O'Connell and the Repeal Party," *Irish Historical Studies* 11 (1958–59): 297–315.

19 Yael Tamir, *Liberal Nationalism* (Princeton, 1993), 60; D. George Boyce, *Nationalism in Ireland* (London, 1995), 149; Jacqueline

R. Hill, *From Patriots to Unionists: Dublin Civic Politics and Irish Protestant Patriotism, 1660–1840* (Oxford, 1997), 285–7, 345–8; F.A. D'Arcy, "The Artisans of Dublin and Daniel O'Connell, 1830–47: An Unquiet Liaison," *Irish Historical Studies* 17 (1970–71): 239; F.S.L. Lyons and R.J. Hawkins, eds., *Ireland under the Union: Varieties of Tension* (Oxford, 1980), 35–68; Elliott, *Catholics of Ulster*, 282; John Biggs-Davison and George Chowdharay-Best, *The Cross of St. Patrick: The Catholic Unionists Tradition in Ireland* (Bourne End, 1984), 145–8, 155–7; J.S. Whale, *The Protestant Tradition: An Essay in Interpretation* (Cambridge, 1962), 237–8; Desmond Bowen, *History and the Shaping of Irish Protestantism* (New York, 1995), 191–3, 253; Emmet Larkin, trans. and ed., *Alexis de Tocqueville's Journey in Ireland July–August, 1835* (Washington, D.C., 1990), 47; Desmond Bowen, *Protestant Crusade in Ireland, 1800–70* (Dublin, 1978), 19–20; Ambrose Macaulay, *William Crolly, Archbishop of Armagh 1835–49* (Dublin, 1994), 281, 285; Breuilly, *Nationalism and the State*, 69.

20   Cookson, *Armed Nation*, 177; Thomas N. Brown, "Nationalism and the Irish Peasant, 1800–1848," 406, reprinted in Lawrence J. McCaffrey, ed., *Irish Nationalism and the American Contribution* (New York, 1976); Brockliss and Eastwood, *Union of Multiple Identities*, 163, 166; Alvin Jackson, *Ireland 1798–1998* (Oxford, 1999), 9; Gary Owens, "Visualizing the Liberator: Self-Fashioning, Dramaturgy, and the Construction of Daniel O'Connell, *Eire/Ireland* 33 (1998): 103–30; see also idem "Nationalism without Words: Symbolism and Ritual Behaviour in the Repeal 'Monster Meetings' of 1843–5," in James S. Donnelly and Kerby A. Miller, *Irish Popular Culture 1650–1850* (Dublin, 1998), 245, 261; Peter Alter, "Symbols of Irish Nationalism," *Studia Hibernica* 14 (1974): 104–9; John F. Broderick, *The Holy See and the Irish Movement for the Repeal of the Union with England 1829–1847* (Rome, 1951), 125–35.

21   Quinn, *Father Mathew's Crusade*, 12; Raymond Gillespie, *The Remaking of Modern Ireland 1750–1950* (Dublin, 2004), 73, 75, 85, 92–5; Mac Laughlin, *Reimagining the Nation-State*, 3, 9, 26–7, 97; Macaulay, *William Crolly*, 336.

22   Reynolds, *Catholic Emancipation*, 51; Donal A. Kerr, *Peel, Priests and Politics* (Oxford, 1982), 6; Oliver MacDonagh, "The Politicization of the Irish Catholic Bishops, 1800–1850," *Historical Journal* 18 (1975): 44–5; J.A. Whyte, "The Influence of the Irish Catholic Clergy on Elections in Nineteenth Century Ireland," *English Historical Review* 75 (1960): 241–2; Kenneth

Wilson Underwood, *Protestant and Catholic: Religious and Social Interaction in an Industrial Community*, reprint ed. (Westport, Conn., 1973), 100, 102; S.J. Connolly, *Priests and People in Pre-famine Ireland* (New York, 1982), 13–14, 58; Patrick J. Corish, *The Irish Catholic Experience: A Historical Survey* (Dublin, 1985), 159, 165; R.V. Comerford, Mary Cullen, Jacqueline Hill, and Colin Lennon, eds., *Religion, Conflict and Coexistence in Ireland* (Dublin, 1990), 213; Hoppen, *Elections, Politics and Society*, 198–9; see also Sean Connolly, *Religion and Society in Nineteenth Century Ireland* (Dublin, 1985).

23 Macaulay, *William Crolly*, 271, 277–8; Draft circular by Leahy, 1866, Leahy Papers, reel 6008/51, NLI.

24 Eduardo Posarda-Carbo, ed., *Elections before Democracy: The History of Elections in Europe and Latin America* (London, 1996), 121–2; Hoppen, *Elections, Politics and Society*, 179–80; Larkin, *Alexis de Tocqueville's Journey in Ireland*, 46–7; Cornelius M. Buckley, "French Views of Ireland on the Eve of the Famine," *Journal of Religious History* 8 (1974–75): 240–1, 245; Carroll to Cullen, 13 November 1865, Cullen Correspondence, 1865 Laity 320/4, DDA.

25 Kerr, *Peel, Priests and Politics*, 21–2; *Edinburgh Review* 37 (1828): 482–3; Bernard O'Reilly, *John MacHale, Archbishop of Tuam*, 2 vols. (New York, 1890), 1:72, 75–6, 199–200, 206, 409, 538; Nuala Costello, *John MacHale Archbishop of Tuam* (Dublin, 1939), 15–16, 22–3, 34, 40; Philip H. Bagenal, *The Priest in Politics* (London, 1893), 40; Collins, *Catholic Churchmen and the Celtic Revival*, 30, 62; Broderick, *Holy See and the Irish Movement for Repeal of the Union*, 58–65; Keenan, *Catholic Church in Nineteenth Century Ireland*, 108; Patrick Ward, *Exile, Emigration and Irish Writing* (Dublin, 2002), 78; Buckley, *Journal of Religious History* 8:245; Bowen, *Protestant Crusade*, 71–2.

26 O'Reilly, *MacHale*, 1:72; Hilary Andrews, *The Lion in the West: A Biography of John MacHale* (Dublin, 2001), 35, 97; Collins, *Catholic Churchmen and the Celtic Revival*, 81–3, 15; Kerr, *Peel, Priests and Politics*, 21–7; Bowen, *Protestant Crusade*, 8, 16; Colm Kerrigan, *Father Mathew and the Irish Temperance Movement 1838–1849* (Cork, 1992), 158–9; Broderick, *Holy See and the Irish Movement for Repeal of the Union*, 83–95, 121–2; Comerford, Cullen, Hill, and Lennon, *Religion, Conflict and Coexistence in Ireland*, 214; Keenan, *Catholic Church in Nineteenth Century Ireland*, 189; Macaulay, *William Crolly*, 274–5; MacDonagh, *Historical Journal* 18:47; Donal Kerr, "Peel and the

Political Involvement of the Priests," *Archivium Hibernicum/Irish Historical Records* 36 (1981): 21, 19; Jacqueline R. Hill, "Nationalism and the Catholic Church in the 1840s: Views of Dublin Repealers," *Irish Historical Studies* 19 (976): 373, 390–1; Connor, *Ethnonationalism*, 153.

27 Broderick, *Holy See and the Irish Movement for Repeal of the Union*, 218; Evelyn Bolster, *A History of the Diocese of Cork,* vol. 4: *The Episcopate of William Delany 1847–1888* (Cork, 1993), 19; MacDonagh, *Historical Journal* 18:49–50; Bowen, *History and the Shaping of Irish Protestantism*, 256; Ciaran Brady, ed., *Interpreting Irish History: The Debate on Historical Revisionism 1938–1994* (Dublin, 1994), 14.

28 Lawrence J. McCaffrey, *Daniel O'Connell and the Repeal Year* (Lexington, 1965), 26–8; Miles, *British Journal of Sociology* 38:28; Richard Davis, *The Young Ireland Movement* (Dublin, 1987), 242, 234; Nicholas Canny, "The Formation of the Irish Mind: Religion, Politics and Gaelic Irish Literature 1580–1750," *Past and Present* 95 (1982): 106–7; Colin Kidd, *British Identities before Nationalism: Ethnicity and Nationhood in the Atlantic World, 1600–1800* (Cambridge, 1999), 151; Clare O'Halloran, "Irish Re-Creations of the Gaelic Past: The Challenge of McPherson's Ossian," *Past and Present* 124 (1989): 72, 93; Foster, TRHS, 5th ser., 33:173–4; Norman Vance, "Celts, Carthaginians and Constitutions: Anglo-Irish Literary Relations, 1780–1820," *Irish Historical Studies* 2 (1980–81): 237–8; Hachey and McCaffrey, *Perspectives on Irish Nationalism*, 42–3; John Hutchinson, *The Dynamics of Cultural Nationalism: The Gaelic Revival and the Creation of the Nation State* (London, 1987), 75; Gabriel Doherty, "National Identity and the Study of Irish History," *English Historical Review* 111 (1996): 348; Terry Eagleton, *Heathcliff and the Great Hunger: Studies in Irish Culture* (New York, 1995), 246; Eagleton, *Scholars and Rebels*, 18; Maurizio Vitoli, *For Love of Country: An Essay on Patriotism and Nationalism* (Oxford, 1995), 2; Mary Helen Thuente, *The Harp Restrung: The United Irishmen and the Rise of Literary Nationalism* (Syracuse, 1994), 3, 9–10, 26, 89–90.

29 Mulvey, *Thomas Davis*, 115; Ward, *Exile, Emigration and Irish Writing*, 94; Foley and Ryder, *Ideology and Ireland in the Nineteenth Century*, 173–7; W.E. Vaughan, *A New History of Ireland,* vol. 6: *Ireland under the Union, II 1870–1921* (Oxford, 1996): 386, 391, 393.

30 Hachey and McCaffrey, *Perspectives on Irish Nationalism*, 53; Mulvey, *Thomas Davis*, 105, 209, 236–7; Brendan O Cathaoir,

John Blake Dillon: Young Irelander (Dublin, 1980), 10; Davis, *Revolutionary Imperialist*, 165; Cronin, *Irish Nationalism*, 68; Joep Leerssen, *Remembrance and Imagination: Patterns in the Historical and Literary Representation of Ireland in the Nineteenth Century* (Cork, 1996), 4, 147; John Neylon Molony, *A Soul Came into Ireland: Thomas Davis, 1841–1845: A Biography* (Dublin, 1995), 48; Damien Murray, *Romanticism, Nationalism and Irish Antiquarian Societies 1840–1880* (Dublin, 2000), 1, 5, 9, 46; David N. Buckley, *James Fintan Lalor: Radical* (Cork, 1990), 50; Rothschild, *Ethnopolitics*, 2, 11, 15; Thomas Francis Meagher, *Speeches on the Legislative Independence of Ireland* (New York, 1853), 32, 83.

31 Buckley, *Lalor*, 55; Hutchinson, *Dynamics of Cultural Nationalism*, 12–19; Molony, *A Soul Came into Ireland*, 30; Hill, *Studia Hibernica* 20:73–109; Steven R. Knowlton, "The Enigma of Sir Charles Gavan Duffy: Looking for Clues in Australia," *Eire/Ireland* 31 (1996): 190–1; Hutchinson, *Modern Nationalism*, 59; Mulvey, *Thomas Davis*, 52, 55–8, 63, 65; Thuente, *The Harp Restrung*, 193–4, 214–15, 225; Laurence M. Geary, *Rebellion and Remembrance in Modern Ireland* (Dublin, 2004), 135, 143–4; Hachey and McCaffrey, *Perspectives on Irish Nationalism*, 55, 57; J.E. Pigot to Smith O'Brien, 17 December 1858, Smith O'Brien Papers, MS 446, NLI; Leerssen, *Remembrance and Imagination*, 148–9; Malcolm Brown, *The Politics of Irish Literature* (Seattle, 1972), 68.

32 Mulvey, *Thomas Davis*, 65; Leerssen, *Remembrance and Imagination*, 148–9; Brown, *Politics of Irish Literature*, 68; Lawrence W. McBride, ed., *Reading Irish Histories: Texts, Contexts, and Memory in Modern Ireland* (Dublin, 2003), 19–21.

33 Colm Kerrigan, *Father Mathew and the Irish Temperance Movement 1838–1849* (Dublin, 1992), 23–5, 32, 34, 155–6, 161–2; Colm Kerrigan, "The Social Impact of the Irish Temperance Movement, 1839–1845," *Irish Economic and Social History* 14 (1987): 20–38; Quinn, *Father Mathew's Crusade*, 53, 56, 34–5, 38, 8, 83–4, 92, 80–1; P.C. to Fawcett, 27 September 1838, Colonial Office (CO), 904/7, PRO.

34 Quinn, *Father Mathew's Crusade*, 82, 111, 8, 101; McBride, *Reading Irish Histories*, 21–2, 26–7; George Bretherton, "The Battle between Carnival and Lent: Temperance and Repeal in Ireland, 1829–1845," *Histoire Sociale/Social History* 29 (1994): 295–320; Elizabeth Malcolm, *'Ireland Sober, Ireland Free': Drink and Temperance in Nineteenth Century Ireland* (Dublin, 1986), 127, 130; Dye, *Journal of British Studies* 40:387.

35 Leslie A. Williams, *Daniel O'Connell, The British Press and the Irish Famine*, ed. by William H.A. Williams (Aldershot, 2003), 73, 79–80, 85–6, 88.

36 Davis, *Revolutionary Imperialist*, 157, 181; Crossman, *Politics, Law and Order*, 77; Brian Jenkins, *Sir William Gregory of Coole* (Gerrards Cross, 1986), 60–2; Jenkins, *Henry Goulburn*, 317; Mulvey, *Thomas Davis*, 139, 150.

37 Kerr, *Archivium Hibernicum* 36:23; Nowlan, *Politics of Repeal*, 20–86; Macaulay, *William Crolly*, 306–7, 322, 329, 435; Andrews, *Lion in the West*, 118–20; Brockliss and Eastwood, *Union of Multiple Identities*, 41; Collins, *Catholic Churchmen and the Celtic Revival*, 82–3, 86; Mulvey, *Thomas Davis*, 178.

38 Brian Jenkins, *Henry Goulburn 1784–1856: A Political Biography* (Montreal and Liverpool, 1996), 318; Cronin, *Irish Nationalism*, 71; Hutchinson, *Dynamics of Cultural Nationalism*, 76; Hill, *Studia Hibernica* 20:108; Maurice O'Connell, "Young Ireland and the Catholic Clergy in 1844: Contemporary Deceit and Historical Falsehood," *Catholic Historical Review* 74 (1988): 199–225; Mulvey, *Thomas Davis*, 176.

39 Molony, *A Soul Came into Ireland*, 76; Denis Gwynn, *Young Ireland and 1848* (Cork, 1949), 23, 57; Hill, *Irish Historical Studies*, 19:382–3; Lyons and Hawkins, *Ireland under the Union*, 80–1; Davis, *Revolutionary Imperialist*, 207; O'Connell, *Correspondence of O'Connell*, 7:237; Donal A. Kerr, *'A Nation of Beggars?' Priests, People and Politics in Famine Ireland 1846–1852* (Oxford, 1994), 12.

CHAPTER THREE

1 Leslie Williams, *Daniel O'Connell, the British Press and the Irish Famine* (Aldershot, 2000), 80; Joseph Rothschild, *Ethnopolitics: A Conceptual Framework* (New York, 1981), 22–3; *Times*, 6 November 1866; David Thornley, *Isaac Butt and Home Rule*, reprint ed. (Westport, Conn., 1976), 17–18; D. George Boyce and Alan O'Day, *Defenders of the Union: A Survey of British and Irish Unionism since 1801* (London, 2001), 85, 77; James H. Murphy, *Ireland: A Social, Cultural and Literary History 1791–1891* (Dublin, 2003), 80.

2 Emmet O'Connor, *A Labour History of Ireland 1824–1960* (Dublin, 1992), 21–3; Liam Kennedy, *Colonialism, Religion and Nationalism in Ireland* (Belfast, 1996), 40–3; Frank Geary, "The Act of Union, British-Irish Trade, and Pre-Famine Industrialization," *Economic History Review* 48 (1995): 68–88; Frank Geary,

"Regional Industrial Structure and Labour Force Decline in Ireland between 1841 and 1851," *Irish Historical Studies* 30 (1996): 193; L.M. Cullen, *An Economic History of Ireland Since 1660* (London, 1972) 121; Joel Mokyr, "Industrialization and Poverty in Ireland and the Netherlands," *Journal of Interdisciplinary History* 10 (1980): 455; Cormac O Grada, *Ireland: A New Economic History 1780–1939* (Oxford, 1994), 23, 87; J.M. Goldstrom and L.A. Clarkson, eds., *Irish Population, Economy and Society: Essays in Honor of the Late K.H. Connell* (Oxford, 1981), 31; Colm Kerrigan, *Father Mathew and the Irish Temperance Movement 1838–1849* (Cork, 1992), 71; Cormac O Grada, ed., *Famine 150: Commemorative Lecture Series* (Dublin, 1997), 16–17, 19–20, 32, 34–7, 39; K.D.M. Snell, ed., *Letters from Ireland during the Famine of 1847: Alexander Somerville* (Dublin, 1994), 84–5; Cormac O Grada, *Black '47 and Beyond: The Great Irish Famine in History, Economy, and Memory* (Princeton, 1999), 26, 30, 33.

3 Colm Toibin and Diarmaid Ferriter, *The Irish Famine: A documentary* (New York, 2001), 47–8, 58; Michael de Nie, *The Eternal Paddy: Irish Identity and the British Press, 1798–1882* (Madison, 2004), 93; Williams, *Daniel O'Connell*, 126, 139; Melissa Fegan, *Literature and the Irish Famine 1845–1919* (Oxford, 2002), 36.

4 Toibin and Ferriter, *Irish Famine*, 73–5; Robin Haines, *Charles Trevelyan and the Great Irish Famine* (Dublin, 2004), 250.

5 Haines, *Charles Trevelyan*, 85, 271, 502; Joel Mokyr, *Why Ireland Starved: A Quantitative and Analytical History of the Irish Economy, 1800–1850* (London, 1985), 268; O'Grada, *Black '47*, 156ff., 85; Mokyr, *Journal of Interdisciplinary History*, 10:433; Joseph Robins, *The Miasma: Epidemic and Panic in Nineteenth Century Ireland* (Dublin, 1995), 34–5, 43, 119; Catharine Anne Wilson, *A New Lease on Life: Landlords, Tenants and Immigrants in Ireland and Canada* (Kingston, 1994), 85.

6 Haines, *Charles Trevelyan*, 13, 203, 302; Toibin and Ferriter, *Irish Famine*, 13, 89; John F. Quinn, *Father Mathew's Crusade: Temperance in Nineteenth-Century Ireland and Irish America* (Amherst, 2002), 136; Brian Jenkins, *Henry Goulburn 1784–1856: A Political Biography* (Montreal and Liverpool, 1996), 337–8.

7 Quinn, *Father Mathew's Crusade*, 136, 141; Williams, *Daniel O'Connell* 195; Snell, *Alexander Somerville*, 187; Fegan, *Literature and the Irish Famine*, 62–3; Haines, *Charles Trevelyan*, 258,

85; James H. Murphy, *Abject Loyalty: Nationalism and Monarchy in Ireland during the Reign of Queen Victoria* (Washington, D.C., 2001), 63–4.

8 Robins, *The Miasma*, 124, 132; *Parliamentary Debates*, 3rd ser., 93: 1014; O Grada, *Ireland*, 191.

9 Haines, *Charles Trevelyan*, 375; Donal Kerr, *The Catholic Church and the Famine* (Dublin, 1996), 55–6; Donal Kerr, *'Nation of Beggars'? Priests, People and Politics in Famine Ireland 1846–1852* (Oxford, 1994), 96, 83; Bernard O'Reilly, *John MacHale Archbishop of Tuam*, 2 vols. (New York, 1890), 1:623, 614; Peadar MacSuibhne, ed., *Paul Cullen and His Contemporaries with Their Letters from 1820–1902*, 5 vols. (Naas, 1961–77), 1:293; Ambrose Macaulay, *William Crolly, Archbishop of Armagh 1835–49* (Dublin, 1994), 337–9.

10 Fegan, *Literature and the Irish Famine*, 36, 54, 59, 63.

11 Donald MacKay, *Flight from Famine: The Coming of the Irish to Canada* (Toronto, 1990), 223, 225; Thomas Francis Meagher, *Speeches on the Legislative Independence of Ireland* (New York, 1853), 38, 102, 128; Williams, *Daniel O'Connell*, 102–3, 144–7, 157; Toibin and Ferriter, *Irish Famine*, 17–18, 40; Fegan, *Literature and the Irish Famine*, 44; de Nie, *Eternal Paddy*, 108.

12 De Nie, *Eternal Paddy*, 108; John Killen, ed., *The Famine Decade: Contemporary Accounts 1841–1851* (Belfast, 1995), 41, 71–2, 100–1, 131–2, 145–7, 200–2; R.L. Sheil to A. Sheil, n.d. [1846], MS 11, 138, NLI; Williams, *Daniel O'Connell*, 199; Kathleen Villiers-Tuthill, *Patient Endurance: The Great Famine in Connemara* (Dublin, 1997), 46.

13 Chris Morash and Richard Hayes, eds., *Fearful Realities: New Perspectives on the Famine* (Dublin, 1996), 52, 154; Killen, *Famine Decade*, 132; Arthur Gribben, ed., *The Great Famine and the Irish Diaspora in America* (Amherst, 1999), 181–2; Haines, *Charles Trevelyan*, 22–3; K. Theodore Hoppen, *Ireland since 1800* (London, 1989), 56–7; O Grada, *Ireland*, 202; Goldstrom and Clarkson, *Irish Population, Economy and Society*, 169; O Grada, *Black '47*, 124–5, 85; Seamus O'Brien, *Famine and Community in the Mullingar Poor Law Union, 1845–1849: Mud Huts and Fat Bullocks* (Dublin, 1999), 28; O Grada, *Famine 150*, 82–4, 144, 146, 151; Marianne Elliott, *The Catholics of Ulster* (London, 2001), 306–7.

14 Snell, *Alexander Somerville*, 187; Mokyr, *Why Ireland Starved*, 289; Patrick O'Sullivan, ed., *The Meaning of the Famine* (London, 1997), 31; Toibin and Ferriter, *Irish Famine*, 7, 83; Kerrigan, *Father Mathew*, 171–2; Villiers-Tuthill, *Patient Endurance*,

45–6; Brendan O Cathaoir, *Famine Diary* (Dublin, 1999), 82; Kerr, *Catholic Church and the Famine*, 14–15.

15 Morash and Hayes, *Fearful Realities*, 167–9; *Fraser's Magazine* 72 (1865): 412; O'Sullivan, *Meaning of the Famine*, 32; Timothy P. O'Neill, "Clare and Irish Poverty, 1815–1851," *Studia Hibernica* 14 (1974): 22–3; Desmond Bowen, *Protestant Crusade in Ireland, 1800–70* (Dublin, 1978), 184; Marcus Tanner, *Ireland's Holy Wars: The Struggle for a Nation's Soul, 1500–2000* (New Haven, 2001), 243; D. George Boyce, *Nineteenth Century Ireland: The Search for Stability* (Dublin, 1990), 110; James H. Murphy, *Ireland: A Social, Cultural and Literary History 1791–1891* (Dublin, 2003), 68; Marilyn Silverman and P.H. Gulliver, eds., *Approaching the Past: Historical Anthropology through Irish Studies* (New York, 1992), 78; O'Brien, *Famine and Community in Mullingar Poor Law Union*, 21; Elliott, *Catholics of Ulster*, 309; Desmond Bowen, *History and the Shaping of Irish Protestantism* (New York, 1995), 266; Macaulay, *William Crolly*, 455; Eduardo Posarda-Carbo, ed., *Elections before Democracy* (London, 1996), 121; Evelyn Bolster, *A History of the Diocese of Cork*, vol. 4 (Cork, 1993), 24; Kerr, *Catholic Church and the Famine*, 22, 35–40.

16 O Grada, *Ireland*, 204; O'Brien, *Famine and Community in Mullingar Poor Law Union*, 32, 34, 37, 41, 39, 47; Robins, *Miasma*, 115, 137–40, 148, 130–1; Haines, *Charles Trevelyan*, 521–2; Sheil to A. Sheil, 10 August 1848, 11, 138, NLI; O Grada, *Famine 150*, 156; Kennedy, *Colonialism, Religion and Nationalism*, 68.

17 James E. Thorold Rogers, ed., *Speeches on Questions of Public Policy by John Bright, M.P.*, 2 vols. (London, 1868), 1:320, 305–6.

18 Richard Davis, *Revolutionary Imperialist: William Smith O'Brien* (Dublin, 1998), 194–5; W.L. Morton, "Lord Monck and Nationality in Ireland and Canada," *Studia Hibernica* 13 (1973): 80–1; Brian Jenkins, *Sir William Gregory of Coole* (Gerrards Cross, 1986), 69–70.

19 Jenkins, *Gregory*, 70–4; Jim Smyth, "'An Entirely Exceptional Case': Ireland and the British Problem," *Historical Journal* 34 (1991): 1003–4; W.E. Vaughan, *A New History of Ireland*, vol. 5: *Ireland under the Union, 1: 1801–1870* (Oxford, 1989), 362; Denis Gwyn, *Young Ireland and 1848* (Cork, 1949), 110; Oliver MacDonagh, "The Irish Catholic Clergy and Emigration during the Great Famine," *Irish Historical Studies* 5 (1946–47): 287–302; Patrick Ward, *Exile, Emigration and Irish Writing* (Dublin, 2002), 109–10; Richard Kearney, ed., *Migrations: The Irish at Home and Abroad* (Dublin, 1990), 96; O Grada, *Ireland*, 204;

Walker Connor, *Ethnonationalism: The Quest for Understanding* (Princeton, 1994), 154.

20 Kevin B. Nowlan, *The Politics of Repeal: A Study in the Relations between Great Britain and Ireland 1841–50* (London, 1965), 108–10; Davis, *Revolutionary Imperialist*, 175; Brendan O Cathaoir, *John Blake Dillon: Young Irelander* (Dublin, 1980), 52; John Augustus O'Shea, *Leaves from the Life of a Special Correspondent*, 2 vols. (London, 1885), 1:15, 18; Laurence M. Geary, *Rebellion and Remembrance in Modern Ireland* (Dublin, 2004), 149–50; John Newsinger, "John Mitchel and Irish Nationalism," *Literature and History* 6:184, 193–4; Leon O Broin, *Charles Gavan Duffy, Patriot and Statesman: The Story of Charles Gavan Duffy (1816–1903)* (Dublin, 1967), 29–32.

21 John Neylon Molony, *A Soul Came into Ireland: Thomas Davis, 1841–1845* (Dublin, 1995), 33; Terry Eagleton, *Heathcliff and the Great Hunger Studies in Irish Culture* (New York, 1995), 228; Laurence Brockliss and David Eastwood, eds., *Union of Multiple Identities: The British Isles c.1750–c.1850* (Manchester, 1997), 147, 156–9; Maurice O'Connell, ed., *Daniel O'Connell: Political Pioneer* (Dublin, 1991), 5, 43; Kevin B. Nowlan and Maurice R. O'Connell, eds., *Daniel O'Connell: Portrait of a Radical* (Belfast, 1984), 18; Boyce, *Nationalism in Ireland*, 167–9; Richard Davis, *The Young Ireland Movement* (Dublin, 1987), 248–50; L. Perry Curtis Jr, "Moral and Physical Force: The Language of Violence in Irish Nationalism," *Journal of British Studies* 27 (1988): 164–5; Gary Owens, "Visualizing the Liberator: Self-fashioning, Dramaturgy, and the Construction of Daniel O'Connell," *Eire/Ireland*, 33 (1998): 115–16; James S. Donnelly and Kerby Miller, eds., *Irish Popular Culture 1650–1850* (Dublin, 1998), 251; Lawrence J. McCaffrey, *Daniel O'Connell and the Repeal Year* (Lexington, 1966), 76–7; Charles Chenevix-Trench, *The Great Dan: A Biography of Daniel O'Connell* (London, 1984), 275–7; Tom Garvin, *The Evolution of Irish Nationalist Politics* (Dublin, 1981), 46–7; John F. Broderick, *The Holy See and the Irish Movement for Repeal of the Union with England 1829–1847* (Rome, 1951), 141, 216; Geary, *Rebellion and Remembrance*, 149; Oliver MacDonagh, *States of Mind: A Study of Anglo-Irish Conflict 1780–1980* (London, 1983), 90–103.

22 Kerr, *'A Nation of Beggars,'* 126–7; Davis, *Revolutionary Imperialist*, 208–11; O'Connor, *Labour History of Ireland*, 26; Bolster, *Diocese of Cork*, 4:18; Garvin, *Evolution of Irish Nationalist Politics*, 51; Boyce, *Nineteenth Century Ireland*, 115; Nowlan, *Politics of Repeal*, 111–14; Meagher, *Speeches*, 91.

23 Lawrence J. McCaffrey, " Irish Nationalism and Irish Catholi-
    cism: A Study in Cultural Identity," *Church History* 42 (1973):
    527; Jacqueline R. Hill, "The Intelligentsia and Irish Nationalism
    in the 1840s," *Studia Hibernica*, 20 (1980): 84–5; O'Connor,
    Labour History of Ireland, 26; O Broin, *Charles Gavan Duffy*,
    44; Davis, *Revolutionary Imperialist*, 224, 226, 231; Kerr, 'A
    Nation of Beggars,' 74, 79; Nowlan, *Politics of Repeal*, 142.
24 See L. Fogarty, *James Fintan Lalor: Patriot and Political Essayist
    (1807–1849)* (Poole, 1997); David N. Buckley, *James Fintan
    Lalor: Radical* (Cork, 1990), 32, 65.
25 Geary, *Rebellion and Remembrance*, 51–3, 145, 64; Nowlan,
    Politics of Repeal, 143–7, 150, 171–2; Maurice O'Connell, "John
    O'Connell and the Great Famine," *Irish Historical Studies* 25
    (1986): 139–41; Boyce, *Nationalism in Ireland*, 172–3; Graham
    Walker, "Irish Nationalism and the Uses of History," *Past and
    Present* 126 (1990): 206; Davis, *Revolutionary Imperialist*,
    234–7; Robert Sloan, *William Smith O'Brien and the Young Ire-
    land Rebellion of 1848* (Dublin, 2000), 208.
26 Steven R. Knowlton, "The Quarrel between Gavan Duffy and
    John Mitchel: Implications for Ireland," *Albion* 21 (1989): 582;
    Boyce, *Nationalism in Ireland*, 173–5; Sean Cronin, *Irish Nation-
    alism: A History of Roots and Ideology* (New York, 1981),
    79–80; O Broin, *Charles Gavan Duffy*, 51; Nowlan, *Politics of
    Repeal*, 172; D.N. Petler, "Ireland and France in 1848," *Irish
    Historical Studies* 24 (1985): 493–505; R.V. Comerford, "France,
    Fenianism and Nationalist Strategy," *Etudes Irlandaises* 7 (1982):
    116–17; Davis, *Revolutionary Imperialist*, 238–45; Dorothy
    Thompson, *Outsiders: Class, Gender and Nation* (London,
    1993), 159–61; Dublin Metropolitan Police Reports, 9 June
    1841, 14 August 1841, 6 October 1841, CO 904/8; Sloan,
    William Smith O'Brien, 216, 225–7.
27 O Cathaoir, *John Blake Dillon*, 69–71; Davis, *Revolutionary
    Imperialist*, 252–5; John Mitchel's Jail Memoir; O Broin, *Charles
    Gavan Duffy*, 60; Sloan, *William Smith O'Brien*, 230.
28 R.V. Comerford, *The Fenians in Context: Irish Politics and Soci-
    ety 1848–82* (Dublin, 1985), 15, 18; Vaughan, *Ireland under the
    Union*, 1:368; Nowlan, *Politics of Repeal*, 211–14.
29 Nowlan, *Politics of Repeal*, 211–14; O Cathaoir, *John Blake Dil-
    lon*, 78–9; Thomas G. McAllister, *Terence Bellew McManus
    1811(?)-1861: A Short Biography* (Maynooth, 1972), 11–12;
    O'Connor, *Labour History of Ireland*, 27–8; Sloan, *William
    Smith O'Brien*, 257–8, 262, 288–9.

30 Desmond Bowen, *Paul, Cardinal, Cullen and the Shaping of Modern Irish Catholicism* (Dublin, 1983), 97; Kerr, 'A Nation of Beggars,' 58, 73–6, 82–3, 123, 128, 132–40, 144, 151–60; Redmond to Cullen, 5 February 1868, Cullen Correspondence 1868, 341/1/I, DDA; Geary, *Rebellion and Remembrance*, 59.

31 Rothschild, *Ethnopolitics*, 86, 88, 96; Jim Mac Laughlin, *Reimagining the Nation-State: The Contested Terrains of Nation-building* (London, 2001), 265; Kevin Nowlan, "The Catholic Clergy and Irish Politics in the Eighteen Thirties and Forties," *Historical Studies* 9 (1974): 119–35; O Cathaoir, *Famine Diary*, 115; Cornelius M. Buckley, "French Views of Ireland on the Eve of the Famine," *Journal of Religious History* 8 (1974–75): 245; Tim Pat Coogan, *The Troubles: Ireland's Ordeal 1966–1996 and the Search for Peace*, rev. ed. (London, 1996), 104; John Newsinger, "Revolution and Catholicism in Ireland, 1848–1923," *European Studies Review* 9 (1979): 461; W.E.H. Lecky, *Leaders of Public Opinion in Ireland*, 2 vols. (London, 1903), 2:229; Macaulay, *William Crolly*, 453; Yonah Alexander and Alan O'Day, *Terrorism in Ireland* (Beckenham, 1984), 123.

32 Martin E. Marty and R. Scott Appleby, eds., *Religion, Ethnicity, and Self-Identity: Nations in Turmoil* (Hanover, N.H., 1997), 8; Guenter Lewy, *Religion and Revolution* (New York, 1974), 583–4, 546, 551, 553, 42, 554, 566, 568; Salo Wittmayer Baron, *Modern Nationalism and Religion* (New York, 1960), 98, 105.

33 Alexander and O'Day, *Terrorism in Ireland*, 122–3; D.G. Boyce, ed., *The Revolution in Ireland 1879–1923* (London, 1988), 158–9; Daire Keogh, *The French Disease: The Catholic Church and Radicalism in Ireland 1790–1800* (Dublin, 1993), 142, 127, 159; S.J. Connolly, *Priests and People in Pre-Famine Ireland* (Dublin, 1982), 220–3, 225, 233–5, 237; David C. Rapoport and Yonah Alexander, eds., *The Morality of Terrorism: Religious and Secular Justifications* (New York, 1982), 101; Donal A. Kerr, "England, Ireland, and Rome, 1847–1848," *Studies in Church History* 21 (1989): 271; Buckley, *Journal of Religious History* 8:246–7.

34 Kerr, *Studies in Church History* 21:270–4; Buckley, *Journal of Religious History* 8:248; Macaulay, *William Crolly*, 334–5; Mac-Suibhne, *Paul Cullen and His Contemporaries*, 1:312.

35 Kerr, *Studies in Church History* 21:275; John O'Mahony recollections, MS 868, NLI; Mary E. Daly, "Recent Writings on Modern Irish History: The Interaction of Past and Present," *Journal of Modern History* 69 (1997): 521; Cyril Pearl, *The Three Lives of*

Gavan Duffy (Kensington, N.S.W., 1979), 103; O Cathaoir, *Famine Diary*, 169–70; Kerr, *Catholic Church and the Famine*, 64; Newsinger, *European Studies Review* 9:464–6; Denis Gwyn, "The Priests and Young Ireland in 1848," *Irish Ecclesiastical Record* 70 (1948): 598, 601, 609; McAllister, *McManus*, 15.

36 Kerr, '*Nation of Beggars*,' 125; Donal A. Kerr, ed., *Religion, State and Ethnic Groups* (New York, 1992), 287; MacSuibhne, *Paul Cullen and His Contemporaries*, 1: 387; Mitchel to Thomson, 26 August 1854, John Mitchel Papers, T413/5, PRONI; Kerrigan, *Father Mathew*, 130; McCaffrey, *Church History* 42:533; Redmond to Cullen, 13 November 1863, Cullen Correspondence 1863, 340/8/I, DDA; Redmond to Cullen, 8 March 1867, Cullen Correspondence 1867, 334/5/I, DDA; Philip H. Bagenel, *The Priest in Politics* (London, 1893), vi, 39.

CHAPTER FOUR

1 *Irish Catholic Banner*, 14 March 1868; S.J. Connolly, *Religion and Society in Nineteenth Century Ireland* (Dundalk, 1985), 35, 31.

2 D. George Boyce, *Nineteenth-Century Ireland: The Search for Stability* (Dublin, 1990), 122–3; Kevin B. Nowlan, *The Politics of Repeal: A Study of the Relations between Great Britain and Ireland, 1841–50* (London, 1965), 218–19; Michael Gallagher, "Socialism and the Nationalist Tradition in Ireland, 1798–1918," *Eire/Ireland* 12 (1977): 74; Tom Garvin, *Evolution of Irish Nationalist Politics* (Dublin, 1981), 52; Graham Walker, "Irish Nationalism and the Uses of History," *Past and Present* 126 (1990): 207; Joep Leerssen, *Remembrance and Imagination: Patterns in the Historical and Literary Representation of Ireland in the Nineteenth Century* (Cork, 1996), 22; Damien Murray, *Romanticism, Nationalism and Irish Archeological Societies 1840–1880* (Dublin, 2000), 52, 75, 77, 122–3, 131–2; Raymond Gillespie, *The Remaking of Modern Ireland 1750–1950* (Dublin, 2004), 140–1.

3 Murray, *Romanticism, Nationalism and Irish Archeological Societies*, 57, 77; Donal A. Kerr, '*Nation of Beggars*'? *Priests, People and Politics in Famine Ireland 1846–1852* (Oxford, 1994), 189; Emmet Larkin, "Church, State, and Nation in Modern Ireland," *American Historical Review* 80 (1975): 1256–7; *Fortnightly Review* 4 (1866): 288; Peter Alter, *Nationalism* (London, 1985), 68.

4 P.T. Phillips, ed., *The View from the Pulpit: Victorian Ministers and Society* (Toronto, 1978), 273–4; Desmond Bowen, *Paul Cardinal Cullen and the Shaping of Modern Irish Catholicism* (Dublin, 1983), 5–16, 31; Donal Kerr, *Peel, Priests and Politics: Sir Robert Peel's Administration and the Roman Catholic Church in Ireland, 1841–6* (Oxford, 1982), 62–4; Cullen to Kenrick, 17 August 1843, 28-S-3, Kenrick Papers, Archives of Archdiocese of Baltimore (AAB); Cullen to Hughes, 10 January 1851, Archbishop Hughes MSS, reel 3, Catholic University of America (CUA); Peadar MacSuibhne, ed., *Paul Cullen and His Contemporaries with Their Letters from 1820–1902*, 5 vols. (Naas, 1961–77), 1:176, 194, 2:119.

5 Bowen, *Cullen*, 46, 60–1, 70–1, 97; Kevin Collins, *Catholic Churchmen and Celtic Revival in Ireland 1848–1916* (Dublin, 2002), 99–101; Ambrose Macaulay, *William Crolly, Archbishop of Armagh 1835–49* (Dublin, 1994), 373, 452; Leon O Broin, *Charles Gavan Duffy, Patriot and Statesman* (Dublin 1967), 83; D. George Boyce, *Nationalism in Ireland* (London, 1995), 180; Phillips, *View from the Pulpit*, 276–7; Sheridan Gilley, "The Roman Catholic Church and the Nineteenth-Century Irish Diaspora," *Journal of Ecclesiastical History* 35 (1984): 195; Steven R. Knowlton, *Popular Politics and the Irish Catholic Church: The Rise and Fall of the Independent Irish Party* (New York, 1991), 158; MacSuibhne, *Paul Cullen and His Contemporaries*, 3:131; Cullen to Kenrick, 4 August 1849, 28-S-10, Kenrick Papers, AAB.

6 MacSuibhne, *Paul Cullen and his Contemporaries*, 1:251; Bowen, *Cullen*, 101; Kerr, 'Nation of Beggars,' 221, 311; Oliver MacDonagh, "The Politicization of the Irish Catholic Bishops, 1800–1850," *Historical Journal* 18 (1975):51; Emmet Larkin, *The Making of the Roman Catholic Church in Ireland 1850–1860* (Chapel Hill, 1980), 8–9; Knowlton, *Popular Politics and the Irish Catholic Church*, 54; Patrick J. Corish, *Irish Catholic Experience: A Historical Survey* (Dublin, 1985), 218.

7 Cullen to Kenrick, 9 December 1833, 28-R-3, Kenrick Papers, AAB; Bowen, *Cullen*, 103, 106; Corish, *Irish Catholic Experience*, 210, 221; Daly, *Journal of Modern History* 69:521; Larkin, *Making of the Roman Catholic Church*, 15; Patrick Carey, "Voluntaryism: An Irish Catholic Tradition," *Church History* 48 (1979): 50; Kerr, 'Nation of Beggars,' 207–14; Alvin Jackson, *Ireland 1798–1998: Politics and War* (Oxford, 1999), 59–67; Phillips, *View from the Pulpit*, 17–44; S.J. Connolly, *Priests and People in Pre-Famine Ireland* (New York, 1982), 15; Cullen to Hughes, 10

January 1851, Hughes MSS, reel 3, 21 July 1854, reel 4, CUA; Desmond J. Keenan, *Catholic Church in Nineteenth Century Ireland: A Sociological Study* (Dublin, 1983), 32; Brendan O Cathaoir, *John Blake Dillon: Young Irelander* (Dublin, 1980), 150.

8 Eugene Hynes, "The Great Hunger and Irish Catholicism," *Societas* 8 (1978): 137–56; David W. Miller, "Irish Catholicism and the Great Famine," *Journal of Social History* 9 (1975–76): 81–97; Connolly, *Religion and Society in Nineteenth Century Ireland*, 12, 14–15, 54–5; Larkin, *Making of the Roman Catholic Church*, 400; Emmet Larkin, *The Consolidation of the Roman Catholic Church in Ireland, 1860–1870* (Chapel Hill, 1987), 180–1; K. Theodore Hoppen, *Elections, Politics and Society in Ireland 1832–1885* (Oxford, 1984), 186; Cullen to Kenrick, 21 January 1843, 28-S-2, Kenrick Papers, AAB; Larkin, *American Historical Review* 80:1260; John Fulton, *The Tragedy of Belief: Division, Politics and Religion in Ireland* (Oxford, 1991), 73–6.

9 Ambrose Macaulay, *Dr. Russell of Maynooth* (London, 1983), 119ff.; Hoppen, *Elections, Politics and Society*, 187; Collins, *Catholic Churchmen and Celtic Revival*, 100; MacSuibhne, *Paul Cullen and His Contemporaries*, 2:319; Gilley, *Journal of Ecclesiastical History* 35:205.

10 Patrick O'Farrell, *Ireland's English Question: Anglo-Irish Relations 1534–1970* (London, 1971), 89; Cullen to Hughes, 10 January 1851, Hughes MSS, reel 3; MacSuibhne, *Paul Cullen and His Contemporaries*, 3:247–8; Keenan, *Catholic Church in Nineteenth Century Ireland*, 190–1; Larkin, *Making of the Roman Catholic Church*, 238; Charles Stephen Dessain, ed., *The Letters and Diaries of John Henry Newman* (London, 1972), 22:291; Chris Morash and Richard Hayes, eds., *'Fearful Realities,' New Perspectives on the Famine* (Dublin, 1996), 171; Gilley, *Journal of Ecclesiastical History* 35:205.

11 Napoleon Roussell, *Catholic and Protestant Nations Compared in Their Threefold Relations to Wealth, Knowledge, and Morality* (Boston, 1855), 78–9; O'Farrell, *Ireland's English Question*, 89; Larkin, *Consolidation of the Roman Catholic Church in Ireland*, 182; Larkin, *Making of the Roman Catholic Church in Ireland*, 34; Phillips, *View from the Pulpit*, 286; MacSuibhne, *Paul Cullen and His Contemporaries*, 3:135; E.D. Steele, "Cardinal Cullen and Irish nationality," *Irish Historical Studies* 19 (1975): 246–7.

12 Kerr, *'Nation of Beggars,'* 251, 264–5, 267, 269, 273–5, 278, 281; Cullen to Hughes, 10 January 1851, Hughes MSS, reel 3;

Nuala Costello, *John MacHale Archbishop of Tuam* (Dublin, 1939), 105; Brian Jenkins, *Sir William Gregory of Coole* (Gerrards Cross, 1986), 112–13.

13 Knowlton, *Popular Politics and the Irish Catholic Church*, 97–8, 139; Jenkins, *Gregory*, 119; Hoppen, *Elections, Politics and Society*, 286.

14 Hoppen, *English Historical Review* 92:775–6; Whyte, *English Historical Review* 75:244–5; Roussell, *Catholic and Protestant Nations Compared*, 79; C.H.E. Philpin, ed., *Nationalism and Popular Protest in Ireland* (Cambridge, 1987), 306; Hoppen, *Elections, Politics and Society*, 34, 37–8; K. Theodore Hoppen, "The Franchise and Electoral Politics in England and Ireland 1832–1885," *History* 70 (1985): 209–10; K. Theodore Hoppen, "Roads to Democracy: Electioneering and Corruption in Nineteenth Century England and Ireland," *History* 81 (1996): 566; J.H. Whyte, "Landlord Influence and Elections in Ireland 1760–1885," *English Historical Review* 80 (1965): 749, 755.

15 Kenneth Wilson Underwood, *Protestant and Catholic: Religious and Social Interaction in an Industrial Community* (1957), 117; Hoppen, *Elections, Politics and Society*, 232–3; Whyte, *English Historical Review* 75:246–7; Eduardo Posarda-Carbo, ed., *Elections before Democracy* (London, 1996), 122–3; Steven R. Knowlton, "The Quarrel between Gavan Duffy and John Mitchel: Implications for Ireland," *Albion* 21 (1989): 581; Knowlton, *Popular Politics and the Irish Catholic Church*, 37–9; O Broin, *Charles Gavan Duffy*, 86; Whyte, *English Historical Review* 80:748.

16 Joel Mokyr, *Why Ireland Starved* (London, 1985), 81, 99; Oliver Rafferty, *Catholicism in Ulster 1603–1983: An Interpretive History* (London, 1994), 161; Knowlton, *Popular Politics and the Irish Catholic Church*, 31, 36, 5, 78–9; Larkin, *Making of the Roman Catholic Church in Ireland*, 86; Emmet O'Connor, *A Labour History of Ireland 1824–1960* (Dublin, 1992), 28; R.V. Comerford, *The Fenians in Context: Irish Politics and Society 1848–82* (Dublin, 1985), 18.

17 Steven R. Knowlton, "The Enigma of Sir Charles Gavan Duffy: Looking for Clues in Australia," *Eire/Ireland* 31 (1996): 193; Jackson, *Ireland*, 90; Patrick J. Corish, ed., *A History of Irish Catholicism*, vol. 5, pt 2 (Dublin, 1967), 14–15, 23; Whyte, *Irish Historical Studies* 11:315; Knowlton, *Popular Politics and the Irish Catholic Church*, 254, 115–17, 138; Phillips, *View from the Pulpit*, 286–7.

18 Knowlton, *Popular Politics and the Irish Catholic Church*, 49, 81–5, 90–1; Larkin, *Making of the Roman Catholic Church in Ireland*, 108; O Broin, *Charles Gavan Duffy*, 85–7.

19 Thomas Francis Meagher, *Speeches on the Legislative Independence of Ireland* (New York, 1853), 14; Knowlton, *Popular Politics and the Irish Catholic Church*, 27, 19, 25; Hoppen, *Elections, Politics and Society*, 100–2; James O'Shea, *Priests, Politics and Society in Post-Famine Ireland: A Study of County Tipperary 1850–1891* (1983), 58, 119ff.; Knowlton, *Albion* 21:584; Knowlton, *Eire/Ireland* 31:193; Larkin, *Making of the Roman Catholic Church in Ireland*, 220.

20 Mitchel to Thomson, 4 October 1852, John Mitchel MSS, T413/2, PRONI; Melissa Fegan, *Literature and the Irish Famine* (Oxford, 2002), 27; Knowlton, *Popular Politics and the Irish Catholic Church*, 41, 146, 256, 172; Larkin, *Making of the Roman Catholic Church in Ireland*, 200, 244–5; Whyte, *English Historical Review* 75:246–50; Kerr, *'Nation of Beggars,'* 293; Diaries of 15th Earl of Derby, 26 July 1868, Derby MSS, 920 DER(15), Liverpool Central Library; Bowen, *Cullen*, 249; Philpin, *Nationalism and Popular Protest in Ireland*, 308; John Biggs-Davison and George Chowdharay-Best, *The Cross of St. Patrick: The Catholic Unionists Tradition in Ireland* (Bourne End, 1984), 174; Posarda-Carbo, *Elections before Democracy*, 124–30.

21 Knowlton, *Popular Politics and the Irish Catholic Church*, 187; Knowlton, *Eire/Ireland*, 31:194; Phillips, *View from the Pulpit*, 287; Corish, *History of Irish Catholicism*, vol. 5, pt. 2, 29–32; Larkin, *Making of the Roman Catholic Church in Ireland*, 261–3, 317, 319.

22 Corish, *History of Irish Catholicism*, vol. 5, pt. 2, 35; Knowlton, *Popular Politics and the Irish Catholic Church*, 201, 209–11; Spencer to O'Hagan, 10 March 1873, O'Hagan MSS, D2777/8/222, PRONI; Larkin, *Making of the Roman Catholic Church*, 386; Steele, *Irish Historical Studies* 19:252; Kerr, *'Nation of Beggars,'* 340.

23 C.T. McIntire, *England against the Papacy 1858–1861: Tories, Liberals, and the Overthrow of Papal Temporal Power during the Italian Risorgimento* (Cambridge, 1983), 20, 73–7, 106–8; Odo Russell to Malmesbury, 26 March, 16 April 1859, FO 918/6, Odo Russell Papers.

24 K. Theodore Hoppen, "Tories, Catholics, and the General Election of 1859," *Historical Journal* 13 (1970): 51–3; Jenkins, *Gregory*, 135, 167.

25 Jenkins, *Gregory*, 135, 138; McIntire, *England against the Papacy*, 109–10, 112; Hilary Andrews, *The Lion of the West: A Biography of John MacHale* (Dublin, 2001), 84; Hoppen, *Historical Journal* 13:54, 56–62, 65.

26 McIntire, *England against the Papacy*, 49, 184–5, 219–20; Odo Russell to Russell, 6 July, 16 September 1859, FO 918/10; Russell to Odo Russell, 12 December 1859, FO 918/6; John M. Prest, *Lord John Russell* (London, 1972), 392.

27 McIntire, *England against the Papacy*, 171, 191; Bowen, *Cullen*, 277; Phillips, *Views from the Pulpit*, 290; Anon., "The Irish Question" (Paris, 1860), 46; Janet Fyfe, "The North British Review – Advocate of Italian Independence," *Scottish Tradition* 6 (1976): 64; Cullen to Spalding, 10 November 1866, 33-0-9, Spalding Papers, AAB; E.R. Norman, *The Catholic Church and Ireland in the Age of Rebellion 1859–1873* (London, 1965), 40, 44–5; Larkin, *Consolidation of the Roman Catholic Church*, 6.

28 Cullen to Kenrick, 9 May 1860, 28-T-7, Kenrick Papers, AAB; ibid., 12 June 1860, 28-T-8; Larkin, *Consolidation of the Roman Catholic Church*, 13, 48–50, xvi; Norman, *Catholic Church and Ireland*, 48–9, 51, 81; Margot C. Finn, *After Chartism: Class and Nation in English Radical Politics 1848–1874* (Cambridge, 1993), 206; McIntire, *England against the Papacy*, 202–4, 211.

29 Cullen to Kenrick, 26 March 1853, 28-T-5, Kenrick Papers, AAB; James H. Murphy, *Ireland: A Social, Cultural and Literary History 1791–1891* (Dublin, 2003), 75; Collins, *Catholic Churchmen and Celtic Revival*, 105; Nuala Costello, *John MacHale Archbishop of Tuam* (Dublin, 1939), 64; Larkin, *Making of the Roman Catholic Church*, 400; Larkin, *Consolidation of the Roman Catholic Church*, 113–14, 132–3, 141–3; Liam O'Dowd, ed., *On Intellectuals and Intellectual Life in Ireland* (Belfast, 1996), 104–8.

30 Barry M. Coldrey, *Faith and Fatherland: The Christian Brothers and the Development of Irish Nationalism 1838–1921* (Dublin, 1988); Ruth Schurmann, "The Catholic Priesthood of South Australia, 1844–1915," *Journal of Religious History* 16 (1990): 71; John Denvir, *The Life Story of an Old Rebel*, reprint ed. (Shannon, 1972), 14; Per Bauhn, *Nationalism and Morality* (Lund, 1995), 39; Doherty, *English Historical Review* 111:334; *A Digest of Evidence Taken Before Select Committees ... Appointed to Inquire into the State of Ireland 1824–1825* (London, 1826), 259; Barry M. Coldrey, "Socialisation into Revolution: The Educational Dimension. The Christian Brothers and Irish Revolution-

ary Nationalism," *Irish-Australian Studies*, ed. by Oliver Mac-
Donagh and W.F. Mandle (1989), 74; Cullen to Kenrick, 21 January 1843, 28-S-2, Kenrick Papers, AAB; Conor Cruise O'Brien,
Ancestral Voices: Religion and Nationalism in Ireland (Dublin,
1994), 25; Collins, *Catholic Churchmen and Celtic Revival*,
106–8.

31 Aaron T. Beck, *Prisoners of Hate: The Cognitive Basis of Anger,
Hostility, and Violence* (New York, 1999), 36; Niall O Cosain,
Print and Popular Culture in Ireland 1750–1850 (New York,
1997), 51; Martin Dillon, *God and the Gun: The Church and
Irish Terrorism* (London, 1997), 150; Thomas Keneally, *The
Great Shame: A Story of the Irish in the Old World and the New*
(London, 1998), 418; Terry Golway, *Irish Rebel: John Devoy and
America's Fight for Ireland's Freedom* (New York, 1998), 24;
Marie-Louise Legg, *Newspapers and Nationalism: The Irish
Provincial Press 1850–1892* (Dublin, 1999), 95–6, 66; Kevin
Whelan, *The Tree of Liberty: Radicalism, Catholicism and the
Construction of Irish Identity 1760–1830* (Notre Dame, 1994),
82; Robert James Scally, *The End of Hidden Ireland: Rebellion,
Famine and Emigration* (New York, 1995), 136–7; Donal A.
Kerr, *Religion, State and Ethnic Groups* (New York, 1992), 13;
Rosalind Mitchison, ed., *The Roots of Nationalism: Studies in
Northern Europe* (Edinburgh, 1980), 101–3; *Parliamentary
Papers*, House of Commons, 1866, LVIII:475.

32 Coldrey, *Faith and Fatherland*, 63; MacDonagh, *Hereditary
Bondsman*, 1:208; Boyce, *Nationalism in Ireland*, 159; Whelan,
Tree of Liberty, 62, 64; Joel Mokyr and Cormac O Grada, "Poor
and Getting Poorer? Living Standards in Ireland before the
Famine," *Economic History Review*, 2nd ser., 41 (1988): 225–6;
O Cosain, *Print and Popular Culture*, 29, 43, 163, 166, 185–7;
Kerr, *Religion, State and Ethnic Groups*, 299–300.

33 O Cosain, *Print and Popular Culture*, 188–9; Legg, *Newspapers
and Nationalism*, 16, 21, 30–3, 46, 41; Jim Mac Laughlin,
*Reimagining the Nation-State: The Contested Terrains of Nation-
building* (London, 2001), 207, 187; Doherty, *English Historical
Review* 111: 335; Knowlton, *Popular Politics and the Irish
Catholic Church*, 267–9, 105, 188; Colm Kerrigan, *Father Mathew and the Irish Temperance Movement 1838–1849* (Dublin,
1992), 54; Murray, *Romanticism, Nationalism and Irish Archeological Societies*, 78.

34 Larkin, *Consolidation of the Roman Catholic Church*, 51–4;
James S. Donnelly, Jr, "The Irish Agricultural Depression of
1859–64," *Irish Economic and Social History* 3 (1976): 33–54;

Cormac O Grada, *Ireland: New Economic History 1780–1939* (Oxford, 1994), 236–42; Thomas E. Jordan, *Ireland and the Quality of Life: The Famine Era* (Lampeter, 1997), 299–303; W.E. Vaughan, *Landlords and Tenants in Mid-Victorian Ireland* (Oxford, 1994), 23–4, 80; Paul Bew, *Land and the National Question in Ireland 1858–82* (Dublin, 1978), 4–5.

35 *Irish Canadian*, 5 August 1863, 21 January 1863, 11, 25 February 1863; Donald MacKay, *Flight from Famine: The Coming of the Irish to Canada* (Toronto, 1990), 241; D.J. Oddy, "Urban Famine in Nineteenth Century Britain: The Effect of the Lancashire Cotton Famine on Working-Class Diet and Health," *Economic History Review*, 2nd ser., 36 (1983): 68–86; Cullen to Hughes, 14 December 1862, Hughes MSS, reel 5, CUA.

36 *Irish Canadian*, 5 April 1865, 23 March 1864, 22 April 1863; *Nation*, 30 June 1860, 25 May 1861, 20 July 1861; John Augustus O'Shea, *Leaves from the Life of a Special Correspondent*, 2 vols. (London, 1885), 1:14; *Irish Canadian*, 1, 29 July 1863.

37 *Irish Canadian*, 11 February 1863, 26 August 1863, 28 January 1863, 8 July 1863, 5 August 1863.

38 Assaf Likhovski, "Tyranny in Nineteenth-Century American Legal Discourse: A Rhetorical Analysis," *Journal of Interdisciplinary History* 28 (1997): 205; Adolphe Perraud, *Ireland in 1862* (Dublin, 1863), 22; Vaughan, *Landlords and Tenants*, 219.

39 *Nation*, 28 April 1860, 30 June 1860; Perraud, *Ireland in 1862*, 2–68; Brendan O Cathaoir, *Famine Diary* (Dublin, 1999), 36; John F. Kutolowski, "Mid-Victorian Public Opinion, Polish Propaganda, and the Uprising of 1863," *Journal of British Studies* 8 (1969): 86–110; Joseph John Parot, *Polish Catholics in Chicago 1850–1920: A Religious History* (DeKalb, Ill., 1981), 13; *Irish Canadian*, 5 August 1863, 22 April 1863.

40 *Nation*, 28 April 1860; *Irish Canadian*, 29 July 1863; W.R. Le Fanu, *Seventy Years of Irish Life: Being Anecdotes and Reminiscences* (London, 1894), 301; Larkin, *Consolidation of the Roman Catholic Church*, 54–61; A.M. Sullivan, *New Ireland* (Philadelphia, 1878), 327–30; *Limerick, Tipperary and Waterford Examiner*, 14 July 1860; *Irish Canadian*, 21 October 1863, 13 January 1864.

41 *Irish Canadian*, 16 November 1864; Curtis, *Journal of British Studies* 27:172; Beck, *Prisoners of Hate*, x, 13, 26, 69, 157; Ivo Feierabend, Rosalind N. Feierabend, and Ted Robert Gurr, eds., *Anger, Violence and Politics: Theories and Research* (Englewood Cliffs, N.J., 1972), 62–5; Le Fanu, *Seventy Years*, 299; Joseph Rothschild, *Ethnopolitics: A Conceptual Framework* (New York,

1981), 45; Mitchel to Thomson, 1 November 1855, D/249, Mitchel Papers, PRONI; Oliver MacDonagh, *States of Mind: Two Centuries of Anglo-Irish Conflict 1780–1980* (London, 1992), 98; Kevin Nowlan and Maurice O'Connell, *Daniel O'Connell: Portrait of a Radical* (1984), 27; Peter Marsh and Anne Campbell, eds., *Aggression and Violence* (Oxford, 1982), 6–24; J. Bronowski, *The Face of Violence: An Essay with a Play* (London, 1954), 42, 55, 61–2; Ted Honderich, *Three Essays in Political Violence* (Oxford, 1976), ix, 60–1, 109–10; Peter Gay, *The Cultivation of Hatred: The Bourgeois Experience, Victoria to Freud* (New York, 1993), 553; Sean Farrell Moran, *Patrick Pearse and the Politics of Redemption: The Mind of the Easter Rising, 1916* (Washington, D.C., 1994), 92.

42 Thomas MacNevin, ed., *Speeches of the Right Honourable Richard Lalor Sheil* (Dublin, 1865), 59; Kerrigan, *Father Mathew*, 100; Connolly, *Priests and People*, 264–5; Emmet Larkin, trans. and ed., *Alexis de Tocqueville's Journey in Ireland July–August, 1835* (Washington, D.C., 1990), 62–3, 41; Cormac O Grada, *Famine 150* (Dublin, 1997), 67–91; Anne Coleman, *Riotous Roscommon: Social Unrest in the 1840s* (Dublin, 1999), 27; Seamus O'Brien, *Famine and Community in Mullingar Poor Law Union, 1845–1849* (Dublin, 1999), 23–6, 15, 18; Kathleen Villiers-Tuthill, *Patient Endurance: The Great Famine in Connemara* (Dublin, 1997), 32–3; Anton Blok, "The Peasant and the Brigand: Social Banditry Reconsidered," *Comparative Studies in Society and History* 14 (1972): 494–505; *Parl. Deb.*, 3rd ser., 152:232–7; John Saville, *1848: The British State and the Chartist Movement* (Cambridge, 1987), 48; James S. Donnelly Jr, "The Terry Alt Movement 1829–1831," *History Ireland*, Winter, 1994: 35; Robert Sloan, *William Smith O'Brien and the Young Ireland Rebellion of 1848* (Dublin, 2000), 197.

43 O'Hagan to Monsell, 29 May 1862, MIC 562/27, O'Hagan Papers, PRONI; Charles Townshend, *Making the Peace: Public Order and Public Security in Modern Britain* (Oxford, 1993), 24; Stephen Randolph Gibbons, *Captain Rock, Night Errant: The Threatening Letters of Pre-Famine Ireland, 1801–1845* (Dublin, 2004), 10–25, 30–40; Samuel Clark and James S. Donnelly, Jr, *Irish Peasants: Violence and Political Unrest 1780–1914* (Manchester, 1983), 25, 9; Coleman, *Riotous Roscommon*, 54–5; Philpin, *Nationalism and Popular Protest*, 264–80; E. Steele, *Irish Land and British Politics: Tenant-Right and Nationality, 1865–1870* (Cambridge, 1974), 16; Hoppen, *Elections, Politics and Society*, 341–56.

44 Hoppen, *Elections, Politics and Society*, 385; Clark and Donnelly, *Irish Peasants*, 16, 33; Steele, *Irish Land and British Politics*, 23–4; James S. Donnelly and Kerby Miller, eds., *Irish Popular Culture 1650–1850* (Dublin, 1998), 223, 235; Villiers-Tuthill, *Patient Endurance*, 136; O Grada, *Ireland*, 335; D'Arcy, *Irish Historical Studies* 17:228–33, 240–1; John Darby, Nicholas Dodge, and A.C. Hepburn, *Political Violence: Ireland in Comparative Perspective* (Belfast, 1990), 18–19; D.G. Boyce and Roger Swift, eds., *Problems and Perspectives in Irish History since 1800: Essays in Honour of Patrick Buckland* (Dublin, 2004), 54–77.

45 K. Theodore Hoppen, "Grammars of Political Violence in Nineteenth-Century England and Ireland," *English Historical Review* 109 (1994): 610–19; Hoppen, *Elections, Politics and Society*, 388–416; Lawrence McCaffrey, ed., *Irish Nationalism and the American Contribution* (New York, 1976), 426–7.

46 Jim Smyth, *The Men of No Property: Irish Radicals and Popular Politics in the late Eighteenth Century*, pb ed. (London, 1998), 39, 83, 34; Oliver MacDonagh and W.F. Mandle, *Ireland and Irish-Australia: Studies in Cultural and Political History* (London, 1986), 75, 64; Scally, *End of Hidden Ireland*, 12; Gale E. Christianson, "Secret Societies and Agrarian Violence in Ireland, 1790–1840," *Agricultural History* 46 (1972): 369–84; Charles Townshend, *Political Violence in Ireland: Government and Resistance since 1848*, pb. ed. (Oxford, 1984), 20; Maurice O'Connell, ed., *Daniel O'Connell: Political Pioneer*, 41.

47 Marianne Elliott, "The Origins and Transformation of Early Irish Republicanism," *International Review of Social History* 23 (1978): 421; Coleman, *Riotous Roscommon*, 30–49; Philpin, *Nationalism and Popular Protest*, 219–44; M.R. Beames, "The Ribbon Societies: Lower-Class Nationalism in Pre-Famine Ireland," *Past and Present* 97 (1982): 128–43; Michael Beames, "Peasant Disturbances, Popular Conspiracies and Their Control: Ireland, 1798–1852," Ph.D. thesis, University of Manchester (1975), 59, 156–7; Wolfgang J. Mommsen and Gerhard Hirschfeld, eds., *Social Protest, Violence and Terror in Nineteenth-and Twentieth-Century Europe* (London, 1982), 137–42; Fegan, *Literature and the Irish Famine*, 64.

48 Lucas to O'Brien, 25 January 1842, CO 904/9; Memorandum on Ribbonism, CO 904/8; Dublin Metropolitan Police Report, 27 October 1841, CO 904/8; Ray to O'Connell, 15 November 1837, CO 904/7; Beames, "Peasant Disturbances," 157; Haly to Drummond, 20 May 1839, CO 904/7; O'Brien to Drummond, 29 May 1839, CO 904/7.

49 Haly to Drummond, 29 May 1839, CO 904/7; Drummond Memorandum, 19 December 1839, CO 904/7; Memorandum to Lord Roden, n.d., CO 904/7; Matheson to McGloin, 17 December 1840, CO 904/8; Murray to Drummond, 12 March 1837, 9 June 1839, CO 904/7; Lucas to O'Brien, 25 January 1842, CO 904/9.

50 O'Malley to Drummond, 26 May 1839, CO 904/7; Matheson to Drummond, 27 December 1839, CO 904/7; Murray to Lord Lieutenant, 12 July 1839, CO 904/7; Memorandum on Ribbonmen, CO 904/8; Hamilton to Lucas, 10 January 1842, CO 904/9; Lucas to O'Brien, 25 January 1842, CO 904/9; Clarendon to Grey, CO 904/9; Nowlan, *Politics of Repeal*, 228; S.J. Connolly, R.A. Houston, and J.R. Morris, eds., *Conflict, Identity and Economic Development: Ireland and Scotland, 1600–1939* (Preston, 1985), 181–2; Scally, *End of Hidden Ireland*, 84; Le Fanu, *Seventy Years*, 299; Anthony Denholm, *Lord Ripon 1827–1909: A Political Biography* (London, 1982), 172.

51 Ted Robert Gurr, *Why Men Rebel* (Princeton, 1970), 172; David D. Laitin, "National Revivals and Violence," *European Journal of Sociology* 20 (1995): 18, 20, 14–15; Sheldon Hackney, "Southern Violence," *American Historical Review* 74 (1969): 924; Clark and Donnelly, *Irish Peasants*, 10; Mommsen and Hirschfeld, *Social Protest, Violence and Terror*, 142; Pigot to Smith O'Brien, 3 January 1860, MS. 447, Smith O'Brien Papers, NLI.

52 Paul Wilkinson, *Terrorism and the Liberal State*, 2nd ed. (London, 1986), 37; Singer, *History and Theory* 35:312, 324.

CHAPTER FIVE

1 *Times*, 31 January 1867; Patrick Maume, "Young Ireland, Arthur Griffith, and Republican Ideology: The Question of Continuity," *Eire/Ireland* 34 (1999): 160.

2 John Denvir, *The Life Story of an Old Rebel*, reprint ed. (Shannon, 1972), 62; James E. Thorold Rogers, ed., *Speeches on Questions of Public Policy by John Bright, M.P.*, 2 vols. (London, 1868), 1:356; *Times*, 6 November 1866; Pigot to Smith O'Brien, 4 September 1860; Smith O'Brien to Cork Reading Room, 20 October 1860, Smith O'Brien Papers, MS 447, NLI; Per Bauhn, *Nationalism and Morality* (Lund, 1995), 56; Charles P. Cozic, ed., *Nationalism and Ethnic Conflict* (San Diego, 1994), 119; Adolphe Perraud, *Ireland in 1862* (Dublin, 1863), 271.

3 See Leslie Page Moch, *Moving Europeans: Migration in Western Europe since 1650* (Bloomington, 1992); Maldwyn A. Jones, "The Background to Emigration from Great Britain in the Nine-

teenth Century," *Perspectives in American History* 7 (1973): 3–77; Charlotte Erickson, "Emigration from the British Isles to the U.S.A. in 1831," *Population Studies* 35 (1981): 178, 196; Charlotte Erickson, ed., *Emigration from Europe 1815–1914* (London, 1976), 10; Dudley Baines, *Emigration from Europe 1815–1930* (London, 1991), 11, 14, 33, 44; Dudley Baines, "European Emigration, 1815–1930: Looking at the Emigration Decision Again," *Economic History Review* 47 (1994): 525–44; Peter Dunkley, "Emigration and the State, 1803–1842: The Nineteenth Century Revolution in Government Reconsidered," *Historical Journal* 23 (1980): 353–80; William E. Van Vugt, "Running from Ruin? The Emigration of British Farmers to the U.S.A. in the wake of the Repeal of the Corn Laws," *Economic History Review*, 2nd ser., 41 (1988): 411–28; William E. Van Vugt, "Prosperity and Industrial Emigration from Britain during the early 1850s," *Journal of Social History* 22 (1988–89): 339–54; Raymond L. Cohn, "Occupational Evidence on the Cause of Immigration to the United States, 1836–1853," *Explorations in Economic History* 32 (1995): 383–408.

4 Leo Grinberg and Rebecca Grinberg, *Psychoanalytic Perspectives on Migration and Exile* (New Haven, 1989), 2, 8–9, 15, 17–18, 26–7, 63, 157–9; Perraud, *Ireland in 1862*, 241; MacDonagh, *Irish Historical Studies* 5:289–93; Cullen to Kenrick, 19 April 1852, 28-T-3, Kenrick Papers, AAB.

5 Jones, *Perspectives in American History*, 7:77–82; William E. Van Vugt, "Welsh Emigration to the U.S.A. during the Mid-Nineteenth Century," *Welsh Historical Review* 15 (1990–91): 545–61; Alan Conway, "Welsh Emigration to the United States," *Perspectives in American History* 7 (1973): 178, 193, 207, 266–71.

6 Malcolm Gray, "Scottish Emigration: The Social Impact of Agrarian Change in the Rural Lowlands, 1775–1875," *Perspectives in American History* 7 (1973): 95–174; Jones, *Perspectives in American History* 7:82–90; Eric Richards, *A History of Highland Clearances*, vol. 2: *Emigration, Protest, Reasons* (London, 1985), 181; James Hunter, *A Dance Called America: The Scottish Highlands the United States and Canada* (Edinburgh, 1994), 40; Marjorie Harper, *Emigration from North-East Scotland*, vol. 1: *Willing Exiles* (Aberdeen, 1988), 7; Marianne McLean, "Peopling Glengarry County: The Scottish Origins of a Canadian Community," *Historical Papers* (Montreal: Canadian Historical Association, 1982), 165.

7 T.M. Devine, *The Great Highland Famine: Hunger, Emigration and the Scottish Highlands in the Nineteenth Century* (Edinburgh,

1988), 197; T.M. Devine, *The Scottish Nation 1700–2000* (London, 1999), 471, 479, 483–4, 191; T.M. Devine, *Clanship to Crofters' War: The Social Transformation of the Scottish Highlands* (Edinburgh, 1994), 177–83; James Hunter, *The Making of the Crofting Community* (Edinburgh, 1976), 15, 26; Richards, *History of Highland Clearances*, 2: 7, 49, 53.

8 Richards, *History of Highland Clearances*, 2:192, 211, 217, 233, 249, 250, 252, 264–5; Hunter, *Dance Called America*, 107–12; Hunter, *Making of the Crofter Community*, 37–8, 41, 50; Harper, *Emigration from North-East Scotland*, 1:8, 17; P.M. Toner, ed., *New Ireland Remembered: Essays on the Irish in New Brunswick* (Frederickton, 1988), 15.

9 Hunter, *Making of the Crofter Community*, 54; Devine, *Clanship to Crofters' War*, 158–9, 164, 170; Devine, *Great Highland Famine*, 100–1.

10 Devine, *Clanship to Crofters' War*, 148–56; Devine, *Scottish Nation*, 414–15; Devine, *Great Highland Famine*, 111–23, 196.

11 Richards, *History of Highland Clearances*, 2:301, 321, 335–6, 267–9; Devine, *Clanship to Crofters' War*, 210, 187–91; Devine, *Scottish Nation*, 418–20, 264; Devine, *Great Highland Famine*, 72–4, 176–99, 217–18, 223, 200, 202; Harper, *Emigration from North-East Scotland*, 1:18; Hunter, *Making of the Crofter Community*, 81–2; Hunter, *Dance Called America*, 132; Perraud, *Ireland in 1862*, 221; Catherine Kerngain, ed., *The Immigrant Experience* (Guelph, 1992), 15; W. Stanford Reid, ed., *The Scottish Tradition in Canada* (Toronto, 1976), 93–110, 239; Reginald Coupland, *Welsh and Scottish Nationalism: A Study* (London, 1954), 251, 279; Terrence Murphy and Gerald Stortz, eds., *Creed and Culture: The Place of English-Speaking Catholics in Canadian Society, 1750–1930* (Montreal and Kingston, 1993), 81.

12 David Mills, *The Idea of Loyalty in Upper Canada 1784–1850* (Montreal and Kingston, 1988), 130, 133–4.

13 *Times*, 11 December 1866; Robert S. Fortner, "The Culture of Hope and the Culture of Despair: The Print Media and 19th-Century Irish Emigration," *Eire/Ireland* 13(1978):33, 39; Gerard Moran, *Sending Out Ireland's Poor: Assisted Emigration to North America in the Nineteenth Century* (Dublin, 2004), 17; Erickson, *Population Studies* 35:182, 188; Vaughan, *Ireland under the Union* 1:565, 575–6; Kerby A. Miller, *Emigrants and Exiles: Ireland and the Irish Exodus to North America* (New York, 1985), 137, 193–8, 200, 226, 248, 258, 274; Wendy Cameron, "Selecting Peter Robinson's Irish Emigrants," *Histoire Sociale/Social History* 9 (1976): 29–46; Joel Mokyr and Cormac

O Grada, "Emigration and Poverty in Prefamine Ireland," *Explorations in Economic History* 19 (1982): 360–84; Raymond L. Cohn, "Occupational Evidence on the Causes of Immigration to the United States, 1836–1853," *Explorations in Economic History* 32 (1995): 391, 395, 402–4.

14 Miller, *Emigrants and Exiles*, 280–97; David A. Wilson, *The Irish in Canada* (Saint John, 1989), 7; Oliver MacDonagh, "The Irish Famine Emigration to the United States," *Perspectives in American History* 10 (1976): 418, 421, 423, 426, 429; Donald Harman Akenson, *Irish Diaspora: A Primer* (Toronto, 1993), 20, 47; Maldwyn A. Jones, *Destination America* (New York, 1976), 69, 71–2; Donald MacKay, *Flight from Famine: The Coming of the Irish to Canada* (Toronto, 1990), 281; Cormac O Grada, *Ireland: A New Economic History, 1780–1939* (Oxford, 1994), 177; Margaret Crawford, ed., *The Hungry Stream: Essays on Emigration and Famine* (Belfast, 1997), 77, 79, 88, 92; Vaughan, *Ireland under the Union* 1: 577, 587; Moran, *Sending Out Ireland's Poor*, 38–9, 45, 48, 54, 63, 59.

15 Twenty-Seventh General Report of the Emigration Commissioners, 29 April 1867, *British Parliamentary Papers: Emigration*, vol. 17 (Shannon, 1969), 1–9; *Times*, 11 December 1866; MacDonagh, *Perspectives in American History* 10:394, 402; Toner, *New Ireland Remembered*, 17; Thomas P. Power, ed., *The Irish in Atlantic Canada 1780–1900* (Frederickton, 1991), 125.

16 Edward Laxton, *The Famine Ships: The Irish Exodus to America 1846–51* (New York, 1996), 7; MacKay, *Flight from Famine*, 215; David Hollett, *Passage to the New World: Packet Ships and Irish Famine Emigrants 1845–1851* (Abergavenny, 1995), 121–2, 145, 176; Joseph Robins, *The Miasma: Epidemic and Panic in Nineteenth Century Ireland* (Dublin, 1995), 159; Robert Scally, "Liverpool Ships and Irish Emigrants in the Age of Sail," *Journal of Social History* 17 (1983–84): 5–30; Vaughan, *Ireland under the Union*, 1: 582, 588; Robert O'Driscoll and Lorna Reynolds, eds., *The Untold Story: The Irish in Canada*, 2 vols. (Toronto, 1988), 1:155–69, xx; Daly, *Irish Historical Studies* 30:598; Patrick O'Sullivan, ed., *The Meaning of the Famine* (London, 1997), 81; Terry Coleman, *Going to America* (New York, 1972), 134–5; Raymond L. Cohn, "The Determinants of Individual Mortality on Sailing Ships, 1836–1853," *Explorations in Economic History* 24 (1987): 371–91; Raymond L. Cohn, "Mortality on Immigrant Voyages to New York, 1836–1853," *Journal of Economic History* 44 (1984): 289–300.

17 MacKay, *Flight from Famine*, 284, 290, 296; Minutes of Evidence before the select committee of the House of Lords on colonization from Ireland, Second Report, 4 August 1848, *British Parliamentary Papers: Emigration*, vol. 5 (Shannon, 1969), 286, 338–9; Coleman, *Going to America*, 153; Cecil Houston and William J. Smyth, *Irish Emigration and Canadian Settlement: Patterns, Links, and Letters* (Toronto, 1990), 27, 25, 73; *British Parliamentary Papers*, vol. 17: 47; William M. Nolte, "The Irish in Canada, 1815–1867," Ph.D thesis, 1975, University of Maryland, iii-iv.

18 O'Driscoll and Reynolds, *Untold Story*, 1:30, 17, 178, 197, 206; Wilson, *Irish in Canada*, 11, 13; Nolte, "Irish in Canada," 76; Houston and Smyth, *Irish Emigration and Canadian Settlement*, 4, 8, 127, 188, 204, 17; Power, *Irish in Atlantic Canada*, 86–8.

19 O'Driscoll and Reynolds, *Untold Story*, 1:203–5; Peter McGuigan, "From Wexford and Monaghan: The Lot 22 Irish," *Abegweit Review* 5 (1985): 63, 65; Brendan O'Grady, "The Heritage of New Ireland," *Abegweit Review* 5:99–100; G. Kevin Farmer, "Making Community in Kinkora," *Abegweit Review* 5:52; Power, *Irish in Atlantic Canada*, 97–103; Brendan O'Grady, "Where Were the Irish in 1864?" *Abegweit Review* 6 (1988): 157–8, 162–3; Peter McGuigan, "The Lot 61 Irish: Settlement and Stabilization," *Abegweit Review* 6:34, 41–3.

20 O'Driscoll and Reynolds, *Untold Story*, 1:28–30, 215–24; Terrence Murphy, "The Emergence of Maritime Catholicism, 1781–1830," *Acadiensis* 13 (1984): 31.

21 Leo J. Hynes, *Catholic Irish in New Brunswick, 1783–1900* (Moncton, 1992), 161; MacKay, *Flight from Famine*, 154, 158–9, 162; Toner, *New Ireland Remembered*, 113–14, 123, 128, 10–11, 15; *British Parliamentary Papers, Emigration*, 5:126, 129–30.

22 Houston and Smyth, *Irish Emigration and Canadian Settlement*, 205, 189, 210; Nolte, "Irish in Canada," 142, 148, 154–5; Donald H. Akenson, *The Irish in Ontario: A Study in Rural History* (Kingston, 1984), 15, 27; Gerald Tulchinsky, ed., *Immigration in Canada: Historical Perspectives* (Toronto, 1994), 103, 112; Herbert J. Mays, "'A Place to Stand': Families, Land and Permanence in Toronto Gore Township, 1820–1890," *Historical Papers* (Montreal: Canadian Historical Association, 1980): 193–5; J.K. Johnson and Bruce G. Wilson, eds., *Historical Essays on Upper Canada: New Perspectives* (Ottawa, 1989), 217; Pauline Ryan, "A Study of Irish Immigration to North Hastings County," *Ontario History* 83 (1991): 32; O'Driscoll and Reynolds, *Untold Story*, 1:374–5.

23 Akenson, *Irish in Ontario*, 42, 46; Johnson and Wilson, *Historical Essays on Upper Canada*, 264; Kenneth Duncan, "Irish Famine Immigration and the Social Structure of Canada West," *Canadian Review of Sociology and Anthropology* 2 (1965): 25; Philip Currie, "Reluctant Britons: The Toronto Irish, Home Rule, and the Great War," *Ontario History* 87 (1995): 66; Nolte, "Irish in Canada," 166–7; O'Driscoll and Reynolds, *Untold Story*, 1: 66–7; Brian P. Clarke, *Piety and Nationalism: Lay Voluntary Associations and the Creation of an Irish Catholic Community in Toronto, 1850–1895* (Montreal, 1993), 16–17, 25; Murray W. Nicolson, "Ecclesiastical Metropolitanism and the Evolution of the Catholic Diocese of Toronto," *Histoire Sociale/Social History* 15 (1982): 142; Michael B. Katz, *The People of Hamilton, Canada West: Family and Class in a Mid-Nineteenth Century City* (Cambridge, Mass., 1975), 26–7, 62, 64–5, 68, 173, 110.

24 O'Driscoll and Reynolds, *Untold Story*, 1:263–4, 255–7; Houston and Smyth, *Irish Emigration and Canadian Settlement*, 210–11, 215, 228; Nolte, "Irish in Canada," 81, 88, 93, 95, 116, 119, 126; David de Brou, "The Rose, the Shamrock and the Cabbage: The Battle for Irish Votes in Upper-Town Quebec, 1827–1836," *Histoire sociale/Social History* 24 (1991): 321.

25 Terence J. Fay, *A History of Canadian Catholics: Gallicanism, Romanism, and Canadianism* (Montreal and Kingston, 2002), 35–6; John P. Greene, *Between Damnation and Starvation: Priests and Merchants in Newfoundland Politics, 1745–1855* (Montreal and Kingston, 1999), 270; Terrence Murphy and Cyril J. Byrne, eds., *Religion and Identity: The Experience of Irish and Scottish Catholics in Atlantic Canada* (St John's, 1987), 39; O'Driscoll and Reynolds, *Untold Story*, 1:178, 225–6; O'Grady, *Abegweit Review*, 5:59; Toner, *New Ireland Remembered*, 53, 23, 72–4; Akenson, *Irish in Ontario*, 271; Nolte, "Irish in Canada," 103, 195, 197; MacKay, *Flight from Famine*, 296, 146–7; Murphy and Stortz, *Creed and Culture*, 28–9, 4.

26 Power, *Irish in Atlantic Canada*, 117; Nolte, "Irish in Canada," 61–2, 64; Ryan, *Ontario History* 83:25; G.J. Parr, "The Welcome and the Wake, Attitudes in Canada West toward the Irish Famine Migration," *Ontario History* 66 (1974): 107.

27 Parr, *Ontario History* 66:103–5, 109–10; Houston and Smyth, *Irish Emigration and Canadian Settlement*, 62–3; Mark George McGowan and Brian P. Clarke, eds., *Catholics at the 'Gathering Place': Historical Essays on the Archdiocese of Toronto 1841–1991* (Toronto, 1993), 1; Ryan, *Ontario History* 83: 26–30.

28 Clarke, *Piety and Nationalism*, 29; Frances Morehouse, "Canadian Migration in the Forties," *Canadian Historical Review* 9 (1928): 325; MacKay, *Flight from Famine*, 114, 118, 162; Power, *Irish in Atlantic Canada*, 21, 112; Parr, *Ontario History* 66:113; O'Driscoll and Reynolds, *Untold Story*, 1:330, 206; John Weaver, "Crime, Public Order, and Repression: The Gore District in Upheaval, 1832–1851," *Ontario History* 78 (1986): 198; Duncan, *Canadian Review of Sociology and Anthropology* 2:32; Bishop Lynch to Clergy of Ireland, 1864, LAE 06.01, Lynch Papers, Archives of the Archdiocese of Toronto (AAT).

29 Power, *Irish in Atlantic Canada*, 16–20; Toner, *New Ireland Remembered*, 79; Katz, *People of Hamilton*, 68; Clarke, *Piety and Nationalism*, 28; Lynch to Clergy of Ireland, 1864, LAE 06.01, Lynch Papers, AAT; Weaver, *Ontario History* 78:191, 177; Harvey J. Graff, "'Pauperism, Misery, and Vice': Illiteracy and Criminality in the Nineteenth Century," *Journal of Social History* 11 (1978): 246–7, 257–9; O'Grady, *Abegweit Review* 5:109; James M. Clemens, "Taste Not; Touch Not; Handle Not: A Study of the Social Assumptions of Temperance Literature and Temperance Supporters in Canada West between 1839 and 1859," *Ontario History* 64 (1972): 142–60; Lynch to Bishop of Minnesota, 2 May 1864, AE 06.02, Lynch Papers, AAT.

30 O'Driscoll and Reynolds, *Untold Story*, 1:176, 182, 196, 211, 268, 338; MacKay, *Flight from Famine*, 162; Toner, *New Ireland Remembered*, 25, 55, 57; Hynes, *Catholic Irish in New Brunswick*, 223; Nolte, "Irish in Canada," 83–4, 103–4; Peter Wray, *Common Labour: Workers and the Digging of North American Canals 1780–1860* (Cambridge, 1993), 246–7; Johnson and Wilson, *Historical Essays on Upper Canada*, 261, 268; Michael S. Cross, "The Shiners' War: Social Violence in the Ottawa Valley in the 1830s," *Canadian Historical Review* 54 (1973): 1–26; Duncan, *Canadian Review of Sociology and Anthropology* 2:24, 29, 39; Weaver, *Ontario History* 78:182, 186, 189.

31 O'Driscoll and Reynolds, *Untold Story*, 1: 177, 179, 218–19, 221, 223; Murphy and Stortz, *Creed and Culture*, 52, 54; Power, *Irish in Atlantic Canada*, 28, 14; Toner, *New Ireland Remembered*, 29, 1; Nolte, "Irish in Canada," v, 170.

32 Power, *Irish in Atlantic Canada*, 60, 10–11; MacKay, *Flight from Famine*, 26; Toner, *New Ireland Remembered*, 31–2, 56, 115, 2, 4–5; Houston and Smyth, *Irish Emigration and Canadian Settlement*, 57, 79; O'Driscoll and Reynolds, *Untold Story*, 1:326, 222–3, 269, 234, 266–9; Clarke, *Piety and Nationalism*, 24, 129, 131; McGowan and Clarke, *Catholics at the 'Gathering Place,'*

20; Farmer, *Abegweit Review* 5:69, 53; Nolte, "Irish in Canada," 103, 124, 173, 175; O'Grady, *Abegweit Review* 6:157.

33 O'Driscoll and Reynolds, *Untold Story*, 1: 178, 223; Murphy and Stortz, *Creed and Culture*, 111, 85; Murphy and Byrne, *Religion and Identity*, 31; Toner, *New Ireland Remembered*, 64–9, 53; O'Grady, *Abegweit Review* 5:110; Terrence Murphy, "The Emergence of Maritime Catholicism, 1780–1830," *Acadiensis* 13 (1984): 29–49; Power, *Irish in Atlantic Canada*, 11, 91; Houston and Smyth, *Irish Emigration and Canadian Settlement*, 169.

34 Murray W. Nicolson, "The Catholic Church and the Irish in Victorian Toronto," Ph.D. thesis, 1980, University of Guelph, 5, 160; Nolte, "Irish in Canada," 109, 111, 125, 119, 92, 112; Robert Choquette, *L'Église catholique dans l'Ontario français du dix-neuvième siecle* (Ottawa, 1984), 29–30; O'Driscoll and Reynolds, *Untold Story*, 1:258–9, 266–8, 297; Houston and Smyth, *Irish Emigration and Canadian Settlement*, 174–5.

35 Fay, *History of Canadian Catholics*, 39, 50; John Webster Grant, *A Profusion of Spires: Religion in Nineteenth Century Ontario* (Toronto, 1988), 27–8, 38–9, 43–4, 81; Nolte, "Irish in Canada," 129; Franklin A. Walker, *Catholic Education and Politics in Upper Canada* (Toronto, 1955), 21; McGowan and Clarke, *Catholics at the 'Gathering Place,'* 27.

36 Murray Nicolson, "Ecclesiastical Metropolitanism and the Evolution of the Catholic Diocese of Toronto," *Histoire Sociale/Social History* 15 (1982): 133–5, 144–5; Grant, *A Profusion of Spires*, 81; Choquette, *L'Église catholique*, 38, 41; McGowan and Clarke, *Catholics at the 'Gathering Place,'* 23–40; Houston and Smyth, *Irish Emigration and Canadian Settlement*, 175; Akenson, *Irish in Ontario*, 229.

37 Grant, *A Profusion of Spires*, 119; Murphy and Stortz, *Creed and Culture*, 154; Choquette, *L'Église catholique*, 50, 107–15, 101, 20; Mark G. McGowan, *Michael Power: The Struggle to Build the Catholic Church on the Canadian Frontier* (Montreal and Kingston, 2005), 3, 12, 212; Houston and Smyth, *Irish Emigration and Canadian Settlement*, 175, 173; Michael S. Cross, "Stony Monday, 1849: The Rebellion Losses Riots in Bytown," *Ontario History* 63 (1971): 178; Nolte, "Irish in Canada," 174–5, 261; Thomas Gerald John Stortz, "John Joseph Lynch, Archbishop of Toronto: A Biographical Study of Religious, Political and Social Commitment," Ph.D. thesis, 1980, University of Guelph, 6; Nicolson, *Histoire Sociale/Social History* 15:137, 139; Clarke, *Piety and Nationalism*, 8; McGowan and Clarke, *Catholics at the 'Gathering Place,'* 73, 77–9.

38 McGowan and Clarke, *Catholics at the 'Gathering Place,'* 6, 20, 43–4, 76, 90; McGowan, *Michael Power*, 261; Clarke, *Piety and Nationalism*, 13, 49, 90, 127, 138; Nicolson, *Histoire Sociale/Social History* 15:136–7, 146, 149; O'Driscoll and Reynolds, *Untold Story*, 2:778, 760–1, 766, 769, 854, 772.

39 O'Driscoll and Reynolds, *Untold Story*, 2:759; Murray W. Nicolson, "The Catholic Church and the Irish in Victorian Toronto," Ph.D. thesis, 1980, University of Guelph, 364; Walker, *Catholic Education and Politics*, 33, 22–3; Murray W. Nicolson, "Irish Catholic Education in Victorian Toronto: An Ethnic Response to Urban Conformity," *Histoire Sociale/Social History* 17 (1984): 292–5; Clarke, *Piety and Nationalism*, 40.

40 Murphy, *Acadiensis* 13:41; O'Driscoll and Reynolds, *Untold Story*, 2:815, 819, 821, 791–6; Murphy and Stortz, *Creed and Culture*, 127; Frederick Jones, "Bishops in Politics: Roman Catholic v Protestant in Newfoundland, 1860–2," *Canadian Historical Review* 55 (1974): 408–21; Fay, *History of Canadian Catholics*, 82–4; Murphy and Byrne, *Religion and Identity*, 81–94; Greene, *Between Damnation and Starvation*, 273.

41 McGowan and Clarke, *Catholics at the 'Gathering Place,'* 54–7; O'Driscoll and Reynolds, *Untold Story*, 1:257–60; G.R.C. Keep, "The Irish Adjustment in Montreal," *Canadian Historical Review* 31 (1950): 42; Choquette, *L'Église catholique*, 106; Walker, *Catholic Education and Politics*, 47–51, 68, 139, 163, 169; O'Grady, *Abegweit Review* 6:157.

42 Clarke, *Piety and Nationalism*, 41, 31; Mills, *Idea of Loyalty in Upper Canada*, 52, 57; Walker, *Catholic Education and Politics*, 56–9, 148; Akenson, *Irish in Ontario*, 16, 270–1, 275, 277; Nicolson, *Histoire Sociale/Social History* 17:287, 295; Graff, *Journal of Social History* 11:245–6, 253; Nicolson, "The Catholic Church and the Irish in Victorian Toronto," 378; Nolte, "Irish in Canada," 172, 175; Toner, *New Ireland Remembered*, 38–9; Ian Ross Robertson, "Party Politics and Religious Controversialism in Prince Edward Island from 1860 to 1863," *Acadiensis* 7 (1978): 55; William M. Baker, *Timothy Warren Anglin 1822–96: Irish Catholic Canadian* (Toronto, 1977), 18.

43 John S. Moir, *Church and State in Canada West: Three Studies in the Relation of Denominationalism and Nationalism, 1841–1867* (Toronto, 1959), 152, 12–13; Wilson, *Irish in Canada*, 16; McGowan and Clarke, *Catholics at the 'Gathering Place,'* 20, 53; Walker, *Catholic Education and Politics*, 164–5; Toner, *New Ireland Remembered*, 53; William Westfall, *Two Worlds: The*

Protestant Culture of Nineteenth-Century Ontario (Montreal and Kingston, 1989), 10–11, 106, 123, 22.

44 Grant, *A Profusion of Spires*, 127–8; for an analysis of anti-Catholicism, see J.R. Miller, "Anti-Catholic Thought in Victorian Canada," *Canadian Historical Review* 66 (1985): 474–94; J.R. Miller, "Bigotry in the North Atlantic Triangle: Irish, British and American Influences on Canadian Anti-Catholicism, 1850–1900," *Studies in Religion* 16 (1987): 293; Murphy and Stortz, *Creed and Culture*, 31–4; Walker, *Catholic Education and Politics*, 82; Moir, *Church and State in Canada West*, 17–19.

45 Hereward Senior, "The Genesis of Canadian Orangeism," *Ontario History* 60 (1968): 13–14; H. Senior, "Ogle Gowan, Orangeism, and the Immigrant Question 1830–1833," *Ontario History* 66 (1974): 193–5; Patrick O'Sullivan, ed., *Irish World Wide History, Heritage, Identity*, vol. 5: *Religion and Identity* (London, 1996), 48; Moir, *Church and State in Canada West*, 17; Clarke, *Piety and Nationalism*, 43–4; Duncan, *Canadian Review of Sociology and Anthropology* 2:27; McGowan and Clarke, *Catholics at the 'Gathering Place,'* 15; O'Driscoll and Reynolds, *Untold Story*, 2:792, 838–40; Robertson, *Acadiensis* 7:57; O'Grady, *Abegweit Review* 6:165; Toner, *New Ireland Remembered*, 43; Cross, *Ontario History* 63:179; Victor L. Russell, ed., *Forging a Consensus: Historical Essays on Toronto* (Toronto, 1984), 76; Tulchinsky, *Immigration in Canada*, 120; Cecil J. Houston and William J. Smyth, "Transferred Loyalties: Orangeism in the United States and Ontario," *American Review of Canadian Studies* 14 (1984): 196–7; Cecil J. Houston and William J. Smyth, *The Sash Canada Wore: A Historical Geography of the Orange Order in Canada* (Toronto, 1980), 143.

46 Akenson, *Irish in Ontario*, 280–1; Ryan, *Ontario History* 83:32; Robertson, *Acadiensis* 7:57; McGuigan, *Abegweit Review* 6:45–6; O'Grady, *Abegweit Review* 6:165–6; MacKay, *Flight from Famine*, 172; O'Driscoll and Reynolds, *Untold Story*, 2:xiii; Walker, *Catholic Education and Politics*, 224; Nolte, "Irish in Canada," 271; Franca Iacovelta and Paula Draper, eds., *A Nation of Immigrants: Women, Workers and Communities in Canadian History, 1840–1860s* (Toronto, 1998), 38; Houston and Smyth, *The Sash Canada Wore*, 27–8; Russell, *Forging a Consensus*, 51–4; O'Driscoll and Reynolds, *Untold Story*, 2:841.

47 Kenneth McNaught, "Violence in Canadian History," in John S. Moir, ed., *Character and Circumstance: Essays in Honor of Donald Grant Creighton* (Toronto, 1970), 66–84; Cross, *Ontario History* 63:182; Duncan, *Canadian Review of Sociology and*

Anthropology 2:29; Moir, *Church and State in Canada West*, 19–21; Houston and Smyth, *The Sash Canada Wore*, 149, 49–54; Nolte, "Irish in Canada," 277–9; O'Driscoll and Reynolds, *Untold Story*, 2:794; Clarke, *Piety and Nationalism*, 154; MacKay, *Flight from Famine*, 307; Russell, *Forging a Consensus*, 57, 65, 71.

48 O'Driscoll and Reynolds, *Untold Story*, 2:842–3; Russell, *Forging a Consensus*, 42; Toner, *New Ireland Remembered*, 47; Scott W. See, "The Orange Order and Social Violence in Mid-Nineteenth Century St. John," *Acadiensis* 13 (1984): 68, 77, 81; Scott W. See, "'Mickeys and Demons' v. 'Bigots and Boobies': The Woodstock Riot of 1847," *Acadiensis* 21 (1991): 110–31; Scott W. See, *Riots in New Brunswick: Orange Nativism and Social Violence in the 1840s* (Toronto, 1993), 56, 64–5, 75, 88–9, 21, 191; Gordon M. Winder, "Trouble in the North End: The Geography of Social Violence in St. John, 1840–1860," *Acadiensis* 29 (2000): 47, 56; Murray Barkley, "The Loyalist Tradition in New Brunswick: The Growth and Evolution of an Historical Myth, 1825–1914," *Acadiensis* 4 (1975): 12–20.

49 Clarke, *Piety and Nationalism*, 41; Paul O'Leary, *Immigration and Integration: The Irish in Wales, 1798–1922* (Cardiff, 2000), 113; Gale Stokes, "Cognition and the Function of Nationalism," *Journal of Interdisciplinary History* 4 (1974): 525, 530, 536, 539; O'Driscoll and Reynolds, *Untold Story*, 2:871; Johnson and Wilson, *Historical Essays on Upper Canada*, 271–2; Greene, *Between Damnation and Starvation*, 57; Murphy and Byrne, *Religion and Identity*, 81, 86; McGowan, *Michael Power*, 232; Nicolson, "The Catholic Church and the Irish in Victorian Toronto," 160.

50 Clarke, *Piety and Nationalism*, 41, 160–1; Nicolson, *Histoire Sociale/Social History* 17:296, 298, 300, 304, 299; McGowan and Clarke, *Catholics at the 'Gathering Place,'* 54, 58; O'Driscoll and Reynolds, *Untold Story*, 2:609–16, 811–14; McGowan, *Michael Power*, 210, 231–2; Keep, *Canadian Historical Review*, 31:41.

51 Nicolson, "The Catholic Church and the Irish in Victorian Toronto," 160, 175; McGowan, *Michael Power*, 233–4, 247; McGowan and Clarke, *Catholics at the 'Gathering Place,'* 43–4; Kenneth Moss, "St. Patrick's Day Celebrations and the Formation of Irish-American Identity, 1845–1875," *Journal of Social History* 29 (1995): 130–1, 142; see also Michael Cottrell, "St. Patrick's Day Parades in Nineteenth-Century Toronto: A Study of Immigrant Adjustment and Elite Control," in Iacovelta and Draper, *Nation of Immigrants*, 35–54.

52 David De Brou, "The Rose, the Shamrock and the Cabbage: The Battle for Irish Voters in Upper-Town Quebec, 1827–1836," *Histoire Sociale/Social History* 24:316–17, 323–4; Nolte, "Irish in Canada," 195, 207, 210–11, 224–9, 231, 234–7, 239; O'Driscoll and Reynolds, *Untold Story*, 1:257–8, 2: 816; Hereward Senior, *The Fenians and Canada* (Toronto, 1974), 17.

53 Fay, *History of Canadian Catholics*, 75; McGowan, *Michael Power*, 96; Allen Greer and Ian Radforth, eds., *Colonial Leviathan: State Formation in Mid-Nineteenth Century Canada* (Toronto, 1992), 58–9; Ramsay Cook, *Canada, Quebec, and the Uses of Nationalism*, 2nd ed. (Toronto, 1995), 87–90; O'Driscoll and Reynolds, *Untold Story*, 1:297–300; Nolte, "Irish in Canada," 109, 111.

54 Tulchinsky, *Immigration in Canada*, 97; Wilson, *Irish in Canada*, 20; Clarke, *Piety and Nationalism*, 43; Currie, *Ontario History* 87:65; O'Driscoll and Reynolds, *Untold Story*, 2:816; Power, *Irish in Atlantic Canada*, 91, 25, 11, 27; Toner, *New Ireland Remembered*, 65–8, 4, 59, 36; O'Driscoll and Reynolds, *Untold Story*, 1:177; Connolly to Lynch, 12 March 1866, Lynch Papers, AE 02.14, AAT.

55 Arthur G. Doughty, ed., *Elgin-Grey Correspondence 1846–1852*, 4 vols. (Ottawa, 1937), 1:144–5, 149, 265; 4:1479; 2:411; O'Driscoll and Reynolds, *Untold Story*, 2:817–18.

56 O'Driscoll and Reynolds, *Untold Story*, 1:466; Currie, *Ontario History* 87:65–6; O'Driscoll and Reynolds, *Untold Story*, 2:821, 796, 800, 759, 764, 778; Clarke, *Piety and Nationalism*, 161; Nolte, "Irish in Canada," 261; Nicolson, *Histoire Sociale/Social History* 15:146.

57 Clarke, *Piety and Nationalism*, 11, 161–3; McGowan and Clarke, *Catholics at the 'Gathering Place,'* 44–5; Michael Cottrell, "Irish Catholic Political Leadership in Toronto, 1855–1882: A Study in Ethnic Politics," Ph. D. thesis, 1988, University of Saskatchewan, 155; Russell, *Forging a Consensus*, 75.

58 O'Driscoll and Reynolds, *Untold Story*, 1:xviii, 453–61, 465–73, 481–3; Michael Brown, Patrick M. Geoghegan, James Kelly, eds., *The Irish Act of Union, 1800: Bicentennial Essays* (Dublin, 2003), 22; Keep, *Canadian Historical Review* 31:42, 46; Currie, *Ontario History* 87:67; Nolte, "Irish in Canada," 150.

59 Baker, *Timothy Warren Anglin*, 9–10, 16, 24, 35–6, 4–5, 15, 21, 37, 46–9, 58; O'Driscoll and Reynolds, *Untold Story*, 1:60–1, 481–5.

60 Baker, *Anglin*, 46; Toner, *New Ireland Remembered*, 66–7; Connolly to Lynch, 12 March 1866, Lynch Papers, AE 02.14, AAT;

See, *Riots in New Brunswick*, 194; Murphy and Byrne, *Religion and Identity*, 114–25.

61 O'Driscoll and Reynolds, *Untold Story*, 1:510–11; Thomas Gerald John Storz, "John Joseph Lynch Archbishop of Toronto: A Biographical Study of Religious, Political and Social Commitment," Ph.D. thesis, 1980, University of Guelph.

62 Currie, *Ontario History* 87:68; Storz, "John Joseph Lynch," 204; Lynch to Barnabo, 29 September 1864, AE 06.03; Lynch to Leahy, 8 October 1864, AE 07.06, Lynch Papers, AAT.

63 Lynch to Leahy, 8 October 1864, AE 07.06; Lynch to Barnabo, 29 September 1864, AE 06.03; Lynch to Archbishop (unidentified), 7 June 1864, AE 07.04; Lynch Papers, AAT; Gerald J. Stortz, ed., "Archbishop Lynch's *The Evils of Wholesale and Improvident Emigration from Ireland* (1864)," *Eire/Ireland* 18 (1983): 7; Lynch to the Clergy of Ireland Only, [1864], AE 06.01; Lynch to Crawford, 23 December 1864, AE 06.05, Lynch Papers, AAT.

64 Storz, "John Joseph Lynch," 23; Lynch to The Clergy of Ireland Only, [1864], AE 06.01, Lynch Papers, AAT; McGowan and Clarke, *Catholics at the 'Gathering Place,'* 48; Clarke, *Piety and Nationalism*, 164–5; Cottrell, "Irish Political Leadership in Toronto," 168; Iacovelta et al., *Nation of Immigrants*, 35–6, 43; O'Driscoll and Reynolds, *Untold Story*, 2:874; *Irish Canadian*, 30 March 1864.

65 George Sheppard, "'God Save the Green,' Fenianism and Fellowship in Victorian Ontario," *Histoire Sociale/Social History* 20 (1987): 131; Northgraves to Lynch, 19 November 1863, AE 02.01, Lynch papers, AAT; O'Driscoll and Reynolds, *Untold Story*, 2:802–4; *Irish Canadian*, 4, 18 March, 11 November 1863, 25 May, 23 November, 1864, 23 August 1865; Nicolson, "The Catholic Church and the Irish in Victorian Toronto," 180, 183; Murphy and Byrne, *Religion and Identity*, 120.

CHAPTER SIX

1 W.E. Vaughan, ed., *A New History of Ireland*, vol. 6: *Ireland under the Union, 1:1801–1870* (Oxford, 1989), 354; Robert Toombs, "Emigrants to America," *Broadway Annual* 1868: 437–44; Bruce Levine, *The Spirit of 1848: German Immigrants, Labor Conflict and the Coming of the Civil War* (Chicago, 1992), 2; David Noel Doyle and Owen Dudley Edwards, eds., *America and Ireland 1776–1976: The American Identity and the Irish Connection* (Westport, 1976), 204, 94, 98, 100; MacDonagh, *Perspectives in American History* 10:426–9; Vaughan, *Ire-*

land under the Union, 1:606; S.H. Cousens, "Emigration and Demographic Change in Ireland, 1851–1861," *Economic History Review*, 2nd ser., 14 (1961–62): 275; Timothy J. Hatton and Jeffrey G. Williamson, "After the Famine: Emigration from Ireland, 1850–1913," *Journal of Economic History* 53 (1993): 579, 587; John Bodner, *The Transplanted: A History of Immigrants in Industrial America* (Bloomington, 1987), 2; Cormac O Grada, *Ireland: New Economic History 1780–1939* (Oxford, 1994), 227; William D. Griffin, ed., *The Irish in America* (New York, 1973), 41–2; Hasia A. Diner, *Erin's Daughters in America: Irish Immigrant Women in the Nineteenth Century* (Baltimore, 1983), 42.

2   Diner, *Erin's Daughters*, xiv, 71–2; Levine, *Spirit of 1848*, 53; Kerby Miller and Bruce D. Boling, "Golden Streets, Bitter Tears: The Irish Image of America during the Era of Mass Migration," *Journal of American Ethnic History* 10 (1990–91): 18–19, 22–4; Arnold Schrier, *Ireland and the American Emigration 1850–1900* (Minneapolis, 1958), 18–30; Robert S. Fortner, "The Culture of Hope and the Culture of Despair: The Print Media and 19th Century Irish Emigration," *Eire/Ireland* 13 (1978): 48; Edward J. Maguire, ed., Reverend John O'Hanlon's *The Irish Emigrant's Guide for the United States* (New York, 1976), 12; J.J. Lynch, "For the Clergy of Ireland Only," LAE 0601, Lynch Papers, AAT; *Broadway Annual*, 1868: 444; Griffin, *Irish in America*, 75.

3   Robert Ernst, *Immigrant Life in New York City 1825–1862*, reprint ed. (New York, 1979), 27–9, 31–2, 34; Ronald H. Bayor and Timothy J. Meagher, eds., *The New York Irish* (Baltimore, 1996), 19; Charlotte Erickson, *American Industry and the European Immigrant 1860–1885* (New York, 1957), 69, 96; Mary Gilbert Kelly, *Catholic Immigrant Colonization Projects in the United States 1815–1860* (New York, 1939), 5–6.

4   Lawrence J. McCaffrey, *The Irish Diaspora in America* (Bloomington, 1976), 63; P.J. Drudy, ed., *The Irish in America: Emigration, Assimilation and Impact* (Cambridge, 1985), 21; Bayor and Meagher, *New York Irish*, 3, 18; Oliver MacDonagh and W.F. Mandle, *Ireland and Irish-Australia: Studies in Cultural and Political History* (London, 1986), 11; Stuart M. Blumn, *The Urban Threshold: Growth and Change in a Nineteenth Century Community* (Chicago, 1976), 75, 79–80, 82; David Noel Doyle, "The Irish as Urban Pioneers in the United States, 1850–1870," *Journal of American Ethnic History* 10 (1990–91): 36–43; Donald B. Cole, *Immigrant City: Lawrence, Massachusetts, 1845–1921* (Chapel Hill, 1963), 10; William F. Hartford, *Working*

People of Holyoke: Class and Ethnicity in a Massachusetts Mill Town 1850-1960 (New Brunswick, N.J., 1990), 35; Gene Sessions, "'Years of Struggle': The Irish in the Village of Northfield, 1845-1900," *Vermont History* 55 (1987): 70, 75; Stanley Nadel, *Little Germany: Ethnicity, Religion and Class in New York City, 1845-1880* (Urbana, 1990), 22.

5 Ronald Takaki, *A Different Mirror: A History of Multicultural America* (Boston, 1993), 146-7; Stephen Thernstrom, *Poverty and Progress: Social Mobility in a Nineteenth Century City*, pb. ed. (New York, 1977); J.P. Dolan, *The Immigrant Church: New York's Irish and German Catholics, 1815-1865* (Baltimore, 1975), 34; Richard A. Meckel, "Immigration, Mortality, and Population Growth in Boston, 1840-1880," *Journal of Interdisciplinary History* 15 (1985): 413-14; Diner, *Erin's Daughters*, 106-9; Howard I. Kushner, "Immigrant Suicide in the United States: Toward a Psycho-Social History," *Journal of Social History* 18 (1984): 11.

6 Lee Soltow, *Men and Wealth in the United States 1850-1870* (New Haven, 1975), 44, 150, 171-2; Florence E. Gibson, *The Attitudes of the New York Irish to State and National Affairs 1848-1892* (New York, 1951), 16, 7; Michael F. Funchion, *Chicago's Irish Nationalists, 1881-1890* (New York, 1976), 13; Priscilla Ferguson Clement, *Welfare and the Poor in the Nineteenth Century City: Philadelphia, 1800-1854* (London, 1985), 28-31; McCaffrey, *Irish Diaspora in America*, 66; Tyler Anbinder, "Lord Palmerston and the Irish Famine Emigration," *Historical Journal* 44 (2001): 447; Drudy, *Irish in America*, 96-7, 100; Tyler Anbinder, "From Famine to Five Points: Lord Lansdowne's Irish Tenants Encounter North America's Most Notorious Slum," *American Historical Review* 107 (2002): 376; Oscar Handlin, *Boston's Immigrants 1790-1865: A Study in Acculturation* (Cambridge, Mass., 1941), 126; Sam Bass Warner, Jr., and Colin Burke, "Cultural Change and the Ghetto," *Journal of Contemporary History* 4 (1969): 173-87; Sam Bass Warner, *The Private City: Philadelphia in Three Periods of Its Growth* (1968), 56-7; Allen F. David and Mark H. Haller, eds., *The Peoples of Philadelphia: A History of Ethnic Groups and Lower Class Life, 1790-1940* (Philadelphia, 1973), 136-7; Kenneth Wilson Underwood, *Protestant and Catholic: Religious and Social Interaction in an Industrial Community* (1957), 209; Tamara K. Hareven, ed., *Anonymous Americans: Explorations in Nineteenth Century Social History* (Englewood Cliffs, 1971), 32-4; Thomas Hylland Eriksen, *Ethnicity and Nationalism* (London, 2002), 134; Dolan, *Immigrant Church*, 37; Ernst, *Immigrant Life in New York*, 25;

Thomas Sowell, *Ethnic America* (New York, 1981), 25; Maguire, O'Hanlon's *Irish Emigrant's Guide*, 232.

7 Thernstrom, *Poverty and Progress*, 59; Anbinder, *American Historical Review* 107:381; Howard Harris, "'The Eagle to Watch and the Harp to Tune the Nation': Irish Immigrants, Politics and Early Industrialization in Paterson, New Jersey, 1824–1836," *Journal of Social History* 23 (1989–90): 574–8; Susan E. Hirsch, *Roots of the American Working Class: The Industrialization of Crafts in Newark, 1800–1860* (Philadelphia, 1978), 48; Denis Clark, *The Irish Relations: Trials of an Immigrant Tradition* (East Brunswick, 1982), 28; David and Haller, *The Peoples of Philadelphia*, 136; Sessions, *Vermont History* 55:73; Richard L. Erlich, ed., *Immigrants in Industrial America 1850–1920* (Charlottesville, 1977), 145; Victor A. Walsh, "'A Fanatic Heart': The Cause of Irish-American Nationalism in Pittsburg during the Gilded Age," *Journal of Social History* 15 (1981–82): 195, 197; Noel Ignatiev, *How the Irish Became White* (London, 1995), 116–17; Takaki, *A Different Mirror*, 162; Ernst, *Immigrant Life in New York*, 73, 75, 87, 89, 98; Dennis Clark, *Hibernia America: The Irish and Regional Cultures* (1986), 56; Dennis P. Ryan, *Beyond the Ballot Box: A Social History of the Boston Irish, 1845–1917* (1983), 83–7; Bayor and Meagher, *New York Irish*, 20; Anbinder, *Historical Journal* 44:443.

8 Maguire, O'Hanlon's *Irish Emigrant's Guide*, 114; Peter Wray, *Common Labour: Workers and the Digging of North American Canals 1780–1860* (Cambridge, 1993), 142; Bruce Laurie, Theodore Hershberg, and George Alter, "Immigrants and Industry: The Philadelphia Experience, 1850–1880," *Journal of Social History* 9 (1975–76): 242–3; Drudy, *Irish in America*, 119; Clark, *Irish Relations*, 88; Peter R. Knights, *The Plain People of Boston, 1830–1860: A Study in City Growth* (New York, 1971), 123; Brian C. Mitchell, *The Paddy Camps: The Irish of Lowell 1821–1861* (Urbana, 1988), 89, 94; Richard Stott, "British Immigrants and the American 'Work Ethic' in the Mid-Nineteenth Century," *Labor History* 26 (1985): 95, 99, 100–1; McCaffrey, *Irish Diaspora in America*, 62.

9 Glenn C. Altschuler and Stuart M. Blumin, "Limits of Political Engagement in Antebellum America: A New Look at the Golden Age of Participatory Democracy," *Journal of American History* 87 (1997): 855, 877; Stephen P. Erie, *Rainbow's End: Irish-Americans and the Dilemmas of Urban Machine Politics, 1840–1985* (Berkeley, 1988), 31–3, 27–8; Edward M. Levine, *The Irish and Irish Politicians: A Study of Social and Cultural Alienation*

(Notre Dame, 1966), 41–51; Doyle and Edwards, *America and Ireland*, 139; Gibson, *Attitudes of the New York Irish*, 18.

10 Erie, *Rainbow's End*, 26–7, 53, 57–8, 61–2, 64; W. J. Rorabaugh, "Rising Democratic Spirits: Immigrants, Temperance, and Tammany Hall, 1854–1860," *Civil War History* 22 (1976): 141, 152–3, 155; Levine, *The Irish and Irish Politicians*, 117; Ernst, *Immigrant Life in New York*, 162–6; Clark, *Hibernia America*, 53; Harris, *Journal of Social History* 23:585–6; Erlich, *Immigrants in Industrial America*, 90–1.

11 Takaki, *A Different Mirror*, 162; Philip Bagenal, *The American Irish and Their Influence on Irish Politics* (London, 1882), 48; Wray, *Common Labour*, 96; Underwood, *Protestant and Catholic*, 208–9; Estelle F. Feinstein, *Stamford in the Gilded Age: The Political Life of a Connecticut Town, 1868–1893* (Stamford, 1973), 10; Mitchell, *Paddy Camps*, 105–7; Cole, *Immigrant City*, 27; Handlin, *Boston's Immigrants*, 100; Ernst, *Immigrant Life in New York*, 39; J.P. Dolan, "Immigrants in the City: New York's Irish and German Catholics," *Church History* 4 (1972): 354–5; David and Haller, *Peoples of Philadelphia*, 56; Patrick J. Blessing, "Ethnicity: Perspectives in History and Sociology. A Review Article," *Comparative Studies in Society and History* 22 (1980): 454.

12 Hartford, *Working People of Holyoke*, 49; Denis Clark, *Erin's Heirs: Irish Bonds of Community* (Lexington, 1991), 3, 22–5; Erlich, *Immigrants in Industrial America*, 46; Drudy, *Irish in America*, 126; Diner, *Erin's Daughters*, 50–1; Takaki, *A Different Mirror*, 154; Mitchell, *Paddy Camps*, 22, 34; Feinsten, *Stamford in the Gilded Age*, 5; Handlin, *Boston's Immigrants*, 156–7; Ernst, *Immigrant Life in New York*, 125; David and Haller, *Peoples of Philadelphia*, 136–7; Eriksen, *Ethnicity and Nationalism*, 21; Kushner, *Journal of Social History* 18:18–19; Dolan, *Immigrant Church*, 20.

13 Ira Berlin and Herbert G. Gutman, "Natives and Immigrants, Free Men and Slaves: Urban Workingmen in the Antebellum American South," *American Historical Review* 88 (1983): 1178; Randall M. Miller and Jon L. Wakelyn, eds., *Catholics in the Old South: Essays on Church and Culture* (Macon, 1983), 197–8, 201; Dennis C. Rousey, "Aliens in the WASP Nest: Ethnocultural Diversity in the Antebellum Urban South," *Journal of American History* 79 (1992): 157; Fred Siegel, "Artisans and Immigrants in the Politics of Late Antebellum Georgia," *Civil War History* 27 (1981): 226–7, 223; Richard C. Wade, *Slavery in the Cities: The South 1820–1860* (New York, 1964), 274–5; Earl F. Niehaus, *The Irish in New Orleans 1800–1860* (Baton Rouge, 1965), 38–9, 41–2, 45–9, 28–30, 12, 22, 98.

14 Niehaus, *Irish in New Orleans*, 35; William Pencak, Selma
   Berrol, and Randall M. Miller, eds., *Immigration to New York*
   (London, 1991), 40; Henry J. Browne, "Archbishop Hughes and
   Western Colonization," *Catholic Historical Review* 36 (1950):
   260–1; M. Justine McDonald, *History of the Irish in Wisconsin
   in the Nineteenth Century* (Washington, 1954), 24; Mary Gilbert
   Kelly, *Catholic Immigrant Colonization Projects in the United
   States 1815–1860* (New York, 1939), 5–6, 13, 42, 145, 178, 185,
   198–9; James P. Shannon, *Catholic Colonization on the Western
   Frontier* (New Haven, 1957), 15–19.

15 Pencak, Berrol, and Miller, *Immigration in New York*, 40, 48–9,
   52–3; John Gjerde, *The Minds of the West: Ethnocultural Evolution in the Rural Middle West, 1830–1917* (Chapel Hill, 1997),
   42; Kelly, *Catholic Immigrant Colonization Projects*, 213; Shannon, *Catholic Colonization on the Western Frontier*, 21–2;
   Thomas T. McAvoy, "Orestes A. Brownson and Archbishop John
   Hughes in 1860," *Review of Politics* 24 (1962): 22–3; Browne,
   Catholic Historical Review 36:263, 268, 271–2, 275, 283; Griffin, *Irish in America*, 77.

16 Browne, *Catholic Historical Review* 36:274; Charles E. Orser, Jr,
   "The Illinois and Michigan Canal: Historical Archeology and the
   Irish Experience in America," *Eire/Ireland* 27 (1992): 122–34;
   Levine, *Spirit of 1848*, 2; David Noel Doyle and Owen Dudley
   Edwards, eds., *America and Ireland 1776–1976: The American
   Identity and the Irish Connection* (1980), 165–6, 169; McDon-
   ald, *History of the Irish in Wisconsin*, 9, 22, 39, 41, 121; James
   P. Walsh, "American-Irish: West and East," *Eire/Ireland* 6
   (1971): 25–32; see also David A. Gerber, *The Making of Ameri-
   can Pluralism: Buffalo, New York, 1825–1860* (Urbana, 1989);
   JoEllen Vinyard, *The Irish on the Urban Frontier: Nineteenth
   Century Detroit, 1850–1880* (New York, 1976); David Noel
   Doyle, "The Irish in Chicago," *Irish Historical Studies* 26
   (1989): 293–303; Peter d'A. Jones and Melvin G. Holli, eds.,
   Ethnic Chicago (Grand Rapids, 1981); Kathleen Neils Conzen,
   *Immigrant Milwaukee 1836–1860: Accommodation and Com-
   munity in a Frontier City* (Cambridge, Mass., 1976); R.A.
   Burchell, *The San Francisco Irish 1848–1880* (Berkeley, 1980);
   Erie, *Rainbow's End*, 33; Timothy J. Meagher, *From Paddy to
   Studs: Irish American Communities in the Turn of the Century
   Era, 1880–1920* (New York, 1986), 5–6, 9; Funchion, *Chicago's
   Irish Nationalists*, 15.

17 David H. Bennett, *The Party of Fear: From Nativist Movements
   to the New Right in American History* (Chapel Hill, 1988),
   29–30; Forrest G. Wood, *The Arrogance of Faith: Christianity*

and Race in America from the Colonial Era to the Twentieth Century (New York, 1990), 354–5; Dolores Liptak, *Immigrants and Their Church* (New York, 1989), 59; Kenrick to Cullen, 28 March 1843, 7 December 1846, Irish College MSS, microfilm 109/1, Catholic University of America (CUA); Hughes to Cullen, 24 January 1845, Hughes MSS, reel 3, CUA; Sandra Yocum Mize, "Defending Roman Loyalties and Republican Values: The 1848 Revolution in American Catholic Apologetics," *Church History* 60 (1991): 481–3, 490, 487; Maurice R. O'Connell, "Daniel O'Connell and Irish-Americans," *Eire/Ireland* 16 (1981): 11.

18 Thomas T. McAvoy, *A History of the Catholic Church in the United States* (Notre Dame, 1969), 124, 136; John Tracy Ellis, ed., *The Catholic Priest in the United States: Historical Investigations* (Collegeville, Minn., 1971), 397, 21, 29.

19 McAvoy, *History of the Catholic Church in the United States*, 131, 139, 152; Ellis, *Catholic Priest in the United States*, 116, 300, 304; Vaughan, *Ireland under the Union*, 1: 714; Olson, *Catholic Immigrants in America*, 29; Liptak, *Immigrants and Their Church*, 59.

20 Harold J. Abramson, *Ethnic Diversity in Catholic America* (New York, 1973), 19; James Stuart Olson, *Catholic Immigrants in America* (Chicago, 1987), 1; John Hutchinson and Anthony D. Smith, eds., *Ethnicity* (Oxford, 1996), 187, 197; Randall M. Miller and Thomas D. Marzik, *Immigrants and Religion in Urban America* (Philadelphia, 1977), xv; Wood, *Arrogance of Faith*, 346; Harry S. Stout, "Ethnicity: The Vital Center of Religion in America," *Ethnicity* 2 (1975): 207, 210; Dolan, *Church History* 41:360; McAvoy, *History of the Catholic Church in the United States*, 137; Conzen, *Immigrant Milwaukee*, 36; Coleman J. Barry, *The Catholic Church and German Americans* (Milwaukee, 1953), 19; John P. Marschall, "Kenrick and the Paulists: A Conflict of Structures and Personalities," *Church History* 38 (1969): 89.

21 Rudolph J. Vecoli, "Prelates and Peasants: Italian Immigrants and the Catholic Church," *Journal of Social History* 2 (1968–69): 220–1; Underwood, *Protestant and Catholic*, 215; Miller and Marzik, *Immigrants and Religion in Urban America*, xvii; Gilley, *Journal of Ecclesiastical History* 35:202; Dolan, *Church History* 41:357; Ernst, *Immigrant Life in New York*, 137; Dolan, *Immigrant Church*, 71; Lawrence J. McCaffrey, Ellen Skerrett, Michael Funchion, and Charles Fanning, eds., *The Irish in Chicago* (Urbana, 1987), 23–5; Charles Shanabruch, *Chicago's Catholics: The Evolution of an American Identity* (Notre Dame, 1981), 6,

8–13; F.E.T., ed., *The Kenrick-Frenaye Correspondence 1830–1862* (Philadelphia, 1920), 356; Hughes to Kenrick, 30 August 1852, 29-I-2, Kenrick Papers, AAB; Barry, *Catholic Church and German Americans*, 13.

22 Henry B. Leonard, "Ethnic Conflict and Episcopal Power: The Diocese of Cleveland, 1847–1870," *Catholic Historical Review* 62 (1976): 388–407; Ronald C. Murphy and Jeffrey Potash, "The 'Highgate Affair': An Episode in Establishing the Authority of the Roman Catholic Diocese of Burlington," *Vermont History* 52 (1984): 33–43; Dolan, *Immigrant Church*, 86; Nadel, *Little Germany*, 94; Purcell to Spalding, 7 September 1866, 35-R-23, Spalding Papers, AAB.

23 MacDonagh, *Irish Historical Studies* 5:302; *Cork Examiner*, 16 September 1867; Jones and Holli, *Ethnic Chicago*, 219; Barron to Cullen, 6 July 1838, Irish College MSS, reel 109/2, CUA.

24 Owen Dudley Edwards, "The Irish Priest in North America," *Studies in Church History* 21 (1989): 336, 332, 346; Dolan, *Immigrant Church*, 64; Jim Obelkevich, *Disciplines of Faith: Studies in Religion, Politics and Hierarchy* (London, 1987), 341; Lawrence J. McCaffrey, "Irish Textures in American Catholicism," *Catholic Historical Review* 78 (1992): 11; Thernstrom, *Poverty and Progress*, 175; Gerber, *Making of American Pluralism*, 334; Hartford, *Working People of Holyoke*, 50–1.

25 Hynes, *Societas* 8:145; Dolan, *Immigrant Church*, 57–8; Miller and Marzik, *Immigrants and Religion in Urban America*, 73; Glanmor Williams, ed., *Merthyr Politics: The Making of a Working Class Tradition* (Cardiff, 1966), 52; Dolan, *Church History* 41:365–7; Bodner, *Transplanted*, 151–2; Jay P. Dolan, *Catholic Revivalism: The American Experience 1830–1900* (Notre Dame, 1978), 196–7; Patrick Carey, "Voluntaryism: An Irish Catholic Tradition," *Church History* 48 (1979): 56–7.

26 Gjerde, *Minds of the West*, 104–5; Conzen, *Immigrant Milwaukee*, 167, 170; Mitchell, *Paddy Camps*, 39, 56; Gerber, *Making of American Pluralism*, 151, 147; Vinyard, *Irish on the Urban Frontier*, 110–11; Abramson, *Ethnic Diversity in Catholic America*, 66; Burchell, *San Francisco Irish*, 85; Kerby A. Miller, *Emigrants and Exiles: Ireland and the Irish Exodus to North America* (New York, 1985), 333.

27 Drudy, *Irish in America*, 131; McDonald, *History of the Irish in Wisconsin*, 252; Cole, *Immigrant City*, 139; Gjerde, *Minds of the West*, 108; Dolan, *Immigrant Church*, 128; David and Haller, *Peoples of Philadelphia*, 139–40; Timothy Walch, "Catholic Social Institutions and Urban Development: The View from Nine-

teenth-Century Chicago and Milwaukee," *Catholic Historical Review* 64 (1978): 16–32; Robert Francis Hueston, *The Catholic Press and Nativism 1840–1860* (New York, 1976), 19; Burchell, *San Francisco Irish*, 94–5; Gerber, *Making of American Pluralism*, 151, 154.

28 James W. Sanders, *The Education of an Urban Minority: Catholics in Chicago, 1833–1965* (New York, 1977), 13, 18, 22–3, 42; Thernstrom, *Poverty and Progress*, 50–1; Stout, *Ethnicity*, 2: 213–14; Kenrick to Cullen, 28 March 1843, Irish College MSS, reel 109/1, CUA; Jones and Holli, *Ethnic Chicago*, 15; Vincent P. Lannie, "Alienation in America: The Immigrant Catholic and Public Education in Pre-Civil War America," *Review of Politics* 32 (1970): 515.

29 David W. Galenson, "Ethnic Differences in Neighborhood Effects on the School Attendance of Boys in Early Chicago," *History of Education Quarterly* 38 (1998): 26, 29; Gerber, *Making of American Pluralism*, 152; Ernst, *Immigrant Life in New York*, 141, 150; Donna Merwick, *Boston's Priests, 1848–1900: A Study in Social and Intellectual Challenge* (Cambridge, Mass., 1973), 68; Shanabruch, *Chicago's Catholics*, 22; David W. Galenson, "Determinants of the School Attendance of Boys in Early Chicago," *History of Education Quarterly* 35 (1995): 400; Olson, *Catholic Immigrants in America*, 38; Levine, *Irish and Irish Politicians*, 82–3; McCaffrey et al., *Irish in Chicago*, 47; Ryan, *Beyond the Ballot Box*, 68–9; Dolan, *Immigrant Church*, 118; Liptak, *Immigrants and Their Church*, 66; Hueston, *The Catholic Press and Nativism*, 99, 100, 310; Gjerde, *Minds of the West*, 242; Handlin, *Boston's Immigrants*, 171.

30 William Leonard Joyce, *Editors and Ethnicity: A History of the Irish-American Press 1848–1883* (New York, 1976), 54, 59; Bayor and Meagher, *New York Irish*, 23–4; Gerber, *Making of American Pluralism*, 153; McAvoy, *History of the Catholic Church in the United States*, 202; Vaughan, *Ireland under the Union*, 1:714; Burchell, *San Francisco Irish*, 13; *Kenrick-Frenaye Correspondence*, 163; Vinyard, *Irish on the Urban Frontier*, 291; McDonald, *History of the Irish in Wisconsin*, 251; Thomas D'Arcy McGee, *A History of the Irish Settlers in North America*, reprint ed. (Bowie, Md, 1989), 132.

31 Hughes to Potts, 2 May 1846, Hughes MSS, reel 3, CUA; Ernst, *Immigrant Life in New York*, 150–1; Joyce, *Editors and Ethnicity*, 59, 64, 77; Gerber, *Making of American Pluralism*, 160–1; Hueston, *Catholic Press and Nativism*, 309; Handlin, *Boston's Immigrants*, 145.

32 Hueston, *Catholic Press and Nativism*, 139–40, 124; Joyce, *Editors and Ethnicity*, 74–5, 53–4, 84, 60–2; Sally M. Miller, *The Ethnic Press in the United States: A Historical Analysis and Handbook* (New York, 1987), 178–9, 182; Thomas O'Connor, *Boston Irish: A Political History* (Boston, 1995), 44; Francis R. Walsh, "Who Spoke for Boston's Irish? The Boston *Pilot* in the Nineteenth Century," *Journal of Ethnic Studies* 10 (1982): 21–2; Ryan, *Beyond the Ballot Box*, 102–3; Handlin, *Boston's Immigrants*, 173–4.

33 Merwick, *Boston's Priests*, 23–5; Ryan, *Beyond the Ballot Box*, 101; Joyce, *Editors and Ethnicity*, 63, 84; Miller, *Ethnic Press in the United States*, 183; Ernst, *Immigrant Life in New York*, 158; McAvoy, *History of the Catholic Church in the United States*, 176.

34 Richard Shaw, *Dagger John: The Unquiet Life and Times of Archbishop John Hughes of New York* (New York, 1977), 13–16, 18, 23–4, 56; Bayor and Meagher, *New York Irish*, 87; McAvoy, *History of the Catholic Church in the United States*, 149, 176, 190; Edward K. Spann, *The New Metropolis: New York City, 1840–1857* (New York, 1981), 29; Browne, *Catholic Historical Review* 36:310; Miller, *Emigrants and Exiles*, 334; Pencak, Berrol, and Miller, *Immigration to New York*, 32–3.

35 John R.G. Hassard, *Life of John Hughes, First Archbishop of New York*, reprint ed. (New York, 1969), 220–1, 270, 304–7; John Hughes, "Reflections and Suggestions in Regard to What Is Called the Catholic Press in the United States," Pamphlet no. 848, American Catholic Historical Association (ACHA), Philadelphia, 23; Lawrence Kehoe, ed., *Complete Works of the Most Reverend John Hughes, D.D., Archbishop of New York*, 2 vols. (New York, 1864), 1:544, 548, 552, 556; Shaw, *Dagger John*, 235; Handlin, *Boston's Immigrants*, 137, 153; Edwards, *Studies in Church History* 21:323; Rudolph J. Vecoli, "Prelates and Peasants: Italian Immigrants and the Catholic Church," *Journal of Social History* 2 (1968–69): 221–2; Joseph George, Jr, "'A Catholic Family Newspaper' Views the Lincoln Administration: John Mullaly's Copperhead Weekly," *Civil War History* 24 (1978): 113–15.

36 Jones and Holli, *Ethnic Chicago*, 21; McAvoy, *Review of Politics*, 24:21; Ellis, *Catholic Priest in the United States*, 299; Lannie, *Review of Politics* 32:509; Pencak, Berrol, and Miller, *Immigration to New York*, 37; Edwards, *Studies in Church History* 21:323; Stout, *Ethnicity* 2:207; Cole, *Immigrant City*, 144; Michael Cottrell, "St. Patrick's Day Parades in Nineteenth-

Century Toronto: A Study of Immigrant Adjustment and Elite
Control," *Histoire Sociale/Social History*, 25 (1992): 58, 62; *New
York Times*, 18 March 1854; John F. Delury, "Irish Nationalism
in the Sacramento Region (1850–1890)," *Eire/Ireland* 21 (1986):
39; Timothy J. Meagher, "'Why Should We Care for a Little
Trouble or a Walk in the Mud': St. Patrick's and Columbus Day
Parades in Worcester, Massachusetts, 1845–1915," *New England
Quarterly* 58 (1985): 7; Charles J. O'Fahey, "Reflections on the
St. Patrick's Day Orations of John Ireland," *Ethnicity* 2 (1975):
244–57; Moss, *Journal of Social History* 29:130; Oliver Mac-
Donagh, *States of Mind: Two Centuries of Anglo-Irish Conflict,
1780–1980* (London, 1992), 98.

37 Edwards, *Studies in Church History* 21:336; Levine, *Irish and
Irish Politicians*, 79; Delury, *Eire/Ireland* 21:31; O'Fahey, *Ethnici-
ty* 2:247; Moss, *Journal of Social History* 29:133; MacDonagh,
Irish Historical Studies 5:296; *New York Times*, 18 March 1853,
18 March 1854, 19 March 1855; P.E. Moriarty, "What Right
Has England to Rule in Ireland ?" Pamphlet no. 1075, ACHA.

38 Stout, *Ethnicity* 2:207; Moss, *Journal of Social History* 29:127–8;
Gerber, *Making of American Pluralism*, 334; Miller, *Journal of
Social History* 9:88; Hutchinson and Smith, *Ethnicity*, 211; Erik-
sen, *Ethnicity and Nationalism*, 107; Olson, *Catholic Immigrants
in America*, 11; Miller and Marzik, *Immigrants and Religion in
Urban America*, 77; Laurence J. McCaffrey, *Textures of Irish
America* (Syracuse, 1992), 72; Underwood, *Protestant and
Catholic*, 210; James A. Reynolds, *The Catholic Emancipation
Crisis in Ireland, 1823–1829* (New Haven, 1954), 85; Conzen,
Immigrant Milwaukee, 160; Vinyard, *Irish on the Urban
Frontier*, 304; McCaffrey, Skerritt, Funchion, and Fanning, *Irish
in Chicago*, 42; Obelkevich, *Disciplines of Faith*, 341; McCaffrey,
Catholic Historical Review 78:5.

39 Timothy L. Smith, "Religion and Ethnicity in America," *Ameri-
can Historical Review* 83 (1978): 1156, 1158; Eriksen, *Ethnicity
and Nationalism*, 105; Paul Brass, "Ethnicity and Nationality
Formation," *Ethnicity* 3 (1976): 234–5; Rodolfo Stavenhagen,
The Ethnic Question: Conflicts, Development and Human Rights
(Tokyo, 1990), 78.

40 Joseph P. Ferrie, "The Wealth Accumulation of Antebellum European Immigrants to the United States, 1840–60," *Journal of Economic History* 54 (1994): 5, 21; Joseph P. Ferrie, "Up and Out or
Down and Out? Immigrant Mobility in the Antebellum United
States," *Journal of Interdisciplinary History* 26 (1995): 52; Raymond L. Cohn, "The Occupations of English Immigrants to the

United States, 1836–1853," *Journal of Economic History* 52 (1992): 384; Charlotte Erickson, *Invisible Immigrants: The Adaptation of English and Scottish Immigrants in Nineteenth-Century America* (Coral Gables, 1972), 41–3, 51, 70–5, 258–9, 69; Rowland Berthoff, *British Immigrants in Industrial America, 1790–1950,* reprint (New York, 1968), 211–12.

41 Clark, *Erin's Heirs,* 25–6, 29; David A. Wilson, *United Irishmen, United States: Immigrant Radicals in the Early Republic* (Dublin, 1998), 9–10, 13, 61, 89, 137–40, 157–9, 163, 168–70; Kevin Whelan, *The Tree of Liberty: Radicalism, Catholicism and Construction of Irish Identity, 1760–1830* (Notre Dame, 1996), 167–8.

42 McGee, *History of the Irish Settlers,* 133; Bayor and Meagher, *New York Irish,* 68, 27; Thomas Moriarty, "The Irish American Response to Catholic Emancipation," *Catholic Historical Review,* 66 (1980): 372; McDonald, *History of the Irish in Wisconsin,* 241; David T. Gleeson, "Parallel Struggles: Irish Republicanism in the American South, 1798–1876," *Eire/Ireland* 34 (1999): 107; Ignatiev, *How the Irish Became White,* 21.

43 Gleeson, *Eire/Ireland* 34:102–3; John Belchem, "Republican Spirit and Military Science: The Irish Brigade and Irish-American Nationalism in 1848," *Irish Historical Studies* 29 (1994): 46; Ignatiev, *How the Irish Became White,* 29; Arthur G. Doughty, *Elgin-Grey Correspondence 1846–1852,* 4 vols. (Ottawa, 1937), 1:165; Brian Jenkins, *Fenians and Anglo-American Relations during Reconstruction* (Ithaca, 1969), 13.

44 O'Connell, *Eire/Ireland* 16:13–15; Gleeson, *Eire/Ireland* 34:103, 107–8; Ignatiev, *How the Irish Became White,* 7–13, 19–21, 23–4, 26–9; Douglas C. Riach, "Daniel O'Connell and American Anti-slavery," *Irish Historical Studies* 20 (1976): 21, 11.

45 McDonald, *History of the Irish in Wisconsin,* 241–2; McGee, *History of the Irish Settlers,* 133, 139; Conzen, *Immigrant Milwaukee,* 171; Gleeson, *Eire/Ireland* 34:103–4; Niehaus, *Irish in New Orleans,* 150; Patrick O'Sullivan, ed., *The Meaning of the Famine* (London, 1997), 114.

46 McGee, *History of the Irish Settlers,* 133–4; Niehaus, *Irish in New Orleans,* 151–2; Gleeson, *Eire/Ireland* 34:104; Belchem, *Irish Historical Studies* 29:44–54; John Belchem, "Nationalism, Republicanism and Exile: Irish Emigrants and the Revolutions of 1848," *Past and Present* 146 (1995): 103–18; Doughty, *Elgin-Grey Correspondence,* 1:1477–8, 408–9, 411.

47 Wilson, *United Irishmen, United States,* 7; McGee, *History of the Irish Settlers,* 174, 177; Handlin, *Boston's Immigrants,* 138;

Meagher, *From Paddy to Studs*, 13; Niehaus, *Irish in New Orleans*, 154; Doyle and Edwards, *America and Ireland*, 111; James S. Donnelly, Jr, "The Construction of the Memory of the Famine in Ireland and the Irish Diaspora, 1850–1900," *Eire/Ireland* 31 (1996): 33.

48 Mitchel to Thomson, n.d., Mitchel Papers, T413/3, PRONI; Thomas Keneally, *The Great Shame: A Story of the Irish in the Old World and the New* (London, 1998), 275, 289, 311; John Mitchel, *Jail Journal: With Introductory Narrative of Transactions in Ireland*, reprint ed. (London, 1983), 359–62, 379–81.

49 Patrick Ward, *Exile, Emigration and Irish Writing* (Dublin, 2002), 116; Mitchel, *Jail Journal*, 362; Mitchel to Thomson, 26 August 1854, Mitchel Papers, T413/5, PRONI; Steven R. Knowlton, "The Politics of John Mitchel: A Reappraisal," *Eire/Ireland* 22 (1987): 39–41, 43; Mitchel to Thomson, 4 October 1852, Mitchel Papers, T413/2, PRONI.

50 Malcolm Brown, *The Politics of Irish Literature* (Seattle, 1972), 138–9; Knowlton, *Eire/Ireland* 22:40–2; Mitchel, *Jail Journal*, 365–6, 161, 206, 226, 244; Peter O'Shaughnessy, ed., *The Gardens of Hell: John Mitchel in Van Dieman's Land 1850–1853* (Sydney, 1988), 6, 14–15; Mitchel to Thomson, 4 October 1852, Mitchel Papers, T413/2, PRONI.

51 Mitchel, *Jail Journal*, xx, xxv–xxix, xxxii, 5, 67.

52 Chris Morash and Richard Hayes, eds., *'Fearful Realities': New Perspectives on the Famine* (Dublin, 1996), 136; Morash, *Writing the Famine*, 60–3, 68, 144–5; O'Sullivan, *Meaning of the Famine*, 16–17; Donnelly, *Eire/Ireland* 31:28–39; Mitchel, *Jail Journal*, xxxii; Cormac O Grada (Dublin, 1997), *Famine 150*, 167–73; Vaughan, *Ireland under the Union*, 1: 371.

53 Joyce, *Editors and Ethnicity*, 80; Ernst, *Immigrant Life in New York*, 128–9; McGee, *History of the Irish Settlers*, 176; Knowlton, *Eire/Ireland* 22:50–1; Mitchel to Thomson, 1 November 1855, Mitchel Papers, D/249, PRONI; Deegee Lester, "John Mitchel's Wilderness Years in Tennessee," *Eire/Ireland* 25 (1990): 7–13; Gleeson, *Eire/Ireland* 34:106, 108–9; Niehaus, *Irish in New Orleans*, 158.

54 *Irish Canadian*, 4 February 1863; O'Sullivan, *Meaning of the Famine*, 33; Kerby A. Miller, "Emigrants and Exiles: Irish Cultures and Irish Emigration to North America, 1790–1922," *Irish Historical Studies* 22 (1980): 97–125; Miller, *Emigrants and Exiles*, 103–30; Miller and Boling, *Journal of American Ethnic History* 10:32; Margaret Crawford, ed., *The Hungry Stream: Essays on Emigration and Famine* (Belfast, 1997), 72; Paula M.

Kane, *Separatism and Subculture: Boston Catholicism,*
1900–1920 (Chapel Hill, 1994), 50; Jim MacLaughlin, ed., *Loca-*
tion and Dislocation in Contemporary Irish Society: Emigration
and Irish Identities (Cork, 1997), 9; David Fitzpatrick, "The Irish
in America: Exiles or Escapers?" *Reviews in American History* 15
(1987): 277–8; Victor A. Walsh, "The Great Famine and Its Consequences," *Eire/Ireland* 23 (1988): 13–14, 6; Paul Tabori, *The*
Anatomy of Exile: A Semantic and Historical study (London,
1972), 33–8; Griffin, *Irish in America,* 39.
55 Miller, *Emigrants and Exiles,* 119; Tabori, *Anatomy of Exile,* 38;
Kane, *Separatism and Subculture,* 2; O Grada, *Famine 150,* 169.

CHAPTER SEVEN

1 Edward J. Maguire, ed., Reverend John Hanlon's *The Irish Emi-*
grant Guide for the United States (New York, 1976), 108–9, 226,
230–1.
2 J.P. Dolan, "Immigrants in the City: New York City's Irish and
German Catholics," *Church History* 41 (1972): 359; Earl F.
Niehaus, *The Irish in New Orleans 1800–1860* (Baton Rouge,
1965), 113; Robert Ernst, *Immigrant Life in New York City*
1825–1862 (New York, 1972), 102–3; Ronald H. Bayor and
Timothy J. Meagher, *The New York Irish* (Baltimore, 1996), 19;
Brian C. Mitchell, *The Paddy Camps: The Irish in Lowell*
1821–1861 (Urbana, 1988), 9; Priscilla Ferguson Clement, *Wel-*
fare and the Poor in the Nineteenth Century City: Philadelphia
1800–1854 (London, 1985), 112; Susan E. Hirsch, *Roots of the*
American Working Class: The Industrialization of Crafts in
Newark, 1800–1860 (Philadelphia, 1978), 106; Joan Underhill
Hannon, "Poverty in the Antebellum Northeast: The View from
New York State's Poor Relief Rolls," *Journal of Economic*
History 44 (1984): 1008; Glenn C. Altschuler and Jan M. Saltz-
gaber, "Clearinghouse for Paupers: The Poorfarm of Seneca
County, New York, 1830–1860," *Journal of Social History* 17
(1983–84): 584; David A. Gerber, *The Making of American Plu-*
ralism: Buffalo, New York, 1825–1860 (Urbana, 1989), 85.
3 Gene Sessions, "'Years of Struggle': The Irish in the Village of
Northfield, 1845–1900," *Vermont History* 55 (1987): 72; Hasia
A. Diner, *Erin's Daughters in America: Irish Immigrant Women*
in the Nineteenth Century (Baltimore, 1983), 112; Jill Siegel
Dodd, "The Working Classes and the Temperance Movement in
Ante-Bellum Boston," *Labor History* 19 (1978): 512, 520, 530;
John F. Quinn, "Father Mathew's American Tour, 1849–1851,"

Eire/Ireland 30 (1995–96): 95–9, 101–4; John F. Quinn, *Father Mathew's Crusade: Temperance in Nineteenth Century Ireland and Irish America* (Amherst, 2002), 149, 155, 168–71; Stuart Blumin, *The Urban Threshold: Growth and Change in a Nine-teenth Century Community* (Chicago, 1976), 96; Dolan, *Church History* 41:363; Thomas H. O'Connor, *The Boston Irish: A Polit-ical History* (Boston, 1995), 65; Mitchell, *Paddy Camps*, 111; Richard L. Ehrlich, ed., *Immigrants in Industrial America 1850–1920* (Charlottesville, 1977), 87; Bayor and Meagher, *New York Irish*, 114.

4 David J. Rothman, *The Discovery of the Asylum: Social Order and Disorder in the New Republic*, pb. ed. (Boston, 1990), 254–5, 283–5; Bayor and Meagher, *New York Irish*, 154–6, 158, 160; Mitchell, *Paddy Camps*, 99.

5 Rothman, *Discovery of the Asylum*, 261–2; O'Connor, *Boston Irish*, 64; Harry S. Stout, "Ethnicity: The Vital Center of Religion in America," *Ethnicity* 2 (1975): 214; Lannie, *Review of Politics* 32:508, 512, 515; James W. Sanders, *The Education of an Urban Minority: Catholics in Chicago, 1833–1965* (New York, 1977), 18, 21–3; Robert Dunne, *Antebellum Irish Immigration and Emerging Ideologies of 'America': A Protestant Backlash* (Lewis-ton, 2002), 58, 90; Carey, *Church History* 48:58.

6 Stanley Nadel, *Little Germany: Ethnicity, Religion and Class in New York City, 1845–1880* (Urbana, 1990), 87; John Gjerde, *The Minds of the West: Ethnocultural Evolution in the Rural Middle West, 1830–1917* (Chapel Hill, 1997), 241; Peter Way, "Shovel and Shamrock: Irish Workers and Labor Violence in the Digging of the Chesapeake and Ohio Canal," *Labor History* 30 (1989): 490–1, 507, 516; William A. Gudelunas and William G. Shade, *Before the Molly Maguires: The Emergence of the Ethno-Religious Factor in the Politics of the Lower Anthracite Region 1844–1872* (New York, 1976), 68–9; Grace Palladino, *Another Civil War: Labor, Capital and the State in the Anthracite Regions of Pennsylvania 1840–68* (Chicago, 1990), 49, 51, 54; Edward G. Quinn, "Of Myths and Men: An Analysis of Molly Maguireism in Nineteenth-Century Pennsylvania," *Eire/Ireland* 23 (1988): 52–61; Kevin Kenny, *Making Sense of the Molly Maguires* (New York, 1998), 44–5; Gerber, *Making of American Pluralism*, 255; David Grimsted, "Ante-Bellum Labor: Violence, Strike, and Communal Arbitration," *Journal of Social History* 19 (1985–86): 8–12; Diner, *Erin's Daughters*, 112.

7 Peter Wray, *Common Labour: Workers and the Digging of North American Canals, 1780–1860* (Cambridge, 1993), 173, 179, 201;

Michael A. Gordon, *The Orange Riots: Irish Political Violence in New York City 1870 and 1871* (Ithaca, 1993), 9–10; Niehaus, *Irish in New Orleans*, 29, 46; Siegel, *Civil War History* 27:226; Hirsch, *Roots of the American Working Class*, 106; Roger Lane, *Policing the City: Boston 1822–1885* (Cambridge, Mass., 1967), 120; Wilbur R. Miller, *Cops and Bobbies: Police Authority in New York City and London, 1830–1870* (Chicago, 1973), 23, 30–1; Paul O. Weinbaum, "Temperance, Politics, and the New York City Riots of 1857," *New York Historical Society Quarterly* 59 (1975): 246–70.

8 Mitchell, *Paddy Camps*, 98–9; Gerber, *Making of American Pluralism*, 95, 186–7; Joseph Duffy, "19th-Century Images of Hartford's Irish Catholic Community (1827–1861)," *Eire/Ireland* 21 (1986): 7; George E. Ryan, "Shanties and Shiftlessness: The Immigrant Irish of Henry Thoreau," *Eire/Ireland* 13 (1978): 54–78; Patrick O'Sullivan, ed., *The Creative Immigrant* (New York, 1994), 44–8.

9 Carl Van Doren, *Benjamin Franklin*, pb. ed. (New York, 1956), 390–1; Owen Dudley Edwards, "The American Image of Ireland: A Study of its Early Phases," *Perspectives in American History* 4 (1970): 199–251; Thomas Bartlett, David Dickson, Dáire Keogh, and Kevin Whelan, eds., *1798: A Bicentennial Perspective* (Dublin, 2003), 621–30.

10 Edwards, *Perspectives in American History* 4:203–4; O'Sullivan, *Creative Immigrant*, 70; Dennis Clark, *Erin's Heirs: Irish Bonds of Community* (Lexington, 1991), 39; Robert K. Dodge, "The Irish Comic Stereotype in the Almanacs of the Early Republic," *Eire/Ireland* 19 (1984): 111–20; Dale T. Knobel, "A Vocabulary of Ethnic Perception: Content Analysis of the American Stage Irishman, 1820–1860," *Journal of American Studies* 15 (1981): 46–66; Dale T. Knobel, *Paddy and the Republic: Ethnicity and Nationality in Antebellum America* (Middletown, 1986), 46–7, 65, 10; Bayor and Meagher, *New York Irish*, 161–2.

11 John Higham, *Strangers in the Land: Patterns of American Nativism 1860–1925* (New York, 1965), preface to 2nd ed.; Dale T. Knobel, '*America for Americans': The Nativist Movement in the United States* (New York, 1996), 11; Martin E. Marty, "Ethnicity: The Skeleton of Religion in America," *Church History* 41 (1972): 12, 20; Ernst, *Immigrant Life in New York*, 168; Edward M. Levine, *The Irish and Irish Politicians: A Study in Social and Cultural Alienation* (Notre Dame, 1966), 91; Mary E. Wilkie, "Colonials, Marginals and Immigrants: Contributions to a Theory of Ethnic Stratification," *Comparative Studies in Society and*

History 19 (1977): 88–9; Dunne, *Antebellum Irish Immigration,* 91; Knobel, *Paddy and the Republic,* 42, 65, 55.

12 Max Berger, "The Irish Emigrant and American Nativism as Seen by British Visitors, 1836–1860," *Pennsylvania Magazine of History and Biography* 70 (1946): 146–55.

13 Bartlett et al., *1798,* 621–30; David H. Bennett, *The Party of Fear: From Nativist Movements to the New Right in American History* (Chapel Hill, 1988), 22–3, 53–4; Gerber, *Making of American Pluralism,* 375; Thomas J. Curran, *Xenophobia and Immigration, 1820–1930* (Boston, 1975), 31; Melvin G. Holli and Peter d'A. Jones, eds., *Ethnic Chicago: A Multicultural Portrait,* 4th ed. (Grand Rapids, 1995), 214; Allan Nevins, ed., *The Diary of Philip Hone 1828–1851,* 2 vols., reprint ed. (New York, 1969), 1:190; Harris, *Journal of Social History* 23:586; Niehaus, *Irish in New Orleans,* 71; William Cullen Bryant II, "No Irish Need Apply: William Cullen Bryant Fights Nativism, 1836–1845," *New York History* 74 (1993): 36–8; Jean A. Baker, *Ambivalent Americans: The Know-Nothing Party in Maryland* (Baltimore, 1977), 4.

14 Bennett, *Party of Fear,* 18–19, 21; James S. Olson, *Catholic Immigrants in America* (1987), 1, 5; Ray Allen Billington, *The Protestant Crusade 1800–1860: A Study of the Origins of American Nativism,* pb ed. (Chicago, 1964), 8–11, 21; Eric Kaufmann, "American Exceptionalism: Anglo-Saxon Ethnogenesis in the 'Universal' Nation, 1776–1850," *Journal of American Studies* 33 (1999): 439–42; Dorothy Ross, "Historical Consciousness in Nineteenth Century America," *American Historical Review* 89 (1984): 912; Gerber, *Making of American Pluralism,* 281.

15 Ross, *American Historical Review* 89:913; Gerber, *Making of American Pluralism,* 281–2; Bennett, *Party of Fear,* 36–7; Dunne, *Antebellum Irish Immigration,* 33; Clifford S. Griffin, "Converting the Catholics: American Benevolent Societies and the Ante-Bellum Crusade against the Church," *Catholic Historical Review* 47 (1961–62): 325–30; D. Gregory Van Dussen, "American Methodism's *Christian Advocate* and Irish Catholic Immigration, 1830–1870," *Eire/Ireland* 26 (1991): 79–81, 86; Berger, *Pennsylvania Magazine of History and Biography* 70:155; Jay P. Dolan, *Catholic Revivalism: The American Experience, 1830–1900* (Notre Dame, 1978), 20–1; Barron to Cullen/Kirby, 27 July 1846, Irish College MSS, 109/1, CUA; Nevins, *Diary of Philip Hone,* 2:660.

16 Robert Francis Hueston, *The Catholic Press and Nativism, 1840–1860* (New York, 1976), 82; Van Dussen, *Eire/Ireland*

26:87; Griffin, *Catholic Historical Review* 47:331; Mize, *Church History* 60:489; Dolan, *Catholic Revivalism*, 34–5; Gerber, *Making of American Pluralism*, 283; Lawrence Kehoe, *Complete Works of The Most Reverend John Hughes D.D. Archbishop of New York*, 2 vols. (New York, 1864), 1:101.

17 Thomas T. McAvoy, "Orestes A. Brownson and Archbishop John Hughes in 1860," *Review of Politics* 24 (1962): 19; Arthur M. Schlesinger, Jr, *Orestes A. Brownson: A Pilgrim's Progress*, reprint ed. (New York, 1963), 214–15; Carl F. Krummel, "Catholicism, Americanism, Democracy and Orestes Brownson," *American Quarterly* 6 (1954):21; Brownson to Hecker [c. 1 June 1855], 29 August 1855, in Joseph F. Gower and Richard M. Leliaert, eds., *The Brownson-Hecker Correspondence* (Notre Dame, 1979), 182–3, 186; Walsh, *Journal of Ethnic Studies* 10:25–6, 28; Albert J. Von Frank, *The Trials of Anthony Burns: Freedom and Slavery in Emerson's Boston* (Cambridge, Mass., 1998), 245.

18 Thomas J Curran, *Xenophobia and Immigration 1820–1930* (New York, 1975), 54–5; Billington, *Protestant Crusade*, 289–312, 326, 331; Howard R. Marraro, "Italians in New York in the Eighteen Fifties, Part II," *New York History* 30 (1949): 277, 280–1; Richard Carwardine, "The Know-Nothing Party, the Protestant Evangelical Community and American National Identity," *Studies in Church History* 18 (1982): 453; William Pencak and Selma Berrol, *Immigration to New York* (1991), 43; Thomas M. Keefe, "The Catholic Issue in the Chicago Tribune before the Civil War," *Mid-America* 57 (1975): 230–1; Knobel, 'America for Americans,' 44; Michael F. Holt, "The Origins of Know Nothingism," *Journal of American History* 60 (1973): 323–4; Holli, *Ethnic Chicago*, 215.

19 William G. Bean, "Puritan versus Celt 1850–1860," *New England Quarterly* 7 (1934): 70–2, 77, 81; Ronald Takaki, *A Different Mirror: A History of Multicultural America* (Boston, 1993), 150–2; Levine, *Irish and Irish Politicians*, 91–4; Gilbert Osofsky, "Abolitionists, Irish Immigrants, and the Dilemmas of Romantic Nationalism," *American Historical Review* 80 (1975): 896–7; Douglas C. Riach, "Blacks and Blackface on the Irish Stage, 1830–60," *Journal of American Studies* 7 (1973): 231–41; Ernst, *Immigrant Life in New York*, 104–5; John L. Stanley, "Majority Tyranny in Tocqueville's America: The Failure of Negro Suffrage in 1846," *Political Science Quarterly* 34 (1967): 433; Noel Ignatiev, *How the Irish Became White* (London, 1995), 120–1, 111, 40–1; Dennis P. Ryan, *Beyond the Ballot Box: A Social History of the Boston Irish 1845–1917* (1983), 130; Von Frank,

Trial of Anthony Burns, 137; Bayor and Meagher, *New York Irish*, 129-30, 124, 114-5; Berlin and Gutman, *American Historical Review* 88:1196-9; Holli and Jones, *Ethnic Chicago*, 214.

20 Bean, *New England Quarterly* 7:81; Ryan, *Beyond the Ballot Box*, 131; Joseph P. Hernon, Jr, *Celts, Catholics, and Copperheads: Ireland Views the American Civil War* (Columbus, 1968), 66; Forrest G. Wood, *Arrogance of Faith* (New York, 1990), 358-60; Walter G. Sharrow, "Northern Catholic Intellectuals and the Coming of the Civil War," *New York Historical Society Quarterly* 58 (1974): 44-5; Dolan, *Immigrant Church*, 24-5.

21 Hernon, *Celts, Catholics, and Copperheads*, 65; Marty, *Church History* 41:20; Higham, *Strangers in the Land*, 10; Reginald Horsman, *Race and Manifest Destiny: The Origins of Racial Anglo-Saxonism* (Cambridge, Mass., 1981), 116-17, 137, 155-7, 160-1, 164, 252-3; Bayor and Meagher, *New York Irish*, 146, 162; Duffy, *Eire/Ireland* 21:4; Knobel, *Paddy and the Republic*, 75-123; Knobel, *Journal of American Studies* 15:67, 71; Charles E. Rosenberg, *No Other Gods: On Science and American Social Thought*, 3rd ed. (Baltimore, 1976), 67.

22 Rosenberg, *No Other Gods*, 67; O'Connor, *Boston Irish*, 70-1; Robert P. Swierenga, ed., *Beyond the Civil War Synthesis: Political Essays of the Civil War Era* (Westport, Conn., 1975), 245-54; Kevin Sweeney, "Rum, Romanism, Representation, and Reform: Coalition Politics in Massachusetts, 1847-1853," *Civil War History* 22 (1976): 126-8; Dale Baum, "Know Nothingism and the Republican Majority in Massachusetts: The Political Realignment of the 1850s," *Journal of American History* 64 (1977): 962-3, 966; Holt, *Journal of American History* 60:328-30; Tyler Anbinder, *Nativism and Slavery: The Northern Know Nothings and the Politics of the 1850s* (New York, 1992), 19, 104-7; Elliot J. Gorn, "'Good-Bye Boys, I die a true American': Homicide, Nativism, and Working Class Culture in Antebellum New York City," *Journal of American History* 74 (1987): 394-5, 397; Knobel, *'America for the Americans,'* 100-2; Palladino, *Another Civil War*, 73; Michael A. Bellesiles, *Arming America: The Origins of a National Gun Culture* (New York, 2000), 397-8; Donald Harman Akenson, *The Irish Diaspora: A Primer* (Toronto, 1993), 241.

23 Curran, *Xenophobia and Immigration*, 67; Anthony Gene Carey, "Too Southern to Be Americans: Proslavery Politics and the Failure of the Know Nothing Party in Georgia, 1854-1856," *Civil War History* 41 (1995): 28-9, 33; Bennett, *Party of Fear*, 141-55; Osofsky, *American Historical Review* 80:910-11; David A. Gerber, "Ambivalent Anti-Catholicism: Buffalo's Protestant

Elite Faces the Challenge of the Catholic Church, 1850–1860," *Civil War History* 30 (1984): 135; Carwardine, *Studies in Church History* 18:456–63; Richard Carwardine, "The Religious Revival of 1857–58 in the United States," *Studies in Church History* 15 (1978): 397–405.

24 Roy P. Basler, ed., *Collected Works of Abraham Lincoln*, 8 vols. (New Brunswick, N.J., 1953), 2:285, 287, 316, 323, 333n., 373; 3: 108, 173, 329; Palladino, *Another Civil War*, 72–3, 79, 81–2; Michael Holt, *Political Parties and American Political Development from the Age of Jackson to the Age of Lincoln* (Baton Rouge, 1992), 79; Anbinder, *Nativism and Slavery*, 46, 240, 255, 269; Bennett, *Party of Fear*, 154.

25 Kirby A. Miller, *Emigrants and Exiles: Ireland and the Irish Exodus to North America* (New York, 1985), 334; Hughes to Brownson, 1 July 1854, Hughes MSS, reel 4, CUA; Brownson to Hecker, 29 September 1857, *Brownson-Hecker Correspondence*, 129–30; Philip H. Bagenal, *The American Irish and Their Influence on Irish Politics* (London, 1882), 60; Nevins, *Diary of Philip Hone*, 2:660; Michael Feldberg, *The Philadelphia Riots of 1844: A Study in Ethnic Conflict* (Westport, 1975), 28–9; Van Dussen, *Eire/Ireland* 26:89; Philip Gleason, "Coming to Terms with American Catholic History," *Societas* 3(1973):287.

26 Lynch to the Clergy of Ireland Only, Lynch MSS, LAE 0601, AAT; Carwardine, *Studies in Church History* 18:460; Gale Stokes, "Cognition and the Function of Nationalism," *Journal of Interdisciplinary History* 4 (1974): 538–9; Thomas N. Brown, "The Origins and Character of Irish-American Nationalism," *Review of Politics* 18 (1956): 332, 341–2; Bagenal, *American Irish*, 60; *Irish Canadian*, 7 February 1863; P.M. Gill to Rossa, 25 February 1871, box 2/24, O'Donovan Rossa MSS, CUA.

27 Bagenal, *American Irish*, 33, 107, 109, 111, 116–17, 119, 122, 131–2, 218.

28 Arthur Gribben, *The Great Famine and the Irish Diaspora in America* (Amherst, 1999), 184, 189; Miller, *Emigrants and Exiles*, 342; Brown, *Review of Politics* 18:333; Thomas N. Brown, *Irish-American Nationalism* (Philadelphia, 1966), 20–4; Joseph P. O'Grady, *How the Irish Became Americans* (New York, 1973), 41; Hartford, *Working People of Holyoke*, 66–7; Larcom to Mayo, 21 March 1867, Mayo MSS, 11, 191, NLI; William H. A. Williams, "From Lost Land to Emerald Isle: Ireland and the Irish in American Sheet Music, 1800–1920," *Eire/Ireland* 26 (1991): 23–4; David Noel Doyle and Owen Dudley Edwards, eds., *America and Ireland 1776–1976: The American Identity and the Irish Connection* (Westport, 1976), 169.

29 Doyle and Edwards, *America and Ireland*, 127; Robert M. Senkewicz, *Vigilantes in Gold Rush San Francisco* (Stanford, 1985), 134–5, 138; Miller, *Emigrants and Exiles*, 335; Diner, *Erin's Daughters*, 25; Drudy, *Irish in America*, 259–60.

30 *Daily Telegraph*, 16 December 1867.

31 Hugh Davis Graham and Ted Robert Gurr, *The History of Violence in America: Historical and Comparative Perspectives*, pb. ed. (New York, 1969), 4–36; *Daily Telegraph*, 16 December 1867.

32 Neal Garnham, "How Violent Was Eighteenth Century Ireland," *Irish Historical Studies*, 30 (1997): 392; Bellesiles, *Arming America*, 81, 175, 177; Richard Maxwell Brown, *Strain of Violence: Historical Studies of American Violence and Vigilantism* (New York, 1975), 5, 21–2; Alexander DeConde, *Gun Violence in America: The Struggle for Control* (Boston, 2001), 23; Graham and Gurr, *History of Violence*, 53; Richard Slotkin, *Regeneration through Violence: The Mythology of the American Frontier, 1600–1800* (Middletown, 1973), 5, 18.

33 Graham and Gurr, *History of Violence*, 62–4; Brown, *Strain of Violence*, 22; J.C. Furnas, *A Social History of the United States 1587–1914* (New York, 1969), 521–2, 529–31; Niehaus, *Irish in New Orleans*, 62; Michael A. Bellesiles, "The Origins of Gun Culture in the United States, 1760–1865," *Journal of American History* 83 (1996): 448; DeConde, *Gun Violence in America*, 55, 58–61; William Cooper, Jr, Michael F. Holt, and John McCardell, eds., *A Master's Due: Essays in Honor of David Herbert Donald* (Baton Rouge, 1985), 112–37; Bellesiles, *Arming America*, 349; David T. Courtwright, *Violent Land: Single Men and Social Disorder from the Frontier to the Inner City* (Cambridge, Mass., 1996), 2–3, 9, 30.

34 Paul A. Gilje, *Rioting in America* (Bloomington, 1996), 75–80; Graham and Gurr, *History of Violence*, 150.

35 David Grimsted, *American Mobbing 1828–1861: Toward Civil War* (New York, 1998), viii, 218; Theodore M. Hammett, "Two Mobs of Jacksonian Boston: Ideology and Interest," *Journal of American History* 62 (1975–76): 845–68; Allen F. David and Mark H. Haller, eds., *The Peoples of Philadelphia: A History of Ethnic Groups and Lower Class Life, 1790–1940* (Philadelphia, 1973), 77–82, 99–100; Emma Jones Lapsansky, "'Since They Got Those Separate Churches': Afro-Americans and Racism in Jacksonian Philadelphia," *American Quarterly* 32 (1980): 54–78; Elizabeth M. Geffen, "Violence in Philadelphia in the 1840's and 1850's," *Pennsylvania History* 36 (1969): 381–410; David Mont-

gomery, "The Shuttle and the Cross: Weavers and Artisans in the Kensington Riots of 1844," *Journal of Social History* 5 (1971–72): 411–46; Ignatiev, *How the Irish Became White*, 152; see also Feldberg, *The Philadelphia Riots of 1844*.

36 Paul O. Weinbaum, *Mobs and Demagogues: The New York Response to Collective Violence in the Early Nineteenth Century* (New York, 1979), 37–9; Gilje, *Rioting in America*, 74–5; Bayor and Meagher, *New York Irish*, 17; David A. Johnson, "Vigilance and the Law: The Moral Authority of Popular Justice in the Far West," *American Quarterly* 33 (1981): 558–86; Graham and Gurr, *History of Violence*, 188–98; Senkewicz, *Vigilantes in Gold Rush California*, 173–5.

37 Roy P. Basler, ed., *Collected Works of Abraham Lincoln*, 8 vols. (Springfield, 1953), 1:111, 114; Sowell, *Ethnic America*, 40; Bellesiles, *Arming America*, 362; Michael Feldberg, *The Turbulent Era: Riot and Disorder in Jacksonian America* (New York, 1980), 100, 105, 127; Niehaus, *Irish in New Orleans*, 65, 94; Feldberg, *The Philadelphia Riots of 1844*, 34; Grimsted, *American Mobbing*, 227; David Grimsted, "Rioting in Its Jacksonian Setting," *American Historical Review* 77 (1972): 391–2.

38 Feldberg, *The Philadelphia Riots of 1844*, 22; Bayor and Meagher, *New York Irish*, 81; Bellesiles, *Arming America*, 371; Kenny, *Making Sense of the Molly Maguires*, 7–9, 18, 29, 62–3, 65–6, 70.

CHAPTER EIGHT

1 John O'Leary, *Recollections of Fenians and Fenianism*, reprint ed., 2 vols. (New York, 1969), 1:8, 79; Richard Davis, *The Young Ireland Movement* (Dublin, 1987), 257, 259, 264; Sean Cronin, "'The Country Did Not Turn Out': The Young Ireland Rising of 1848," *Eire/Ireland* 11 (1976): 11–13; James H. Billington, *Fire in the Minds of Men: Origins of the Revolutionary Faith*, pb. ed. (New York, 1980), 6, 33, 45, 86, 127, 132, 134, 160–1, 164–6, 170–1.

2 T.W. Moody, ed., *The Fenian Movement* (Cork, 1968), 64–8; James Stephens's American Diary, MIC 15D/1, PRONI; John O'Mahony Manuscript, MSS 868, NLI; Desmond Ryan, *The Fenian Chief: A Biography of James Stephens* (Coral Gables, 1967), 63, xxiii.

3 John Hutchinson and Anthony D. Smith, *Ethnicity* (New York, 1996), 317–18; *Irish Catholic Banner*, 14 March 1868; Gorn, *Journal of American History* 74:409; William D'Arcy, *The Fenian*

Movement in the United States 1858–1886, reprint ed. (New York, 1971), 5–8, 314; Hereward Senior, *The Last Invasion of Canada: The Fenian Raids, 1866–1870* (Ottawa, 1991), 19: Robert Francis Hueston, *The Catholic Press and Nativism 1840–1860* (New York, 1976), 148; Oliver MacDonagh, *States of Mind* (London, 1983), 82; Thomas N. Brown, *Irish-American Nationalism 1870–1890* (New York, 1966), 28; Ryan, *Fenian Chief*, 61–2; Joseph Denieffe, *A Personal Narrative of the Irish Revolutionary Brotherhood*, reprint ed. (Shannon, 1969), 3.

4 Denieffe, *Personal Narrative*, 14; Ryan, *Fenian Chief*, 1–5, 57–9, 74, 80; O'Mahony Manuscript, MSS 868, NLI.

5 John Augustus O'Shea, *Leaves from the Life of a Special Correspondent*, 2 vols. (London, 1885), 1:101–3; Ryan, *Fenian Chief*, 84; Stephens to Doheny, 1 January 1858, O'Donovan Rossa Papers, Margaret McKim Maloney Collection, New York Public Library, microfilm copies, P740, NLI.

6 Denieffe, *Personal Narrative*, 25; R.V. Comerford, *Charles J. Kickham: A Biography* (Dublin, 1979), 50, 17–19, 24; John Devoy, *Recollections of an Irish Rebel*, reprint ed. (Shannon, 1969), 375–8; Terry Golway, *Irish Rebel: John Devoy and America's Fight for Irish Freedom* (New York, 1998), 13–14, 31, 33, 37–9, 42–3; Marcus Bourke, *John O'Leary: A Study in Irish Separatism* (Tralee, 1967), 4–5, 10, 14–17, 36; Moody, *Fenian Movement*, 54–9.

7 Denieffe, *Personal Narrative*, 25, 45; Billington, *Fire in the Minds of Men*, 130, 182, 178–80; MacDonagh, *States of Mind*, 80–1, 84; John Newsinger, *Fenianism in Mid-Victorian Britain* (London, 1994), 25; Peter H. Merkl, ed., *Political Violence and Terror: Motifs and Motivations* (Berkeley, 1986), 53; Walter Laqueur, *Terrorism* (Boston, 1977), 26; David C. Rapoport, *Assassination and Terror* (Toronto, 1971), 56; Edward Price Jr, "The Strategy and Tactics of Revolutionary Terrorism," *Comparative Studies in Society and History* 19 (1977): 56–7.

8 R.V. Comerford, "France, Fenianism, and Irish Nationalist Strategy," *Etudes Irlandaises* 7 (1982): 118; F.S.L. Lyons and R.A.J. Hawkins, eds., *Ireland under the Union: Varieties of Tension. Essays in Honour of T.W. Moody* (Oxford, 1980), 149–55; Denieffe, *Personal Narrative*, 27–8.

9 James Stephens's American Diary, MIC 15D/1, PRONI; Seamus Pender, ed., "Fenian Papers in the Catholic University of America: A Preliminary Survey," 123–4, Department of Archives, CUA; R.V. Comerford, *The Fenians in Context: Irish Politics and Society, 1848–1882* (Dublin, 1985), 51; James Stephens on "Fenianism: Past and Present," MS 10, 492, NLI; *Notes and Queries*, 21

March 1868; Damien Murray, *Romanticism, Nationalism and Irish Antiquarian Societies 1840–1880* (Dublin, 2000), 108–9.

10 Comerford, *Etudes Irlandaises* 7:120; Lyons and Hawkins, *Ireland under the Union*, 155; Wendy Hinde, *Richard Cobden: A Victorian Outsider* (New Haven, 1987), 294–9; Denieffe, *Personal Narrative*, 46–7; Ryan, *Fenian Chief*, 91–2.

11 Denieffe, *Personal Narrative*, 28–30, 36; O'Leary, *Recollections of Fenians and Fenianism*, 1:111; Michael Beames, "Peasant Disturbances, Popular Conspiracies and Their Control: Ireland, 1798–1852," Ph.D. thesis, 1975, University of Manchester, 269; Beames, *Past and Present* 97:142; K. Theodore Hoppen, "Grammars of Electoral Violence in Nineteenth-Century England and Ireland," *English Historical Review* 109 (1994): 613; K. Theodore Hoppen, *Elections, Politics and Society in Ireland, 1832–1885 (Oxford, 1984)*, 358–61; W. Mommsen and G. Hirschfeld, *Social Protest, Violence and Terror in Nineteenth and Twentieth Century Europe* (London, 1982), 149; Alfred P. Smyth, *Faith, Famine and Fatherhood in the Irish Midlands: Perceptions of Priest and Historian Anthony Cogan 1826–1872* (Dublin, 1992), 80; C.H.E. Philpin, ed., *Nationalism and Popular Protest in Ireland* (Cambridge, 1987), 243; Comerford, *Fenians in Context*, 34, 41–2; Desmond Ryan, *The Phoenix Flame: A Study of Fenianism and John Devoy* (London, 1937), 54; Ira B. Cross, ed., *Frank Roney, Irish Rebel and California Labor Leader: An Autobiography* (Berkeley, 1931), 3–4, 6, 12–13, 16, 52–3, 57–8; Charles Townshend, *Political Violence in Ireland: Government and Resistance since 1848* pb. ed. (Oxford, 1984), 25.

12 Jeremiah O'Donovan Rossa, *Irish Rebels in English Prisons* (1991), 22–3; W.E. Vaughan, ed., *Ireland under the Union* (Oxford, 1989), 1:418; Murray, *Romanticism, Nationalism and Irish Antiquarian Societies*, 109; Richard Pigott, *Personal Recollections of an Irish Nationalist Journalist* (Dublin, 1882), 81; Ryan, *Fenian Chief*, 94; Leon O Broin, "The Phoenix Conspiracy," *Irish Sword* 14 (1980): 25–8; Lawrence W. McBride, ed., *Reading Irish Histories: Texts, Contexts and Memory in Modern Ireland* (Dublin, 2003), 30; Pigot to O'Brien, 15 December 1858, MS 446, Smith O'Brien Papers, NLI.

13 Confidential Cabinet Memorandum, 10 November 1858, MS 7793, Larcom Papers, NLI; O Broin, *Irish Sword* 14:29–33; Papers Relating to the Phoenix Society, box 2/31, O'Donovan Rossa Papers, CUA.

14 O Broin, *Irish Sword* 14:35–38, 158–61; *Parl. Deb.* 3rd ser., 152:1384; Pender, "Fenian Papers," 131; Phoenix Society Prosecutions, box 2/23, Rossa Papers, CUA; J. Pope Hennessy to

Edward O'Sullivan, 3 May 1859, box 2/23, Rossa Papers, CUA.

15 Larcom to Commissioners of National Education, 6 April 1859, MS 7793, NLI; O Broin, *Irish Sword* 14:45.

16 Lyons and Hawkins, *Ireland under the Union*, 157–9; Shin-ichi Takagami, "The Dublin Fenians 1858–79," Ph.D. thesis, 1990, Trinity College Dublin, 19–20; Tom Garvin, *The Evolution of Irish Nationalist Politics* (Dublin, 1981), 60; Moody, *Fenian Movement*, 18; Malcolm Brown, *The Politics of Irish Literature* (Seattle, 1972), 161–3; Comerford, *Fenians in Context*, 73–4; Denieffe, *Personal Narrative*, 56, 165.

17 M.J. Egan, *Life of Dean O'Brien* (Dublin, 1949), 11–12, 17, 20, 23, 29, 36, 94, 110.

18 Stephens to O'Mahony, 5 March 1860, Rossa Papers, P740, NLI; Pender, "Fenian Papers," 126; Bourke, *John O'Leary*, 37; Ryan, *Fenian Chief*, 159; O'Leary, *Recollections of Fenians and Fenianism*, 1:109–10, 113.

19 O'Leary, *Recollections of Fenians and Fenianism*, 1:129–30; Ryan, *Fenian Chief*, 167; Pender, "Fenian Papers," 127.

20 Comerford, *Fenians in Context*, 67; Emmet O'Connor, *Labour History of Ireland 1824–1960* (Dublin, 1992), 31; Ryan, *Fenian Chief*, 167–8; Allan Nevins, *The Emergence of Lincoln*, 2 vols. (New York, 1950), 1:193, 2:482–3; William Brock, "The Image of England and American Nationalism," *Journal of American Studies* 5 (1971): 227, 237; David Gerber, *The Making of American Pluralism: Buffalo, New York, 1825–1860* (1989), 390; Martin Crawford, *The Anglo-American Crisis of the Mid-Nineteenth Century: 'The Times' and America, 1850–1862* (Athens, Ga, 1987), 48; Stanley Weintraub, *Edward the Caresser: The Playboy Prince Who Became Edward VII* (New York, 2001), 77; Martin Crawford, "Anglo-American Perspectives: J.C. Bancroft Davis, New York Correspondent of *The Times*, 1854–61," *New York Historical Society Quarterly* 62 (1978): 191; *Illustrated London News*, 25 August, 13 October 1860.

21 Denieffe, *Personal Narrative*, 60; Comerford, *Fenians in Context*, 68; Comerford, *Kickham*, 55; O'Leary, *Recollections of Fenians and Fenianism*, 1:140; Joseph M. Hernon Jr, *Celts, Catholics, and Copperheads: Ireland Views the American Civil War* (Columbus, 1968), 35.

22 Dale T. Knobel, *Paddy and the Republic: Ethnicity and Nationalism in Antebellum America* (Middletown, 1986), 180–1; Kevin Kenny, *Making Sense of the Molly Maguires* (New York, 1998), 96–7; Grace Palladino, *Another Civil War: Labor, Capital and*

the State in the Anthracite Regions of Pennsylvania 1840–68 (Chicago, 1990), 114; Lawrence Frederick Kohl, ed., *Irish Green and Union Blue: The Civil War Letters of Peter Welsh* (New York, 1986), 62; Clark, *Irish Relations*, 105.

23 Michael A. Bellesiles, *Arming America: The Origins of a National Gun Culture* (New York, 2000), 430; Hernon, *Celts, Catholics, and Copperheads*, 11; Florence E. Gibson, *The Attitudes of the New York Irish toward State and National Affairs, 1848–1892* (New York, 1951), 124; Justille Macdonald, *History of the Irish in Wisconsin in the Nineteenth Century* (Washington, D.C., 1954), 142; Kohl, *Irish Green and Union Blue*, 65, 79, 102–3; Richard Schneirov, "Political Cultures and the Rule of the State in Labor's Republic: The View from Chicago, 1848–1877," *Labor History* 32 (1991): 386–7.

24 Macdonald, *Irish in Wisconsin*, 143; D'Arcy, *Fenian Movement*, 32–8; W.S. Niedhardt, *Fenianism in North America* (University Park, 1975), 12–13; Pender, "Fenian Papers," 128–31.

25 Joseph M. Hernon, Jr, "The Irish Nationalists and Southern Secession," *Civil War History* 12 (1966): 44–8; Hernon, *Celts, Catholics, and Copperheads*, 97; Charles P. Cullop, "An Unequal Duel: Union Recruiting in Ireland, 1863–1864," *Civil War History* 13 (1967): 101–13; Joseph M. Hernon, Jr, "Irish Religious Opinion on the American Civil War," *Catholic Historical Review* 49 (1963–64): 509–13.

26 Hernon, *Catholic Historical Review* 49:510; Hernon, *Celts, Catholics, and Copperheads*, 100–2, 55, 75–6, 15, 35, 99, 119.

27 Louis B. Bisceglia, "The Fenian Funeral of Terence Bellew McManus," *Eire/Ireland* 14 (1979): 45–57; O'Connell to Moriarty, 27 June 1853, San Francisco 13, Archives of All Hallows College (AAHC), Dublin; Thomas G. McAllister, *Terence Bellew McManus 1811(?)-1861: A Short Biography* (Maynooth, 1972), 40–3.

28 Iorwerth Prothero, *Radical Artisans in England and France* (Cambridge, 1997), 205; Bisceglia, *Eire/Ireland* 14:58–64; McAllister, *McManus*, 44–7; Denieffe, *Personal Narrative*, 64; Comerford, *Fenians in Context*, 75–9; MacDonagh, *States of Mind*, 85; Stephens to O'Mahony, 25 February [1862], P740, O'Donovan Rossa Papers, NLI; Devoy, *Recollections of an Irish Rebel*, 25.

29 Denieffe, *Personal Narrative*, 72; Stephens to O'Mahony, 25 February [1862], P740, Rossa Papers, NLI; Stephens to O'Mahony, 11 December 1864, box 2/17, Rossa Papers, CUA.

30 Comerford, *Fenians in Context*, 83, 89–92; Hernon, *Celts,*

Catholics, and Copperheads, 50; Lawrence Kehoe, ed., *Complete Works of the Most Reverend John Hughes D.D., Archbishop of New York* 2 vols. (New York, 1864), 1: 527–8.

31 Kehoe, *Complete Works of Archbishop John Hughes*, 1: 529–38; Cullen to Hughes, 14 December 1862, reel 5, Hughes MSS, CUA; Alan O'Day, *Reactions to Irish Nationalism* (London, 1987), 10–11.

32 Tom Garvin, *Nationalist Revolutionaries in Ireland 1858–1928* (Oxford, 1987), 35; Stephens to O'Mahony, 13 March 1863, P740, Rossa Papers, NLI; Denieffe, *Personal Narrative*, 77–8; Pender, "Fenian Papers," 17, 22; Rossa, *Irish Rebels in English Prisons*, 44; Devoy, *Recollections of an Irish Rebel*, 42.

33 Bourke, *John O'Leary*, 71, 50, 53; Mary Leó, "The Influence of the Fenians and their Press on Public Opinion in Ireland, 1863–70," M.Litt. thesis, TCD, iv, 2–3, 5; Stephens, "Fenianism: Past and Present," Ms. 10, 492, NLI; Comerford, *Kickham*, 69; Comerford, *Fenians in Context*, 98, 109; Pender, "Fenian Papers," 17; A.M. Sullivan, *New Ireland* (1878), 338; D'Arcy, *Fenian Movement*, 57.

34 John P. Huttman, "Fenians and Farmers: The Merger of the Home-Rule and Owner-Occupancy Movements in Ireland, 1850–1915," *Albion* 3 (1971): 183; Takagami, "Dublin Fenians," 80, 96; Leo, "The Influence of Fenians and Their Press," 12–19; O'Leary, *Recollections of Fenians and Fenianism*, 2:43–4; James Stephens, American Diary, MIC 15D/1, PRONI; Michael Gallagher, "Socialism and the Nationalist Tradition in Ireland, 1798–1918," *Eire/Ireland* 12 (1977): 76; John W. Boyle, "Ireland and the First International," *Journal of British Studies* 11 (1972): 45–6; the articles from the *Irish People* were reprinted in the *Irish Canadian*, 27 July, 17 August, 5 October 1864; E. Steele, *Irish Land and British Politics: Tenant-Right and Nationality, 1865–1870* (Cambridge, 1974), 30; Philip Bull, *Land, Politics and Nationalism: A Study of the Irish Land Question* (Dublin, 1996), 40; Philpin, *Nationalism and Popular Protest in Ireland*, 339; Paul Bew, *Land and the National Question in Ireland 1858–82* (Dublin, 1978), 40.

35 *Irish Canadian*, 11 November 1863, 20 July, 13 January 1864, 30 December 1863.

36 Comerford, *Fenians in Context*, 100–1; Sullivan, *New Ireland*, 336, 339; *Irish Canadian*, 14 December, 23 March, 21 December 1864; *Second Annual Report of the Irish National League* (Dublin, 1866), 9, LAE 0611, Lynch Papers, AAT.

37 Hernon, *Celts, Catholics, and Copperheads*, 36; Sullivan, *New*

Ireland, 342–6; *Irish Canadian*, 31 August 1864; Oliver Mac-
Donagh and W.F. Mandle, *Ireland and Irish-Australia: Studies in
Cultural and Political History* (London, 1986), 130; Tadgh Foley
and Sean Ryder, *Ideology and Ireland in the Nineteenth Century*
(Dublin, 1998), 55–67.

38 Kevin B. Nowlan and Maurice O'Connell, eds., *Daniel O'Connell: Portrait of a Radical* (Belfast, 1984), 20; O'Leary, *Recollections of Fenians and Fenianism*, 2:31–8.

39 Denieffe, *Personal Narrative*, 183–5; Pender, "Fenian Papers,"
18–20; Comerford, *Fenians in Context*, 120–1.

40 O'Day, *Reactions to Irish Nationalism*, 117–40; Emmet Larkin,
*Consolidation of the Roman Catholic Church in Ireland,
1860–1870* (Dublin, 1987), 275–347; *Irish Canadian*, 21 December 1864.

41 Leo, "The Influence of the Fenians and Their Press," 7; *Irish
Canadian*, 19 April, 23 August 1865.

42 Larkin, *Consolidation of the Roman Catholic Church*, 280–1; J.
Herbert Stack, "The New Irish Difficulty," *MacMillan's Magazine*
13 (1865–66): 507.

43 John Darby, Nichlas Dodge, and A.C. Hepburn, eds., *Political
Violence: Ireland in a Comparative Perspective* (Belfast, 1990),
174; Pender, "Fenian Papers," 21; O'Leary, *Recollections of Fenians and Fenianism*, 2:2; T.P.O'Connor to Rossa, 15 April 1903,
P740, Rossa Papers, NLI; Ryan, *Fenian Chief*, 188: A.T.Q. Stewart, *The Summer Soldiers: The 1798 Rebellion in Antrim and
Down* (Belfast, 1995), 39–40; A.J. Semple, "The Fenian Infiltration of the British Army," *Journal of the Society for Army Historical Research* 52 (1974): 139; Hernon, *Celts, Catholics, and Copperheads*, 36; *MacMillan's Magazine* 13:507.

CHAPTER NINE

1 William D'Arcy, *The Fenian Movement in the United States
1858–1886*, reprint ed. (New York, 1971), 47–8, 50–1; Mabel
Gregory Walker, *The Fenian Movement* (Colorado Springs,
1969), 36–9; P.M. Toner, "The 'Green Ghosts': Canada's Fenians
and the Raids," *Eire/Ireland* 16 (1981): 28–9; George Sheppard,
"'God Save the Green': Fenianism and Fellowship in Victorian
Ontario," *Histoire Sociale/Social History* 20 (1987): 132; Hereward Senior, *The Last Invasion of Canada: The Fenian Raids
1866–1870* (Toronto, 1991), 32–4.

2 Hereward Senior, "Quebec and the Fenians," *Canadian Historical
Review* 48 (1967): 30–1; Senior, *Last Invasion of Canada*, 38;

Toner, *Eire/Ireland* 16:29–32; Michael Cottrell, "St. Patrick's Day Parades in Nineteenth-Century Toronto: A Study in Immigrant Adjustment and Elite Control," *Histoire Sociale/Social History* 25(1992):66–7; *Irish Canadian*, 27 September 1865.

3 Walsh to Lynch, 8 November 1864, AE06.04, Lynch Papers, AAT; Brian Clarke, *Piety and Nationalism: Lay Volunteer Associations and the Creation of an Irish Catholic Community in Toronto, 1850–1895* (Montreal, 1993), 187; C.P. Stacey, "A Fenian Interlude: The Story of Michael Murphy," *Canadian Historical Review* 15 (1934): 139; Hereward Senior, *The Fenians in Canada* (Toronto, 1978), 68–9, 71; William Nolte, "The Irish in Canada, 1815–1867," Ph.D. thesis, 1875, University of Maryland, 303; Sheppard, *Histoire Sociale/Social History* 20:132–3; Jeff Keshen, "Cloak and Dagger: Canada West's Secret Police, 1864–1867," *Ontario History* 79 (1987): 354–64.

4 P.M. Toner, ed., *New Ireland Remembered: Essays on the Irish in New Brunswick* (Fredericton, 1988), 137; Cottrell, *Histoire Sociale/Social History* 25:66–7; W.S. Niedhardt, *Fenianism in North America* (University Park, 1975), 26; Nolte, "Irish in Canada," 305; Robert O'Driscoll and Lorna Reynolds, eds., *Untold Story: The Irish in Canada*, 2 vols. (Toronto, 1988), 1:462, 471–4, 514; Senior, *Fenians in Canada*, 72–3.

5 *Irish Canadian*, 10, 17 February, 2 March, 15, 29 June, 1864.

6 John S. Moir, *Church and State in Canada West: Three Studies in the Relation of Denominationalism and Nationalism, 1841–1867* (Toronto, 1959), 23; Thomas Gerald John Stortz, "John Joseph Lynch, Archbishop of Toronto: A Biographical Study of Religious, Political and Social Commitment," Ph.D. thesis, 1980, University of Guelph, 221–3; Lynch to Cullen, 28 September 1864, 320/3/II, Cullen Correspondence, AAD; Clarke, *Piety and Nationalism*, 185, 189; Michael Cottrell, "Irish Catholic Political Leadership in Toronto, 1855–1882: A Study in Ethnic Politics," Ph.D. thesis, 1988, University of Saskatchewan, 152, 155, 168, 174, 187; McGee to Northgraves, 27 December 1864, AE02.04, Lynch Papers, AAT; *Irish Canadian*, 12 April 1865.

7 Clarke, *Piety and Nationalism*, 190–2; Senior, *Canadian Historical Review* 48:31; Stortz, "John Joseph Lynch," 223; Lynch to Farrell, 1 August 1865, AE06.08, Lynch Papers, AAT; *Irish Canadian*, 23, 30 August 1865.

8 Lynch to Connolly, 1 February 1866, AE02.09, Lynch Papers, AAT; Terrence Murphy and Cyril J. Byrne, eds., *Religion and Identity: The Experience of Irish and Scottish Catholics in Atlantic Canada* (St John's, 1987), 120.

9 Connolly to Lynch, 12 March 1866, AE02.14, Lynch Papers, AAT.

10 Lynch to Connolly, 1 February 1866, AE02.09; "Loyal Petition," AE02.06; Connolly to Lynch, 12 March 1866, AE02.14; McGee to Lynch, 19 February 1866, AE02.10, Lynch Papers, AAT; Stortz, "John Joseph Lynch," 224; Lynch to O'Donohoe, 28 February 1866, AE02.12, Lynch Papers, AAT; Lynch to Cullen, 24 March 1866, 327/5/II, Cullen Correspondence, Foreign Bishops, 1866, AAD.

11 Sheppard, *Histoire Sociale/Social History* 20:136-7, 141; Victor L. Russell, ed., *Forging a Consensus: Historical Essays on Toronto* (Toronto, 1984), 76; Connolly to Lynch, 12 March 1866, AE02.14; Lynch to O'Donohoe, 28 February 1866, AE06.12, Lynch Papers, AAT.

12 Kevin Kenny, *Making Sense of the Molly Maguires* (New York, 1998), 100-1; Jay P. Dolan, *Catholic Revivalism: The American Experience 1830-1900* (Notre Dame, 1978), 174; Dennis Clark, *The Irish Relations: Trials of an Immigrant Tradition* (1982), 107; Wood to Cullen, 7 November 1864; Duggan to Cullen, 9 March 1864, 320/3/II, Cullen Correspondence, Foreign Bishops, 1864, AAD; Fergus Macdonald, *The Catholic Church and Secret Societies in the United States* (Washington, D.C., 1946), 35, 26-7; Kevin Kenny, "The Molly Maguires and the Catholic Church," *Labor History* 37 (1995): 349; *Irish Canadian*, 2 March 1864.

13 Purcell to Spalding, 7 September 1864, 35-Q-11; 20 February 1865, 35-R-13, Spalding Papers, AAB; Macdonald, *Catholic Church and Secret Societies*, 35, 37, 39, 44; William L. Joyce, *Editors and Ethnicity: A History of the Irish-American Press, 1848-1883* (New York, 1976), 85-6; Oliver Rafferty, "Fenianism in North America in the 1860s: The Problems of Church and State, *History* 84 (1999): 267; John R.G. Hassard, *Life of John Hughes, First Archbishop of New York* (New York, 1969), 258; Bisceglia, *Eire/Ireland* 14:55-6; David O'Brien, *Public Catholicism*, 2nd ed. (New York, 1996), 101; McCloskey to Leahy, 21 August 1867, 6008, Leahy Papers, NLI; *Irish Canadian*, 30 September 1863; Walker, *Fenian Movement*, 28.

14 Peter Kenrick to Spalding, 27 February 1866, 34-N-23, Spalding Papers, AAB; Duggan to Cullen, 12 February, 9 March 1864; Wood to Cullen, 7 November 1864, 320/3/II, Cullen Correspondence, AAD; Cullen to Spalding, 20 August 1864, 33-O-2; Cullen to Spalding, 17 September 1864, 33-O-3; Purcell to Spalding, 27 June 1864, 35-Q-10, Spalding Papers, AAB; Duggan to Cullen, 26 July 1864, 320/3/II, Cullen Correspondence, AAD; Russell to Odo

Russell, 16 March 1863, FO 918/8, Odo Russell Papers; McCloskey to Spalding, 25 August 1864, 35-D-10, Spalding Papers, AAB.

15 Kenrick to Spalding, 18 August 1864, 34-M-5, 25 October 1864, 34-M-7, Spalding Papers, AAB; Spalding to Kenrick, 2 October 1865, Spalding Letterpress Books, 1:163, AAB; Walker, *Fenian Movement*, 27; Spalding to Cullen, 18 November 1865, Spalding Letterpress Books, 1:720; Spalding to Cullen, 7 May 1866, Spalding Letterpress Books, 1:734; O'Connor to Leahy, 28 October 1867, Leahy Papers, 6008, NLI.

16 Thomas W. Spalding, *The Premier See: A History of the Archdiocese of Baltimore, 1789–1989* (Baltimore, 1989), 197; Kenrick to Spalding, 7 November 1864, 34–M-8, Spalding Papers, AAB; Thomas W. Spalding, *Martin John Spalding: American Churchman* (Washington, D.C., 1973), 247–8; Duggan to Spalding, 23 September 1864, 33-S-13, Spalding Papers; Spalding to Bayley, 3 March 1865, Spalding Letterpress Books, 1: 61; Spalding to McCloskey, 5 June 1865, Spalding Letterpress Books, 1:120; Timon to Spalding, 13 February 1865, 36-F-6; 9 March 1865, 36-F-7, Spalding Papers; Bayley to Spalding, 1 March 1865, 33-D-2, Spalding Papers; Purcell to Spalding, 23 June 1865, 35-R-14, Spalding Papers, AAB; Finbar Kenneally, ed., *United States Documents in the Propaganda Fide Archives*, 5th ser., 3 (Washington, D.C., 1971): 69; 5:173; 8 (Washington, D.C., 1980): 93.

17 Purcell to Spalding, 17 August 1865, 35-R-16, Spalding Papers; Timon to Spalding, 13 August 1865, 36-F-15, Spalding Papers, AAB; Spalding, *Spalding*, 249–50; Kenrick to Spalding, 25 February 1866, 34-N-23, Spalding Papers, AAB; O'Connor to Leahy, 28 October 1867, Leahy Papers, 6008, NLI; Purcell to Cullen, 17 October 1865, 327/1/II, Cullen Correspondence, AAD; Kenneally, *Propaganda Fide*, 8:49.

18 Spalding to Cullen, 18 November, 14 December, Spalding Letterpress Books, 1:720, 722; Wood to Spalding, 14 August 1865, 36-S-20, Spalding Papers, AAB; Wood to Cullen, 11 December 1865, 327/1/II, Cullen Correspondence, AAD; Spalding to Cullen, 7 May 1866, Spalding Letterpress Books, 1:734, AAB; Spalding, *Spalding*, 250; Spalding to Cullen, 10 December 1866, Spalding Letterpress Books, 1: 740, AAB.

19 Cullen to Spalding, 20 August 1864, 33-0-2, Spalding Papers, AAB; Seamus Pender, ed., "Fenian Papers in the Catholic University of America: A Preliminary Survey," 26, Department of Archives, CUA; D'Arcy, *Fenian Movement*, 52; Marcus Bourke, *John O'Leary: A Study in Irish Separatism* (Tralee, 1967), 87;

Charles Townshend, *Political Violence in Ireland: Government and Resistance since 1848* (Oxford, 1983), 29; R.V. Comerford, *Fenians in Context: Irish Politics and Society, 1848–82* (Dublin, 1985), 126–7, 122; Desmond Ryan, *The Fenian Chief: A Biography of James Stephens* (Dublin, 1987), 205.

20 Richard L. Blanco, "Army Recruiting Reforms, 1861–1867," *Journal of the Society for Army Historical Research* 46 (1968): 217–24; William O'Brien, *Recollections* (London, 1905), 52; A.J. Semple, "The Fenian Infiltration of the British Army 1864–1867," M.Litt. thesis, 1971, TCD, 15, 25, 30, 36; Ted Gurr, *Why Men Rebel* (Princeton, 1970), 253, 271.

21 F.S.L. Lyons and R.J. Hawkins, *Ireland under the Union: Varieties of Tension* (Oxford, 1980), 85, 90; James S. Donnelly and Kerby Miller, *Irish Popular Culture, 1650–1850* (Dublin, 1998) 51–2; K. Theodore Hoppen, *Elections, Politics and Society in Ireland, 1832–1885* (Oxford, 1984), 52; Semple, *Journal of the Society of Army Historical Research* 52:133–60; Comerford, *Fenians in Context*, 125; Semple, "Fenian Infiltration," 63–4, 81.

22 O'Mahony to Stephens, 14 April 1865, Rossa Papers, P740, NLI; W.E. Vaughan, ed., *Ireland under the Union* (Oxford, 1989), 1:429; Comerford, *Fenians in Context*, 123; Joseph Denieffe, *A Personal Narrative of the Irish Revolutionary Brotherhood*, reprint ed. (Shannon, 1969), 90–2; John Devoy, *Recollections of an Irish Rebel*, reprint ed. (Shannon, 1969), 57; D'Arcy, *Fenian Movement*, 44, 52–60, 69–70.

23 Stewart J. Brown and David M. Miller, eds., *Piety and Power in Ireland 1760–1960: Essays in Honour of Emmet Larkin* (Belfast, 2000), 27; Conor Cruise O'Brien, *Ancestral Voices: Religion and Nationalism in Ireland* (Chicago, 1995), 118; Emmet Larkin, *Consolidation of the Roman Catholic Church in Ireland, 1860–1870* (Dublin, 1987), 105, 112.

24 Steele, *Irish Historical Studies* 19:256; Hoppen, *Elections, Politics and Society*, 189; Cullen to Spalding, 17 September 1864, 33-0-3, Spalding Papers, AAB; Peadar MacSuibhne, ed., *Paul Cullen and His Contemporaries with Their Letters from 1820–1902*, 5 vols. (Naas, 1961–77), 4:162; Cullen to Spalding, 12 November 1864, 33-0-4; Cullen to Spalding, 2 March 1865, 33-0-5, Spalding Papers, AAB.

25 Larkin, *Consolidation of the Roman Catholic Church*, 77, 96–7; John J. Silke, "The Roman Catholic Church in Ireland 1800–1922: A Survey of Recent Historiography," *Studia Hibernica* 15 (1975): 84; Cullen to Spalding, 17 September 1864, 33-0-3; Cullen to Spalding 12 November 1864, 33-0-4, Spalding

Papers, AAB; MacSuibhne, *Paul Cullen and His Contemporaries*, 4:158; Patrick J. Corish, ed., *A History of Irish Catholicism*, vol. 5, pt 3 (Dublin, 1967): 7; Marcus Tanner, *Ireland's Holy Wars: The Struggle for a Nation's Soul, 1500–2000* (New Haven, 2001), 250–1; Steven R. Knowlton, *Popular Politics and the Irish Catholic Church: The Rise and Fall of the Independent Irish Party* (New York, 1991), 58–9; Brown and Miller, *Piety and Power in Ireland*, 34.

26 Larkin, *Consolidation of the Roman Catholic Church*, 258–9; Corish, *History of Irish Catholicism*, vol. 5, pt 3: 8.

27 Bernard O'Reilly, *John MacHale, Archbishop of Tuam: His Life, Times and Correspondence*, 2 vols. (1890), 2:533; Tomas O Fiaich, "The Clergy and Fenianism," *Irish Ecclesiastical Record* 109 (1968): 87–8; Redmond to Cullen, 13 November 1863, 340/8/I, Cullen Correspondence, AAD; D. George Boyce, ed., *The Revolution in Ireland 1879–1923* (London, 1988), 163; Patrick J. Corish, "Irish College, Rome: The Kirby Letters," *Archivium Hibernicum/Irish Historical Records* 30 (1972): 34, 39; Larkin, *Consolidation of the Roman Catholic Church*, 258; MacHale to Lavelle, 9 August 1860, w3/37/28, Wiseman Papers, Westminster Diocesan Archive (WDA); *Irish Canadian*, 24 June 1863, 24 February 1864; Ira B. Cross, ed., *Frank Roney, Irish Rebel and California Labor Leader: An Autobiography* (Berkeley, 1931), 72.

28 Corish, *Archivium Hibernicum* 30:32, 45; Furlong to Cullen, 7 November 1861; Gillooly to Cullen, 16 November 1861, 337/7/1, Cullen Correspondence, AAD; Ambrose Macaulay, *Patrick Dorrian: Bishop of Down and Connor 1865–85* (Dublin, 1987), 176.

29 Alan O'Day, *Reactions to Irish Nationalism* (London, 1987), 122–3; Liam Bane, *The Bishop in Politics: Life and Career of John MacEvilly* (Westport, 1993), 10; MacEvilly to Cullen, 11 April 1862, 340/3/I, Cullen Correspondence, AAD; Corish, *Archivium Hibernicum* 30:35; E.R. Norman, *Catholic Church and Ireland in the Age of Rebellion, 1859–1873* (London, 1965), 94–5; *Irish Canadian*, 21 October 1863; *Blackwood's Magazine* 54 (1843): 772.

30 Kieran O'Shea, "David Moriarty (1814–77), I: The Making of a Bishop," *Journal of the Kerry Archeological Society* 3 (1970): 84–98; ibid., "II: Reforming a Diocese," 4 (1971): 107–26; ibid., "III: Politics," 5 (1972): 86–102; Corish, *Archivium Hibernicum* 30:41; Larkin, *Making of the Roman Catholic Church*, 210–18; Norman, *Catholic Church and Ireland in the Age of Rebellion*, 93.

31 J. O'Shea, *Priests, Politics and Society in Post Famine Ireland: A Study of County Tipperary* (Dublin, 1983), 139, 137; Hoppen, *Elections, Politics and Society*, 187; Corish, *Archivium Hibernicum* 30:33; Oliver Rafferty, *The Church, the State and the Fenian Threat 1861–75* (London, 1999), 40; Redmond to Cullen, 13 November 1863, 340/8/1, Cullen Correspondence, AAD; Alfred P. Smyth, *Faith, Famine and Fatherland in the Irish Midlands: Perceptions of a Priest and Historian, Anthony Cogan 1826–1872* (Dublin, 1992), 80, 82–3; O'Brien to Cullen, 24, 31 March, 11, 16 April 1862, 340/4/1, Cullen Correspondence, AAD; M.J. Egan, *Life of Dean O'Brien* (Dublin, 1949), 94; *Irish Canadian*, 18 May 1864; Carroll to Cullen, 13 November 1865, 320/4, Cullen Correspondence, AAD.

32 Maurice Harmon, ed., *Fenians and Fenianism* (Seattle, 1970), 17; Desmond Bowen, *Paul Cardinal Cullen and the Shaping of Modern Irish Catholicism* (Dublin, 1983), 266; *Irish Canadian*, 9 March 1864, 15 March 1865; Yonah Alexander and Alan O'Day, eds., *Terrorism in Ireland* (Beckenham, 1984), 126, 128–30; Gerald Moran, *A Radical Priest in Mayo: Fr. Patrick Lavelle: The Rise and Fall of an Irish Nationalist, 1825–86* (Dublin, 1994), 1–15, 43; MacHale to Lavelle, 9 August 1860, w3/37/28, Wiseman Papers, WDA; R.A.J. Walling, ed., *The Diaries of John Bright* (London, 1930), 104; M.L.R. Smith, *The Military Strategy of the Irish Republican Movement* (London, 1995), 14.

33 Alexander and O'Day, *Terrorism in Ireland*, 131–3; Corish, *History of Irish Catholicism*, 5, pt. 3: 10; Dixon to Cullen, 1 February 1862, 340/3/1, Cullen Correspondence, AAD; *Irish Canadian*, 25 February, 23, 17 June, 5 August 1863, 6, 27 April 1864; Marie-Louise Legg, *Newspapers and Nationalism: The Irish Provincial Press 1850–1892* (Dublin, 1999), 103–7; MacSuibhne, *Paul Cullen and His Contemporaries*, 4:116; Corish, *Archivium Hibernicum* 30:41.

34 *Irish Canadian*, 24 June 1863; Alexander and O'Day, *Terrorism in Ireland*, 135; Bowen, *Cullen*, 265.

35 Larkin, *Consolidation of the Roman Catholic Church*, 260, 399, 319–20, 348–9; Brendan Ó Cathaoir, *John Blake Dillon: Young Irelander* (Dublin, 1990), 155, 164; Newsinger, *European Studies Review* 9:473; Fiaich, *Irish Ecclesiastical Record* 109:89; Corish, *Archivium Hibernicum* 30:48.

36 *Fortnightly Review* 3 (1868): 319; Alexander Grant and Keith J. Stringer, eds., *Uniting the Kingdom? The Making of British History* (London, 1995), 196; *Trans. R.H.S.*, 6th ser., 4 (1994): 12; Hugh Kearney, *The British Isles: A History of Four Nations*

(Cambridge, 1989), 108; Matthew Cragoe, *Culture, Politics, and National Identity in Wales 1832–1886* (Oxford, 2004), 2; Bill Schwarz, ed., *The Expansion of England: Race, Ethnicity and Cultural History* (London, 1996), 172; Lawrence Brockliss and David Eastwood, eds., *A Union of Multiple Identities: The British Isles c.1750–c.1850* (Manchester, 1997), 94–5; Murray G.H. Pittock, *Celtic Identity and the British Image* (Manchester, 1999), 3, 29; *Blackwood's Magazine* 66 (1849): 335–6; John S. Ellis, "Reconciling the Celt: British National Identity, Empire, and the 1911 Investiture of the Prince of Wales," *Journal of British Studies* 37 (1998): 398; Glanmor Williams, *Religion, Language, and Nationality in Wales: Historical Essays* (Cardiff, 1979), 195.

37 Kearney, *British Isles*, 165–6; Ivor Wilks, *South Wales and the Rising of 1839: Class Struggle as Armed Struggle* (London, 1984), 11, 249–50; Charles R. Foster, ed., *Nations Without a State: Ethnic Minorities in Western Europe* (New York, 1980), 45; Kenneth O. Morgan, *Wales in British Politics 1868–1922* (Cardiff, 1963), 5, 9: F.M.L. Thompson, *Cambridge Social History of Britain*, 3 vols. (Cambridge, 1990), 1:287–97; David V. Jones, *Rebecca's Children* (Oxford, 1989), 342–3; Matthew Cragoe, "Welsh Electioneering and the Purpose of Parliament: 'From Radicalism to Nationalism' Reconsidered," *Parliamentary History*, vol. 17 pt 1 (1998): 121; K. Theodore Hoppen, *Mid-Victorian Generation 1846–1886* (Oxford, 1998), 550–1.

38 Thompson, *Cambridge Social History* 1:300–23; Williams, *Religion, Language, and Nationality*, 141; Kearney, *British Isles*, 166; Wilks, *South Wales and the Rising of 1839*, 73, 81–3, 25, 53; Reginald Coupland, *Welsh and Scottish Nationalism: A Study* (London, 1954), 176–8.

39 Brendan Bradshaw, ed., *British Consciousness and Identity: The Making of Britain 1533–1707* (Cambridge, 1998), 219; Grant and Stinger, *Uniting the Kingdom?* 200; *Trans. R.H.S.*, 6th ser., 4:19; *Trans. R.H.S.*, 6th ser., 7 (1997): 20; Victor Durkacz, *The Decline of the Celtic Languages: A Study of Linguistic and Cultural Conflict in Scotland, Wales and Ireland from the Reformation to the Twentieth Century* (Edinburgh, 1983), 82–3, 108–9, 190; Eric Hobsbawm and Terence Ranger, eds., *The Invention of Tradition* (Cambridge, 1983), 56–8, 79, 90; Cragoe, *Culture, Politics, and National Identity*, 40; R.R. Davis, Ralph A. Griffiths, Ieuan Gwynedd Jones, and Kenneth O. Morgan, eds., *Welsh Society and Nationhood: Historical Essays Presented to Glanmor Williams* (Cardiff, 1984), 208–9, 215.

40 *Trans. R.H.S.*, 6th ser., 7: 10, 15; Wilks, *South Wales and the Rising of 1839*, 26; *Blackwood's Magazine* 66:328; Keith Robbins, *Nineteenth-Century Britain: England, Scotland and Wales: The Making of a Nation* (Oxford, 1989), 31; Williams, *Religion, Language, and Nationality*, 25, 143; *North London News*, 13 October 1866; *Blackwood's Magazine* 54:776; Schwarz, *Expansion of England*, 185; Brockliss and Eastwood, *Union of Multiple Identities*, 93; Pittock, *Celtic Identity and the British Image*, 64, 125.

41 Thompson, *Cambridge Social History* 1:329; Bradshaw *British Consciousness and Identity*, 45, 73–81; Niall O Cosain, *Print and Popular Culture in Ireland 1750–1850* (London, 1997), 163; Glanmor Williams, "Language, Literacy and Nationality in Wales," *History* 56 (1971): 6–8; Durkacz, *Decline of the Celtic Languages*, 34–6, 81–8; Pittock, *Celtic Identity and the British Image*, 30; *Blackwood's Magazine* 66:327, 333–4; Derby to Cairns, 25 April 1859, PRO 30/51/8, Cairns Papers.

42 *Blackwood's Magazine* 66:327; Durkacz, *Decline of the Celtic Languages*, 99; Williams, *Religion, Language, and Nationality*, 25; Morgan, *Wales in British Politics*, 11, 15; Richard Carwardine, "The Welsh Evangelical Community and 'Finney's Revival,'" *Journal of Ecclesiastical History* 29 (1978): 465–6; Jim Obelkevich, Lyndal Roper, and Raphael Samuel, eds., *Disciplines of Faith: Studies in Religion, Politics and Patriarchy* (New York, 1987), 311–12, 318, 320–1.

43 Cragoe, *Culture, Politics, and National Identity*, 182, 175, 181, 191, 199, 171; E.T. Davies, *A New History of Wales: Religion and Society in the Nineteenth Century* (Llandybie, 1981), 18, 20–3, 25; Robbins, *Nineteenth-Century Britain*, 85; David L. Adamson, *Class, Ideology and Nation: A Theory of Welsh Nationalism* (Cardiff, 1991), 105; Williams, *History* 56:12; Donal A. Kerr, ed., *Religion, State and Ethnic Groups* (New York, 1992), 265–6, 271–2.

44 Bradshaw, *British Consciousness and Identity*, 215; Pittock, *Celtic Identity and the British Image*, 21, 93, 102; Linda Colley, *Britons: Forging the Nation, 1707–1837* (New Haven, 1992), 13; Davis et al., *Welsh Society and Nationhood*, 199–215; J.C.D. Clark, "English History's Forgotten Context: Scotland, Ireland, Wales," *Historical Journal* 32 (1989): 224; David Hempton, *Religion and Political Culture in Britain and Ireland: From the Glorious Revolution to the Decline of Empire* (Cambridge, 1996), 71; Williams, *Religion, Language, and Nationality*, 144;

Cragoe, *Culture, Politics, and National Identity*, 38; Brockliss and Eastwood, *Union of Multiple Identities*, 105; D.W. Bebbington, "Religion and National Feeling in Nineteenth-Century Wales and Scotland," *Studies in Church History* 18 (1982): 495; Grant and Stringer, *Uniting the Kingdom?* 241.

45 *Fortnightly Review* 3 (1868): 319; Coupland, *Welsh and Scottish Nationalism*, 245, 248–51; Colin Kidd, *Subverting Scotland's Past: Scottish Whig Historians and the Creation of an Anglo-British Identity, 1689–c.1830* (Cambridge, 1993), 71; Grant and Stringer, *Uniting the Kingdom?* 196; Wilson McLeod, *Divided Gaels: Gaelic Cultural Identities in Scotland and Ireland c.1200–c.1650* (Oxford, 2004), 20; Linda Colley, "Britishness and Otherness: An Argument," *Journal of British Studies* 31 (1992): 314; E.W. McFarland, *Ireland and Scotland in the Age of Revolution: Planting the Green Bough* (Edinburgh, 1994), 41; Thompson, *Cambridge Social History* 1:155; Pittock, *Celtic Identity and the British Image*, 26–7; John F. McCaffrey, *Scotland in the Nineteenth Century* (London, 1998), 1–3, 30–2.

46 Coupland, *Welsh and Scottish Nationalism*, 251, 259–64; Kearney, *British Isles*, 168, 171–2; Bradshaw, *British Consciousness and Identity*, 239, 247–8, 299; Durkacz, *Decline of the Celtic Languages*, 49–52, 111; Bebbington, *Studies in Church History*, 18:498–9; Dauvit Broun, R.L. Finlay, and Michael Lynch, eds., *Image and Identity: The Making and Re-making of Scotland through the Ages* (Edinburgh, 1998), 164, 197, 200–2; Hempton, *Religion and Political Culture*, 69; *Fortnightly Review* 5 (1866): 91.

47 Kidd, *Subverting Scotland's Past*, 98–9, 127; Colin Kidd, "North Britishness and the Nature of Eighteenth-Century British Patriotisms," *Historical Journal* 39 (1996): 363, 366, 373–4; Murray G. H. Pittock, *Scottish Nationality* (New York, 2001), 75; Brockliss and Eastwood, *Union of Multiple Identities*, 110, 117–18; Pittock, *Celtic identity and British image*, 54–6, 115; T. W. Moody, ed., *Nationality and the Pursuit of National Independence* (Belfast, 1978), 94–5; James D. Young, *The Rousing of the Scottish Working Class* (Montreal, 1979), 19.

48 Young, *Rousing of the Scottish Working Class*, 57–62, 110; S.J. Connolly, R.A. Houston, and R.J. Morris, eds., *Conflict, Identity and Economic Development: Ireland and Scotland, 1600–1939* (Preston, 1995), 9; Pittock, *Scottish Nationality*, 88–9; Murray G.H. Pittock, *Inventing and Resisting Britain: Cultural Identities in Britain and Ireland, 1685–1789* (London, 1997), 170; T.M. Devine, *Scottish Nation 1700–2000* (London, 1999), 209–10,

215, 217, 224–9; McCaffrey, *Scotland in the Nineteenth Century*, 25–9; Michael Kealing and Daniel Bleiman, *Labour and Scottish Nationalism* (London, 1979), 26.

49 T.M. Devine, *Clanship to Crofters' War: The Social Transformation of the Scottish Highlands* (Manchester, 1994), 77, 100, 105, 113–17; Robert Clyde, *From Rebel to Hero: The Image of the Highlander, 1745–1830* (East Lothian, 1998), 5, 7, 9–10, 17, 24, 26, 57, 67; Rosalind Mitchison and Peter Roebuck, eds., *Economy and Society in Scotland and Ireland 1500–1939* (Edinburgh, 1988), 126–32; Connolly, Houston, and Morris, *Conflict, Identity and Economic Development*, 177; Napoleon Roussell, *Roman Catholic Ireland and Protestant Scotland Compared* (Boston, 1855), 124–7; Broun, Finlay, and Lynch, *Image and Identity*, 201–2.

50 Pittock, *Celtic Identity and the British Image*, 40, 36, 62–3, 39; Devine, *Scottish Nation*, 242; John Brewer, *The Pleasures of the Imagination: English Culture in the Eighteenth Century* (New York, 1997), 658–9; Durkacz, *Decline of the Celtic Languages*, 190–4; Kidd, *Subverting Scotland's Past*, 233–4; Connolly, Houston, and Morris, *Conflict, Identity and Economic Development*, 150–7; Clyde, *From Rebel to Hero*, 108.

51 Clyde, *From Rebel to Hero*, 150–3, 156–7, 169, 176–7; Pittock, *Celtic Identity and the British Image*, 43; J.E. Cookson, *The British Armed Nation 1793–1815* (Oxford, 1997), 126–9, 146–9; Saree Makdisi, *Romantic Imperialism: Universal Empire and the Culture of Modernity* (Cambridge, 1998), 79; Steve Murdoch and A. MacKillop, eds., *Fighting for Identity: Scottish Military Experience c. 1550–1900* (Boston, 2002), 188, 190, 196–204, 210, 215.

52 Cookson, *Armed Nation*, 151; Clyde, *From Rebel to Hero*, 177; Makdisi, *Romantic Imperialism*, 70, 74–5; Kidd, *Subverting Scotland's Past*, 266–7; Lindsay Paterson, *The Autonomy of Modern Scotland* (Edinburgh, 1994), 59; Pittock, *Scottish Nationality*, 3; Hobsbawm and Ranger, *Invention of Tradition*, 15–31; Devine, *Scottish Nation*, 244–5.

53 Broun, Finlay, and Lynch, *Image and Identity*, 165–6; Robert Robson, *Ideas and Institutions of Victorian Britain: Essays in Honour of George Kitson Clark* (New York, 1967), 144; J.N. Wolfe, ed., *Government and Nationalism in Scotland: An Enquiry* (Edinburgh, 1969), 5; Katie Trumpener, *Bardic Nationalism: The Romantic Novel and the British Empire* (Princeton, 1997), 13, 17, 24–5; Christopher Harvie, *Scotland and Nationalism: Scottish Society and Politics, 1707–1977* (London, 1977), 129; Claudio Veliz, *The Worth of Nations* (Boston, 1993), 23;

Colin Kidd, "Teutonist Ethnology and Scottish Nationalist Inhibition, 1780–1880," *Scottish Historical Review* 74 (1995): 47, 49, 51, 55, 67; Pittock, *Scottish Nationality*, 96; Coupland, *Welsh and Scottish Nationalism*, 273–4; Alice Brown, David McCrone, and Lindsay Paterson, *Politics and Society in Scotland* (London, 1996), 39–40, 48–50; Devine, *Scottish Nation*, 288.

54 McCaffrey, *Scotland in the Nineteenth Century*, 57; Veliz, *Worth of Nations*, 26–8; Harvie, *Scotland and Nationalism*, 39; Wolfe, *Government and Nationalism in Scotland*, 5, 180–6; Pittock, *Scottish Nationality*, 82.

55 Robson, *Ideas and Institutions of Victorian Britain*, 151–62, 173–5; H.J. Hanham, *Scottish Nationalism* (Harvard, 1969), 51–5, 71–81; McCaffrey, *Scotland in the Nineteenth Century*, 57–8; Coupland, *Welsh and Scottish Nationalism*, 282–7; Paterson, *Autonomy of Modern Scotland*, 60; Graeme Morton, *Unionist-Nationalism Governing Urban Scotland, 1830–1860* (Edinburgh, 1999), 138–40; Brockliss and Eastwood, *Union of Multiple Identities*, 118–9.

56 Morton, *Unionist-Nationalism*, 158, 171, 173, 83; Thompson, *Cambridge Social History* 1:269; Kidd, *Historical Journal* 39:377–8; Kidd, *Subverting Scotland's Past*, 206; Bebbington, *Studies in Church History* 18:501–3; *North London News*, 30 September 1865; *Daily Telegraph*, 21 December 1867.

57 *Daily Telegraph*, 21 December 1867; Grant and Stringer, *Uniting the Kingdom?* 241; S.J. Connolly, "Late Eighteenth-Century Irish Politics," *Parliamentary History*, vol. 13 pt 2 (1994): 231.

Index

Act of Union: with Ireland, 4, 8, 10–11, 13, 15, 86; with Scotland, 3–4, 6–7, 12

Acton, John, 47–8, 50–1

All Hallows College, 199, 211, 268, 310

Anglin, Timothy, 170, 183, 289; and Irish nationalism, 184, 289

anglophobia, 33, 35, 64, 142, 208, 211–12, 214, 243, 245–7, 271, 305

Anglo-Saxonism, 239–40, 245, 270–1, 273, 316

anti-Catholicism, 4, 6, 8, 11–12, 26–8, 31, 33–4, 45, 108, 111, 157, 163, 171–2; in British North America, 157, 163, 171–2; in the United States, 227, 230, 232–5, 237, 242–3; anti-English (British) sentiment, 30–2, 46, 52, 55, 65–6, 75, 84, 88, 98, 100, 103, 110, 127, 129, 131–3, 140, 142, 208, 211–12, 216

anti-slavery movement, 214–16, 222, 231, 236–7, 250–1

anti-union sentiment, 13–17, 30–1, 40, 48, 65, 73

Antonelli, Giacomo, Cardinal Secretary of State, 119

Boston, 154, 191, 193, 199, 208, 215, 217, 229, 238, 240, 251, 253, 293

Boston *Pilot*, 200, 208–9, 216, 231, 238, 296

Bright, John, 87, 143, 284

Britishness, 4, 7–8, 43, 46–9, 71, 103, 245, 316, 326, 329, 332

British North America, 150–1, 153–5, 189, 197, 208, 229, 251, 289, 302; and anti-Catholicism, 157, 163, 171–2; Catholic Irish and ethnic community, 162–4, 168, 171, 176–7; Famine refugees, 158–9; growth of Fenianism, 289–90; and Irish nationalism, 176–7, 180–1; Irish nationalism, deterrents to, 179–80; sectarianism, 157, 171, 173, 175; suspicions of Catholic Irish disloyalty, 161–2, 164; unsavoury reputation of Catholic Irish, 160–1; and violence, 174. *See also* Catholic Church

Brown, George, 171, 174

Brownson, Orestes, 235–6, 240, 243

Burns, Robert, 330, 332

Butt, Isaac, 73, 79

Canada East (Lower Canada), 172; Catholic Irish in, 157, 164–5; and ethnic hostility towards, 158; and urbanization, 157. *See also* Catholic Church

Canada West (Upper Canada), 150, 157, 165; Catholic Irish in, 156, 163, 168; concept of loyalty in, 150–1, 294; difficulties of Catholic Irish in, 156–7, 159; Fenian panic, 289; growth of Fenianism, 289; Orange Order, 170, 172–5, 178, 181–2; sectarianism, 158, 171, 173–5, 181–2, 184

Cantwell, John, Bishop of Meath, 62, 70, 85

Catholic Association, 29, 32–4, 37, 56, 68, 215; and peasant grievances, 29–30, 56

Catholic Church
– in British North America), 163–8, 171;

MacHale, John, 38, 64, 67, 70, 97–8, 115–7, 120, 122, 124, 169, 201, 209–10, 265, 278, 284–5, 290, 308, 312, 314–15; anti-English sentiment, 61, 308–9; Archbishop of Tuam, 61, 107, 111–12; background and character, 60–2, 109; Bishop of Killala, 35, 61, 63; critic of government, 80, 100; and Fenianism, 308–9; and nationalism, 60–2, 100–1, 109, 290, 308

McManus, Terence Bellew, 275; and funeral of, 275–7, 283, 297, 301, 307, 309, 313

Maginn, Edward (Bishop of Derry), 62, 70, 88

magistracy (Irish): and reform, 23, 26; and sectarianism, 23, 26

Maguire, John Francis, 121, 126

Martin, John, 96, 129, 131, 273, 281–2, 285; and Irish National League, 282

Massachusetts, 153, 240, 272

Mathew, Father Theobald, 68, 177, 210; background, 67; and Great Famine, 77–8, 84; and temperance movement, 67–8, 204, 226

Maynooth seminary, 25, 31, 52, 60–2, 64, 66, 70–1, 101–2, 104–5, 108–9, 165, 199, 211, 312; and nationalism, 104

Mazzini, Giuseppe, 48, 54, 106, 307–8

Meagher, Thomas Francis, 81, 90, 94–5, 115, 218, 255, 272, 274

Mill, John Stuart, 47–8, 50

Mitchel, John, 71, 89, 96, 102, 116, 132, 143, 181, 217, 222, 245, 255, 257, 261, 273; advocacy of physical force, 94–5, 116, 218, 220–1; anglophobia, 219; and British response to Famine, 221; escape to United States, 115–16, 218; and ideology, 89, 92–5; and *Jail Journal*, 220–1; limits of influence, 222; and transportation, 95, 116

Molly Maguires, 137–8, 254, 295

Montreal, 158, 160, 164, 172, 181, 288, 290

Moriarty, David, 264–6; background, 310; Bishop of Kerry, 120, 310; and Phoenix Society, 264–5, 311; and rebellion, 311; and the Union, 120, 266, 310–11

Moriarty, Father P.E., 212, 297

Murphy, Michael, 186–7, 291–2; Fenian leader in Canada West, 288

Murray, Daniel (Archbishop of Dublin), 63, 70, 97, 107, 109, 139

Musgrave, Richard, 26, 30

Nation, 66–7, 69, 71, 80, 89–90, 94, 101, 108, 113–14, 116, 126–7, 129–32, 137, 259, 264–6, 277, 281; and the Famine, 80–3, 91

National Association, 283–5, 315; and clergy apathy towards, 315

National Brotherhood of St Patrick, 267, 274, 277–81, 296, 308; episcopal condemnation of, 310; Fenian infiltration of, 267, 308

nationalism, 9, 17, 49, 51, 54; development of, 49–51, 53–4; divisiveness of anti-slavery movement, 216; influence of religion, 53–5, 124; Irish American, 207–16, 223; revolutionary, 217–21; and rhetorical violence, 216–18. *See also* Catholic Irish

national schools, 36, 39–40, 65, 122–5, 308; and sectarianism, 40, 122–3

nativism, 207, 220, 224–5, 227, 231–4, 237, 239–41, 243, 245–6, 251, 293

New Brunswick, 153, 155, 170, 289; and Catholic Irish, 156, 163; and Protestant Irish, 155–6; and sectarianism, 158, 173, 175

Newfoundland, 170; and Catholic Irish, 155, 163–4; and clergy in politics, 169, 176; and relief of disabilities, 158

New York, 153, 190–1, 194, 197, 199–200, 218, 232, 250, 297

New York City, 154, 190, 192, 200, 203, 206, 209, 216–17, 222, 229, 240, 252–3, 257, 270–1, 275, 289

New York *Freeman's Journal*, 207, 209, 297

North Britons, 8, 10, 325

Nova Scotia, 268; and Catholic Irish, 155, 163; and relief of disabilities, 158

O'Brien, Richard (Dean of Limerick), 141, 268, 285, 311–12; background, 268; and nationalism, 268, 285, 312; and Young Men's Catholic Society, 141, 311–12

O'Brien, Smith, 87, 92, 94–5, 141, 144,

Irish emigration to, 189–90; Catholic Irish employment and progress, 192–5, 197–8, 202; Catholic Irish political involvement, 193–5, 230, 236, 240, 243; Catholic Irish support of Catholic Church, 203; complexity of racial attitudes of Catholic Irish, 237–8; difficulties encountered by Catholic Irish, 190–2, 225–6; enclave consciousness and self-segregation of Catholic Irish, 194–5, 199, 202, 204, 206, 224–5, 227; and hostility to Catholic Irish, 225–7, 231–3, 235–6, 239–40, 243, 246; and Irish nationalism, 243–7; as Protestant civilization, 233–5, 241; and sectarianism, 233, 236, 244, 253; and tradition of violence, 248–53; and tradition of violence, 228–9, 238, 248 251, 253–4, 257; unsavoury reputation of Catholic Irish, 226–9, 231

violence: agrarian, 12, 20–1, 23, 34, 36, 41, 133–7, 140–1; 313; in Britain, 248–9, 318, 325; political, 136, 138, 140–1; in United States, 248–51; urban, 135–7, 238; in Wales, 317–19

Wales: agrarian distress in, 317; anti-Catholicism, 321–2; cultural nationalism, 318–19, 322; disturbances, 317–18; education and literacy,

318–19; ethnic tension, 318; national consciousness, 322–3; nonconformity and survival of language, 7, 125, 319–23; nonconformist ministers and politics, 321–2; Protestantism, 7, 125; rapid industrialization, 317; secret societies, 317–18; violence, 317–19
Wellesley, Arthur, Duke of Wellington, 16, 22, 33, 35, 49, 90, 221
Welsh, English scorn of, 9, 316, 319
West Britons, 8, 41
Whig-Liberals, 118–9; and Italian nationalism, 119–21
Whigs, 40–1, 43, 45–6, 56, 72, 76, 79, 95, 104, 111–13, 118, 120; and Famine relief, 76–7, 79, 82, 86, 91, 119; and Irish reforms, 35–9, 46
Whiteboys, 19, 21, 34
Wiseman, Nicholas (Cardinal Archbishop of Westminster), 118, 120
workhouses, 77, 82, 127

Young Ireland movement, 63–7, 71, 73, 81, 90, 93, 101, 103, 108–9, 116, 118–19, 125, 132, 143–4, 177, 209-10, 217, 245, 248, 255-6, 267-8, 275, 295; and differences with O'Connell, 72, 89–91; and exiles in United States, 218
Young Men's Catholic Society, 141, 268